8th EDITION

CANADIAN BUSINESS ENGLISH

8th EDITION

CANADIAN BUSINESS ENGLISH

MARY ELLEN GUFFEY
Professor of Business Emerita
Los Angeles Pierce College

CAROLYN M. SEEFER
Professor of Business
Diablo Valley College

CATHY WITLOX
Instructor, Certificate in Publishing
The Chang School at Ryerson University

Australia • Brazil • Canada • Mexico • Singapore • United Kingdom • United States

***Canadian Business English*, Eighth Edition**
Mary Ellen Guffey, Carolyn M. Seefer, and Cathy Witlox

Senior Director, Product: Jackie Wood

Senior Portfolio Manager: Lenore Taylor-Atkins

Product Marketing Manager: Sydney Pope

Director, Content and Production: Toula DiLeo

Senior Content Development Manager: Liisa Kelly

Senior Content Production Manager: Natalia Denesiuk Harris

IP Analyst: Christine Myaskovsky

Production Service: MPS Limited

Copy Editor: Dawn Hunter

Compositor: MPS Limited

Text Designer: Ken Cadinouche

Cover Designer: John Montgomery

For product information and technology assistance, contact us at **Canada Support, canadasupport@cengage.com.**

For permission to use material from this text or product, submit all requests online at **www.cengage.com/permissions.**

Library and Archives Canada Cataloguing in Publication:

Title: Canadian business English / Mary Ellen Guffey (Professor of Business Emerita, Los Angeles Pierce College), Carolyn M. Seefer (Professor of Business Diablo Valley College), Cathy Witlox (The Chang School at Ryerson University)

Names: Guffey, Mary Ellen, author. | Seefer, Carolyn M., author. | Witlox, Cathy, 1969– author.

Description: 8th edition. | Includes index.

Identifiers: Canadiana 20200390570 | ISBN 9780176832193 (softcover)

Subjects: LCSH: English language—Business English. | LCSH: English language—Grammar.

Classification: LCC PE1115 .G83 2021 | DDC 808.06/665—dc23

Print text ISBN-13: 978-0-17-683219-3
Print text ISBN-10: 0-17-683219-X
Ebook ISBN-13: 978-0-17-688761-2
Ebook ISBN-10: 0-17-688761-X

Cengage Canada
333 Bay Street, #2400
Toronto, ON M5H 2T6
Canada

Cengage is a leading provider of customized learning solutions with employees residing in nearly 40 different countries and sales in more than 125 countries around the world. Find your local representative at **www.cengage.com**.

To learn more about Cengage platforms and services, register or access your online learning solution, or purchase materials for your course, visit **www.cengage.ca.**

Printed in Canada
Print Number: 02 Print Year: 2022

CONTENTS

UNIT 5

Punctuating Sentences 281

UNIT 6

Writing With Style 349

Appendices

Self-Help Exercises 449

Answers

PREFACE

Canadian Business English, Eighth Edition, is the Canadian version of Mary Ellen Guffey's well-known and successful *Business English* text. The bold and innovative approach taken by Dr. Guffey in *Business English* continues to appeal to instructors and students in Canada and the United States. Since 1995 *Canadian Business English* has helped thousands of Canadian students improve their language skills. This edition of *Canadian Business English* continues to offer Canadian students the tools they need to reach excellence in language skills while reflecting today's Canadian workplace landscape and the new technologies and challenges facing students in their professional life.

General Revisions

Canadian Business English, Eighth Edition, largely retains the content and sequencing of previous editions, with the notable exception of the reconfiguration of Chapters 7 and 8. Chapter 7 introduces verb tenses and parts to ensure students' comfort with conjugation and helping verbs before moving to Chapter 8, which builds on and references these skills, focusing on the more advanced concepts of verb types, voices, and moods. Because the concepts developed in these chapters are closely linked, we refer students between the chapters often, with page references, and reinforce the lessons learned in each.

As well, this most recent update further considers technological advancements, addresses changes in workplace environments, reflects our Canadian diversity, emphasizes professional vocabulary, and focuses on the employment skills of editing and proofreading. Reinforcing the importance of these professional roles, FAQs have been replaced with "Ask an Editor" boxes, and "Spot the Bloopers" now invite students to "Be the Editor." The Editor's Challenges remain and continue to include the kind of spelling errors spell-checkers do not recognize, common typographical and homophone errors, and sentence faults. These challenges build in other common errors cumulatively as they are studied.

New to this edition is a glossary, providing students a handy quick alphabetical reference of grammar terms defined throughout the text. (These terms appear in boldface type.)

Finally, this text retains its emphasis on reinforcement through exercises. An additional 150 exercise questions have been added, and more than 30 percent of questions from the previous edition have been revised, with an even greater emphasis on business and diversity.

Chapter-Specific Changes to This Edition

- Chapter 1 (Parts of Speech) recognizes some of the struggles of English language learners by elaborating on the use of articles.
- Chapter 3 (Nouns) has a new exercise that reinforces the basic skill of identifying nouns.
- Chapter 4 (Possessive Nouns) introduces students to a style preference of *The Canadian Press Stylebook,* a style guide used by many Canadian corporate communications departments. This guide is referenced in other places throughout the text.

- Chapter 5 (Personal Pronouns) now addresses gender inclusivity.
- Chapter 6 (Pronouns and Antecedents) contains a new lesson on pronouns that can be either singular or plural depending on context.
- Chapter 7 (Verb Tenses and Parts) was Chapter 8 in previous editions. Among the revisions to this chapter are a chart illustrating the use of helping verbs, a reinforcement exercise about helping verbs (particularly useful for ELL students), and a new section that addresses frequently confused verbs, such as *affect/effect* and *compliment/complement.*
- Chapter 8 (Verbs: Kinds, Voices, Moods) was Chapter 7 in previous editions. The revised chapter explains in greater detail why understanding verb types is important, offers a new way of testing for verb type, and reinforces this learning with a new exercise.
- Chapter 16 (Semicolons and Colons) has an added exercise to test students' ability to differentiate the need for a semicolon, colon, or comma.
- Chapter 18 (Capitalization) has a new section that addresses the common error of capitalizing words that have capitalized abbreviations.
- Chapter 20 (Effective Sentences) now includes a chart illustrating some common redundant expressions and further explanation to help students better understand redundancy.

Textbook Features

Many unique features ensure that students will be successful with *Canadian Business English* in the classroom.

PRETEST

Preceding Chapter 1 is a short pretest designed to help students assess their business English strengths and weaknesses. Answer keys for this test and for chapter self-check exercises are available in the Instructor Guide.

WRITER'S WORKSHOPS

Six workshops feature composition tips and techniques. These workshops begin with proofreading skills and progress through the writing of sentences, paragraphs, email messages, memos, letters, short reports, and internal proposals. Frequent skill checks allow students to apply writing principles immediately, and each workshop presents an optional writing assignment. Answers for the Writer's Workshop activities can be found in the Instructor Guide.

THREE-LEVEL APPROACH

Beginning with Chapter 3, language concepts appear in levels. These levels progress from fundamental, frequently used concepts in Level I to more complex concepts in Level III. Each level has its own trial exercises as well as numerous student reinforcement drills.

The three-level approach has distinct advantages. First, the complexities of English are not immediately recognizable, making the subject less intimidating. Second, the three-level approach facilitates comprehension and promotes student confidence by providing small, easily mastered learning segments. Third, this strategy provides convenient blocks of material that allow individual instructors to tailor the content of the course to fit student abilities, institutional goals, and time constraints.

ASK AN EDITOR

One of the most popular features of *Canadian Business English* has been its questions and answers patterned on those from grammar hotline services. These questions—and the answers to them—illustrate everyday communication problems encountered in the work world. In easy-to-read question-and-answer format, the text explains important distinctions in English grammar, usage, style, and vocabulary.

LEARNING OBJECTIVES

Concisely stated learning objectives introduce each chapter. These overtly stated goals summarize the concepts to be presented and facilitate learning by stimulating a student mindset favourable to the learning process.

PRETESTS AND POSTTESTS

Each chapter includes a pretest to preview concepts and to pique student interest. Chapters also provide a posttest to enable students to evaluate their achievement. Answers appear at the back of the book.

SELF-CHECK EXERCISES AND UNIT REVIEWS

The first student exercise in each level of each chapter is self-checked. Students are thereby able to determine immediately whether they comprehend the concepts just presented. At the end of each unit, a self-checked review exercise enables students to test their mastery of the unit. Answers appear at the back of the book.

EDITOR'S CHALLENGE

The Editor's Challenge exercises are packed with grammar and mechanics errors that cover many concepts presented in the textbook. In addition, these editing exercises include spelling and typographical errors. Revising business documents is an excellent technique for helping students become familiar with document formats and for building spelling and grammar skills. Answers can be found in the Instructor Guide.

WRITING COMPONENT

Sentence-writing exercises conclude each chapter. These skill-building opportunities encourage students to apply chapter principles in forming complete sentences. Optional editing and composition unit tests are available in the Instructor Guide, which also includes ideas for incorporating this writing program into the business English course.

SPELLING AND VOCABULARY

For students who desire them and for instructors who have time to include them, optional spelling and vocabulary development materials appear in separate appendixes. Answers to questions in Appendix B: Developing Vocabulary Skills appear at the back of the book.

SELF-HELP EXERCISES

Because business English students need many opportunities to try out their learning, supplementary self-paced exercises for all levels of all chapters appear at the back of the book, along with the exercise answers. This self-help section has perforated pages and its own table of contents so that it can be separated from the text as a supplementary resource.

MARGINAL ANNOTATIONS

Interesting marginal annotations continue to provide stimulus to our students.

Student Resources in the Text

STUDY TIP Memory devices and learning suggestions appear as study tips. They help students understand and retain the many language principles they will be reviewing.

CAREER TIP These tips suggest applications and practical career advice that relate language concepts to students' needs on the job.

BE THE EDITOR To provide comic relief from the sometimes heavy load of grammar and mechanics, these published bloopers demonstrate common language errors and help students understand how faulty expression can destroy a message.

DID YOU KNOW? These tidbits relate interesting trivia to *Canadian Business English* concepts.

Unparalleled Supplements and Instructor Support

Canadian Business English includes a number of supplements to help students learn and instructors teach. Cengage provides the best support for business communication in Canada.

The following instructor resources have been created for *Canadian Business English*, Eighth Edition. Access these ultimate tools for customizing lectures and presentations at **login.cengage.com.**

TEST BANK

This resource was created by Jean Mills and includes over 1,000 multiple-choice and true/false questions written according to guidelines for effective construction and development of higher-order questions.

The Test Bank is available on a cloud-based platform. **Testing Powered by Cognero®** is a secure online testing system that allows instructors to author, edit, and manage test bank content from anywhere Internet access is available. No special installations or downloads are needed, and the desktop-inspired interface, with its drop-down menus and familiar, intuitive tools, allows instructors to create and manage tests with ease. Multiple test versions can be created in an instant, and content can be imported or exported into other systems. Tests can be delivered from a learning management system, the classroom, or wherever an instructor chooses. Testing Powered by Cognero for *Canadian Business English*, Eighth Edition, can also be accessed through **login.cengage.com**.

POWERPOINT®

Microsoft® PowerPoint® lecture slides were revised and updated by Brandon Reece of Sheridan College. There is an average of 50 slides per chapter. Principles of clear design and engaging content have been incorporated throughout, making it simple for instructors to customize the deck for their courses.

INSTRUCTOR GUIDE WITH SOLUTIONS

This resource was updated and revised by author Cathy Witlox of the Chang School at Ryerson University. It is organized according to the textbook chapters and addresses key educational concerns, such as typical stumbling blocks students face and how to address them. The instructor guide also includes solutions and other features to assist instructors in making the most of their classroom time.

MINDTAP

MindTap is the digital learning solution that powers students from memorization to mastery. It gives instructors complete control of their course—to provide engaging content, challenge every individual, and build student confidence. Instructors can customize interactive syllabi to emphasize priority topics as well as add their own material or notes to the ebook as desired. This outcome-driven application gives instructors the tools needed to empower students and boost both understanding and performance.

Cengage
MINDTAP

Student Ancillaries

Modern students require modern solutions. MindTap is a flexible all-in-one teaching and learning platform that includes the full ebook, a customizable learning path, and various course-specific activities that drive student engagement and critical thinking. For the eighth edition of *Canadian Business English*, all textbook exercises have been fully digitized in MindTap so that students can work directly within the ebook. Additional homework and practice exercises have been added to the Learning Path to increase opportunities for students to practise and master the various grammatical concepts.

DOWNLOAD THE CENGAGE MOBILE APP

Get access to a full, interactive ebook, readable online or off; study tools that empower anytime, anywhere learning; and 24/7 course access. The Cengage Mobile app keeps students focused and ready to study whenever it is convenient for them.

Acknowledgments

Teaching business writing and grammar to business professionals has shown me how under-taught these essential skills are in our public education system. People who have studied grammar and business writing in college or university enter today's workforce with a clear advantage. The reality is that workplace technologies expose our communication competencies and deficiencies, so achieving mastery of the written word is more important than ever. This text duly prepares students for that reality.

It has been an honour to follow such strong educators and writers as Mary Ellen Guffey, Carolyn Seefer, and Patricia Burke. I am grateful to Anne-Marie Taylor for putting her trust in me to pick up the baton with the seventh edition and to Alexis Hood and subsequently Lenore Taylor-Atkins for their inspired vision in developing this latest edition. Thanks also to Liisa Kelly, who offered invaluable guidance and encouragement throughout the process. As well, I appreciate copy editor Dawn Hunter's keen eyes and relentless pursuit of consistency. On a personal level, I am grateful to my husband for his patience while I worked on this text while concurrently running my business full-time and also to my employees, who accommodated me when I needed time to write.

The modern textbook is more than just a textbook. It is a system of learning comprising several components—the text, the MindTap website, the Instructor Guide, the Test Bank, the PowerPoint slides, and more. To everyone who contributed to the creation of the supplementary materials, including Jean Mills and Brandon Reece, who revised the materials for this edition, thank you for your efforts in staying true to the text. And to the reviewers of the current and previous edition, the educators who use it and know it best—Maureen Antonio, SIAST; Marina Arkley, Seneca College; Chelsa Budd, SIAST; Janet Charron, Red River College; Nicole Davis, Okanagan College; Lisa Deighan, New Brunswick Community College; Candice Dyck, College of New Caledonia; Edie Lowes, Okanagan College; Maxine Macmillan, New Brunswick Community College; and Sylvia Vrh-Zoldos, Centennial College—I appreciate your valuable insights and hope you find that the eighth edition's revisions further enrich your classroom experience.

Cathy Witlox

INTRODUCTION AND PRETEST

Canadian Business English is the study of the language fundamentals needed to communicate effectively in today's workplace. These basics include grammar, usage, punctuation, capitalization, number style, and spelling. Because business people must express their ideas clearly and correctly, such language basics are critical.

Why Study Business English?

What you learn in this class will help you communicate more professionally when you write and when you speak. These skills will help you get the job you want, succeed in the job you have, or prepare for promotion to a better position. Good communication skills can also help you succeed in the classroom and in your personal life, but we will be most concerned with workplace applications.

Increasing Emphasis on Workplace Communication

In today's workplace you can expect to be doing more communicating than ever before. You will be participating in meetings and webinars, writing business documents and presentations, and using email, instant messaging, and videoconferencing to communicate with others. It's possible that you will telecommute: you may work from a satellite office or from home and conduct all your business remotely, mostly through the Internet. Communication skills, therefore, are more important than they were for previous generations, and the emphasis on writing in particular has increased dramatically. Misspelled words, poor grammar, sloppy punctuation—all of these faults stand out glaringly when they are in print or displayed online. Not only are people writing more, but their messages are seen by larger and larger audiences. Because of the growing emphasis on information exchange, language skills are more relevant today than ever before.

What Does This Mean for You?

As a business person or professional, you will want to feel confident about your writing skills. This textbook and this course can sharpen your skills and greatly increase your confidence in expressing ideas. Improving your language skills is the first step toward success in your education, your career, and your life.

NAME ____________________

PRETEST

In the following sentences, errors in grammar, punctuation, capitalization, or number expression may appear. In each sentence underline any error(s). Then write a corrected form in the space provided. Write *C* if a sentence is correct. *Clue:* One sentence at each level is correct.

Example: The inheritance will be given to my brother and myself on our twenty-first birthdays. ____me____

LEVEL I

1. In today's organizations teams play an increasingly important role, employees must learn to work together. ____________
2. The May 10, 202x edition of the newsletter featured an interview with our CEO. ____________
3. The announcement from our Human Resources Department surprised the other employees as much as I. ____________
4. We were given no notice of your joining us for the event. ____________
5. A list with all our customers' names and addresses were given to the manager and her last week. ____________
6. Every field employee, as well as every manager and certified employee, are eligible for sales discounts. ____________
7. Thank you Margaret for your excellent service to our firm over the past twenty-two years. ____________
8. Under the circumstances, we can give you only 90 days time in which to sell the house and its contents. ____________
9. We normally hire only experienced operators; but we occasionally consider well-trained individuals who lack experience. ____________
10. In the fall Lisa took courses in history, french, and accounting. ____________

LEVEL II

1. More than 500 customers names and confidential information were revealed when hackers broke into the computer records. ________________
2. Either Martin or she will be working at the shop the next two Sunday's. ________________
3. Of the eighty-six email messages he received, Ahmoud said that only nine were legitimate. ________________
4. The candidate hired for the position will report to the District Manager. ________________
5. No one has yet took responsibility for leaving the warehouse door unlocked. ________________
6. Chapter 15, which is titled "Credit Buying," is one of the best chapters in *Today's Consumer.* ________________
7. Before her trip down East last summer, my mother bought a Sony Camera. ________________
8. We need at least one hundred eighty-cent postage stamps. ________________
9. Either the department manager or one of her direct reports are going to work more closely with the intern. ________________
10. I feel badly about your missing the deadline, but the application has been lying on your desk for 15 days. ________________

LEVEL III

1. The award will go to whomever gains the most new business during the fiscal year. ________________
2. All job applicants must comply to the rules printed in our employee handbook. ________________
3. Montréal is larger than any city in Québec. ________________
4. The number of units shipped each month are steadily increasing. ________________
5. The school's alumni are certainly different than its currently enrolled students. ________________
6. Astrid is one of those efficient, competent managers who is able to give sincere praise for work done well. ________________
7. Because she looks like her sister, Mary is often taken to be her. ________________
8. If I was he, I would call the Harrises' lawyer at once. ________________
9. The company only promoted one employee last year. ________________
10. It was definitely she who left the package on the boss's desk. ________________

UNIT 1

Laying a Foundation

CHAPTER 1
Parts of Speech

CHAPTER 2
Sentences: Elements, Patterns, and Faults

CHAPTER

1

PARTS OF SPEECH

OBJECTIVES

When you have completed the materials in this chapter, you will be able to do the following:

- Define the eight parts of speech
- Recognize how parts of speech function in sentences
- Compose sentences showing words playing more than one grammatical role

PRETEST

Study the following sentence and identify the selected parts of speech. Underline the correct part of speech. Compare your answers with those provided on page 526.

We routinely review the services that we offer to customers.

1.	*We*	(a) noun	(b) conjunction	(c) pronoun	(d) adjective
2.	*routinely*	(a) noun	(b) adverb	(c) verb	(d) adjective
3.	*review*	(a) preposition	(b) conjunction	(c) verb	(d) adverb
4.	*the*	(a) adjective	(b) conjunction	(c) preposition	(d) adverb
5.	*services*	(a) interjection	(b) conjunction	(c) verb	(d) noun
6.	*that*	(a) adjective	(b) conjunction	(c) verb	(d) adverb
7.	*we*	(a) noun	(b) pronoun	(c) adjective	(d) adverb
8.	*offer*	(a) verb	(b) adjective	(c) noun	(d) adverb
9.	*to*	(a) adjective	(b) conjunction	(c) preposition	(d) adverb
10.	*customers*	(a) adjective	(b) verb	(c) pronoun	(d) noun

The study of professional-level English logically begins with the eight parts of speech, the building blocks of our language. This chapter provides a brief overview of the parts of speech; the chapters that follow deal with specific parts of speech in greater detail.

CAREER TIP

"Whatever your program in college, be sure to include courses in writing and speaking. Managers must constantly write instructions, reports, memos, letters, and survey conclusions. If this comes hard to you, it will hold you back."
— James A. Newman and Alexander Roy in *Climbing the Corporate Matterhorn*

THE EIGHT PARTS OF SPEECH

Learning the eight parts of speech helps you develop the working vocabulary necessary to discuss and study the language. (You will find these terms and others that are boldfaced throughout the text briefly defined in the glossary starting on page 533.) You need to recognize the parts of speech in the context of sentences especially because many words function in more than one role. Only by analyzing the sentence at hand can you see how a given word functions. Although you probably won't need to identify parts of speech in the workplace, being able to do so will help you avoid grammatical errors, punctuate correctly, choose the most suitable words, and feel confident about your writing. Using the parts of speech correctly will also help you sound more professional and intelligent on the job.

Nouns

In elementary school you probably learned that **nouns** are the names of persons, places, and things. In addition, though, nouns name qualities, concepts, and activities.

Persons:	Maria, Chief Youngblood, sister, trainer
Places:	Canada, Charlottetown, college, park
Things:	chair, invoice, Skechers, motorcycle
Qualities:	dependability, honesty, initiative, warmth
Concepts:	knowledge, freedom, friendship, happiness
Activities:	eating, reading, gaming, management

BE THE EDITOR

Advice from a Canadian telephone company booklet: "Hang up if the caller . . . doesn't identify themself to your satisfaction."

Nouns are important words in our language. Sentences revolve around nouns since these words function both as subjects and as objects of verbs. To determine whether a word is a noun, try using it with the verb *is* (for a singular noun) or *are* (for a plural noun). Notice that all the nouns listed above make sense if used this way: *Maria is young; Charlottetown is in Canada; honesty is important; reading is my favourite hobby;* and so on. In Chapters 3 and 4, you will learn more about nouns.

Question:
My colleague insists that the word *his* is an adjective when it is used in an expression such as *his* car. I learned that *his* is a pronoun. What is it?

Answer:
Although most people consider words such as *his, her, our, your, their,* and *its* to be pronouns, when these words describe nouns, they are functioning as adjectives. Your colleague is right.

Pronouns

Pronouns are words used in place of nouns. As substitutes for nouns, they provide your writing with variety and efficiency. Compare these two versions of the same sentence:

Without pronouns:	Ferenah gave the book to John so that John could use the book to study.
With pronouns:	Ferenah gave the book to John so that he could use it to study.

In sentences pronouns may function as subjects (for example, *I, we, they*) or as objects (*me, us, them*). They may show possession (*mine, ours, his*), and they may act as connectors (*that, which, who*). These are only a few examples. More examples, along with functions and classifications of pronouns, will be presented in Chapters 5 and 6.

Verbs

Verbs express an action, an occurrence, or a state of being. Some action verbs are *run, study, work,* and *dream.* Verbs that join descriptive words to the subject are called "state of being" or "linking" verbs. The most common of these is the verb *be,* which takes the forms *am, is, are, was, were, be, being,* and *been.* Other linking verbs express the senses: *feel, appear, taste, sound, seem, look,* and *smell.*

Verbs will be discussed more fully in Chapters 7 through 10. At this point it is important that you be able to recognize verbs so that you can determine whether sentences are complete. All complete sentences have at least one verb; many sentences have more than one verb. Verbs may be single words or phrases. In verb phrases helping verbs are added.

Stacy *submitted* her application to become a management trainee. (Action verb)
It *is* the newest device on the market. (Linking verb)
I *feel* bad because Karen *worked* so late last night. (Linking verb and action verb)
Our company *will be installing* a new computer system soon. (Action verb in verb phrase; helping verbs are *will* and *be*)

Note that the forms of the verbs indicate tense or time. For example, *submitted* shows past and *is* shows present time.

STUDY TIP

To test whether a word is a verb, try using it with a noun or pronoun: *George eats, she seemed, it was. He food* doesn't make sense because *food* is not a verb.

Adjectives

Adjectives are words that describe nouns or pronouns. They often answer the questions *What kind?, How many?,* or *Which one?* The adjectives in the following sentences are italicized. Observe that the adjectives all answer questions about the nouns or pronouns that they describe.

Small, independent businesses can succeed with *hard* work. (What kinds of businesses? What kind of work?)
We have *fourteen* franchises in *four* provinces. (How many franchises? How many provinces?)
That chain of hotels started as *a small* operation. (Which chain? What kind of operation?)
He is *energetic* and *forceful,* and she is *personable* and *outgoing.* (What pronouns do these adjectives describe?)

Adjectives usually precede nouns. They may, however, follow the nouns or pronouns they describe, especially when used with linking verbs, as in the last example above. Here are a few more examples of words used as adjectives:

bad	French	Métis	successful
effective	helpless	new	terrific
excellent	long	profitable	various

Three words—*a, an,* and *the*—form a special group of adjectives called **articles**. *A* and *an* are called *indefinite articles* because they refer to any one of the item identified. *The* is a *definite article,* used when readers or listeners know which specific item is meant.

We are looking to hire a stylist. (Which stylist is not yet known.)
The stylist we hired has proven very popular with clients. (*The* is used to refer to a specific stylist.)

More information on adjectives appears in Chapter 11.

STUDY TIP

Words such as *his, my,* and *its* are classified as adjectives when they describe nouns (*his car, my desk, its engine*).

STUDY TIP

Articles (*a, an, the*) are sometimes called "noun markers" because they identify, or mark, nouns. Articles are always followed by a noun or noun phrase.

Adverbs

Adverbs are words that describe verbs, adjectives, or other adverbs. Adverbs often answer the questions *When?*, *How?*, *Where?*, or *To what extent?*

> *Today* we must begin work. (Must begin *when*?)
> Mohammed proceeded *rapidly* with the orders. (Proceeded *how*?)
> He seemed *exceedingly* happy. (*How* happy?)
> Did you see the schedule *there?* (*Where*?)
> The prosecutor questioned him *further*. (Questioned him *to what extent*?)

Some commonly used adverbs follow:

after	greatly	often	really
carefully	here	only	too
easily	now	rather	very

Most, but not all, words ending in *ly* are adverbs. Common exceptions are *friendly*, *costly*, and *ugly*, all of which are adjectives.

More information on adverbs appears in Chapter 11.

Prepositions

Prepositions join nouns and pronouns to other words in a sentence. As the word itself suggests (*pre* means "before"), a preposition is a word in a position *before* its object. (The object of a preposition is a noun or pronoun.) The term **prepositional phrase** signifies a group of two words or more that begins with a preposition and ends with its object, for example, *with Mr. Li*. Prepositions are used in phrases to show a relationship between the object of the preposition and another word in the sentence. In the following sentence, notice how the preposition changes the relation of the object (*Mr. Li*) to the verb (*talked*):

> Marina often talked *with* Mr. Li.
> Marina often talked *about* Mr. Li.
> Marina often talked *to* Mr. Li.

Some of the most frequently used prepositions are *at*, *by*, *for*, *from*, *in*, *of*, *to*, and *with*. A more extensive list of prepositions can be found in Chapter 12 (p. 224). Learn to recognize objects of prepositions so that you won't confuse them with sentence subjects.

Conjunctions

Conjunctions are words that connect other words or groups of words. The most common conjunctions are *and*, *but*, *or*, and *nor*. These are called *coordinating conjunctions* because they join grammatically equal (coordinate) parts of sentences. More information on coordinating conjunctions appears in Chapter 13; other kinds of conjunctions are presented in Chapter 14. Study the examples of coordinating conjunctions shown here:

> Koshi, Bill, *and* Amber are looking for jobs. (Joins grammatically equal words)
> You may be interviewed by a personnel officer *or* by a supervising manager. (Joins grammatically equal groups of words)

CAREER TIP

To sound professional, credible, and objective, most writers avoid interjections and exclamation marks in business and professional messages.

Interjections

Interjections are words that express strong feelings. Interjections standing alone are followed by exclamation marks. When woven into a sentence, they are usually followed by commas.

> *Wow*! Did you see the total of our bill?
> *Well*, I guess that means the meeting is over.

SUMMARY

The sentence below illustrates all eight parts of speech.

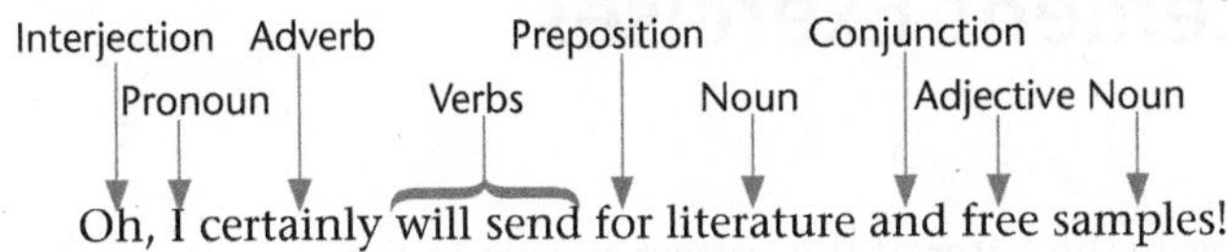

Oh, I certainly will send for literature and free samples!

You need to know the functions of these eight parts of speech so that you will be able to understand the rest of this textbook and profit from your study of English fundamentals. The explanation of the parts of speech has been kept simple so far. This chapter is meant to serve as an introduction to later, more fully developed explorations of each of the parts of speech.

A word of caution: English is a wonderfully flexible language. As we noted earlier, many words in our language serve as more than one part of speech. Notice how flexible the word *mail* is in these sentences:

Our *mail* is late today. (Noun—serves as subject of sentence)
The knight's suit of *mail* protected him. (Noun—serves as object of preposition *of*)
Mail the letter today. (Verb—serves as action word in sentence)
Your *mail* slot is full. (Adjective—used here to describe *slot*, a noun that is subject of sentence)

Now complete the reinforcement exercises for this chapter on pages 8–11.

NAME ____________________

CHAPTER 1 ■ Reinforcement Exercises

A. (**Self-check**) Complete these statements. Write the letter of the correct answer in the space provided.

1. Words that describe nouns and pronouns are
(a) verbs (b) adjectives (c) adverbs (d) pronouns ________

2. Words that have the same functions as and often substitute for nouns are
(a) pronouns (b) interjections (c) adjectives (d) conjunctions ________

3. The part of speech that answers the questions *How?* and *When?* is a/an
(a) adverb (b) adjective (c) interjection (d) conjunction ________

4. Names for persons, places, things, qualities, concepts, and activities are
(a) pronouns (b) adjectives (c) nouns (d) verbs ________

5. *I, us, they,* and *hers* are examples of
(a) nouns (b) pronouns (c) verbs (d) adverbs ________

6. Words that connect words or groups of words are
(a) interjections (b) prepositions (c) adjectives (d) conjunctions ________

7. Words that express an action, an occurrence, or a state of being are
(a) verbs (b) adverbs (c) nouns (d) interjections ________

8. *Wow, well,* and *oh* are examples of
(a) conjunctions (b) adverbs (c) pronouns (d) interjections ________

9. *Beautiful, small, three,* and *shiny* are examples of
(a) nouns (b) verbs (c) adjectives (d) adverbs ________

10. Words such as *by, in,* and *of* that show the relationship of noun or pronoun objects to other words in sentences are
(a) adverbs (b) prepositions (c) interjections (d) adjectives ________

11. Pronouns are often used in place of
(a) prepositions (b) verbs (c) nouns (d) adjectives ________

12. What part of speech might come at the end of a prepositional phrase?
(a) noun or pronoun (b) adjective (c) interjection (d) preposition ________

Check your answers.

B. In each of the following sentences, identify the parts of speech of the underlined words. Keep in mind how each part of speech functions.

1. The boardroom hasn't been used for weeks because of a leak in the ceiling. ____________________

____

____

TEAR HERE

2. Clients often comment on our receptionist's friendly and outgoing nature. ______

______

______

3. We have determined that three new hires are needed. ______

______

______

4. The company is researching how to make its products environmentally safe. ______

______

______

5. My meeting with her ended when the fire alarm sounded. ______

______

______

6. The First Nation hosted a competition powwow. ______

______

______

C. In each of the following groups of sentences, one word is used as an adjective, as a noun, and as a verb. For each sentence indicate the part of speech of the italicized word.

EXAMPLE: Much *work* must be done. noun

Can you *work* overtime? verb

We need two *work* orders. adjective

1. At the *end* of the meeting, the vice president will make an announcement. ______

   The report should *end* with a summary. ______

   The *end* unit will be available next month. ______

2. Please *park* in the lot behind the building. ______

   Park visitors must sign in. ______

   The industrial *park* has two units available. ______

3. Several *test* fabrics were sent for trial. ______

   The human resources manager will have you write a *test*. ______

   We will *test* the new products in the field. ______

TEAR HERE

4. The Hamilton manufacturing *plant* will close during the expansion. ________________

The *plant* manager needs to hire two more supervisors. ________________

As part of its commitment to the environment, the company will *plant* 200 trees. ________________

5. *Report* numbers suggest that sales will increase over the next year. ________________

The sales team will *report* their projected sales volumes quarterly. ________________

Have you read the annual *report* yet? ________________

6. Write complete sentences using the word *file* as the part of speech indicated.

(noun) ____

(adjective) ____

(verb) ____

7. Write complete sentences using the word *cover* as the part of speech indicated.

(noun) ____

(adjective) ____

(verb) ____

D. Read the following sentences. Taking into account the function of the words within each sentence, identify the part of speech of each word shown. Use a dictionary if necessary.

On behalf of her team, the sales manager humbly accepted an award for customer service.

On	________	the	________	an	________
behalf	________	sales	________	award	________
of	________	manager	________	for	________
her	________	humbly	________	customer	________
team	________	accepted	________	service	________

The pharmaceutical company now markets medical and recreational marijuana.

The	________	now	________	and	________
pharmaceutical	________	markets	________	recreational	________
company	________	medical	________	marijuana	________

The local newspaper surveyed community members, and they enthusiastically nominated our team.

The	________	community	________	enthusiastically	________
local	________	members	________	nominated	________
newspaper	________	and	________	our	________
surveyed	________	they	________	team	________

TEAR HERE

E. In each of the following sentences, identify the verb. Each sentence contains only one verb. As an added challenge, try to identify whether the verb is an action verb or a linking verb.

1. Hélène's colleague attended the webinar in her place. ______
2. The parts order arrived late for the second week in a row. ______
3. Managers from across Canada travelled to Montréal for the training. ______
4. The software for the 3-D photocopier looks easy enough to learn. ______
5. The Internet team hosted a lunch-and-learn event for other employees. ______
6. At the end of each month, Accounting needs our business receipts. ______
7. The panelists have nameplates on the table at the front of the conference room. ______
8. The building is currently under renovation. ______
9. Showtime Audio installed a new sound system for the event. ______
10. Make a good first impression at a job interview by looking professional. ______
11. The seats with gift bags are for special guests of the company's president. ______
12. The redesign of the vehicle's instrument panel certainly improved sales. ______

F. **Writing Exercise.** Complete this exercise on a separate sheet.

Write eight sentences, one to illustrate each of the parts of speech: noun, pronoun, verb, adjective, adverb, conjunction, preposition, and interjection. Identify each part of speech by labelling it at the beginning of the sentence and underlining it within the sentence.

EXAMPLES: Noun: I read the article and wrote a summary.

Pronoun: It was a difficult assignment.

POSTTEST

Identify the parts of speech in this sentence by underlining the correct choice. Compare your answers with those on page 526.

Because the building elevator was often broken, our office moved.

1.	Because	(a) adverb	(b) adjective	(c) verb	(d) conjunction
2.	the	(a) pronoun	(b) interjection	(c) adjective	(d) conjunction
3.	building	(a) adverb	(b) verb	(c) preposition	(d) adjective
4.	elevator	(a) noun	(b) pronoun	(c) adjective	(d) verb
5.	was	(a) verb	(b) conjunction	(c) interjection	(d) adjective
6.	often	(a) verb	(b) adverb	(c) noun	(d) adjective
7.	broken	(a) pronoun	(b) verb	(c) noun	(d) adjective
8.	our	(a) adverb	(b) adjective	(c) preposition	(d) interjection
9.	office	(a) adjective	(b) adverb	(c) noun	(d) verb
10.	moved	(a) adverb	(b) verb	(c) pronoun	(d) noun

TEAR HERE

EDITOR'S CHALLENGE

To develop your vocabulary skills, supply a single word for each space in the following memo and letter. The word you supply should represent the part of speech shown.

TO: Caitlyn Abernathy
FROM: Kumar Nugral
DATE: March 30, 202x
SUBJECT: Job Specifications for Duty Manager

Caitlyn, as you (verb) ________________ last week, I am summarizing our department's needs (preposition) ________________ filling the position of duty manager.

The duty manager, reporting to the operations manager, assumes the management of the hotel for the duration of his or her shift. The (adjective) ________________ candidate should have a(n) (noun) ________________ in hospitality or a related field. (Adverb) ________________, the incoming duty manager will have at least one year's front-desk (noun) ________________.

Most important in the candidate (verb) ________________ excellent interpersonal and communication skills, a calm demeanour, the (noun) ________________ to solve problems, and supervisory skills. (Adjective) ________________ duty manager is responsible (preposition) ________________ overseeing the work of up to five staff members on (adjective) ________________ shift.

The job can be (adverb) ________________ demanding at times, requiring the candidate to be on his or her feet for up to nine hours.

I look forward to working with (pronoun) ________________ to find the most suitable person for the position, (conjunction) ________________ I appreciate your expertise in (adjective) ________________ search.

TEAR HERE

Alice Evans
Retail Credit Department
Prairie National Bank
P.O. Box 2051
Edmonton, AB T5W 4B3

Dear Ms. Evans:

SUBJECT: Charges to Credit Account #4002-3422-8910-3299

Because of the wide acceptance of the Visa (adjective) ________ card and because (preposition) __________ the low interest rate at your bank, my wife and I became cardholders two (noun) __________ ago. Recently, however, we had a charge to (adjective) __________ account that we would like to discuss (preposition) __________ you.

Between August 7 (conjunction) __________ September 17, we made 12 small purchases. All of (pronoun) __________ were processed without question. When we (verb) __________ our October statement, we were surprised to see a $10 charge for each of these purchases because our account was over the limit. The total charge (verb) __________ $120.

We (adverb) __________ should have been more aware of the limit and the number of charges we made, (conjunction) __________ we assumed that if our transactions received approval, we were still within (adjective) __________ limit. Upon receiving our October statement, we (adverb) __________ called your (noun) __________ and were referred to Mr. Alan Moore. (Pronoun) __________ said he could do nothing because our purchases had been over the limit of the card.

Please (verb) __________ our account, Miss Evans, and reconsider this penalty. Since we have never before exceeded our credit limit and did receive approval for most of the charges, we (verb) __________ that the $120 charge should be removed. We look forward (preposition) __________ a speedy resolution of this problem.

For additional resources, please visit MindTap at login.cengage.com. Cengage | MINDTAP

TEAR HERE

CHAPTER

SENTENCES: ELEMENTS, PATTERNS, AND FAULTS

2

OBJECTIVES

When you have completed the materials in this chapter, you will be able to do the following:

- Recognize subjects and predicates
- Complete sentences in four basic sentence patterns
- Recognize and correct basic sentence faults such as fragments, comma splices, and run-on sentences

PRETEST

In the space provided, write the correct letter(s) to identify each numbered groups of words.

c = correctly punctuated sentence	cs = comma splice
f = fragment	ro = run-on sentence

1. Although employees can choose their start time. ________
2. Carlos works 30 hours this week, Leona works 32. ________
3. Across the street from our office are a coffee shop and a convenience store. ________
4. Some employers monitor their employees' email others do not want to bother. ________
5. Jessica, who was recently hired on a six-month contract. ________
6. Here we are. ________
7. It's a good time to sell gold, you can benefit from the high market prices. ________
8. Whereas the price of gas continued to rise. ________
9. Each employee received a new identification card last week it is needed to use the elevator. ________
10. For example, Canadian professor Wendy Xiao and American professor Timothy Beal. ________

CAREER TIP

You may be worth an additional $5,000 or more to your employer (and to yourself) if you have writing skills, according to one communications expert. Because companies can no longer afford expensive on-site training, employees with already-developed skills are much more valuable to employers.

To be a good writer, you must be able to construct effective sentences. Sentences are groups of words that express complete thoughts. In this chapter you'll review the basic elements of every sentence, and you'll learn to recognize sentence patterns. This knowledge will help you to punctuate sentences correctly and to recognize and correct common sentence faults. The Writer's Workshop following this chapter introduces proofreading marks, which are helpful in revising messages.

SENTENCE ELEMENTS

Sentences consist of two essential elements: subjects and predicates. In addition, sentences must make sense and express a complete idea. When any one of these elements is missing, readers or listeners are confused. To help you better understand the structure of sentences, you'll learn to distinguish between simple and complete subjects and simple and complete predicates.

Subjects

Every sentence must have a subject. A **simple subject** is a noun or pronoun that tells who or what the sentence is about. The **complete subject** of a sentence includes the simple subject and all of its **modifiers** (words that describe or limit).

> *The new manager of the office* received our cooperation. (Simple subject underscored; complete subject italicized.)

Predicates

Every sentence must have a predicate. A **simple predicate** is a verb or verb phrase that tells what the subject is doing or what is being done to the subject. The **complete predicate** includes the verb or verb phrase and its modifiers, objects, and complements.

> New employees in the company *may choose from several benefits packages*. (Simple predicate underscored; complete predicate italicized.)

Simple Subject	**Simple Predicate (Verb)**
All employees of the company	are linked by an intranet.
Several stores downtown	will be having Canada Day sales.
An Alberta pilot program	will have been launched by the end of the year.
Fast-food restaurant owners	conduct traffic counts.
A review of policies and procedures	was performed by an outside auditor.

STUDY TIP

The helping verbs *have*, *be*, and *do* change forms. Be sure that the helping verb agrees with the subject.

Notice in the previous sentences that the verbs may consist of one word (*conduct*) or several (*will be having*). In a verb phrase such as *will have been launched*, the **principal verb** is the final one (*launched*). The other verbs are **helping**, or **auxiliary**, verbs. Helping verbs can be used to identify the time of occurrence of an action (*was* performed), to create emphasis (*did* perform), or to show necessity or possibility (*would* perform). The most frequently used helping verbs are *am, is, are, was, were, been, have, has, had, must, ought to, may, might, can, could, would, should, will, do, does,* and *did*.

Locating Subjects

You can locate the subject in a sentence by asking, *Who or what [predicate]?*

> *Rebecca* wanted out of her dead-end job. (Who wanted out of her dead-end job? *Rebecca*)

Positions in many companies are advertised online. (What are advertised online? *Positions*)

Don't be misled by prepositional phrases. Subjects are not found in such phrases.

In many companies *employees* must be promoted from within. (Who must be promoted from within? *Employees*. Ignore the prepositional phrase *In many companies*.)

After January 1 *applicants* for all jobs must submit their résumés by email. (Who must submit their résumés by email? *Applicants*. Ignore the prepositional phrases *After January 1* and *for all jobs*.

Sentences may have multiple subjects joined by the conjunctions *and*, *or*, or *nor*.

The *manager* or his *assistant* will conduct the training. (Who will conduct the training? *Manager* or *assistant*)

Artwork, *paint*, and *plants* are great ways to bring colour into an office. (What are great ways to bring colour into an office? *Artwork*, *paint*, and *plants*)

Neither the *boardroom* nor the *break room* is large enough to seat that many people. (What is not large enough to seat that many people? *Boardroom* nor *break room*)

Although a sentence subject usually appears before a verb, there are three instances in which the verb may precede the subject: (1) inverted sentences, (2) sentences beginning with *there* or *here*, and (3) questions.

First on the program was *Jeffrey*. (In this inverted sentence the verb *was* precedes the subject *Jeffrey*.)

There are many *jobs* listed online. (Ignore *There*, which cannot function as a sentence subject. Try reading the sentence as follows: *Many jobs are listed online*. Now the subject *jobs* is obvious because the sentence is in its normal order.)

Are the best *jobs* listed online? (To locate the subject, reword this question: *The best jobs are listed online*.)

You'll learn more about locating subjects in Chapter 9.

Sentence Sense

In addition to a subject and a predicate, a group of words must possess one additional element to qualify as a sentence: *The group of words must be complete and make sense*. Observe that two of the groups of words that follow express complete thoughts and make sense; the third does not.

Jean-Paul built his business through personal contacts. (Subject plus predicate making sense = sentence)

Efficient service ensured return business. (Subject plus predicate making sense = sentence)

When Jean-Paul started his own business (Subject plus predicate but NOT making sense = no sentence)

In the third case, a reader or listener senses that the idea expressed is incomplete. We do not have a sentence; instead, we have a fragment.

Sentence Patterns

One way business communicators can add variety to their writing is to use different sentence patterns. Four basic patterns express thoughts in English sentences:

PATTERN NO. 1: SUBJECT–VERB. In the most basic sentence pattern, the verb follows its subject. The sentence needs no additional words to make sense and be complete.

Subject	Verb
We	worked.
Everyone	is studying.
She	might have called.
Employees	should have been informed.

PATTERN NO. 2: SUBJECT–ACTION VERB–OBJECT. When sentences have an object, the pattern is generally subject, action verb, and object.

Objects of action verbs can be direct or indirect. A **direct object** is a noun or pronoun that answers the question *What?* or *Whom?*

Subject	Action Verb	Direct Object	
Most students	brought	supplies.	(Brought *what?*)
The manager	praised	the employees.	(Praised *whom?*)
Mrs. Chartrand	needed	a new car.	(Needed *what?*)

Pattern No. 2 may also employ an **indirect object**, which answers the question *To whom?*, *To what?*, *For whom?*, or *For what?* Notice that a sentence can have both an indirect object and a direct object.

Subject	Action Verb	Indirect Object	Direct Object
Our company	offers	employees	excellent benefits.
Ren	handed	her	a cheque.
The technician	gave	the vehicle	a tune-up.

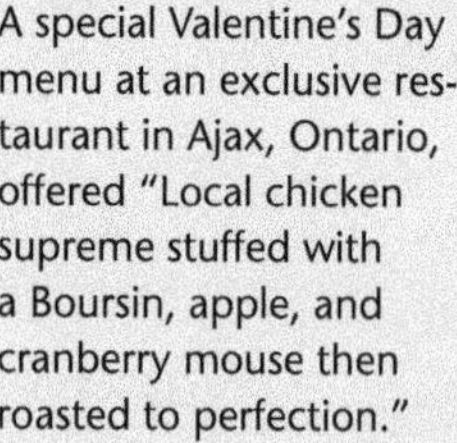
A special Valentine's Day menu at an exclusive restaurant in Ajax, Ontario, offered "Local chicken supreme stuffed with a Boursin, apple, and cranberry mouse then roasted to perfection."

The sentences shown here have been kept simple so that you can recognize their patterns easily. Although most speakers and writers expand these basic patterns with additional phrases and clauses, the basic sentence structure remains the same. Despite its length the following sentence follows the basic subject–action verb–object order:

> Many large *companies*, as well as small companies with sizable real estate holdings, *employ* specialized risk *managers* to handle their insurance problems. (The simple subject is *companies*, the verb is *employ*, and the object of the verb is *managers*.)

PATTERN NO. 3: SUBJECT–LINKING VERB–COMPLEMENT. In Pattern No. 3 the subject comes before a linking verb and its complement. A **complement** is a noun, a pronoun, or an adjective that renames or describes the subject. A complement *completes* the meaning of the subject and always follows a linking verb. Notice that we can often transpose the subject and a noun or pronoun complement without changing the meaning (although by doing so we change the emphasis).

Subject	Linking Verb	Complement	
The author	was	Christine Higdon.	(*Noun complements*)
Christine Higdon	was	the author.	
Our customers	become	friends.	
Your supervisor	is	she.	(*Pronoun complements*)
She	is	your supervisor.	
The callers	might have been	they.	

They	might have been	the callers.	
These data	look	accurate.	(*Adjective complements*)
His report	is	excellent.	

PATTERN NO. 4: INVERTED ORDER. In sentences with **inverted order**, at least one part of the verb comes before the subject.

Sitting in front is Doreen.
Working hardest was the marketing team.

In questions the verb usually comes before the subject or may be interrupted by the subject.

What is the shipment number?
Have the bills been sent?

In sentences beginning with the adverbs *here* or *there*, the word order is also inverted.

Here are the applications.
There was a demand for accountants.

To locate the true subject in any inverted sentence, mentally rearrange the words. Place them in the more common subject–verb order.

Doreen is sitting in front.
The shipment number is what?
The applications are here.

ASK AN EDITOR

Question:
This sentence doesn't sound right to me, but I can't decide how to improve it: *The reason I'm applying is because I enjoy electronics.*

Answer:
The problem lies in this construction: *the reason ... is because.* Only nouns, pronouns, or adjectives may act as complements following linking verbs. In your sentence an adverbial clause follows the linking verb *is.* Instead, substitute a noun clause beginning with *that: The reason I'm applying is that I enjoy electronics.* Better yet, make the sentence a direct statement: *I'm applying because I enjoy electronics.*

SENTENCE FAULTS

To be successful in your career, you must be able to write complete sentences that avoid three common faults: fragments, comma splices, and run-ons. You can eliminate these sentence faults by recognizing them and by applying revision techniques such as the ones described here.

STUDY TIP

In workplace writing you will most often use Patterns 1, 2, and 3 because readers usually want to know the subject first. For variety or emphasis, however, you can use introductory elements and inverted order as in Pattern 4.

Fragments

A **sentence fragment** is an incomplete sentence punctuated as if it were a complete sentence. Fragments are often groups of words that are broken off from sentences preceding or following them. Avoid fragments by making certain that each sentence contains a subject and a verb and makes sense by itself. You can remedy fragments by (a) joining them to complete sentences or (b) adding appropriate subjects and verbs. In the following examples, the fragments are italicized.

Fragment: We're looking for a potential manager. *An individual who can accept responsibility and supervise other employees.*

Revision: We're looking for a potential manager who can accept responsibility and supervise other employees.

Fragment: My research report in business communication took a long time to prepare. *And then turned out badly.*

Revision: My research report in business communication took a long time to prepare and then turned out badly.

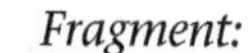

BE THE EDITOR

From a set of bylaws: "Each condominium unit may have a reasonable number of household pets. Which at the desecration of the Association do not create a nuisance to other owners."

Fragment:	*To excel as a knowledge worker in today's digital workplace.* One must know how to find and evaluate information on the Internet.
Revision:	To excel as a knowledge worker in today's digital workplace, one must know how to find and evaluate information on the Internet.

Occasionally, the omission of a small but essential word results in a fragment.

Fragment:	We been looking for an administrative assistant for three weeks. (incomplete verb)
Revision:	We have been looking for an administrative assistant for three weeks.
Fragment:	Sometimes is too cold in our office. (subject missing)
Revision:	Sometimes it is too cold in our office.

Note that commands (imperative sentences) such as *Turn off the photocopier* are not fragments, even though they seem at first glance to have no subject. The subject in all commands is understood to be *you* ([You] turn off the photocopier). Refer to Writer's Workshop for Unit 2, pages 112–118.

Run-On Sentences

A **run-on sentence** fuses two or more complete sentences without punctuation. Run-on sentences can usually be repaired by (a) separating the run-on into two sentences, (b) adding a comma and a conjunction, or (c) adding a semicolon.

Run-On Sentence:	The work ethic in Canada is not dead it is deeply ingrained in most people.
Revision:	The work ethic in Canada is not dead. It is deeply ingrained in most people. (Separate into two sentences.)
Run-On Sentence:	Sachi thought she had passed the exam she was wrong.
Revision:	Sachi thought she had passed the exam, but she was wrong. (Add a comma and a conjunction.)
Run-On Sentence:	Many freelance workers take part in "co-working" this allows them to share office space and socialize with other freelancers.
Revision:	Many freelance workers take part in "co-working"; this allows them to share office space and socialize with other freelancers. (Add a semicolon.)

BE THE EDITOR

From globalnews.ca: "This marks a shift into the spring and summer seasons, our mornings might be darker at first, but in turn we get an extra hour of sunlight just as we're all heading home from work."

You will usually recognize run-on sentences because they are difficult to understand when you proofread. If you are not sure that a group of words is a run-on sentence or you are not sure how to correct it, identifying subjects and verbs can help.

Run-On Sentence:	Every correct sentence must have a subject and verb it must also express a complete thought.
Revision:	Every correct sentence must have a subject and verb. It must also express a complete thought.

(Refer to Writer's Workshop for Unit 2, pp. 112–118.)

Comma Splices

A **comma splice** results when two or more complete sentences are incorrectly joined or spliced together with a comma. A comma alone cannot join two sentences. Comma splices occur far more often than run-on sentences because the pause indicated by the comma makes them easier to read and, therefore, easier to miss during proofreading. Finding a subject and verb combination in each part of the comma splice will help you determine that the group of words contains two complete thoughts:

> Legislation *was enacted* to protect homeowners, victims *will receive* compensation within 90 days.

Comma splices can usually be repaired by (a) adding a conjunction after the comma, (b) separating the comma splice into two sentences, or (c) changing the comma to a semicolon.

Comma Splice:	Muzana is the office manager, Michael is the office assistant.
Revision:	Muzana is the office manager, and Michael is the office assistant. (Add a conjunction.)
Comma Splice:	You must fill one more purchase order, then your work will be finished.
Revision:	You must fill one more purchase order. Then your work will be finished. (Separate into two sentences.)
Comma Splice:	Many applicants responded to our advertisement, however, only one had the required certification.
Revision:	Many applicants responded to our advertisement; however, only one had the required certification. (Change the comma to a semicolon.)

Now complete the reinforcement exercises for this chapter on pages 22–26.

ASK AN EDITOR

Question:
My colleague says that this sentence is correct: *Please complete this survey regarding your satisfaction at our dealership, then return it in the enclosed envelope.* I think something is wrong, but I'm not sure what.

Answer:
You're right! This sentence has two short independent clauses, and the writer attempted to join them with a comma. This construction produces a comma splice. *Then* is an adverb, not a conjunction like *but* or *and*, and cannot join two clauses. You can correct the problem by inserting *and* between the clauses, starting a new sentence, or using a semicolon between the clauses.

NAME ____________________

CHAPTER 2 ■ Reinforcement Exercises

A. (**Self-check**) In the space provided, indicate whether the following statements are true (T) or false (F).

1. In an inverted sentence, the verb comes before the subject. ______
2. A group of words with a subject and a verb is always a complete sentence. ______
3. A run-on sentence can be corrected by inserting a comma. ______
4. Joining two complete sentences with a comma and a conjunction creates a *comma splice.* ______
5. The complete subject of a sentence includes a noun or pronoun and all its modifiers. ______
6. Objects may follow either action verbs or linking verbs. ______
7. The subject of a command or an imperative sentence is always *you.* ______
8. The verb phrase *must have been* is considered to be a linking verb. ______
9. A complement may be a noun, an adjective, or an adverb. ______
10. A comma splice can be corrected by changing the comma to a semicolon. ______
11. In sentences beginning with *there,* the subject comes after the verb. ______
12. A simple predicate is a verb or verb phrase without modifiers. ______

Check your answers.

B. Study the examples shown below. Then fill in the words necessary to complete the four sentence patterns.

Pattern No. 1: Subject–Verb

EXAMPLE: The boss called.

1. The supervisor ____________________.
2. Our department ____________________.
3. Students ____________________.
4. The phone ____________________.
5. The computer ____________________.
6. The email server ____________________.

Pattern No. 2: Subject–Action Verb–Object

EXAMPLE: Administrative assistants use software.

7. Indira answered the ____________________.
8. The report outlines ____________________.
9. Salespeople must record ____________________.
10. The intern has asked ____________________.
11. Students know their ____________________.
12. Lawyers represent ____________________.

TEAR HERE

Pattern No. 3: Subject–Linking Verb–Complement

Fill in noun or pronoun complements.

EXAMPLE: The manager is John.

13. The applicant was ________________.

14. Ms. Beesla may be ________________.

15. The caller could have been ________________.

16. The company president is ________________.

Fill in adjective complements.

EXAMPLE: The salary is fair.

17. Her intentions were ________________.

18. Québec City is ________________.

19. The sales staff was ________________.

20. The report should have been ________________.

Pattern No. 4: Inverted Order

Fill in the missing verb or verb part.

EXAMPLE: Have you seen my stapler?

21. __________ Human Resources distribute the survey?

22. There __________ many options to choose from.

23. __________ in the kitchen is the water cooler.

24. __________ the department recently reorganized?

C. Underline the simple subject (noun or pronoun) once and the simple predicate (verb) twice.

EXAMPLE: She is resigning for personal reasons.

1. The results will be delivered by April 2.
2. Prince George is home to the University of Northern British Columbia.
3. Sales are declining.
4. We will finalize the deal next week.
5. The company has found a replacement for Nica.
6. Beck's Parts may become our new supplier.
7. Andy preferred a handshake to a written contract.
8. The repairs should have been completed already.
9. Excellent communication skills can help you get a job.
10. All interns in our company receive extensive training.

TEAR HERE

D. The following sentences have inverted word order. To help in locating subjects, revise these sentences so that the subject comes first. Then underline the simple subject once and the verb twice.

EXAMPLE: Here are some of the necessary materials. Some of the necessary materials are here.

1. There is no website listed for that organization. ______

2. In Hailun's inbox were nearly 200 emails. ______

3. What is the marketing team working on? ______

4. There were only five board members at Tuesday's meeting. ______

5. Has your support team read the report? ______

6. Where was the computer training held? ______

E. Expand the following sentence fragments into complete sentences.

EXAMPLE: If I had read his speech beforehand, I would have suggested some revisions.

1. By the end of the two-day conference ______.

2. Although I promised to make up the work I'd missed ______.

3. ______ which included flights to Halifax.

4. When a job opens ______.

5. Because I have studied hotel management ______.

6. If the contract terms have been agreed upon ______.

7. ______ so that we will be able to write more effectively in the workplace.

TEAR HERE

8. When visitors enter the building ____

____.

9. ____

and left the office at 2:00 to meet a client.

F. Write the correct letter(s) after each of the following groups of words to indicate whether it represents a correctly punctuated sentence, a fragment, a comma splice, or a run-on sentence.

c = correctly punctuated sentence   cs = comma splice
f = fragment   ro = run-on sentence

EXAMPLE: Because the world seems to be getting smaller. ____f____

1. Anyone doing business in another country should learn what kinds of gifts are expected and under what circumstances to give them. ________
2. The district manager has seven offices to visit in five days, therefore, she will be here for only half a day. ________
3. Although we have a powerful printer capable of producing high-quality graphics. ________
4. Amina wanted a practical spreadsheet program she just didn't know what to purchase. ________
5. In North America, making eye contact is a sign of confidence and sincerity. ________
6. A company newsletter may help keep employees informed, but we may have difficulty getting everyone to read it. ________
7. Some companies may require in-depth personnel investigations. ________
8. Particularly companies that have exceptional security concerns. ________
9. We have tried to collect this account in a friendly manner, our efforts, however, have failed to secure your cooperation. ________
10. Being on time is important in North America in some other countries time is less important. ________
11. Research suggests that stress is associated with ulcers and heart disease. ________
12. Next Monday is Victoria Day, hence all branch offices will be closed. ________
13. Mornings seem to be better than afternoons for catching business executives in their offices. ________
14. Because Canada's dairy industry is protected by a supply-management system that ensures a living wage for dairy farmers. ________
15. The timing is right for expanding into other markets if we have a product that can make an impact. ________
16. The executive teams are finalizing a plan for integration the two companies may both see some layoffs. ________
17. Thank you for your support, the entire neighbourhood benefits from a strong business association. ________

TEAR HERE

18. When the human resources department makes its decision. ______________

For class discussion: In the preceding exercise, how could each of the incorrectly punctuated groups of words be made acceptable?

G. Writing Exercise. Your instructor may ask you to complete this exercise on a separate sheet.

Compose eight original sentences, two for each of the following patterns:

1. Sentence with action verb and object
2. Sentence with linking verb and noun complement
3. Sentence with linking verb and adjective complement
4. Sentence in inverted order

Label each pair of sentences, and underline simple subjects once and verbs twice.

POSTTEST

Write the correct letter(s) after each of the numbered items below.

c = correctly punctuated sentence — cs = comma splice
f = fragment — ro = run-on sentence

1. The computer arrived Monday the printer is expected shortly. ______
2. Down the hall from the director's office sit the sales representatives. ______
3. Since the contract was mailed Monday but not received until late Friday. ______
4. The finance team needs extra help temporarily, otherwise the year-end financial reports will be delayed. ______
5. Because Ahmed, who is one of our best employees, was ill last week. ______
6. For instance, D+H, a multinational company with 5,000 employees in 15 countries. ______
7. The new photocopier works well. ______
8. Earning an average of $7,200 less than their male counterparts, Canadian women are more likely than men to live in poverty, Indigenous women, in particular, are among the most affected by the gender wage gap. ______
9. The online offer was extended through Saturday. ______
10. Simone was in the purchasing division for five years her boss just recommended her for a promotion. ______

TEAR HERE

EDITOR'S CHALLENGE

The following email message contains errors in sentence structure and spelling, as well as other common errors. Make corrections. Your instructor may ask you to read about proofreading marks on page 31 and to use those marks in noting your corrections.

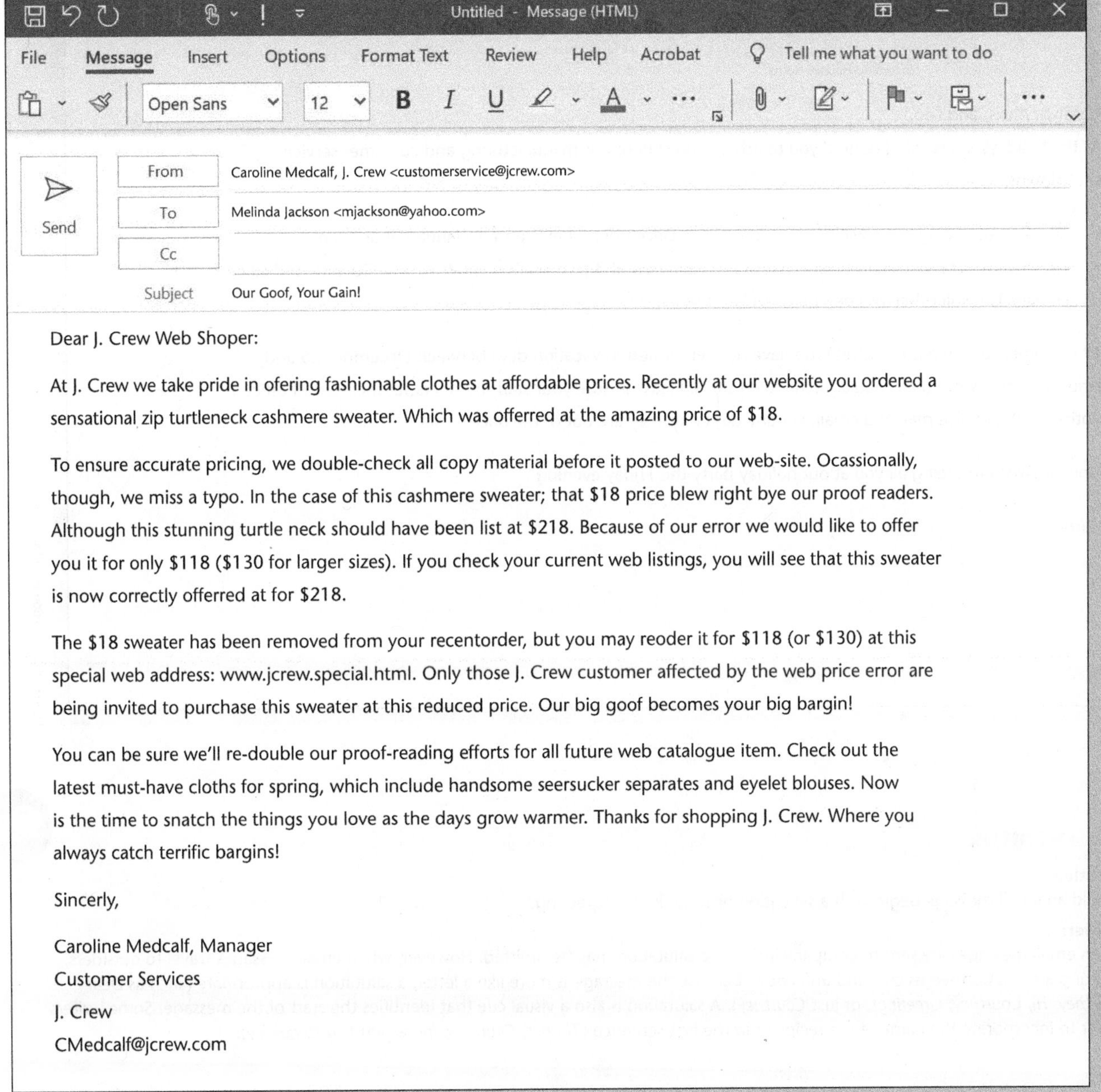

From: Caroline Medcalf, J. Crew <customerservice@jcrew.com>
To: Melinda Jackson <mjackson@yahoo.com>
Cc:
Subject: Our Goof, Your Gain!

Dear J. Crew Web Shoper:

At J. Crew we take pride in ofering fashionable clothes at affordable prices. Recently at our website you ordered a sensational zip turtleneck cashmere sweater. Which was offerred at the amazing price of $18.

To ensure accurate pricing, we double-check all copy material before it posted to our web-site. Ocassionally, though, we miss a typo. In the case of this cashmere sweater; that $18 price blew right bye our proof readers. Although this stunning turtle neck should have been list at $218. Because of our error we would like to offer you it for only $118 ($130 for larger sizes). If you check your current web listings, you will see that this sweater is now correctly offerred at for $218.

The $18 sweater has been removed from your recentorder, but you may reoder it for $118 (or $130) at this special web address: www.jcrew.special.html. Only those J. Crew customer affected by the web price error are being invited to purchase this sweater at this reduced price. Our big goof becomes your big bargin!

You can be sure we'll re-double our proof-reading efforts for all future web catalogue item. Check out the latest must-have cloths for spring, which include handsome seersucker separates and eyelet blouses. Now is the time to snatch the things you love as the days grow warmer. Thanks for shopping J. Crew. Where you always catch terrific bargins!

Sincerely,

Caroline Medcalf, Manager
Customer Services
J. Crew
CMedcalf@jcrew.com

TEAR HERE

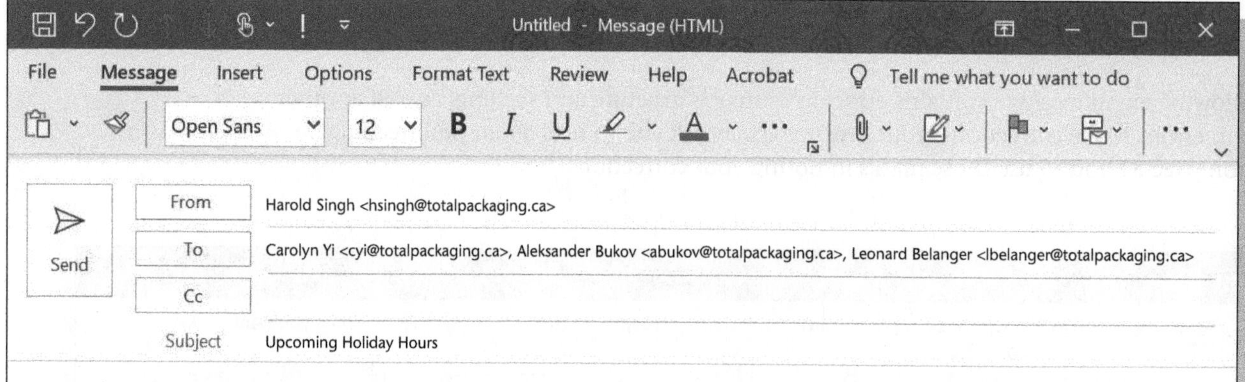
Untitled - Message (HTML)

File Message Insert Options Format Text Review Help Acrobat Tell me what you want to do

From Harold Singh <hsingh@totalpackaging.ca>

To Carolyn Yi <cyi@totalpackaging.ca>, Aleksander Bukov <abukov@totalpackaging.ca>, Leonard Belanger <lbelanger@totalpackaging.ca>

Cc

Subject Upcoming Holiday Hours

Carolyn, Aleks, and Leo,

As the holidays approach, I remind you to advice you staff of our manufacturing and customer service shut-downs.

- All manufactureing shifts will be shut down form December 24 at 3 p.m. to January 4 at 7 a.m.
- The customer service centre will be close December 24 at 3 p.m. to December 27 at 8:30 a.m. and all day January 1, it will otherwise be open regular business hours.

All customer service representives who have not yet requested vacation days between December 26 and January 1 must work their regulary scheduled shifts. Please in sure your staff members set their out of office notice on their voice mail and email. For any days that they are out of the ofice.

I look forword to seeing all you at our holiday party this Friday evening

Harry

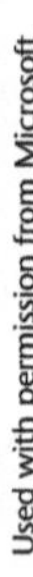

ASK AN EDITOR

Question:
Should an email message begin with a salutation or some kind of greeting?

Answer:
When email messages are sent to company insiders, a salutation may be omitted. However, when email messages travel to outsiders, omitting a salutation seems curt and unfriendly. Because the message is more like a letter, a salutation is appropriate (such as *Dear Courtney; Hi, Courtney; Greetings;* or just *Courtney*). A salutation is also a visual cue that identifies the start of the message. Some writers prefer to incorporate the name of the recipient in the first sentence (*Thanks, Courtney, for responding so quickly*).

TEAR HERE

NAME ______________________

UNIT 1 REVIEW ■ Chapters 1 and 2 (Self-Check)

Begin your review by rereading Chapters 1 and 2. Then check your comprehension of those chapters by completing the exercises that follow. Compare your responses with those provided at the end of the book, page 531.

Read the following sentence carefully. In the spaces provided, identify the parts of speech for the words as they are used in this sentence.

He glanced at the numbers and then announced his relief.

1. *He*	(a) noun	(b) pronoun	(c) adjective	(d) adverb	______
2. *glanced*	(a) conjunction	(b) preposition	(c) verb	(d) adverb	______
3. *at*	(a) conjunction	(b) preposition	(c) adjective	(d) adverb	______
4. *the*	(a) noun	(b) pronoun	(c) adjective	(d) adverb	______
5. *numbers*	(a) noun	(b) pronoun	(c) adjective	(d) adverb	______
6. *and*	(a) noun	(b) pronoun	(c) conjunction	(d) preposition	______
7. *then*	(a) noun	(b) adverb	(c) conjunction	(d) preposition	______
8. *announced*	(a) verb	(b) adjective	(c) adverb	(d) preposition	______
9. *his*	(a) noun	(b) pronoun	(c) adjective	(d) preposition	______
10. *relief*	(a) noun	(b) pronoun	(c) verb	(d) preposition	______

For each of the following statements, determine the word or phrase that correctly completes that statement. Write its letter in the space provided.

11. In the sentence *Excellent communication skills can benefit you in your job search,* the verb is (a) Excellent, (b) communication skills, (c) can benefit, (d) you. ______

12. In the sentence *Here are the requested files,* the simple subject is (a) Here, (b) are, (c) requested, (d) files. ______

13. In the sentence *The applicant for the position was impressive,* the complement is (a) applicant, (b) position, (c) was, (d) impressive. ______

14. In the sentence *We will hire her for the job,* the verb is (a) will, (b) hire, (c) will hire, (d) job. ______

15. In the sentence *All invoices have been paid in full,* the words *in full* constitute a (a) prepositional phrase, (b) complete predicate, (c) complete subject, (d) noun phrase. ______

16. In the sentence *She looked unwell,* the word *looked* is considered a(n) (a) linking verb, (b) helping verb, (c) action verb, (d) subject. ______

TEAR HERE

17. The sentence *She visited the head office last week* represents what sentence pattern? (a) subject–verb, (b) subject–action verb–object, (c) subject–linking verb–complement, (d) subject–linking verb–object. ____________

18. In the sentence *Alistair's manager was absent from the meeting,* the complement is a(n) (a) noun, (b) pronoun, (c) adjective, (d) adverb. ____________

From the list below, select the letter or letters that describe each of the following groups of words. Write it in the space provided.

c = complete sentence f = fragment cs = comma splice ro = run-on sentence

19. Ryan works part-time during the school year, however, he plans to work full-time over the summer. ____________

20. Therefore, the forms must still be filled out. ____________

21. We turned on our computers when we arrived, and we left them on all day. ____________

22. Whatever you need us to do. ____________

23. Many employees have signed up for the in-service training, it is scheduled for February 16. ____________

24. Although the power was off for only six minutes. ____________

25. Complete the form and send it with your cheque. ____________

26. Our corporate headquarters will be moved next year then we expect to be transferred. ____________

27. The letter arrived today, the package should be here next week. ____________

28. Some employers weigh education and grades heavily, others focus more on experience. ____________

29. Sign and return the contract we will be in touch once we receive it. ____________

ASK AN EDITOR REVIEW

Select the word or phrase that correctly completes each statement, and write its letter in the space provided.

30. In the sentence *Please refer all your questions to her,* the word *her* is (a) a pronoun, (b) an adjective. ____________

31. In the sentence *We haven't yet processed his order,* the word *his* is (a) a pronoun, (b) an adjective. ____________

32. The account manager wants to schedule a product demonstration (a), then (b); then he hopes we will place an order. ____________

33. The reason I am late is (a) because, (b) that my car stalled. ____________

34. An email message should (a) always, (b) never, (c) sometimes begin with a salutation. ____________

TEAR HERE

WRITER'S WORKSHOP

DEVELOPING PROOFREADING SKILLS

As you complete each unit, you will find a workshop exercise that introduces various techniques to help you improve your writing skills. This first workshop emphasizes proofreading skills. You will learn about proofreading marks, which are often used to edit printed material. Study the basic symbols shown here. See the inside front cover of your textbook for a more comprehensive list.

≡ Capitalize	Insert apostrophe	Insert period
Delete	Insert comma	/ Lowercase
∧ Insert	Insert hyphen	Close up space

EXAMPLE

Proof reading marks areused by writers an editors too make corrections and revisions in printed copy they use these Standard Marks for clarity and consistency. If you are revising your own work Youll probable use these mark only occasional. In many jobs today however you will be working in a team environment. Where writing tasks are shared. Thats when its important to able to aply these well known marks correctly.

PRACTICE

Now it's your turn! Use the proofreading marks above to edit the following email message. You will insert ten proofreading marks.

Sol,

The meeting agenda is attached, we will begin at 9 a.m. in the executive boardroom on the ninth floor. You and your team should plan to spend most of day. Ill order in lunch.

We look foward to presenting out new products to you we are confident you will find them to meet the needs of your market. And to be at a fair price point.

TEAR HERE

PROOFREADING TIPS

- Use your computer's spell-checker, but do not rely on it solely. It often can't tell the difference, for example, between *effect* and *affect* and many other confusing words.
- Look for grammar and punctuation errors. As you complete this book, you'll become more alert to common problem areas, such as subject–verb agreement and comma placement.
- Double-check names and numbers. Compare all names and numbers with their sources because inaccuracies are not always immediately visible. Verify the spelling of the names of individuals receiving the message. Many people immediately dislike someone who misspells their name.
- When proofreading long or especially important documents that you've written, always print a copy (preferably double-spaced), set it aside for at least a day, and then proofread it when you are fresh.
- Be prepared to find errors. One student confessed, "I can find other people's errors, but I can't seem to locate my own." Psychologically, we don't *expect* to find errors, and we don't *want* to find them. You can overcome this obstacle by anticipating errors and congratulating, not criticizing, yourself each time you find one.

TEAR HERE

Writing Application 1.1

After you read and edit the letter below, your instructor may ask you to write a similar introductory personal business letter to her or him. On a separate sheet of paper, explain why you enrolled in this class, evaluate your present communication skills, name your field of study, describe the career you seek, and briefly tell about your current work (if you are employed) and your favourite activities. Your instructor may ask you to write a first draft quickly, print it, and then use proofreading marks to show corrections. Make a final copy. Double-space the rough draft; single-space the final copy. Turn in both copies. See Appendix C for a model personal business letter.

The following personal business letter contains errors in typing, spelling, capitalization, and sentence punctuation. Use proofreading marks to edit this letter.

810 North Miller Road
Vancouver, BC V6B 4H3
September 8, 202x

Professor Margaret M. Sullivan
Department of Busness Administration
Schoolcraft College
Vancouver, BC V6B 5H6

Dear Professor Sulivan:

I enrolled this class to help me improve the way I use language I know that comunication skills are important, and I'm afraid that my present skills are below average. They're not good enough for me to get the kind of job I want I also enrolled in this class because its required in my program of study.

Accounting is my major I chose this field because I like working with figures. And because I know that many good jobs are available in accounting. Although I thought that accountants worked totaly with figures. My adviser tells me that accountants also need to be able to explain their work to management, to fellow employees, and to clients. My language skills are not terrific, and I want to improve. When I finish my accounting program, I hope to get a job in the entertainment industry as a Junior Accountant.

I have a part time job at Pizza Bob's. Where I deliver pizzas to campus dormitories or to apartments an homes. I like my job because I get to meet people and because it helps me pay for my car and it's insurance.

When I'm not studing or working, I like to surf the internet. My favourite places to visit are websites devoted to unusual hobbys and businesses. Right now I'm interested in "CyberSlice," a site showing the menus of participating pizzerias in a neighbourhood. May be I can get Pizza Bob to participate!

Sincerely,

Mark Avila

Mark Avila

For additional resources, please visit MindTap at login.cengage.com. Cengage | MINDTAP

TEAR HERE

UNIT 2

Knowing the Namers

CHAPTER 3
Nouns

CHAPTER 4
Possessive Nouns

CHAPTER 5
Personal Pronouns

CHAPTER 6
Pronouns and Antecedents

CHAPTER 3

NOUNS

OBJECTIVES

When you have completed the materials in this chapter, you will be able to do the following:

LEVEL I

- Recognize four kinds of nouns
- Follow the basic rules for spelling plural nouns

LEVEL II

- Spell challenging plural nouns ending in *y*, *o*, and *f*
- Form the plurals of proper nouns, surnames, compound nouns, numerals, letters, degrees, and abbreviations

LEVEL III

- Recognize and correctly use foreign plural nouns
- Make special nouns plural

PRETEST

Underline any incorrectly spelled noun in the following sentences. Spell the word correctly in the space provided.

1. Shoppers will need their proof of purchases to get the redemption. ______________
2. BuroCo delivered several boxs of office supplies today. ______________
3. Several Crown attornies requested tax write-offs for books. ______________

(continued)

PRETEST *(CONTINUED)*

4. The Freemans have asked their respective employers for leave of absences in June. ________________

5. Both GPs said there are several possible diagnosis based on the test results. ________________

6. We are considering two logoes for our new business start-up. ________________

7. The restaurateur ordered 9 kilograms of tomatoes and 20 kilograms of potatos. ________________

8. We haven't put skis on sale for three Februaries. ________________

9. Canada's first superstore opened in Montréal in the 1970's. ________________

10. In preparation for his new sales job, Ben bought three new suites. ________________

This business English textbook treats the study of our language *selectively*. We will not consider *all* the rules and conventions of English. Instead, we will focus on those aspects of the language that are often troublesome. Therefore, in this chapter on nouns, the principal emphasis will be on forming and spelling plural nouns, an area of confusion for many business writers.

Beginning with this chapter, we present concepts in levels, progressing from basic, frequently used concepts at Level I to more complex, less frequently used concepts at Level III.

DID YOU KNOW?

A government agency in the United Kingdom reported that the company Taylor & Sons Ltd. was out of business. However, the bankrupt company was actually Taylor & *Son* Ltd. (not *Sons*). As a result of the government error, the company that was called Taylor & Sons Ltd. lost enough business also to end up bankrupt. In 2014, the owners of the irreparably damaged company successfully sued the government agency, claiming damages of £8.8 million.

LEVEL I

One way to ensure that you are writing well is to understand the importance of nouns in sentences. As you will recall from Chapter 1, nouns name persons, places, things, qualities, concepts, and activities.

KINDS OF NOUNS

As the "namers" in our language, nouns perform an important function. They often serve as sentence subjects. In addition, nouns serve as objects of verbs and objects of prepositions. To help you understand nouns better, we will first divide them into four categories: concrete, abstract, common, and proper nouns.

Concrete and Abstract Nouns

Concrete nouns name specific objects that you can actually see, hear, feel, taste, or smell. **Abstract nouns** name qualities and concepts that may be difficult to visualize. Because concrete nouns are precise, they are more forceful and effective in writing and in speech than abstract nouns are.

Concrete Nouns		Abstract Nouns	
dictionary	valley	freedom	happiness
stapler	jasmine	success	accuracy
envelope	laptop	memory	personality
dentist	coffee	ethics	value

Common and Proper Nouns

Common nouns name *generalized* persons, places, and things. Because they are general, common nouns are not capitalized. **Proper nouns**, on the other hand, name *specific* persons, places, and things and are always capitalized. Rules for capitalization are presented in Chapter 18 (pp. 352–359).

Common Nouns		Proper Nouns	
document	town	Charter of Rights and Freedoms	Mabou
organization	computer	United Nations	Dell
chief	cellphone	Chief Charriere	Samsung Galaxy
photocopier	company	Xerox machine	Canadian Tire Corporation
candy	magazine	Smarties	*Canadian House & Home*

CAREER TIP

Successful job applicants fill their résumés with concrete expressions and quantifiable data rather than abstractions. Instead of *Worked as lab assistant*, try *Assisted over 300 students and 25 faculty members using Word, PowerPoint, and Excel in computer lab.*

BASIC PLURALS

Singular nouns name *one* person, place, or thing. Plural nouns name *two* or more. At Level I you will learn basic rules for forming plurals.

Regular nouns form the plural with the addition of *s* or *es*.

Add *s* to most nouns:

advantage, advantages	graphic, graphics	password, passwords
merchant, merchants	house, houses	Tom, Toms
passenger, passengers	issue, issues	Khan, Khans

Add *es* to most nouns ending in *s*, *x*, *z*, *ch*, or *sh*:

brush, brushes	tax, taxes	yes, yeses
business, businesses	wrench, wrenches	Schwartz, Schwartzes

Irregular nouns form the plural by changing the spelling of the word.

child, children	goose, geese	mouse, mice
foot, feet	man, men	ox, oxen

ASK AN EDITOR

Question:
What is the plural of computer *mouse*?

Answer:
Mice refers to both computer devices and rodents. However, some experts prefer *mouse devices*, which is probably less confusing.

Because of space restrictions, most dictionaries do not show plurals of *regular* nouns. Thus, if you look up the plural of *ranch*, you probably will not find it. Dictionaries *do* show the plurals of nouns that might be confusing or difficult to spell.

Apostrophes (') are *not* used to form plural nouns. Reserve the apostrophe to show possession. (Chapter 4 discusses possessive nouns in detail.)

Wrong: Management executive's can earn excellent bonus's.
Right: Management executives can earn excellent bonuses.

Now complete the reinforcement exercises for Level I on pages 44–46.

DID YOU KNOW?

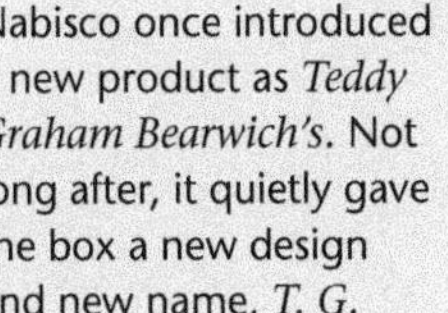

Nabisco once introduced a new product as *Teddy Graham Bearwich's*. Not long after, it quietly gave the box a new design and new name, *T. G. Bearwiches*.

LEVEL II

CHALLENGING NOUN PLURALS

You can greatly improve your ability to spell troublesome noun plurals by studying the following rules and examples.

1. **Common nouns ending in *y*** form the plural in two ways:

   When the letter *y* is preceded by a vowel (*a, e, i, o, u*), form the plural by adding *s* only.

valley, valleys	journey, journeys	buoy, buoys
turkey, turkeys	delay, delays	attorney, attorneys

   When the letter before *y* is a consonant (all letters other than vowels), form the plural by changing the *y* to *ies*.

country, countries	quality, qualities	luxury, luxuries
currency, currencies	company, companies	library, libraries

   Note: This rule does *not* apply to the plural forms of proper nouns: *Camry, Camrys; Landry, Landrys; July, Julys.*

2. **Common nouns ending in *fe* or *f*** follow no standard rules in the formation of plurals, though most simply add *s* to the singular form. Study the examples shown here, and use a dictionary when in doubt. When dictionaries recognize two plural forms for a word, they usually show the preferred form first, as in the third column below.

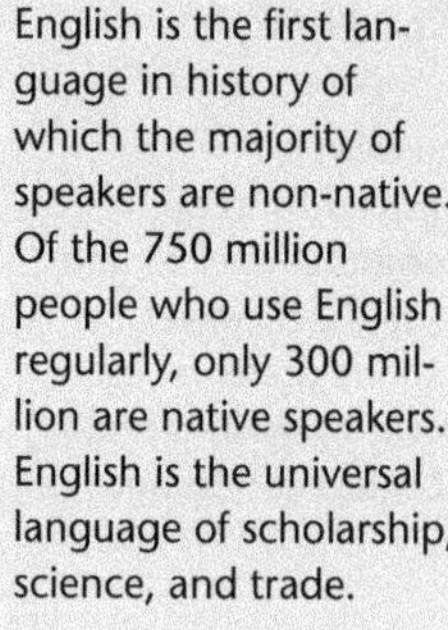

DID YOU KNOW?

English is the first language in history of which the majority of speakers are non-native. Of the 750 million people who use English regularly, only 300 million are native speakers. English is the universal language of scholarship, science, and trade.

Add *s*	**Change to *ves***	**Both Forms Recognized**
chief, chiefs	half, halves	dwarfs, dwarves
cliff, cliffs	knife, knives	scarves, scarfs
proof, proofs	leaf, leaves	wharves, wharfs
safe, safes	shelf, shelves	
sheriff, sheriffs	wife, wives	
tariff, tariffs	wolf, wolves	

Be careful not to confuse plural nouns with verb forms ending in *s*. He *saves* (verb) his money in two *safes* (noun). Be especially aware of the following words:

Nouns	**Verbs**
belief, beliefs	believe, believes
leaf, leaves (foliage)	leave, leaves (to depart)
loaf, loaves (of bread)	loaf, loafs (to be idle)
proof, proofs	prove, proves

3. **Common nouns ending in *o*** may be made plural by adding *s* or *es*.

   a. When the letter before *o* is a vowel, form the plural by adding *s* only.

studio, studios	video, videos	portfolio, portfolios
duo, duos	ratio, ratios	tattoo, tattoos

b. When the letter before *o* is a consonant, form the plural by adding *s* or *es*. Study the following examples, and again use your dictionary whenever in doubt.

Add *s*	**Add *es***	**Both Forms Recognized**
auto, autos	echo, echoes	cargoes, cargos
casino, casinos	embargo, embargoes	ghettos, ghettoes
logo, logos	hero, heroes	innuendoes, innuendos
memo, memos	potato, potatoes	mangoes, mangos
silo, silos	tomato, tomatoes	mosquitoes, mosquitos
typo, typos	veto, vetoes	mottoes, mottos

c. Musical terms ending in *o* form the plural with the addition of *s* only.

alto, altos	contralto, contraltos	solo, solos
cello, cellos	piano, pianos	soprano, sopranos

4. **Proper nouns and surnames** are generally made plural by adding *s* or *es*. When making proper nouns and surnames (last names) plural, don't change the original spelling of the word. Simply add *s* or *es* to the end. Note that when the word *the* appears before a surname, the name is always plural (the *Kennedys*).

a. Most proper nouns become plural by adding *s*.

Khoury, the Khourys	Germany, Germanys	Leno, the Lenos
January, Januarys	Yang, the Yangs	Elizabeth, Elizabeths

b. Proper nouns and surnames that end in *j*, *s*, *x*, *z*, *ch*, or *sh* are made plural by adding *es*.

Rex, Rexes	Ivanovich, the Ivanoviches	Paris, Parises
March, Marches	Hiraj, the Hirajes	Williams, the Williamses

5. **Compound nouns** are formed by joining two or more words. They may be written as single (or solid) words, may be hyphenated, or may appear as separate words.

a. When written as single words, compound nouns usually form the plural by appropriate changes in the final element.

bookshelf, bookshelves	printout, printouts
footnote, footnotes	child, children
photocopy, photocopies	walkway, walkways

Exception: passerby, passersby

b. When written in hyphenated or *open form* (as two or more separate words), compound nouns form the plural by appropriate changes in the principal (most important) noun. Determining which word is made plural can be challenging when the compound includes more than one noun. Logic usually prevails.

editors-in-chief	More than one editor, not more than one chief
bills of lading	More than one bill, not more than one "lading"
mayors-elect	More than one mayor, not more than one "elect"
boards of directors	More than one board (with more than one director on each)
mothers-in-law	More than one mother, not more than one law
leaves of absence	More than one leave, not more than one absence
runners-up	More than one runner, not more than one "up"
paper clips	More than one clip, not more than one paper

c. If a hyphenated compound noun has no principal noun—often the case when the compound is created from words that are not nouns—the final element is made plural.

cure-alls	look-alikes	start-ups
go-betweens	no-shows	trade-ins
know-it-alls	run-ins	write-ups

ASK AN EDITOR

Question:
Could you help me spell the plurals of *do* and *don't*?

Answer:
Formerly, some words that were uncommon to see in the plural took an apostrophe before the *s*. However, the modern way to make any word plural is to add *s* without an apostrophe. Thus, we have *dos* and *don'ts*.

6. **Numerals, alphabet letters, isolated words, and degrees** are made plural by adding *s, es,* or *'s*. Use *'s* only when necessary for clarity (see *d* below).

a. Numerals and uppercase letters (with the exception of *A, I, M,* and *U*) require only *s* in plural formation.

Price trends from the *1980s* continued through the *1990s*.
Her new calculator was not printing *7s* and *9s*.
Narinder received all *Bs* and *Cs* on his report card.

b. Isolated words used as nouns are made plural with the addition of *s* or *es*, generally as needed for pronunciation.

The Speaker of the House took a count of *yeses* and *noes* on the bill.
Numerous *ands, ahs,* and *you knows* made his speech ineffective.
She considered all the *pros* and *cons* before signing the contract.

c. Degrees are made plural with the addition of *s*.

Dr. Helstrum holds two *PhDs* in related fields.
Graduates with *MBAs* are being heavily recruited.

d. Isolated lowercase letters and the capital letters *A, I, M,* and *U* require *'s* for clarity. Without the apostrophe these letters might be confused with words.

Unless she writes more legibly, her *o's* may be mistaken for *a's*.
In preparing the notice for the marquee yesterday, we ran out of *A's* and *I's*.

ASK AN EDITOR

Question:
In the sentence *Please read our FAQs*, does the abbreviation need an apostrophe?

Answer:
No. The abbreviation for *Frequently Asked Questions* is *FAQs*, as you wrote it. Avoid using an apostrophe for plural forms.

7. **Abbreviations** are usually made plural by adding *s* to the singular form.

yr., yrs.	mgr., mgrs.	dept., depts.	wk., wks.
No., Nos.	LSAT, LSATs	DVD, DVDs	bldg., bldgs.

The singular and plural forms of abbreviations or symbols for units of measurement are, however, usually identical (*always* identical in the case of metric units of measurement).

g	(gram or grams)	L	(litre or litres)
km	(kilometre or kilometres)	deg.	(degree or degrees)
cm	(centimetre or centimetres)	ft.	(foot or feet)

Now complete the reinforcement exercises for Level II on pages 47–48.

STUDY TIP

If a word ending in *um, is, us,* or *a* is new to you, you should probably use a dictionary to confirm its plural form. Many have unpredictable plurals.

LEVEL III

FOREIGN NOUNS AND SPECIAL PLURALS

Selected nouns borrowed from foreign languages and other special nouns require your attention because their plural forms can be confusing.

1. Nouns borrowed from foreign languages may retain a foreign plural. A few, however, also have an anglicized plural form, shown second below. Check your dictionary for the preferred or more frequently used form.

Singular	**Plural**
alumna (feminine)	alumnae
alumnus (masculine)	alumni
analysis	analyses
appendix	appendices or appendixes
axis	axes
bacterium	bacteria
basis	bases
crisis	crises
criterion	criteria
curriculum	curricula
datum	data
diagnosis	diagnoses
erratum	errata
formula	formulae or formulas
hypothesis	hypotheses
matrix	matrices or matrixes
memorandum	memoranda or memorandums
parenthesis	parentheses
phenomenon	phenomena
stimulus	stimuli
thesis	theses
vertebra	vertebrae

2. **Special nouns**, many of which may end in *s*, may normally be *only* singular *or* plural in meaning. Other special nouns may be considered *either* singular *or* plural in meaning, whether they end in *s* or not. Notice that many of the nouns that are usually singular refer to games, fields of study, or diseases. Many of the nouns that are usually plural refer to clothing and tools. Those nouns that may be singular or plural often refer to animals or nationalities.

Usually Singular	**Usually Plural**	**May Be Singular or Plural**
billiards	clothes	corps
economics	earnings	deer
genetics	goods	headquarters
mathematics	pants	series
measles	pliers	sheep
mumps	scissors	statistics
news	thanks	Vietnamese

3. **Single-letter abbreviations** may be made plural by doubling the letter.

pp. (pages)	See pp. 18–21 (pages 18 through 21)
ff. (and following)	See p. 18 ff. (page 18 and following pages)

Now complete the reinforcement exercises for Level III on pages 49–51.

ASK AN EDITOR

Question:
One member of our staff consistently corrects our use of the word *data*. He says the word is plural. Is it never singular?

Answer:
The word *data* is indeed plural; the singular form is *datum*. Through common usage, however, *data* has more recently become a collective noun. Collective nouns may be singular or plural depending on whether they are considered as one unit or as separate units. For example, *These data are much different from those findings* (plural) or *This data is conclusive* (singular).

STUDY TIP

Practise these special nouns by using them before the singular verb *is* or the plural verb *are*. Genetics *is* fascinating (singular). Scissors *are* useful (plural).

NAME ____________________

CHAPTER 3 ■ Reinforcement Exercises

LEVEL I

Note: At the beginning of each level, a self-check exercise is provided so that you may immediately check your understanding of the concepts in that level. Do not look at the answers until you have finished the exercise. Then compare your responses with the answers shown in the back of the book. If more than three of your answers do not agree with those shown, reread the level before continuing with the other reinforcement exercises.

A. (Self-check) In the space provided, write the plural form of the singular noun shown in parentheses.

EXAMPLE: Investors purchased numerous rare Chinese (tea). teas

1. The department already has four technical (assistant). ____________
2. Many organizations have procedures in place to prevent (virus) on their office computers. ____________
3. The new sales (pitch) yielded positive responses in the focus group. ____________
4. Several (mouse) have been spotted in the storage room. ____________
5. All sales (tax) are charged at the point of purchase. ____________
6. The company kitchen always has a supply of apples, oranges, and (banana) for employees. ____________
7. One virtual assistant may serve several (business). ____________
8. The nearest coffee shop is two (block) from the office. ____________
9. Most toy manufacturers employ (child) to test new products. ____________
10. The new open-concept office space includes a central lounge with (couch). ____________

Check your answers.

B. Identify the nouns (that are acting as nouns) in each of the following sentences. Note which are common nouns (CN) and which are proper nouns (PN).

EXAMPLE: Every meeting of the town council is aired on the local cable TV station. (3 nouns) meeting (CN) council (CN) station (CN)

1. Invoices are sorted by the due date of the payment. (3 nouns) ____________ ____________ ____________

2. A new personal delivery service is opening in Brandon. (2 nouns) ____________ ____________

TEAR HERE

3. Motion is a mobility company that has locations across Canada. (4 nouns) ____________

____

____

____

4. My accountant says I will have to pay more taxes this year. (3 nouns) ____________

____

____

5. Only service animals are permitted on the premises. (2 nouns) ____________

____

6. More companies are recognizing the benefits of a social media presence. (3 nouns) ____________

____

____

7. A Mi'kmaq entrepreneur provided the site for the children's computer workshop. (3 nouns) ____________

____

____

8. Farouk just became an officer with the Royal Newfoundland Constabulary. (3 nouns) ____________

____

____

C. In the space provided, write the plural form for the noun listed.

1. employee ____________
2. flash ____________
3. villa ____________
4. gas ____________
5. blitz ____________
6. foot ____________
7. kilometre ____________
8. phase ____________
9. guarantee ____________
10. bias ____________
11. franchise ____________
12. key ____________
13. goose ____________
14. quota ____________
15. absence ____________

D. Correct any errors in the use of plural nouns in the following sentences by underlining the incorrect form and writing the correct form in the space provided. Write *C* if a sentence is correct.

EXAMPLE: She has three different account's with her bank. accounts

1. More than 20 men and woman were interviewed for the vacant position. ____________
2. The sketchs for the marketing campaign look promising. ____________

TEAR HERE

3. Having two Jeff's in the department can be confusing. ____________

4. The floores of all business units will be replaced in the spring. ____________

5. After many delays the heavy boxs were delivered. ____________

6. At Vankirk Medical Supplies our employee's are family. ____________

7. Mr. Burtness and his two stepchilds attended the reunion. ____________

8. Veera used two different lens for photographing the products. ____________

9. Nyla was beginning to see there were no quick fixs for her computer issues. ____________

10. Have the Noori's submitted this year's income tax return? ____________

11. The reception room will have two benches and four upholstered chairs. ____________

12. Each employee received two free pass's to the exhibit. ____________

13. The two bus we've chartered will leave at 4 p.m. ____________

14. Only two news dispatches were released concerning the stock split. ____________

15. Close the blindes before leaving for the day. ____________

TEAR HERE

NAME ______________________________

LEVEL II

A. **(Self-check)** In the space provided, write the correct plural form of the noun shown in parentheses.

1. Both (bill of lading) showed excessive shipping charges. ______________
2. A business cannot function with too many (chief) and not enough workers. ______________
3. Our organization is prepared to deal in foreign (currency). ______________
4. Page numbers of a document can also be called (folio). ______________
5. Students had to show their (ID) before they were admitted. ______________
6. We have decided to close on (Sunday) during July and August. ______________
7. In the past, many people spent their (life) working for the same company. ______________
8. We need the ad (proof) by Monday. ______________
9. The (runner-up) for the job heard the disappointing news today. ______________
10. The committee debated the (pro and con) of decentralization. ______________

Check your answers.

B. In the space provided, write the plural form for the noun listed. Use a dictionary if you are unsure of the spelling.

1. line of credit ______________
2. Wednesday ______________
3. bill of sale ______________
4. 100 ______________
5. safe ______________
6. FAQ ______________
7. trolley ______________
8. balance of trade ______________
9. Murray ______________
10. half ______________
11. liability ______________
12. M ______________
13. yes ______________
14. port of entry ______________
15. subsidiary ______________
16. cure-all ______________
17. No. ______________
18. D ______________
19. if ______________
20. premier-elect ______________
21. IPO ______________
22. send-off ______________
23. RSVP ______________
24. dept. ______________

TEAR HERE

C. In the space provided, write the correct plural form of the singular expression shown in parentheses.

1. All that remained standing were two blackened (chimney). __________
2. We compared the liquidity (ratio) of the two companies. __________
3. Several (VIP) are invited to this event. __________
4. As a company, we support a selection of local (charity). __________
5. Both (Lori) are outstanding customer service representatives. __________
6. The creative team presented two very different (motif) for the campaign. __________
7. Do the (Wolf) subscribe to *Canadian Business?* __________
8. City Council awarded medals to three local (hero). __________
9. After the lecture three (hanger-on) remained at the lectern. __________
10. Interest rates were as high as 18 percent in the late (1980). __________
11. Computer users must distinguish between zeros and (O). __________
12. What percentage of (CEO) are women? __________
13. The two (board of directors) voted to begin merger negotiations. __________
14. The cousins are near (look-alike). __________
15. At least two employees have recently taken (leave of absence). __________

D. **Writing Exercise.** In the space provided, write complete sentences using the plural forms of the nouns shown in parentheses.

1. (witness) ____________________.
2. (Spiros [surname]) ____________________.
3. (up and down) ____________________.
4. (MPP) ____________________.
5. (mm) ____________________.
6. (standby) ____________________.
7. (tomato) ____________________.
8. (armoury) ____________________.
9. (typo) ____________________.
10. (BA) ____________________.

TEAR HERE

NAME ______________________________

LEVEL III

A. (Self-check) In the space provided, write the plural form of the singular expression in parentheses.

1. Sensorial (stimulus) should be considered when creating marketing pieces. ____________
2. Creative product videos shared on social media have become marketing (phenomenon). ____________
3. Our retail outlets sell many book (series) that would appeal to young adult readers. ____________
4. The (alumna) of Canada's only women's university are raising funds for the Brescia University College Foundation. ____________
5. The most important (criterion) for making our decisions are expense and safety. ____________
6. An appendix appears on (p.) 535–540. ____________
7. Experts presented conflicting (analysis) of the problem. ____________
8. The (datum) show which campaigns are most effective. ____________
9. Almost all humans are born with 33 (vertebra), but most have only 23 by adulthood. ____________
10. Numerous (crisis) within education will only be worsened by budget cuts. ____________

Check your answers.

B. In the space provided, write the correct plural form of the expression in parentheses.

1. Researchers collected substantial data to support their (hypothesis). ____________
2. The public school (curriculum) for most provinces are available to homeschooling organizations. ____________
3. Our CEO was asked to address the (alumnus) who attended the fundraiser. ____________
4. Improper temperature controls allowed (bacterium) to contaminate some of the restaurant's food. ____________
5. Translations of foreign words are enclosed in sets of (parenthesis). ____________
6. Sales records for the past five years may be found on p. 25 (and following pages). ____________
7. Several (memorandum) have been issued about the privacy laws and how they affect operations. ____________
8. The stems of (cactus) store water, allowing these plants to survive drought. ____________
9. Various members of the IT department have provided different (diagnosis) of our computer problems. ____________
10. Dr. Binsley's master's and doctoral (thesis) are both available online. ____________

TEAR HERE

C. Complete the sentences below. In the space provided, write the singular verb form *is* or the plural verb form *are* to agree with the noun subject of each.

1. Modern genetics (is, are) a dynamic field of study with an expanding array of sub-fields. ____________
2. If the scissors (is, are) sharp enough, we can use them to cut the flower stems. ____________
3. (Is, Are) the proceeds being donated to charity? ____________
4. Thanks (is, are) due to our organizing committee. ____________
5. Max's earnings (is, are) paying next term's tuition. ____________
6. The statistics on social media marketing success (is, are) telling. ____________
7. Deer (is, are) venturing into neighbourhood gardens. ____________
8. Despite near eradication in the early twenty-first century, measles (is, are) regaining prevalence in North America. ____________
9. The job criteria (is, are) outlined in detail on the company intranet. ____________
10. Many sheep (is, are) raised for their wool. ____________

D. **Review of Levels I, II, and III. (Self-check)** In the following sentences, underline any errors in noun plurals. For each sentence write a corrected form in the space provided. Write *C* if a sentence is correct. Then check your answers on page 526.

1. Many restaurant customers find boothes more comfortable than chairs. ____________
2. She received two different diagnosises from two different doctors. ____________
3. Next month franchisee's from across the country are meeting in Vancouver. ____________
4. Two Wilcoxs have applied for the marketing job. ____________
5. A tour of local artists' studioes is one of the highlights of the upcoming company retreat. ____________
6. Leaves of absence for the week of June 7 were granted to both woman. ____________
7. After numerous brushes with the law, Darcy became a consultant to a security company. ____________
8. Our directory lists RN's and NP's separately. ____________
9. Both companies had record earnings last quarter. ____________
10. The Abbases discussed all the in's and out's of the transaction before signing the contract. ____________
11. The Fitch's named three beneficiaries in their insurance policies. ____________
12. Tomatoes are grown to perfection in the interior vallies. ____________
13. The board of directors from the affected companies will vote within the week. ____________

TEAR HERE

14. Despite the new flexible hours for Mondays through Thursdays, all employees must put in a full workday on Fridays. __________

15. The attorneys and judges were advised to place their heaviest books on the lower shelfs. __________

16. Pullies can help prevent back injuries. __________

17. Two Chevy Equinox will be given away. __________

18. The new tariffes will increase prices on several imported goods. __________

19. The highers-up in the company can count on good bonus's this year. __________

20. Tour participants can choose from several interesting journeys. __________

Check your answers.

E. Writing Exercise. Your instructor may ask you to complete this exercise on a separate sheet.

Write ten complete sentences using the plural forms of the following nouns, one per sentence: *belief, CEO, Ruvinsky, datum, process, privilege, father-in-law, 20, phenomenon, tooth.*

POSTTEST

Underline any incorrectly spelled nouns. Write the correct forms in the space provided.

1. The children were warned to be careful of the sharp knifes. __________
2. Before sending out any memoranda, proofread for typoes. __________
3. On either side of the warehouse are allies wide enough for the trucks to park during their deliveries. __________
4. In the 1990s, many companys were searching for graduates with MBAs. __________
5. After several business crisises, we hired two consultants. __________
6. Jason's last name is spelled with two *us*. __________
7. How many sister-in-laws does he have? __________
8. We purchased several DVD's for training purposes. __________
9. Nine woman and three men belong to the book club. __________
10. The Thomas's go on vacation in Cabo San Lucas every year. __________

TEAR HERE

EDITOR'S CHALLENGE

The following letters contain errors in spelling, noun plurals, and sentence structure, as well as other common errors. Use proofreading marks to correct them.

SHEARMAN BROTHERS

415 Yonge Street
Toronto, ON M5B 2E7

Phone: (416) 502-8694 *Fax: (416) 502-7619* *Web: http://www.shearmanbros.com*

April 5, 202x

Ms. Judy B.Bachman
The Daily News
11 Thornhill Drive
Dartmouth, NS B3B 1R9

Dear Ms. Bachman:

Thanks for the oportunity to contribute to the article. That you are writting about fast-food promotions. As an analyst with Shearman Brothers, I specialize in the fast-food and beverage industrys.

You specifically wanted information about what sells fast food. Actually, competition among the fast food giants has always been as much about appearances as reality. Its a lot like a three-ring circus, with flashy new showstoppers needed to keep men, woman, and children coming back. Some promotions by companys have been fiascos. I assume, however, that you are most interested in sucessful stategies such as the following:

- **Giveaways.** Fast-food giants suchas McDonald's use movie tie-ins and toy promotions that appeal children, who then persuade their parents to come into the stores.
- **Advertising.** Companys spend million on ad campaigns promoting expressions that they hope will become part of everyone's speech, such as classics like "You deserve a break today."
- **Food.** Nothing else matters if the food doesn't taste good. McDonald's, for example, grows its own potatos and raises cattle to ensure that its french frys and sandwichs meet rigid specifications.
- **Price.** Cutting prices increases sale, but usually for a short time only. In the end, price-cutting erodes profites. Another strategy is the repackaging of popular items in "value" combinations. Which is an effort to boost sales.
- **Convenience.** People often go to a fastfood restaurant on impulse, the more restaurants that a company has, the likelier that it will make a sale.

I hope theseideas are helpful to you in prepareing your article. If you use any of this material, I must submit your article to our lawyers for approval. Call me when you would like to talk further about this article.

Sincerely,

Paul Lahijanian

Paul Lahijanian
Senior Analyst

TEAR HERE

AAA ADMINISTRATIVE SERVICES

10187 104 St. NW, Unit 301
Edmonton, AB T5J 0Z9
(780) 224-6868
aaaadministrative.com

December 1, 202x

Abigail Wright
Wright Writes
10620 136 Ave. NW
Edmonton, AB T8A 0G2

Dear Ms. Wright:

One of our regular clientes recently informed us of your consultings services. We are working with two other agencys to organize two week's of training seminars for temporary administrative workers, you have been suggested as a good resource for a writing segment.

Our company offer temporary clerical services to local Edmonton business's. Some of our employee's have a lot of expereince in the field, and some have very little. Many are not comfortable with writing or with proofreading written dispatchs, but these are important skills for administrative profesionals.

I have a few idea's of what topics could be covered. To help our office temp's become more valuble to our clients:

- Using dictionaries and thesauris. Many of our employee's are proofreading letters for the organizations they are temporarly employed at. Some seem to need a greater understanding of how to use these tools to do their jobs' better.
- Making writing modern. Some of our staffs cling to old fashion terminology such as "to whom it may concern" and "herewith." You could perhaps present language do's and dont's and introduce options to outdated terms.
- Condensing correspondence. I've noticed repetition and overly wordy expressions used, some helpful hits for getting to the point would be useful.

From my understanding, you have offered simular training for other companys, so you probably have other thoughts about topics to cover. Our training dates are February 6–17, 202x. If you are available to do one-day workshop that week, please present me with a proposal and your fee by December 19.

Sincerely,

N LeBlanc

Naya LeBlanc
Human Resources Manager
nleblanc@aaaadministrative.com

For additional resources, please visit MindTap at login.cengage.com. Cengage | MINDTAP

CHAPTER 4

POSSESSIVE NOUNS

OBJECTIVES

When you have completed the materials in this chapter, you will be able to do the following:

LEVEL I

- Distinguish between possessive nouns and plural nouns
- Follow five steps to ensure the apostrophe is used correctly

LEVEL II

- Make compound nouns, combined ownership nouns, organization names, and abbreviations possessive
- Understand incomplete possessives
- Avoid awkward possessives

LEVEL III

- Make proper nouns possessive

PRETEST

Underline any incorrect possessive forms of nouns. Write correct versions in the spaces provided.

1. Some students loans carried lower interest rates than yours. ____________
2. The runner-ups' prizes were supplied by Everyday Fitness. ____________
3. Most landlords require two months rent in advance. ____________
4. The agent who listed the house has prepared a copy of the properties selling features. ____________
5. Our editor's-in-chief office will remain on the second floor. ____________
6. Our country-wide survey polled many companys officers. ____________

(continued)

PRETEST (CONTINUED)

7. Nadya Assans new tax-preparation practice needs more promotion. ________
8. Our Sale's Department will relocate to the third floor. ________
9. Toni's commute to and from work uses ten dollars worth of gas. ________
10. The Horowitzes real estate holdings are in the eastern townships. ________

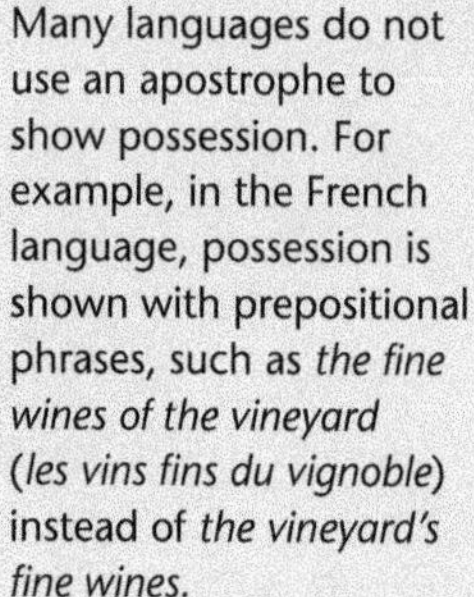

DID YOU KNOW?

Many languages do not use an apostrophe to show possession. For example, in the French language, possession is shown with prepositional phrases, such as *the fine wines of the vineyard* (*les vins fins du vignoble*) instead of *the vineyard's fine wines.*

ASK AN EDITOR

Question:
Where should the apostrophe go in *employee's handbook?*

Answer:
This is tricky. If the writer considers the handbook from one employee's point of view, the expression is singular: *employee's handbook* (similarly, *owner's manual*). If the writer is referring to a group, the references are plural: *employees' handbook* (a handbook for all employees), *owners' manuals* (the manuals of all owners). Alternatively, some organizations use these terms as adjectives: *employee handbook, owner manual.*

Nouns play significant roles in sentences, so being able to use nouns effectively will make you a better writer. Thus far you have studied four kinds of nouns (concrete, abstract, common, and proper), and you have learned how to make nouns plural. In this chapter you will learn how to use the apostrophe to make nouns possessive.

LEVEL I

SHOWING POSSESSION WITH APOSTROPHES

Possession occurs when one noun (or pronoun) possesses another. Notice in the following phrases how possessive nouns show ownership, origin, authorship, or measurement:

Jack's computer (ownership)
Saskatchewan's citizens (origin)
Atwood's writings (authorship)
three years' time (measurement)

In expressing possession, English speakers and writers have a choice. They may show possession with an apostrophe construction, or they may use a prepositional phrase with no apostrophe:

the computer of Jack
the citizens of Saskatchewan
the writings of Atwood
the time of three years

The use of a prepositional phrase to show ownership (usually beginning with *of*) is more formal and tends to emphasize the word that names the owner (the object of the preposition). The use of the apostrophe construction to show ownership is more efficient and more natural, especially in conversation. In writing, however, deciding where to place the apostrophe can be perplexing. Here are five simple but effective steps that will help you write possessives correctly.

Five Steps to Ensure the Apostrophe Is Used Correctly

1. **Look for possessive construction.** Usually two nouns appear together. The first noun shows ownership of (or a special relationship to) the second noun.

the man['s] book
Tita['s] note
the building['s] entrance
a year['s] rent
both doctors['] offices

2. **Reverse the nouns.** Use the second noun to begin a prepositional phrase. The object of the preposition is the ownership word.

book of the *man*
note from *Tita*
entrance to the *building*
rent of a *year*
offices of both *doctors*

3. **Examine the ownership word.** To determine the correct placement of the apostrophe, you must first know whether the ownership word is singular or plural.

4. If the ownership word is singular, add apostrophe and *s*.

the man's book
a witness's testimony
a year's rent

5. If the ownership word is plural,

   a. and it ends in an *s* sound, add only an apostrophe.

   both doctors' offices
   several investors' portfolios

   b. but it does not end in an *s* sound, add an apostrophe and *s*.

   the children's games
   women's health

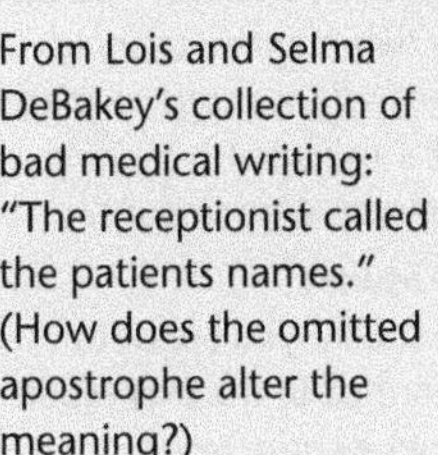

BE THE EDITOR

From Lois and Selma DeBakey's collection of bad medical writing: "The receptionist called the patients names." (How does the omitted apostrophe alter the meaning?)

STUDY TIP

You can't hear apostrophes. For example, *company's*, *companies'*, and *companies* sound identical. For this reason these guidelines are especially important.

Notice that an apostrophe and an *s* are added to make all nouns possessive, unless the noun is plural and ends in *s*. In this case, add an apostrophe only.

A word of caution: Do NOT use apostrophes for nouns that simply show more than one of something. In the sentence *These businesses are opening several new locations*, no apostrophes are required. The words *businesses* and *locations* are plural; they are not possessive. In addition, be careful to avoid changing the spelling of singular nouns when making them possessive. For example, the *secretary's* desk (meaning the desk of one secretary) is *not* spelled *secretaries'*.

Pay particular attention to the following possessive constructions, keeping in mind that time and money can show possession. The explanations and hints in parentheses will help you understand and remember such conventional expressions.

a day's work (the work of one day)
three days' pay (the pay of three days)
a dollar's worth (the worth of one dollar)
your money's worth (the worth of your money)
today's weather (note that only one *today* is possible)
tomorrow's work (note that only one *tomorrow* is possible)

STUDY TIP

Whenever you have any doubt about using an apostrophe, always put the expression into an *of* phrase. You'll immediately recognize the ownership word and see whether it is singular or plural and whether it ends in *s*.

Complete the reinforcement exercises for Level I on pages 61–63.

STUDY TIP

To identify descriptive nouns, ask whether ownership is involved. Is *industry* possessed by *electronics*? Does record belong to *earnings*? When the answer is no, omit the apostrophe.

ASK AN EDITOR

Question:
Our sales manager wrote an announcement about a *two months' training period*. I wanted to make it a *two-month training period*. Who is right?

Answer:
Actually, you are both correct! In the expression *two months' training period, two months'* is possessive (*training period of two months*). In *two-month training period, two-month* is descriptive and no apostrophe is required. Only a slight difference in wording distinguishes a descriptive phrase from a possessive phrase, and sometimes it is hard to tell them apart.

STUDY TIP

Look at the object owned (*rights, business,* etc.). If that object is singular, ownership is usually combined.

BE THE EDITOR

Sign in a Tim Hortons parking lot: "All vehicles other than Tim Horton's 'in-the-store' customers will be towed at owner's expense." (Can you spot more than one error in this sentence?)

LEVEL II

CHALLENGING POSSESSIVE CONSTRUCTIONS

You can greatly improve your skill in using apostrophes by understanding the following additional possessive constructions.

1. **Descriptive versus possessive nouns.** When nouns provide description or identification only, the possessive form is NOT used. Writers have the most problems with descriptive nouns ending in *s*, such as Claims Department. No apostrophe is needed, just as none is necessary in Legal Department.

   Human Resources Department (not Resources' Department)
   the electronics industry (not electronics' industry)
   earnings record (not earnings' record)

2. **Compound nouns.** Make compound nouns possessive by adding an apostrophe or *'s* to the end of the compound word.

   father-in-law's property
   onlookers' interest
   notary public's seal

3. **Incomplete possessives.** When the second noun in a possessive noun construction is omitted, the first noun is nevertheless possessive.

   Let's meet at Patrick's [home] after the game.
   This year's sales are higher than last year's [sales].
   I need to stop at the doctor's [office] to pick up a prescription.

4. **Separate or combined ownership.** When two nouns express separate ownership, make both possessive. When two nouns express combined ownership, make only the second one possessive.

Separate Ownership	**Combined Ownership**
landlords' and tenants' rights	the husband and wife's business
Anya's and Sam's cellphones	Anya and Sam's house

5. **Names of organizations.** Organizations with possessives in their names may or may not use apostrophes. Follow the style used by the individual organization (e.g., Tim Hortons, not Tim Horton's). Consult the organization's website, logo, or directory listing if you are unsure.

Metro Tenants Legal Services	Harvey's Restaurants
Chapters	Ontario Secondary School Teachers' Federation
Tim Hortons	Domino's Pizza

6. **Abbreviations.** Make abbreviations possessive by following the same guidelines as for nouns.

the CMA's ruling	All PhDs' dissertations
the CBC's coverage	Ticketmaster Canada Inc.'s sales

7. **Awkward possessives.** When the addition of an apostrophe results in an awkward construction, show ownership by using a prepositional phrase.

Awkward	**Improved**
my brothers-in-law's opinions	opinions of my brothers-in-law
your neighbour's doctor's telephone number	telephone number of your neighbour's doctor
my professor, Dr. Aller's, office	office of my professor, Dr. Aller

Complete the reinforcement exercises for Level II on pages 64–65.

ASK AN EDITOR

Question:
As the holidays approach, I'm wondering whether I should write *Season's greetings* or *Seasons' greetings*.

Answer:
Because you are referring to one season, it's *Season's greetings* (*greetings of the season*).

LEVEL III

BE THE EDITOR

From an old Sears advertisement: "Are you giving away your kids old clothes as fast as you're buying them new ones?"

ADDITIONAL GUIDELINE

You have learned to follow five steps in identifying possessive constructions and in placing the apostrophe correctly. The guidelines presented thus far cover most possessive constructions. Determining the possessive form of a few proper nouns, however, requires a refinement of Step 4.

Let us briefly review the five-step plan for placing the apostrophe in noun possessives, adding a refinement to the fourth step.

1. Look for possessive construction. (Usually, though not always, two nouns appear together.)
2. Reverse the nouns.
3. Examine the ownership word.
4. If the ownership word is singular, add an apostrophe and *s*. However, if the ownership word is a name ending in an *s* sound, you may choose to add only an apostrophe. (See "Making Difficult Proper Nouns Possessive.")
   a. If the ownership word is plural and ends in an *s* sound, add only an apostrophe.
   b. If the ownership word is plural but does not end in an *s* sound, add an apostrophe and *s*.

ASK AN EDITOR

Question:
I have a problem with the following sentence from a legal document involving a restaurant chain called Denny's: *The plaintiff was in fact fired ostensibly for violating Denny's alcoholic beverage service policy.* How do I make possessive a proper name that is already possessive?

Answer:
As you suspected, you can't add another apostrophe. In the interests of clarity, consider the name descriptive, thus avoiding an additional *'s*, and leave the sentence as written.

Making Difficult Proper Nouns Possessive

Of all possessive forms, individuals' names—especially those ending in *s* sounds—are the most puzzling to students, and understandably so. Even experts don't always agree on the possessive form for singular proper nouns.

Traditionalists, as represented in *The Canadian Press Stylebook, The Chicago Manual of Style*, and *The Modern Language Association Style Manual*, prefer adding an apostrophe and *s* to *singular proper* nouns that end in *s* sounds. This style is used by most Canadian newspapers and many businesses. On the other hand, writers of popular literature often prefer adding just an apostrophe to singular proper nouns that end in *s* sounds. You may apply either style, but you must be consistent. Please note that this style choice applies *only to singular names ending in* s *sounds*. Plural names are always made possessive with the addition of an apostrophe only. Study the examples shown.

BE THE EDITOR

Announcement pasted on top of Domino's Pizza boxes: "We accept all competitors coupons."

STUDY TIP

The word *the* preceding a name is a clue that the name is being used in a plural sense. For example, *the Katzes* means the entire Katz family.

Singular Name	Singular Possessive—Traditional	Singular Possessive—Popular	Plural Possessive
Ms. Jones	Ms. Jones's	Ms. Jones'	the Joneses'
Mr. Santos	Mr. Santos's	Mr. Santos'	the Santoses'
Elder Rais	Elder Rais's	Elder Rais'	the Raises'
Miss Weisz	Miss Weisz's	Miss Weisz'	the Weiszes'

Complete the reinforcement exercises for Level III on pages 66–68.

NAME ______________________

CHAPTER 4 ■ Reinforcement Exercises

LEVEL I

A. (Self-check) Using apostrophes, change the following prepositional phrases into possessive constructions. Ownership words are underlined.

EXAMPLE: compensation of men ____men's compensation____

1. labour of a day ______________________
2. meals for patients ______________________
3. permit for a learner ______________________
4. interest of ten months ______________________
5. office of the purchasing manager ______________________
6. economies of the world ______________________
7. prices of competitors ______________________
8. duties of the treasurer ______________________
9. delay of a month ______________________
10. gift for Heba ______________________

Check your answers.

B. In the space provided, rewrite the following phrases without apostrophes. Use prepositional phrases instead.

EXAMPLE: the trainee's hours ____hours of the trainee____

1. the defendant's pleas ______________________
2. six months' paternity leave ______________________
3. three children's bicycles ______________________
4. our company's policy ______________________
5. the computer's warranty ______________________
6. this client's email message ______________________
7. two years' time ______________________
8. our customers' opinions ______________________
9. society's ills ______________________

TEAR HERE

10. a beginner's luck ______________________

11. for safety's sake ______________________

12. the building's exterior ______________________

C. In the following sentences, determine whether the word in parentheses should be singular or plural, and then provide the correct possessive form in the space provided.

1. Success depends on a (company) capacity to deliver. ____________
2. Many of the job (applicant) résumés have not been proofread. ____________
3. (Customer) opinions affect the bottom line. ____________
4. It is rewarding to do an honest (day) work. ____________
5. Both (clerk) salaries will be reviewed next quarter. ____________
6. New legislation in British Columbia has assured Indigenous (group) participation in environmental assessments. ____________
7. The (speaker) message resonated with many people who attended the dinner. ____________
8. Several (business) payment systems were affected by the Internet outage. ____________
9. The three (economist) theories created international news. ____________
10. My (boss) husband retired last month. ____________
11. The company (car) lease expires in July. ____________
12. The hydro and gas (bill) due dates are the same day every month. ____________

D. Underline the errors in possessive construction in the following sentences. In the space provided, write the correct form. Write *C* if a sentence is correct.

EXAMPLE: The servers uniforms make them look competent and professional. servers'

1. Every employees job description will be reviewed over the coming months. ____________
2. Three month's interest will be due in four days. ____________
3. The picketers message is not being heard. ____________
4. All the candidates platforms were released this week. ____________
5. The consultants fees prohibited our hiring him on a long-term basis. ____________
6. Some companies are cutting expenses by requiring employees, customers, and vendors to communicate by email. ____________
7. Fire department inspectors are checking all of the buildings sprinkler heads. ____________
8. Many chef's work with organic products. ____________
9. Dawn gave two weeks' notice on Monday. ____________

TEAR HERE

10. All taxpayers returns are checked by computer. ______________

11. Many of Disneys' animated films are made in Vancouver, North America's second-largest film production centre. ______________

12. Volunteers duties include participating in fundraising events and hosting social media accounts. ______________

13. Nunavut's Arctic Bay Adventures won the Indigenous Adventure Award in 2018. ______________

14. All managers should be informed of the security alarms code. ______________

15. Police officer's checked all drivers licences at two checkpoints. ______________

16. No smoking is allowed within 3 metres of the employees entrance. ______________

17. Many people think that professional athlete's earnings are too high. ______________

18. The ladies room is closed for cleaning. ______________

19. The profits of all companies are being affected by developing technologies and worldwide competition. ______________

20. New protocols prohibit customer's from using the bathroom facilities. ______________

TEAR HERE

NAME ______________________

LEVEL II

A. (Self-check) Underline the errors in possessive construction in the following sentences. Write the correct form in the space provided. Write *C* if a sentence is correct.

EXAMPLE: The meeting Friday is at Ellens. Ellen's

1. Where can I find the editor-in-chiefs office? ______
2. Thomas's and Mahmoud's presentation was inspiring to all. ______
3. The Jones' brothers both play hockey. ______
4. This company's product line is superior to that companies. ______
5. The first runner-ups prize of $200 went to Chandra Lewis. ______
6. Sales of shares were stimulated by the CRTC's ruling. ______
7. The new hire in the Communications' Department studied journalism. ______
8. We can get that part at the Lowe's store down the street. ______
9. Most ladies and mens raincoats are reduced in price. ______
10. Is your sister-in-laws law firm downtown? ______

Check your answers.

B. Underline the errors in possessive construction in the following sentences. Write the correct form in the space provided. Write *C* if a sentence is correct.

1. The company's year-end barbecue will be held at Annas'. ______
2. The duke and duchess's limousine approached slowly. ______
3. Website designers must consider a wide variety of Web browsers and devices. ______
4. Every summer the company sponsors a local arts and crafts' show. ______
5. All beneficiaries names must be submitted when we issue policies. ______
6. NATOs member countries include Canada and France. ______
7. Please read the term's and condition's outlined in the document. ______
8. This year's computer sales outdistanced last years. ______
9. Selma was hired when she was six months pregnant. ______
10. The new winter uniforms are made from sheeps' wool. ______
11. Both the husband's and wife's signatures must be secured before the sale is valid. ______
12. The Sandinskys took their complaint to small claim's court. ______

TEAR HERE

13. At least a dozen buyers and sellers finances were scrutinized. ____________

14. The last power failure happened on New Years' Eve. ____________

15. Your totals for the last three columns are certainly different from Carols. ____________

16. GMs plant in Oshawa, Ontario, began operations in 1953. ____________

17. Lyon & Co.s annual sale is scheduled to begin in three days. ____________

18. This month's report is similar to previous months. ____________

19. Although I'm interested in the electronics' field, I have not settled on a definite career. ____________

20. Were they at Hassans last Saturday night? ____________

C. Rewrite these sentences to remedy awkward or incorrect possessives. (*Hint:* Start your sentence with the word that is owned.)

EXAMPLE: My brother's friend's car is available. The car of my brother's friend is available.

1. Our CFO's report's summary pointed to some problems we need to address. ____________

2. Dr. Hiyate, my dentist's, practice is flourishing. ____________

3. The two managers-in-training's pass cards were compromised. ____________

4. The board of directors' treasurer's position remains vacant. ____________

5. The engineer's assistant's computer held all the necessary equations. ____________

6. My boss's friend's motorhome is always parked in the company lot. ____________

TEAR HERE

NAME ______________________

LEVEL III

A. **(Self-check)** Select the acceptable possessive form(s), and write its letter in the space provided.

1. Several of the (a) employees', (b) employee's computers were infected by a virus. ______
2. We can't locate (a) Francises', (b) Francis' or Francis's file. ______
3. The (a) Chuks's (b) Chukses' paperwork is ready for their signatures. ______
4. Liane was just following her (a) bosses (b) boss's orders. ______
5. Even the pharmacists had difficulty reading Dr. (a) Fox's or Fox', (b) Foxes prescription. ______
6. All (a) creditor's, (b) creditors' claims will be honoured. ______
7. Have you seen Annie (a) Leibovitz's or Leibovitz', (b) Leibovitzes' photographs? ______
8. Please verify Ms. (a) Davises', (b) Davis's or Davis' hours. ______
9. Have you noticed that the (a) Felizes, (b) Felizes' have a new car? ______
10. Where is (a) Tobias's or Tobias' (b) Tobiases new office? ______

Check your answers.

B. Fill in the singular possessive forms for the two styles shown below.

Name	Traditional Style	Popular Style
EXAMPLE: [Mr. Jones] Suit	Mr. Jones's suit	Mr. Jones' suit
1. [Ms. Reis] laptop		
2. [Abhiz] lawyer		
3. [Dr. Cortez] office		
4. [Glynnis] computer		
5. [Miss Mertz] letter		
6. [Mr. Wilcox] response		

TEAR HERE

C. Review of Levels I, II, and III. Correct any errors in possessives in the following sentences. Write the corrected forms in the space provided. Write *C* if a sentence is correct.

1. Do you feel that you got your moneys worth? ____________
2. His landlord said that four months rent was due. ____________
3. Were the Bikakises' notified of the change in their account status? ____________
4. We were all invited to the party at the Wheatons. ____________
5. The wireless routers reach doesn't cover the entire office. ____________
6. I believe that Russ letter is on the top of the pile. ____________
7. Todays forecast calls for freezing temperatures. ____________
8. Charlie's and Mika's laptops were stolen last week. ____________
9. Are we responding with a tender for Ontario's highways' winter maintenance? ____________
10. The packages were delivered to all but one of the addressees. ____________
11. The Moskowitz two sons are enrolled in a Saskatchewan college. ____________
12. I can find other peoples errors but not my own. ____________
13. After three day's practice, all trainees qualified. ____________
14. The accountant and her assistant's vacation dates cannot overlap. ____________
15. Onex founder and CEO Gerry Schwartz spouse, Heather Reisman, founded Indigo Books & Music. ____________
16. If our departments had been aware of each others' needs, we could have shared our inventories. ____________
17. The Sales Department hosts an awards ceremony every June. ____________
18. Our mens team placed second in the hockey championship. ____________
19. The technicians training session has been rescheduled for Monday. ____________
20. You must examine a contractors licence before agreeing to any work. ____________

TEAR HERE

D. Writing Exercise. Your instructor may ask you to complete one or both of these exercises on a separate sheet.

(a) Write ten original sentences, one to illustrate the possessive form of each of the following: *Idris, two years, driver, Jason and Rena, bus, a dollar, customers, host, mother-in-law, the Lees.* Underline the possessive form in each sentence.

(b) Practise making your own name possessive. Write four complete sentences showing your family name in these formats: singular, singular possessive, plural, plural possessive. (Remember that you must add the word *the* before your last name to make it plural.)

POSTTEST

Underline any incorrect possessive forms. Write the correct version in the space provided.

1. Possible new products were discussed at the managers meeting. ________
2. This month's sales figures were better than last months. ________
3. Three companys tax returns were audited. ________
4. Mr. Nasser's account has been transferred to the Collections' Department. ________
5. Marc makes a point of wishing everyone a happy Valentines Day. ________
6. Three witnesses testimonies required seven court days. ________
7. My father's-in-law birthday is in November. ________
8. In just two years time, your profits will likely double. ________
9. The Lopez's car was towed from the parking lot. ________
10. Both parties signatures are needed to validate the contract. ________

TEAR HERE

EDITOR'S CHALLENGE

The following personal business letter and community announcement contain errors in sentence structure, plural nouns, and possessive nouns, as well as other common errors. Use standard proofreading marks (see the inside front cover) to show your corrections.

2320 Centennial Road
Oshawa, ON L1G 8K7
February 9, 202x

Mr. Jonathon Benson
Benson Brothers Management Services
368 Glenlake Ave.
Toronto, ON M9B 2B4

Dear Mr. Bensen:

SUBJECT: Managing Apartment Complex in Don Mills

Please send me more information about your companys managment service for apartment owners' I especially would like answers to the following questions.

What are your fees to manage an apartment complex with six unit? Do you take care of renting the units when they become vacant? What percentage of all renters payments do you keep?

Will you enforce a list of do's and don't's that the owner provides? Do you require the last months rent in advance, do you maintain lawyers to handle legal problems?

Its now my responsibility to care for my father-in-laws six-unit apartment complex in Don Mills. This complex is 23 years old with all units occupied. Although we expect to have two vacancys in April. Your firms management services' may be exactly what I need. Since I do not live near the apartment complex. Please respond to my questions before March 1. So that I may evaluate the pro's and con's of your services.

Sincerely,

Laura W. Stephens

Laura W. Stephens

TEAR HERE

Town Meeting Notification

The Town of Somerville has recieved an application from Advantage Homes' to develop the vacant area of land on the southeast corner at the juction of Lake Street and Bentley Avenue.

The aplicant proposes building seven individual complex's that will house 27 single-family condominum townhome dwellings. The developers plan also includes the following common elements. A private road, a water meter room, and a mail kiosk. The walking pathes currently in place and the city-planted trees will remain.

We invite you to attend public meeting about this proposal, at the meeting, you will have an opportunity to review the builders' plans, discuss issues it may cause, and raise any concern's you have.

Please contact Bas Jergins's office at (905) 526-6824 if you have question's or require further information.

For additional resources, please visit MindTap at login.cengage.com. Cengage | MINDTAP

TEAR HERE

CHAPTER 5

PERSONAL PRONOUNS

OBJECTIVES

When you have completed the materials in this chapter, you will be able to do the following:

LEVEL I

- Use personal pronouns correctly as subjects and objects
- Distinguish between personal possessive pronouns (such as *its*) and contractions (such as *it's*)

LEVEL II

- Choose the correct pronoun in compound constructions, comparatives, and appositives
- Use reflexive pronouns correctly

LEVEL III

- Use subjective-case pronouns as subject complements following linking verbs
- Select the correct pronouns for use with the infinitive *to be*

PRETEST

Underline the correct pronouns.

1. A blog post written by (she, her) was widely shared on social media.
2. Who will do inside sales while Liv and (I, me, myself) are at the convention?
3. No one other than (her, she) thinks the radio ad is working.
4. Are you sure it was (she, her) who called me yesterday morning?
5. Reliable managers like you and (he, him) are difficult to retain.

(continued)

PRETEST *(CONTINUED)*

6. (Us, We) employees receive additional benefits in September.
7. It wouldn't be a surprise if everyone but (she, her) liked the idea.
8. Inconsiderate people annoy my roommate as much as (I, me, myself).
9. The interview team believed the best candidate to be (he, him).
10. Please contact Allison or (I, me, myself) with any questions.

BE THE EDITOR

From a Reliance Home Comfort radio ad: "No one cares about your comfort more than us."

One area of writing that requires great effort is the correct use of pronouns. As you will remember from Chapter 1 (p. 4), pronouns are words that substitute for nouns and other pronouns. They enable us to speak and write without awkward repetition. Grammatically, pronouns may be divided into seven types: personal, relative, interrogative, demonstrative, indefinite, reflexive, and reciprocal. Rather than consider all seven pronoun types, this textbook will be concerned only with those pronouns that cause difficulty in use.

LEVEL I

GUIDELINES FOR USING PERSONAL PRONOUNS

Personal pronouns indicate the person speaking, the person spoken to, or the person or thing spoken of. Notice in the following table that the personal pronouns change their form (or **case**) depending upon who is speaking or being spoken about (called the **person**), how many the speaker is speaking about (the **number**), and the sex (or **gender**) of the one being spoken about. For example, the third-person feminine singular objective-case pronoun is *her*. Most personal pronoun errors by speakers and writers involve faulty usage of case forms. Referring to the following table as you learn how pronouns function in sentences can help you avoid errors in personal pronoun use.

	Subjective Case*		**Objective Case†**		**Possessive Case**	
	Singular	**Plural**	**Singular**	**Plural**	**Singular**	**Plural**
First person (person speaking)	I	we	me	us	my, mine	our, ours
Second person (person spoken to)	you	you	you	you	your, yours	your, yours
*Third person*** *(person or thing spoken of)*	he, she, it	they	him, her it	them	his, her, hers, its	their, theirs

*Some authorities prefer the term *nominative case.*

†Some authorities prefer the term *accusative case.*

**The chart and the exercises in this chapter reflect traditional grammar. However, when a specific individual prefers to go by a neutral-gender pronoun, *they, them,* and *theirs* can be appropriate singular pronouns.

Basic Use of the Subjective Form

Subjective-case pronouns are used primarily as the subjects of verbs. Every verb or verb phrase, regardless of its position in a sentence, has a subject. If that subject is a pronoun, it must be in the subjective form.

I thought that *he* was texting someone.

They asked if *we* had valid passports.

Once *she* has read the report, *I* will invite her feedback.

Basic Use of the Objective Form

Objective-case pronouns are used most commonly as objects of verbs or objects of prepositions.

OBJECT OF A VERB. As you learned in Chapter 2 (p. 18), objects of action verbs can be direct or indirect. In either case, as objects of verbs, pronouns must be in the objective form.

Bob asked *her* for help. (direct object)

The reporter quoted *us* correctly. (direct object)

The manager gave *them* a building map. (indirect object)

The real estate agent sold *him* a fixer-upper. (indirect object)

OBJECT OF A PREPOSITION. The objective case is used for pronouns that are objects of prepositions.

Just between *you* and *me*, profits are slipping.

A letter signed by all of *us* was sent to *him*.

The meeting will have to begin without *her*.

When the words *between, but, like,* and *except* are used as prepositions, errors in pronoun case are likely to occur. To avoid such errors, isolate the prepositional phrase, and then use an objective-case pronoun as the object of the preposition. Example: *Every employee [but her] completed the form.*

BE THE EDITOR

On a plaque outside the Pigott Building in Hamilton, Ontario: "Here the Canadian Club movement had it's beginning. . . . Erected by the Womens Canadian Club of Hamilton."

Basic Use of the Possessive Form

Possessive pronouns show ownership. Unlike possessive nouns, possessive pronouns never have apostrophes. Study these five common possessive pronouns: *hers, yours, ours, theirs, its*. Notice the absence of apostrophes.

Do not confuse possessive pronouns with contractions. **Contractions** are shortened (contracted) forms of subjects and verbs, such as *it's* (for *it is* or *it has*), *they're* (for *they are*), and *you're* (for *you are*). The apostrophes in these examples indicate omitted letters.

Possessive Pronouns	**Contractions**
The cat is cleaning *its* fur.	*It's* a household pet.
Your presentation will be excellent.	*You're* the next speaker.
Their anniversary is tomorrow.	*They're* going to have a party.
Theirs are the first few seats.	*There's* not an empty seat left.

STUDY TIP

Never use *it's* unless you can substitute *it is* or *it has*; if you cannot, use the pronoun *its*. As you learned in Chapter 1, some possessive forms function as adjectives when they describe nouns (e.g., *its fur, your presentation*).

Complete the reinforcement exercises for Level I on pages 78–79.

LEVEL II

CHALLENGES IN USING PERSONAL PRONOUNS

BE THE EDITOR

Paris Hilton wore a T-shirt that said "Thats hot" on the front and "Your not" on the back.

BE THE EDITOR

From a commercial greeting card: "If the stars were champagne bubbles spilled across the sky . . . that enchanted night would be a toast to you and I. Happy Anniversary!"

ASK AN EDITOR

Question:

On the radio, I recently heard a talk-show host *say, My producer and myself.* A little later the same host said, *Send any inquiries to the station or myself at this address.* Is this correct grammar?

Answer:

No, but the problem is a common one: use of a reflexive pronoun (*myself*) when it has no preceding noun or pronoun on which to reflect. Corrections: *My producer and I* and *Send inquiries to the station or to me.* Reflexive pronouns like *myself* should be used only with obvious antecedents, such as *I myself will take the calls.* Many people misuse reflexive pronouns, perhaps to avoid sounding egocentric with overuse of *I* and *me* or because of a mistaken belief that the reflexive is a more polite form.

Compound Subjects and Objects

When a pronoun appears in combination with a noun or another pronoun, we must give special attention to case selection. Try this technique to help choose the correct pronoun case: Ignore the extra noun or pronoun and its related conjunction, and consider separately the pronoun in question to determine what the case should be.

~~Sanjay and~~ *he* enrolled in the class. (Ignore *Sanjay and.*) (compound subject)
Will you permit ~~Toby and~~ *them* to join you? (Ignore *Toby and.*) (compound object)
Laura asked ~~you and~~ *me* for advice. (Ignore *you and.*) (compound object)

Notice in the first sentence, for example, that when *Sanjay and* is removed, it is much easier to see that the pronoun *he* must be selected because it functions as the subject of the verb.

Comparatives

In **comparative statements**, words are often implied but not stated. To determine pronoun case in partially complete statements of comparison introduced by *than* or *as,* always mentally finish the comparative by adding the implied missing words.

Jon earns as much as *they.* (= Jon earns as much as *they* [not *them*] earn.)
Farah spells better than *he.* (= . . . better than *he* [not *him*] spells.)
Tardiness annoys Mr. Boht as much as *me.* (= . . . as much as it annoys *me* [not *I*].)

In many sentences, either meaning could be accurate. Only the use of the correct pronoun will ensure the reader understands your meaning.

Leo likes his car more than *I.* (= Leo likes his car more than I like it.)
Leo likes his car more than *me.* (= Leo likes his car more than he likes me.)

The examples above illustrate the importance of using the right pronoun.

Appositives

Appositives are words or groups of words that explain or rename previously mentioned nouns or pronouns. A pronoun that has an appositive takes the same case as the noun or pronoun that follows it. To determine more easily what pronoun form to use for a pronoun in combination with an appositive, temporarily ignore the appositive.

We ~~consumers~~ are protected by laws. (Ignore *consumers.*)
Precautions were taken by *us* ~~neighbours~~. (Ignore *neighbours.*)

Reflexive Pronouns

Reflexive pronouns end in *self* or *selves* and emphasize or reflect on their **antecedents** (the nouns or pronouns previously mentioned).

The president *himself* presented the award. (Emphasizes *president*)

We hope the matter will resolve *itself.* (Reflects on *matter*)

Errors result if we use reflexive pronouns when we should use personal pronouns. If a sentence part has no previously mentioned noun or pronoun, use a personal pronoun instead of a reflexive pronoun.

Send the proposed agenda to either Bradley or *me*. (Objective pronoun *me* [not *myself*])
Jee Yun and *I* analyzed the numerous possibilities. (Subjective pronoun *I* [not *myself*])

Complete the reinforcement exercises for Level II on pages 80–82.

STUDY TIP

A pronoun that follows a linking verb acts as a subject complement and, therefore, should be in the subjective form.

LEVEL III

ADVANCED USES OF SUBJECTIVE-CASE PRONOUNS

Although the following applications appear infrequently, careful speakers and writers try to understand why certain pronoun forms are used.

Subject Complement

As we saw earlier in this chapter, subjective-case pronouns usually function as subjects of verbs. Less frequently, subjective-case pronouns also perform as subject complements. A pronoun that follows a linking verb and renames the subject must be in the subjective case. As you learned in Chapter 1, **linking verbs** express a state of being and generally link the subject to words in the predicate that describe or rename it. Be especially alert to the linking verb forms *am, is, are, was, were, be, being,* and *been*. Other linking verbs express the senses: *feel, appear, taste, sound, smell, look, seem*.

It *was I* who placed the order. (Not *me*)
I'm sure it *is she* who usually answers the telephone. (Not *her*)
If you *were I*, what would you do? (Not *me*)

When a sentence includes a verb phrase, look at the final word of the verb phrase. If it is a linking verb, use a subjective-case pronoun.

It *might have been they* who made the bid. (Not *them*)
The driver *could have been he*. (Not *him*)
If the manager *had been I*, your money would have been refunded. (Not *me*)

In casual conversation it is common to say, *It is me* or, more likely, *It's me*. Careful business speakers and writers, though, normally use subjective-case pronouns after linking verbs. If the resulting constructions sound too formal, revise your sentences appropriately. For example, instead of *It is I who placed the order*, use *I placed the order*.

ASK AN EDITOR

Question:
My supervisor corrected me when I said "This is her" on a telephone call. However, *This is she* sounds unnatural to me. How can I sound natural but also professional?

Answer:
To sound natural and professional, try saying *This is . . .* followed by your name.

Infinitive *To Be* With a Subject

An **infinitive** is the base form of a verb, usually preceded by *to*; for example, *to sit, to run,* and *to walk*. An important infinitive is *to be*. Infinitives can have subjects, which normally immediately precede the infinitive. When *to be* has a subject, any pronoun following it will function as an object. Therefore, the pronoun following the infinitive will take the objective case.

The interviewer believed the best candidate to be *her*. (The subject of the infinitive *to be* is *candidate*; therefore, the pronoun functions as an object. Try it another way: *The interviewer believed her to be the best candidate*. You would not say, *The interviewer believed she to be the best candidate*.)
The receptionist expected the caller to be *me*. (The subject of the infinitive *to be* is *caller*; therefore, the pronoun functions as an object.)

Colonel Dunn judged the winner to be *him*. (The subject of the infinitive *to be* is *winner*; therefore, use the objective-case pronoun *him*.)

Infinitive *To Be* Without a Subject

When the infinitive *to be* has no subject, subjective-case pronouns are used after the infinitive. In this instance the infinitive joins a complement (not an object) to the subject. (Linking verbs and complements are discussed more fully on pages 147–148.)

Her twin sister was often taken to be *she*. (The infinitive *to be* has no subject; *she* is the complement of the subject *sister*.)

Darrell was mistakenly thought to be *I*. (The infinitive *to be* has no subject; *I* is the complement of the subject *Darrell*.)

Why would Amal want to be *she*? (The infinitive *to be* has no subject; *she* is the complement of the subject *Amal*.)

DID YOU KNOW?

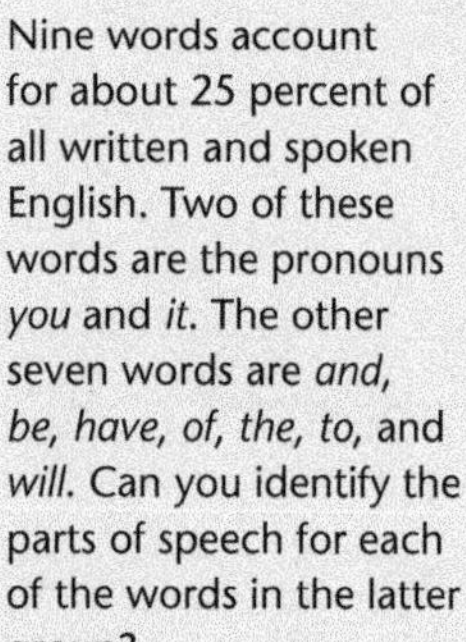

Nine words account for about 25 percent of all written and spoken English. Two of these words are the pronouns *you* and *it*. The other seven words are *and, be, have, of, the, to,* and *will*. Can you identify the parts of speech for each of the words in the latter group?

BE THE EDITOR

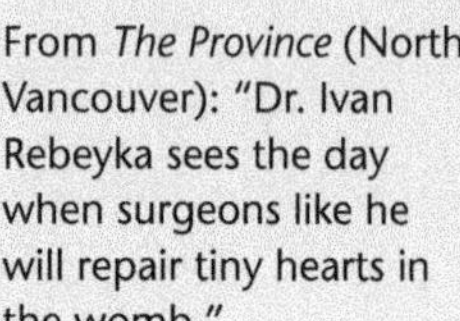

From *The Province* (North Vancouver): "Dr. Ivan Rebeyka sees the day when surgeons like he will repair tiny hearts in the womb."

ASK AN EDITOR

Question:
My boss is ready to send out a letter that says, *I respectfully call you and your client's attention to* . . . What's wrong with this? How can I make *you* possessive?

Answer:
The best way to handle this awkward wording is to avoid using the possessive form. Use a prepositional phrase instead (*I respectfully call to the attention of you and your client . . .*).

Whenever you want to test the correctness of the pronoun you have selected for the infinitive *to be*, try reversing the pronoun and its antecedent. For example, *We thought the winner to be her* (*We thought her* [not *she*] *to be the winner*) or *Cheryl was often taken to be she* (*She* [not *Her*] *was often taken to be Cheryl*). In the first sentence, *the winner* is the subject of *to be*; in the second sentence, *to be* has no subject, so the subjective-case pronoun follows.

SUMMARY OF PRONOUN CASES

The following table summarizes the uses of subjective- and objective-case pronouns.

Subjective Case	
Subject of the verb:	*They* are skydivers.
	We will go together.
Subject complement:	That is *he*.
	The best candidate was *she*.
Infinitive *to be* without a subject:	Ed pretended to be *he*.
	The driver at fault was determined to be *I*.

Objective Case	
Direct or indirect object of a verb:	He interviewed *her*.
	Give *him* another chance.
Object of a preposition:	Send the order to *him*.
	The gift came from *them*.
Object of an infinitive:	Jane promised to call *us*.
	Her manager needs to trust *her*.
Infinitive *to be* with subject:	We thought the guests to be *them*.
	He mistook the server to be *me*.

SUMMARY OF TYPES OF PRONOUNS

For those of you interested in a total view, here is a summary of the seven types of pronouns, with sentences illustrating each type. This list is presented only for your interest, not for potential testing.

1. **Personal pronouns** replace nouns or other pronouns.

Subjective case:	I, we, you, he, she, it, they
Objective case:	me, us, you, him, her, it, them
Possessive case:	my, mine, our, ours, your, yours, his, her, hers, its, their, theirs

Dr. Benton said *she* put *her* signature on *it* yesterday.

2. **Relative pronouns** join subordinate clauses to antecedents. Examples: *who, whose, whom, which, that, whoever, whomever, whichever, whatever.*

   He is the candidate *whom* we all admire.

3. **Interrogative pronouns** replace nouns in a question. Examples: *who, whose, whom, which, what.*

   Who is sitting here?

4. **Demonstrative pronouns** designate specific persons or things. Examples: *this, these, that, those.*

   This must be the work request we need.

5. **Indefinite pronouns** replace nouns in a non-specific way. Examples: *everyone, anyone, someone, each, everybody, anybody, somebody, one, none, some, most, all.*

   Everybody needs adequate nourishment.

6. **Reflexive pronouns** emphasize or reflect on antecedents. Examples: *myself, ourselves, yourself, yourselves, himself, herself, itself, oneself, themselves.*

   The CEO *himself* answered that letter.

7. **Reciprocal pronouns** indicate mutual relationship. Examples: *each other, one another.*

   The three chief executive officers consulted *one another* before making the announcement.

Complete the reinforcement exercises for Level III on pages 83–85.

NAME ______________________

CHAPTER 5 ■ Reinforcement Exercises

LEVEL I

A. **(Self-check)** Select the correct form, and write it in the space provided.

1. We are confident that (he, him) will do a good job. ______
2. Are you sure (there's, theirs, their's) time to complete the form? ______
3. For people like (they, them) who want the best, we have our deluxe model. ______
4. We are very impressed with (your, you're) application. ______
5. Everyone except (she, her) prefers to use instant messaging. ______
6. Please ask (she, her) to meet with us tomorrow morning. ______
7. Jas didn't know that (we, us) in Finance had planned to be there. ______
8. Malia was the one who called the meeting, and then (she, her) had to miss it. ______
9. When you see Dabinder, give (he, him) my email address. ______
10. Don is certain that nobody but (he, him) can access these files. ______

B. In the spaces provided, list five personal pronouns that can be used as subjects of verbs and five that can be used as objects of verbs or objects of prepositions.

As subjects: **1.** ______ **2.** ______ **3.** ______ **4.** ______ **5.** ______

As objects: **1.** ______ **2.** ______ **3.** ______ **4.** ______ **5.** ______

C. In the spaces provided, write *a*, *b*, or *c* to indicate how the italicized pronouns function in these sentences.

a = subject of a verb b = object of a verb c = object of a preposition

EXAMPLE: Please tell *her* that the refund is being processed. b

1. Ms. Larsen asked *me* for my cellphone number. ______
2. *She* and Pooja were late for their counselling appointment. ______
3. When you ship the package, be sure to notify *us* of the tracking number. ______
4. The work the consultant did for *us* has greatly improved our processes. ______
5. *You* made a good impression on the board of directors. ______
6. Who hired *him*? ______
7. Without his support *I* wouldn't be here today. ______

TEAR HERE

8. Pina enjoyed visiting *us* at the cottage. ____________

9. Everyone but *them* invested in technology stocks. ____________

10. Taryn's manager promised *her* a raise if the project launches on time. ____________

11. Because of *it*, the business turned a profit last year. ____________

12. *He* and the project director worked on the program budget. ____________

D. Select the correct pronoun, and write it in the space provided.

1. Please have (he, him) notarize this document. ____________

2. (Your, You're) new office is on the third floor. ____________

3. Nobody but (he, him) has been authorized to use the premises. ____________

4. Only (he, him) has been authorized to use the premises. ____________

5. Between you and (I, me), I think the committee should be dissolved. ____________

6. We have already sent the parts to (they, them) for inspection. ____________

7. Knowing you've done a job well is (it's, its) own reward. ____________

8. If the error is (there's, theirs, their's), they will have to own up to it. ____________

9. A presentation by (he, him) may convince the board to change directions. ____________

10. Which of the options will (she, her) choose? ____________

11. I am pleased to learn that (he, him) will be transferred to our division. ____________

12. Mr. Sandhu asked whether the terms of the contract were satisfactory to (we, us). ____________

13. A customer complaint made (she, her) work harder to be helpful. ____________

14. Employees like (he, him) are hard to come by. ____________

15. The Nanwakolas Council engaged seven participating First Nations in the creation of (it's, its) economic development plan. ____________

E. Change the italicized words in the following paragraph into appropriate pronouns. Add your answers on the space below each.

Several contractors have responded to our request for proposals. However, some of ________ (*the contractors*) already maintain large accounts, raising concerns about ________ (*the contractors'*) ability to manage a larger workload. Ms. Preet Nashir stood out as someone we should consider further. ______ (*Ms. Nashir*) has worked as a copywriter for six years, and ______ (*Ms. Nashir's*) rates are competitive. The human resources representative will contact Ms. Nashir's references tomorrow, and then ________________ (*the human resources representative*) will offer ________________ (*the human resources representative's*) expert opinion on whether we should offer the contract to Ms. Nashir. If all goes well, we will begin working with ______ (*Ms. Nashir*) by next month.

TEAR HERE

NAME ______________________

LEVEL II

A. (Self-check) Select the correct pronoun, and write it in the space provided.

1. The proposals submitted by (she and I, her and me, her and I) were considered first. ______
2. No one knows technical jargon better than (he, him). ______
3. The marketing team and (we, us) need to work together on this. ______
4. A flexible benefits plan was offered to (we, us) employees. ______
5. (Us, We) delegates stayed at the Hotel Dupar during the convention. ______
6. Sacha Ouellet and (myself, I, me) were singled out for commendation. ______
7. The manager would rather see Elio in that role than (she, her). ______
8. No one but my friend and (myself, I, me) spoke up during the discussion. ______
9. Both programmers, Ari and (she, her), are testing spam-blocking software. ______
10. The announcement surprised Professor Einarsson as much as (she, her). ______

B. Write the correct pronoun in the space provided.

1. (Her, She) and a colleague plan to take a college writing course next term. ______
2. I have been with the company six months longer than (she, her). ______
3. Some of (we, us) applicants were interviewed in groups. ______
4. Paul will allow no one but (he, him, himself) to change the account information. ______
5. Our director's presentation on social responsibility inspired Fausto as much as (I, me). ______
6. No other applicants stood out as much as Mr. Rhodes and (he, him). ______
7. It's not often that (us, we) technicians get recognition. ______
8. Will you and (he, him) have time to meet with the delegates? ______
9. The designers' arguing among (they, them, themselves) in front of us seemed unprofessional. ______
10. An IT professional would be better suited than (I, me, myself) to help you. ______
11. The vice president of operations (she, her, herself) told us the plant is relocating. ______
12. A serious disagreement between Ola and (he, him, himself) caused problems in the office. ______
13. Two from our team, (he, him) and Mimi, were selected for the internal focus group. ______
14. Do you think Ambreen can complete the work more quickly than (he, him)? ______
15. In the wilderness survival class, Tsuut'ina students learn to work together to help (them, themselves) thrive. ______

TEAR HERE

16. All employees but Dan Oleniuk and (I, me, myself) agreed to the proposal for a shorter workday. ____________

17. Whether (we, us) franchisees want them or not, we will have to purchase the new signs. ____________

18. The letters appear to have been signed by you and (she, her, herself). ____________

19. The authors typed the manuscripts (themself, themselves). ____________

20. Everyone except two drivers and (he, him) has checked in with the dispatcher. ____________

C. Underline any faulty pronouns in the following sentences. Write the correct form in the space provided. Write *C* if a sentence is correct.

1. Raynard and him had a history that made a positive working relationship unlikely. ____________

2. Please submit your expense claim to Raghad or myself by Friday afternoon. ____________

3. If Matt and I do not receive email confirmations of our itinerary, neither him nor I can make the trip. ____________

4. Business book reviews written alternately by he and she are published in the quarterly newsletter. ____________

5. Just between you and I, neither Kris nor he met the monthly quota. ____________

6. The insurance forms need to be filled out by you and she. ____________

7. Both owners, he and Maris Alikova, will attend to sign the lease agreement. ____________

8. It's surprising that us renters were not consulted about the remodelling. ____________

9. When you, Alexis, and me meet, we will brainstorm ways to improve the process. ____________

10. All students except Ali and she use laptops in class. ____________

11. I think that failing to get to meetings on time is rude, but it angers the boss even more than I. ____________

12. The transition should be an easy one for you and I. ____________

13. Does the yellow Toyota Prius in the employee parking lot belong to yourself? ____________

14. If you and she are selected for the training program, you will both have your tuition paid. ____________

15. Us on the management team congratulate you on this achievement. ____________

16. Her partner doesn't enjoy bookkeeping as much as her. ____________

17. The firm awarded several academic scholarships to we students. ____________

18. Email messages intended for Zola and he were accidentally forwarded to the entire department. ____________

19. Her and the CEO discussed how to improve public relations after customers lost Internet access for 18 hours. ____________

20. The applicant we are offering the job to has more experience than her. ____________

TEAR HERE

D. In the space provided, write complete sentences that begin with the words shown. Supply a pronoun where indicated.

EXAMPLE: Dana Paulson and (pronoun) Dana Paulson and he agreed to market their invention.

1. My supervisor and (pronoun)

2. The two sales reps, Edita and (pronoun),

3. Just between you and (pronoun),

4. Except for Mr. Sanders and (pronoun),

5. The manager expected Yumiko and (pronoun)

6. Yours or (pronoun)

7. Someone other than (pronoun)

8. When the board of directors and (pronoun)

TEAR HERE

NAME ____________________

LEVEL III

A. (Self-check) Select the correct pronoun, and write it in the space provided.

1. The new vice president of purchasing is (she, her). ____________
2. If you were (he, him), would you make the same decision? ____________
3. Ramco asked my partner and (I, me) to write a proposal. ____________
4. It might have been (she, her) who recommended our new paralegal. ____________
5. Was it (they, them) who redesigned the company website? ____________
6. We all assumed the new head of marketing would be (him, he). ____________
7. Gilbert said that it was (he, him) who used the printer last. ____________
8. The audience didn't discover that Marcelle was (she, her) until the final act. ____________
9. No one had thought Marcelle to be (she, her). ____________
10. If the caller had been (he, him), Raja would have left the meeting to take the call. ____________

B. Write the correct pronoun in the space provided.

1. Whether it is you or (I, me) who gets the promotion, I will be pleased. ____________
2. Do you think it was (they, them) who left the door unlocked last night? ____________
3. The committee chair asked Ely and (I, me) to serve on a special task force. ____________
4. Almost everyone expected the successful applicant to be (her, she). ____________
5. If you were (I, me), would you apply for additional financing? ____________
6. We are unsure whether the supervisor will be (he, him). ____________
7. It was (she, her) who called this morning. ____________
8. The person who reported the safety issue was thought to be (he, him). ____________
9. If the newly elected council member had been (he, him), our worst fears might have been realized. ____________
10. We could not expect (she, her) to have read the entire manual already. ____________
11. We hope to book Professor Wells and (he, him) to be keynote speakers. ____________
12. The keynote speakers turned out not to be (they, them). ____________
13. Adam and Tanisha were certain it was not (they, them) who caused the network to crash. ____________
14. The committee declared the scholarship recipient to be (her, she). ____________
15. When Asha opened the door, she expected to see you and (he, him). ____________
16. It must have been (they, them) who reported the missing funds. ____________
17. If it had been (we, us) who filed the complaint, would the result be different? ____________
18. If the caller is (he, him), ask him for his cellphone number. ____________

TEAR HERE

19. The whistleblower was suspected to be (she, her). ____________

20. Will it be (she, her) who represents the company at the convention? ____________

C. Review of Levels I, II, and III. Underline any errors in personal pronouns, and write a correct form in the space provided. Write *C* if a sentence is correct.

1. His mentor and him plan to meet weekly. ____________
2. If the task had been given to anyone but her to do, I would be more concerned. ____________
3. Do you know whose working on the final version of the JetCom proposal? ____________
4. Because of it's success, our cultural awareness training program is being expanded. ____________
5. Was it him who notified the company of the defective batteries? ____________
6. The wage discussions between Mr. O'Donnell and they appear to be progressing smoothly. ____________
7. Send a message to Gene or myself once you've arrived. ____________
8. We believe that no one is more familiar with the situation than him. ____________
9. Us investors, of course, expect to make at least a minimal profit. ____________
10. Travis wouldn't have done the job any better than me. ____________
11. Jensen assumed it was they who made the initial report. ____________
12. To get us candidates to agree on anything will take a miracle. ____________
13. The insurance salespeople, Mr. Zhang and her, made several appointments for evening interviews. ____________
14. Everyone except he took part in the videoconference. ____________
15. The inventor credited with the idea was thought to be he. ____________
16. All software technicians except Fatima and she were transferred. ____________
17. We would like to know more about how your addressing the situation. ____________
18. Jean Powers and me completed our project on time. ____________

D. Review of Chapters 4 (Possessive Nouns) and 5 (Personal Pronouns). Underline any errors in possessive nouns or personal pronouns in the following sentences. For each sentence write a corrected form in the space provided. Be alert! Some sentences need more than one correction. Write *C* if a sentence is correct.

1. Many small business owners like Asmon and I work in home office's. ____________
2. On the way to the airport, Lila and me passed a white stretch limousine that was stalled at the side of the road with it's hood up. ____________
3. Do you want to carpool to the award's ceremony with the Jenkins's and I? ____________
4. Even if it was him who borrowed the laptop overnight, it should have been signed for in the book on Rose's desk. ____________
5. Neither Mr. Persaud nor I could believe that Jeff was taken to be him. ____________
6. Between you and me, I think your going to be promoted. ____________
7. Of all the professionals in our IT department, Craig and her are the one's I find most helpful. ____________

TEAR HERE

Making Pronouns Agree With Their Antecedents in Number

Pronouns must agree in number with the nouns they represent. For example, if a pronoun replaces a singular noun, that pronoun must be singular.

> *Michelangelo* felt that *he* was a failure. (Singular antecedent and pronoun)
>
> Great *artists* often doubt *their* success. (Plural antecedent and pronoun)

If a pronoun refers to two nouns joined by *and*, the pronoun must be plural.

> The *president* and the *shareholders* discussed *their* differences. (Plural antecedent and pronoun)
>
> *Warren* and *Jerome* asked that suggestions be sent to *them*. (Plural antecedent and pronoun)

Pronoun–antecedent agreement can be complicated when words or phrases come between the pronoun and the word to which it refers. Disregard phrases such as those introduced by *as well as, in addition to, together with, of,* and other prepositions. Find the true antecedent, and make the pronoun agree with it.

> The *general*, together with the chiefs of staff, is considering *his* strategy carefully. (Singular antecedent and pronoun)
>
> The *chiefs* of staff, along with the general, have submitted *their* plans. (Plural antecedent and pronoun)
>
> A female *member* of the group of protesting students demanded that *she* be treated fairly. (Singular antecedent and pronoun)

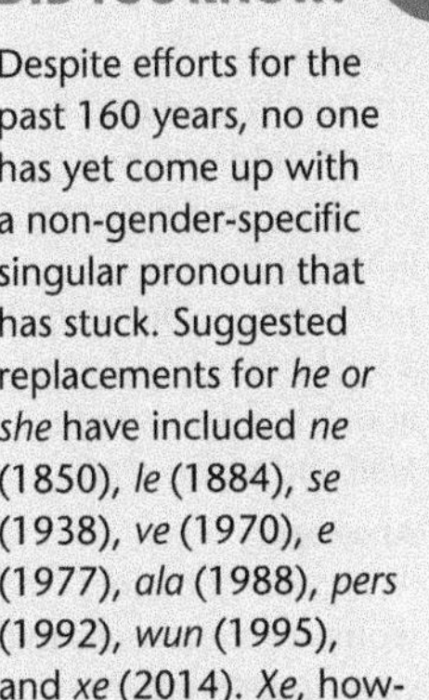

DID YOU KNOW?

Despite efforts for the past 160 years, no one has yet come up with a non-gender-specific singular pronoun that has stuck. Suggested replacements for *he or she* have included *ne* (1850), *le* (1884), *se* (1938), *ve* (1970), *e* (1977), *ala* (1988), *pers* (1992), *wun* (1995), and *xe* (2014). *Xe*, however, gained traction in 2014, when a Vancouver school board officially approved its use.

Making Pronouns Agree With Their Antecedents in Gender

A pronoun exhibits one of three **genders**: masculine (male), feminine (female), or neuter (neither masculine nor feminine). Pronouns must agree with their antecedents in gender.

> John read *his* assignment. (Masculine gender)
>
> Nancy prepared for *her* trip. (Feminine gender)
>
> The idea had *its* limits. (Neuter gender)

CHOOSING ALTERNATIVES TO SINGULAR COMMON-GENDER PRONOUNS. Occasionally, writers and speakers face problems in choosing pronouns of appropriate gender. Although first-person (*I*) and second-person (*you*) singular pronouns may be used to refer to either gender, third-person singular pronouns (*he, she, it*) refer to specific genders. English has no all-purpose singular pronoun that can represent or refer to nouns of unclear gender such as *student* or *employee*.

For this reason writers and speakers in the past used masculine pronouns, then deemed common-gender, to refer to nouns that might be either masculine or feminine. For example, in the sentence "A student has *his* rights," the pronoun *his* referred to its antecedent, *student*, which might name either a female or male person.

Today this use of masculine pronouns is considered sexist or gender biased because the speaker or writer appears to exclude women. Modern business communicators, therefore, should rewrite sentences to avoid using masculine pronouns (*he, him, his*) when referring to

CAREER TIP

Business and professional people strive to avoid sexist and biased language. For example, they use parallel terms (*men and women* instead of *men and ladies*) and neutral titles (*salesperson* instead of *salesman*, *server* instead of *waitress*). They also avoid implied gender (*lawyers and their spouses* instead of *lawyers and their wives*).

ASK AN EDITOR

Question:
I'm totally confused by job titles for women. What do I call a woman who is a *fireman*, a *policeman*, a *chairman*, or a *spokesman*? And what about the words *mankind* and *manpower*?

Answer:
As more and more women enter careers that were traditionally the domain of men, and vice versa, job designations are being replaced by neutral, inclusive titles, such as the following:

actor, not *actress*

chair, not *chairman*

firefighter, not *fireman*

flight attendant, not *stewardess*

mail carrier, not *mailman*

nurse, not *male nurse*

police officer, not *policeman*

reporter or journalist, not *anchorman* or *newsman*

server, not *waitress*

spokesperson, not *spokesman*

As for *mankind* and *manpower*, how about *humankind* and *workforce*? It isn't difficult to be gender-inclusive, but it can take some thought until the more modern terminology becomes second nature. Many readers will appreciate that you've made the effort.

BE THE EDITOR

Television commercial for *Encyclopedia Britannica*: "Every parent has a wish list for their child."

nouns (or pronouns) that could refer to either men or women. Although many alternatives exist, here are three ways to avoid the masculine pronoun:

Traditional common gender:	An employee wants his job to be easy.
Alternative No. 1:	Employees want their jobs to be easy.
Alternative No. 2:	An employee wants a job to be easy.
Alternative No. 3:	An employee wants his or her job to be easy.
Less accepted:	An employee wants their job to be easy.

In Alternative No. 1, the subject has been made plural to avoid the need for a singular common-gender pronoun. In Alternative No. 2, an article is substituted for the pronoun, although at the cost of making the original meaning less emphatic. In Alternative No. 3, both masculine and feminine references (*his or her*) are used. Because this construction is wordy and rather clumsy, avoid using it frequently. Note that the plural pronoun *their* does not agree with the singular antecedent *employee* in the final example. In the absence of a gender-neutral singular pronoun, what's often dubbed "the singular *they*" is gaining acceptance, even among grammarians. However, business communicators should recognize that many people will still consider its use to be erroneous or lazy, especially when there are other more widely accepted ways to ensure agreement.

Now complete the reinforcement exercises for Level I on pages 97–99.

LEVEL II

SPECIAL PRONOUN–ANTECEDENT AGREEMENT CHALLENGES

The following guidelines will help you avoid several common errors in pronoun–antecedent agreement. These special instances include sentences in which the antecedents are (a) nouns or pronouns joined by *or* or *nor*, (b) indefinite pronouns, (c) collective nouns or company names, or (d) nouns preceded by *each* or *every*.

Antecedents Joined by *or* or *nor*

When antecedents are joined by *or* or *nor*, the pronoun should agree in number with the closer antecedent. The closer antecedent will be the one that comes after the *or* or *nor*.

Either Alice or *Vicki* left *her* coat in the office.

Neither the manager nor the *employees* objected to *their* salary cuts.

If, however, the antecedents are of different gender, recast the sentence to avoid the awkward construction.

Awkward:	Jake or *Mirela* just had her red Hyundai towed.
Better:	A red Hyundai, either Jake's or Mirela's, was just towed.

You may be wondering why antecedents joined by *and* are treated differently from antecedents joined by *or* or *nor*. The conjunction *and* joins one plus one to make two antecedents; therefore, a plural pronoun makes sense. The conjunctions *or* and *nor*, on the other hand, require a choice between two antecedents.

Indefinite Pronouns as Antecedents

Indefinite pronouns include pronouns such as *anyone, something,* and *everybody*. These pronouns are called indefinite because they refer to no specific person or object. Some indefinite pronouns are always singular; others are always plural.

Always Singular		Always Plural	Singular or Plural
anybody	everything	both	all
anyone	neither	few	any
anything	nobody	many	more
each	no one	several	most
either	nothing		none
everybody	somebody		some
everyone	someone		

When an indefinite pronoun functions as an antecedent of a personal pronoun, make certain that the personal pronoun agrees with its antecedent. And do not let a prepositional phrase obscure the true antecedent.

Somebody in the men's league left *his* lights on.

Each of the corporations had *its* own private plane.

Few of our employees use *their* work computers for personal tasks.

Several of our branches list *their* job openings on the company intranet.

The words *either* and *neither* can be confusing. When these words stand alone and function as subjects, they are always singular. When they are joined with *or* or *nor* to form the conjunctions *either/or* and *neither/nor*, however, they may connect plural subjects. These plural subjects may act as antecedents to plural pronouns.

Either of the women is able to see *her* personnel file. (*Either* is a singular pronoun and functions as the subject of the sentence. It is the antecedent of the pronoun *her* and also controls the singular verb *is*.)

Either the woman or her friends left *their* packages. (*Either/or* is used as a conjunction to join the two subjects, *woman* and *friends*. The pronoun *their* agrees with its plural antecedent, *friends*, which is the closer antecedent.)

The words *all, any, most, none,* and *some* can also trip up speakers and writers. These words may be plural or singular; their number depends on the word to which they refer, which often follows in an *of* phrase.

If *any* of the elk *burgers* are left after the ceremony, you can take *them* home.

If *any* of the *bannock* is left after the ceremony, you can take *it* home.

Collective Nouns as Antecedents

Words such as *jury, faculty, committee, staff, community, union, team, herd,* and *group* are called **collective nouns** because they refer to a collection of people, animals, or objects. Such words may be either singular or plural depending on whether the members of the group perform the action in the sentence jointly or individually. When the elements of the collective operate as a unit, the collective noun is singular. When the elements of the collective operate separately, the collective noun is plural.

BE THE EDITOR

From an American Express print ad: "Every ten minutes someone travelling in America loses their cash."

STUDY TIP

When followed by an *of* phrase, *either* or *neither* is functioning as a singular pronoun. (For example, *Neither of the books is available.*)

BE THE EDITOR

From *The New York Times:* "Neither Gore nor Bush could bring themselves to utter a word in defense of scientific truth."

Our *staff* reaffirmed *its* position on bargaining. (*Staff* operating as one unit)
Our *staff* enjoy *their* jobs. (*Staff* operating as individuals)
The *jury* rendered *its* verdict. (*Jury* operating as one unit)
The *jury* were divided in *their* opinions. (*Jury* operating as individuals)

However, if you want to use a collective noun in a plural sense, the sentence will seem less awkward if you add a plural noun.

The jury <u>members</u> were divided in their opinions.

Company and Organization Names as Antecedents

Company and organization names, including names of musical groups, are generally considered singular. Unless the actions of the organization are attributed to individual representatives of that organization, pronouns referring to organizations should be singular.

The *United Nations*, in addition to other organizations, is expanding *its* campaign to fight hunger.
Maclean Hunter Limited can trace *its* roots back to the nineteenth century.
Tim Hortons has started *its* Roll Up the Rim to Win contest again.
U2 is known throughout the world for *its* humanitarian efforts.

The Antecedents *Each* and *Every*

When *each* or *every* comes before a compound subject joined by *and*, that compound subject is considered singular.

Every player and coach on the men's team has *his* assigned duties.
Each daughter and mother will receive *her* award at the banquet.

Complete the reinforcement exercises for Level II on pages 100–101.

ASK AN EDITOR

Question:
I believe it is correct to ask, "To whom am I speaking?" but it seems very stiff-sounding. Is it ever acceptable instead to say, "Whom am I speaking to?"

Answer:
In Shakespeare's time prepositions often fell at the ends of sentences; about a century later some writers put forth the idea that English sentences shouldn't end with prepositions, as modelled by Latin sentence structure. Although grammarians dating as far back as the early 1900s have asserted that ending a sentence with a preposition is grammatical, many readers find the construction clunky. In speech, however, there's little harm in ending a sentence with a preposition.

LEVEL III

ADVANCED PRONOUN USE

The use of *who* and *whom* presents a continuing dilemma for speakers and writers. In conversation the correct choice of *who* or *whom* is often especially difficult because of the mental gymnastics necessary to locate subjects and objects. In writing, however, an author has ample time to analyze a sentence carefully and make a correct choice—if the author understands the traditional functions of *who* and *whom*.

The Challenge of *Who* and *Whom*

Who is the subjective-case form. Like other subjective-case pronouns, *who* may function as the subject of a verb or as the subject complement of a noun following a linking verb. *Whom* is the objective-case form. It may function as the object of a verb or as the object of a preposition.

Who do you think will be chosen as director? (*Who* is the subject of *will be chosen.*)
Lebron asked me *who* my boss is. (*Who* is the complement of *boss.*)
Whom should we hire? (*Whom* is the object of *should hire.*)
Alicia is the one to *whom* I spoke. (*Whom* is the object of the preposition *to.*)

How to Choose Between *Who* and *Whom*

The choice between *who* and *whom* becomes easier if the sentence in question is approached using the following three steps:

1. Isolate the *who/whom* clause, the part of the sentence to which the pronoun belongs.
2. Invert the clause, if necessary, to restore normal subject–verb–object order.
3. Try substituting the *who* or *whom* with the subjective pronoun form *he* (or *she* or *they*) and the objective pronoun form *him* (or *her* or *them*). If the sentence sounds correct with *him* (or *her* or *them*), use *whom* in the original sentence. If the sentence sounds correct with *he* (or *she* or *they*), choose *who*.

Study the following sentences, and notice how the choice of *who* or *whom* is made:

Here are the records of the man (who/whom) we have selected.

Isolate:	___________ we have selected
Invert:	we have selected ___________
Substitute:	we have selected him
Equate:	we have selected whom
Complete:	Here are the records of the man whom we have selected.

Do you know (who/whom) his doctor is?

Isolate:	___________ his doctor is
Invert:	his doctor is ___________ (or ___________ is his doctor)
Substitute:	his doctor is he (or he is his doctor)
Equate:	his doctor is who (or who is his doctor)
Complete:	Do you know who his doctor is?

When studying this example, remember from Chapter 5 that subjective-case pronouns follow linking verbs.

In choosing *who* or *whom*, ignore extra expressions such as *I hope, we think, I believe,* and *you know*.

Matthew is the candidate (who/whom) we believe is best.

Isolate:	___________ we believe is best
Ignore:	___________ [we believe] is best
Substitute:	he is best
Equate:	who is best
Complete:	Matthew is the candidate who we believe is best.

EXAMPLES:

Whom do you think we should call? (*Invert:* We should call her/*whom*)

The person to *whom* the article referred was Mr. Stein. (*Invert:* The article referred to him/*whom*)

Do you know *who* the manager is? (*Invert:* The manager is she/*who*)

Whom would you like to see appointed to that position? (*Invert:* You would like to see him/*whom* appointed to that position)

BE THE EDITOR

Famous singer on NBC's *Today* show: "I began to recognize whom I am, and I wasn't afraid of whom I was."

BE THE EDITOR

An article in *The Economist:* "In the past two years police have rescued 251 women whom they believe were trafficked to Britain."

ASK AN EDITOR

Question:
I'm disgusted with and infuriated by an advertisement I just saw for a university. It says, *It's not just who you know. . . .* Why would a leading institution of learning use such poor grammar?

Answer:
Because it sounds familiar—but familiarity doesn't make it correct. You're right in recognizing that the proper form is *whom* (isolate the clause *you know him* or *whom*). The complete adage—or more appropriately, cliché—correctly stated is *It's not what you know but whom you know.*

The Use of *Whoever* and *Whomever*

As with *who* and *whom*, *whoever* is subjective and *whomever* is objective. The selection of the correct form in clauses is sometimes complicated. You must determine how *whoever* or *whomever* is functioning (either as subject or object) within the clause. Note that clauses that feature these words may act as objects of prepositions, objects of verbs, or subjects of verbs. Study the following examples and explanations:

Issue a password to whoever needs one. (The entire clause *whoever needs one* is the object of the preposition *to*. Within the clause itself, *whoever* acts as the subject of *needs* and is therefore in the subjective form. Think: he needs one.)

Sadie will train whoever covers her parental leave. (The clause *whoever covers her parental leave* is the object of the verb *will train*. Within the clause, *whoever* acts as the subject of *covers* and is therefore in the subjective form. Think: he covers her parental leave.)

Whomever they nominate will have our support. (The clause *whomever they nominate* is the subject of the verb *will have*. Within the clause, *whomever* is the object of *they nominate* and is therefore in the objective form. Think: they nominate him.)

The Use of *Whose*

The pronoun *whose* functions as a possessive pronoun or an adjective. Like other possessive pronouns, *whose* has no apostrophe. Do not confuse it with the contraction *who's*, which means "who is" or "who has."

We haven't decided *whose* proposal will be accepted.
Whose applications were submitted by the deadline?
Please let me know *who's* on call this evening.
Do you know *who's* scheduled to give the keynote address?

Complete the reinforcement exercises for Level III on pages 102–105 and the unit review exercises on pages 109–111.

NAME ______________________

CHAPTER 6 ■ Reinforcement Exercises

LEVEL I

A. **(Self-check)** Select the correct word(s) to complete the following sentences.

1. A snow plow driver with (his, her, his or her, their) own truck is required for the overnight shift. ______
2. Every applicant must submit (his, her, his or her, their) résumé by email. ______
3. Jaime as well as his brother found (his, their) calling in engineering. ______
4. (They, Human resources experts) say that the prevalence of cellphones in the workplace is decreasing production by more than a third. ______
5. One of the men asked whether (he, they) could use (his, their) cellphone during the meeting. ______
6. Every nurse must perfect (his, her, his or her, their) bedside manner. ______
7. The furniture designer puts (his, her, his or her, their) vision on paper, and the carpenter builds it. ______
8. All flight attendants must have (her, his, his or her, their) uniforms cleaned regularly. ______
9. Miss Shapiro, after consulting the production staff and others, made (her, his or her, their) pricing decision. ______
10. No employee is forced to retire when (he reaches, it reaches, he or she reaches, they reach) the age of 65. ______

Check your answers.

B. Select the correct word(s) to complete the following sentences. Write it in the space provided.

1. A judge must deliver (his, her, his or her, their) instructions in plain English. ______
2. A shift supervisor, along with the other members of management, must do (his, her, his or her, their) best to exhibit strong ethics. ______
3. Workers in the largest plant asked that (his, his or her, their) working conditions be improved. ______
4. A nutritionist and a fitness instructor are hosting a lunch and learn today to share (his, her, his or her, their) tips for healthy living. ______
5. An employee should know what rights (he has, she has, he or she has, they have) in the workplace. ______

TEAR HERE

6. (You, Commuters) aren't allowed to drive in the carpool lane with fewer than three passengers. __________

7. Bob Eustes, one of our top chefs, entered (his, his or her, their) signature dish in the competition. __________

8. Any IT manager would be pleased to have Val on (his, her, his or her, their) team. __________

9. If the insured party causes an accident, (he, she, it, he or she, they) will be charged a higher premium. __________

10. The human resources manager advised each candidate of (his, her, his or her, their) opportunities for advancement within the organization. __________

C. In the space provided, rewrite the following sentences to avoid the use of gender-biased pronouns. Show three versions of each sentence.

1. Every shift supervisor must meet his production quota.

   a. __________

   b. __________

   c. __________

2. Be sure that each new employee has received his orientation packet.

   a. __________

   b. __________

   c. __________

3. The on-duty manager must use his pass card to void transactions.

   a. __________

   b. __________

   c. __________

4. A carpenter uses his tape measure several times a day.

   a. __________

   b. __________

   c. __________

5. Any salesperson who sells $10,000 of product in a month gets his picture on the "wall of fame."

   a. __________

   b. __________

   c. __________

TEAR HERE

D. In the space provided, rewrite these sentences to make the pronoun references clear.

1. They examine your gait at that shoe store.

2. Mr. Bhang told Mr. Vaccaro that he was the right person for the job.

3. Fatima asked Courtney if her job could be done from home.

4. Recruiters like to see job objectives on résumés; however, they may restrict their chances.

5. The article reported that Google had acquired Image America and that it planned to use its aerial photography technology.

E. Underline the errors in the following sentences, and then write a correction in the space provided. Write *C* if a sentence is correct.

1. At month end, each manager must submit their budget for the next month. ____________
2. A work-at-home employee is often more productive than his in-office counterparts. ____________
3. A consultant will oversee the survey process and share their recommendations with each department head. ____________
4. Two marketing consultants left their positions on the same day. ____________
5. Any administrative assistant we hire will need to prove that she has completed a college program. ____________

TEAR HERE

NAME ______________________________

LEVEL II

A. (Self-check) Select the correct word(s) to complete the following sentences.

1. Everyone in the department is encouraged to share (his, her, his or her, their) suggestions for increasing sales. ____________
2. Apparently, neither the email nor the printed letters had (its, their) contents proofread very carefully. ____________
3. Gold, Steinmetz, & Burns Inc. held an open house in honour of (its, their) anniversary. ____________
4. The radio spots and the print ad will be worth (its, their) money. ____________
5. Each man, woman, and child who attended the game made (his, her, his or her, their) own contribution to the food drive. ____________
6. Either Ms. Huang or Ms. Snyder will attend the meeting to share (his, her, his or her, their) experience in company restructurings. ____________
7. No one who attended the training seminars has submitted (his, her, his or her, their) feedback form yet. ____________
8. The Chamber of Commerce shared with the town council the views of (his or her, its, their) members concerning holiday lighting. ____________
9. Neither of the men would admit (his, their) part in causing the accident. ____________
10. The Coast Guard has five regional offices, but (his or her, its, their) headquarters is in Ottawa. ____________

Check your answers.

B. Select the appropriate pronoun(s) to complete the following sentences.

1. Every company laptop will have (its, their) software updated over the next several weeks. ____________
2. Dun and Bradstreet bases (its, their) financial ratings on accounting reports. ____________
3. Each of the managers has (his, her, his or her, their) own methods for motivating and rewarding staff. ____________
4. Some of the speakers shared (his or her, their) advice on improving morale. ____________
5. The CRTC uses (its, their) influence to increase the proportion of Canadian content in the media. ____________
6. Someone in this office reported that (his, her, his or her, their) computer had a virus. ____________
7. Neither of Gila's speaking events met (its, their) attendance goals. ____________

TEAR HERE

8. The inspection team will give (its, their) feedback by May 1. ____________

9. A committee of our colleagues will form and submit (its, their) recommendations for cost savings throughout the department. ____________

10. Any new subscriber may cancel (his, her, his or her, their) subscription within the first ten days. ____________

C. Underline any errors, and write a correct form in the space provided. Write *C* if a sentence is correct.

1. Each of the supermarkets featured their specials in Thursday's free newspaper. ____________

2. Every one of the 14 Inuit designers was paid a commission from Canada Goose for their parka design. ____________

3. A group of tourists missed the bus because they were delayed in the souvenir shop. ____________

4. Every employee should take the vacation time they earn. ____________

5. Most of the inventory has been accounted for and put in their place on the shelves. ____________

6. The Cheer Committee has chosen the charity they will raise funds for this holiday season. ____________

7. Either of the potential locations would need their parking lot resurfaced. ____________

8. *Consumer Reports* announced a plan to change its method of distribution. ____________

9. Union members elected their officers by electronic ballot. ____________

10. Not one of the employees cast his vote in approval of the new union contract. ____________

11. Neither the father nor his sons wanted to sell his shares. ____________

12. None of the marketing photography is in the file they are supposed to be in. ____________

TEAR HERE

NAME ____________________

LEVEL III

A. (Self-check) Select the correct word, and write it in the space provided.

1. (Who's, Whose) car is blocking the entry? ____________
2. This is the applicant (who, whom) impressed the hiring committee. ____________
3. (Who, Whom) do you think we should hire for the data communications analyst position? ____________
4. For (who, whom) were these messages intended? ____________
5. The contract will be awarded to (whoever, whomever) submits the lowest bid. ____________
6. When I return the call, for (who, whom) should I ask? ____________
7. Jackie Wong is the contractor (who, whom) Mr. Olson recommended. ____________
8. Is the woman (who, whom) audited the report a chartered accountant? ____________
9. Do you know (who's, whose) been invited to give the keynote address? ____________
10. (Whoever, Whomever) passes the communications test will be granted an interview. ____________

Check your answers.

B. Write the correct word in the space provided.

1. Evie, (who, whom) left last week, was our most experienced automotive service technician. ____________
2. An Anishinaabe Qwe elder (who, whom) is accessible through our employee assistance program has both Aboriginal and non-Aboriginal clients. ____________
3. Please tell us (who, whom) you recommend for the position. ____________
4. The company's lawyer would like to talk to (whoever, whomever) witnessed the accident. ____________
5. He is the graphic designer (who, whom) we believe will revitalize the company's image. ____________
6. The person (who's, whose) desk this is needs better organizational skills. ____________
7. Internal mail should be delivered into the hands of (whoever, whomever) it is addressed to. ____________
8. The "Father of Accounting" to (who, whom) the professor referred is Luca Pacioli. ____________
9. Ms. Silva is the one (who, whom) we think should be made supervisor. ____________
10. Vita needs to know (who's, whose) taking vacation next month. ____________

TEAR HERE

11. (Who, Whom) have you asked to research promotion of our products on the Internet? ____________

12. In making introductions, (who, whom) should be introduced to (who, whom)? ____________

13. Hamid will help (whoever, whomever) is next in line. ____________

14. Do you know (who, whom) will be taking your place? ____________

15. The front-desk employees are the ones (who, whom) have to deal with the complaints. ____________

16. I have hotel recommendations for (whoever, whomever) plans to travel to the trade show. ____________

17. Once candidates are selected for further screening, please let Ben know (who, whom) he will interview. ____________

18. (Who, Whom) shall I say is calling? ____________

19. Charles Gennaro, (who, whom) we thought should be appointed, was not among the final candidates. ____________

20. The decision to diversify will be made by (who, whom)? ____________

C. In the following sentences, determine whether to use *whose* or *who's*. Write it in the space provided.

1. Rose Kessler was nominated by her students for the "(Who's, Whose) Who of Professors" list. ____________

2. Psychologists have found that someone (who's, whose) handshake is firm is more likely to be socially dominant. ____________

3. The committee chair asked (who's, whose) recommendation we plan to adopt. ____________

4. (Who's, Whose) had a chance to study the brief? ____________

5. We are not sure (who's, whose) name will be called for the award. ____________

6. Looking for volunteers, the office manager asked, "(Who's, Whose) it going to be?" ____________

7. It is unclear (who's, whose) planning to take part in tomorrow's walkout. ____________

8. (Who's, Whose) car is parked in front of the No Parking sign? ____________

9. Management hasn't yet notified us of (who's, whose) required to attend the conference. ____________

10. (Who's, Whose) on first? ____________

TEAR HERE

D. Review of Levels I, II, and III. Underline any errors, and write a correction in the space provided. Write *C* if the sentence is correct.

1. The door or the windows need their seals replaced. ________________
2. Whomever is in charge of finances should receive the bill. ________________
3. Someone in the office left their radio on. ________________
4. Have you decided whom the winner is? ________________
5. Every union member is expected to give at least 20 hours of their time per week to picketing during a strike. ________________
6. The representative from our Kelowna branch, whom was due to arrive today, missed her connecting flight in Winnipeg. ________________
7. The task force submitted their recommendation a week early. ________________
8. Do you know who's phone was ringing during the meeting? ________________
9. Anyone in the department who needs a computer upgrade should submit their request form by Friday. ________________
10. Chapman's has to increase their staff every summer. ________________
11. Each of the companies calculated their assets and liabilities before the merger. ________________
12. Whom is sending all these email messages? ________________
13. Whoever you choose to replace Alain will have big shoes to fill. ________________
14. Everyone is responsible for their own happiness. ________________
15. Neither of the seamstresses has had their machine repaired yet. ________________

E. Cumulative Review. (Self-check) These sentences review Chapters 1 through 6. Underline any errors. Then write corrected forms in the spaces provided. Be alert! Some sentences contain more than one correction. If a sentence is correct, write *C* in the space. Then check your answers on page 527.

1. Pfizer Canada hired a Toronto ad agency to create there TV campaign for Viagra. ________________
2. Would one of the VP's give their time to speak to a class of MBA candidates? ________________
3. Itinerarys of all employees travel plans must be sent to Rick or myself before any reservations are made. ________________
4. No one knew it was her because she didn't introduce herself. ________________
5. How many faxs do you and him normally receive in one business day? ________________
6. Advocates for both tenants and landlords rights brought their arguments to the weekly meeting of the city council. ________________

TEAR HERE

7. Whether us Canadians like it or not, our economic health will always be affected by Americas. ____________

8. Two lawyers are needed to handle my father's-in-laws business transactions, one works with real estate, and the other deals with asset protection. ____________

9. Each contest winner received season tickets for his personal use. ____________

10. Breach of contracts are taken very seriously and may result in the contracts termination. ____________

11. If you were him, would you disregard five years experience and switch careers? ____________

12. Several business's computers were hacked, resulting in customers information being compromised. ____________

13. As soon as Naila Gould passes the bar exam. She will hang out her shingle. ____________

14. In some companys its standard practice to distribute a weeks extra pay in December as a holiday bonus. ____________

15. Just between you and me, who do you think will be named CEO? ____________

16. Drug maker Bayer cut 6,100 jobs, half were in Europe. ____________

17. They will generally grant interviews to whomever applies to work at that company. ____________

18. The police wanted to know whether either of the women had their seat belt on. ____________

19. We have two Weisz's on our executive team. ____________

20. Nearly all libraries offer computerized indexes and databases to whoever needs it. ____________

Check your answers.

F. **Writing Exercise.** Your instructor may ask you to complete this exercise of ten sentences on a separate sheet.

Write seven original sentences in which the following words function as subjects: *either, everybody, both, someone, staff, team,* and *McDonald's*. In each of the sentences, the main verb should be either *is* or *are*. You may add phrases for clarity, such as *Either of the two choices . . .*

In addition, write sentences showing *who* as the subject of a verb, *whom* as the object of a preposition, and *whoever* as the subject of a clause. Label the last three sentences.

POSTTEST

Underline the correct word.

1. Of the three women we talked to, only one was willing to have (her, their) story shared.
2. Everyone in the orchestra played (his, his or her, their) best during the performance.
3. Neither of the companies could identify (its, their) equipment.
4. (Who, Whom) do you feel deserves the promotion most?
5. We will give a bonus to (whoever, whomever) reaches the sales goal first.
6. A rider must show (his, his or her, their) ticket before boarding the bus.
7. Neither the CEO nor the department heads have yet uploaded (his, his or her, their) speech transcripts onto the shared drive.
8. The entire faculty voted to give (its, their) support to the president.
9. Hudson's Bay advertised (its, their) end-of-season sale in today's newspaper.
10. (Who's, Whose) bid is most cost-effective?

TEAR HERE

EDITOR'S CHALLENGE

The following business letter and email message contain errors reflecting the concepts you have studied thus far, as well as other common errors. Use standard proofreading marks (see the inside front cover) to show your corrections.

❖ BENSON BROTHERS MANAGEMENT SERVICES ❖

368 Glenlake Ave.
Toronto, ON M9B 2B4
(416) 358-2249 Email: bensonbros@world.com Web: www.bensonbros.com

February 9, 202x
Ms. Laura W. Stephens
2320 Centennial Road
Oshawa, ON L1G 8K7

Dear Ms. Stephens:

My partner and myself are certain that our rental management service can help you care for your fathers-in-law apartment complex in Don Mills, here are answers to you're questions.

To manage a clients rental units, we charge 10 percent of all fees' collected, we will advertise whenever a unit becomes vacant. We charge an additional 10 percent on the first years rent whenever we fill a vacant unit. Whether we charge the last months rent in advance is between you and I. Our firms lawyers is available to assist both you and I. If necessary.

During the 1990's we expanded, our's is now the only firm to offer maintenance and cleaning services to their customers.

Ms. Stephens, we now manage over 75 rental propertys in the greater Toronto area. We are available to whomever needs rental assistance. Either for private residences or for multiple unit. One client wrote to us saying, "You've managed my units much better than I, and you're firm has made life much easier for my husband and I." Not one of our costumers has ever cancelled their contract with us, and we are convinced that we can ease the burden of your responsibilitys also, please call my partner or myself at 416-358-2249 to arrange an appointment this week.

Sincerely yours,

Jonathon Benson

Jonathon Benson

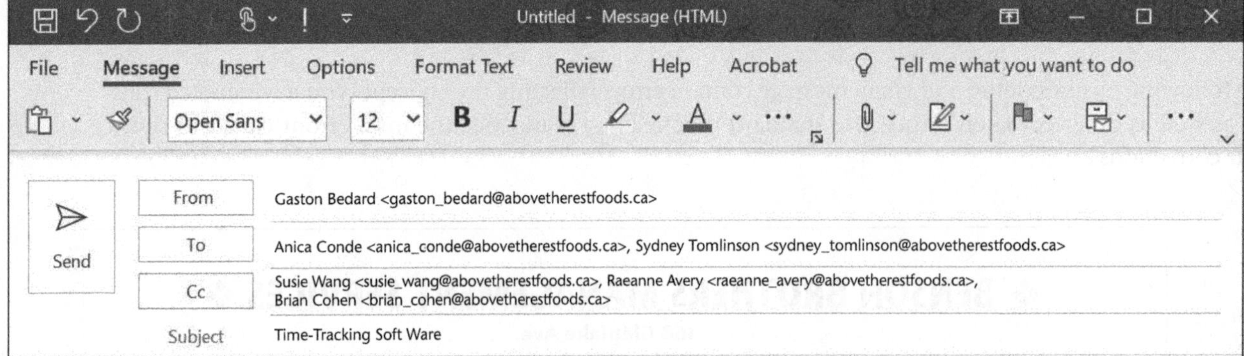

Untitled - Message (HTML)

File Message Insert Options Format Text Review Help Acrobat Tell me what you want to do

Open Sans 12

Send

From Gaston Bedard <gaston_bedard@abovetherestfoods.ca>

To Anica Conde <anica_conde@abovetherestfoods.ca>, Sydney Tomlinson <sydney_tomlinson@abovetherestfoods.ca>

Cc Susie Wang <susie_wang@abovetherestfoods.ca>, Raeanne Avery <raeanne_avery@abovetherestfoods.ca>, Brian Cohen <brian_cohen@abovetherestfoods.ca>

Subject Time-Tracking Soft Ware

Us in Human Resource's have been investigating ways to collect information that will help us to find efficiencys.

One method we have found is time tracking, which has been proven to motivate employees to be more productive. Over the next two weeks', Clock-It time-tracking software will be roled out across several departments, including your's. Its easy to use and will require little training, however, we'd like you to attend a managers informaton session on Tuesday, July 19, 202x, from 9 to 9:30 a.m., so that your able to answer your employee's questions should they have any.

With this time-tracking solution, you can monitor how much time is spent on certain projects and even on certain task's toward the completion of projects. Depending on the level of detail you want employees to provide. With the press of a button, employees can start an stop the clock as they change tasks, attend meetings, or take part in other activities. Clock-It also requires they to record vacation days, sick days, and overtime hours, then, at the end of each week, every employees' computer will produce a report of their hours spent on each project or task, and the report will automatically arrive in your inbox as a Excel spreadsheet once its set up.

Rest assured that the software will be installed on employees computers after hours so as not to disrupt there workdays.

Please contact Brian or I if you have any questions, otherwise, him and I will see you at the meeting on Tuesday.

Gaston

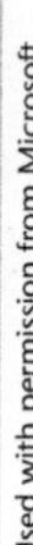

TEAR HERE

NAME ____________________

UNIT 2 REVIEW ■ Chapters 3–6 (Self-Check)

Begin your review by rereading Chapters 3 through 6. Then check your comprehension of those chapters by completing the exercises that follow. Compare your responses with those provided at the end of the book, page 531.

LEVEL I

For each of the following sentences, determine the word or phrase that correctly completes that statement and write its letter in the space provided.

1. Payroll mixed up the cheques for the two (a) Sarah's, (b) Sarahs in the company. ____________

2. An unusual number of (a) virus's (b) viruses (c) viruses' have been detected on our computers in the past week. ____________

3. We have purchased two new (a) couches, (b) couchs, (c) couch's for the waiting room. ____________

4. In seven (a) days, (b) day's, (c) days' time, Hasan will retire. ____________

5. We are giving careful consideration to each (a) company's, (b) companies', (c) companys shares. ____________

6. We will call you in if (a) you're, (b) your needed. ____________

7. The committee completed (a) it's, (b) its work last week. ____________

8. Some industry leaders have collaborated to publish some of (a) their, (b) they're, (c) there insights on various management styles. ____________

9. Ask both of the designers when (a) she, (b) he, (c) he or she, (d) they can give us estimates. ____________

10. When a customer complains, (a) his, (b) her, (c) his or her, (d) their complaint must be taken seriously. ____________

11. Mark, along with several other VPs, has not submitted (a) their, (b) his, (c) his or her direct reports' performance evaluation forms. ____________

12. *I, we, he, she,* and *they* are (a) subjective-case, (b) objective-case pronouns. ____________

LEVEL II

13. Our (a) attorneys, (b) attornies have been notified. ____________

14. Theo and Madra follow two different (a) school of thoughts, (b) schools of thought about interview techniques. ____________

15. The applicants for the graphic design job should be asked to bring their (a) portfolioes, (b) portfolio's, (c) portfolios to the interview. ____________

TEAR HERE

16. The committee is waiting for (a) Diane and Kiran's, (b) Diane's and Kiran's proposal before making a decision. ________

17. The convenience store owned by the (a) Ramirezes, (b) Ramirez, (c) Ramirez's is for sale. ________

18. I certainly hope that today's weather is better than (a) yesterday, (b) yesterday's, (c) yesterdays. ________

19. Insincerity irritates Mr. Sanchez as much as (a) I, (b) me, (c) myself. ________

20. If it weren't for you and (a) me, (b) I, the presentation wouldn't have been ready on time. ________

21. Neither the foreman nor the jury members wanted (a) his name, (b) their names to be released by the media. ________

22. Every clerk and every administrative assistant signed (a) his, (b) her, (c) his or her, (d) their name to the card for Jim. ________

23. Marsten, Xiao, and Jackson Inc. plans to move (a) it's, (b) its, (c) their offices in September. ________

24. Over the next week, (a) visitors, (b) visitor's, (c) visitors' passes will be unavailable. ________

LEVEL III

25. Following several financial (a) crisis, (b) crises, (c) crisises, the corporation was forced to declare bankruptcy. ________

26. Several of the (a) series' or series's, (b) serieses, (c) series have been discontinued. ________

27. Have you seen the (a) Williamses, (b) Williamses', (c) William's account file? ________

28. Do you know (a) whose, (b) who's doing the photography for the brochure? ________

29. (a) Who, (b) Whom is available to work overtime this weekend? ________

30. We chose not to ask (a) whose, (b) who's job may be affected by the cutbacks. ________

31. The employee who offered the suggestion was thought to be (a) he, (b) him. ________

32. If I were (a) her, (b) she, I would decline the offer. ________

33. To (a) who, (b) whom did you send your application? ________

34. Please read the privacy policy on (a) pp., (b) p. 22–24. ________

35. Give the extra supplies to (a) whoever, (b) whomever needs them. ________

36. (a) Who, (b) Whom would you prefer to see in that job? ________

37. You'll never guess (a) who, (b) whom I saw today. ________

38. It is usually (a) her, (b) she who arrives first. ________

TEAR HERE

ASK AN EDITOR REVIEW

39. How many (a) RFQ's, (b) RFQs has the company put out this year? __________

40. Check your (a) owners, (b) owners' warranty carefully. __________

41. The policies and procedures manual outlines the (a) dos and don'ts, (b) do's and don't's, (c) dos and dont's regarding using social media sites. __________

42. Once you have made the decision, you will have to notify Human Resources and (a) me, (b) myself, (c) I. __________

43. The company has purchased larger monitors and new computer (a) mouses, (b) mice for all employees. __________

TEAR HERE

TECHNIQUES FOR EFFECTIVE SENTENCES

The basic unit in writing is the sentence. Sentences come in a variety of sizes, shapes, and structures. As business and professional communicators, we are most interested in functional sentences that say what we want to say correctly and concisely. In this workshop you will concentrate on two important elements: writing complete sentences and writing concise sentences.

WRITING COMPLETE SENTENCES

To be complete, a sentence must have a subject and a predicate, and it must make sense. As you learned in Chapter 2, incomplete sentences are fragments. Let's consider four common fragment errors you will want to avoid.

1. The fragment contains a subject and a predicate, which make it a **clause**, but it begins with a subordinate word (such as *because, although, since,* or *if*) and so fails to express a complete thought. You can correct this problem by joining the fragment to a relevant main clause.

Fragment:	Because world markets and economies are becoming increasingly intermixed.
Revision:	Because world markets and economies are becoming increasingly intermixed, Canadians are doing more business with people from other cultures.
Fragment:	Although North Americans tend to come to the point directly.
Revision:	Although North Americans tend to come to the point directly, people from some other cultures prefer indirectness.

2. The fragment does not contain a subject and a predicate, but a nearby sentence completes its meaning.

Fragment:	In the spring of every year in Las Vegas. That's when computer vendors stage a huge show.
Revision:	In the spring of every year in Las Vegas, computer vendors stage a huge show.

3. The fragment starts with a relative pronoun such as *which, that,* or *who.* Join the fragment to a main clause to form a complete sentence.

Fragment:	Which is a precious item to North Americans and other Westerners.
Revision:	Concise business letters save time, which is a precious item to North Americans and other Westerners.

4. The fragment starts with a noun followed by a *who, that,* or *which* clause. Add a predicate to form a complete sentence.

Fragment:	The visiting Asian executive who was struggling to express his idea in English.
Revision:	The visiting Asian executive who was struggling to express his idea in English appreciated the patience of his listener.

TEAR HERE

Skill Check 2.1: Eliminating Sentence Fragments

Each of the following consists of a fragment and a sentence, not necessarily in that order. Use proofreading marks to eliminate the fragment.

EXAMPLE: Speak in short sentences and use common words. If you want to be understood abroad.

1. Although you should not raise your voice. You should speak slowly and enunciate clearly.
2. A glazed expression or wandering eyes. These alert a speaker that the listener is lost.
3. In speaking with foreign business people, be careful to avoid jargon. Which is special terminology that may confuse listeners.
4. Gayle Cotton, who is an executive coach and cultural diversity expert. She said that someone who starts a conversation with chit-chat may not want to dive into a business conversation.
5. Graciously accept the blame for not making your meaning clear. If a misunderstanding results.

Skill Check 2.2: Making Sentences Complete

Expand the following fragments into complete sentences, adding your own ideas and placing the fragments appropriately. Be ready to explain why each fragment is incomplete and what you did to remedy the problem.

EXAMPLE: If we keep in mind that North Americans abroad are often accused of talking too much.

REVISION: If we keep in mind that North Americans abroad are often accused of talking too much, we'll become better listeners.

1. The business person who engages a translator for important contracts ____________

____

____

2. Assuming that a nod, a yes, or a smile indicates agreement ____________

____

____

3. If you learn greetings and a few phrases in the language of the country you are visiting,

____

____

4. Although global business transactions are often conducted in English ____________

____

____

TEAR HERE

5. Which is why we sometimes put words in the mouths of foreign colleagues struggling to express an idea ______________________________

____

____

AVOIDING RUN-ON (FUSED) SENTENCES AND COMMA SPLICES

In Chapter 2, you learned to recognize run-on sentences and comma splices. Remember that locating subjects and verbs may help in identifying and correcting run-ons and comma splices.

A run-on sentence consists of two or more complete thoughts without punctuation to separate them. A comma splice consists of two or more complete thoughts with only a comma between them. The simplest way to correct both these errors is to separate complete thoughts.

Run-on sentence:	Profit for the second quarter rose to $24.1 million sales rose to $151.9 million.
Revision:	Profit for the second quarter rose to $24.1 million. Sales rose to $151.9 million.
Comma splice:	Analysts expected a decline of 2.3 percent in sales, the decline was actually 5 percent.
Revision:	Analysts expected a decline of 2.3 percent in sales. The decline was actually 5 percent.

Note that other methods of correcting run-ons or comma splices can be used.

Analysts expected a decline of 2.3 percent in sales, but the decline was actually 5 percent. (Coordinating conjunctions are discussed in Chapter 13.)

Analysts expected a decline of 2.3 percent in sales; the decline was actually 5 percent. (Semicolons are discussed in Chapter 16.)

Skill Check 2.3: Correcting Comma Splices and Run-On Sentences

Use proofreading marks to correct any comma splices or run-ons in the following items. *Note:* Not all sentences contain errors.

1. Canadians take fewer sick days in summer than in winter, one reason may be the prevalence of winter colds and flu.
2. At Amazon.com all employees, including the CEO, work in customer service every so often so that they understand the customer service process.
3. Although Singapore Airlines announced that it was the first airline to offer in-flight web browsing, it had to admit that the service was initially quite limited.
4. The tour operator offers motor coach tours throughout Europe participants choose from a variety of itineraries, activities, and accommodations.
5. Québec City was founded by Champlain in 1608, its historic district was named a UNESCO World Heritage Site in 1985.
6. After September 11, 2001, tourism fell sharply in the US capital, and within two months an estimated 17,000 Washington residents had lost jobs related to the tourism industry.
7. Studies show that the most productive day of the workweek is Tuesday, the least productive is Friday.
8. It may surprise you to learn that the bestselling product online is clothing trips and tourism are second and tech products are third.

TEAR HERE

9. Nicholas checked his email then he checked his voice mail.

10. The Japanese delicacy fugu, or blowfish, is known for its exorbitant price, furthermore, it is well known for being extremely poisonous.

11. One minute he was there the next minute he was gone.

12. Many people believe that the daughter of Dave Thomas, founder of Wendy's restaurants, is named Wendy, in fact, her name is Melinda, but her nickname is Wendy.

WRITING CONCISE SENTENCES

Business people and professionals value concise, economical writing. Wordy communication wastes the reader's time and sometimes causes confusion. You can make your sentences more concise by avoiding opening fillers, revising wordy phrases, and eliminating redundant words.

AVOIDING OPENING FILLERS. Openers such as there is, it is, and this is to inform you that fill in sentences but generally add no meaning. Train yourself to question these constructions. About 75 percent can be eliminated, almost always resulting in more concise sentences.

Wordy:	*There are* three students who volunteered to help.
Revised:	Three students volunteered to help.
Wordy:	*This is to inform you that* our offices will be closed on Monday.
Revised:	Our offices will be closed on Monday.

REVISING WORDY PHRASES. Some of our most common and comfortable phrases are actually full of "word fat." When examined carefully, these phrases can be pared down considerably.

Wordy Phrases	**Concise Substitutes**
as per your suggestion	as you suggested
at this point in time	now
due to the fact that	because
for the purpose of	to
give consideration to	consider
in all probability	probably
in spite of the fact that	even though
in the amount of	for
in the event that	if
in the near future	soon
in the neighbourhood of	about
in view of the fact that	because, since
with reference to	about

Notice how you can revise wordy sentences to make them more concise:

Wordy:	*Due to the fact that* fire damaged our distribution centre, we must delay some shipments.
Revised:	*Because* fire damaged our distribution centre, we must delay some shipments.
Wordy:	The cost for the entire system is *in the neighbourhood of* $18,000.
Revised:	The cost for the entire system is *about* $18,000.

TEAR HERE

ELIMINATING REDUNDANT WORDS. Words that are needlessly repetitive are said to be redundant. Writers must be alert to eliminating redundant words and phrases, such as the following:

advance warning	few in number	positively certain
assemble together	free and clear	potential opportunity
basic fundamentals	grateful thanks	proposed plan
collect together	integral part	reason why
consensus of opinion	last and final	refer back
contributing factor	midway between	return back
dollar amount	new changes	today's modern world
each and every	past history	true facts
end result	perfectly clear	very unique
exactly identical	personal opinion	visible to the eye

Wordy: We studied the *past* history of *each and every* potential donor.
Revised: We studied the history of every potential donor.
Wordy: Please collect *together* all the *true* facts before proceeding.
Revised: Please collect all the facts before proceeding.

Skill Check 2.4: Writing Concise Sentences

In the space provided, rewrite the following sentences to make them more concise.

1. In view of the fact that health care benefits are being drastically altered, there is a free booklet that shows all the new changes in employee benefits.

____

____

2. This is to inform you that a meeting will be scheduled in the near future in hopes of coming to a consensus of opinion.

____

____

3. My personal opinion is that you do not yet understand the basic fundamentals of our operations.

____

____

4. In the event that McDonald's offers new menu items for the purpose of increasing sales, experts think that there is every reason to believe that the effort will be successful.

____

____

5. There will be a second showing of the orientation training film at 10 a.m. due to the fact that there were so few in number who were able to attend the first showing.

____

____

TEAR HERE

6. The reason why Ray and I were given advance warning of the proposed plan is because we were tasked with gathering together customer opinions on our current service model.

____

____

Skill Check 2.5: Proofreading a Memo

In the following memo, we have deliberately introduced sentence fragments and wordy writing. Use proofreading marks to make all sentences complete and concise.

BECKTELMAN WORLDWIDE CONTRACTORS

Interoffice Memo

TO: Natasia Kozlov
FROM: Jason Corzo
DATE: August 20, 202x
SUBJECT: Congratulations on Your Assignment to Japan

Your assignment to Kansai, Japan, as office manager of our International Business Relations Department. That's cause for celebration! This is to inform you that although I'm a little late in responding to your request, I have assembled together some experiences and advice that may interest you.

When I was on assignment for our firm in Japan. My job was to help us break into the construction business. I found it very difficult to locate a Japanese construction firm. That would act as a subcontractor for us. In time I did find a company, and eventually over time we began to win contracts. In spite of the fact that the process was slow and frustrating.

Despite the slow pace of qualifying for and winning contracts. I am optimistic with regard to expanding our business in Asian countries. In my personal opinion, an important contributing factor in our successful entrance into Pacific Rim markets is how willing we are to play the game according to Asian rules. In the event that we are willing to work from the inside and show our long-term commitment. I am positively certain that we can succeed in gaining a great majority of Asia's construction business in the near future.

On a personal level, Natasia, there are a few things that really helped me in communicating with the Japanese. I learned to smile a lot due to the fact that a smile is perfectly clear to everyone. I also learned to listen without interrupting, and I learned to accept blame each and every time a communication misunderstanding occurred.

Due to the fact that you are in all probability midway between assignments. This message may take a while to catch up with you. Regardless, I congratulate you on this promotion, Natasia. It is the consensus of opinion in our office that you will be very successful in managing our Kansai office in Japan.

TEAR HERE

Writing Application 2.1

After you edit the memo on page 117, your instructor may ask you to respond to it. In a memo on a separate sheet, assume that you have received this memo. Show your appreciation to Jason Corzo for his advice. Explain that you are both excited and worried about your new assignment. Use your imagination to tell why. Describe how you expect to prepare for the new assignment. You might say that you plan to start learning the language, to read about the culture, and to talk with colleagues who have worked in Japan. Put this in your own words and elaborate.

For additional resources, please visit MindTap at login.cengage.com. Cengage | MINDTAP

TEAR HERE

Present Participle

The **present participle** of regular and irregular verbs is formed by adding *ing* to the root verb. When used in a sentence as part of a verb phrase, the present participle must be preceded by one or more helping verbs, usually forms of *to be*, such as *am, is, are, was, were, been*. The combination of a form of *to be* and a present participle creates a verb phrase in the *progressive tense* (explained below).

I *am changing* jobs. (Helping verb *am*; present participle *changing*)
You *were sitting* at the wrong desk. (Helping verb *were*; present participle *sitting*)

Past Participle

The **past participle** of a regular verb is usually formed by adding a *d* or *ed* to the root verb. (As you will learn in Level III, the past participles of irregular verbs are formed differently.) Like present participles, past participles may function as parts of verb phrases when preceded by one or more helping verbs, usually forms of *to have*, such as *has, have,* or *had*. The combination of a form of *to have* and a past participle creates a verb phrase in the *perfect tense* (explained on p. 126).

Ryan *has checked* the inventory. (Helping verb *has*; past participle *checked*)
The visitors *had finished* their factory tour. (Helping verb *had*; past participle *finished*)

CAREER TIP

In employment interviews, recruiters listen carefully to a candidate's spoken English. One quick way to be eliminated is to use a past participle in the place of a past tense. WRONG: *He come over last night* or *I seen them.*

PROGRESSIVE AND PERFECT TENSES

Most native speakers and writers of English have little difficulty controlling the progressive and perfect tenses (although the names of these forms are possibly unfamiliar) because they have frequently heard them used correctly. This largely descriptive section is thus presented for those who are not native speakers and for those who are eager to study the entire range of verb tenses.

Progressive Tenses

Progressive tenses generally indicate action in progress now, in progress in the past, or in progress in the future. Form the progressive tenses by adding a form of *to be* to the present participle (*ing* form) of a verb, as demonstrated in the following table.

Present Progressive Tense

	First Person	Second Person	Third Person
Active:	I am calling	you are calling	he, she, it is calling
	we are calling		they are calling
Passive (discussed in Chapter 8):	I am being called	you are being called	he, she, it is being called
	we are being called		they are being called

Past Progressive Tense

	First Person	Second Person	Third Person
Active:	I was calling	you were calling	he, she, it was calling
	we were calling		they were calling
Passive:	I was being called	you were being called	he, she, it was being called
	we were being called		they were being called

Future Progressive Tense

	First Person	Second Person	Third Person
Active:	I will be calling	you will be calling	he, she, it will be calling
	we will be calling		they will be calling
Passive:	I will be being called	you will be being called	he, she, it will be being called
	we will be being called		they will be being called

EXAMPLES:

We *are exporting* grain to numerous countries. (Present progressive tense expresses action currently in progress.)

Many textile companies *were sending* delegates to the government conference. (Past progressive tense indicates action in progress in the past.)

The sun *was shining* when the company golf tournament began. (Past progressive indicates one action going on when another action started.)

We expect that the Bank of Canada *will be raising* interest rates. (Future progressive indicates action in the future.)

STUDY TIP

If you are an English language learner, try searching the web for *ESL verbs*. Grammar books specifically for English language learners are also widely available, including the texts by Betty Schrampfer Azar.

Perfect Tenses

The **perfect tenses** show actions that are already completed, or *perfected*. The present perfect tense describes actions that began in the past and have been completed in the present. The past perfect tense describes past actions that took place before other past actions. The future perfect tense describes actions that will take place before other future actions. Form perfect tenses by adding a form of *to have* to the past participle of a verb, as shown in the following table.

Present Perfect Tense

	First Person	Second Person	Third Person
Active:	I have called	you have called	he, she, it has called
	we have called		they have called
Passive (discussed in Chapter 8):	I have been called	you have been called	he, she, it has been called
	we have been called		they have been called

Past Perfect Tense

	First Person	Second Person	Third Person
Active:	I had called	you had called	he, she, it had called
	we had called		they had called
Passive:	I had been called	you had been called	he, she, it had been called
	we had been called		they had been called

Future Perfect Tense

	First Person	Second Person	Third Person
Active:	I will have called	you will have called	he, she, it will have called
	we will have called		they will have called
Passive:	I will have been called	you will have been called	he, she, it will have been called
	we will have been called		they will have been called

BE THE EDITOR

From an interview with Kanye West after he nearly interrupted Beck onstage at the Grammys: "Taylor Swift came up to me right afterwards . . . and tells me that I should've went onstage." (Can you find more than one error in this quotation?)

EXAMPLES:

He *has* just *received* the news. (Present perfect tense expresses action recently completed.)

We *have had* an office in North Bay since 1998. (Present perfect expresses action begun in the past and continuing to the present.)

The cheque *had cleared* the bank before I cancelled payment. (Past perfect tense shows an action finished before another action in the past.)

The polls *will have closed* by the time we get home. (Future perfect tense indicates action that will be completed by a time in the future and, in this case, before another future action.)

Perfect Progressive Tense

Perhaps the most complex tense in English, the perfect progressive tense combines forms of the helping verbs *have* and *be* (always *been*) with the progressive form of the main verb. This verb tense denotes continuous action over a period of time in the present, past, or future.

Everyone *has been gathering* feedback from end users. (Present perfect progressive)
Economists *had been warning* of a downturn for some time. (Past perfect progressive)
By July Ilsa *will have been working* here for 20 years. (Future perfect progressive)

SUMMARY OF VERB TENSES

Primary Tenses	Progressive Tenses (use form of *be* + progressive participle)	Perfect Tenses (use form of *have* + past participle)	Present Progressive Tenses (use form of *have* + *been* + progressive participle)
present	present progressive	present perfect	present perfect progressive
past	past progressive	past perfect	past perfect progressive
future	future progressive	future perfect	future perfect progressive

Complete the reinforcement exercises for Level II on pages 135–136.

LEVEL III

IRREGULAR VERBS

Up to this point, we have considered only regular verbs. Regular verbs form the past tense by the addition of *d* or *ed* to the root. **Irregular verbs**, however, form the past tense with *t* or by varying the root vowel and, commonly, adding *en* to the past participle. A list of frequently used irregular verbs follows. Learn the forms of these verbs by practising them aloud in patterns such as the following:

Present tense:	Today I drive.
Past tense:	Yesterday I drove.
Past participle:	In the past I have driven.

Frequently Used Irregular and/or Problematic Verbs

Present	**Past**	**Past Participle**
arise	arose	arisen
be (*am, is, are*)	was, were	been
bear (to carry)	bore	borne
become	became	become
begin	began	begun
bite	bit	bitten
blow	blew	blown
break	broke	broken
bring	brought	brought
build	built	built
buy	bought	bought
catch	caught	caught
choose	chose	chosen
come	came	come
do	did	done
draw	drew	drawn
drink	drank	drunk
drive	drove	driven
eat	ate	eaten
fall	fell	fallen
fly	flew	flown
forbid	forbade	forbidden
forget	forgot	forgotten
forgive	forgave	forgiven
freeze	froze	frozen
get	got	gotten *or* got
give	gave	given
go	went	gone

grow	grew	grown
hang (an object)	hung	hung
hang (a person)	hanged	hanged
hide	hid	hidden
know	knew	known
lay (to place)	laid	laid
lead	led	led
leave	left	left
lend	lent	lent
lie (to rest)	lay	lain
lie (to tell a falsehood)	lied	lied
lose	lost	lost
make	made	made
pay	paid	paid
prove	proved	proven *or* proved
raise (to lift)	raised	raised
ride	rode	ridden
ring	rang	rung
rise (to move up)	rose	risen
run	ran	run
see	saw	seen
seek	sought	sought
set (to place)	set	set
shake	shook	shaken
shrink	shrank	shrunk
sing	sang	sung
sink	sank	sunk
sit (to rest)	sat	sat
speak	spoke	spoken
spring	sprang	sprung
steal	stole	stolen
strike	struck	struck *or* stricken
swear	swore	sworn
swim	swam	swum
take	took	taken
teach	taught	taught
tear	tore	torn
throw	threw	thrown
wear	wore	worn
write	wrote	written

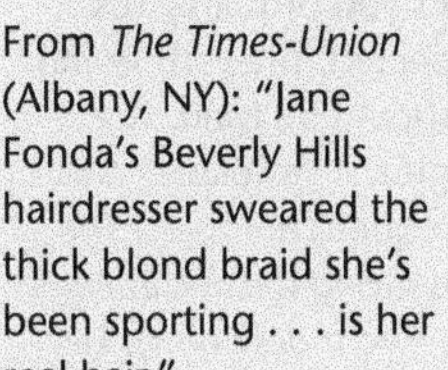

BE THE EDITOR

From *The Times-Union* (Albany, NY): "Jane Fonda's Beverly Hills hairdresser sweared the thick blond braid she's been sporting . . . is her real hair."

SOME FREQUENTLY MISUSED IRREGULAR VERBS

Three pairs of verbs often cause confusion: *lie–lay*, *rise–raise*, and *sit–set*. The secret to using them correctly lies in recognizing their tense forms.

BE THE EDITOR

From a CNN interview: "The warden has came out and gave us his view of the execution."

Lie–Lay

These two verbs can be confusing because the past tense of *lie* is spelled the same way as the present tense of *lay*. Memorize these verb forms:

Present	Past	Past Participle	Present Participle
lie (to rest)	lay	lain	lying
lay (to place)	laid	laid	laying

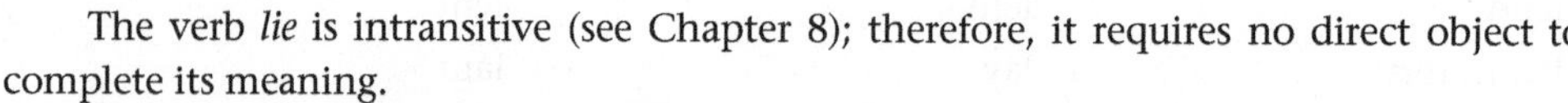

The verb *lie* is intransitive (see Chapter 8); therefore, it requires no direct object to complete its meaning.

I *lie* on the sofa on Sunday afternoons when I can. (Present tense)
"Lie down," Frank told his dog. (Commands are given in the present tense. Note that *down* is not a direct object.)
Yesterday I *lay* down for a nap. (Past tense)
The originals have *lain* in the copy machine for some time. (Past participle)
The papers are *lying* on the desk. (Present participle)

STUDY TIP

Whenever you use a form of the verb *lay* in the sense of "placing" something, you must provide a receiver (object) of the action: *Please lay the book down.* If nothing receives action, you probably want a form of the verb *lie*, which means "rest."

The verb *lay* is transitive (see Chapter 8) and must have a direct object to complete its meaning. The objects in the following examples are underlined.

A bricklayer *lays* bricks. (Present tense)
Lay the report over there. (Command in the present tense)
He *laid* the handouts on the conference table. (Past tense)
He has *laid* tile for 20 years. (Past participle)
The contractor is *laying* new flooring in the hallway. (Present participle)

ASK AN EDITOR

Question:
I'm editing a screenplay for a studio, and I know something is grammatically wrong with this sentence: *The old man left the room hurriedly after discovering a body laying near the window.*

Answer:
As you probably suspected, the verb *laying* should be *lying*. *Lay* means "to place" and requires an object (*he is laying the document on your desk now*). *Lie* means "to rest" and requires no object (*the document is lying on your desk*).

Rise–Raise

The intransitive verb *rise* (past tense, *rose*; past participle, *risen*) means "to go up" or "to ascend" and requires no direct object.

The sun *rises* every morning in the east. (*Every morning* is an adverbial phrase, not an object.)
Yesterday the bread dough *rose* nicely. (Past tense)
Prices have *risen* substantially. (Past participle)
The elevator is *rising* to the seventh floor. (Present participle)

The transitive verb *raise* (past tense, *raised*; past participle, *raised*) means "to lift up" or "to elevate" and, in this sense, must have a direct object. The objects in the following examples are underlined.

Please *raise* the window. (Present tense)
The nonprofit organization *raised* substantial funds during its annual campaign. (Past tense)
Airlines have *raised* fares over the past year. (Past participle)
Enbridge is *raising* prices next month. (Present participle)

BE THE EDITOR

From a Dunkin' Donuts advertisement: "The trouble with supermarket doughnuts is there's no telling how long they've been laying around."

Present	Past	Past Participle	Present Participle
rise (to ascend)	rose	risen	rising
raise (to elevate)	raised	raised	raising

Sit–Set

Less troublesome than *lie–lay* or *rise–raise*, the combination of *sit–set* can nevertheless be perplexing because the sounds of the verbs are similar. The intransitive verb *sit* (past tense, *sat*; past participle, *sat*) means "to rest" and requires no direct object.

I always *sit* in the front row. (Present tense)
They had *sat* in the waiting room for two hours before they decided to leave. (Past participle)
Will you be *sitting* here tomorrow? (Present participle)

The verb *set* (past tense, *set*; past participle, *set*) usually means "to place" and, when transitive, must have a direct object. The objects in the following examples are underlined.

Letty usually *sets* her books there. (Present tense)
The CEO had *set* the deadline before conferring with his managers. (Past participle)
The committee is *setting* the ground rules. (Present participle)

STUDY TIP

To help you remember that these verbs are intransitive, look at the second letter of each:
l*i*e
s*i*t
r*i*se
Associate *i* with intransitive.

ASK AN EDITOR

Question:
I learned that the verb *set* requires an object. If that's true, how can we say that the sun *sets* in the west?

Answer:
Good question! While the verb *set* generally requires an object, some standardized uses do not require one, such as the one you mention. Here's another: *Glue sets quickly.* I doubt that anyone would be likely to substitute *sit* in either of these unusual cases. The verb *sit* also has some exceptions. Although generally it requires no object, *sit* has a few uses that require objects, such as *Sit yourself down* and *The server sat us at Table 1.*

SOME FREQUENTLY CONFUSED VERBS

Several verbs in English sound similar but have different meanings. The list below is by no means exhaustive; however, we have chosen a select few verb pairs used often in business contexts that you should recognize as troublesome and confirm before using. (While spelling and vocabulary are topics outside of grammar, this text aims to help you become a better business communicator, so this list is presented to that end.)

Affect–Effect

Affect and *effect* are among the most commonly confused words in English. Each of these words can function as both a verb and a noun. Study the definitions of the verbs and the examples so that you always use the correct word.

	Affect*	**Effect**†
Definition	To influence or produce an effect on	To bring about or result in
Examples	Having more employees *affects* our bottom line.	A bigger profit *effects* higher taxes.
	Government policies *affect* citizens.	Small cars *effect* gasoline savings.

*Note that the direct object that follows *affect* does not describe a result but only names what is influenced or what an effect is produced on.
†Note that the direct object that follows *effect* describes a result.

Complement–Compliment

	Complement	**Compliment**
Definition	To add to	To express approval or admiration
Example	The new products *complement* our existing line.	Juby *complimented* me on a job well done.

Perhaps this memory device will help you keep these words straight: *I* like compl*i*ments. A com*ple*ment com*ple*tes something.

Disburse–Disperse

	Disburse	Disperse
Definition	To pay out	To scatter
Example	Bonus cheques will be *disbursed* in November.	Information will be *dispersed* to all divisions.

Imply–Infer

	Imply	Infer
Definition	To suggest indirectly	To understand from context
Example	My manager *implied* I have been doing a good job.	I *inferred* from the email that my manager thinks I have been doing a good job.

Complete the reinforcement exercises for Level III and cumulative review on pages 137–140.

NAME ______________________

CHAPTER 7 ■ Reinforcement Exercises

LEVEL I

A. **(Self-check)** Select the correct verb. Use your dictionary to verify spelling if necessary.

1. We (carried, carryed) insurance from that company for 20 years. ______________
2. What (is, was) your maiden name? ______________
3. The printer (jamed, jammed) because the paper was too heavy. ______________
4. Mr. Milne said that the distance between Calgary and Edmonton (is, was) 300 kilometres. ______________
5. What (is, was) the name of Lululemon's former CEO? ______________
6. We (transferred, transfered) several inventory items from our Park Street location to our Island Drive location. ______________
7. Miriam (submited, submitted) her monthly expenses late. ______________
8. This product (sell, sells) itself. ______________
9. The department manager (want, wants) us to track our time on individual tasks. ______________
10. The researcher (tried, tryed) to get her findings published. ______________

Check your answers.

B. Provide three tenses for each verb in the following sentences.

EXAMPLE: She (arrive) at the office at 7:45 a.m.

Past arrived Present arrives Future will arrive

1. The interviewers (prefer) candidates with excellent communication skills.

   Past __________ Present __________ Future __________

2. Our supervisor (copy) us on every email message related to the pending merger.

   Past __________ Present __________ Future __________

3. The competitor (push) continually for more information.

   Past __________ Present __________ Future __________

4. The Royal Bank (open) its new branch office downtown today.

   Past __________ Present __________ Future __________

TEAR HERE

5. Professor Coolidge (cover) the same material in her class.

Past ___________ Present ___________ Future ___________

6. Abi (label) the file folders related to the Remax account.

Past ___________ Present ___________ Future ___________

7. Donald (plan) to major in finance.

Past ___________ Present ___________ Future ___________

8. Yuri (press) us to rush through the job.

Past ___________ Present ___________ Future ___________

9. Jun (apply) for any job in the Shipping Department.

Past ___________ Present ___________ Future ___________

10. Questionnaires (gauge) customers' reactions to our new products.

Past ___________ Present ___________ Future ___________

C. Compose sentences using the verbs shown.

1. (Past tense of *ship*) ____

____

____

2. (Present tense of *try*) ____

____

____

3. (Past tense of *study*) ____

____

____

4. (Past tense of *cancel*) ____

____

____

5. (Future tense of *delay*) ____

____

____

TEAR HERE

NAME ______________________

LEVEL II

A. (Self-check) In the space provided, indicate the tense of each of the italicized verbs. Some of these verbs are also in the passive voice. Refer to the tables on pages 125–127 to guide you.

EXAMPLE: IT *had recovered* the files before most people knew they were lost. past perfect

1. Our supervisor *will have made* a decision by the end of the month. ______
2. The Edmonton branch *is fulfilling* all Western Canada orders. ______
3. The advertisement *will be featured* on 20 websites. ______
4. We are impressed by what we *are hearing*. ______
5. Charles *had been told* to send the payroll reports to the auditor. ______
6. We *will be increasing* security at all locations. ______
7. All employees *have been following* the manager's suggestions for reducing paper use. ______
8. Once we *had investigated* the matter, we had to make some difficult decisions. ______
9. By next year, the company *will have been reducing* its emissions for a decade. ______
10. We *are* now *experiencing* the effects of the last cutback. ______

Check your answers.

B. In the spaces provided, write the correct helping verb(s).

1. A task list (was, has, will) provided to each committee member. ______
2. The event (is, had, will) take place Thursday. ______
3. Several entrepreneurs within the area (are, have, will) helped with the school program. ______
4. Job descriptions (are being, have been, will have) revised over the next few months. ______
5. Sohail (is, has, will) completed his WHMIS training. ______

TEAR HERE

C. In the spaces provided, indicate whether the italicized verbs include a (a) present participle or (b) past participle.

EXAMPLE: The federal government *is using* the Web to communicate with citizens. ___a___

1. A focus group *is offering* feedback on our new online products. ______
2. One person *has commented* that our website is not user friendly. ______
3. Fortunately, many others *have indicated* that they find the site easy to navigate. ______
4. In fact, we *are considering* redesigning the site. ______
5. Students *are preparing* to start the new semester. ______
6. Many students *have packed* basics, including clothing, toiletries, and books. ______
7. Some students *are* also *packing* TVs, laptops, and espresso machines. ______
8. Some Canadian investors *are benefiting* from Italy's emerging biotechnology sector. ______
9. Italy *has become* home to more than 220 biotechnology companies. ______
10. Many of Italy's biotechnology companies *have gone* public. ______

D. Write the correct form of the tense indicated in the spaces provided.

1. Many purchasers (return) the faulty product. (Present perfect) ______
2. Our advertising dollars (spend) online only. (Present progressive, passive) ______
3. The company (want) to focus on business-to-business sales. (Past perfect) ______
4. We (remove) summer stock from the shelves. (Present perfect progressive) ______
5. The vice president of sales (manage) the Shoppers Drug Mart account until recently. (Past progressive) ______
6. By next April, RamCo (open) four branch outlets. (Future perfect) ______
7. We (learn) that about 94 percent of Canadian adults who are online use social media. (Present perfect) ______
8. The Human Resources Department (develop) a plan to reduce administrative costs. (Present progressive) ______
9. By 5 p.m. the contract (finish) and faxed to our client. (Past perfect, passive) ______
10. You (arrive) in Shanghai before I even board my flight. (Future perfect) ______

TEAR HERE

NAME ____________________

LEVEL III

A. (Self-check) Write the correct verb form. Do not add a helping verb.

EXAMPLE: He should have (eat) before he left. eaten

1. Steam has (rise) from the pot on the stove. ________
2. Has she (see) the changes we made to the website? ________
3. That helicopter has (fly) over the intersection twice. ________
4. The economy has (begin) to recover. ________
5. Our email manual was (write) more than ten years ago. ________
6. The mild earthquake (shake) the windows in the conference room. ________
7. Yesterday IBM (break) the news that it will lay off 4,600 employees. ________
8. Have you (speak) with the supervisor yet? ________
9. A person who shops in thrift stores is (know) as a "recessionista." ________
10. All employees should have (go) to the emergency procedures demonstration. ________

Check your answers.

B. Underline any verb errors you find in the following sentences. Write the correct forms in the spaces provided. Do not add helping verbs or change the verb tense. Write *C* if a sentence is correct.

EXAMPLE: Janet claimed that she <u>seen</u> the accident. saw

1. The world has shrank considerably as a result of new communication technologies. ________
2. The business had to close because the owner run it like a not-for-profit company. ________
3. The office staff must chose new letterhead stationery. ________
4. Insulation was blown into the ceiling for added R value. ________
5. Found as a stray in the truck yard, that cat has rode along on Chuck's long-haul drives for years. ________
6. The accounting fraud investigation lead to several arrests. ________
7. Guillaume in Accounting has broke local records in the Scotiabank marathon. ________
8. A lot of work has went into scheduling training sessions at the conference. ________
9. She payed a premium to get a copy of the book signed by the author. ________
10. Have many people bit into our new gluten-free muffins? ________

TEAR HERE

11. Claudia brang some product samples to the meeting. ____________

12. The telephone has rung only twice in the past hour. ____________

13. Because of daylight savings time, many people arose late on Monday. ____________

14. Prices on the stock exchange sunk to a new low. ____________

15. Has much inventory been stole? ____________

C. Write the proper verb forms according to the specifications in parentheses.

EXAMPLE: They (drive) all night before they found a motel. (Past perfect) had driven

1. Trish (meet) with dozens of recruiters before she found the perfect job. (Past perfect) ____________
2. Since the company expanded nationally, warehousing (prove) to be a big challenge. (Past progressive) ____________
3. Our company (think) about offering on-site child care. (Present progressive) ____________
4. A visitor's pass (give) to you upon arrival, allowing you access to our fifth-floor boardroom. (Future perfect, passive) ____________
5. Though not yet 30 years old, the entrepreneur (sell) two online businesses for six figures each. (Present perfect) ____________
6. The CEO said that the corporation (lose) money in six divisions. (Past progressive) ____________
7. A For Lease sign (hang) on that building for years before Tharsana rented it for her business. (Past perfect) ____________

D. *Lie–lay.* Select the correct verb.

1. Last night the documents (lay, layed, laid) on the printer unclaimed. ____________
2. In fact, they have (laid, lain) there for more than a week. ____________
3. Some people risk getting skin cancer because they insist on (laying, lying) in the sun. ____________
4. Scott (layed, laid, lay) the mail on Ms. Moorjani's desk. ____________
5. Every day at 2 p.m., Mr. Tomas (lies, lays) down to rest. ____________
6. If the book will not (lay, lie) flat, do not use force to open it further. ____________
7. The terms of her contract were (laid, lain) out for her. ____________
8. In this meeting we will be (lying, laying) the foundation for several new projects. ____________
9. Iain Grant (lay, laid) some of the blame on management policies. ____________
10. He was accused of (lying, laying) down on the job. ____________

TEAR HERE

E. *Sit–set; rise–raise.* Select the correct verb.

1. The world literacy rate has (rose, risen, raised) over the past few decades, especially for women. ____________
2. How can we finish if Roland (sits, sets) there all day? ____________
3. Telling staff about the sale of the company may (raise, rise) concerns about layoffs. ____________
4. The temperature (raises, rises) rapidly in a room filled with people. ____________
5. Consumer prices have (raised, risen, rose) faster than consumer income. ____________
6. I (sat, set) my briefcase on the table for inspection. ____________
7. Ms. Tibari (raised, rose) the question of retroactive benefits. ____________
8. Several of us have (raised, risen) the issue of poor employee benefits. ____________
9. Our office building (sits, sets) at the corner of Front and Pine. ____________
10. No one (raised, rose) when the speaker had finished. ____________

F. Choose the correct verb to complete the following sentences.

1. Once we arrived at the conference, we (disbursed, dispersed) to attend separate events. ____________
2. Online sessions have been planned to (complement, compliment) the conference program. ____________
3. Did you (imply, infer) from that conversation that a merger may occur? ____________
4. Customers have been as (affected, effected) as employees by the new regulations. ____________
5. Funds have already been (disbursed, dispersed) for overnight accommodations. ____________
6. Everyone (complemented, complimented) Moumen's work on the project. ____________
7. The open-concept layout has (affected, effected) more communication among departments. ____________
8. However, several managers have (implied, inferred) that productivity is suffering. ____________

G. Compose original sentences using the verb forms shown. Add helping verbs as needed.

1. drawn ____________
2. sung ____________
3. shrank ____________
4. lent ____________
5. shaken ____________
6. caught ____________
7. grown ____________
8. lay ____________

TEAR HERE

H. Cumulative Review. These sentences review Chapters 1 through 7. Underline any errors and write corrected forms in the spaces provided. Some sentences require more than one correction. Write *C* if a sentence is correct.

1. The number of spam messages has raised steadily over the past few years. ______
2. Ongoing shortages of personal protective equipment has drove more Canadian companies to find way's to manufacture locally. ______
3. Sera and me could have forgiven her if she had softened her tone. ______
4. The company hided it's losses by inflating sales. ______
5. Every employee must name a beneficiary on their life insurance forms. ______
6. The contract should be awarded to whomever offers the best warranty for their work. ______
7. You and me need to work hard to make sure that we don't loose this opportunity. ______
8. Many larger facilitys can recycle at no net cost because there haulers are taking away less trash. ______
9. Everyone except Helena and myself seemed impressed by last month's sales volume. ______
10. Mr. Sanchez contract, which is laying on the desk, must be delivered immediately. ______
11. The vice president has swore that no one would work harder than him to meet the deadline. ______
12. Not one of the job candidates who we interviewed has wrote a thank-you letter. ______
13. Eventually everyone in attendance lay down their phone's and payed attention. ______
14. How long have you know that you're application was accepted? ______
15. The plan for the products re-launch was mistakenly emailed to Claudette and I. ______
16. The meeting begun before the CEO's staff arrived. ______
17. Our research shows that the average part-time retail employee will have stole over $300 worth of merchandise in a years time. ______
18. You may set the printer on this desk until a better location is found. ______
19. Cheryl said she seen you and him at Omars party. ______
20. Navdeep has wore his lucky tie to every interview so far. ______

I. Writing Exercise. Your instructor may ask you to complete this exercise on a separate sheet. Write ten original sentences, one for each of the following verb forms: *chose, driven, drunk, given, lying* (resting), *raise, ran, sank, spoke,* and *worn.*

TEAR HERE

POSTTEST

Underline the correct answers.

1. In the sentence *Every day at 5 p.m., a convoy of vehicles files out of the parking lot*, the verb is in the (a) present, (b) past, (c) future tense.
2. In the sentence *Riva joined Toastmasters International to improve her speaking skills*, the verb is in the (a) present, (b) past, (c) future tense.
3. In the sentence *Several employees have felt unwell this week*, the verb is in the (a) present perfect, (b) past perfect, (c) future perfect tense.
4. In the sentence *One in eight Canadians has worked at a fast-food restaurant, worked* is a (a) past participle, (b) present participle.
5. In the sentence *Both Canadians and Americans are fighting the problem of obesity, fighting* is a (a) present participle, (b) past participle.
6. If you had (saw, seen) how professional she looked, you would have been impressed too.
7. Has the school bell (rung, rang) yet?
8. The report has (laid, lain) on your desk for over a week.
9. Soil temperatures will slowly (raise, rise) during the spring.
10. If you had (sat, set) in your department head's chair, you might realize you don't want his job.

TEAR HERE

EDITOR'S CHALLENGE

The following memo and letter contain errors reflecting the concepts you have studied thus far, as well as other common errors. Use standard proofreading marks to show your corrections.

DATE: January 21, 202x

TO: All Employees

FROM: Vice President, Human Resources

SUBJECT: Change in Floating Holiday Policy

The senior executive staff has approve a change in the companys floating holiday plan. Employees in the past vote on a single date to be took by all workers as there floating holiday, now, however, each employee will be allowed to chose the date that they wish to use as a floating holiday.

To reserve your floating holiday. Please notify your supervisor or I. Approval will be base on your units staffing needs. If a supervisor or myself receive several requests for the same date, employment seniority will govern.

A question has arose about how to record these holidays. I have spoke to Payroll, and they say you should use the Attendance Bonus code on your time card. This method will be used until Payroll has went over all employees records and modified it.

We wish it was possible for everyone to have their holiday exactly when desired, but we must urge you to be flexible. Our principle concern is that a reduced workforce may have a negative affect on our service. Because your supervisor has all ready began a schedule of employees floating holidays. It's not too early for you to submit your request.

TEAR HERE

Rehabilitation for Life

November 24, 202x

Mr. Erik Saari

3250 Maple Way

Surrey, BC V4A 5G4

Dear Mr. Saari:

Thank you for you're recent donation to the Riverview Rehabilitation Hospital Foundation. It is because of assistence from donors like yourself that this years program has been even better than previous years. We are happy to share with our supporters a recent happy outcome for one of the many child and young adults who have seeked our services.

When 13-year-old Lucy was tole that she might loose the use of one of her legs after a skying accident, this lively, bright girl shed no tears, she just asked what had to be did next.

And what come next was not easy. Lucy worked hard over eight month's. She started by swiming; she done strength-training with several different trainers; and just a few weeks ago she begun re-learning how to walk using both legs, she did all this while keepping up with her study's! Lucys goal is to be able to dance at her grade-eight graduation in June. And we think she'll do it!

As you know, our hospital offered patients the latest in rehabilitation equipment. The children and young adult's in our care work hard to improve their lifes, but they also get to play hard. Inside our state-of-the-art virtual reality laboratory, Lucy and pateints like she live through adventurous scenario's. While remaining secure in a harness and traveling over different terrains. In our lab Lucy will eventually walk along a suspension bridge, through a forest, and up a hill. She hopes that once she's ready, the lab will even allow her ski again virtually before hiting the real slope's.

So we—including Lucy—thank you for you're donation and request that you consider enroling in our monthly donor program. As a monthly contributer, you will receive regular updates and get to share in the success's of our patients. If you became a gold-level donor, you will even recieve a personal guided tour of our facility and have your name added to a donor's plaque at the hospital entry. We are greatful for your continued support.

Cordially,

Gayle Newbank

Gayle Newbank

Fundraising Manager

Enclosure

2400 Kamloops Street, Vancouver, BC V5M 9P1 250.316.2828

For additional resources, please visit MindTap at login.cengage.com. Cengage | MINDTAP

VERBS: KINDS, VOICES, MOODS

CHAPTER

8

OBJECTIVES

When you have completed the materials in this chapter, you will be able to do the following:

LEVEL I

- Distinguish between transitive and intransitive verbs
- Identify the functions and specific uses of at least eight linking verbs

LEVEL II

- Recognize active- and passive-voice verbs
- Convert sentences written in the passive voice to sentences in the active voice

LEVEL III

- Recognize sentence constructions requiring the subjunctive mood
- Use subjunctive forms correctly

PRETEST

Underline the appropriate answers.

1. In the sentence *Vito scheduled a web conference*, the verb *scheduled* is (a) transitive, (b) intransitive, (c) linking.
2. In the sentence *Allie seems excited about her upcoming vacation*, the verb *seems* is (a) transitive, (b) intransitive, (c) linking.
3. In the sentence *A select few were chosen to respond to the survey*, the verb phrase *were chosen* is in the (a) active voice, (b) passive voice, (c) subjunctive mood.
4. In the sentence *An employee manual was provided*, the verb phrase *was provided* is in the (a) active voice, (b) passive voice, (c) subjunctive mood.

(continued)

PRETEST (CONTINUED)

5. In the sentence *Haddin taught the class*, the verb *taught* is in the (a) active voice, (b) passive voice, (c) subjunctive mood.

6. In the sentence *Ian wishes he were rich*, the verb *were* is in the (a) indicative mood, (b) imperative mood, (c) subjunctive mood.

7. Jackie acts as if she (a) was, (b) were the manager.

8. A shareholder moved that the meeting (a) is, (b) be adjourned.

9. If it (a) was, (b) were my company, you would get double pay for overtime.

10. If there (a) was, (b) were an alarm last night, we didn't hear it.

Verbs express an action, an occurrence, or a state of being.

Abu wrote an excellent proposal. (Action)

The winter holidays end the fall term. (Occurrence)

Sandee is the new technical writer. (State of being)

In relation to subjects, verbs generally tell what the subject is doing or what is being done to the subject. Verbs may also link the subject to words that describe the subject or identify it.

In this chapter you'll learn about kinds of verbs, verb voices, and verb moods.

LEVEL I

KINDS OF VERBS

BE THE EDITOR

From a card sent by a Saturn dealer to customers: "Thank you. . . . Your Special!"

We'll begin our discussion of verbs by focusing on the ones that express action. These verbs may be divided into two categories: *transitive* and *intransitive*. Some verbs may have both a transitive and an intransitive sense; the verb type depends on how the verb functions in a particular sentence, as you will see below.

As you read about transitive and intransitive verbs, you may wonder how to apply the information we are sharing or even why it is important. As discussed in Chapter 7, some verbs are close in meaning and in sound (*lie–lay, rise–raise, sit–set*). Recognizing how a verb is functioning helps you ensure that you are using the correct verb and communicating your meaning clearly. As well, a single verb can have more than one definition, depending on whether it is transitive or intransitive. To be sure you are using a verb correctly, refer to the dictionary for the transitive and intransitive definitions.

Transitive Verbs

When a verb expresses an action that is directed toward or received by a person or thing, the verb is said to be **transitive**. A transitive verb needs, in addition to its subject, a noun or pronoun to complete its meaning. This noun or pronoun functions as the direct object of the transitive verb. Notice in the following sentences that the verbs direct action toward objects (shown in italics).

Objects usually answer the questions *What?* or *Whom?*

Employees made *suggestions*.	Employees made *what?*
We sold the *shares* at a profit.	We sold *what?*
Lana drove *him* to work all week.	Lana drove *whom?*
The author's appearance increased book *sales*.	The author's appearance increased *what?*

STUDY TIP

Remember that *trans*itive verbs *trans*fer action onto an object (a noun or pronoun that receives the action of the verb).

Intransitive Verbs

An action verb that does not require an object to complete its action is said to be **intransitive**.

Rami interned in our Human Resources Department.

The driver listened carefully to the directions.

Lana drove to work all week.	Compare: Lana drove *him* to work all week.
Our sales increase every summer.	Compare: The author's appearance increased book *sales*.

Notice that the verbs in these sentences do not express actions directed toward persons or things. Prepositional phrases (*in our Human Resources Department, to the directions, to work*) and adverbial phrases (*every summer, carefully*) do not receive the action expressed by the verbs, nor do they answer the questions *What?* or *Whom?* That is because prepositional and adverbial phrases do not function as objects of verbs. Rami didn't *intern the department*; the driver didn't *listen the directions*, Lana didn't *drive work*, and the sales didn't *increase summer*.

Linking Verbs

You will recall from Chapter 5 that **linking verbs** express a state of being, rather than an action. They *link* the subject to words that rename or describe the subject. A noun, a pronoun, or an adjective that renames or describes the subject is called a *complement* because it *completes* the meaning of the subject.

Nevinka is the *manager*. (*Manager* is a noun complement that completes the meaning of the sentence by renaming *Nevinka*, the subject.)

Her salary is *excellent*. (*Excellent* is an adjective complement that completes the meaning of the sentence by describing *salary*, the subject.)

The caller was he. (*He* is a pronoun complement that completes the meaning of the sentence by identifying *caller*, the subject.)

STUDY TIP

Here's a mnemonic (memory) device to help you remember the verbs of the senses. Call them the FATS verbs, an **acronym** (word formed of initials) made from the first letters of *feel*, *appear*, *taste*, and *seem*.

Notice in the preceding sentences that the noun, pronoun, or adjective complements following the linking verbs do not receive action from the verb; instead, the complements *complete* the meaning of the subject.

Many linking verbs are derived from the verb *to be*: *am, is, are, was, were, be, being, been*. Other words that often serve as linking verbs are *feel, appear, taste, seem, sound, look,* and *smell*. Notice that many of these words describe sensory experiences. Verbs expressing sensory experiences may be followed by complements just as the *to be* linking verbs are.

They feel bad about the sale of the company. (*Bad* is an adjective complement following the linking verb *feel*. An adjective—not the adverb *badly*—is needed here to describe the senses.)

Jay appears sad. (*Sad* is an adjective complement following the linking verb *appears*.)

The use of adjectives following such verbs is discussed in more detail in Chapter 11.

BE THE EDITOR

Advice in Harvard Medical School's *Heart Letter*: "Do not feel too badly about missing dosages of your pills."

Review of Verb Functions

The function of a verb in a sentence determines its classification. The action verb *write*, for example, is intransitive when it has no object (*Ernie writes*). The same verb, however, is transitive when an object follows (*Ernie writes reports*). The verb *felt* is linking when it is used to connect a complement describing the subject (*Devon felt marvellous*). The same verb is transitive when it directs action to an object (*Devon felt the wet sand beneath his feet*). To distinguish between classifications, study carefully the constructions in which the verbs appear.

To review briefly:

1. Action verbs—two kinds:
   a. Transitive: need objects to complete their meaning
   b. Intransitive: do not need objects to complete their meaning
2. Linking verbs: form a link to words that rename or describe the subject

Complete the reinforcement exercises for Level I on pages 151–153.

LEVEL II

VERB VOICES

You will recall that a verb expressing an action directed toward a person or thing is said to be transitive. Transitive verbs fall into two categories depending upon whether the subject performs or receives the action of the verb.

Active Voice

When the subject of a sentence performs an action, the verb is said to be in the **active voice**.

Ada answered the telephone.

Our department uses Excel.

Edmund speaks confidently.

Verbs in the active voice are direct and forceful; they clearly identify the doer of the action. For these reasons, writing that uses mostly the active voice is vigorous and effective. Writers of business and professional communications strive to use the active voice; in fact, it is called the *voice of business*.

STUDY TIP

Passive-voice verbs are made up of a helper, usually *is, are, was, were, being,* or *been*, and a past participle (see Chapter 7). For example, *Repairs were made by the manufacturer.*

Passive Voice

When the action of the verb is received by the sentence's subject, rather than directed by the subject, the verb is said to be in the **passive voice**. Study the following pairs:

Passive Voice	Active Voice
The figures are totalled daily.	We total the figures daily.
The machines are being sold by Mr. Chawla.	Mr. Chawla is selling the machines.
Three errors were found in the report.	The auditor found three errors in the report.
The order was submitted after the deadline.	You submitted the order after the deadline.

STUDY TIP

A clue to passive voice is a prepositional phrase beginning with *by*: *That film was seen by millions of viewers.* Note, however, that not all passive voice sentences include *by* phrases.

Note that in the second pair of examples, the verb *is selling* is in the active voice, even though a form of *to be* appears in the verb. This verb is in the present progressive tense (discussed in Chapter 7), denoted by the *ing* suffix.

Because the passive voice can be used to avoid mentioning or to de-emphasize the performer of the action, the passive voice is sometimes called the *voice of tact.* Notice how much more tactful the passive versions of the last two examples are. Although directness in business writing is generally preferable, in certain instances we use the passive voice because indirectness is desired.

Complete the reinforcement exercises for Level II on pages 154–156.

ASK AN EDITOR

Question:
My word-processing program flags every passive-voice verb and tells me to consider using an active-voice verb. Are passive-voice verbs totally forbidden in business and professional writing?

Answer:
Certainly not! Computer style-checkers capitalize on language areas that can be detected mechanically, and a passive-voice verb is easily identified by a computer. Although active-voice verbs are considered more forceful, passive-voice verbs have a genuine function. Because they hide the subject and diffuse attention, passive verbs are useful in sensitive messages where indirect language can develop an impersonal, inconspicuous tone. For example, when a lower-level employee must write a persuasive and somewhat negative message to a manager, passive-voice verbs are quite useful.

LEVEL III

VERB MOODS

Three verb moods are available to enable a speaker or writer to express an attitude toward a subject: (1) the **indicative mood** is used to express a fact (*We need a contract*); (2) the **imperative mood** is used to express a command or give advice (*Read any contract before signing it*); (3) the **subjunctive mood** is used to express a doubt, a conjecture, or a suggestion (*If the contract were ready, we could review it*). The subjunctive mood may cause speakers and writers difficulty and therefore demands special attention.

Subjunctive Mood

The subjunctive in English is formed in three ways: using the base form of the verb (not the conjugated form); using *were* in place of *was;* and using the modal verbs *would, could,* and *should.*

Careful speakers and writers use the subjunctive mood in the following constructions.

1. ***If* and *wish* clauses.** When a statement that is doubtful or contrary to fact is introduced by *if, as if, as though,* or *wish,* use the subjunctive form *were* in place of the indicative form *was.*

   If Lori *were* here, we could proceed. (Lori is *not* here.)
   She acts as if she *were* the boss. (She is *not* the boss.)
   He spends money as though he *were* a millionaire. (He is *not* a millionaire.)
   George wishes he *were* able to snowboard. (George is *not* able to snowboard.)

   If the statement could possibly be true, however, use the indicative form.

   If Chris was in the audience, I missed him. (Chris might have been in the audience.)

2. ***That* clauses.** When a *that* clause follows a verb expressing a command, recommendation, request, suggestion, or requirement, use the subjunctive verb form *be* for *to be* verbs. For other third-person singular verbs, use the base form of the verb instead of the present tense form ending in *s* or *es.*

   The doctor recommended that everyone *be* [not *is*] inoculated.
   Our manager ordered that all reports *be* [not *are*] proofread twice.
   Test Centre rules require that every student *show* [not *shows*] photo ID.
   It is important that Val *attend* [not *attends*] the conference.

3. **Motions.** When a motion is stated, use a subjunctive verb form in the *that* clause that follows it.

   Abdul moved that a vote *be* [not *is*] taken.
   Jeremy seconded the motion that the meeting *be* [not *is*] adjourned.

CAREER TIP

To be an effective communicator, use the subjunctive correctly. A well-spoken business person would avoid saying *If I was you,* for example.

BE THE EDITOR

The title of a *True Blood* episode: "I Wish I Was the Moon."

ASK AN EDITOR

Question:
What's the correct verb in this sentence? *Tim recognized that if his company (was or were) to prosper, it would require considerable capital.*

Answer:
The verb should be *were* because the clause in which it functions is not true. Statements contrary to fact that are introduced by words like *if* and *wish* require subjunctive-mood verbs.

Caution: In a sentence without *that* clauses, do not mix subjunctive and indicative verbs.

Right: If she *were skilled,* she *would receive* job offers. (Both verbs subjunctive)

Right: If she *is skilled,* she *will receive* job offers. (Both verbs indicative)

Wrong: If she *were skilled,* she *will receive* job offers. (One subjunctive verb and one indicative verb)

Complete the reinforcement exercises for Level III on pages 157–158.

NAME ____________________

CHAPTER 8 ■ Reinforcement Exercises

LEVEL I

A. **(Self-check)** In the space provided, indicate whether the italicized verbs are transitive (*T*), intransitive (*I*), or linking (*L*).

EXAMPLE: Elvira *is* our team leader. L

1. Ava *seems* happier in her new position. ____
2. Canada *exports* products to numerous countries. ____
3. Before the conference, delegates *met* in the foyer. ____
4. Some of us *are* more prepared for retirement than others. ____
5. The customer *felt* all the fabrics before making her choice. ____
6. It *was* he who devised the current work schedule. ____
7. The production manager *called* more than four hours ago. ____
8. Last year's sales *appear* useful for estimating this year's inventory needs. ____
9. Well-written business letters *get* results. ____
10. We job candidates *waited* impatiently for a response. ____

Check your answers.

B. Each of the following sentences contains a verb that is either transitive or intransitive. If the verb is intransitive, underline it and write *I* in the space provided. If the verb is transitive, underline it, write *T* in the space provided, and also write its direct object.

EXAMPLE: After her presentation the salesperson <u>left</u>. I

Employees <u>brought</u> their lunches. T (lunches)

1. Jaspreet Kaur designed the website for her new business. ____
2. Our suppliers raised their prices. ____
3. Canada Post delivers packages seven days a week in December. ____
4. Many employees take the subway to work. ____
5. Only two of us remained. ____
6. Over the years our assets increased. ____
7. Many businesses receive more email messages than phone calls. ____
8. The network connection failed repeatedly. ____
9. The proposal interested us. ____
10. The customer returned yesterday for her lost credit card. ____

TEAR HERE

Linking verbs are followed by complements that identify, rename, or describe the subjects. The most common linking verbs are the forms of *to be* (*am, is, are, was,* etc.) and the verbs of the senses (*feel, appear, taste, smell,* etc.). The following sentences all contain linking verbs. For each sentence underline the linking verb and write its complement in the space provided.

EXAMPLE: Joanna feels confident in her abilities. confident

Our new director is Dave Johnson. Dave Johnson

11. The employees are happy about the pay increases. ______

12. He sounds unconvinced. ______

13. Your lunch smells fantastic! ______

14. His presentation was professional and convincing. ______

15. Priya appears knowledgeable about the improvement plan. ______

16. Mr. Flores was our representative for two years. ______

17. She feels comfortable buying items online. ______

18. LeRoy Haitz is their wedding photographer. ______

19. The new menu items taste great. ______

20. The product seems successful. ______

C. In the following sentences, select verbs are italicized. For each sentence indicate whether the italicized verb is transitive (*T*), intransitive (*I*), or linking (*L*). In addition, if the verb is transitive, write its object; if the verb is linking, write its complement.

EXAMPLE: The new sales rep *is* Janet Oso. L (Janet Oso)

Our computer *stores* the mailing list. T (list)

1. His uniform *is* wrinkled. ______

2. That hallway *leads* to the executives' offices. ______

3. General Motors *offered* an extended warranty on certain engine parts. ______

4. Urban reserves *create* revenue for First Nations communities. ______

5. This software *identifies* almost any malware. ______

6. Her report *appears* accurate, but we must verify some data. ______

7. Her report appears accurate, but we *must verify* some data. ______

8. Mitchell *feels* relieved to have submitted the project. ______

9. Please *check* the links to make sure that they are working. ______

10. Before ordering lunch for the meeting, the assistant *tasted* every dish. ______

11. It *was* he who sent the memo. ______

12. We *listened* to the presentation with great interest. ______

13. Although consumers protested, the airline *ended* its meal service. ______

14. PayPal *is* a useful tool for online companies. ______

15. Your report *was lying* on the boss's desk. ______

16. Everyone *felt* the tension in the room throughout the annual meeting. ______

TEAR HERE

17. Our website *generates* many hits each day. ____________

18. The world's highest tides *happen* twice a day in the Bay of Fundy. ____________

19. Please *smile* at customers as soon as they enter. ____________

20. The call *seemed* important. ____________

D. Look up the following words in a dictionary and write a sentence using each transitively and a sentence using each intransitively. In your transitive sentences, underline the object of the verb.

1. set (transitive) ____________

   (intransitive) ____________

2. run (transitive) ____________

   (intransitive) ____________

3. pass (transitive) ____________

   (intransitive) ____________

TEAR HERE

NAME ______________________

LEVEL II

A. **(Self-check)** Transitive verbs in the following sentences are italicized. For each sentence write *active* or *passive* in the space provided to indicate the voice of the italicized verb.

EXAMPLE: Several building code violations *were found* by the home inspector. ___passive___

1. The Internet activity of all employees *is monitored* by our company. ______________
2. Our company *monitors* the Internet activities of all employees. ______________
3. Sixty employees *were laid off.* ______________
4. Many hiring companies *require* good written and oral communication skills. ______________
5. Our business insurance premium nearly *doubled* after the break-in. ______________
6. Our insurance premium *is withdrawn* automatically each month. ______________
7. The new office furniture *was delivered* on Friday. ______________
8. The cleansers that *are used* by Happy Home Cleaning Service are organic. ______________
9. Ileana D'Angelo *prepared* the certified cheque. ______________
10. The superintendent *is adjusting* the temperature. ______________

Check your answers.

B. Underline the verb in the sentence, and then in the space provided, write *active* or *passive* to indicate the voice of the verb.

1. Canadian regulations restrict the advertising of cannabis products. ______________
2. The flight left 15 minutes later than scheduled. ______________
3. Many small businesses have been listed for sale in recent years. ______________
4. You withdrew the funds in question on May 29. ______________
5. Intranets are used in many companies to provide information to employees. ______________
6. Arthur Haig was asked to give the commencement address. ______________
7. Contract arbitration will be conducted by the union and the manufacturer. ______________
8. Citizens often apply for government jobs online. ______________
9. Researchers have found a correlation between meaningful work and employee loyalty. ______________
10. A sense of contributing to the greater good of others was found to make work meaningful. ______________

TEAR HERE

C. Careful writers use the active voice in business and professional communications when they want to identify the "doer" of the action. To practise this skill, rewrite the following sentences, changing their passive-voice verbs to active voice. Normally, you can change a verb from passive to active voice by making the doer of the action—usually contained in a *by* phrase—the subject of the sentence.

EXAMPLE: *Passive:* Production costs must be reduced by manufacturers.
Active: Manufacturers must reduce production costs.

1. Pollution was greatly reduced by Chrysler Canada when the company built its new plant. (*Hint:* Who greatly reduced pollution? Start your sentence with that name.)

___

___

___

2. All receipts and invoices were carefully reviewed by investigators during the audit.

___

___

___

3. Online entrepreneurship is being used to great effect by Indigenous Canadians to sidestep obstacles and discriminatory hiring practices.

___

___

___

4. A car with solar panels that will power the air conditioning system was designed by Toyota.

___

___

___

D. Some sentences with passive-voice verbs do not identify the doer of the action. Before these sentences can be converted to active voice, a subject must be provided.

EXAMPLE: *Passive:* New subscribers will be offered a bonus.

(By whom?—let's say by *Maclean's*)

Active: Maclean's will offer new subscribers a bonus.

In each of the following sentences, first answer the question *By whom?* Then rewrite the sentence, beginning with your answer as the subject.

TEAR HERE

1. Our website was recently redesigned to incorporate an online store.

(By whom?) ______________________________

____

____

2. Net income before taxes must be calculated carefully when you fill out your tax return.

(By whom?) ______________________________

____

____

3. Only a few of the many errors were detected during the first proofreading.

(By whom?) ______________________________

____

____

4. A cellphone tower was constructed in their neighbourhood.

(By whom?) ______________________________

____

____

TEAR HERE

NAME ________________

LEVEL III

A. (Self-check) Select the correct word, and write it in the space provided.

1. If Ray Cortez (was, were) our union rep, he would not approve these work rules. ________
2. Was it suggested that the next scheduled meeting (is, be) cancelled? ________
3. If I (was, were) Mrs. Prashad, I'd buy medical insurance for the trip abroad. ________
4. If Mr. McHenry (was, were, be) at the opening session, he did not announce himself. ________
5. Sandi Woodruff recommended that additional chairs (are, be) set up for the afternoon session. ________
6. The supervisor ordered that everyone (attend, attends) one of the training sessions. ________
7. If you were in my place, I'm sure you (will, would) agree. ________
8. Did your doctor advise that you (be, are) excused from heavy duty? ________
9. He acts as if he (was, were) the only employee who had to work overtime. ________
10. It is necessary that the accountant (receive, receives) all the documents by June 30. ________

Check your answers.

B. Underline verbs that are incorrectly used in the following sentences. Write correct forms in the spaces provided. Write *C* if a sentence is correct.

1. William Harris wishes that he was able to retire by age 50. ________
2. I move that Mira remains chair of the hiring committee. ________
3. The HR manager recommended that each employee is given his or her birthday off. ________
4. I wish that there was an IT help desk professional available now so that I could finish that report. ________
5. A suggestion was made that employees are allowed to telecommute one day a week. ________
6. If he was in that position, he will be more understanding. ________
7. If a better employee benefit program was available, recruiting would be easier. ________
8. Suyin Cheng, our IT manager, strongly advised that computer firewalls are installed. ________
9. Henri said he wished that Luce were able to join him for lunch. ________
10. If Sam were in the office that day, I did not see him. ________

TEAR HERE

C. Choose the correct verb form, and complete the following sentences in the space required.

1. I wish that I (was, were) ____.
2. If my boss (was, were) ____.
3. It was recommended that the school (implements, implement) ____________________.
4. If anyone famous (was, were) at the premiere, ____________________________.

D. **Writing Exercise.** Your instructor may ask you to complete this exercise on a separate sheet.

Write sentences containing the following: transitive verb (two sentences), intransitive verb (two), linking verb (one), active-voice verb (two), passive-voice verb (two), and verb in the subjunctive mood (one). Label each of the ten sentences.

POSTTEST

Underline the appropriate answers.

1. In the sentence *He tasted the cookies while they were still warm*, the verb *tasted* is (a) an action verb, (b) a linking verb.
2. In the sentence *The cookies tasted delicious*, the verb *tasted* is (a) an action verb, (b) a linking verb.
3. In the sentence *The accounting firm released the report*, the verb *released* is (a) transitive, (b) intransitive, (c) subjunctive, (d) passive.
4. In the sentence *The workers have left for the day*, the verb phrase *have left* is (a) transitive, (b) intransitive, (c) subjunctive, (d) passive.
5. In the sentence *Lucy Xing hired four employees*, the verb *hired* is in the (a) active voice, (b) passive voice, (c) subjunctive mood.
6. In the sentence *Angelo Clouse was given the award*, the verb phrase *was given* is in the (a) active voice, (b) passive voice, (c) subjunctive mood.
7. In the sentence *Ruth insisted that the blog post be taken down*, the verb *be taken* is in the (a) active voice, (b) passive voice, (c) subjunctive mood.
8. If Mr. Pataky (a) was, (b) were the instructor, the class would be full.
9. Professor St. Clair recommended that students (a) are, (b) be admitted free.
10. If I (a) was, (b) were in your shoes, I would be thrilled.

TEAR HERE

EDITOR'S CHALLENGE

The following email message and memo contain errors in spelling and grammar principles you have studied thus far, as well as other common errors. Use proofreading marks to correct the errors.

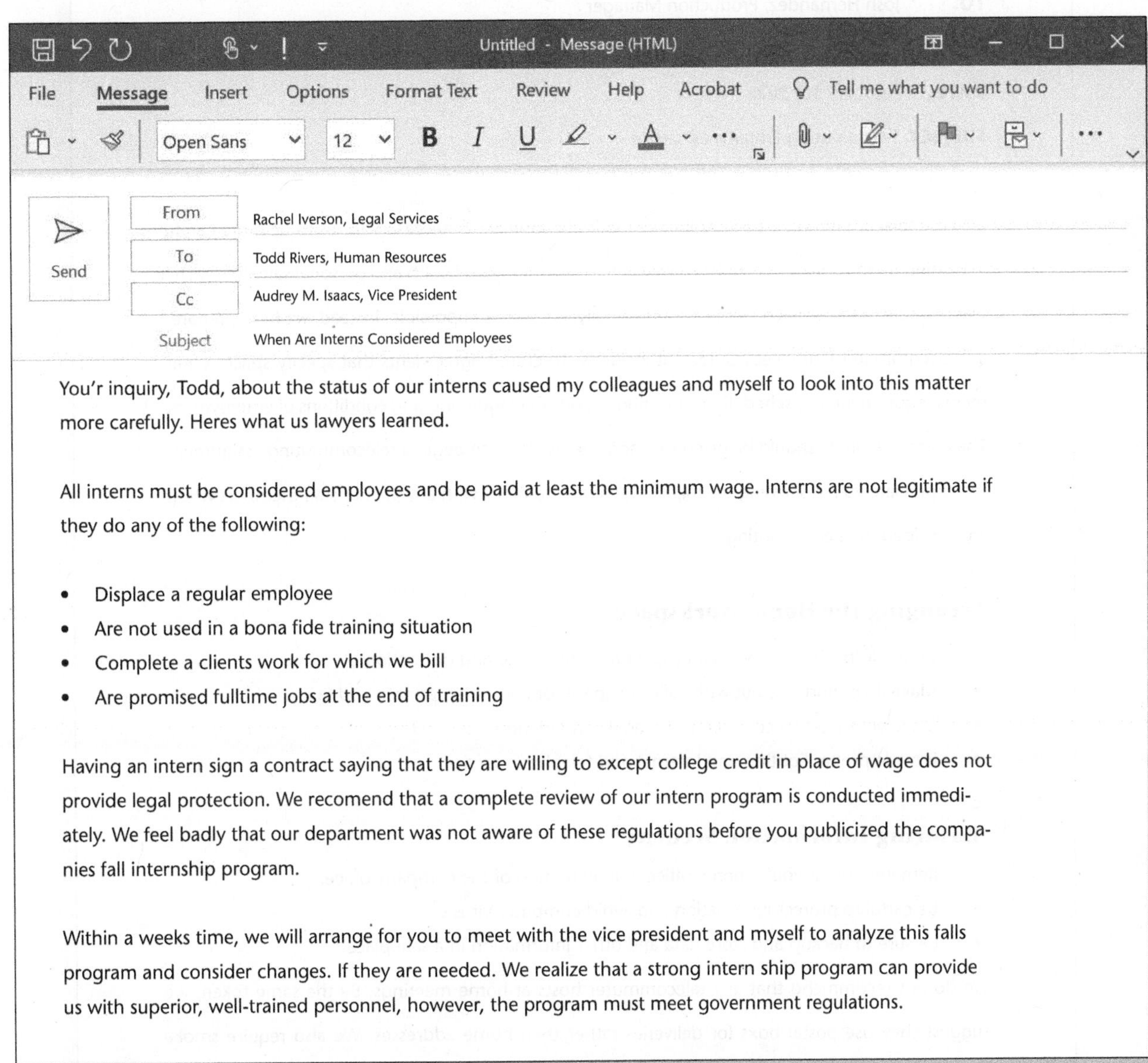
Untitled - Message (HTML)

From: Rachel Iverson, Legal Services
To: Todd Rivers, Human Resources
Cc: Audrey M. Isaacs, Vice President
Subject: When Are Interns Considered Employees

You'r inquiry, Todd, about the status of our interns caused my colleagues and myself to look into this matter more carefully. Heres what us lawyers learned.

All interns must be considered employees and be paid at least the minimum wage. Interns are not legitimate if they do any of the following:

- Displace a regular employee
- Are not used in a bona fide training situation
- Complete a clients work for which we bill
- Are promised fulltime jobs at the end of training

Having an intern sign a contract saying that they are willing to except college credit in place of wage does not provide legal protection. We recomend that a complete review of our intern program is conducted immediately. We feel badly that our department was not aware of these regulations before you publicized the companies fall internship program.

Within a weeks time, we will arrange for you to meet with the vice president and myself to analyze this falls program and consider changes. If they are needed. We realize that a strong intern ship program can provide us with superior, well-trained personnel, however, the program must meet government regulations.

GRADIENT RESEARCH INC.

INTEROFFICE MEMORANDUM

TO: Josh Hernandez, Production Manager

FROM: Edward J. Juralski, CEO

DATE: February 16, 202x

SUBJECT: Telecomuting Employees' Guide

Because telecommuting is becomming increasingly popular, its neccesary for us to be more careful in planing for information security. As well as for our employees health and personal safty. We wish it was feasable to talk to each employee individually, but that is impossible. Instead, we have prepared a "Telecommuter Employees Guide," it includes structured agreements that specify space requirments, equipment use, scheduling, communications management, and conditions of employment. The complete guide should be given to whomever is about to begin a telecommuting assignment. We appreciate your discussing the following recomendations with any of your staff members whom are considering telecommuting.

Arranging the Home Workspace

- Create a space where you can expect minimal traffic and distraction.
- Make it comfortable but with suficient space for computer, printer, and fax.
- Make your workspace off-limits to family and friend's.
- Provide proper lighting and Internet and telephone service.

Ensuring Information Security

- Remember that you're home office is an extention of the company office.
- Be carful to protect information and avoid computer virus's.
- Be sure to backup and store data and other information in a safe place.

We do not recommend that any telecommuter hosts at-home meetings. By the same token, we suggest they use postal boxs for deliveries rather then home addresses. We also require smoke detector's in home work areas.

To have any questions answered, contact my assistant or I at Ext. 310.

For additional resources, please visit MindTap at login.cengage.com. Cengage | MINDTAP

TEAR HERE

CHAPTER 9

SUBJECT–VERB AGREEMENT

OBJECTIVES

When you have completed the materials in this chapter, you will be able to do the following:

LEVEL I

- Locate the subjects of verbs despite intervening elements and inverted sentence structure
- Make verbs agree with subjects joined by *and* and with company names and titles

LEVEL II

- Make verbs agree with subjects joined by *or* or *nor*
- Select the correct verbs to agree with indefinite pronouns and collective nouns

LEVEL III

- Make verbs agree with *the number/a number*, quantities and measures, and fractions and portions
- Achieve subject–verb agreement with phrases and clauses as subjects and with subject complements

PRETEST

Underline the correct verb form.

1. There (is, are) six items on today's agenda.
2. Having to learn how to use a professional camera and its various lenses (intimidates, intimidate) some real estate agents.
3. McDonald's (has, have) seen decreasing sales.
4. One of the plant supervisors (plans, plan) to implement a new safety program.

(continued)

PRETEST *(CONTINUED)*

5. The director of fulfillment, along with her entire department, (was, were) given training on the new shipping system.

6. Neither the supervisor nor the members of his team (is, are) satisfied with the level of service.

7. Hassan is the only one of the engineers who (understands, understand) what our priorities are.

8. Behind our building (lies, lie) the parking lot and an outdoor recreation area.

9. The number of email messages (is, are) increasing daily.

10. Everyone (is, are) welcome to attend the grand opening ceremony.

Writing isn't brain surgery, but at times it can seem every bit as difficult. Fortunately, you have the ability to edit your writing. One important item to test for during editing is subject–verb agreement. Subjects must agree with verbs in number and person. Beginning a sentence with, for example, *He don't* damages the credibility and effectiveness of a speaker or writer.

An error in subject–verb agreement can generally be attributed to one of three lapses: (1) failure to locate the subject, (2) failure to recognize the number (singular or plural) of the subject after locating it, or (3) failure to recognize the number of the verb. Suggestions follow for locating the true subject and determining the number of the subject and its verb.

LEVEL I

LOCATING SUBJECTS

All verbs have subjects. Locating these subjects can be difficult, particularly when (a) a prepositional phrase comes between the verb and its subject, (b) an intervening element separates the subject and verb, (c) sentences begin with *there* or *here*, and (d) sentences are inverted. You practised locating subjects in Chapter 2; because this is such an important skill, we provide additional instruction here.

Prepositional Phrases

Subjects of verbs are not found in prepositional phrases. Therefore, you must learn to ignore such phrases in identifying subjects of verbs. Some of the most common prepositions are *of, to, in, from, for, with, at,* and *by*. (See a more complete list on page 224.) Notice that the italicized prepositional phrases in these sentences do not contain the subjects of the verbs:

Only one *of the company executives* has insurance. (The verb *has* agrees with its singular subject, *one*, not with *executives*, the object of the preposition.)

We wonder if the invoice *for the two shipments* is lost. (The verb *is* agrees with its singular subject, *invoice*.)

The range *of tasks and skill requirements* allows for upward growth potential. (The verb *allows* agrees with its singular subject, *range*.)

BE THE EDITOR

On the label of Heinz 57 sauce: "Its' unique tangy blend of herbs and spices bring out the natural taste of steak." [Did you spot two errors?]

Some of the less easily recognized prepositions are *except, but* (when it is used to mean *except*), *like*, and *between*. In the following sentences, distinguish the subjects from the italicized prepositional phrases:

All employees *but Tom* are to report early. (The verb *are* agrees with its plural subject, *employees*.)

Everyone *except the managers* is in the union. (The verb *is* agrees with its singular subject, *everyone*.)

Engineers *like me* enjoy complex math equations. (The verb *enjoy* agrees with its plural subject, *engineers*.)

Intervening Elements

Groups of words introduced by expressions such as *as well as, in addition to, such as, including, plus, together with*, and *other than* do NOT contain sentence subjects.

The priceless book, *as well as other valuable documents*, was lost in the fire.

In this sentence the writer has elected to emphasize the subject *book* and to de-emphasize *other valuable documents*. The writer could have given equal weight to these elements by writing *The priceless book* and *other valuable documents were lost in the fire*. Notice that the number (singular or plural) of the verb changes when both *book* and *documents* are given equal emphasis. Here are additional examples involving intervening elements:

Our president, *together with her entire staff of 12 employees*, believes that the company will rebound. (The singular subject *president* agrees with the singular verb *believes*.)

Other pianists, *such as Pennario*, appear on the program. (The plural subject *pianists* agrees with the plural verb *appear*.)

Sentences Beginning with *There* and *Here*

In sentences beginning with *there* or *here*, look for the true subject AFTER the verb. *Here* and *there* cannot function as subjects.

There are four candidates for the position. (The plural subject *candidates* follows the verb *are*.)

Here is the fuel oil consumption report. (The singular subject *report* follows the verb *is*.)

Be especially careful when using contractions. Remember that *here's* is the contraction for *here is*; therefore, it should be used only with singular subjects. Likewise, *there's* is the contraction for *there is* or *there has* and should also be used only with singular subjects.

Incorrect:	Here's the documents you requested. (The plural subject *documents* does not agree with the verb *is*.)
Correct:	Here are the documents you requested. (The plural subject *documents* agrees with the verb *are*.)
Incorrect:	There's three reasons you should hire me for the proofreader position. (The plural subject *reasons* does not agree with the verb *is*.)
Correct:	There are three reasons you should hire me for the proofreader position. (The plural subject *reasons* agrees with the verb *are*.)

ASK AN EDITOR

Question:
Please help me with this sentence that I'm transcribing for a medical laboratory: *A copy of our analysis, along with our interpretation of its results, (has* or *have) been sent to you.*

Answer:
The subject of your sentence is *copy*; thus the verb must be *has*. Don't let interrupting elements obscure the real sentence subject.

CAREER TIP

Skilful writers avoid starting sentences or clauses with *there*, a word-wasting filler. Sentences can usually be rewritten and made stronger without it.

Inverted Sentence Order

In inverted sentences, including questions, look for the subject after the verb or after the first element of a verb phrase.

How important are salary, benefits, and job security? (Verb precedes subjects.)

On our board of directors are three prominent scientists. (Verb precedes subject.)

Have the product specifications been submitted? (Subject interrupts verb phrase.)

STUDY TIP

Remember that, although the ending *s* makes a noun plural, it makes a verb singular (*The students come from Alberta; the student comes from Alberta*).

BASIC RULES FOR SUBJECT–VERB AGREEMENT

Once you have located the sentence subject, decide whether the subject is singular or plural and select a verb that agrees in number. The table on page 123 of Chapter 7 will remind you that the third-person singular form of present-tense verbs requires an *s*.

Subjects Joined by *and*

BE THE EDITOR

Message printed on a Gap T-shirt: "The days of this society is numbered."

When the conjunction *and* joins one subject to another, the result is a compound subject. The subject is usually plural and thus requires a plural verb.

Mark Zuckerberg and Tom Anderson are two influential people in the world of social networking.

The proposed law and its amendment are before the legislature.

BE THE EDITOR

From *The St. John's Evening Telegram*: "It's important that we have in that position someone who's judgment, integrity, and incompetence is beyond question." (Did you spot three errors?)

Company and Organization Names

Even though they may appear to be plural, company and organization names are generally considered singular; therefore, they require singular verbs.

Manitobah Mukluks makes boots rated to –32 degrees Celsius.

Richards, Bateman, and Richards is offering the bond issue.

Titles

Titles of publications and artistic works such as songs are singular; therefore, they require singular verbs.

Seven Secrets to Successful Investing was an instant bestseller.

Leonard Cohen's *Songs of Love and Hate* (1971) is the third-bestselling Canadian album of all time.

Complete the reinforcement exercises for Level I on pages 168–170.

LEVEL II

SPECIAL RULES FOR SUBJECT–VERB AGREEMENT

Making sure your subjects agree with your verbs sometimes requires the application of special rules. This is especially the case when dealing with subjects joined by *or* or *nor*, indefinite pronouns as subjects, and collective nouns as subjects.

Subjects Joined by *or* or *nor*

When two or more subjects are joined by *or* or *nor*, the verb should agree with the closer subject (usually the subject that follows *or* or *nor*).

Neither the supervisor nor the clerks know the order number.

Either Leslie or you are responsible for ordering supplies.

The distributors or the manufacturer carries spare parts.

STUDY TIP

Unlike subjects joined by *and*, subjects joined by *or* or *nor* require a choice between Subject No. 1 and Subject No. 2. Always choose the subject closer to the verb to determine the correct verb form.

Indefinite Pronouns as Subjects

As you may recall from Chapter 6 (p. 93), some indefinite pronouns are always singular, whereas other indefinite pronouns are always plural. In addition, some may be either singular or plural, depending on the words to which they refer.

Always Singular	**Always Plural**	**Singular or Plural**
anyone, anybody, anything,	both, few,	all, any, more,
each, either, every, everyone,	many, several	most, none, some
everybody, everything,		
neither, nobody, nothing,		
somebody, someone, something		

Either of the two applicants *is* suitable.
Everybody in the lottery *has* an equal chance.
A *few* of the employees *are* applying for shares.
Neither of the websites *is* particularly helpful.

Some indefinite pronouns can be singular or plural, depending on context. These indefinite pronouns, including *all, more,* and *most,* provide one of the few instances when prepositional phrases become important in determining agreement. Although the prepositional phrase does not contain the subject of the sentence, it may contain the noun to which the indefinite pronoun refers. If that noun is singular, use a singular verb; if the noun is plural, use a plural verb.

Most of the letters *are* finished. (*Most* is plural because it refers to the plural noun *letters.*)

Most of the work *is* completed. (*Most* is singular because it refers to the singular noun *work.*)

None presents an interesting case. Traditionally, *none* was almost always used in a singular sense. Over time, through usage, *none* has become accepted as either singular or plural depending on what you want to emphasize.

None of the students *are* failing.
None of the students *is* failing. (The singular use emphasizes "not even one.")

If *each* or *every* is used to describe two or more subjects joined by *and*, the subjects are considered singular.*

Each semicolon and colon *was* misused.
Every man, woman, and child *is* affected by the tax cut.

Anyone and *everyone* are spelled as two words when followed by *of* phrases.

Any one of those websites can be used to book hotel reservations.
Every one of the candidates has a campaign committee.

*This use of a singular verb for two or more subjects joined by *and* is the main exception to the general rule presented in Level I.

Collective Nouns as Subjects

Collective nouns such as *faculty, class, committee, council,* and *team* may be singular or plural, depending on how they are used in a sentence. Usually a collective noun operates as a single unit, so its verb should be singular. If the elements of a collective noun operate separately, however, the verb should be plural.

Our faculty *has* approved the proposal. (*Faculty* has operated as a single unit.)

The city council *were* sharply divided over appropriations. (*Council* members were acting separately. While technically correct as it stands, the sentence would be less awkward if it read, *The council members were sharply. . . .*)

The city council *has* voted in favour of the zoning change. (*Council* is operating as a single unit.)

Our faculty *disagree* on the need for a strike. (*Faculty* members are acting separately.)

Complete the reinforcement exercises for Level II on pages 171–172.

LEVEL III

ADDITIONAL RULES FOR SUBJECT–VERB AGREEMENT

In some instances it is difficult to know whether a subject is singular or plural. Here are a few additional rules to guide you in selecting appropriate verbs for such subjects.

The Distinction Between *the number* and *a number*

When the word *number* is the subject of a sentence, its article (*the* or *a*) becomes significant. *The* is specific and therefore implies *singularity*; *a* is general and therefore implies *plurality*. This means that *the number* is singular and *a number* is plural. Ignore any prepositional phrases that follow.

The number of managers *is* declining. (Singular)

A number of orders *were* lost. (Plural)

Quantities and Measures

When they refer to *total* amounts, quantities and measures are singular. If they refer to individual units that can be counted, quantities and measures are plural.

Forty points is all you need to win.

Five points were awarded for each email response.

Fractions, Portions, and Percentages

Fractions, portions, and percentages may be singular or plural, depending on the nouns to which they refer.

Only a *third* of the students' reading scores are satisfactory.

Over *half* of the contract was ratified.

A *majority* of employees agree with the proposal.

A small *percentage* of the delegates are in favour of the plan.

Part of the proposal is ambiguous.

Who, That, and *Which* Clauses

Verbs in *who, that,* and *which* clauses (known as **relative pronoun clauses**) must agree in number and person with the nouns to which these relative pronouns refer.

A book of poems that were written in the seventeenth century is on display at my college.

A book of poems that was published by my professor is on display at my college.

All uses of the company's 3-D printer—which is not a toy, according to a note on the unit—must be approved by management.

The prototype, which was created using a 3-D printer, has received positive reviews.

It is you who are responsible for security.

Could it be I who am to blame?

In *who* clauses introduced by *one of*, the verb is plural because *who* refers to a plural antecedent. In *who* clauses introduced by *the only one of*, the verb is singular because *who* refers to *one*.

Mrs. Tam is *one of* those managers who always support their employees.

Eli is *one of* those people who are late sleepers.

Margaret is *the only one* of the girls who is prepared.

STUDY TIP

For sentences with *one of those who* clauses, begin reading with the word *of*: *Of those people who are late sleepers, Eli is one.* The verb is always plural. However, if the sentence is limited by the word *only* before *one*, the verb is always singular: *Of the girls, Margaret is the only one who is prepared.*

Phrases and Clauses as Subjects

Use a singular verb when the subject of a sentence is an entire phrase or clause.

Learning about the stock market is fascinating.

That verbs must agree with subjects is accepted.

Subject Complements

Previously you learned that linking verbs are followed by complements. Although the complement may differ from the subject in number, the linking verb should always agree with the subject.

The best part of the show is the *singing and dancing*. (The singular subject *part* agrees with the singular verb *is* despite the plural complement *singing and dancing*.)

The reason for his bankruptcy is poor *investments*.

If such a sentence seems awkward, you may reconstruct it so that the plural element is first: *Poor investments are the reason for his bankruptcy.*

Complete the reinforcement exercises for Level III on pages 173–175.

BE THE EDITOR

From an Associated Press article: "Education and employer training is often the biggest need in an independently owned business."

NAME ______________________________

CHAPTER 9 ■ Reinforcement Exercises

LEVEL I

A. **(Self-check)** Select the correct word to complete each sentence below. Write it in the space provided.

1. Presenting today (is, are) two well-known investment experts. ____________
2. Our local manufacturer, as well as our overseas manufacturer, (is, are) looking at ways to help us reduce costs without affecting quality. ____________
3. There (is, are) several industries whose workforces are growing across Canada. ____________
4. (Has, Have) the title page and bibliography been completed yet? ____________
5. A set of procedures for protecting network security (seems, seem) necessary. ____________
6. One of the first computer viruses (was, were) the "elk cloner," which was written by a Grade 9 student in 1982. ____________
7. Sampling our new line of seasonings (is, are) a group of students from the culinary arts program at Bonne Cuisine. ____________
8. We understand that Porter Airlines (provides, provide) excellent benefits. ____________
9. No one but Lena and Max (has, have) opened the file. ____________
10. *Freakonomics* by Steven D. Levitt and Stephen J. Dubner (appear, appears) to be one of the bestselling economics books of all time. ____________

Check your answers.

B. Assume that the following phrases serve as sentence subjects. Underline the simple subject(s) in each item. Then indicate whether the subject is singular or plural.

	Singular	**Plural**
EXAMPLE: the controller and the treasurer of the county	____	✓
1. a directory of email addresses	____	____
2. the time and money involved in the project	____	____
3. her department manager, as well as other managers	____	____
4. each of our employees	____	____
5. the production cost and the markup of each item	____	____
6. one of the most successful e-commerce sites in the industry	____	____
7. current emphasis on product safety and consumer protection	____	____

TEAR HERE

8. the network administrator, together with her staff ______ ______

9. Madison, Lee, & Cassidy, an executive placement service ______ ______

10. the anger and frustration of the passengers ______ ______

C. For each of the following sentences, cross out any phrases that separate the verb from its simple subject. Underline the subject. Then choose the correct verb, and write it in the space provided.

EXAMPLES: The supervisor, ~~together with two of his assistants~~, (is, are) here. is

Our catalogue ~~of gift ideas~~ (is, are) being sent to you. is

1. Our company's full range of products and services (is, are) available through our new online store. ______
2. Compensation, along with benefits and vacation time, (is, are) generally discussed after a job offer is made. ______
3. All manufacturing divisions except one (has, have) newly updated safety standards. ______
4. The delivery of the parts (needs, need) to be made by Friday. ______
5. Only one of the major North American automobile manufacturers (has, have) been able to show profits. ______
6. Not in every workplace (does, do) non-binary people feel accepted as they are. ______
7. A contest like ones we've done in previous years (seems, seem) unlikely to boost sales. ______
8. One of your duties, in addition to the tasks already described, (is, are) the budgeting of funds for both departments. ______
9. A diploma from a reputable college and three years of experience (is, are) required for this position. ______
10. (Has, Have) the charges claimed on your expense form been approved? ______

D. Select the correct verb and write it in the space provided.

1. Of the traits we're looking for in a candidate, flexibility and an understanding of our industry (counts, count) among the most important. ______
2. Sam and Roshani (is, are) unable to attend today's meeting. ______
3. Iconic Canadian company Roots (was, were) founded in 1973 by Michael Budman and Don Green. ______
4. Canoe tours that teach about Nuu-Chah-Nulth culture (is, are) among the offerings of T'ashii Paddle School in Tofino. ______
5. T'ashii (employs, employ) several Nuu-Chah-Nulth youths, who learn much about their own culture and history through their work. ______
6. There (is, are) a buyer and her assistant waiting in your office. ______
7. How essential (is, are) experience and education in this field? ______

TEAR HERE

8. Our president, as well as the general manager and three salespeople, (plan, plans) to attend the conference. ______________

9. Not one of our four service representatives (is, are) available. ______________

10. Seated next to the al-Sahilis (is, are) Joe Miranda. ______________

11. Cisco Systems (has, have) found a way to restructure its finances. ______________

12. Lying on my desk (is, are) my itinerary and plane tickets. ______________

13. Here (is, are) a complete list of product features. ______________

14. Considerable time and money (was, were) spent on the final product. ______________

15. Tim Ferriss's *Tools of Titans* (is, are) among the most recommended books for entrepreneurs. ______________

TEAR HERE

NAME ______________________

LEVEL II

A. (Self-check) Write the correct form in the space provided.

1. A task force of four men and five women (were, was) appointed. ______

2. Either Facebook or Instagram (is, are) the best source of new customers for our online store. ______

3. Each clerk, administrative assistant, and data entry specialist (attend, attends) the training sessions. ______

4. Each of the websites (provide, provides) live support. ______

5. Every workshop participant and facilitator (is, are) to be served lunch. ______

6. Nothing but old catalogues and sales sheets (is, are) in this box. ______

7. (Everyone, Every one) of the sales reps made quota this month. ______

8. A committee of executives (do, does) the final interviewing of candidates for jobs at this level. ______

9. Both the research and the feedback (is, are) going into the report. ______

10. Everyone except a few employees (admit, admits) that the new CEO is doing a good job. ______

Check your answers.

B. Write the correct form in the space provided.

1. Each quarter 100 Women Who Care (select, selects) a local charity to support. ______

2. A selection of sandwiches, pastries, and beverages (was, were) ordered for the meeting. ______

3. (Everyone, Every one) of the résumés contained grammatical errors. ______

4. Most of the blog (is, are) dedicated to sharing online marketing strategies. ______

5. Either the owner or her partners (is, are) responsible for the taxes. ______

6. Either the partners or the owner (was, were) contacted by the Canada Revenue Agency. ______

7. The group of executives, sales representatives, and clients (plan, plans) to charter a plane. ______

8. The group (is, are) choosing their seats on the plane now. ______

9. (Anyone, Any one) on the contact list may be called upon to fill in. ______

10. Every year at the conference, a panel of industry insiders (discusses, discuss) issues the industry is facing. ______

11. Management (forbid, forbids) employees to access social media on their work computers. ______

12. Some of the drop-down menu items (is, are) unclear. ______

TEAR HERE

13. (Was, Were) any of the members of the organization present that afternoon? ____________________

14. Neither the president nor the VPs (favour, favours) the proposed cutbacks. ____________________

15. Most of the adults using Twitter (is, are) urban and educated. ____________________

16. (Do, Does) the team of lawyers think the case is winnable? ____________________

17. Every one of the employees who attended the meeting (was, were) opposed to the reductions in benefits. ____________________

18. None of the research (deals, deal) with television advertising. ____________________

19. Either computer malware or corrupted files (has, have) prevented us from accessing the information we need. ____________________

20. A 24-pack of bottled water (cost, costs) nearly $30 in Iqaluit. ____________________

21. Most of the cost of groceries (relates, relate) to high transportation fees. ____________________

22. As well, most of the communities in Nunavut (is, are) not connected to the electricity grid, incurring high energy costs for preserving food. ____________________

23. A group of researchers (has, have) reviewed grocery store financial records. ____________________

24. Every dollar of sales (net, nets) four cents in profit, in line with the rest of the industry in Canada. ____________________

25. While Iqaluit residents with credit cards can access lower priced groceries through Amazon, any of Nunavut's smaller communities (lacks, lack) an Amazon delivery option. ____________________

C. Writing Exercise. Use your imagination to complete the sentences started below, choosing the correct verb form from the choices in parentheses.

1. The staff (is, are) ____________________

2. Our city council (has, have) ____________________.

3. Every executive, manager, and worker (values, value) ____________________.

4. Many of the reviewers (states, state) ____________________.

5. Somebody in the theatre filled with patrons (was, were) ____________________.

6. The audience (was, were) ____________________.

7. Some of the proposal (needs, need) ____________________.

8. Either Anne or you (is, are) ____________________.

TEAR HERE

NAME ______________________________

LEVEL III

A. (Self-check) For each sentence write the correct verb in the space provided.

1. The number of companies using social media to perform background checks on potential employees (is, are) growing. ____________
2. She is the only one of the service reps who (speak, speaks) both French and English fluently. ____________
3. Part of the reason for declining sales (is, are) poor customer service. ____________
4. Laurie McDonough is one of those professors who (has, have) earned the respect of students. ____________
5. Fourteen metres of pipe (is, are) exactly what was specified. ____________
6. About one-third of the records stored on microfiche (has, have) been transferred to the computer. ____________
7. A number of companies (is, are) choosing to advertise on social media instead of on television. ____________
8. The people in line who (has, have) reserved seats can enter now. ____________
9. Two cups of water (is, are) mixed with half a cup of sugar to make hummingbird food. ____________
10. The hardest part of the job (is, are) the bending and lifting. ____________

Check your answers.

B. Select the correct verb and write it in the space provided.

1. One hundred pennies (is, are) needed to make one dollar. ____________
2. Five hundred dollars (is, are) required as a deposit to hold the conference facility. ____________
3. Only a fraction of the conference room (was, were) set up by the time the meeting was scheduled to begin. ____________
4. Didn't you know that it is you who (has, have) been chosen for the promotion? ____________
5. Why they were absent (remains, remain) a mystery. ____________
6. Please review the enclosed portfolio of our designs that (has, have) won awards. ____________
7. A number of productivity experts (recommends, recommend) using a paper planner to schedule tasks. ____________
8. Ibrahim is the only one of the lab assistants who (was, were) able to repair the malfunctioning machine. ____________
9. Our updated policies and procedures (is, are) the next item on the agenda. ____________
10. Sixty days (is, are) the period of the loan. ____________
11. In our agency the number of highly successful marketers (is, are) steadily increasing. ____________

TEAR HERE

12. Exactly what answers the hiring committee wanted to hear (is, are) anyone's guess.

13. Over 80 percent of the individuals attending the lecture series (is, are) college students.

14. Michael is one of those people who always (get, gets) along well with fellow workers.

15. Keeping your skills up to date (is, are) important in today's economy.

16. The documents related to the sale, which (was, were) signed by both parties, are legally binding.

17. A full three-quarters of our employees (contributes, contribute) to RRSPs through the company.

18. Is Mr. Gouveia one of the executives who (is, are) being investigated?

19. That the letters went out without having been proofread (is, are) indisputable.

20. An RBC report says women who (has, have) children earn less than their childless counterparts for up to five years after giving birth.

C. Review of Levels I, II, and III. Underline any subject–verb agreement problem, and write an improved form or forms in the space provided. Write *C* if the sentence is correct.

1. Ultimately, business is business, even though every industry and every profession have some unique elements.
2. *Stumbling Giants* by Patricia Meredith and James L. Darroch argue that Canadian banks are risking irrelevance by not changing with the times.
3. The use of UPC scanning devices, computer databases, and thermal-imaging receipts is almost universal in the retail industry.
4. Every one of the meters has been giving a faulty reading.
5. Mike is one of those accountants who works day and night until the financial statements are ready.
6. There's many advantages to earning a college degree.
7. Representing our office is several men and women who are well respected in the industry.
8. Trimark Mutual Funds, with headquarters in Toronto, often advertise in *The Globe and Mail.*
9. Are either of the applicants available to interview on Friday?
10. Was any of the members of the organization present for the final vote?
11. After several days of deliberation, the jury has announced its verdict.
12. Containers will not be moved until the negotiations or the strike have ended.
13. Persistent inflation and interest rate worries often causes share prices to drop.
14. Globalization, the fluidity of Canada's ethnic composition, and the introduction of a third gender designation is encouraging more organizations to embrace diversity programs.
15. The committee have shared its findings and recommendations.

TEAR HERE

D. Writing Exercise. Your instructor may ask you to complete this exercise on a separate sheet.

Write ten original sentences, one for each of the following expressions. Use the words as subjects of present-tense verbs: *anyone, any one, everyone, every one, committee, most, the number, a number, five days,* and *a majority of the students.*

POSTTEST

Underline the correct verb.

1. Neither the transportation costs nor the storage fee (was, were) accounted for in the budget.
2. Our recipes use a variety of wholesome products that (has, have) not been processed.
3. The cost of materials, along with manufacturing expenses, (dictates, dictate) how we need to price the product.
4. Everyone except the president and other senior managers (qualifies, qualify) for early retirement.
5. Appearing next on the program (was, were) Dr. Gwen Hester and Professor Michele Koci.
6. The research team (has, have) determined that the number one feature women want in a vehicle is extra storage.
7. Five centimetres (makes, make) a significance difference in the size of a computer screen.
8. There (is, are) always other options if one fails.
9. Featuring suggested wine pairings on the menu (has, have) increased the restaurant's wine sales.
10. A number of surprising events (is, are) creating spikes in the stock market.

TEAR HERE

EDITOR'S CHALLENGE

The following letter proposal and email contain errors in spelling and grammar principles you have studied thus far, as well as other common errors. Use proofreading marks to show your corrections.

Wright Research Consultants

385 Eglinton Ave. West
Toronto, ON M4T 2H9

Web: http://www.wrightresearch.com Phone: (416) 220-9184 Email: lwright@wrightresearch.com

April 15, 202x

Mr. Morris Edelson
Consumer Credit Service
1021 Birchmount Road
Toronto, ON M1K 5G3

Dear Mr. Edelson:

At your request my staff and myself is submitting the following proposal regarding a survey of university students credit habits in southern Ontario.

Problem

As you point out, credit purchase's among university students is burdening them with to much debt, more than half of full-time undergraduate students now has at least one major credit card. Although students account for less than 3 percent of the domestic credit card business, a significant number of these students is having more trouble than other borrowers in repaying. Credit card use among students have rose dramatically in the past decade.

Background

We understand that your non-profit organizations principle goal is to open a credit counselling service aimed at university students in southern Ontario. Specifically, you want to investigate (1) credit card habit's among university students in general, (2) credit card habits among students in your area, and (3) the affectiveness of student counselling services in other parts of the country.

Proposed Plan

On the basis of our experience in conducting many local and national surveys. Wright Research propose to develop a short but thorough questionnaire probing the data you desire. We will submit the questionnaire for you approval, and we will consult with you regarding the exact sample and it's demographics. Data from the surveywill be analyze by our experienced team of experts. Using the latest computer systems and advanced statistical measures.

TEAR HERE

Consumer Credit Service   Page 2   April 15, 202x

Staffing and Budget

Wright Research Consultants are a nationally recognized, experienced research consulting firm specializing in survey investigation. My staff has assigned your survey to Dr. Rebecca Horne, whom is our director of research. Dr. Horne was trained at the University of Alberta and has successfully supervise our research program for the past nine years. Further information about her qualifications and our staffs training are provided in the attached brochure. Everyone of the members of our staff are experienced in survey research. Budget figures for this proposed survey is shown in the attach brochure.

Authorization

My staff and myself sincerely believe that our profesionally designed and administered survey are exactly what you need to enable you to make a decision about the establishment of a student credit counselling service in southern Ontario. Wright Research can have the results for you by July 2. If you sign the enclosed duplicate copy of this letter and return them immediately to Dr. Horne or I with a retainer of $3000. The prices in this offer is in affect only until September 1.

Sincerely,

Lawrence R. Wright

Lawrence R. Wright
President
Enclosure

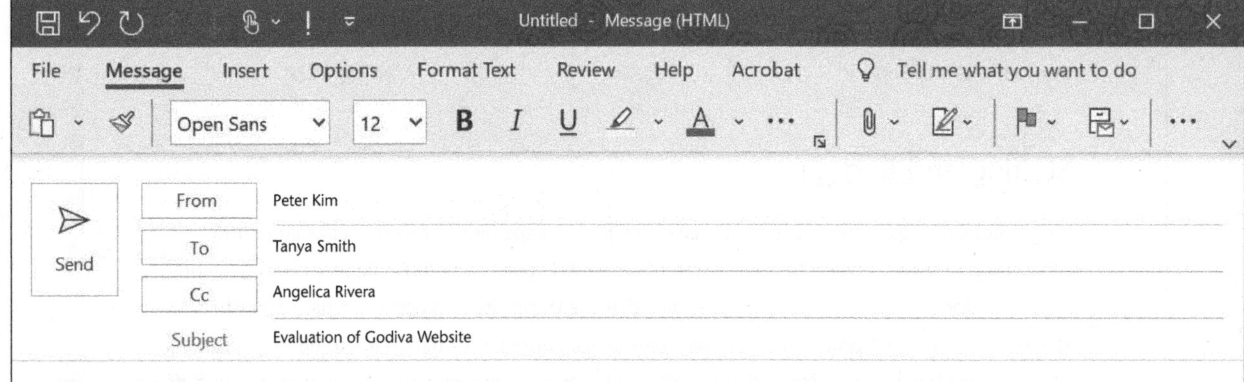

Tanya,

As you requested, I have complete my research on the website of our principle competitor, Godiva Chocolatier. This website, along with the sites of many other chocolate entrepreneurs, are intended primarily to sell quality chocolate online. The range of clever features and activitys from the Godiva site are extensive.

Although selling chocolates online are very important, advertising and customer service is also important at *Godiva.com*. Stylish graphics and a gold back ground reminiscent of Godivas gold packaging makes the site one of the most attractive I have saw.

Navigating the site seems easy. Clear links take visitors to different parts of the site, allowing them to order chocolate, learn about Godiva products, or work with a customer service representative. Although the link's change frequently. Here is a few typical links:

- **Shopping Online.** This link enables the web cruiser to search for and purchase Godiva chocolates via an online catalogue. Customers may search for chocolates by price, by type, or even by holiday. The selections they have chose are collected in a shopping basket and purchase with a credit card.
- **Recipes.** A number of mouth-watering recipes featuring Godiva chocolates are posted on this link. However, if you have ever ate Godiva chocolates, you would wonder why any one would ever ruin them by cooking them!
- **Business Gift-Giving.** One of the best links for companies describe corporate incentive programs, custom packaging, and volume discounts.
- **What's New?** A collection of new items are features, including Godiva biscuits, gifts, recipes, and new products. Although prices are raising, Godiva's seems reasonable.
- **Spotlight.** This link describes an online sweepstakes, a soap opera, Godiva kosher products, and *Chocolatier Magazine*. I will send printouts of several of *Godiva.coms* best web pages. Visitors' may also access the site directly at **www.godiva.com**.

If you have began to think seriously about redesigning our companys Website, I am eager to help. Please write or call me at Ext. 388 to let me know how I may assist.

Peter

For additional resources, please visit MindTap at login.cengage.com. Cengage | MINDTAP

TEAR HERE

CHAPTER

10

VERBALS

OBJECTIVES

When you have completed the materials in this chapter, you will be able to do the following:

LEVEL I

- Recognize gerunds and supply appropriate modifiers of gerunds
- Use infinitives correctly and avoid awkward split infinitives

LEVEL II

- Correctly punctuate introductory and other verbal phrases
- Use participles correctly

LEVEL III

- Spot dangling verbal phrases
- Rewrite sentences to avoid misplaced verbal phrases

PRETEST

Write *a*, *b*, or *c* in the space provided to describe the following sentences.

a = contains no errors
b = contains error in use of verbal form
c = contains error in punctuation of verbal form

1. We appreciate you bringing the matter to our attention. ________
2. Galen Weston Jr. having been educated at Harvard, returned to Canada to work in his father's business, Loblaw Companies Ltd. ________
3. When you visit the Sault Ste. Marie office, be sure and check that employees follow the same procedures as we do here. ________

(continued)

PRETEST *(CONTINUED)*

4. When preparing my report, the Internet provided me with the best information. ___________
5. After considering the project carefully the vice president gave his approval. ___________
6. To register by mail, return the enclosed application form. ___________
7. Announced in August, CEO Milton explained details of the payout plan. ___________
8. To finish the report on time the staff had to put in many extra hours of effort. ___________
9. Sarah deposited nearly $800 into her savings account made during her weekend garage sale. ___________
10. The surgeon unexpectedly found a tumour, operating on Mr. Khan's heart. ___________

As you learned earlier, English is a highly flexible language in which a given word may have more than one grammatical function. In this chapter you will study verbals. Derived from verbs, verbals are words that function as nouns, adjectives, or adverbs. The three kinds of verbals we will study are gerunds (verbal nouns), infinitives, and participles (verbal adjectives).

LEVEL I

GERUNDS

A **gerund** is a verb form that ends in *ing* and is used as a noun. Gerunds often name activities.

> *Advertising* is necessary. (Gerund used as subject)
> Dale enjoys *skiing*. (Gerund used as direct object of verb)
> Indira insisted on *revealing* the code. (Gerund used as object of preposition)

Using Gerunds Correctly

In using gerunds, follow this rule: Make any noun or pronoun that modifies a gerund possessive.

> *Karen's keyboarding* | *his father's remarrying*
> *the Hoseins' purchasing* | *their visiting*

Because we sometimes fail to recognize gerunds as nouns, we fail to make their modifiers possessive.

> *Incorrect:* The staff objects to Kevin smoking.
> *Correct:* The staff objects to Kevin's smoking.

The staff does not object to Kevin, as the first version states; it objects to his smoking. If we substitute a more easily recognized noun for *smoking*, the possessive form seems more natural: *The staff objects to Kevin's behaviour. Behaviour* is a noun, just as *smoking* is a noun; the noun or pronoun modifiers of both must be possessive.

Jennie resented *his* calling during lunch. (The gerund *calling* requires the possessive pronoun *his*, not the objective-case pronoun *him*.)
We appreciate *your* bringing this matter to our attention. (Not *you bringing*)

Of course, not all verb forms ending in *ing* are gerunds. Some are participles acting either as elements in verb phrases or as adjectives. Compare these three sentences:

I saw Monica typing. (The word *typing* functions as an adjective describing Monica.)
I admired Monica's typing. (As the object of the verb, *typing* acts as a gerund.)
Monica is typing. (Here, *typing* is part of a verb phrase.)

INFINITIVES

When the present form of a verb is preceded by *to*, the most basic verb form results: the **infinitive**. A sign of the infinitive is the word *to*.

Try *to sign* the papers immediately.
To write clearly and concisely requires skill.

Using Infinitives Correctly

Observe the use of the word *to* in the following infinitive phrases. Do not commit the common error of substituting the conjunction *and* in place of the *to* of the infinitive.

Try *to call* when you arrive. (Not *Try and call*)
Be sure *to speak* softly when you use your cellphone in public. (Not *Be sure and speak*)
Check *to see* when your appointment is. (Not *Check and see*)

When any word appears between *to* and the verb (*to* carefully *prepare*), an infinitive is said to be split. At one time split infinitives were considered great grammatical sins. Today most authorities agree that infinitives may be split if necessary for clarity and effect. However, avoid split infinitives that result in awkward sentences.

Awkward:	Mr. Stokes wanted to, if he could find time, *recheck* his figures.
Better:	If he could find time, Mr. Stokes wanted to *recheck* his figures.
Awkward:	Our company has *to*, when the real estate market returns to normal, *consider* purchasing an office building.
Better:	Our company has *to consider* purchasing an office building when the real estate market returns to normal.
Acceptable:	*To* wilfully *lie* under oath is perjury. (No awkwardness results from this split infinitive.)
Acceptable:	Mrs. Higgins expects you *to* really *concentrate* when you proofread. (No awkwardness results from this split infinitive.)

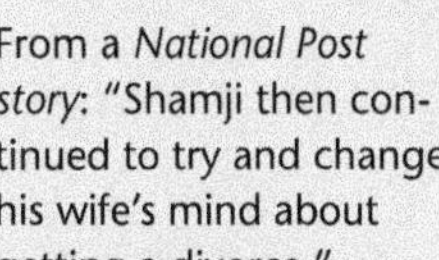

BE THE EDITOR

From a *National Post* story: "Shamji then continued to try and change his wife's mind about getting a divorce."

Complete the reinforcement exercises for Level I on pages 185–187.

LEVEL II

PARTICIPLES

STUDY TIP

To distinguish between *ing* forms used as nouns and those used as adjectives, remember that nouns answer the questions *What?* or *Who(m)?* In the sentence *I admired Monica's handwriting,* ask, "I admired *what?*" Answer: "I admired (Monica's) *handwriting.*" Therefore, *handwriting* is the object and is functioning as an *ing* noun.

In Chapter 7, you studied the present and past forms of participles functioning as parts of verb phrases. You will recall that in such constructions present and past participles always require helping verbs: *is typing, was seen, has been, had broken.*

In this chapter we are concerned with a second function of participles: participles as adjectives. As adjectives, participles modify nouns or pronouns and do not require helping verbs. These adjectives are unusual because they, like verbs, can appear in the passive voice, preceded by a form of *be*, or in a perfect form, preceded by a form of *have*. Here are sentences that illustrate the five forms of the participle.

Present participle, active:	Starting her new job, Lena looked forward to the challenge. (The participle *Starting* modifies *Lena.*)
Present participle, passive:	Lena felt that the new job being started would give her better opportunity for advancement. (*Being started* is a participle that describes *job.*)
Past participle, passive:	Once started, the new job was more challenging than Lena expected. (The participle *started* functions as an adjective to describe *job.*)
Perfect participle, active:	Having started the new job, Lena felt rewarded. (The participle *Having started* describes *Lena.*)
Perfect participle, passive:	The new job having been started, Lena had less free time. (The participle *having been started* functions as an adjective to describe *job.*)

CAREER TIP

You'll win the respect of your colleagues if you avoid using *being, being as,* or *being that* when you mean *since* or *because* (*Being it was hot . . .*). These substandard usages create the impression of poor education and can limit a career.

Using Participles Correctly

Avoid using participles that sound awkward, such as the following:

Awkward:	Pam having been promoted to office manager was cause for celebration.
Better:	Pam's promotion to office manager was cause for celebration.
Awkward:	Being as you have arrived early, may I leave now?
Better:	Since you have arrived early, may I leave now?

PUNCTUATING VERBAL FORMS

Determining whether verbal forms require commas sometimes causes difficulty. Let's try to clear up this difficulty with explanations and examples.

Punctuating Introductory Verbal Forms

When verbal forms are used in introductory words or expressions, there's no question about punctuating them. A comma should always be placed between an introductory verbal form or phrase and the main clause of a sentence.

Astonished, the lawyer turned to the jury. (Introductory verbal form)
To improve product distribution, Samuel hired a traffic manager. (Introductory verbal phrase)

Receiving too many email messages, Rajesh established filters. (Introductory verbal phrase)

Having merged with First Air, Canadian North serves 24 northern communities. (Introductory verbal phrase)

Not all verbal phrases that begin sentences, however, are introductory. If the verbal phrase represents the subject or part of the verb of the sentence, no comma should separate it from the rest of the sentence.

Preparing a budget is Reid's responsibility. (Verbal phrase used as subject; no comma)

To change our budget at this time is almost impossible. (Verbal phrase used as subject; no comma)

Located in the other building is our Shipping Department. (Verbal phrase used as part of verb *is located*; no comma)

Punctuating Non-essential Verbal Phrases

Essential (restrictive) information is needed for the reader to understand the sentence. Verbal phrases often serve to identify the subject; these phrases require no commas. On the other hand, non-essential (non-restrictive) information could be omitted without altering the basic meaning of the sentence, so non-essential phrases are set off by commas.

Ms. Lanier, *working late at the office,* was able to meet the deadline. (The verbal phrase *working late at the office* adds additional information, but it is not essential because the subject is fully identified by name. Use commas to set off the non-essential phrase.)

The woman *working late at the office* was able to meet the deadline. (In this sentence the verbal phrase *working late at the office* is essential; it is needed to identify the subject. *Which* woman was able to meet the deadline? The woman *working late at the office*. No commas set off this essential verbal phrase.)

TD Canada Trust, *opening a new branch in St. John's,* offered gifts to attract customers. (The verbal phrase is not essential because there is only one TD Canada Trust. Commas enclose this non-essential verbal phrase.)

A company *opening a new branch in St. John's* offered gifts to attract customers. (This verbal phrase is essential to identify *which* company offered gifts. No commas are needed. *Note:* Even if you pause when you reach the end of the verbal phrase, don't be tempted to add a comma.)

Note that in the preceding sentences, whenever a non-essential verbal phrase interrupts the middle of a sentence, *two* commas set it off.

Complete the reinforcement exercises for Level II on pages 188–190.

STUDY TIP

To help you understand the use of commas in dealing with non-essential information, think of the commas as perforations. If you tear along the perforated lines and take out the words between the commas, will the meaning of the sentence remain intact? If yes, the commas are used correctly.

LEVEL III

AVOIDING MISPLACED VERBAL MODIFIERS

Used correctly, verbal modifiers and phrases add clarity and description to your writing. Used incorrectly, they may be confusing or even humorous. Let's consider the best way to position them within sentences.

Introductory Verbal Phrases

Introductory verbal phrases must be followed by words they can logically modify. Such phrases can create confusion or unintended humour when placed incorrectly in

BE THE EDITOR

As heard during an Ontario radio station's newscast: "A large black bear was reported by concerned citizens rummaging through garbage."

BE THE EDITOR

From *Country Collectibles*: "Sitting by a blazing fire, reading a good mystery novel, a dog can jump into your lap and beg for a few playful pats on the head."

a sentence. Consider this sentence: *Sitting in the car, the mountains were breathtaking.* The introductory participial phrase in this sentence is said to *dangle* or to be a **dangling modifier** because it is not followed immediately by a word it can logically modify. This sentence says the mountains are sitting in the car. The sentence could be improved by adding a logical subject: *Sitting in the car, we saw the breathtaking mountains.* (*We*, a word logically modified by the verbal phrase, now comes directly after the phrase.)

See how the following illogical sentences have been improved:

Illogical:	Slipping on the ice, his back was injured.
Logical:	Slipping on the ice, *he* injured his back.
Illogical:	Stopped at a red light, a handheld phone still must not be used.
Logical:	Stopped at a red light, drivers still must not use a handheld phone.
Illogical:	After answering the telephone, the doorbell began to ring insistently.
Logical:	After answering the telephone, *Jeremy* heard the doorbell ring insistently.
Illogical:	To earn a certificate, completion of five courses is necessary.
Logical:	To earn a certificate, *students* must complete five courses.
But:	To master a language, listen carefully to native speakers. (In commands, the understood subject is *you*. Therefore, this verbal phrase is correctly followed by the word to which it refers: *To master a language, [you] listen carefully to native speakers.*)

STUDY TIP

After reading an introductory verbal phrase, ask the question *Who?* or *What?* The answer to that question must immediately follow the introductory phrase. For example, *To find a good job, who?* Answer: *To find a good job,* Derek *wrote to many companies.*

Verbal Phrases in Other Positions

In other positions within sentences, verbal phrases must also be placed in logical relation to the words they modify—in other words, as close as possible to those words.

Illogical:	The missing purchase orders were found by Ms. Seldon's assistant lying in the top desk drawer.
Logical:	Ms. Seldon's assistant found the missing purchase orders lying in the top desk drawer.
Illogical:	Emma met many women who were planning weddings while working at Sunnylea Bridal.
Logical:	While working at Sunnylea Bridal, Emma met many women who were planning weddings.

Complete the reinforcement exercises for Level III on pages 191–194.

NAME ____________________

CHAPTER 10 ■ Reinforcement Exercises

LEVEL I

A. (Self-check) In the following sentences gerunds are italicized. The *ing* words that are not italicized are not functioning as gerunds. Select the appropriate word in parentheses and write it in the space provided.

1. We appreciate (you, your) *sending* us your résumé. ____________
2. I saw (Mardi, Mardi's) leaving the office early. ____________
3. The manager was upset about (Mardi, Mardi's) *leaving* early. ____________
4. The auditor questioned (his, him) *travelling* first class. ____________
5. Did Esme tell you about the (company, company's) *opening* another branch? ____________
6. The (clerk, clerk's) making the sale receives the commission. ____________
7. Will your (colleagues, colleagues') *embracing* the new process change your opinion of it? ____________
8. The sales team wasn't happy to hear about Mr. (Hepler, Hepler's) *reconsidering* the need to hire another associate. ____________
9. I appreciate (them, their) *responding* to my emails so quickly. ____________
10. We noticed (Rachel, Rachel's) driving past the office. ____________

Check your answers.

B. Gerunds are not italicized this time. Choose the correct word and write it in the space provided.

1. Prasong's future at Dunbarton & Associates depends on (him, his) making a good impression in the interview. ____________
2. The HR (manager, manager's) organizing the interviews will phone the successful candidate. ____________
3. Ciara wasn't pleased about (others, others') having heard about her written warning. ____________
4. They said (you, your) printing of the brochures was excellent. ____________
5. We must try to win back the (customers, customers') raising concerns about our prices. ____________
6. Our success depends on (you, your) choosing the best investments. ____________
7. A highlight of the team-building event was (us, our) winning the escape room challenge. ____________

8. The manager didn't approve of (them, their) handling of the situation. ____________

9. The (person, person's) picking up Hamza's retirement gift can use the company van. ____________

10. (Him, His) being on time for the interview is very important. ____________

C. From each of the pairs of sentences shown, select the more acceptable version. Write its letter in the space provided.

1. (a) Emilio was asked to, as soon as possible, correct the pricing on the website.
   (b) Emilio was asked to correct the pricing on the website as soon as possible. ____________

2. (a) I think their being present at the hearing is crucial.
   (b) I think them being present at the hearing is crucial. ____________

3. (a) Be sure and arrive at the interview on time.
   (b) Be sure to arrive at the interview on time. ____________

4. (a) Everyone was shocked to learn of Doug's accepting the competitor's job offer.
   (b) Everyone was shocked to learn of Doug accepting the competitor's job offer. ____________

5. (a) The public relations team tried, unsuccessfully, to prevent the media from getting the story.
   (b) The public relations team tried to, unsuccessfully, prevent the media from getting the story. ____________

6. (a) Try and find out when the meeting is scheduled.
   (b) Try to find out when the meeting is scheduled. ____________

7. (a) A power outage led to Luke's missing the deadline.
   (b) A power outage led to Luke missing the deadline. ____________

8. (a) Please check to see whether the contract is ready.
   (b) Please check and see whether the contract is ready. ____________

9. (a) You may wish to, if you have time, contact your broker.
   (b) You may wish to contact your broker if you have time. ____________

10. (a) He has to, if he wants to keep his job, start showing up on time.
    (b) He has to start showing up on time if he wants to keep his job. ____________

D. **Writing Exercise.** Rewrite the following sentences to remedy any gerund or infinitive faults.

1. We plan to, if all the papers have been signed, initiate proceedings tomorrow.

____

____

____

TEAR HERE

2. If you haven't made other arrangements, be sure and call us for a ride to your hotel.

3. I think you should try and sell your idea to the advertising team.

4. The office environment was improved by several colleagues forming a spirit committee.

5. This patented technology should result in the company cornering the market.

6. Sanjiv's promotion depends largely on him doing a good job on this account.

7. Serona Software requires employees to, every Friday, spend an hour networking on Facebook.

NAME ____________________

LEVEL II

A. (Self-check) Verbal phrases in the following sentences are shown in italics. All the sentences have been punctuated correctly. Study each sentence, select the letter that explains the reason for including or omitting commas, and write it in the space provided .

a = introductory verbal phrase, comma necessary
b = essential verbal phrase, no commas necessary
c = non-essential verbal phrase, commas necessary
d = verbal phrase used as a subject, no comma necessary

EXAMPLE: *To settle the matter* is extremely difficult. ____d____

Vince manning, *to settle the matter,* flipped a coin. ____c____

1. *Neglecting to proofread an email message* can reveal a writer's weaknesses. ________
2. Leeta, *having neglected to proofread an email message,* worried about her tone. ________
3. *Randomly selected from hundreds of entrants,* the winner will get a weekend for two in Banff. ________
4. *Reporting a sharp climb in quarterly earnings,* the bank greatly exceeded analysts' expectations. ________
5. *Volunteering in the community* can open up job opportunities. ________
6. *Ordered by the government,* the investigation found proof of more than $15 million in illegal profits. ________
7. The employee *caught in a lie* was called to the Human Resources Department. ________
8. Dee Calder, *caught in a lie,* was called to the Human Resources Department. ________
9. Anyone *looking at the trade show schedule* can see when demonstrations are happening. ________
10. The event planner, *looking at the trade show schedule,* noticed a scheduling error. ________

Check your answers.

B. Select verbals and verbal phrases have been italicized in the sentences below. Insert commas if needed. In the space provided at the right, write the number of commas that you insert for each sentence. If no commas are needed, write *0*.

EXAMPLE: To complete the job before the deadline, we worked late. ____1____

1. *To be eligible for the contest* like us on Facebook and share this post. ________
2. *Participating in the Great Canadian Shoreline Cleanup* has been a tradition for scores of volunteer groups since 2003. ________
3. *Inspired* the entrepreneur signed his company up to participate in the cleanup efforts. ________

TEAR HERE

4. Retailers *wanting to avoid single-use plastic bags* need to find suitable replacements. __________

5. *Called in for second interviews* were two candidates with quite varied experiences. __________

6. *Travelling frequently for work* the manager could not get along without her laptop. __________

7. *To improve the writing of government employees* we hired consultants. __________

8. *Daydreaming* Inga lost her train of thought. __________

9. H. J. Heinz *having begun as a sole proprietor* eventually built a large corporation. __________

10. *To visit all provincial offices within the first quarter* was a key initiative of the new district manager. __________

C. Underline the verbals and verbal phrases in the following sentences. Every sentence is punctuated correctly. Study each sentence, select the letter that explains the reason for including or omitting commas, and write it in the space provided . (Don't forget the infinitive phrases!)

a = introductory verbal phrase, comma necessary
b = essential verbal phrase, no commas necessary
c = non-essential verbal phrase, commas necessary
d = verbal phrase used as a subject, no comma necessary

1. Facebook, known for microtargeting advertising, is seeking ways to prevent employers from discriminating against certain job seekers. __________

2. The tour operator teaching Indigenous children about hunting and gathering is facing a large increase in the leasing fees for Crown land. __________

3. Responding to consumers' feedback, the company changed the name of the product a few months after its release. __________

4. Any student enrolled in the fourth year of this degree program will have a 14-week paid work term. __________

5. The latest company contract provides additional benefits to employees participating in our profit-sharing plan. __________

6. Enrolling in continuing education courses can improve an employee's chances for promotion. __________

7. The Canadian Federation of Independent Business, having advocated for small businesses for 50 years, now offers its members educational opportunities through free webinars. __________

8. The money being raised by the local cadet troupe will be donated to the veteran's family. __________

9. Featuring Viola Desmond, the $10 bill is Canada's first vertical banknote. __________

10. Bates' Fine Jewellery, opening this week, advertised in the local paper. __________

TEAR HERE

D. If necessary, insert commas to punctuate verbal forms in the following sentences. In the space provided, indicate the number of commas added.

1. To plan effectively management must have a realistic picture of production. __________
2. The Lawsons' home situated on a 20- by 70-metre lot sold quickly. __________
3. Explaining the failure of the merger negotiations proved a difficult task for the business reporters. __________
4. Our Canadian Consumers' Survey undertaken every February shows continual increases in online shopping. __________
5. Anyone having worked for more than six months is eligible for benefits. __________
6. Our CEO facing another year of intense pressure resigned his post. __________
7. Found beside the sink in the ladies' room was a white-gold ring with a blue gem. __________
8. Human resources director Lyall Higgins hoping to help employees improve their job skills organized an in-service training class. __________
9. To enrol in any of the programs employees must sign up immediately. __________
10. All employees interested in improving their job skills are invited to attend the in-service programs. __________

TEAR HERE

NAME ______________________

LEVEL III

A. (Self-check) From each of the pairs of sentences that follow, select the sentence that is stated in the more logical manner. Write its letter in the space provided.

1. (a) To use this new service, the updated software must be downloaded.
(b) To use this new service, you must download the updated software. ______________

2. (a) Sold at most newsstands, get a copy of *Canadian Business* today.
(b) Get a copy of *Canadian Business*, sold at most newsstands, today. ______________

3. (a) To be sure of a table on Friday or Saturday, you must make dinner reservations at least a week in advance.
(b) To be sure of a table on Friday or Saturday, it is necessary to make dinner reservations at least a week in advance. ______________

4. (a) Before crossing the border, identification must be shown.
(b) Before crossing the border, drivers must show identification. ______________

5. (a) While sorting the names and addresses, Gilda discovered an error.
(b) While sorting the names and addresses, an error was discovered. ______________

6. (a) Discounted by nearly 50 percent, sales of the starburst chandeliers still weren't meeting expectations.
(b) Discounted by nearly 50 percent, the starburst chandeliers still weren't meeting sales expectations. ______________

7. (a) After collecting author references on note cards, write the bibliography.
(b) After collecting author references on note cards, the bibliography should be written. ______________

8. (a) Having graduated at the top of his class, Randall was given numerous job interviews.
(b) Having graduated at the top of his class, numerous job interviews were given to Randall. ______________

9. (a) Selected from more than 100 candidates, the job was awarded to Ms. Jinnah.
(b) Selected from more than 100 candidates, Ms. Jinnah was awarded the job. ______________

10. (a) To qualify for the certificate, perfect attendance must be maintained.
(b) To qualify for the certificate, students must maintain perfect attendance. ______________

Check your answers.

B. Each of the following sentences has an illogical introductory verbal phrase. Maintaining that introductory phrase, rewrite each sentence so that it is followed by a word it can logically modify. You may need to invent an appropriate subject.

EXAMPLE: Driving through the hills, the city came into view.

Driving through the hills, we saw the city come into view.

TEAR HERE

1. By answering the telephone on the first ring, goodwill is created by our staff.

2. Driving to the sales meeting, her radio was tuned to CBC Radio One.

3. To retire by age 65, RRSP contributions should be started when you're young.

4. Having been returned, employees examine each pair of shoes.

5. Selected as Employee of the Year, the CEO presented an award to Cecile Chang.

6. Having forgotten the pass code, the alarm sounded when I entered the office.

7. To be promoted, your performance appraisal must be excellent.

8. Averaging more than 100 online orders a day, our shipping costs exceeded our rent.

TEAR HERE

The preceding sentences had misplaced introductory verbal phrases. The next sentences have misplaced verbal phrases in other positions. Rewrite these sentences so that the verbal phrases are close to the words they can logically modify.

9. If you bake, you most likely already have the ingredients to make these cookies sitting in your pantry.

10. His wallet was found by Dave Evola lying under the front seat of his car.

11. A guest said someone stole a necklace from her closet valued at $4000.

12. Agnes Macphail became the first female parliamentarian in the British Empire elected to the House of Commons in 1921.

13. I overheard that Telisa got a promotion while waiting in line at the cafeteria.

14. Officials did not disclose the name of the man who died honouring the request of his family.

15. The man pleaded guilty while standing before the judge facing five counts of first-degree murder.

C. Writing Exercise. Compose an appropriate sentence to follow each introductory verbal phrase below.

1. To get better photographs, ________________________________.
2. Practising his presentation, ________________________________.
3. Having checked email, ________________________________.
4. Based in Québec, ________________________________.
5. Sent through Canada Post, ________________________________.
6. Playing in her first international competition, ________________________________.

D. Writing Exercise. Your instructor may ask you to complete this exercise on a separate sheet.

Write ten original sentences, two for each of the following verb forms: gerund, infinitive, present participle, past participle, and perfect participle. Label each sentence.

POSTTEST

Write *a*, *b*, or *c* in the space provided to describe the following sentences.

a = contains no error
b = contains error in use of verbal form
c = contains error in punctuation of verbal form

1. We are worried about Patrick's vaping. __________
2. To supervise effectively a manager must have excellent communication skills. __________
3. A manager must have excellent communication skills to supervise effectively. __________
4. Deciding that his first letter was unclear, a second letter was written by Mr. Holmes. __________
5. Improving health and dental benefits for all employees is our primary goal. __________
6. Having submitted a claim form, payment should be forthcoming immediately. __________
7. Stapled to the report, were Rodney's receipts for his expenses. __________
8. If you would try and make it to the meeting, we'd appreciate your input. __________
9. Journalist Elijah Omondi travelling through Kenya on assignment, saw hippos and crocodiles up close. __________
10. We appreciated him designing the brochure for us. __________

TEAR HERE

EDITOR'S CHALLENGE

The following letter and email contain errors in spelling and language principles covered thus far, as well as other common errors. Use proofreading marks to show your corrections.

Mr. Michael K. Topton
455 Zionsville Road
Corner Brook, NL A2H 4G1

Dear Mr. Toptan:

At the suggestion of your former partner, Ms. Molly Harned. I am submiting this application for the position of legal secertary in your office. I understand that you are seeking an individual whom has communication, transcription, and microcomputer skills. Both my education and my experience, I believe, qualifies myself for this position.

Having finish two years of schooling at Valley Community College. My skills include word processing, machine transcription, and business letter writing. To learn about working for a lawyer, a course in legal procedures was completed. Being that we studied personal injury, dissolution, and unlawful detainer procedures, I now have skill in these areas. Moreover, I have took a course in legal terminology.

In addition to my education, I have complete a six-month internship with two lawyers, Mr. Ronald W. Schultz and Ms. Robin Sawicki, in Halifax. Keyboarding legal documents and updating a client database in Mr. Schultz office, has helped me learn current computer software program.

Please study the enclosed resumé to review my complete educational and employment background. Ms. Harned said that you needed some one immediately, if I was hired for this position, I would be able to start in June, after giving two weeks notice to my present employer. If I meet your requirements, I would appreciate you calling me at 389-5910 to arrange a interview at a time convenent to you.

Sincerely,

Michelle A. Robinson

Michelle A. Robinson

Enclosure

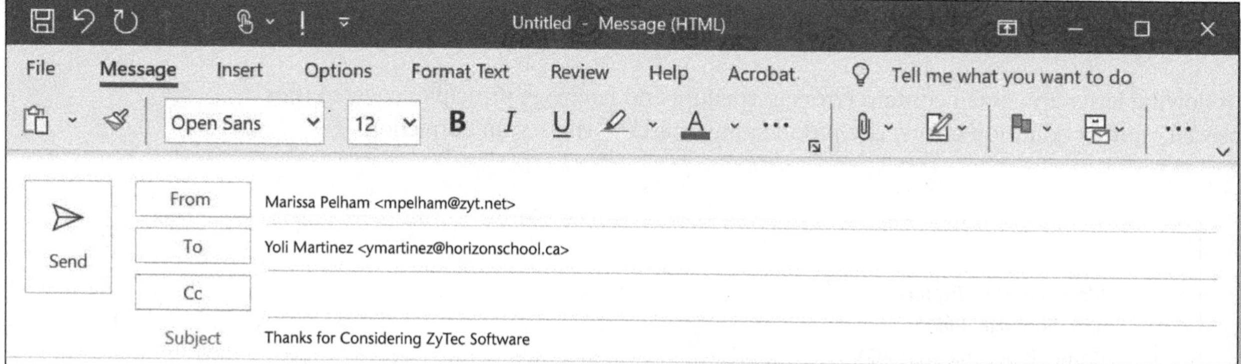

We are happy to learn from your recent massage that Horizon School is considering ZyTec Software Systems as it's source for educational software. Designed to be especially user-friendly many schools and businesses are successfully using our software.

When we sell a software system to a school, we take great care to provide suitable training for the school staff. Some companys provide a short training course for there school staff; however, we recognize that most questions arise long after training sessions are completed. Rather than providing the the superficial training that has became common in the industry, we've learned that the best way to train school staff is to provide in-depth training for two teachers from each school. After these two teachers work with our training consultant, they are formerly equip to act as teacher-trainers who can expertly train your teachers and staff.

Unlike trainers who are available for only a few ours, your teacher-trainers would be able to, whenever questions and concerns arise, deal with them. Furthermore, ZyTec establish ongoing relationships with teacher-trainers so that your teachers will always have the software support they need.

You will soon be receiving a copy of ZyTecs educational software training program guide, as well as a copy of one of our training CD's. I hope you will find these recourses helpful as you consider our educational software. Inasmuch as a number of neighbouring schools is using ZyTec software, you might find it useful to speak with a teacher-trainer from a near by school district. To let me know whether such a meeting is feasible please call or write me.

All the best,

Marissa Pelham

Senior Marketing Manager

ZyTec Software Systems

Phone: (514) 921-1489

Email: mpelham@zyt.net

TEAR HERE

NAME ______________________________

UNIT 3 REVIEW ■ Chapters 7–10 (Self-Check)

Begin your review by rereading Chapters 7 through 10. Then test your comprehension of those chapters by completing the exercises that follow. Compare your responses with those provided at the end of the book on page 531.

LEVEL I

In the space provided, write the letter of the word or phrase that correctly completes each of the following sentences.

1. The department (a) relyed, (b) relied heavily upon Martin's expertise. ________
2. In the sentence *Maggie booked her flight*, the verb *booked* is (a) transitive, (b) intransitive, (c) linking. ________
3. In the sentence *Reshma Khan is our agent*, the word *agent* is a(n) (a) object, (b) linking verb, (c) complement. ________
4. In the sentence *Reshma Khan requested a new agent*, the word *agent* is a(n) (a) object, (b) linking verb, (c) complement. ________
5. There (a) is, (b) are a motion light and a security camera installed outside the warehouse for safety. ________
6. The president, together with all the employees, (a) wish, (b) wishes you well. ________
7. The president and her entire staff (a) wish, (b) wishes you well. ________
8. Be sure (a) and write, (b) to write the name and address legibly. ________
9. When we arrived, there were several (a) students, (b) students' waiting for interviews for the internship. ________
10. Davis, Crowley, and Kovacs, Inc. (a) is, (b) are expecting an increase in profits this quarter. ________
11. The shipping statement for the equipment and supplies (a) was, (b) were delayed. ________
12. Nearly everyone objected to (a) Sara, (b) Sara's using her iPhone during the meeting. ________
13. How effective (a) is, (b) are the company guidelines on Internet use? ________
14. Downsizing could result in (a) me, (b) my losing my job. ________
15. What (a) is, (b) was the name of the sales rep who offered the discount? ________

LEVEL II

In the space provided, write the letter of the word or phrase that correctly completes each of the following sentences.

16. In the sentence *The gross daily sales have improved since April,* the verb is in the (a) simple present, (b) present perfect, (c) past perfect tense. ____________

17. In the sentence *Before April, our sales were falling each month,* the verb is in the (a) simple present, (b) present progressive, (c) past progressive. ____________

18. In the sentence *The contract was approved yesterday,* the verb is in the (a) active, (b) passive voice. ____________

19. In the sentence *The courier delivered the package late,* the verb is in the (a) active, (b) passive voice. ____________

20. Neither the computers nor the printer (a) is, (b) are working. ____________

21. We think that (a) anyone, (b) any one of our IT specialists could fix the issue. ____________

22. Each of our IT specialists (a) is, (b) are capable of fixing the issue. ____________

Insert commas where necessary in the next group of sentences. In the space provided, indicate the number of commas added. Write *0* for none.

23. We were very pleased to see that Rebecca working until 10 p.m. was able to complete the job. ____________

24. Working until 10 p.m. is not routine. ____________

25. Working until 10 p.m. Rebecca was able to complete the job. ____________

LEVEL III

In the space provided, write the letter of the word or phrase that correctly completes each sentence.

26. Many letters and packages have (a) laid, (b) lain, (c) lay unopened on that desk for the past week. ____________

27. If you had (a) rode, (b) ridden the subway to work, you would have arrived on time. ____________

28. Have all of the safety inspectors (a) went, (b) gone for the additional training? ____________

29. He acts as if he (a) was, (b) were the only employee who had to work overtime. ____________

30. She suggested that everyone (a) meet, (b) meets at the café after work. ____________

31. The number of taxpayers who file online (a) is, (b) are growing rapidly. ____________

32. It is you who (a) is, (b) are to do the judging tomorrow. ____________

33. She told me that two-thirds of the proposal (a) has, (b) have yet to be written. ____________

TEAR HERE

34. Ours is one of the vacation packages that (a) includes, (b) include meals and unlimited golf. ______

35. The renovations being done on the building were (a) affecting, (b) effecting employees' productivity. ______

For each sentence below, indicate in the space provided whether (a) the sentence is written correctly or (b) the sentence has a verbal phrase placed illogically. Rewrite illogical sentences.

36. To qualify for a full scholarship, applications must be submitted by January 1. ______

37. The burglar was about 180 centimetres, weighed about 60 kilograms, and had shoulder-length brown hair, wearing a blue denim jacket and blue jeans. ______

38. Skilled at troubleshooting network problems, the human resources manager hired Hans instantly. ______

39. Reorganizing the archived personnel files, Mr. Leggatt's file went missing. ______

40. Containing jewellery and clothing, thieves stole a suitcase from Mrs. Mercier's car in broad daylight. ______

ASK AN EDITOR REVIEW

Select the word or phrase that correctly completes each statement, and write its letter in the space provided.

41. All employees (a) may, (b) can take a half-hour lunch break. ______

42. The papers (a) laying, (b) lying in that folder need to be signed. ______

43. If she (a) was, (b) were to apply for the job, she might get it. ______

44. Copies of the document, distributed throughout the company, (a) contain, (b) contains embarrassing errors. ______

TEAR HERE

ASK AN EDITOR

Question:
When writing email messages, I often type in all lowercase letters. It's my style. My boss just told me that I should stop this practice. Why?

Answer:
Your boss is correct. Messages written in all lowercase or all capital letters are difficult to read and look unprofessional. On the job, business communicators want their messages to be as professional and as easy to read as possible. Therefore, always use standard upper- and lowercase letters when writing your email messages.

TECHNIQUES FOR EFFECTIVE PARAGRAPHS

As you learned in the Writer's Workshop for Unit 2, the basic unit in writing is the sentence. The next unit is the paragraph. Although no rule regulates the length of paragraphs, business writers recognize the value of short paragraphs. Paragraphs with fewer than eight printed lines look inviting and readable, whereas long, solid chunks of print appear formidable. In this workshop you will learn writing techniques for organizing sentences into readable, coherent, and clear paragraphs. The first very important technique involves topic sentences.

ORGANIZING PARAGRAPHS AROUND TOPIC SENTENCES

A well-organized paragraph has two important characteristics. First, it covers just one subject. For example, if you are writing about your booth at a computer show, you won't throw in a sentence about trouble with your taxes. Keep all the sentences in a paragraph related to one topic. Second, a well-organized paragraph begins with a **topic sentence** that summarizes what the paragraph is about. A topic sentence helps readers by preparing them for what follows.

Consider the following scenario. Let's say your company promotes an extensive schedule of team sports for employees after hours. One group enjoys weekend bicycling. You've been assigned the task of writing an email message to the members of this group stating that they must wear helmets when cycling. One paragraph of your memo covers statistics about cycling accidents and the incidence of brain injury for unhelmeted riders. Another paragraph discusses the protection offered by helmets:

> *Helmets protect the brain from injury.* They spread the force of a crash from the point of impact to a wider area. When an accident occurs, an unhelmeted head undergoes two collisions. The first occurs when the skull slams into the ground. The second occurs when the brain hits the inside of the skull. A helmet softens the second blow and acts as a shock absorber. Instead of crushing the brain, the impact crushes the foam core of the helmet, often preventing serious brain injury.

Notice how the preceding paragraph focuses on just one topic: how helmets protect the brain from injury. Every sentence relates to that topic. Notice, too, that the first sentence functions as a topic sentence, informing the reader of the subject of the paragraph.

The best way to write a good paragraph is to list all the ideas you may include. Here's a rough draft of ideas for the preceding paragraph. Notice that the fourth item doesn't relate to the topic sentence. By listing the ideas to be included in a paragraph, you can immediately see what belongs—and what doesn't. Once the list is made, you can easily write the topic sentence.

PARAGRAPH IDEA LIST

1. Helmets spread the force of impact.
2. Crashes cause two collisions, the first when the skull hits ground and the second when the brain hits skull.
3. The foam core of helmets absorbs impact.
4. ~~The federal government has issued biking regulations requiring helmets.~~

Topic Sentence: Helmets protect the brain from injury.

TEAR HERE

Skill Check 3.1: Organizing a Paragraph

In a letter to the college president, the athletic director is arguing for a new stadium scoreboard. One paragraph will describe the old scoreboard and why it needs to be replaced. Study the following list of ideas for that paragraph.

1. The old scoreboard was originally constructed in the 1970s.
2. It's now hard to find replacement parts for it when something breaks.
3. The old scoreboard is not energy-efficient.
4. Coca-Cola has offered to buy a new sports scoreboard in return for exclusive rights to sell soft drinks on campus.
5. The old scoreboard should be replaced for many reasons.
6. It shows scores only for football games.
7. When we have soccer games or track meets, we're without any functioning scoreboard.

(a) Which sentence should be the topic sentence? __________

(b) Which sentence(s) should be developed in a different paragraph? __________

(c) Which sentences should follow the topic sentence? __________

WRITING COHERENT PARAGRAPHS

Effective paragraphs are coherent; that is, they hold together. **Coherence** is a quality of good writing that doesn't happen accidentally. It is consciously achieved through effective organization and through skilful use of three writing devices. These devices are (a) repetition of key ideas or key words, (b) use of pronouns that refer clearly to their antecedents, and (c) use of transitional expressions.

REPETITION OF KEY IDEAS OR KEY WORDS. Repeating a key word or key thought from a preceding sentence helps guide a reader from one thought to the next. This redundancy is necessary to build cohesiveness into writing. Notice how the word *deal* is repeated in the second sentence below.

> For the past six months, college administrators and Coca-Cola have been working on a *deal* in which the college would receive a new sports scoreboard. The *deal* would involve exclusive rights to sell soft drinks on the 12,000-student campus.

USE OF PRONOUNS THAT REFER CLEARLY TO THEIR ANTECEDENTS. Pronouns such as *this, that, they, these, those,* and *it* help connect thoughts in sentences; but these pronouns are useful only when their antecedents are clear. Often it's better to make the pronoun into an adjective joined with its antecedent to ensure that the reference is absolutely clear. Notice how the pronoun *this* is clearer when it is joined to its antecedent *contract.*

Confusing: The Coca-Cola offer requires an exclusive contract committing the college for ten years without any provision preventing a price increase. *This* could be very costly to students, staff, and faculty.

Improved: The Coca-Cola offer requires an exclusive contract committing the college for ten years without any provision preventing a price increase. *This contract* could be very costly to students, staff, and faculty.

TEAR HERE

Avoid vague or inaccurate pronouns, such as *it* in the following example.

Confusing: Both Coca-Cola and Pepsi offered to serve our campus, and we agreed to allow *it* to submit a bid.

Improved: Both Coca-Cola and Pepsi offered to serve our campus, and we agreed to allow Coca-Cola to submit a bid.

USE OF TRANSITIONAL EXPRESSIONS. One of the most effective ways to achieve paragraph coherence is through the use of transitional expressions. These expressions act as road signs. They indicate where the message is headed, and they help the reader anticipate what is coming. Some common transitional expressions follow:

also	hence	moreover
as a result	however	nevertheless
consequently	in addition	of course
for example	instead	on the other hand
for this reason	in this way	therefore
furthermore	meanwhile	thus

Other words that act as connectives are *first, second, finally, after, next, after all, although, specifically, likewise, as,* and *as if.*

The following paragraph achieves coherence through use of all three techniques. (1) The key idea of *surprising battle* in the first sentence is echoed in the second sentence with repetition of the word *battle* coupled with *unexpected*, a synonym for *surprising*. (2) The use of *this* in the second sentence connects the second sentence to the first. (3) The transitional expressions *however* and *as a result* in the sentences that follow continue to build coherence.

> A *surprising battle* between two global cola giants was fought in Venezuela. *This battle* was *unexpected* because Venezuelans had always been loyal Pepsi drinkers. *However,* when the nation's leading bottler sold half of its interest to Coca-Cola, everything changed. *As a result,* Coca-Cola turned the Pepsi-drinking nation of Venezuela into Coke drinkers almost overnight.

Skill Check 3.2: Improving Paragraph Coherence

On a separate sheet of paper, use the information from Skill Check 3.1 to write a coherent paragraph about replacing the sports scoreboard. Remember that this paragraph is part of a letter from the athletic director to the college president. Include a topic sentence. Strive to illustrate all three techniques to achieve coherence.

DEVELOPING PARALLEL CONSTRUCTION

You can improve paragraph clarity by expressing similar ideas with similar grammatical structures. For example, if you are listing three ideas, do not use *ing* words for two of the ideas and a *to* verb with the third idea: *reading, eating,* and *studying* (not *to study*). Use adjectives with adjectives, verbs with verbs, phrases with phrases, and clauses with clauses. In the following list, use all verbs: *the machine sorted, stamped, and counted* (not *and had a counter*). For phrases, the wording for all parts of the list should be matched; *safety must be improved in the home, in the classroom, and on the job* (not *for office workers*).

Poor: Miss Tanaga is energetic, resourceful, and she can be relied on.

Improved: Miss Tanaga is energetic, resourceful, and reliable. (Matching adjectives)

Poor: The new shredder helped us save money, reduce pollution, and paper could be recycled.

Improved: The new shredder helped us to save money, reduce pollution, and recycle paper. (Matching verb–noun construction)

Skill Check 3.3: Improving Parallel Construction

Revise each of the following sentences to improve parallel construction.

1. Some airlines offer frequent fliers free upgrades, priority boarding, and they can call special reservation numbers.

____

____

2. Your job is to research, design, and the implementation of a diversity program.

____

____

3. The report should be concise, thorough, and written clearly.

____

____

4. The new software totals all balances, gives weekly reports, and statements are printed.

____

____

5. She proofread for errors in spelling, punctuation, and the use of capital letters.

____

____

For further practice, see Chapter 20 (Exercises A and B on pp. 399–400).

Writing Application 3.1

On a separate sheet, revise the following paragraph. Add a topic sentence and improve the organization. Correct wordiness, misplaced verbal modifiers (which you learned about in Chapter 10), and pronouns with unclear antecedents. Add transitional expressions, if appropriate.

> You may be interested in applying for a new position within the company. The Human Resources Department has a number of jobs available immediately. The positions are at a high level. Current employees may apply immediately for open positions in production, for some in marketing, and jobs in administrative support are also available. To make application, these positions require immediate action. Come to the Human Resources Department. We have a list showing the open positions, what the qualifications are, and job descriptions are shown. Many of the jobs are now open. That's why we are sending this now. To be hired, an interview must be scheduled within the next two weeks.

Writing Application 3.2

On a separate sheet, revise the following poorly written paragraph. Add a topic sentence and improve the organization. Correct misplaced modifiers, unclear pronouns, wordiness, and any other writing faults. Add transitional expressions, if appropriate.

> As you probably already know, this company (Lasertronics) will be installing new computer software shortly. There will be a demonstration April 18, which is a Tuesday. We felt this was necessary because this new software is so different from our previous software. It will be from 9 to 12 a.m. in the morning. This will show employees how the software programs work. They will learn about the operating system, and this should be helpful to nearly everyone. There will be information about the new word processing program, which should be helpful to administrative assistants and product managers. For all you people who work with payroll, there will be information about the new database program. We can't show everything the software will do at this one demo, but for these three areas there will be some help at the Tuesday demo. Oh yes, Paula Roddy will be presenting the demonstration. She is the representative from Quantum Software.

Writing Application 3.3

Assume you work in the Human Resources Department of Imperial Trust. You must write an email announcement describing a special program of classes for your employees. Use the following information to write a well-organized paragraph announcement. The information is purposely disorganized; you must decide how best to organize it. Add any information needed for clarity.

> Explain that Imperial Trust will reimburse any employee the full cost of tuition and books if that employee attends classes. Describe the plan. Skyline Community College, in co-operation with Imperial Trust, will offer a group of courses for college credit at very convenient locations for our employees. Actually, the classes will be offered at your downtown and East Bay branches. Tell employees that they should call Jean Fujimoto at Ext. 660 if they are interested. You'd better mention the tuition: $230 for a semester course. Explain that we (Imperial Trust) are willing to pay these fees because we value education highly. However, make it clear that employees must receive a grade of C or higher before they are eligible for reimbursement of course and book fees. It might be a good idea to attach a list of the courses and the times that they will be offered. Include a deadline date for calling Jean.

Note: You can refer to an attached list of courses and times, but you needn't prepare the actual attachment.

TEAR HERE

UNIT 4

Modifying and Connecting Words

CHAPTER 11

MODIFIERS: ADJECTIVES AND ADVERBS

OBJECTIVES

When you have completed the materials in this chapter, you will be able to do the following:

LEVEL I

- Form the comparative and superlative degrees of regular and irregular adjectives and adverbs
- Use articles and demonstrative adjectives correctly
- Avoid double negatives

LEVEL II

- Decide whether to use adjectives or adverbs in sentences
- Punctuate compound and successive independent adjectives correctly
- Master the correct usage of commonly confused adjectives and adverbs

LEVEL III

- Make comparisons within a group
- Place adverbs and adjectives close to the words they modify

PRETEST

Underline the correct answer.

1. Of the two proposals, Mr. Shankar liked this one (better, best).
2. When it is raining, people should drive (careful, carefully).
3. (This sort, These sorts) of meetings can be very productive.
4. We (couldn't, could) hardly believe the news.
5. It wasn't a great meeting, but it could have been (worse, worst).
6. (A, An) exceptional job was done on the website redesign.

(continued)

PRETEST *(CONTINUED)*

7. If you did (good, well) in the interview, you will be hired.
8. The company is offering employees (less, fewer) personal days this year than it did last year.
9. Our (six-year-old, six year old) lease must be renegotiated.
10. The (newly repaired, newly-repaired) copier seems to be working well.

You can use adjectives and adverbs to add character to your writing. Both adjectives and adverbs act as modifiers; that is, they describe or limit other words. Many of the forms and functions of adjectives and adverbs are similar. Because of this similarity, these two parts of speech may be confused. That is why we will treat adjectives and adverbs together in this chapter.

CAREER TIP

Good writers avoid vague and overworked adverbs and adjectives (such as *interesting, good, nice, great, really,* and *bad*). Strive to use precise words that say exactly what you mean.

BASIC FUNCTIONS OF ADJECTIVES AND ADVERBS

Adjectives describe or limit nouns and pronouns. As you learned in Chapter 1, they often answer the questions *What kind?*, *How many?*, and *Which one?* Adjectives in the following sentences are italicized.

> *Short* visits are *the best* visits. (Adjectives answer *What kind?*)
> *The Innovacorp* grant was awarded to *two emerging* companies.
> (Adjectives answer *Which one?*, *How many?*, and *What kind?*)

Question:
One of my favourite words is *hopefully*, but I understand that it's often used improperly. How should it be used?

Answer:
Language purists insist that the word *hopefully* be used to modify a verb (*we looked at the door hopefully, wishing that Mr. Gross would return*). In formal English, the word *hopefully* should not be used as a substitute for *I hope that* or *we hope that*. Instead of saying, *hopefully, interest rates will decline*, one should say *I hope that interest rates will decline.*

Adverbs usually describe or limit verbs, adjectives, or other adverbs. They often answer the questions *When?*, *How?*, *Where?*, and *To what extent?*

> *Yesterday* our work went *slowly*. (Adverbs answer *When?* and *How?*)
> Please take a seat *there*. (Adverb answers *Where?*)
> He cooperated *fully*. (Adverb answers *To what extent?*)

Comparative and Superlative Forms

Most adjectives and adverbs have three **degrees**, or **forms**: positive, comparative, and superlative. The examples below illustrate how the comparative and superlative degrees of regular adjectives and adverbs are formed.

	Positive	**Comparative**	**Superlative**
Adjective	warm	warmer	warmest
Adverb	warmly	more warmly	most warmly
Adjective	careful	more careful	most careful
Adverb	carefully	more carefully	most carefully

The positive degree of an adjective or an adverb is used in simply describing or limiting another word. The comparative degree is used to compare two persons, things, or actions. The superlative degree is used to compare three or more persons, things, or actions.

The comparative degree of short adjectives (nearly all one-syllable adjectives and most two-syllable adjectives ending in *y*) is formed by adding *er* (*warmer*). The superlative degree of short adjectives is usually formed by the addition of *st* or *est* (*warmest*). Long adjectives and those that are difficult to pronounce form the comparative and superlative degrees, as do adverbs, with the addition of *more* and *most* (*more careful, most careful*). The following sentences illustrate degrees of comparison for adjectives and adverbs.

Adjectives	Sales are unusually *high*.	(Positive degree)
	Sales are higher than ever before.	(Comparative degree)
	Sales are the *highest* in years.	(Superlative degree)
Adverbs	He drives *carefully*.	(Positive degree)
	He drives more *carefully* now.	(Comparative degree)
	He drives most *carefully* at night.	(Superlative degree)

Do *not* create a double comparative form by using *more* and the suffix *er* together (such as *more neater*) or by using *most* and the suffix *est* together (such as *most fastest*).

Adjectives that end in *e* or *y* require special treatment. To those that end in *e*, simply add an *r* for the comparative and an *st* for the superlative (*purer, purest*). For those that end in *y*, change the *y* to *i* and then add the ending (*lovelier, loveliest*). As well, a few adjectives and adverbs form the comparative and the superlative degrees irregularly. Common irregular adjectives include *good* (*better, best*), *bad* (*worse, worst*), *little* (*less, least*), and *many* (*more, most*). Common irregular adverbs include *well* (*better, best*) and *much* (*more, most*).

Modifiers That Deserve Special Attention

A few adjectives and adverbs require special attention because they can cause difficulty for writers and speakers.

ARTICLES. The articles *a, an,* and *the* make up a special category of adjectives, and these words must be used carefully. When describing specific persons or things, use the definite article *the*, as in *the film*. When describing persons or things in general, use the indefinite article *a* or *an*, as in *a film* (meaning *any film*). Indefinite articles are used only with singular nouns. The choice of *a* or *an* is determined by the initial sound of the word modified. Use *a* before consonant sounds; use *an* before vowel sounds.

Before Vowel Sounds		**Before Consonant Sounds**	
an operator		a shop	
an elder		a plan	
an hour an honour	*h* is not voiced; vowel is heard	a hook a hole	*h* is voiced
an office an onion	a vowel	a one-man show a one-week trip	*o* sounds like the consonant *w*
an understudy an umbrella	a vowel	a union a unit	*u* sounds like the consonant *y*
an X-ray an MD	*X* and *M* sound like vowels ("ex" and "em")	a xylophone a meteor	*x* sounds like the consonant *z*; *m* consonant sound is heard

DOUBLE NEGATIVES. When a negative adverb (*no, not, scarcely, hardly, barely*) is used in the same sentence as a negative verb (*didn't, don't, won't*), a substandard construction called a double negative results. Among professionals such constructions are considered illogical. In the following examples, notice that eliminating one negative corrects the double negative.

STUDY TIP

The sound of a word, not the spelling, governs the choice between *a* and *an*. For example, when the letter *u* sounds like a *y*, treat it as a consonant and use *a*: *a utility, a used car.*

ASK AN EDITOR

Question:
Is *every day* one word or two in this case? *We encounter these problems (every day or everyday).*

Answer:
In your sentence it is two words. When it means "ordinary," it is a one-word adjective (*She wore everyday clothes*). If you can insert the word *single* between *every* and *day* without altering your meaning, as in your sentence, you should use two words. (In such a case, *every* is an adjective, and *day* is the noun it is modifying.)

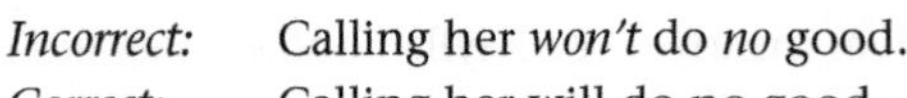

DID YOU KNOW?

At one time in the history of the English language (going back farther than Chaucer), multiple negatives were used to emphasize an idea. (*Don't never say nothing wicked!*) But in the eighteenth century, grammarians adopted Latin logic and decreed that two negatives created a positive.

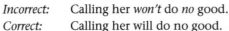

Incorrect:	Calling her *won't* do *no* good.
Correct:	Calling her will do no good.
Correct:	Calling her won't do any good.
Incorrect:	We *couldn't hardly* believe the news report.
Correct:	We could hardly believe the news report.
Correct:	We couldn't believe the news report.
Incorrect:	Drivers *can't barely* see in the heavy fog.
Correct:	Drivers can barely see in the heavy fog.
Correct:	Drivers can't see in the heavy fog.

THE DEMONSTRATIVE ADJECTIVES *THIS/THAT* AND *THESE/THOSE*. Demonstrative adjectives indicate whether a noun is singular or plural and whether the item or person is located nearby or farther away. The demonstrative adjective *this* and its plural form *these* indicate something nearby. The adjective *that* and its plural form *those* indicate something at a distance. Be careful to use the singular forms of these words with singular nouns and the plural forms with plural nouns (*this shoe, that road, these accounts, those records*) even if a later word isn't of the same number (*this calendar of events*). Pay special attention to the nouns *kind, type,* and *sort*. Match singular adjectives to the singular forms of these nouns and plural adjectives to the plural forms.

CAREER TIP

The misuse of *badly* for *bad* is one of the most frequent errors made by educated persons. Following the linking verb *feel*, use the adjective *bad*, not the adverb *badly*.

Incorrect:	Job candidates should be prepared for these type of questions.
Correct:	Job candidates should be prepared for this type of question.
Correct:	Job candidates should be prepared for these types of questions.

Complete the reinforcement exercises for Level I on pages 214–215.

ASK AN EDITOR

Question:
In my writing I want to use *firstly* and *secondly*. Are they acceptable?

Answer:
Both words are acceptable, but most writers prefer *first* and *second* because they are more efficient and equally accurate.

ASK AN EDITOR

Question:
How should I write *industry wide*? It's not in my dictionary.

Answer:
A word with the suffix *wide* is used as either an adjective or an adverb. Most often, it is written solid: *industrywide, nationwide, countrywide, statewide, worldwide* (but *province-wide*).

LEVEL II

ADJECTIVE AND ADVERB CHALLENGES

In the following discussion, you will learn not to confuse adjectives with adverbs. You will also learn to express compound adjectives and independent adjectives.

Deciding Whether to Use Adjectives or Adverbs

Because they are closely related and both serve to describe, adjectives are sometimes confused with adverbs. Here are guidelines that will help you choose the appropriate adjective or adverb.

WHEN TO USE ADJECTIVES. Use adjectives to modify, or describe, nouns and pronouns. Note particularly that adjectives (not adverbs) should follow linking verbs. (For a refresher on linking verbs, see Chapter 8.)

The actors gave *incredible* performances.

This corn soup tastes *delicious*. (*Tastes* is a linking verb here relating the subject, *soup*, to the adjective *delicious* to describe its taste.)

I feel *bad* about the loss. (*Feel* is a linking verb here relating the subject, *I*, to the adjective *bad* to describe a feeling.)

She looks *good* in her business suit. (*Looks* is a linking verb here relating the subject, *she*, to the adjective *good* to describe appearance.)

WHEN TO USE ADVERBS. Use adverbs to modify, or describe, verbs, adjectives, or other adverbs.

> The engine runs *smoothly*. (Use *smoothly*, not *smooth*, because the word is describing *how* it runs.)
>
> The band office runs *more smoothly* now than before. (Remember to maintain the adverb form in the comparative.)
>
> Listen *carefully* to the directions. (Not *careful*)

A few adverbs have two acceptable forms: *slow, slowly; deep, deeply; direct, directly; close, closely*. Check your dictionary for the uses of such forms.

> Drive *slowly*. (Or, less formally, *slow*)
> You may dial us *directly*. (Or, less formally, *direct*)

BE THE EDITOR

From a full-page IBM advertisement: "Can you really buy a computer that makes someone feel differently about their job?" (Do you see two problems?)

Compound Adjectives

Writers may form their own adjectives by joining two or more words. When these words act as a single modifier preceding a noun, they are temporarily hyphenated. If these same words appear after a noun, they are generally not hyphenated. (A reference manual can provide more guidance than we have space for in this text.)

Words Temporarily Hyphenated Before a Noun	Same Words Not Hyphenated After a Noun
never-say-die attitude	attitude of never say die
eight-storey building	building of eight storeys
a case-by-case analysis	analysis that is case by case
four-year-old child	child who is four years old
out-of-warranty repair	repair that is out of warranty
follow-up appointment	an appointment to follow up

BE THE EDITOR

Headline in a Florida newspaper: "Man Eating Piranha Sold as Pet Fish."

Compound adjectives shown in your dictionary with hyphens are considered permanently hyphenated. Regardless of whether such a compound adjective appears before or after a noun, it retains the hyphen(s). Use a current dictionary or reference manual to determine what expressions are always hyphenated. Be sure that you find the dictionary entry that is marked *adjective*. Here are samples:

Permanent Hyphens Before Nouns	Permanent Hyphens After Nouns
old-fashioned attitude	attitude that is old-fashioned
short-term loan	loan that is short-term
well-behaved child	child who is well-behaved
well-rounded program	program that is well-rounded
first-class service	service that is first-class
part-time worker	worker who is part-time

ASK AN EDITOR

Question:
Why are these two expressions treated differently: *two-week vacation* and *two weeks' vacation*?

Answer:
Although they express the same idea, they represent two different styles. If you omit the *s*, *two-week* is hyphenated because it is a compound adjective. If you add the *s*, as in *two weeks' vacation*, the expression becomes possessive and requires an apostrophe. Either is correct; just don't use both styles together (not *two-weeks' vacation*).

When a compound adjective is interrupted by the addition of other modifiers linked to the first part of the compound, it is important to retain the hyphen, called a *hanging* or *suspended hyphen*. Note that if no punctuation is necessary, a space follows the hanging hyphen.

> The *three-*, *four-*, and *five-year* terms offer better interest rates. (Not *three, four, and five-year terms*)

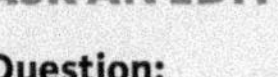

ASK AN EDITOR

Question:
Is it necessary to hyphenate a *25 percent discount*?

Answer:
No. Percentages are not treated in the same way as numbers appearing in compound adjectives. Thus, you would not hyphenate *15 percent loan*, but you would hyphenate *15-year loan*.

We have several *full-* and *part-time* positions open. (Not *full and part-time positions*)

When considering hyphenation, be sure to differentiate between adverbs ending in *ly* and compound adjectives. Constructions such as *newly decorated office* (adverb *newly* + adjective *decorated*) and *highly regarded architect* (adverb *highly* + adjective *regarded*) are not hyphenated because they are not compound adjectives.

In some cases, hyphens are not used. When two-word, easily recognizable compound nouns written as separate words (e.g., *income tax, community college*) are used as adjectives and would not create any confusion in the context of the sentence, they are not hyphenated. Proper names used as adjectives are not hyphenated either. Here are some examples:

car insurance policy	real estate agent
charge account customer	St. Lawrence Seaway locks
home office staff	Royal Bank account
data processing centre	Steven Stamkos poster

STUDY TIP

To determine whether successive adjectives are independent, mentally insert the word *and* between them. If the insertion makes sense, the adjectives are probably independent and require a comma.

Independent (Coordinate) Adjectives

Independent adjectives occur when two or more adjectives appearing before a noun independently modify the noun. In most cases writers must separate such independent adjectives with commas. No comma is needed, however, when the first adjective modifies the combined idea of the second adjective and the noun.

Two Adjectives Independently Modifying a Noun	**First Adjective Modifying a Second Adjective Plus a Noun**
confident, self-reliant individual	efficient administrative assistant
attractive, efficient car	blue sports car
stimulating, provocative book	luxurious mobile home

ASK AN EDITOR

Question:
In a business report is it acceptable to write the following: *Most everyone agrees . . .* ?

Answer:
In this construction *most* is a shortened form of *almost*. Although such contractions are heard in informal speech, they should not appear in business writing. Instead, use the longer form: *Almost everyone agrees . . .*

Commonly Confused Adjectives and Adverbs

The following adjectives and adverbs cause difficulty for many writers and speakers. With a little study, you can master their correct usage.

almost (adv.—nearly):	*Almost* (not *Most*) all students study hard.
most (adj., adv.—greatest in amount):	*Most* students study hard.
farther (adj., adv.—actual distance):	How much *farther* is the airport?
further (adj., adv.—more, additionally):	I won't argue the matter *further*.
sure (adj.—certain):	He is *sure* of victory.
surely (adv.—undoubtedly):	He will *surely* be victorious.
later (adv.—after expected time):	The contract arrived *later* in the day.
latter (adj.—the second of two things):	Of the two options, I prefer the *latter*.
fewer (adj.—refers to number, used with plural noun):	*Fewer* requests for tours were granted this year.
less (adj.—refers to amount, used with singular noun):	*Less* time remains than we anticipated.
real (adj.—actual, genuine):	The *real* power in the company lies with the treasurer.
really (adv.—actually, truly):	Jan wondered if she could *really* learn the system in five hours.
good (adj.—desirable):	His is a *good* plan.
well (adv.—satisfactorily)	Faraz did *well* on his performance evaluation.
well (adj.—healthy)	Deborah feels *well* despite having a fever.

BE THE EDITOR

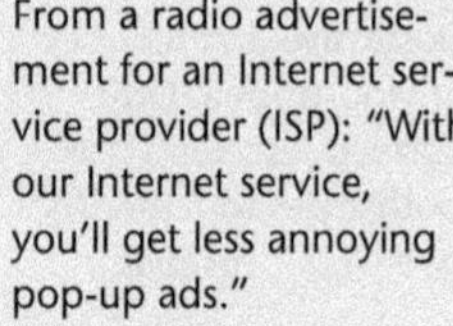

From a radio advertisement for an Internet service provider (ISP): "With our Internet service, you'll get less annoying pop-up ads."

Complete the reinforcement exercises for Level II on pages 216–218.

LEVEL III

USING ADJECTIVES AND ADVERBS LOGICALLY

BE THE EDITOR

From a radio commercial for The Club, a device to prevent auto theft: "The Club works where other cheap imitations fail."

In this section you will learn how to make comparisons within a group and how to place adjectives and adverbs appropriately in sentences.

Comparisons Within a Group

When the word *than* is used to compare a person, place, or thing with other members of a group to which it belongs, be certain to include the word *other* or *else* in the comparison. This inclusion ensures a clear and logical comparison.

Illogical: Calgary is larger than any city in Alberta. (This sentence suggests that Calgary is larger than itself or that it is not a city in Alberta.)
Logical: Calgary is larger than any other city in Alberta.
Illogical: Our team had more points than any league team. (Implies that our team does not belong to the league.)
Logical: Our team had more points than any other league team.
Illogical: Alex works harder than anyone in the office. (Implies that Alex doesn't work in the same office.)
Logical: Alex works harder than anyone else in the office.

Placing Adverbs and Adjectives

The position of an adverb or adjective can seriously affect the meaning of a sentence. Study these examples:

Only I can change the password. (No one else can change it.)
I can *only* change the password. (I can't do anything else.)
I can change *only* the password. (I can't change anything else.)

To avoid confusion, you should place adverbs and adjectives close to the words they modify. In this regard, special attention should be given to the words *first, only, just, even, almost, merely,* and *last.* These modifiers limit the meaning of the word or phrase that follows, so if they are misplaced, your sentence may be unclear to some readers.

BE THE EDITOR

Headline from *The Concord* [New Hampshire] *Monitor*: "How Can You Expect a Child Who Can't Tell Time to Only Get Sick During Office Hours?"

Confusing: Even if the float is a little short, you might not be able to make change.
Clear: If the float is even a little short, you might not be able to make change.
Confusing: Seats in the five first rows have been reserved.
Clear: Seats in the first five rows have been reserved.

Complete the reinforcement exercises for Level III on pages 219–220.

NAME ______________________

CHAPTER 11 ■ Reinforcement Exercises

LEVEL I

A. (Self-check) Write the correct form in the space provided.

1. Business is the (worse, worst) it has been since 2008. __________
2. The company's sales are (worse, worst) this year than last year. __________
3. The blades on (this, these) pair of scissors need sharpening. __________
4. The catering company will need at least (a, an) hour to prepare the room. __________
5. We (can, can't) hardly work in this room with the air conditioning system down. __________
6. This is the (hottest, most hot) day we've had all year. __________
7. (This, These) types of computer viruses can be difficult to detect. __________
8. Our part-time workers are trying to form (a, an) union. __________
9. Rainfall for this year (has, hasn't) been barely 22 centimetres. __________
10. Of the two tests you took this fall, which did you find (harder, hardest)? __________

Check your answers.

B. Write the correct form in the space provided.

1. (That sort, Those sorts) of businesses have been asked to restrict exports. __________
2. Malala Yousafzai is the world's (famousest, most famous) advocate of education for girls. __________
3. The wealthy financier left everything to (a, an) heir he had never met. __________
4. There wasn't (nothing, anything) that could be done to save jobs. __________
5. The company (has, hasn't) barely begun to see the benefits of the retrofitting. __________
6. The biotechnology industry is growing at (a, an) unusually fast pace. __________
7. Of the four interns, he is the (younger, youngest). __________
8. The architect sent over (this, these) set of drawings for our review. __________
9. Susan said she couldn't see (no, any) other way to install the program. __________
10. We will sign a contract with whichever of the two cellphone companies offers the (more, most) comprehensive package. __________

TEAR HERE

C. Can you find and correct 12 errors in this paragraph? *Hint:* Eight errors involve adverbs and adjectives from Level I.

In Winnipeg a officer of a bank was involved in one of the worse embezzlement schemes in the banks history. Because of lax bank controls, the embezzler was able to withdraw hundreds of thousands of dollars in a unprecedented banking loss. To avoid detection by the banks computer-fraud defences, the embezzler took advantage of his position as an bank officer. The scheme involved making debit and credit transactions in two offices, but the embezzler found the Winnipeg office was best for withdrawals. As the size of the theft grew, the bank officer couldn't hardly conceal it any longer. The bank discovered it's loss when the embezzler made a error, filling out a credit slip instead of a debit slip. Embarrassed bank officials have announced there intention to set up new operational controls to prevent these kind of fraudulent scheme in the future.

D. In the space provided, supply the proper article (*a* or *an*) for the following words:

EXAMPLE: __an__ adjustment

1. ________ year
2. ________ honour
3. ________ email message
4. ________ RRSP
5. ________ activity
6. ________ warehouse
7. ________ hotel
8. ________ iPhone
9. ________ utility
10. ________ human cost
11. ________ insult
12. ________ X-ray
13. ________ illegible letter
14. ________ one-year lease
15. ________ eight-year lease
16. ________ upload

E. In the space provided, write the correct comparative or superlative form of the adjective.

EXAMPLE: Of the three software packages, which is (good)? __best__

1. Yasmin is the (creative) member of the team. ________
2. She did (well) on the certification exam than she had expected. ________
3. Where is the (recent) forecast for this fiscal year? ________
4. Nearly everyone is (happy) in his or her job since the change in management. ________
5. Farah was asked to research group insurance plans with (good) dental coverage than our current plan. ________
6. Of all the employees, Richard is the (shy). ________
7. Ms. Qamut is (businesslike) than the office manager she replaced. ________
8. That business is known to be the (respectful) of Treaty Day in the town. ________
9. This is the (bad) winter we've had in years. ________
10. Which is the (little) expensive of the two advertising packages? ________

TEAR HERE

NAME ______________________________

LEVEL II

A. (Self-check) Write the correct form in the space provided.

1. Nearly everything I've had at that restaurant tastes (good, well). __________
2. The lighthouse is (farther, further) away than it first appeared. __________
3. Better service is ensured if a purchaser has (face-to-face, face to face) dealings with the manufacturer. __________
4. Companies have reported (fewer, less) security breaches this year. __________
5. Mr. Lee looked (nervous, nervously) during the interview. __________
6. Mr. Burton (sure, surely) made his personal feelings apparent when he announced the policy change. __________
7. Paul feels (bad, badly) that he has to miss the ceremony. __________
8. Of probationary and permanent employees, only the (later, latter) are eligible for tuition reimbursement. __________
9. Some small businesses barely exist from (year-to-year, year to year). __________
10. Knowing someone had reported his transgression, Jim looked (suspicious, suspiciously) at his colleagues. __________

Check your answers.

B. Write the correct word in the space provided. Be prepared to explain your choices.

1. Manuel feels (insecure, insecurely) about his transfer to the Winnipeg office. __________
2. Because of the construction decline, (fewer, less) housing is available. __________
3. Saima knows the government funding conditions (real, really) well. __________
4. Apples and brie cheese taste (good, well) on pizza. __________
5. Thunderchild First Nation acted (prompt, promptly) to become the largest investor in Westleaf. __________
6. Since its tune-up, the engine runs (smoother, more smoothly). __________
7. His acceptance of responsibility for the error suggests that Peter can be considered (genuine, genuinely). __________
8. Please don't take her comments (personal, personally). __________
9. Of Yuko and Irina, the (later, latter) has more direct experience. __________
10. Your new job certainly suits you (good, well). __________
11. It is (certain, certainly) a breach of privacy to access employees' personal email accounts. __________
12. She wanted to debate the question (further, farther). __________
13. Unless online orders can be processed more (efficient, efficiently), we will lose business to our competitors. __________

TEAR HERE

14. The airport is (farther, further) away than it appears on the map. ________

15. Henry feels (sure, surely) that part-time salaries will improve. ________

16. (Most, Almost) everyone agreed that work is the price one pays for a good lifestyle. ________

17. Most tech companies allow employees to dress (casual, casually). ________

18. The buyers want the deal to close as (quick, quickly) as the sellers do. ________

19. Our new (ergonomic, ergonomically) designed office furniture should help prevent undue strain on employees. ________

20. Having recovered from his illness, Luis said he feels (good, well) enough to return to work. ________

C. Select the correct group of words below. Write its letter in the space provided.

1. (a) coast to coast contest
(b) coast-to-coast contest ________

2. (a) well-prepared presentation
(b) well prepared presentation ________

3. (a) building that is eight-years-old
(b) building that is eight years old ________

4. (a) right or left brain activities
(b) right- or left-brain activities ________

5. (a) locally sourced foods
(b) locally-sourced foods ________

6. (a) state of the art technology
(b) state-of-the-art technology ________

7. (a) data-processing service
(b) data processing service ________

8. (a) no-fault insurance
(b) no fault insurance ________

9. (a) last-minute preparations
(b) last minute preparations ________

10. (a) widely-accepted policy
(b) widely accepted policy ________

11. (a) Canada-Post depot
(b) Canada Post depot ________

12. (a) direct-to-consumer marketing
(b) direct to consumer marketing ________

Are any of the above in your dictionary?

TEAR HERE

Place commas where needed in the following groups of words.

13. honest fair appraisal

14. innovative software program

15. skilled financial analyst

16. diverse equal-opportunity workplaces

17. concise courteous letter

18. disappointing quarterly results

19. imaginative daring designer

20. efficient clerical employee

21. 18-foot extension ladder

22. solid wood furniture

23. hand-made slip-on moccasins

24. thoughtful proactive response

D. Writing Exercise. Compose sentences using the following words as compound adjectives. Be sure that the compound adjectives precede nouns, and add hyphens as needed.

EXAMPLE: (on the spot) We offer on-the-spot appraisals.

1. (first class) ______

2. (smart home) ______

3. (two year) ______

4. (once in a lifetime) ______

5. (community college) ______

6. (work related) ______

7. (limited time) ______

8. (energy efficient) ______

TEAR HERE

NAME ______________________

LEVEL III

A. **(Self-check)** Underline any errors in the following sentences, and write corrections in the space provided. Write *C* if a sentence is correct.

EXAMPLE: Her three last books have been bestsellers. last three

1. The 50 first customers will receive a gift bag. ______
2. Indira is the most supportive manager in the company. ______
3. She is more supportive than any manager I've ever had. ______
4. We don't even think our IT department would be able to fix that issue. ______
5. We just want to hire two more clerks. ______
6. The 12 last people in line were unable to get tickets. ______
7. He merely thought you wanted one page copied. ______
8. Updating the software nearly cost the company $10,000. ______
9. We are only concerned with your welfare and happiness. ______
10. Apple is worth more than any business. ______

Check your answers.

B. Underline errors, and write corrected forms in the space provided. Write *C* if the sentence is correct.

1. We merely have three weeks left before the budget deadline. ______
2. Simi is taking vacation during the two last weeks of August. ______
3. Air Canada beat out all North American airlines in 2018 to win a Skytrax award. ______
4. The workplace accident didn't only harm Karl's wrist; his shoulder was also injured. ______
5. I have just one idea for solving the security problem. ______
6. Halifax is the largest city in Nova Scotia. ______
7. Halifax is larger than any city in Nova Scotia. ______
8. That particular product is only sold on our website. ______
9. Joka seems to be more skilled than anyone at jamming the photocopier. ______
10. The two first applicants presented excellent résumés. ______

C. **Review of Levels I, II, and III.** For each sentence below, underline any errors. Then write a corrected form in the space provided. Write *C* if the sentence is correct.

1. The new product line, which was only launched a year ago, is already our most profitable. ______
2. Which of the three new colour choices do you like better? ______

TEAR HERE

3. Reka said that she couldn't barely hear you on your cellphone. ____________

4. Because of excessive costs, designer Donna Karan made less trips to the Far East and Africa in search of "creative inspiration." ____________

5. We can better judge our inventory value once we have conducted our end of year stock count. ____________

6. I hope we can discuss this farther at our next meeting. ____________

7. The latest advertising campaign is the most cleverest the agency has come up with to date. ____________

8. The designer attempted to create an attractive functional working environment. ____________

9. I like this job better than any job I've ever had. ____________

10. Hawkins interviewed a Canadian official and an European diplomat concerning the proposed two-year trade program. ____________

11. Juanita didn't feel well about having passed the blame. ____________

12. The executive team thought most everyone would like the change in work hours. ____________

13. The pre and post conference events have nearly sold out. ____________

14. The distribution manager only requested a quotation from one transportation company. ____________

15. You shouldn't have spoken so rude during the meeting. ____________

D. Writing Exercise. Your instructor may ask you to complete this exercise on a separate sheet.

Write five original sentences using the following as adjectives: *federally funded, fewer, less, top of the line,* and *step by step*. In addition, write five sentences using the following as adverbs: *already, better, further, only,* and *well*.

POSTTEST

Underline the correct word or words.

1. Orders are processed (smoother, more smoothly) using this new software.
2. Steve feels (bad, badly) about having to reduce employee benefits.
3. (This kind, These kinds) of employees help to make a company successful.
4. If you had read (farther, further) in the manual, you would have found the instructions.
5. We (could, couldn't) hardly believe the change in her personality.
6. Gelato has (fewer, less) calories than ice cream.
7. (A, An) euphemism often used to mean *fired* is *laid off*.
8. Mrs. Sherman said she felt (good, well) following her surgery.
9. Yusef completed a (page by page, page-by-page) review of the document.
10. It's always nice to work with an (enthusiastic hard-working; enthusiastic, hard-working) trainee.

TEAR HERE

EDITOR'S CHALLENGE ■

The following memo proposal and letter contain errors in spelling and language principles covered thus far, as well as other common errors. Use standard proofreading marks to show your corrections.

DATE: June 5, 202x

TO: Larry LaGrange, Vice President, Operations

FROM: Elyse Ellerman, Manager, Accounting

SUBJECT: Installation of Undercarpet Wiring

Proposal

Because the Accounting Department needs a flexible economical wiring system that can acommodate our ever changing electrical needs. I propose that we install a flat undercarpet wiring system.

Present System

At this time the Accounting Department has an out of date system of floor wiring and power poles that limit us to surface wiring. This network of surface wiring appear to be totally overwhelmed by the demands we are now placing on them. The operation of 27 pieces of equipment in addition to 34 telephone lines require extensive electrical circuits and cabling. Moreover, our overhead lighting, which consist of fluorescent fixtures in a suspended egg crate structure, contains excessive wiring above the ceiling. Technicians whom have came to our office have said that its the worse system they've ever saw.

Advantages of Proposed System

Cabling for telephone, power, and data are now available in a flat form only 1 mm thick. This flat flexible cable can be install underneath existing carpeting. Thus preventing costly and disruptive renovation. Undercarpet wiring would mean less office power poles. Moreover, flat cables can be moved easy, giving we accountants greater flexibility when we need to add equipment. Having a undercarpet wiring system all ready installed in the Accounting Department would also enable the company to evaluate the systems effectiveness before considering it for other departments.

Cost and Savings

The suppliers and our consultant estimates that an undercarpet wiring system for the Accounting department would cost about $75,000. If we was to use conventional methods to install round wiring, we would have to renovate our entire department, costing over $300,000. Equally important, however, is the savings in terms of productivity and employee satisfaction. Which would decline if renovation was required.

Please let me know by June 10 whether you want me to precede with this project.

TEAR HERE

Speedy Courier

8567 Sheppard Ave.
Suite 2398
Toronto, ON M3L 2Z9

Phone: 416-545-6886
Fax: 416-545-6887
Website: http://www.speedycourier.com

November 2, 202x

Ms. Jessica Stoudenmire
World Decor
520 West Hickmore
St. Laurent, QC H3T 1K2

Dear Ms. Stoudemire:

As a result of the possible rail strike, you may have full or partially-full shipping containers' waiting in Vancouver for cross-country shipment to your stores. Without another solution, these containers may be delayed for weeks or months. While rail workers strike or negotiations are in process. In the meantime, you sure will incur costly storage and other fees that you couldn't hardly have anticipated.

Speedy Courier can help, offering Canada's most wide delivery network. We transport your goods by truck, shipping them direct to your stores or to local, distribution centres for later delivery to market. We even have convenient cost effective warehousing solutions available to you in the vicinity of Edmonton, Winnipeg, Toronto, Montreal, and Halifax. The transit time to Halifax or any of these centres via road only is three to four days.

If you have time sensitive goods sitting in Vancouver—or just if you don't want to waist money on unexpected storage fees—call you account executive or I today. With Speedy's help, you can count on your customers receiving there orders in less then five days, just tell us were the shipments needs to go, and we'll get it there!

Sincerely,

Roshani Wallani
Manager, Marketing

TEAR HERE

PREPOSITIONS

CHAPTER

12

OBJECTIVES

When you have completed the materials in this chapter, you will be able to do the following:

LEVEL I

- Use objective-case pronouns as objects of prepositions
- Avoid using prepositions in place of verbs and adverbs

LEVEL II

- Use challenging prepositions correctly
- Omit unnecessary prepositions and retain necessary ones
- Construct formal sentences that avoid terminal prepositions

LEVEL III

- Recognize words and constructions requiring specific prepositions (idioms)
- Use idioms involving prepositions correctly

PRETEST

Underline the correct word(s).

1. All managers except Phil and (she, her) have completed the training.
2. Where did those photocopies (go, go to)?
3. Lydia is frustrated because she receives (to, too) much spam.
4. She feels (as if, like) these spam messages are affecting her productivity.
5. This plan is different (from, than) the one I suggested.
6. Management and workers alike agreed (to, with) the contract.
7. The printer should be placed (beside, besides) the computer.

(continued)

PRETEST (CONTINUED)

8. Divide the work evenly (among, between) the four administrative assistants.
9. Please turn this form (into, in to) your supervisor by Friday.
10. Will someone be available to speak (to, about) the issue of computer misuse?

Prepositions are connecting words that show the relationship of a noun or pronoun to other words in a sentence. This chapter focuses on common problems that communicators have with troublesome prepositions. It also reviews the use of objective-case pronouns following prepositions. Finally, this chapter presents many idiomatic expressions that require specific prepositions to sound correct.

LEVEL I

COMMON USES OF PREPOSITIONS

STUDY TIP

The most commonly used prepositions are *of* and *for*. Remember that any nouns or pronouns following these or other prepositions in prepositional phrases are serving as objects. Objects of prepositions cannot be subjects of sentences.

This list contains the most commonly used prepositions. Notice that prepositions may consist of one word or more than one word.

about	beneath	in spite of	through
above	beside	into	to
according to	between	like	toward
after	but	near	under
alongside	by	of	until
along with	down	off	up
among	during	on	upon
around	except	on account of	with
at	for	opposite	within
before	from	outside	without
behind	in addition to	over	
below	inside	since	

A preposition usually appears in a **prepositional phrase**, which consists of the preposition followed by the object of the preposition. The **object of a preposition** is a noun or a pronoun. In the following sentences, prepositional phrases are italicized. Notice that a sentence can contain more than one prepositional phrase.

Some *of our greatest innovations* were launched *during tough times.*
The most important ideas *in business* were developed *over the past 120 years.*
The assembly line, created *in 1910 by Henry Ford,* had a positive effect *on the economy.*

Objective Case Following Prepositions

As you learned in Chapter 5, pronouns that are objects of prepositions must be in the objective case. Objective-case pronouns include *me, us, you, him, her, it,* and *them.*

We received pledges *from him and her* for the charity bike ride.
Give the account balances *to us.*
Marian, *along with them,* arrived later.

Some often troublesome prepositions are *like, between, except,* and *but* (meaning "except"). These prepositions may lead to confusion in determining pronoun case. Consider the following examples.

Strictly *between you* and *me* (not *I*), the contract has already been signed.
Applications from individuals *like* Mr. Sheldon and *him* (not *he*) are rare.
Recommendations from everyone *but them* (not *they*) have arrived.

CAREER TIP

"You are the same today as you are going to be five years from now except for two things: the people with whom you associate and the books you read."
—Charles Jones

Typical Problems With Prepositions

In even the most casual speech or writing, you should avoid the following misuses of prepositions.

***OF* FOR *HAVE*.** The verb phrases *should have, would have, could have, must have,* or *might have* should never be written as *should of, would of, could of, must of,* or *might of.* The word *of* is a preposition and cannot be used as part of a verb phrase.

Zainab *should have* (not *should of*) called first.
He *could have* (not *could of*) renewed his commercial fishing licence.

***OFF* FOR *FROM*.** The preposition *from* should never be replaced by *off* or *off of.*

My friend borrowed money *from* (not *off* or *off of*) me.
Doreen said she got the book *from* you.

***TO* FOR *TOO*.** The preposition *to* means "in a direction toward." The word *to* may also be part of an infinitive construction. Do not use the word *to* in place of the adverb *too,* which means "additionally," "also," or "excessively."

Dividends are not distributed *to* shareholders unless declared by the directors.
Because profits were *too* small, we declared no dividends.
Contributions of services will be accepted *too.*
She is learning *to* program in Python and JavaScript.

Complete the reinforcement exercises for Level I on pages 229–230.

ASK AN EDITOR

Question:
Another employee and I are collaborating on a report. I wanted to write this: *Money was lost due to poor attendance.* She says the sentence should read *Money was lost because of poor attendance.* My version is more concise. Which of us is right?

Answer:
Many language authorities agree with your co-author. Historically, *due to* was considered acceptable only as part of a phrase modifying a specific noun or pronoun, for example, after a linking verb, as in *Success was due to proper timing.* In this sentence *due to proper timing* describes *success. Because of,* on the other hand, has always been able to introduce adverbial phrases and modify verbs, as it does in *Money was lost because of poor attendance.* In the twenty-first century most authorities have accepted *due to* as a legitimate preposition, but many writers and readers may take issue with it because of the historical debate.

LEVEL II

CHALLENGING PREPOSITIONS

Use special caution with the following prepositions.

***AMONG, BETWEEN*.** *Among* is used to speak of three or more persons or things. *Between* is usually used for two persons or things.

The disagreement was *between* Stipchek and his partner.
Profits were distributed *among* the four partners.

***BESIDE, BESIDES*.** *Beside* means "next to"; *besides* means "in addition to."

Please sit *beside* me at the assembly.
Besides a preface, you must write an introduction.

BE THE EDITOR

Colorado Springs traffic sign: "Following to close." (City officials blamed the sign company, which had shortened "Following too closely" because it didn't fit.)

EXCEPT. The preposition *except*, meaning "excluding" or "but," is sometimes confused with the verb *accept*, which means "to receive."

Everyone *except* Melanie was able to come.
Please *accept* this gift of tobacco.

IN, INTO, IN TO. *In* indicates a position or location. *Into* can mean several things, including (1) entering something, (2) changing form, or (3) making contact. Some constructions may employ *in* as an adverb preceding an infinitive (which begins with *to*).

We store copy paper *in* the supply cabinet. (Preposition *in* indicates location.)
Bring the boxes *into* the storeroom. (Preposition *into* indicates movement to an interior location.)
They went *in* to see the manager. (Adverb *in* precedes infinitive *to see*.)

BE THE EDITOR

From a job applicant's cover letter: "I would be prepared to meet with you at your earliest convenience to discuss what I can do to your company."

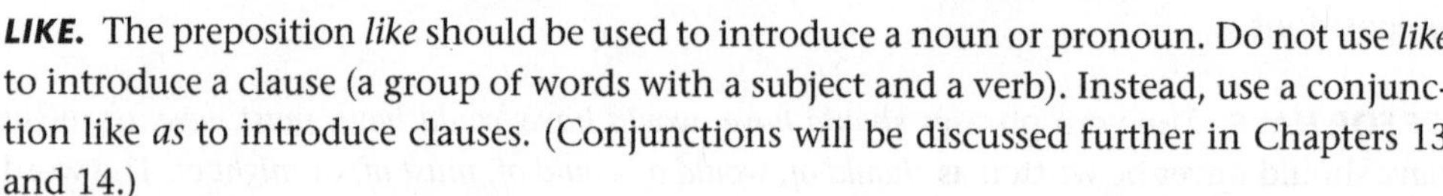

LIKE. The preposition *like* should be used to introduce a noun or pronoun. Do not use *like* to introduce a clause (a group of words with a subject and a verb). Instead, use a conjunction like *as* to introduce clauses. (Conjunctions will be discussed further in Chapters 13 and 14.)

The copy looks very much *like* the original. (*Like* is used as a preposition introducing the object *original*.)
It looks *as if* (not *like*) it may rain soon. (*As if* is a conjunction used to introduce the clause *it may rain soon*.)
As (not *like*) I said earlier, the order was sent. (Do not use *like* to introduce the clause *I said earlier*.)

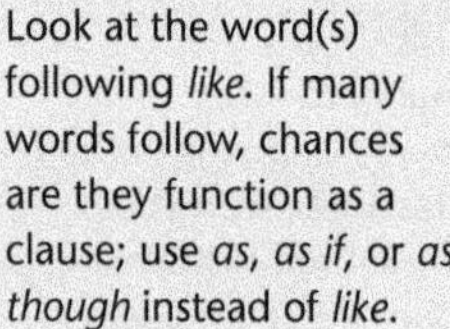

STUDY TIP

Look at the word(s) following *like*. If many words follow, chances are they function as a clause; use *as*, *as if*, or *as though* instead of *like*.

USING PREPOSITIONS EFFICIENTLY

Necessary Prepositions

Don't omit those prepositions that are necessary to clarify a relationship. Be particularly careful when two prepositions are necessary with a single object.

We have every desire *for* and hope *of* an early settlement. (Do not omit *for*.)
What type *of* coupler do you need? (Do not omit *of*.)
Mr. Munoz is unsure *of* where to place the machine. (Do not omit *of*.)
Salaries seem to be higher for temporary positions than *for* permanent positions. (Do not omit second *for*.)
When did you graduate *from* high school? (Do not omit *from*.)

ASK AN EDITOR

Question:
What's wrong with saying *Lisa graduated college last year*?

Answer:
Interestingly, in the nineteenth century, *graduated* was preferred to be used in a transitive sense, as it is in your sentence. However, since the twentieth century, grammarians have opted for the intransitive form, with the addition of *from* for syntactical fluency.

Unnecessary Prepositions

Omit unnecessary prepositions that clutter sentences.

The book fell *off* the desk. (Not *off of*)
He met *with* the new manager at lunch. (Not *met up with*)
Leave the package *inside* the door. (Not *inside of*)
Both websites are useful. (Not *of the websites*)
All the letters require signatures. (Not *of the letters*)
Where is the meeting? (Not *meeting at*)
She could not help laughing. (Not *help from*)
Keep the paper *near* the printer. (Not *near to*)

Ending a Sentence With a Preposition

In the past, language authorities warned against ending a sentence (or a clause) with a preposition. In formal writing today, most careful authors continue to avoid terminal prepositions. In conversation and informal writing, however, terminal prepositions are acceptable.

Informal Usage	**Formal Usage**
What organization is he a member *of*?	*Of* what organization is he a member?
What is the medicine prescribed *for*?	*For* what is the medicine prescribed?
We don't know whom you spoke *to* when you called.	We don't know *to* whom you spoke when you called.
We missed the television news program she appeared *on*.	We missed the television news program *on* which she appeared.

Complete the reinforcement exercises for Level II on pages 231–233.

BE THE EDITOR

From an Ann Landers advice column: ". . . [They] might get their eyes opened up."

ASK AN EDITOR

Question:
What's the difference between *toward* and *towards*?

Answer:
None. They are interchangeable. However, it is more efficient to use the shorter word *toward*. Of most importance is to use one or the other consistently within your document. If your company has a style guide, it is best to consult it for a preferred term.

LEVEL III

IDIOMATIC USE OF PREPOSITIONS

Every language has **idioms**, which are word combinations unique to that language. These combinations have developed over time through usage and often cannot be explained rationally. Native speakers usually are unaware of idiom usage until a violation jars their ear, such as "He is capable *from* (rather than *of*) violence."

The following list shows words that require specific prepositions to denote precise meanings. This group is just a sampling of the large number of English idioms involving prepositions. Consult a dictionary when you are unsure of the correct preposition to use with a particular word.

acquaint with	Are you *acquainted with* the new president?
adept in (*or* at)	Are you *adept in* negotiation tactics?
adhere to	All employees must *adhere to* certain office rules.
agree on (*or* upon) (mutual ideas)	Our team members *agree on* nearly everything.
agree to (a proposal)	Did they *agree to* the plan for splitting shifts?
agree with (a person)	I *agree with* you on this issue.
angry at (a thing)	Customers are understandably *angry at* the delay.
angry about (a situation or condition)	Employees are *angry about* the reduction in benefits.
angry with (a person)	How can you be *angry with* the child?
bored with (*not* of)	Terry became *bored with* his repetitive duties.
buy from	You may *buy from* any one of several wholesalers.
capable of	She is *capable of* remarkable accomplishments.
comply with	We must *comply with* government regulations.
conform to	These machine parts do not *conform to* the specifications.
contrast with	The white boat *contrasts* sharply *with* the blue ocean.

(continued)

correspond to (match)	A bird's wing *corresponds to* a person's arm.
correspond with (write)	We *correspond with* our clients regularly.
desire for	A *desire for* wealth may create greed.
desirous of	Rogers was *desirous of* acquiring blue-chip investments.
differ from (things)	Debit cards *differ from* credit cards.
differ with (a person)	I *differ with* you in small points only.
different from (followed by word or phrase)	This product is *different from* ours.
different than (followed by clause)	Our processes now are quite *different than* they were in the early 2000s.
disagree with	Do you *disagree with* him?
expert in	Dr. Rand is an *expert in* electronics.
guard against	*Guard against* infection by washing hands frequently.
identical with (*or* to)	Our strategy is *identical with* (or *to*) our competitor's.
independent of	Living alone, the young man was *independent of* his parents.
infer from	I *infer from* your remark that you are dissatisfied.
interest in	Jan has a great *interest in* the bond market.
negligent of	*Negligent of* his diet, the old man became ill.
oblivious to (*or* of)	McClain was *oblivious to* (or *of*) his surroundings.
plan to (*not* on)	We *plan to* expand our target market.
prefer . . . to	I *prefer* a laptop *to* a desktop computer.
reason with	Mr. Miller tried to *reason with* the unhappy customer.
reconcile with (match)	QuickBooks figures must be *reconciled with* bank statements.
reconcile to (accept)	He has never become *reconciled to* retirement.
responsible for	William is *responsible for* locking the building.
retroactive to	The salary increase is *retroactive to* July 1.
sensitive to	Ms. Choy is unusually *sensitive to* her employees' needs.
similar to	Your term paper topic is *similar to* mine.
speak about (*not* to)	The director of marketing will *speak about* the organizational changes.
stand in (*not* on) line	How long have you been *standing in* line?
talk to (tell something)	The speaker *talked to* the large group.
talk with (exchange remarks)	After his lecture, the speaker *talked with* club members informally.
tired of	The receptionist gets *tired of* hearing the telephone ring.
wait for (expect)	Mark is *waiting for* the bus.
wait on (serve)	We left a tip for the person who *waited on* us at the restaurant.

Complete the reinforcement exercises for Level III on pages 234–235.

NAME ____________________

CHAPTER 12 ■ Reinforcement Exercises

LEVEL I

A. (Self-check) Select the correct word, and write it in the space provided.

1. We were able to get her email address (off of, from) Kathleen. ____________
2. Jasdeep thought that he (should of, should have) been allowed extra time. ____________
3. Many believe that corporate annual reports are (to, too) cryptic to understand. ____________
4. Anyone but (she, her) will provide you with a reference. ____________
5. The commission will be split between you and (I, me). ____________
6. The thank-you note is addressed to Susy and (he, him). ____________
7. With more experience Luc (would of, would have) landed the job. ____________
8. Did you get a user name and password (from, off) the IT department? ____________
9. Everyone is expected to go (to, too) the meeting. ____________
10. All employees except (they, them) must submit self-evaluations at review time. ____________

Check your answers.

B. Underline any errors you find in the following sentences. Write the correct form in the space provided. Write *C* if a sentence is correct.

EXAMPLE: Performers like Tao and she are crowd-pleasers. her

1. Everyone in the office except she has a PC. ____________
2. Bill Gates could of kept his fortune, but he chose to give much of it to a charitable foundation. ____________
3. Warren Buffett and Carlos Slim donate large amounts to charity to. ____________
4. Many customers have already made appointments with LaShawn or him. ____________
5. Patience is not the kind of skill you're likely to learn off of others. ____________
6. No one could of known we'd sell out in our first week. ____________
7. It's never to late to learn to write well. ____________
8. Except for Tim and I, the department consists of only new graduates. ____________
9. If the company agrees, the junior designer job could be shared between Odette and he. ____________
10. If you had attended the reception, you would of had a preview of the competitors' new products. ____________

TEAR HERE

11. With you and me managing the product launch, it can't fail. ______

12. You can always rely on coworkers like Renée and she when you need help to meet a deadline. ______

13. The e-newsletter open rate might have been higher with a clearer subject line. ______

14. Everyone except he and I received the announcement too late to respond. ______

15. I am going to try to get the price quotation off of Ric. ______

16. We have received several emails commending the work of Mohammad, Tariq, and her. ______

17. Feedback has been received from everyone but them. ______

18. The car's windows are to darkly tinted to see inside. ______

19. It has been years since we tried to order supplies off of them. ______

20. We couldn't of hoped for better from them. ______

NAME ______________________________

LEVEL II

A. (Self-check) Select the correct word(s) and write it in the space provided.

1. The operating expenses will be divided equally (between, among) the six departments. ________________
2. None of the local lunch caterers (beside, besides) Food-A-Go-Go offer sushi. ________________
3. We engraved identification serial numbers (inside, inside of) all new equipment. ________________
4. Because children can go (in, into) variety stores, the First Nations Council wants to ban the sale of cannabis and liquor in such establishments. ________________
5. It looks (like, as if) our firm will get the government contract. ________________
6. Have you decided whether you will (accept, except) the position? ________________
7. Despite her salary and new title, Helen feels (as, like) a technician. ________________
8. The differences (between, among) the two customer relationship management systems were negligible. ________________
9. The contracts blew (off, off of) the desk when the door was opened. ________________
10. The desk (beside, besides) Thien's is vacant. ________________

Check your answers.

B. In the following sentences, delete unnecessary prepositions and insert any necessary ones.

EXAMPLES: What type ^of wheel bearings are needed?

Where are you going (to)?

1. The time for submitting resumes is over with.
2. A new Tim Hortons is opening opposite to our office building.
3. Where is the conference being held at?
4. Management has asked Claire to provide feedback and a summary of the training session.
5. Do you know if all of the orders have been filled?
6. Oversized printing jobs must be done outside of the office.
7. What type credit card do you accept?
8. The cashier will take 30 percent off of the price at checkout.
9. When not in use, sensitive documents should be placed inside of file folders.
10. Our appreciation and interest in the program remain strong.
11. Despite the company rules for computer use, Davina couldn't stop from checking Facebook a few times a day.

TEAR HERE

12. Where shall I send the application form to?

13. Both of the company websites were down for routine maintenance.

14. We would rather you wait in the foyer than Mr. Lunds's office.

15. Farrokh graduated college with a diploma in graphic design.

C. Select the correct word(s).

1. She hopes to go (in to, into) construction management.

2. Every floor has a gender-neutral washroom (near, near to) the elevator.

3. All funds raised during the charity drive will be divided (among, between) three local charities.

4. (As, Like) we discussed last week, Friday will be a half day.

5. Has anyone been (in to, into) see me this morning?

6. Once (all the, all of the) current orders have been shipped, we should review our process.

7. (Like, As) many employees, Isabel continuously looks for career development opportunities.

8. (Beside, Besides) the marketing and advertising teams, whom have you invited?

9. This weekend, get up to 50% (off, off of) the regular price.

10. All sites (accept, except) ours offer real-time technical support.

11. After the interview, Lee felt (like, as if) he would be offered the position.

12. If he (accepts, excepts) the position, he will have to move to Calgary.

13. The security guard saw several people go (in, into) the building after hours.

14. Anita (met, met up) with her boss this morning.

15. Employees are required to turn expense reports (in to, into) their supervisors within one week.

D. Write original sentences using these prepositions correctly.

1. (among) ______________________________

____

2. (into) ______________________________

____

3. (except) ______________________________

____

4. (like) ______________________________

____

5. (besides) ______________________________

____

E. The following sentences have prepositions that end clauses. Rewrite the sentences so that the prepositions come before their objects.

EXAMPLES: Here is the information you asked about.

Here is the information about which you asked.

1. What warehouse was the shipment delivered to? ______

2. Please locate the file you put the contract in. ______

3. We have a number of loyal members we can rely on. ______

4. What company did you purchase these supplies from? ______

5. Whom did you attend the conference with? ______

TEAR HERE

NAME ________________________________

LEVEL III

A. **(Self-check)** Underline any errors in the use of prepositions in the following sentences, and write a correction in the space provided. Write *C* if a sentence is correct. Refer to the list in Level III (pp. 227–228) or to a dictionary, if necessary.

1. How long do you plan on staying at the conference? ____________
2. We find it impossible to comply to the latest safety regulations. ____________
3. In a televised address at 6 p.m., the prime minister will talk with the nation. ____________
4. The new department head doesn't care to conform with procedures used in the past. ____________
5. Mrs. Reich's management philosophy is quite different from mine. ____________
6. Every holiday season customers wanting deals on the latest electronics stand on line from early morning. ____________
7. Jordan is an expert at bioengineering. ____________
8. Citizens must adhere with all provincial and federal laws. ____________
9. Kay prefers taking the train over driving to work. ____________
10. Are you angry at me for disagreeing with you during the meeting? ____________

Check your answers.

B. Underline any errors in the use of prepositions in the following sentences, and write a correction in the space provided. Write *C* if a sentence is correct.

1. Once I become bored of my job, I will look for another. ____________
2. Our new office building is convenient to many restaurants and cafés. ____________
3. Wei's salary increase will be retroactive from January 1. ____________
4. Ben was surprisingly sensitive about my feelings after I was overlooked for the promotion. ____________
5. It was a pleasure talking to you yesterday about your role in the company. ____________
6. Mr. Colotti described how common stock differs to preferred stock. ____________
7. Because she was negligent to her duties, Shanese received a poor performance review. ____________
8. How long should we wait on the others before beginning the meeting? ____________
9. At the meeting Eleanor was asked to speak to the subject of employee morale. ____________
10. The successful candidate must be adept with collections. ____________
11. The font colour on the web page contrasts nicely against the background. ____________

TEAR HERE

12. Do you hire a translator when your company corresponds to Chinese suppliers? ______

13. Because the franchise is completely standardized, a fast-food restaurant in Saskatchewan may be identical to one in California. ______

14. A firewall will help guard against unauthorized access to our intranet. ______

15. After the poor service I got, I will never buy anything off that company again. ______

16. We cannot possibly agree with a contract that we have not yet read. ______

17. If Ishana isn't capable to train others on the job, we will have to hire a professional trainer. ______

18. I differ from Reina about the important takeaways of the sales report. ______

19. Your ethics do not conform with our expectations. ______

20. We had to wait on feedback from a few key people before we could make our decision. ______

C. Writing Exercise. Your instructor may ask you to complete this exercise on a separate sheet.

Write ten original sentences, one using each of the following expressions: *agree to, agree with, capable of, contrast with, differ from, graduate from, identical to, independent of, retroactive to,* and *similar to.* Use a dictionary if necessary.

POSTTEST

Underline the correct word(s).

1. There is no one else quite like (he, him).
2. No one (accept, except) our controller was aware of the accounting discrepancies.
3. The new independent market (could of, could have) survived with better management.
4. Please turn your uniform (into, in to) your supervisor on your last day.
5. Management encourages employees to take their lunch break (outside, outside of) the office.
6. It looks (like, as if) we will be able to avoid layoffs.
7. Is it necessary for all documents to comply (to, with) the new guidelines?
8. Dividends will be distributed (between, among) shareholders.
9. (Beside, Besides) Ann, who is able to work Saturday?
10. Employees have respect (for, in) leaders who exhibit ethical behaviour.

TEAR HERE

EDITOR'S CHALLENGE

The following report and memo contain errors in spelling and concepts you have studied thus far, as well as other common errors. Use proofreading marks to show your corrections.

RESULTS OF SMOKING POLICY SURVEY

by Ewa Poul, Human Resources

Background

Second hand smoke represents a health risk with significant compensation implications for our company and it's shareholders. After a number of requests was received from employees asking that smoking is banned from all company property, Human Resources distributed a questionnaire to 58 managerial and supervisory personnel, a total of 52 responses were received.

Findings

A tally of the returned surveys show that a clear majority of our managerial employees favours a complete non-smoking policy. A total of 42 employees, or nearly 80 percent of those whom took the survey, indicated there approval for such a policy. To introduce this policy, excellent suggestions were made by respondents. Which have been documented within the attached printout and are summarized below.

Conclusion

The results of this survey suggests that our managers and supervisors would support an extended non-smoking policy.

Summary of Recommendations

Overall, most employees feel that careful planning and sensitive implementation is essential to gaining employee's support and adherence to the new policy. Offering a well managed cessation program to provide support and practical advice to smokers who want to use the opportunity to quit is recommended. High visibility displays should promote participation, and those employees who are interested should be allowed sometime to take part in group counselling activities. Whether to provide any outdoor smoking areas for those employees who do not stop are a matter a committee must be formed to research about.

TEAR HERE

High-Tech Solutions

Interoffice Memo

DATE: July 1, 202x

TO: All Employees

FROM: Craig Abrams, Human Resources

SUBJECT: New Email and Web Policy

Over the past few month's, all of our supervisors have provided datum about email and web use to top management and I. Beside using email and the web for work related purposes, some employees are useing these tools for personal bussiness. This, of course, is having serious implications for our company and its productivity. Improper use can also led to larger problems such as lawsuits. We have, therefore, hired two lawyers who is expert at writing email and web policies to help write a policy for our firm. We plan on implementing the policy on September 1.

During the month of August, workshops will be given by my staff and I to help employees learn how to comply to the new policy. You can also schedule an appointment with your immediate supervisor to talk to them about the new policy. In addition, you can turn any comments or suggestions into me before September 1. Finally, you can obtain a rough draft of the policy off of my receptionist after July 31. She can also let you know where training sessions will be held at.

Because to much personnel email and web use can negatively affect our company. This policy is needed, and we are confident that you will all except it's provisions. The policy we develop will be similar as policies used by other companies in our industry. As we develop the policy, we will remain sensitive of the needs of all employees to make sure that the policy is something to which everyone can agree. If you have an interest in assisting us with this important task, please contact my assistant or I at Ext. 452 or Ext. 464 before August 15.

CHAPTER

13

CONJUNCTIONS TO JOIN EQUALS

OBJECTIVES

When you have completed the materials in this chapter, you will be able to do the following:

LEVEL I

- Distinguish between simple and compound sentences
- Punctuate compound sentences using coordinating conjunctions such as *and*, *or*, *nor*, and *but*

LEVEL II

- Punctuate compound sentences using conjunctive adverbs such as *therefore*, *however*, and *consequently*
- Punctuate sentences using parenthetical (interrupting) adverbs such as *therefore*, *however*, and *consequently*

LEVEL III

- Recognize correlative conjunctions such as *either . . . or*, *not only . . . but also*, and *neither . . . nor*
- Use parallel construction in composing sentences with correlative conjunctions

PRETEST

Insert commas and semicolons to punctuate the following sentences correctly. Write *C* if a sentence is correct.

1. Michael Paez attended the design competition in Toronto and brought home several awards.
2. As many as 20 agents will relocate nevertheless the office will remain open for walk-in business.
3. Eleanor Uyeda prefers to remain in Kitchener but Lu Yi is considering accepting a transfer to the Windsor office.

(continued)

PRETEST (CONTINUED)

4. All employees must be able to communicate effectively consequently we evaluate communication skills during employment interviews.

5. Performance reviews therefore include discussion about employees' communication skills.

6. It is important, however, that employees also have excellent computer skills.

7. The change in start time was communicated two months ago therefore employees have no excuse for lateness.

8. We contacted the supplier about the defect then we notified our customers of it.

Circle the letter of the sentence that is more effective.

9. (a) This wireless service is not only more reliable, but it is also cheaper than the other.
(b) This wireless service is not only more reliable but also cheaper than the other.

10. (a) Either Michelle was flying into Vancouver or into Seattle.
(b) Michelle was flying either into Vancouver or into Seattle.

This chapter and the next cover a very important part of speech: conjunctions. Conjunctions are connecting words. They may be separated into two major groups: those that join grammatically equal words or word groups and those that join grammatically unequal words or word groups. This chapter will focus on those conjunctions that join equals. Recognizing conjunctions and understanding their patterns of usage will, among other things, enable you to use commas and semicolons more appropriately.

LEVEL I

CAREER TIP

Understanding the differences among types of conjunctions will help you use proper sentence structure and punctuate correctly.

COORDINATING CONJUNCTIONS

Coordinating conjunctions connect words, phrases, and clauses of equal grammatical value or rank. The most common coordinating conjunctions are *and*, *or*, *but*, *so*, and *nor*. Notice in these sentences how coordinating conjunctions join grammatically equal elements.

We think your action is *illogical*, *unfair*, and *arbitrary*. (Here the conjunction *and* joins adjectives, which are grammatically equal words.)
Give serious thought *to your letters* and *to reader reaction*. (Here *and* joins prepositional phrases, which are grammatically equal phrases.)
Mr. Freeman opens the mail, but *Ms. Chen fills the orders*. (Here *but* joins independent clauses, which are grammatically equal clauses.)

Phrases and Clauses

A group of related words without a subject and a verb is called a **phrase**. You are already familiar with verb phrases and prepositional phrases. It is not important that you be able to identify the other kinds of phrases (such as infinitive, gerund, and participial), but it is very important that you be able to distinguish phrases from clauses.

The alarm was coming from another part of the building.

phrase phrase phrase

A group of related words that include a subject and a verb is a **clause**.

We interviewed three applicants, and we decided to hire Mr. Lee.

clause clause

Karen is interested in a job in accounting, but she wants to travel also.

clause clause

phrase phrase

Salaries begin at $35,000 annually, and they can reach over $70,000.

clause clause

Clauses often contain phrases, as illustrated in the last sentence.

STUDY TIP

Clauses have both subjects and verbs. Phrases do not. Clauses may have phrases within them.

Simple and Compound Sentences

A **simple sentence** has one independent clause—that is, a clause that can stand alone. A **compound sentence** has two or more independent clauses.

We agreed to lease the equipment. (Simple sentence)

Our Travel Services Department planned the sales trip, but some salespeople also made private excursions. (Compound sentence)

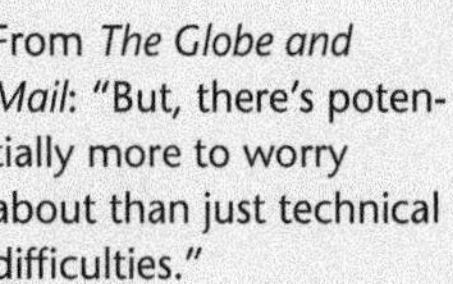

BE THE EDITOR

From *The Globe and Mail*: "But, there's potentially more to worry about than just technical difficulties."

Punctuating Compound Sentences Using Coordinating Conjunctions

When coordinating conjunctions (*and, or, but, nor, for, yet, so*) join clauses in a compound sentence, place a comma before the conjunction.

We can handle our employee payroll internally, *or* we can outsource it to a reputable firm. (Use a comma before *or* to join two independent clauses.)

You can check your account balances online, *and* you can pay your bills electronically. (Use a comma before *and* to join two independent clauses.)

STUDY TIP

An easy way to remember the seven coordinating conjunctions is to think of the acronym *FANBOYS*. Each letter stands for one of the coordinating conjunctions: *for, and, nor, but, or, yet,* and *so*.

When a coordinating conjunction connects short compound sentences, you may omit the comma. Consider a sentence short when each clause contains no more than five words.

Stephanie received the message *and* she responded immediately.

Do not use commas when coordinating conjunctions join compound verbs, objects, or phrases.

The bank will notify you of each transaction and will send you a monthly statement. (No comma needed because *and* joins the compound verbs of a single independent clause.)

Thomas Edison said that colleges should not have to choose between lighting their buildings *and* enlightening their students. (No comma needed because *and* joins the compound objects of the prepositional phrase beginning with *between*.)

Shareholders are expected to attend the meeting *or* to send in their proxies. (No comma needed because *or* joins two infinitive phrases.)

Complete the reinforcement exercises for Level I on pages 244–245.

LEVEL II

CONJUNCTIVE ADVERBS

Conjunctive adverbs may also be used to connect equal sentence elements. Because conjunctive adverbs are used to effect a transition from one thought to another and because they may consist of more than one word, they are also often called **transitional expressions**. The most common conjunctive adverbs and adverb phrases follow.

accordingly	however	on the contrary
also	in fact	on the other hand
consequently	in other words	otherwise
for example	in the meantime	that is
for instance	likewise	then
furthermore	moreover	therefore
hence	nevertheless	thus

In the following compound sentences, observe that conjunctive adverbs join clauses of equal grammatical value. Note that semicolons (not commas) are used before conjunctive adverbs that join independent clauses. Commas should immediately follow conjunctive adverbs of two or more syllables. Note also that the word following a semicolon is not capitalized (unless, of course, it is a proper noun).

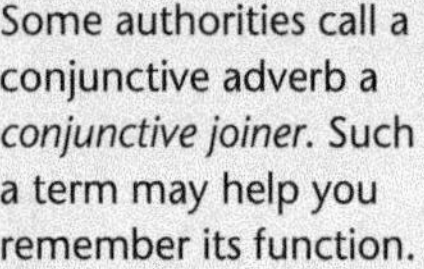

STUDY TIP

Some authorities call a conjunctive adverb a *conjunctive joiner*. Such a term may help you remember its function.

Electricians rewired the equipment room; *nevertheless,* fuses continued to blow.

Some equipment requires separate outlets; *consequently,* we installed new outlets.

Equipment expenditures are high this quarter; *on the other hand,* the new equipment will reduce labour costs.

Generally, no comma is used after one-syllable conjunctive adverbs such as *hence, thus,* and *then.*

Competition among computer manufacturers is intensive; *hence* prices have decreased over the years.

The use of handheld phones while driving endangers safety; *thus* many countries have passed legislation forbidding their use.

STUDY TIP

Use a semicolon with a conjunctive adverb ONLY when you are joining two complete sentences.

Distinguishing Conjunctive Adverbs From Parenthetical Adverbs

Many words that function as conjunctive adverbs may also serve as parenthetical (interrupting) adverbs. **Parenthetical adverbs**, such as *however, therefore,* and *consequently,* may be used to effect transitions from one thought to another within a clause. Use semicolons only with conjunctive adverbs that join independent clauses. Use commas to set off parenthetical adverbs that interrupt the flow of a sentence.

The chief is, *however,* an excellent administrator. (Adverb used parenthetically)

The chief is an excellent administrator; *however,* he does not tell others of his strengths. (Adverb used to join two independent clauses)

The discount will, *furthermore,* be increased after six years.

Policyholders are eligible for a discount only after three years; *furthermore,* the discount will be increased after six years.

We believe, *on the other hand,* that our sales will only continue to grow.

We believe that our sales will continue to grow; *on the other hand,* our costs will simultaneously increase.

Complete the reinforcement exercises for Level II on pages 246–248.

LEVEL III

CORRELATIVE CONJUNCTIONS

So far we have studied two kinds of conjunctions used to join grammatically equal sentence elements: coordinating conjunctions (used to join equal words, phrases, and clauses) and conjunctive adverbs (used to transition between grammatically equal clauses in compound sentences). Correlative conjunctions form the third and final group of conjunctions that join grammatically equal sentence elements.

Correlative conjunctions are always paired: *both . . . and, not only . . . but (also), either . . . or, neither . . . nor.* When greater emphasis is desired, these paired conjunctions are used instead of coordinating conjunctions. Notice the difference in these examples when correlative conjunctions are used:

Your iPhone is on the counter *or* on the desk.

Your iPhone is *either* on the counter *or* on the desk. (More emphatic)

Birks offers excellent customer service *and* a lenient return policy.

Birks offers *not only* excellent customer service *but also* a lenient return policy. (More emphatic)

When you use correlative conjunctions, place them so that the words, phrases, or clauses being joined are **parallel** in construction (have the same grammatical form).

Not parallel:	Either he was working in Victoria or in Nanaimo.
Parallel:	He was working *either* in Victoria *or* in Nanaimo. (Prepositional phrases after both *either* and *or*)
Not parallel:	She was not only gracious, but she was also kind.
Parallel:	She was *not only* gracious *but also* kind. (Adjectives after both *not only* and *but also*)
Not parallel:	I neither have the time nor the energy for this.
Parallel:	I have *neither* the time *nor* the energy for this. (Noun phrases after both *neither* and *nor*)

Complete the reinforcement exercises for Level III on pages 249–250.

BE THE EDITOR

From the *Toronto Star*: "Toronto Hydro said the initial outages were caused by both weather-related issues as well as transmission problems with Hydro One."

NAME ______________________

CHAPTER 13 ■ Reinforcement Exercises

LEVEL I

A. **(Self-check)** Write *a*, *b*, or *c* in the space provided to describe the following sentences.

a = A comma correctly punctuates a compound sentence.

b = The sentence is not compound; thus the comma should be omitted.

c = Although the sentence is compound, the clauses are too short to require a comma.

EXAMPLE: It rained most of the morning, but stopped in the afternoon. ____b____

1. A job opportunity has come open in Operations, but it requires someone with more experience. ______
2. I didn't expect a profit, nor fear a loss. ______
3. Product specialists must know how to use all our products, and should be familiar with how to maintain them. ______
4. The photocopier isn't working right, yet the technician couldn't find anything wrong with it. ______
5. Thank you for applying for admission, and for sending us your résumé. ______
6. Our radio ad is airing four times a day, but none of us has heard it yet. ______
7. Email your résumé, or drop it off. ______
8. Ed worked at a courier company for four years before he started here, and at a construction company for three years before that. ______
9. One upscale restaurant received so many complaints about cellphone use that it set up a cellphone lounge, and banished the use of cellphones elsewhere. ______
10. Our online store accepts Apple Pay, but our brick-and-mortar store does not. ______

Check your answers.

B. A simple sentence has one independent clause. A compound sentence has two or more independent clauses. Indicate with a check mark whether the following sentences, all of which are punctuated correctly, are simple or compound. *Hint:* A sentence is not compound unless the words preceding and following a conjunction form independent clauses. If these groups of words could not stand alone as sentences, the sentence is not compound.

	Simple	Compound
1. The flights have been scheduled and the hotel rooms are booked.	______	______
2. James Thomas conducted research on blogs and shared his findings with other department members.	______	______
3. The hotel restaurant is providing one free meal to conference attendees, and some downtown restaurants are offering discounts.	______	______

TEAR HERE

4. The recently constructed corporate headquarters contains attractive executive offices, but the structure has few support facilities for employees. ____________ ____________

5. The recently constructed corporate headquarters contains attractive executive offices but few support facilities for employees. ____________ ____________

6. Our controller is looking for ways to cut costs, so only two company representatives will attend this year's trade show. ____________ ____________

7. Management trainees are sent to all our branch offices in this country and to some of the branch offices in South America and Europe. ____________ ____________

8. Research the target company, and then decide what to wear to the interview. ____________ ____________

9. Some small-business owners are unhappy with the tax increases and plan to protest. ____________ ____________

10. Sonia will speak to the committee on Friday and hopes to persuade its members to adopt her conservation plan. ____________ ____________

C. Add any necessary commas in the following sentences. In the space provided, write the number of commas you inserted. Write *0* if no commas are needed.

EXAMPLE: Keegan was in the office on Monday, but he worked from home the rest of the week. ____1____

1. Some employees think their email should be confidential but courts generally uphold an employer's right to monitor messages. ____________

2. A 2019 report showed that Indigenous-owned businesses contribute over $30 billion a year to Canada's gross domestic product and estimated annual contributions would grow to $100 billion by 2024. ____________

3. Lionel left work an hour early Monday and he was absent Tuesday. ____________

4. He received a call and then he left. ____________

5. The website's advertising revenue must increase this year or we will have to re-evaluate our strategy. ____________

6. Sole proprietors file only personal taxes but they also must collect and remit HST if they earn $30,000 or more. ____________

7. Periods of stock market growth are called *bull markets* and periods of stock market decline are known as *bear markets*. ____________

8. Some raw materials will have to be imported and we'll have to hire skilled equipment operators but then production can begin. ____________

9. Some software can detect potentially troublesome words or even identify high-pressure sales tactics in email messages. ____________

10. Charles Goodyear invented a process leading to the manufacture of rubber but he failed to benefit from it and died in poverty. ____________

TEAR HERE

NAME ____________________

LEVEL II

A. **(Self-check)** Select adverbs and conjunctions have been italicized in the following sentences. Add any necessary commas and semicolons. In the space provided, write the number of punctuation marks you inserted. Be prepared to explain your choices.

EXAMPLE: Some loans must be secured; *therefore*, the borrower must supply collateral. ___2___

1. At 33, Grand Chief Billy Morin brings to the role his youth as well as a strong business background *thus* he hopes to be a bridge between generations. ________
2. New ergonomic workstations *consequently* have been ordered. ________
3. Bill Gates believes in giving back *therefore* he created the Bill & Melinda Gates Foundation. ________
4. People are increasingly taking precautions to avoid identity theft *however* having any online presence increases identity theft risk. ________
5. Some people are surprised to learn *however* that children are among those most targeted by identity thieves. ________
6. Revised employee manuals should be distributed *on the other hand* the manual could just be posted on the intranet. ________
7. Devi did *nevertheless* pick up the printed copies she needed immediately. ________
8. Your payment is now three months overdue *hence* we are terminating your account. ________
9. Liam *on the other hand* changed jobs whenever the urge struck. ________
10. Acquiring a new customer costs a business six to seven times more than retaining a current one *nevertheless* many businesses don't prioritize customer service. ________

Check your answers.

B. Add any necessary commas and semicolons. In the space provided, write the number of punctuation marks you inserted. Be prepared to explain your choices.

EXAMPLE: Too many staff members missed the seminar; therefore, attendance will be mandatory in the future. ___2___

1. People new to supervisory roles in fact often struggle to balance personal and professional relationships in the workplace. ________
2. The First Nation is accepting applications for the lease of some of its land furthermore the community is open to new business development. ________
3. Attendance at the meeting was good nevertheless many residents were opposed to the plan. ________
4. I can check my account balance online and then pay my bills electronically. ________
5. A recent report shows that more than 60 percent of Canadian companies have boards without female members in fact only 18.1 percent of director seats were held by women in 2017. ________

TEAR HERE

6. The new company car has better-than-average gas mileage but costs more to run than a hybrid would have. ______

7. We are moreover pleased with its manoeuvrability and handling. ______

8. A detailed sales sheet will be released next week in the meantime you will find the information you need in the product manual. ______

9. Automobile repair costs are skyrocketing consequently car insurance premiums are rising sharply. ______

10. Please place your order immediately or you will not be eligible for the discount. ______

11. Our loyalty program requires customers to choose between using their points sooner and saving their points for a higher discount. ______

12. Bell Mobility needed data concerning cellphone use therefore the company conducted a survey. ______

13. Several employees were using business cellphones for personal use thus the company clarified its policies regarding company-issued cellphones. ______

14. A new building can likely be constructed to house the equipment otherwise we'll have to rewire the store room for it. ______

15. Some companies require employees to carry wireless devices with location-tracking software however many employees find this practice intrusive. ______

16. The companies however say that they have the right to monitor their employees' whereabouts during work hours. ______

17. Tim Hortons' rewards program has reduced overall company profits for several quarters but the franchise's new offerings are expected to increase sales. ______

18. The parent company is making plans nevertheless to expand its operations in Asia. ______

19. Not all employees are allowed to book days off this summer for example new hires don't acquire vacation time for three months. ______

20. Two-thirds of our current jobs in progress for example were contracted more than a year ago. ______

C. Write compound sentences using the conjunctions and conjunctive adverbs shown below. Be sure to punctuate each sentence correctly.

1. however ______

______

______

2. but ______

______

______

3. therefore ______

______

______

TEAR HERE

4. otherwise ______

5. and ______

6. meanwhile ______

7. or ______

8. then ______

TEAR HERE

NAME ______________________________

LEVEL III

A. **(Self-check)** Select the more effective version of each of the following sentence pairs. Write its letter in the space provided.

1. (a) She sent the letter either on Monday or Tuesday.
(b) She sent the letter on either Monday or Tuesday. ____________

2. (a) Alex Gores did not attend the meeting, and neither did Adanna Jordan.
(b) Neither Alex Gores nor Adanna Jordan attended the meeting. ____________

3. (a) Our objectives are both to improve customer relations and increase sales.
(b) Our objectives are both to improve customer relations and to increase sales. ____________

4. (a) She neither called nor emailed to say she would be absent.
(b) Neither did she call nor email to say she would be absent. ____________

5. (a) The front seats are reserved for either family members or close friends.
(b) The front seats are either reserved for family members or close friends. ____________

6. (a) The new network is not only faster but also more efficient.
(b) Not only is the new network faster but also more efficient. ____________

7. (a) Neither did the staff finish the proposals nor the contracts.
(b) The staff finished neither the proposals nor the contracts. ____________

8. (a) The agent cannot act on the behalf of both the buyer and the seller.
(b) The agent cannot act both on the behalf of the buyer and of the seller. ____________

9. (a) My sister will look for either a marketing job this summer or go back to school for an MBA.
(b) My sister will either look for a marketing job this summer or go back to school for an MBA. ____________

10. (a) We need signatures not only on the contract but also on the waiver.
(b) We need signatures on not only the contract but also on the waiver. ____________

Check your answers.

B. Which of these sentence pairs is more effective? Write its letter in the space provided.

1. (a) The company will either open a branch in Calgary or in Edmonton.
(b) The company will open a branch in either Calgary or Edmonton. ____________

2. (a) The head office's travel counsellor will not only plan your trip but also make your reservations.
(b) Not only will the head office's travel counsellor plan your trip, but also your reservations will be made. ____________

3. (a) The sign and the awning above the door both need to be replaced this summer.
(b) Both the sign and the awning above the door need to be replaced this summer. ____________

4. (a) Not only does a product carry an expressed warranty but also an implied warranty.
(b) A product carries not only an expressed warranty but also an implied warranty. ____________

5. (a) We must receive either your payment or a reason for nonpayment.
(b) Either we must receive your payment or a reason why you cannot pay. ____________

TEAR HERE

C. Rewrite the following sentences to make them more effective.

1. Either shares can be purchased online, or they can be purchased from a broker.

2. Neither the employees were happy with the proposed cutbacks in benefits, and nor were the managers.

3. Self-governing agreements give First Nations not only the rights to enact laws within their communities, but they also allow for independent management and zoning of their land.

4. Our customer service rep will process your return, and she will ship out replacements too.

5. Foto-Nation not only patented red-eye detection for cameras but also software that detects smiles.

D. **Writing Exercise.** Your instructor may ask you to complete this exercise on a separate sheet.

Write four original sentences, one to illustrate each of the following: a simple sentence, a compound sentence, a parenthetical adverb, and a pair of correlative conjunctions. Label each sentence. Then write six sentences using different conjunctive adverbs from the list on page 242.

E. **Review of Levels I, II, and III.** Select the most suitable conjunction or conjunctive adverb to complete each of the sentences below. Write its letter in the space provided.

1. The standard warranty on the watch has expired, (a) and, (b) but an extended warranty wasn't purchased. ______
2. Huan has responded to neither my emails (a) or, (b) nor my voice messages. ______
3. Tammy doesn't like to exercise, (a) so, (b) yet she is disciplined enough to go to the gym three times a week. ______
4. The introduction of electronic mail was expected to make employees more productive; (a) nevertheless, (b) however, on average, employees spend 28 percent of their time responding to email. ______
5. Crowdfunding has become a primary source of startup funds; (a) furthermore, (b) therefore, entrepreneurs are using it to get a measure of demand for the product. ______

TEAR HERE

POSTTEST

Add any necessary commas or semicolons to the following sentences. Write *C* if a sentence is correct.

1. We are opening seven positions this month then we'll open eight more in January.
2. We are posting the job announcement online and also asking for employee referrals.
3. The cost of our raw materials is increasing consequently the price of our product must also increase.
4. We are convinced nevertheless that our products will continue to be competitive in today's market.
5. The store is relocating so we are limiting orders of new inventory.
6. We are not sure however whether the new location will be ready on schedule.
7. Technology is changing rapidly therefore most employees need regular retraining.
8. Editing skills are now in great demand throughout the media industry hence we are developing courses to meet this demand.

Circle the letter of the sentence that is more effective.

9. (a) Neither can we assemble the desk nor set up the workstation until April 1.
   (b) We can neither assemble the desk nor set up the workstation until April 1.
10. (a) Malware not only includes viruses but also spyware.
    (b) Malware includes not only viruses but also spyware.

EDITOR'S CHALLENGE

The following email message and memo contain errors in spelling, punctuation, and language principles covered thus far, as well as other common errors. Use standard proofreading marks to show necessary corrections.

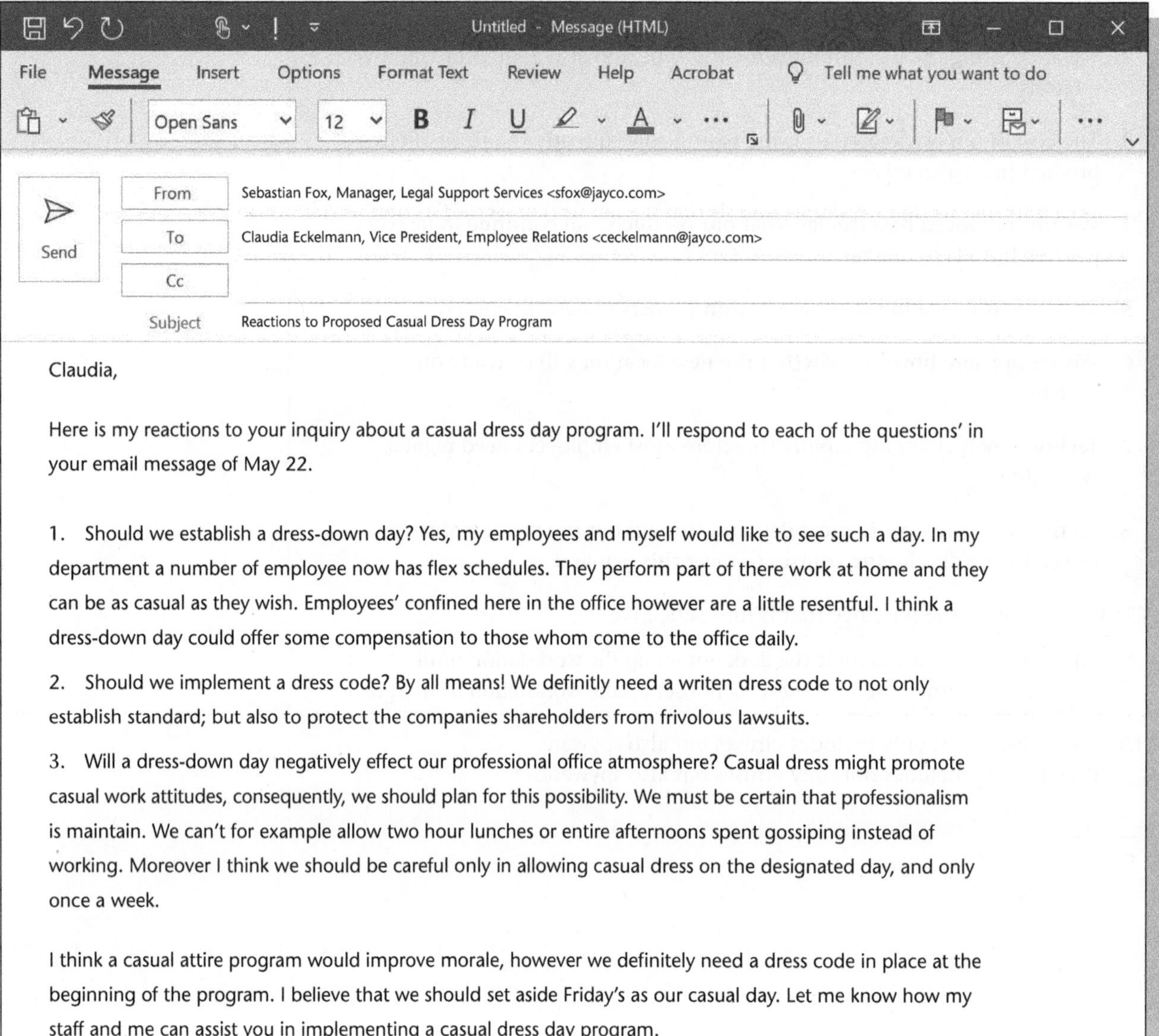

Untitled - Message (HTML)

From: Sebastian Fox, Manager, Legal Support Services <sfox@jayco.com>

To: Claudia Eckelmann, Vice President, Employee Relations <ceckelmann@jayco.com>

Cc:

Subject: Reactions to Proposed Casual Dress Day Program

Claudia,

Here is my reactions to your inquiry about a casual dress day program. I'll respond to each of the questions' in your email message of May 22.

1. Should we establish a dress-down day? Yes, my employees and myself would like to see such a day. In my department a number of employee now has flex schedules. They perform part of there work at home and they can be as casual as they wish. Employees' confined here in the office however are a little resentful. I think a dress-down day could offer some compensation to those whom come to the office daily.

2. Should we implement a dress code? By all means! We definitly need a writen dress code to not only establish standard; but also to protect the companies shareholders from frivolous lawsuits.

3. Will a dress-down day negatively effect our professional office atmosphere? Casual dress might promote casual work attitudes, consequently, we should plan for this possibility. We must be certain that professionalism is maintain. We can't for example allow two hour lunches or entire afternoons spent gossiping instead of working. Moreover I think we should be careful only in allowing casual dress on the designated day, and only once a week.

I think a casual attire program would improve morale, however we definitely need a dress code in place at the beginning of the program. I believe that we should set aside Friday's as our casual day. Let me know how my staff and me can assist you in implementing a casual dress day program.

Sebastian

TEAR HERE

CONSOLIDATED INDUSTRIES

Interoffice Memo

Date: January 28, 202x

To: All Employees

FROM: Brandon George, Manager

SUBJECT: Reducing Overnight Delivery Costs

Overnight delivery services are speedy but they costing us too much money. Here at Consolidated we have see our use of these services increasingly devour a major portion of our shipping budget. It seems that any one who wants to send something to a customer or a vendor automatically send it by FedEx. We have corporate rates with FedEx, however, we are still spending too much on overnight deliveries.

To avoid future restrictions imposed by the CEO I'm asking you to voluntarily reduce your use of these delivery services by 50 percent in the next two month period.

Rather then face a ban on all delivery services, let's work together to reduce our costs. Here's some suggestions:

1. Ask yourself weather the recipient will require the material immediately. If not, use a cheaper method.
2. Send messages either by fax or email. A long distance fax costs only about 35 cents and local messages and email messages cost nothing.
3. Use the FedEx or UPS account number off the recipient whenever posible.
4. Plan ahead so that you can use FedEx, or UPS ground service. These ground services usually take three to five days.

Some overnight shipments, of course are critical. However to retain our budget for those essential shipments, we must reduce our overall use by one half before April 1. If you can think of other ways to reduce overnight shipments, please call me at Ext. 213. I appreciate you helping to solve this problem.

For additional resources, please visit MindTap at login.cengage.com. Cengage | MINDTAP

TEAR HERE

CHAPTER 14

CONJUNCTIONS TO JOIN UNEQUALS

OBJECTIVES

When you have completed the materials in this chapter, you will be able to do the following:

LEVEL I

- Distinguish among dependent clauses, independent clauses, and phrases
- Recognize subordinating conjunctions and relative pronouns functioning as conjunctions

LEVEL II

- Punctuate introductory and terminal dependent clauses
- Punctuate parenthetical, essential, and non-essential dependent clauses

LEVEL III

- Recognize simple, compound, complex, and compound–complex sentences
- Convert simple sentences into a variety of more complex patterns

PRETEST

In the following sentences, add any necessary commas. Write *C* if a sentence is correct.

1. When you receive an email attachment be sure to check it for a virus.
2. Management hasn't yet spoken to the employees who were involved in the incident.
3. We hope to move to new facilities next year although no definite plans have yet been made.
4. While we were studying at college we lived in residence.
5. If possible the marketing intern should spend a day in the Art Department.

(continued)

PRETEST *(CONTINUED)*

6. Sherilyn said that Kala who works in our Marketing Department will be leaving next month.
7. The AG Equipment account which was opened just last month has already been closed.
8. Although several applicants passed the test no one has been hired yet.
9. We will make a decision as soon as the interviews are finished.
10. The process that we have in place is quite efficient.

In Chapter 13 we studied conjunctions that joined equal sentence elements such as words, phrases, and clauses. These equal sentence parts were joined by coordinating conjunctions (such as *and, or, but*), conjunctive adverbs (such as *therefore, however, consequently*), and correlative conjunctions (such as *either . . . or, not only . . . but also*). Now let's look at a group of conjunctions that join unequal sentence parts.

LEVEL I

BE THE EDITOR

An ad for Swiffer: "This Swiffer duster starter kit . . . [leaves] floors up to three times cleaner than a mop or broom."

SUBORDINATING CONJUNCTIONS

To join unequal sentence elements (i.e., an independent clause and a dependent clause), use a **subordinating conjunction**. A list of the most common subordinating conjunctions follows.

after	because	since	until
although	before	so (that)	when
as	if	that	where
as if	in order that	though	whether
as though	provided (that)	unless	while

You should become familiar with this list of conjunctions, but do not feel that you need to memorize them. You can generally recognize a subordinating conjunction by the way it limits, or subordinates, the clause it introduces. In the clause *because he always paid with cash*, the subordinating conjunction *because* limits the meaning of the clause it introduces. The clause beginning with *because* is incomplete and could not stand alone as a sentence.

INDEPENDENT AND DEPENDENT CLAUSES

Clauses that can stand alone are said to be **independent**. They have subjects and verbs and make sense by themselves. In other words, they are sentences.

Business writing should be concise. (One main clause)
Business writing should be concise, and it should be clear as well. (Two main clauses)
Shauna Croix writes many email messages, but Kathleen Young prefers to make a phone call. (Two main clauses)

Clauses that cannot stand alone are said to be **dependent**. They have subjects and verbs, but they depend upon other clauses for the completion of their meaning. Dependent clauses are often introduced by subordinating conjunctions and may either precede or follow independent clauses.

When Sequoia wants a quick reply, she sends an email message. (The dependent clause, *When Sequoia wants a quick reply*, precedes the main clause.)

Since Sequoia writes many emails, she keeps her contacts file current. (The dependent clause, *Since Sequoia writes many emails*, precedes the main clause.)

Business emails are important because they represent the company. (The dependent clause, *because they represent the company*, comes after the main clause.)

STUDY TIP

Dependent clauses should never be written or punctuated as if they were complete sentences.

RELATIVE CLAUSES

The **relative pronouns** *who, whom, whose, which,* and *that* function just like conjunctions when they introduce dependent clauses. *Who, whom,* and *whose* are used to refer to persons. These pronouns may introduce either essential or non-essential clauses. *Which* refers to animals, things, or persons within a collective and introduces non-essential clauses (however, some professional writers will allow it to introduce some essential clauses, too). *That* refers to animals, things, or persons within a collective and introduces only essential clauses.

The part that is sometimes tricky is deciding whether a clause is essential or non-essential. An essential clause is one that is needed to identify the noun to which it refers (called its *antecedent*—see Chapter 5); therefore, no commas should separate an essential clause from its antecedent. Non-essential clauses contain information that the reader does not need to know; the main clause is understandable without this extra information. In some cases only the writer knows whether a clause is intended to be essential or non-essential. If a clause is non-essential, it should be set off from the rest of the sentence by commas. You'll learn more about punctuating these sentences in Level II.

Anyone *who* has a computer can create a website. (The relative pronoun *who* refers to a person, and it introduces an essential clause that limits the meaning of *Anyone*.)

A company *that* values its employees is likely to succeed. (The relative pronoun *that* refers to a thing and introduces an essential clause that limits the meaning of *company*.)

Bionym, *which* is based in Toronto, has created wearable technology that could replace passwords and personal identification numbers. (The relative pronoun *which* introduces a non-essential clause, which is set off by commas.)

Bionym is the company *that* introduced the Nymi. (The relative pronoun *that* introduces an essential clause and requires no commas.)

John Sylvan, *who* invented the Keurig coffeemaker, regrets creating the environmentally disastrous K-Cups. (The relative pronoun *who* introduces a non-essential clause and is set off by commas.)

Complete the reinforcement exercises for Level I on pages 261–263.

STUDY TIP

That and *which*, not *who* or *whom*, are used to refer to a business or a group of people acting as a unit (e.g., a committee).

ASK AN EDITOR

Question:
Can the word *that* be omitted from sentences? For example, *She said [that] she would come.*

Answer:
The conjunction *that* is frequently omitted in conversation and casual writing. However, it is important for writers to recognize that a missing *that* can make a sentence difficult to read or even make its meaning ambiguous. For absolute clarity, therefore, skilled writers include it.

LEVEL II

PUNCTUATION OF SENTENCES WITH DEPENDENT CLAUSES

Business and professional writers are especially concerned with clarity and accuracy. A misplaced or omitted punctuation mark can confuse a reader by altering the meaning of a sentence. The following guidelines for using commas help ensure clarity and consistency in writing. Some professional writers, however, take liberties with accepted conventions of

BE THE EDITOR

From classified ads in local newspapers: "LAWNMORE SHOP" and a house for sale with "walking closets."

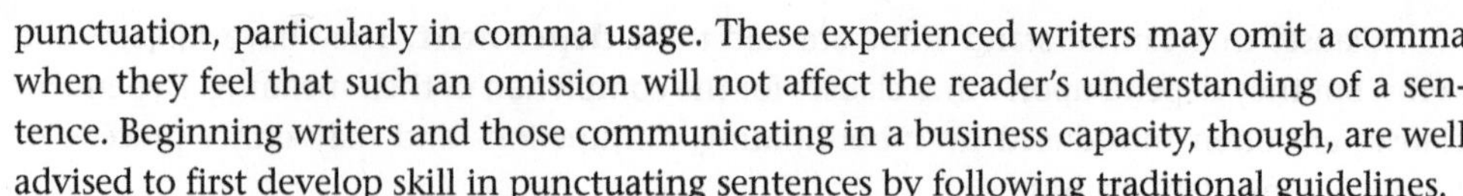

punctuation, particularly in comma usage. These experienced writers may omit a comma when they feel that such an omission will not affect the reader's understanding of a sentence. Beginning writers and those communicating in a business capacity, though, are well advised to first develop skill in punctuating sentences by following traditional guidelines.

Introductory Dependent Clauses

Use a comma after a dependent (subordinate) clause that precedes an independent clause.

> *Before* they left the office, they finished the proposal.
> *Until* he returns, we cannot continue.
> *When* you are ready to start, let me know.

Use a comma after an introductory dependent clause even though the subject and verb may not be stated.

> *As* [it was] expected, the shipment is overdue.
> *If* [it is] possible, send a replacement immediately.
> *When* [they are] printed, your brochures will be distributed.

Terminal Dependent Clauses

Generally, a dependent clause introduced by a subordinating conjunction does not require a comma when the dependent clause is **terminal**, meaning that it falls at the end of a sentence.

> They finished the proposal *before* they left the office.
> We cannot continue *until* he returns.
> Let me know *when* you are ready to start.
> We will meet in person *so that* we can discuss some sensitive issues.

If, however, the dependent clause at the end of a sentence interrupts the flow of the sentence, provides non-essential information, and sounds as though it is an afterthought, use a comma.

> I know the cancelled cheque was returned, *although* I cannot find it now.
> We will ship the goods within the week, *if* that is satisfactory to you.

ASK AN EDITOR

Question:
I don't seem to be able to hear the difference between *than* and *then*. Can you explain it to me?

Answer:
The two words sound similar in ordinary speech, but they function quite differently. The conjunction *than* is used to make comparisons (*your phone rings more than mine*). The adverb *then* means "at that time" (*we must complete this task; then we will take our break*) or "as a consequence" (*if all the angles of the triangle are equal, then it must be equilateral*).

Parenthetical Clauses

A **parenthetical clause** adds additional information to a sentence. Within a sentence, dependent clauses that interrupt the flow of the sentence and are not necessary for the grammatical completeness of the sentence are set off by commas.

> The motion, *unless* you want further discussion, will be tabled at our next meeting.
> At our next meeting, *as long as* we have a quorum, the motion will be reconsidered.

Relative Clauses

You learned earlier that dependent clauses introduced by relative pronouns such as *who*, *that*, and *which* may be essential (restrictive) or non-essential (non-restrictive).

An **essential clause** is needed to clearly identify the noun to which it refers; therefore, no commas should separate this clause from its antecedent.

> Any employee *who missed the training* must attend a later session. (Relative pronoun *who* introduces an essential clause needed to identify *which* employee or employees must attend a later session.)

Parking permits *that were issued in the fall* must be validated for the spring. (Relative pronoun *that* introduces an essential clause needed to identify which parking permits must be validated.)

A **non-essential clause** contains information that is not needed to identify its antecedent. The main clause is understandable without this extra information. If the clause is non-essential, set it off from the rest of the sentence with commas. Notice that *two* commas are used to set off internal non-essential dependent clauses.

Amy Kertesz, *who missed the training*, must attend a later session. (Dependent clause not needed; the antecedent of the clause, *Amy Kertesz*, is clearly identified.)

Lot C parking permits, *which were issued in the fall*, must be validated for the spring. (Dependent clause not needed; the antecedent of the clause, *Lot C parking permits*, is clearly identified.)

Punctuation Review

The following three common sentence patterns are very important for you to study and understand. Notice particularly how the sentences are punctuated.

Independent clause(,) +	{ and / or / nor / but }	+ *Independent clause.*	(A comma is used when a coordinating conjunction joins independent clauses.)
Independent clause(;) +	{ therefore, / consequently, / however, / nevertheless, }	+ *Independent clause.*	(A semicolon is used when a conjunctive adverb joins independent clauses.)
{ Since / If / As / When }	*Dependent clause*(,)	+ *Independent clause.*	(A comma is used when a dependent clause precedes an independent clause.)

Now complete the reinforcement exercises for Level II on pages 264–265.

LEVEL III

SENTENCE VARIETY

To make their messages more interesting, good writers strive for variety in sentence structure. Notice the monotony and choppiness of a paragraph made up entirely of simple sentences:

The United States purchased Alaska from Russia in 1867. The exact boundary of the "panhandle" strip of coastline seemed fairly unimportant. The 1898 Gold Rush made this boundary significant. Both Canadians and Americans wanted to profit from the prospectors and their gold. The boundary dispute became extremely serious. A court of six judges was chosen. It decided 4 to 2 against Canada's version of the boundary. The decision outraged Canadians. One good consequence of this controversy was the International Joint Commission. It was set up in 1909 to settle boundary disputes.

Compare the following version of this paragraph, which uses dependent clauses and other structures to achieve greater sentence variety:

STUDY TIP

Relative clauses introduced by *that* are always essential; they require no commas.

ASK AN EDITOR

Question:
I have a lot of trouble with verbs in sentences like this: *She was one of approximately 20,000 Canadian women who (was or were) diagnosed with breast cancer last year.*

Answer:
You're not alone. Make your verb agree with its antecedent (*women*). One easy way to work with sentences like this is to change the order of the two clauses: *Of those Canadian women who were diagnosed with breast cancer last year, she was one.*

ASK AN EDITOR

Question:
I've often heard *so* and *so that* used interchangeably. Is it incorrect to use *so* to mean *so that*?

Answer:
Speakers and casual writers often use *so* as both the coordinating conjunction and the subordinating conjunction. For clarity, however, it is good practice to write *so that* when that is what you mean. Writing *so that* also helps you to identify its function in the sentence and, therefore, how to punctuate. The coordinating conjunction *so*, when it joins two independent clauses, requires a comma before it; the subordinating conjunction *so that* does not.

BE THE EDITOR

From a 1914 brochure quoted in *The National Post*: "Its streams that have run idly to the sea since the dawn of creation, will supply inexhaustible water-power."

When the United States purchased Alaska from Russia in 1867, the exact boundary of the "panhandle" strip of coastline seemed fairly unimportant. However, the 1898 Gold Rush made this boundary significant since both Canadians and Americans wanted to profit from the prospectors and their gold. After the boundary dispute had become extremely serious, a court of six judges was chosen and decided 4 to 2 against Canada's version of the boundary. Although the decision outraged Canadians, one good outcome of this controversy was the International Joint Committee, which was set up in 1909 to settle boundary disputes.

Recognizing the kinds of sentence structures available to writers and speakers is an important step in achieving effective expression. Let's review the three kinds of sentence structures that you have been studying and include a fourth category as well. In the examples below, independent clauses are marked by boldface type and dependent clauses by italic type.

Kind of Sentence	Minimum Requirement	Example
Simple	One independent clause	**The United States purchased Alaska from Russia in 1867.**
Compound	Two independent clauses	**The exact boundary of the "panhandle" strip of coastline seemed fairly unimportant**, but **the 1898 Gold Rush made this boundary significant**.
Complex	One independent clause and at least one dependent clause	*After the boundary dispute had become extremely serious,* **a court of six judges was chosen**.
Compound–complex	At least two independent clauses and one dependent clause	*When the United States purchased Alaska from Russia in 1867,* **the exact boundary of the "panhandle" strip of coastline seemed fairly unimportant**; however, **the 1898 Gold Rush made this boundary significant**.

Developing the ability to use a variety of sentence structures to facilitate effective communication takes practice and writing experience.

Start sharpening your skills with the Level III reinforcement exercises on pages 266–268.

NAME ______________________

CHAPTER 14 ■ Reinforcement Exercises

LEVEL I

A. **(Self-check)** In the space provided, indicate whether the following word groups are phrases (*P*), independent clauses (*I*), or dependent clauses (*D*). (Remember that phrases do not have both subjects and verbs.)

EXAMPLE: in the spring of the previous year ___P___

1. in the absence of further information ________
2. Microsoft and Google approved of the new Internet regulations ________
3. for the benefit of everyone affected by the merger ________
4. since the store was permanently closing ________
5. she agreed ________
6. yesterday customers were notified ________
7. before anyone had an opportunity to examine it carefully ________
8. when Hewlett-Packard was creating Silicon Valley ________
9. except for the Corporate Communications Department ________
10. our new pricing schedule takes effect January 1 ________

Check your answers.

B. In the space provided, indicate whether the following word groups are phrases (*P*), independent clauses (*I*), or dependent clauses (*D*). For clauses underline the subjects once and the verbs twice, and circle any subordinating conjunctions.

EXAMPLE: (until) we are able to assess the damage ___D___

1. after packages were lost this spring ________
2. so that employees may attend ________
3. then we were without Internet service for a full day ________
4. the link on the home page of the website ________
5. when he complimented Anuja's work ________
6. since Charles began working as a marketing representative ________
7. the conference attended by nine manufacturers and seventy retailers ________

TEAR HERE

8. she laid the employment contract on the desk ____________________

9. individual results are sent separately ____________________

10. during the final briefing last week ____________________

C. For the following sentences, determine the word that correctly completes each and write it in the space provided. Use the relative pronoun *which* only to introduce non-essential clauses (clauses that require commas) that refer to things.

1. We're seeking an e-commerce platform (who, which, that) integrates with Canada Post's shipping software. ____________________

2. The receptionist on the seventh floor, (who, which, that) answers the main phone line, is retiring in July. ____________________

3. T4 slips, (who, which, that) show employees' income and contributions, have to be delivered by employers by the end of February. ____________________

4. The data plan (who, which, that) best meets our company's needs will cost more than we budgeted. ____________________

5. Are you the one (who, which, that) processes refunds? ____________________

6. Is Stefan's computer the one (who, which, that) has AutoCAD on it? ____________________

7. Our team, (who, which, that) has authority to set its own work schedules, tries to rotate the overtime hours. ____________________

8. Any technology company (who, which, that) we partner with will help us improve our online customer experience. ____________________

9. The city council needs to come up with a plan (who, which, that) will satisfy all residents. ____________________

10. Employers are looking for workers (who, which, that) have good manners and communication skills. ____________________

D. For each sentence below, select a suitable subordinating conjunction from the list: *so that, although, unless, after, because*. Use each only once.

1. The company won't award bonuses this year ____________________ it sees an increase in profit over last year.

2. ____________________ Kobo is considered Canadian, it is a subsidiary of the Japanese company Rakuten.

3. Google's Toronto office is set up to encourage socializing ____________________ employees in different departments will talk to one another.

4. Fewer employees are driving their cars to work ____________________ the company is offering incentives for environmental consciousness.

5. ____________________ news of the companies' merger was leaked, the corporate communications department had to field many calls from the media.

TEAR HERE

E. Sort this group of words into three lists, and write them in the spaces below: *although, and, before, but, however, if, nor, or, then, therefore, thus, unless.*

Coordinating Conjunctions	**Conjunctive Adverbs**	**Subordinating Conjunctions**
______________	______________	______________
______________	______________	______________
______________	______________	______________
______________	______________	______________

F. Use your imagination to write complete sentences according to the following directions. Remember that clauses must contain subjects and verbs.

1. A sentence using *or* to connect two independent clauses ______________________________

____

____

2. A sentence using *although* to introduce a dependent clause ______________________________

____

____

3. A sentence using *when* to introduce a dependent clause ______________________________

____

____

4. A sentence using *until* to introduce a dependent clause ______________________________

____

____

5. A sentence using *and* to join two phrases ______________________________

____

____

NAME ______________________________

LEVEL II

A. **(Self-check)** Add any necessary commas in the following sentences. In the space provided, write the number of commas you inserted. Write *0* if no commas are needed. Do not add any commas that you cannot justify.

EXAMPLE: After we hiked to the summit, we pitched our tent. ___1___

1. Hugh Fishbourne who used to work for Manulife recently accepted a job at Allstate. ______
2. Before we make an investment decision we should do more research. ______
3. We should do more research before we make an investment decision. ______
4. A magazine that is featuring the 100 best places to work is now on the newsstands. ______
5. The latest production model unless it is altered drastically looks as if it will be a winner. ______
6. Any salesperson who sells more than the weekly quota will receive a bonus. ______
7. If desired custom finishes can be applied for a fee. ______
8. No decisions will be made until the executives analyze the fourth-quarter results. ______
9. National Public Relations which is Canada's largest public relations firm was consulted. ______
10. A profit-sharing plan for employees is now available although I believe the announcement will not be made until next week. ______

Check your answers.

B. Add any necessary commas in the following sentences. In the space provided, write the number of commas you inserted. Write *0* if no commas are needed. Be prepared to discuss the reasons for the commas you use.

1. Companies that offer good benefits packages attract more job applicants. ______
2. Amazon which offers excellent benefits attracts numerous job applicants. ______
3. If merchant fees weren't so high more small businesses would accept American Express credit cards. ______
4. The offering of company cars which has been a mainstay of executives' compensation packages will be discontinued in the new year. ______
5. I will process the 3M order tomorrow morning if that is soon enough. ______
6. When completed the newly created website will enable customers to track shipments. ______

TEAR HERE

7. In the coming fiscal year provided that enough funds are available we hope to expand our employee fitness program. ____________

8. Because many people are interested in Canadian Indigenous culture the Wei Wai Kum Nation's Thunderbird RV Park and Resort is 95 percent booked in its high season. ____________

9. The warranty that you refer to in your recent letter covers only merchandise brought to our shop for repair. ____________

10. Ray Rampersad who works in the Traffic Department received last month's merit award. ____________

11. A secretary who joined our staff only six months ago received this month's merit award. ____________

12. Although you said my order was shipped ten days ago I have not yet received it. ____________

13. I would like to give your suggestion more thought when I am not quite so preoccupied. ____________

14. Incorporation which can be done at either the federal level or the provincial or territorial level limits the liability of a business's shareholders. ____________

15. If you would like to apply for the position please contact me immediately. ____________

16. Please contact me immediately if you would like to apply for the position. ____________

17. A trade name although it is commonly mistaken for a trademark is not protected. ____________

18. We have received a directive to hold all shipments although I do not know why. ____________

19. Ellie Chang was asked to contact the person who is teaching the Lunch and Learn workshop. ____________

20. The walk-in fridge that was ordered last week will be delivered by the end of the month. ____________

TEAR HERE

NAME ______________________________

LEVEL III

A. **(Self-check)** Indicate the structure of the following sentences by writing the appropriate letter in the space provided:

a = simple sentence c = complex sentence

b = compound sentence d = compound–complex sentence

EXAMPLE: Because the systems were not connected and could not share information with each other, data had to be entered many times. ____c____

1. Mobile phone and data communication has transformed from a luxury into a necessity. ________
2. Since it passed the controversial ordinance, the city council has been besieged by calls. ________
3. Because a decision had to be announced quickly, a shareholders' meeting was scheduled for Monday, and a managers' meeting was arranged for Tuesday. ________
4. We are short-staffed, and other departments face a similar problem. ________
5. Allen was offered a sales position in Fredericton; therefore, he eagerly made plans to travel to New Brunswick, where he looked forward to beginning his sales career. ________
6. We will contact you only if you are selected for an interview. ________
7. The cost of the product increased, but sales continued to climb. ________
8. SecureDrop is an encrypted technology that some news outlets have adopted to allow people to share information with the media confidentially. ________
9. A dedicated employee who is well regarded by his or her peers should receive the award. ________
10. Your report should include photos or graphics and have plenty of white space. ________

Check your answers.

TEAR HERE

B. Rewrite the following groups of simple sentences into *one* sentence for each group. Add coordinating conjunctions, conjunctive adverbs, and subordinating conjunctions as needed to create more effective complex, compound, and compound–complex sentences. Identify the type of sentence you have created.

EXAMPLE: Canadian Tire needed an executive assistant. It advertised online. It finally hired a recent graduate. The graduate had excellent skills.

After advertising online for an executive assistant, Canadian Tire finally hired a recent graduate who had excellent skills. (complex sentence)

1. The Osoyoos band owns and operates Nk'Mip Cellars. Nk'Mip Cellars is the first Indigenous-owned winery in North America. Nk'Mip Cellars is situated in the Sonoran Desert. The Sonoran is Canada's only desert.

2. Skilled writers save time for themselves. They also save time for their readers. They organize their ideas into logical patterns. They organize their ideas before sitting down at their computers.

3. No cases of COVID-19 have been proven to be transmitted through cash. The trend toward using apps such as Apple Pay and Google Pay has accelerated in the wake of the pandemic. Public concerns have central banks looking more closely at digital currencies.

4. My coworker has been off work for six weeks. She has been ill. I have had to work some extra shifts.

5. Farrah Gashi is a single parent. She has merchandising experience. Farrah started a mall-based chain of stores. These stores sell fashionable, durable children's clothing.

6. Lily studied geology. She quit her job to follow her passion making and selling one-of-a-kind jewellery. She hasn't looked back.

7. Your account with us has been inactive for several years. We cannot extend credit to you. We have expressed this in previous letters.

____

____

____

C. Writing Exercise. Your instructor may ask you to complete this exercise on a separate sheet.

First, write four original sentences to illustrate these patterns: simple sentence, compound sentence, complex sentence, and compound–complex sentence. Then write a sentence using each of these subordinating conjunctions: *if, after, as,* and *unless*. In addition, write one sentence in which *who* introduces an essential clause and one in which *who* introduces a non-essential clause.

POSTTEST

Add any necessary commas in the following sentences. In the space provided, write the number of commas you inserted. Write *C* if a sentence is correct.

1. Please email Kris Bertrand if you have any questions. ________
2. Because quick turn-around is important in our industry we require employees to use text messaging to communicate. ________
3. When necessary we make rush shipments of products that we have in our current inventory. ________
4. The software demonstration by Mali Kaul who represents DataTech Products will be Friday. ________
5. Any manager or employee who is unable to attend the Friday demonstration should call me. ________
6. Ever since the manager position opened department employees have shown much more initiative. ________
7. "Green entrepreneurs" are people who create businesses that work toward a more environmentally friendly world. ________
8. Scientists have created lab-grown meat which is intended to reduce some of the greenhouse gas emissions of traditional farming. ________
9. After the company announced its first-quarter profit shares rose almost 10 percent. ________
10. Joe DiPasqua whom Serena hired to fill the management trainee position used to work at an elite golf course. ________

TEAR HERE

EDITOR'S CHALLENGE

The following memo and email message contain errors in spelling, punctuation, and language principles covered thus far, as well as other common errors. Use proofreading marks to show all necessary corrections.

Dee Kirkland Modelling and Dance Studios

MEMORANDUM

DATE: February 21, 202x

TO: Karen Archer, Stacy Janisse, Eduardo Solano, Robin Haynes, Mayer Rubin, Tom Winters

FROM: Dee Kirkland

SUBJECT: March 1 Fashion Show at Westland Plaza Hotel

Thanks to you acceptional students for agreeing to participate in this years fashion show at the Westland Plaza Hotel.

Show time is 8:15 p.m., if possible you should be there at 6:30 to prepare. Rehearsals is scheduled for Tuesday, February 25, and Thursday, February 27, from 5 to 6:15 p.m. Its important for you to be prompt!

Participants in the fashion show will not be payed but we have a bonus for you. Mr. Lon McHenry who is this years sponsor is one of those people who likes to encourage young models, therefore he will allow you to by any of the item in the show at 20 percent below his cost. The cloths are all from CAL SPORT. Which specializes in informal fashions. Since shoes are not supplied everyone should bring there own casual shoes or running shoes.

Of all the students in the school, you were chosen to participate in the show because you have exhibit excellent potential and professionalism. I want you to treat this show like it was any paid professional job. This fashion show is bigger than any show in the area, please consider it a extension of your training. If you succeed here you can count on farther success as you grow in your career.

TEAR HERE

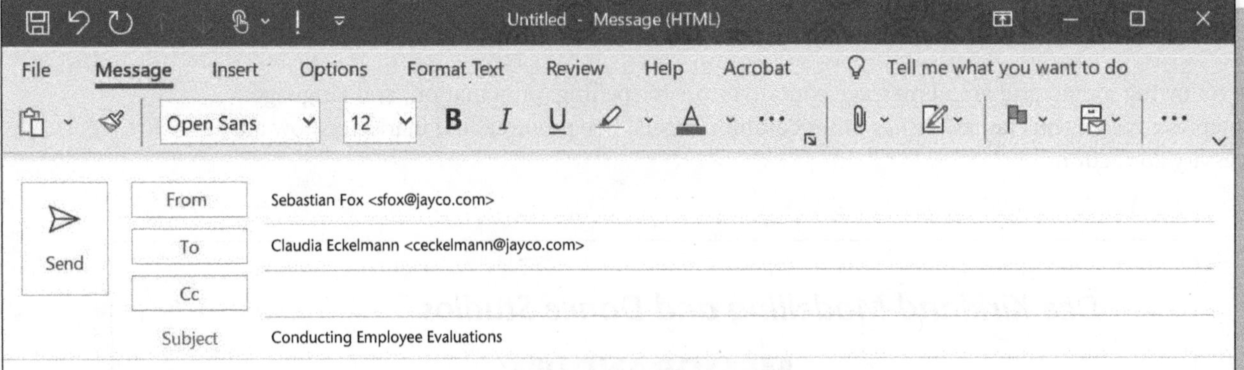

From: Sebastian Fox <sfox@jayco.com>

To: Claudia Eckelmann <ceckelmann@jayco.com>

Cc:

Subject: Conducting Employee Evaluations

Claudia,

I recently learn that one of our employee's has filed a law suit against the company because of comments a supervisor made during a performance evaluation. This is a unfortunate even that could of been prevented. Here are a list of tips that you should share with all manager's.

1. Before you can accurately evaluate an employees performance you need to establish a system to measure that performance. Therefore; you need to develop performance standards and goals for each employee. Remember to remain sensitive of the employees needs. Plan on sharing these standards and goals in writeing with the employee.

2. Monitor the preformance of each employee throughout the year. Keep a log for each worker and note memorable incidents of projects involving that worker. Although many managers are understandably adverse to placing negative comments in files, such comments must be included as part of the evaluation process. Any employee, who does something exceptional, should be given immediate feed back. If you give this feedback orally make a written note of the conversation for the employees personnell file.

3. At least once a year, formally evaluate the worker by writing a performance appraisal and by meeting with the worker. At the meeting let your employee know what you think they did good, and which areas the employee maybe able to improve. Be sure and discuss the standards and goals you set earlier. Listen carefully to your employee's comments and take good notes.

Giving evaluations can be difficult, however, careful planning and preparation will make the process go smooth. Be specific, give deadlines, be honest, and be realistic. Following these steps is an excellent way to help the company avoid legal problems. Please email me with any questions.

Sebastian
Manager, Legal Support Services

NAME ______________________

UNIT 4 REVIEW ■ Chapters 11–14 (Self-Check)

Begin your review by rereading Chapters 11 through 14. Then check your comprehension of those chapters by completing the exercises that follow. Compare your responses with those provided at the end of the book, page 531.

LEVEL I

For the following sentences, write the letter of the correct answer in the space provided.

1. I've never read a (a) worse, (b) worst sell sheet. ____
2. In comparing the three shipping companies, we decided that Purolator is (a) most, (b) more economical. ____
3. Siti was asked to present on behalf of Jim with only (a) a, (b) an hour's notice. ____
4. The committee members (a) should have, (b) should of voted to adopt the proposal. ____
5. The service contract is (a) to, (b) too expensive. ____
6. No one but Patricia and (a) him, (b) he has a key to the executive boardroom. ____
7. Can I borrow some change (a) off of, (b) from you? ____
8. We're seeking a bright young person (a) that, (b) whom we can train. ____
9. The group of words *if you will include us* is a(n) (a) phrase, (b) independent clause, (c) dependent clause. ____

In the following sentences, add any necessary commas. In the space provided, write the number of commas you inserted. Write *0* if no commas are needed.

10. Kristen first took a job in Moose Jaw but later decided to move to Regina. ____
11. Gianni will review the books with the accountant or he will review them on his own and then meet with the accountant. ____
12. WestJet scheduled new flights on its Vancouver–Edmonton route and also lowered Calgary–Vancouver fares. ____
13. Women have made significant progress toward equality but a lot of work remains to be done. ____

LEVEL II

For the following sentences, write the letter of the correct answer in the space provided.

14. The salesperson clearly feels (a) bad, (b) badly that the warranty expired just before the motor failed. ____
15. We hear complaints on a (a) case-by-case, (b) case by case basis. ____

TEAR HERE

16. If you have (a) less, (b) fewer than ten items, you may use the express checkout. ________

17. He's acting (a) as if, (b) like he never wanted the job anyway. ________

18. The inventory that is on sale must be divided (a) among, (b) between our three locations. ________

19. We are looking for an (a) affordable, efficient (b) affordable efficient heating system. ________

In the following sentences, select words have been underlined. Using the letters below, indicate what punctuation should precede and follow the underlined words.

(a) ,________ (c) ________, (e) no punctuation

(b) , ________, (d) ; ________,

20. Miss Daily's payroll service was a huge success consequently she is opening a second office. ________

21. Thus the shipment was accidentally cancelled. ________

22. Tyana's youngest brother who just earned his MBA has applied for a position in the Finance Department. ________

23. Our new building houses underground employee parking which is a benefit the old one didn't offer. ________

24. As reported our division shows declining sales and dwindling profits. ________

25. Once the contract was signed by both parties revisions could not be made. ________

26. Some big-box stores threatened to stop accepting the credit card if fees were not lowered. ________

27. Ms. Ramden's statement is what annoyed a number of those who attended the lunch. ________

LEVEL III

For the following sentences, write the letter of the correct answer in the space provided.

28. Vancouver is larger than (a) any other city, (b) any city on the West Coast. ________

29. The engineer (a) only said that, (b) said that only slight modifications would have to be made. ________

30. The study was done independent (a) of, (b) from big players in the industry. ________

31. The approved contract is not very different (a) than, (b) from the first version. ________

32. The union asked that the wage increase be retroactive (a) to, (b) from the first of the year. ________

33. The Downtown Business Association (a) plans to promote, (b) plans on promoting the event provincially. ________

TEAR HERE

34. (a) You can either be transferred to Winnipeg or to Edmonton.

(b) You can be transferred either to Winnipeg or to Edmonton. ____________

35. (a) He is not only qualified but also fully certified.

(b) He not only is qualified but also fully certified. ____________

ASK AN EDITOR REVIEW

For each of the following statements, select the word or phrase that correctly completes it, and write its letter in the space provided.

36. Ed has visited the new building (a) so that, (b) , so he knows who has the corner offices. ____________

37. If Manny doesn't start taking school seriously, he won't (a) graduate college, (b) graduate from college this year. ____________

38. (a) Every day, (b) Everyday I park in the same spot. ____________

39. Policy changes have been made (a) industrywide, (b) industry wide. ____________

40. She is hoping to get (a) three weeks' vacation, (b) three-weeks vacation next year. ____________

TEAR HERE

EMAIL MESSAGES AND MEMOS

Email messages and memos are vital forms of internal communication for most companies today. Organizations are downsizing, flattening chains of command, forming work teams, and empowering rank-and-file employees. Given more power in making decisions, employees find that they need more information. They must collect, exchange, and evaluate information about the products and services they offer. Management also needs input from employees to respond rapidly to local and global market actions. This unprecedented demand for information results in the daily use of email and memos. Anyone entering the business world today must know how to write good email messages and memos.

CHARACTERISTICS OF EMAIL MESSAGES AND MEMOS

Email messages and memos have a number of characteristics in common:

They begin with the headings *To, From, Date,* and *Subject.*
They generally cover just one topic.
They are informal without being casual.
They are concise.

Email messages and memos use efficient standard formats, such as you see in Figure 4.1 (p. 275). Email messages and memos should discuss only one topic so that each message or memo can be acted on separately. Let's say you send your supervisor an email message requesting a copier repair. You add a comment about an article you want to appear in the company newsletter. The supervisor may act on one item and overlook the other. She might also want to forward your request for a copier repair directly to the operations manager, but she has to edit or rekey the message because of the second topic. Thus email messages and memos are most helpful when they cover just one subject.

Because they replace conversation, these messages tend to be informal. They may include first-person pronouns, such as *I* and *me,* as well as contractions, such as *can't* or *haven't.* The tone, however, should not become familiar or unbusinesslike. Moreover, email messages and memos should not be wordy. Concise messages save time and often are more easily understood than longer documents.

TEAR HERE

Figure 4.1

Comparing Email Messages and Memos

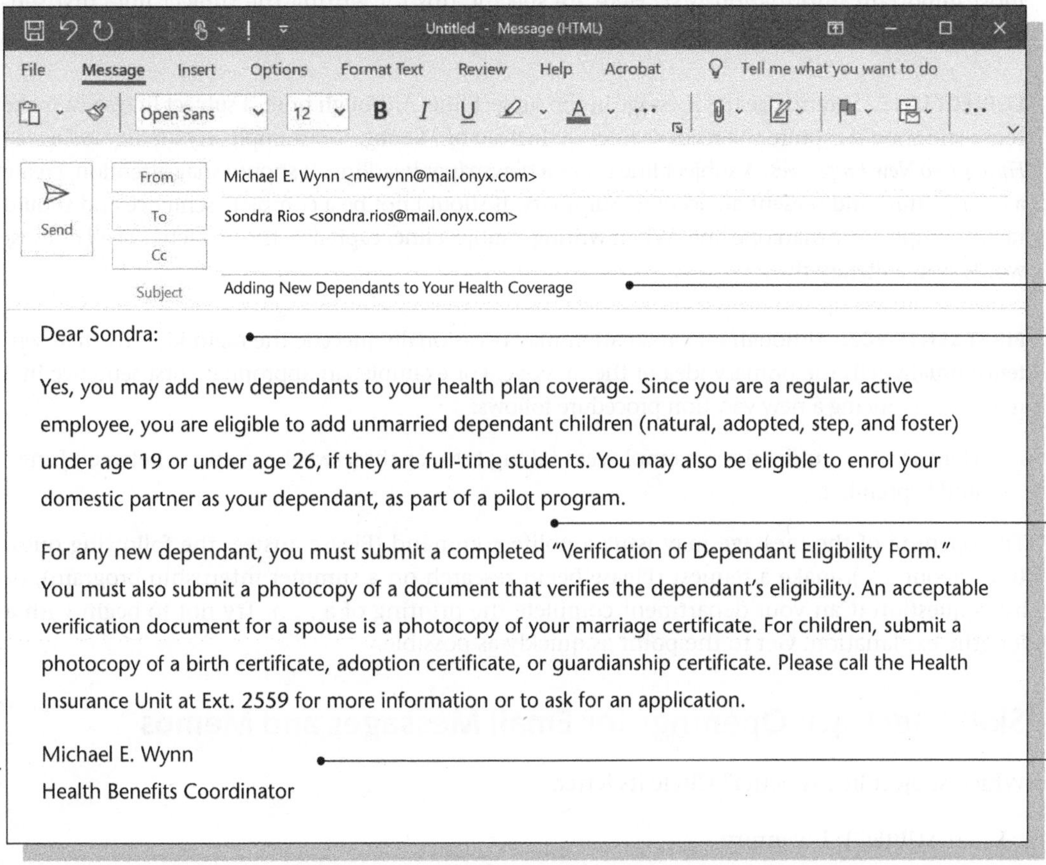

Untitled - Message (HTML)

File | Message | Insert | Options | Format Text | Review | Help | Acrobat | Tell me what you want to do

Open Sans | 12

Send

From: Michael E. Wynn <mewynn@mail.onyx.com>

To: Sondra Rios <sondra.rios@mail.onyx.com>

Cc:

Subject: Adding New Dependants to Your Health Coverage

Dear Sondra:

Yes, you may add new dependants to your health plan coverage. Since you are a regular, active employee, you are eligible to add unmarried dependant children (natural, adopted, step, and foster) under age 19 or under age 26, if they are full-time students. You may also be eligible to enrol your domestic partner as your dependant, as part of a pilot program.

For any new dependant, you must submit a completed "Verification of Dependant Eligibility Form." You must also submit a photocopy of a document that verifies the dependant's eligibility. An acceptable verification document for a spouse is a photocopy of your marriage certificate. For children, submit a photocopy of a birth certificate, adoption certificate, or guardianship certificate. Please call the Health Insurance Unit at Ext. 2559 for more information or to ask for an application.

Michael E. Wynn

Health Benefits Coordinator

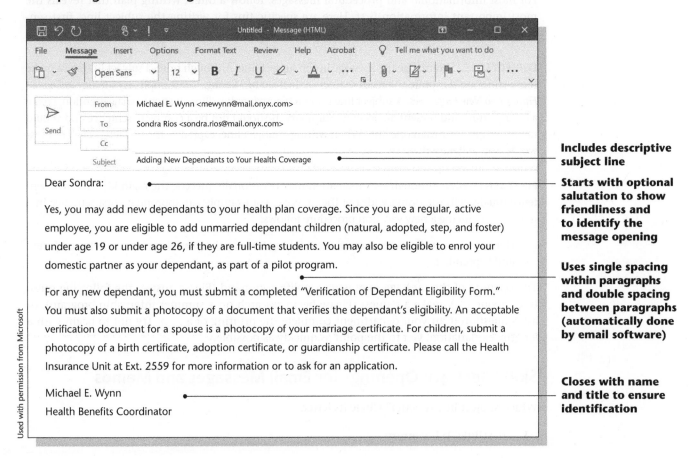

Includes descriptive subject line

Starts with optional salutation to show friendliness and to identify the message opening

Uses single spacing within paragraphs and double spacing between paragraphs (automatically done by email software)

Closes with name and title to ensure identification

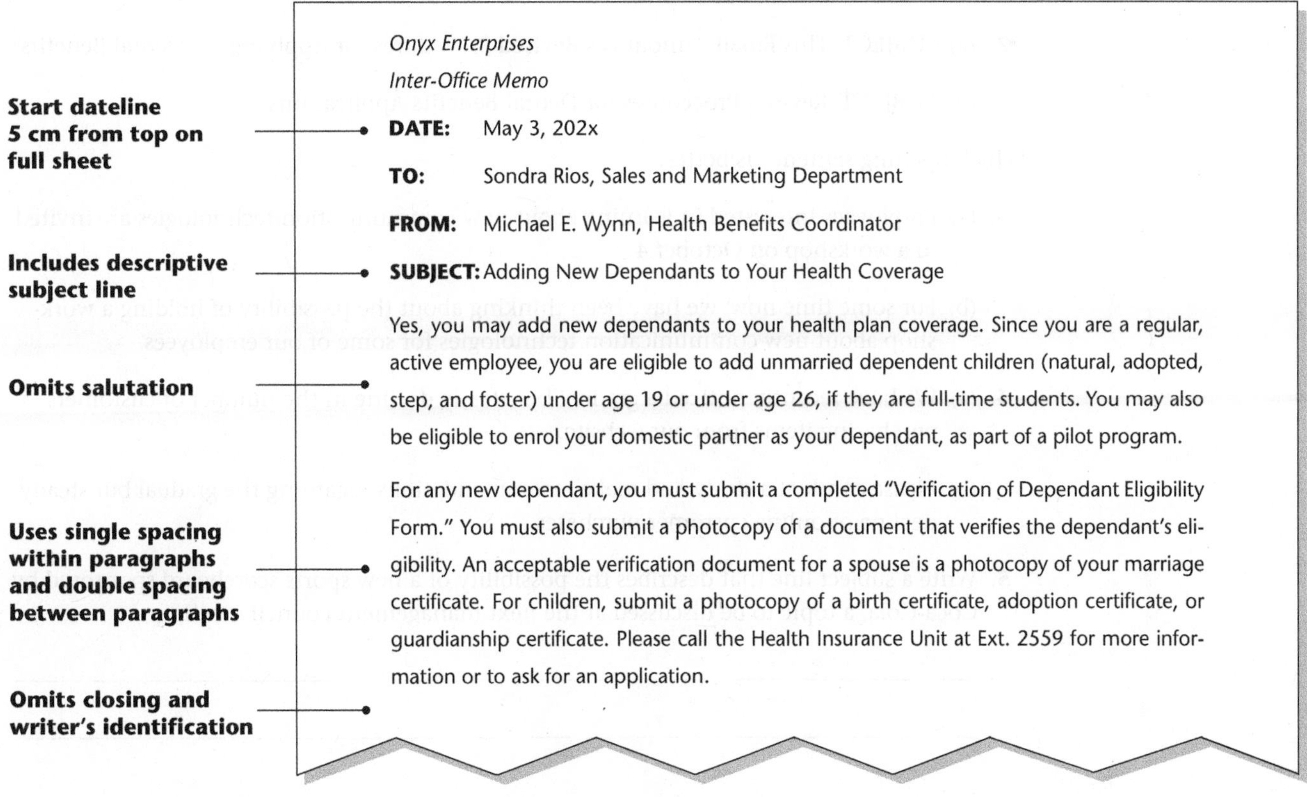

Onyx Enterprises

Inter-Office Memo

DATE: May 3, 202x

TO: Sondra Rios, Sales and Marketing Department

FROM: Michael E. Wynn, Health Benefits Coordinator

SUBJECT: Adding New Dependants to Your Health Coverage

Yes, you may add new dependants to your health plan coverage. Since you are a regular, active employee, you are eligible to add unmarried dependent children (natural, adopted, step, and foster) under age 19 or under age 26, if they are full-time students. You may also be eligible to enrol your domestic partner as your dependant, as part of a pilot program.

For any new dependant, you must submit a completed "Verification of Dependant Eligibility Form." You must also submit a photocopy of a document that verifies the dependant's eligibility. An acceptable verification document for a spouse is a photocopy of your marriage certificate. For children, submit a photocopy of a birth certificate, adoption certificate, or guardianship certificate. Please call the Health Insurance Unit at Ext. 2559 for more information or to ask for an application.

TEAR HERE

WRITING PLAN

For most informational and procedural messages, follow a direct writing plan that reveals the most important information first. Here are specific tips for writing the subject line, first sentence, body, and closing of email messages and memos.

SUBJECT LINE. Summarize the message in the subject line. Although brief, a subject line must make sense and should capture the reader's interest. Instead of *Meeting,* for example, try *Meeting to Discuss Hiring Two New Employees.* A subject line is like a newspaper headline. It should snag attention, create a clear picture, and present an accurate summary. It should not be a complete sentence and should rarely occupy more than one line. When writing a subject line, capitalize the first letter of all or most words as in a literary title.

FIRST SENTENCE. Although an explanation may occasionally precede the main idea, the first sentence usually tells the primary idea of the message. For example, an appropriate first sentence in a memo announcing a new vacation procedure follows:

> Here are new guidelines for employees taking two- or three-week vacations between June and September.

The opening of the message may issue a polite command (Please answer the following questions about . . .), make a request (Please begin research on a summer internship program), or ask a question (Can your department complete the printing of a . . .). Try not to begin with a lengthy explanation. Get to the point as quickly as possible.

Skill Check 4.1: Openings for Email Messages and Memos

Which subject line is better? Circle its letter.

1. (a) SUBJECT: Inventory

(b) SUBJECT: Annual Pharmacy Inventory Scheduled for June 2

2. (a) SUBJECT: This Email Announces Revised Procedures for Applying for Dental Benefits

(b) SUBJECT: Revised Procedures for Dental Benefits Applications

Which opening sentence is better?

3. (a) Employees interested in learning about new communication technologies are invited to a workshop on October 4.

(b) For some time now, we have been thinking about the possibility of holding a workshop about new communication technologies for some of our employees.

4. (a) We have recently noticed a gradual but steady decline in the number of customers purchasing items from our website.

(b) Please conduct a study and make recommendations regarding the gradual but steady decline of online customer purchases.

5. Write a subject line that describes the possibility of a new sports scoreboard sponsored by Coca-Cola, a topic to be discussed at the next management council meeting.

____

____

6. Write a subject line announcing a demonstration of new software for all employees, to be given Thursday, November 16.

____

____

BODY OF MESSAGE. Provide details of the message in the body. If you are asking for information, arrange your questions in a logical order. If you are providing information, group similar information together. Think about using side headings in bold print, such as you see in these paragraphs. They help readers understand, locate, and reference information quickly. You can also improve the readability of any message by listing items with numbers or bullets. Compare the two sets of instructions that follow:

Hard to Read

The instructions for operating our copy machine include inserting the pages to be copied into the document feeder, pressing the number of copies you want, and then the paper size is selected and the *Start Copy* button is pressed, and you collect your copies from the document tray.

Improved

Here are instructions for using the copy machine:

1. Insert the pages to be copied into the document feeder.
2. Press the number of copies you want.
3. Select the paper size.
4. Press the *Start Copy* button.
5. Collect your copies from the document tray.

Notice that all the items in the preceding bulleted list are parallel in construction, meaning that each item uses the same grammatical form. All begin with verbs. This kind of balanced writing helps readers anticipate and understand information more readily.

Skill Check 4.2: Listing Information

In the space provided, revise the following paragraph so that it includes an introductory sentence and a list of four items.

We are trying to improve budget planning, and we would also like to control costs. To accomplish these goals, we must change our procedures for submitting requests in the future for outside printing jobs. The new procedures include first determining your exact printing specifications for a particular job. Then we want you to obtain two estimates for the job. These estimates should be submitted in writing to Kelly. Finally, you may place the outside print order—but only after receiving approval.

____

____

____

____

____

____

CLOSING AN EMAIL MESSAGE OR A MEMO. Email messages and memos frequently end with (a) a request for action, (b) a summary of the message, or (c) a closing thought. If you are seeking action on the part of the recipient, be sure to spell out that action clearly. A vague request such as *Drop by to see this customer sometime* is ineffective because the reader may not understand exactly what is to be done. A better request might be worded as follows: *Please make an appointment to see Vicky Liang before June 2, when she will be leaving to attend a conference.* Notice that an end date is given. This technique, particularly when coupled with a valid reason, is effective in prompting people to act.

Another way to close an internal message is by summarizing its major points. A closing summary is helpful if the message is complicated. When no action request is made and a closing summary is unnecessary, the writer may prefer to end the memo with a simple closing thought, such as *I'd appreciate your assistance, What do you think of this proposal?,* or *Call me if you have questions.* Avoid tired, mechanical phrases such as *Don't hesitate to call on me* or *Thank you for your cooperation.* If you wish to express these thoughts, find a fresh way to say them.

Figure 4.1 (p. 275) shows how the four parts of a writing plan combine to create readable, efficient email messages and memos. For more information on email and memo formats, see Appendix C.

SPECIAL TIPS FOR SENDING EMAIL MESSAGES

To make the best use of email, consider the following suggestions:

- **Compose offline.** Instead of dashing off hasty messages online, take the time to compose offline. Consider using your word processing program and then cutting and pasting your message to the email compose box. This technique also avoids "self-destructing" online (losing all your writing through some glitch or pressing the wrong key).
- **Get the address right.** Email addresses are sometimes complex, often illogical, and always unforgiving. Omit one character or misread the letter *l* for the number *1*, and your message bounces or reaches the wrong inbox. Solution: Use your electronic address book for people to whom you write frequently, and double-check every address that you key in manually. Also, be sure that you don't reply to a group when you intend to answer only the sender. Before hitting *Send*, always confirm the right recipient or recipients are in the *To* line.
- **Keep paragraphs and messages short.** Try to keep your paragraphs no longer than three or four sentences. Above all, keep your message short. If an email message requires scrolling, consider sending the message in hard-copy form.
- **Care about correctness.** Senders and receivers of email tend to be casual about spelling, grammar, and usage. People are still judged by their writing, however, and you never know how far your message will travel. Read and edit any message before hitting the Send button!
- **Don't send anything you wouldn't want published.** Because email seems like a telephone call or a person-to-person conversation, writers sometimes send sensitive, confidential, inflammatory, or potentially embarrassing messages. Beware! Email creates a permanent record that often does not go away even when deleted, and every message is a corporate communication that can be used against you or your employer. Don't write anything that you wouldn't want your boss, your family, or a judge to read.

SPECIAL TIPS FOR REPLYING TO EMAIL MESSAGES

Before replying to an email message, think about some of the suggestions provided here. You can save yourself time and heartache by developing good reply procedures.

- **Scan all messages in your inbox before replying to each individually.** Because subsequent messages often affect the way you respond, read them all first (especially all those from the same individual).

- **Revise the subject line if the topic changes.** When replying or continuing an email exchange, revise the subject line as the topic changes.
- **Don't automatically forward the sender's complete message.** When forwarding information for another party's input, use discretion. Cut any irrelevant parts.
- **Never respond when you are angry.** Always allow some time to cool down before sending a response to an upsetting message. You often come up with different and better alternatives after thinking about what was said. If possible, iron out differences in person.
- **Present your message professionally.** Avoid using emoticons, texting abbreviations (such as LOL or TTYL), and all-caps (to represent shouting) in your business communications.
- **Office computers are meant for work-related communication.** Unless your company specifically allows it, never use your employer's computers for personal messages, personal shopping, or entertainment. Assume that all email is monitored. Employers legally have the right to eavesdrop on employee email messages, and many do.

Writing Application 4.1

Revise the following poorly written message. It suffers from wordiness, indirectness, and confusing instructions. Include a numbered list in your revised memo, and be sure to improve the subject line. Prepare this as an email message or as an internal memo.

TO:	All Staff Members
FROM:	Roy Minami, Manager
DATE:	July 11, 202x
SUBJECT:	Copier Rules

Some of you missed the demonstration of the operation of our new Turbo X copier last week. I thought you might appreciate receiving this list of suggestions from the salesperson when she gave the demonstration. This list might also be helpful to other employees who saw the demo but didn't take notes and perhaps can't remember all these pointers. It's sometimes hard to remember how to operate a machine when you do it infrequently. Here's what she told us to do. There are two paper loading trays. Load 8 1/2- × 11-inch or 8 1/2- × 14-inch paper in the two loading trays. The paper should curve upward in the tray. You should take your copy and feed it into the machine face up. However, if you have small sheets or book pages or cut-and-pasted copy, lift the copier lid and place your copy face down on the glass.

Before you begin, select the number of copies to be made and the paper size by pressing the touch selector panel. Don't push too hard. If copies become jammed, open the front door and see where the paper got stuck in the feed path. Remove jammed paper. Oh yes, your meter must be inserted before the machine will operate. We urge you, of course, to make only as many copies as you really need. Keep this list to use again.

Don't hesitate to call on me if you need a demonstration.

Writing Application 4.2

As the manager of Reprographic Services, write an email message to Kevin Suzuki, manager, Technical Services. You are concerned that the computer of one of your operators may be infected with a virus. The computer belongs to Isabella Jimenez. Isabella says that each time she opens a previously stored document in her Word program, the contents of the document are immediately deleted. Fortunately, because Isabella has backup files, she hasn't lost anything yet, but obviously she can't go on using this computer. You plan to assign Isabella some temporary tasks for the rest of the day; however, she must have her computer up and running by tomorrow. You want a technician to inspect her machine before 5 p.m. today. You know that Kevin likes to learn as much about a computer problem as possible before he sends a technician, so include sufficient details to help him identify the problem.

Writing Application 4.3

As the manager of the Customer Services Division, Molson Breweries, write an email message to Melissa Miller, Supervisor, Customer Services. Ask Melissa to draft a form letter that can be sent to groups requesting plant tours.

In your message, explain that the brewery has always encouraged tour groups to see your home plant brewery. However, you cannot sponsor tours at this time because of extensive remodelling. You are also installing a new computer-controlled bottling system. Tours are expected to resume in September. You need a form letter that can be sent to all groups but that can be personalized for each response. You want the letter draft by Monday, April 6.

The letter should build good customer relations, a primary goal of your tour policy. The letter might enclose a free product coupon and a brochure picturing your operations. Tell Melissa to add any information that she feels would improve the letter.

UNIT 5

Punctuating Sentences

CHAPTER 15

COMMAS

OBJECTIVES

When you have completed the materials in this chapter, you will be able to do the following:

LEVEL I

- Use commas correctly in series, direct address, and parenthetical expressions
- Use commas correctly in punctuating dates, addresses, geographical items, and appositives

LEVEL II

- Place commas correctly in punctuating independent adjectives, introductory verbal phrases, and introductory prepositional phrases
- Use commas correctly in punctuating independent, introductory, terminal, and non-essential clauses

LEVEL III

- Use commas correctly in punctuating degrees, abbreviations, and numerals
- Use commas correctly with omitted words and contrasting statements, for clarity, and with short quotations

PRETEST

Add any necessary commas in the following sentences.

1. Johanna will travel to trade shows in Cleveland Chemnitz and Cologne this year.
2. Galen Weston Jr. executive chairman of Loblaw Companies was born in Dublin Ireland but grew up in Toronto Ontario.
3. Your interview Ms. Cordero will take place Tuesday June 9 at 10 a.m.

(continued)

PRETEST *(CONTINUED)*

4. If consumers purchase insurance from agents or insurers that are not licensed in their province the consumers are not protected.
5. After the breakfast meeting we will leave for the airport.
6. The International System of Units is contrary to what one might expect abbreviated SI.
7. The information revolution began several decades ago and it has brought us into an age of digital interconnectivity.
8. Although tired employees preferred the evening not the morning in-service training programs.
9. The job in Iqaluit Nunavut was offered to Vlad Minkevich MBA who has agreed to a start date of Monday April 8.
10. Patricia T. O'Conner said "When a tiny word gives you a big headache it's probably a pronoun."

DID YOU KNOW?

Some writers of other languages envy those who write in English. Our systematic use of commas and other punctuation marks makes it easy to signal pauses, to emphasize ideas, and to enhance readability.

When you talk with a friend, you are probably unaware of the "invisible" commas, periods, and other punctuation marks that you are using. In conversation your pauses and voice inflections punctuate your thoughts and clarify your meaning. In writing, however, you must use a conventional set of symbols—punctuation marks—to help your reader understand your meaning, just as traffic signs help guide drivers.

Over the years we have gradually developed a standardized pattern of usage for all punctuation marks. This usage has been codified (set down) in rules that are observed by writers who want to make their writing as precise as possible. As noted earlier, some professional writers may deviate from conventional punctuation practices. In addition, some organizations, particularly newspapers and publishing houses, maintain their own style manuals to establish a consistent "in-house" style.

The punctuation guidelines presented in this book represent a consensus about punctuation styles that are acceptable in business and professional writing. Following these guidelines will help you to write with clarity, consistency, and accuracy.

LEVEL I

BASIC GUIDELINES FOR USING COMMAS

DID YOU KNOW?

Serial commas have actually played roles in court cases. For example, the will of a deceased man left everything to *John, Phil and Mary.* John's lawyers argued that John received half and Phil and Mary had to share the other half. What do you think?

The most used and misused punctuation mark, the **comma**, indicates a pause in the flow of a sentence. *Not all sentence pauses, however, require commas.* It is important for you to learn the standard rules for the use of commas so that you will not be tempted to clutter your sentences with needless, distracting commas. Here are the guidelines for basic comma usage.

Series

Commas are used to separate three or more equally ranked, or coordinate, elements (words, phrases, or clauses) in a series. While it is not incorrect to omit the comma before the conjunction connecting the last item to the series (e.g., words, *phrases or* clauses), we do recommend its use. This comma, called a **serial comma**, ensures separation of the last two items and adds clarity. Note that no commas are used when conjunctions join all the items in a series.

Only in June, July, and August is a lifeguard on duty. (Series of words. Notice that a comma precedes *and* but no comma follows the last item, *August*.)
Marta conducted the research, organized the data, and wrote the report. (Series of phrases)
Mrs. Horton is the president, Mr. Wong is the marketing manager, and Miss Zavala is the executive assistant. (Series of clauses)
We need wireless access to email and websites and the company intranet. (No commas are needed when conjunctions are repeated.)

Direct Address

Direct address occurs when a person is being addressed or spoken to directly, rather than being spoken about. Words and phrases of direct address, including names, affiliations, and titles, are set off with commas.

Mr. Lee, you must agree that Ingrid has done outstanding work. (At beginning of sentence)
I respectfully request that I be transferred, *sir.* (At end of sentence)
Are you, *members of the class of 2022,* ready to go out and take on the world? (Within sentence)

Parenthetical Expressions

Parenthetical words, phrases, and clauses may be used to create transitions between thoughts. These expressions interrupt the flow of a sentence and are unnecessary for its grammatical completeness. These commonly used expressions, many of which are listed below, are considered non-essential because they do not specifically answer questions such as *When?*, *Where?*, *Why?*, or *How?* Set off these expressions with commas when they are used parenthetically.

accordingly	hence	nevertheless
after all	however	no
all things considered	in addition	no doubt
as a matter of fact	incidentally	of course
as a result	in conclusion	on the contrary
as a rule	in fact	on the other hand
at the same time	in my opinion	otherwise
by the way	in other words	that is
consequently	in the first place	therefore
finally	in the meantime	under the circumstances
for example	moreover	unfortunately
fortunately	namely	yes
furthermore	needless to say	

Yes, his computer skills are excellent. (At beginning of sentence)
This report is not, *however,* one that must be classified. (Within sentence)
You have checked with other suppliers, *no doubt.* (At end of sentence)

The words in question are set off by commas only when they are used parenthetically and actually interrupt the flow of a sentence.

However the vote goes, we will abide by the result. (No comma needed after *however*, which introduces a dependent clause.)

ASK AN EDITOR

Question:
My boss always leaves out the comma before the word *and* when it precedes the final word in a series of words. Should the comma be used?

Answer:
Although some writers omit this comma, present practice favours its use so that the last two items in the series cannot be misread as one item. For example, *The departments participating are Engineering, Accounting, Marketing, and Advertising.* Without that final comma, the last two items might be read as being one item.

STUDY TIP

As you begin to learn about commas, try to name a rule or guideline for every comma you insert. For example, *comma/series, comma/parenthetical,* and so forth. This practice will help you avoid inserting unnecessary (and often incorrect) commas.

We have *no doubt* our selling techniques must be revamped. (No commas needed to set off *no doubt*, which is object of the verb.)

Don't confuse short introductory essential prepositional phrases functioning as adverbs with parenthetical expressions. Notice that the following short phrases are essential and, therefore, require no commas.

In the summer more rental units become available. (No comma is needed because the short prepositional phrase answers the question *When?*)

In Cambridge Bay researchers are needed. (No comma is needed because the short prepositional phrase answers the question *Where?*)

For this reason we will be lowering our wholesale prices. (No comma is needed because the short prepositional phrase answers the question *Why?*)

With your help our production team can meet its goal. (No comma is needed because the short prepositional phrase answers the question *How?*)

Dates, Addresses, and Geographical Items

STUDY TIP

In separating cities and provinces and dates and years, many writers remember the initial comma but forget the final one, as in *My friend from Chateauguay, Québec, called.*

When dates, addresses, and geographical items contain more than one element, the second and succeeding elements are normally set off by commas. Study the following illustrations.

DATES.

On November 8 we opened for business. (No comma is needed for one element.)

On November 8, 2017, we opened for business. (Two commas set off the second element.)

On Wednesday, November 8, 2017, we opened for business. (Commas set off the second and third elements.)

In November 2017 we opened for business. (Commas are not used with the month and year only.)

ADDRESSES.

Send the software to Mr. Chun Wong, 1639 Carling Avenue, Ottawa, Ontario K1A 0G5, before Tuesday. (Commas are used between all elements except the province or territory and postal code, which are considered a single unit.)

GEOGRAPHICAL ITEMS.

He moved from St. John's, Newfoundland, to Sydney, Nova Scotia. (Two commas set off the province, territory, or state unless it appears at the end of the sentence.)

Our flight from Shanghai, China, to Moscow, Russia, will take 13 hours. (Two commas set off the country unless it appears at the end of the sentence.)

APPOSITIVES. You will recall that appositives rename, describe, or explain preceding nouns or pronouns (Chapter 5). An appositive that provides information that is not essential to the identification of its antecedent should be set off by commas.

Debbie Robinson, *the DataMax sales representative,* is here. (The appositive adds non-essential information; commas set it off.)

The sales representative *Debbie Robinson* is here to see you. (The appositive is needed to identify which sales representative has arrived; therefore, no commas are used.)

Closely related one-word appositives read as a unit with the preceding item do not require commas.

My husband *Kevin* sometimes uses my computer.

Complete the reinforcement exercises for Level I on pages 291–293.

LEVEL II

SPECIAL GUIDELINES FOR USING COMMAS

At this level we will review comma usage guidelines that you studied in previous chapters, and we will add one new guideline.

Independent Adjectives

Separate two or more adjectives that equally modify a noun (Chapter 11).

We're looking for an *industrious, ambitious* person to hire.
Online customers can conduct *secure, real-time* banking transactions.

Introductory Verbal Phrases

Verbal phrases that precede main clauses should be followed by commas (Chapter 10).

To qualify for the position, you must have two years' experience. (Infinitive verbal phrase)
Climbing quickly, the hikers reached the summit by noon. (Participial verbal phrase)

Prepositional Phrases

One or more introductory prepositional phrases totalling four or more words should be followed by a comma.

In the spring of next year, we will move to a new building.
During the winter months, production usually declines.

Introductory prepositional phrases of fewer than four words require *no* commas.

In August that stock reached its highest price.
In some instances it will be necessary to increase our price.

Do NOT use commas to set off prepositional phrases in other positions when the phrases are essential and do not interrupt the flow of the sentence.

The sales figures of our branches in British Columbia have improved.
We do not at this time anticipate any unusual expenses.

Independent Clauses

When a coordinating conjunction joins independent clauses, use a comma before the coordinating conjunction, unless the clauses are very short, that is, six or fewer words in each (Chapter 13).

Income tax preparation fees for sole proprietors can be high, but the fees charged to incorporated companies are often ten times as high.
James uses an iPhone and Jan prefers her Samsung Galaxy. (No comma needed since both clauses are short.)

Introductory Dependent Clauses

Dependent clauses that precede independent clauses are followed by commas (Chapter 14).

When you have finished, please return the style manual.
If you need help, please call me at Ext. 2306.
Since we need more clerks, we will begin advertising.

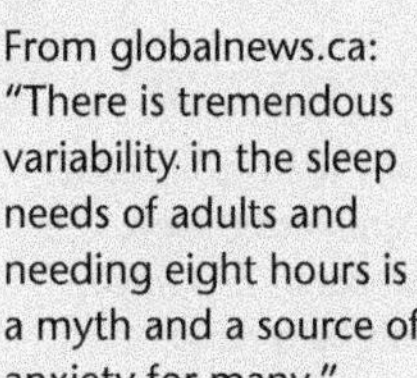

BE THE EDITOR

From globalnews.ca: "There is tremendous variability in the sleep needs of adults and needing eight hours is a myth and a source of anxiety for many."

ASK AN EDITOR

Question:
When the word *too* appears at the end of a sentence, should it be preceded by a comma?

Answer:
When the adverb *too* (meaning "also") appears at the end of a clause, it requires no comma (*his friend is coming too*). However, when *too* appears in the middle of a sentence, particularly between the subject and the verb, it requires two commas to set it off (*his friend, too, is coming*). When *too* means "to an excessive extent," it requires no commas (*the speech was too long*).

STUDY TIP

The comma after an introductory clause may be the most frequently missed comma in student writing. Be sure to insert a comma after clauses beginning with *If, When, As, Since,* and so forth.

Terminal Dependent Clauses

A dependent clause at the end of a sentence is usually not preceded by a comma (Chapter 14). The need for a comma to set off a dependent clause at the end of a sentence depends on whether the added information is essential to the meaning. Generally, terminal clauses add information that answers questions such as *When?*, *Why?*, and *How?* Such information is essential; thus no comma is necessary. Only when a terminal clause adds unnecessary information or an afterthought should a comma be used.

Please return the style manual *when you have finished with it.* (No comma needed because the terminal dependent clause provides essential information and answers the question *When?*)

Please call me at Ext. 2306 *if you have any questions.* (No comma needed because the terminal clause provides essential information and answers the question *Why?*)

I plan to leave at 3:30, *although I could stay if you need me.* (A comma is needed because the terminal clause provides additional and unnecessary information.)

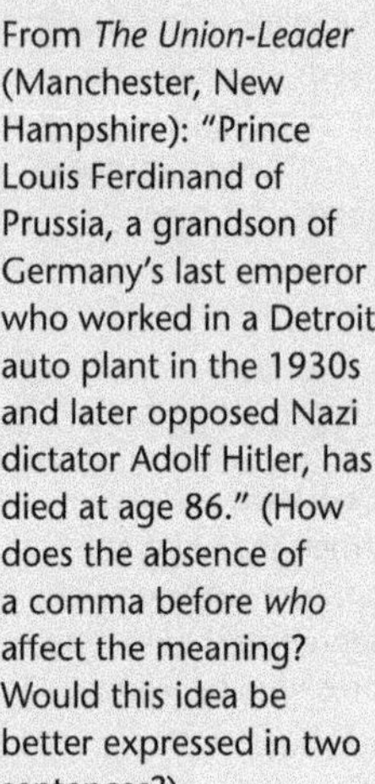

BE THE EDITOR

From *The Union-Leader* (Manchester, New Hampshire): "Prince Louis Ferdinand of Prussia, a grandson of Germany's last emperor who worked in a Detroit auto plant in the 1930s and later opposed Nazi dictator Adolf Hitler, has died at age 86." (How does the absence of a comma before *who* affect the meaning? Would this idea be better expressed in two sentences?)

Non-Essential Clauses

Use commas to set off clauses that are used parenthetically or that supply information not needed for the grammatical completeness of a sentence (Chapter 14). When this information falls in the middle of a sentence, the information presented before the first comma and after the second fits together to make logical and grammatical sense.

An increase in employee salaries, *as you can well understand,* must be postponed until profits improve. (Without the parenthetical clause, the sentence would read *An increase in employee salaries must be postponed until profits improve.*)

The product launch on March 9, which was the day after Daylight Saving Time began, was strategically scheduled. (Without the parenthetical clause: *The product launch on March 9 was strategically scheduled.*)

We received a letter from Anne Diga, *who is now living in Red Deer, Alberta.*

Do NOT use commas to set off clauses that contain essential information.

A student *who is studying English* certainly needs an up-to-date dictionary. (No commas are necessary because the italicized clause is essential; it tells which student needs an up-to-date dictionary.)

Complete the reinforcement exercises for Level II on pages 294–296.

BE THE EDITOR

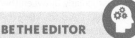

From *National Post*: "Transworld's managing director Larry Finlay said 'the world has lost one of its brightest, sharpest minds.'" (Do you spot more than one error?)

LEVEL III

ADDITIONAL GUIDELINES FOR USING COMMAS

The final guidelines for commas include suggestions for punctuating degrees, abbreviations, numerals, omitted words, contrasting statements, and short quotations.

Degrees and Abbreviations

Degrees and professional designations following individuals' names are set off by commas. The abbreviations *Jr.* and *Sr.* and Roman numerals added to a person's name are not set off by commas unless the person chooses to include them.

Nel Wieman, MD, is Canada's first female Indigenous psychiatrist.
Nalifah Rehman, PhD, applied for the position of college president.

John T. O'Dell Jr. is frequently confused with John T. O'Dell Sr.

Only Gregory Stoddard, Jr., is unable to participate. (Individual prefers having *Jr.* set off by commas.)

Company abbreviations such as *Inc.* and *Ltd.* are not set off by commas unless the company's legal name includes the commas. When referencing a specific company, it is always best to look up the treatment of its name.

DMR Group Inc. is based in Montréal. (Canadian companies' legal names do not as a rule include commas before *Inc.* or *Ltd.*)

The US firm of Blackstone & Smythe, Inc., exports goods worldwide. (Since this company name includes a comma before *Inc.*, a second comma must follow *Inc.* when it appears in the middle of a sentence, similar to the style used for provinces, territories, or states with city names.)

ASK AN EDITOR

Question:
When the company name *Halperin, Inc.*, appears in the middle of a sentence, is there a comma following *Inc.*?

Answer:
Current authorities recommend the following practice in punctuating *Inc.* and *Ltd.*: Do not use commas to set off such expressions unless the company does so itself. Canadian companies, unlike American companies, seldom use commas in this position. If the company does use a comma before an expression like *Inc.*, however, then a comma also follows *Inc.* whenever it is followed by other words in a sentence (*We received from Halperin, Inc., its latest catalogue*).

Numerals

Try to avoid writing a sentence with two numbers side by side. Sometimes, however, adjacent numbers cannot be avoided. If a pause would be natural between the numbers, add a comma. If there is no legitimate reason for a comma, spell out the shorter of the two numbers.

The client has ordered 150 nineteen-inch computer monitors. (A pause would be unnatural, so it's better to spell out *nineteen*.)

By 2014, 258 million people were accessing mobile broadband services wirelessly through their laptops. (The pause is natural after a prepositional phrase.)

We were expecting eight participants; of the eight, three arrived late.

Four-digit numbers can be written with or without a comma. Numbers with five digits or more require commas.

2,760 (or 2760) 47,950 6,500,000

A commonly accepted alternative style, especially when using the International System (SI) of measurement, is to use spaces rather than commas.

2760 47 950 6 500 000

House numbers, decimals, serial numbers, contract numbers, and US zip codes are written without commas within the numerals.

20586 Victory Avenue	(House number)
0.98651	(Decimal)
36-5710-1693285763	(Serial number)
No. 359063420	(Contract number)
46201	(Zip code)

Omitted Words

A comma is used to show the omission of words that are understood.

Last summer we hired 12 interns; this summer, only 3 interns. (Comma shows omission of *we hired* after *summer*.)

Contrasting Statements

Commas are used to set off contrasting or opposing expressions for emphasis or clarity. These expressions are frequently introduced by such words as *not, never, rather than,* and *as opposed to.*

The nominating committee selected Mr. Cardinal, not Mr. Monroe, as its representative. (Two commas set off a contrasting element that appears in the middle of a sentence.)

The riskier the investment, the greater the potential return. (One comma sets off a contrasting element that appears at the end of a sentence.)

Our budget for equipment this year is reduced, yet quite adequate.

STUDY TIP

Here's a good rule to follow in relation to the comma: When in doubt, leave it out!

Clarity

Commas are used to separate words repeated for emphasis and words that may be misread if not separated.

Susan Long said it was a very, very complex contract.
Whoever goes, goes at his or her own expense.
No matter what, you know you have our support.

Short Quotations

Use a comma to separate a short quotation from the rest of a sentence. If the quotation is divided into two parts, use two commas. (Quotation marks are discussed in Chapter 17, Level III.)

Mrs. Lara said, "The deadline for the McBride contract is June 6."
"The deadline for the McBride contract," said Mrs. Lara, "is June 6."

Complete the reinforcement exercises for Level III on pages 297–299.

NAME ______________________________

CHAPTER 15 ■ Reinforcement Exercises

LEVEL I

A. (Self-check) In the following sentences, add any necessary commas. In the space provided, indicate briefly the reason for the comma(s). Write *C* if a sentence is correct.

EXAMPLE: He stated, on the contrary, that he would decline the offer. parenthetical

1. Tuesday September 11 2001 is a date that most North Americans will never forget. ______
2. Under the circumstances we will be closed for an unknown length of time. ______
3. Please see the large selection of trunks briefcases airplane luggage and other travel items in our store. ______
4. Brad Duncan grew up in Kingston Ontario before he moved to Gatineau Quebec to start a business. ______
5. Please contact manager Maurits Racz to discuss your request. ______
6. An extension was requested by Sarah Bernstein the art director's assistant. ______
7. In the winter we always hire additional personnel in the warehouse and in the office. ______
8. Your item has been shipped Ms. Stillwater and should arrive by Friday. ______
9. We have no doubt that such practices are widespread. ______
10. We were all asked to bring paper and a pen and a decorated box of any size to the brainstorming meeting. ______

Check your answers.

B. Add any necessary commas in the sentences below. In the space provided, indicate briefly the reason for the comma(s). Write *C* if a sentence is correct.

1. Our office building has as a matter of fact been designated a heritage building. ______
2. Send the book order to Mrs. Sheila Maynard 4692 Oak Drive Etobicoke Ontario M9B 1L8 before Friday. ______
3. Cynthia Felix the former office manager now has a similar job in Winnipeg Manitoba. ______
4. Hotels restaurants and other hospitality businesses have seen a sharp decline in income this year. ______
5. Most businesses in Montréal Québec closed on Monday March 16 2020 to help stop the spread of coronavirus. ______

TEAR HERE

6. Strict rules are needed however to make sure that companies don't start charging for access to public information. __________

7. Business partners Joe and Amir are looking to open a second location in April 2022. __________

8. Our new online store offers shipping local delivery and on-site pickup options. __________

9. The issue with your order Ms. Riley is that the options you selected are not available on that model. __________

10. We have had applications from people who have worked with such companies as Gillette Norwegian Cruise Line Arby's and General Motors. __________

11. Mike David an Indigenous Canadian entrepreneur hosts a podcast promoting Web-based businesses. __________

12. Having a business online can among other things expand the pool of potential customers. __________

13. In addition our sales letter must include facts testimonials and guarantees. __________

14. The famous investor Warren Buffett agreed to give $37 million to charity. __________

15. Andrea Collins is president Qaasim Jackson is vice president and Robert Chevrier is secretary. __________

C. In the following sentences, add any necessary commas. In the space provided, indicate briefly the reason for the comma(s). Write *C* if a sentence is correct.

1. I hope Cito that you will consider the position in Regina Saskatchewan with an open mind. __________

2. Our sales rep Paul will arrive Monday July 17 from Chicoutimi Québec. __________

3. Bennie Porter the mall's chief security officer responded to an alarm at the store at 1:30 a.m. __________

4. The company's 3-D printer as a rule should not be used for personal projects. __________

5. We have no doubt that we will complete the project by Friday September 9. __________

6. Members may choose from many martial arts Pilates aqua fitness and Zumba classes offered at Bally Total Fitness. __________

7. Incidentally I feel that we should get an outside opinion. __________

8. Our analysis shows that your company could make better use of Twitter Instagram and Facebook. __________

9. I noticed on our company's intranet by the way that your friend Charles was promoted. __________

10. Adam Adler the eminent Toronto architect studied our needs developed a plan and designed our office complex. __________

11. The architect Adam Adler was recently featured in *Architectural Digest.* __________

12. Popular places for destination weddings include Hawaii Mexico and the Caribbean because of their warm weather. ____________

13. Brothers J. W. and A. J. Billes bought a small garage and tire company in Toronto Ontario in 1922. ____________

14. They chose to call their company Canadian Tire because of course it made it sound big. ____________

15. The first gas bar opened at Yonge and Church Streets in Toronto in 1958. ____________

16. A. J. Billes co-founder of Canadian Tire became a member of the Order of Canada in 1976. ____________

TEAR HERE

NAME ______________________________

LEVEL II

A. **(Self-check)** In the following sentences, add any necessary commas. In the space provided, indicate briefly the reason for the comma(s). Write *C* if a sentence is correct.

EXAMPLE: If I were you, I would take a part-time job and continue school. intro. dependent clause

1. We expect honest thorough answers during the interview. ______________
2. To succeed in life find a career that you are passionate about. ______________
3. In 1983 the company enacted a program of energy conservation. ______________
4. After Will quit the department started to fall apart. ______________
5. A visit to your doctor who has been sent the incident form is required before you submit the insurance paperwork. ______________
6. Beginning June 15 the interest on your savings account will be non-taxable. ______________
7. Our annual physical inventory is scheduled for this weekend so our storefront will be closed. ______________
8. The work in this office is strictly confidential as I am sure you are well aware. ______________
9. The person who does our books recommends that we incorporate. ______________
10. Once you've packed the orders call the shipper for pickup immediately. ______________

Check your answers.

B. In the following sentences, add any necessary commas. In the space provided, indicate briefly the reason for the comma(s). Write *C* if a sentence is correct.

1. If I had enough money I would buy instead of lease. ______________
2. The company hired a new graphic designer to bring a fresh more youthful feel to the website. ______________
3. Whether you buy our face cream or not we will be happy to advise you about skin care. ______________
4. Dan Bricklin who created the first spreadsheet has developed a multi-user wiki spreadsheet program. ______________
5. The man who created the first spreadsheet has developed a multi-user wiki spreadsheet program. ______________
6. Restarting her computer Leslie worried that all her work would be lost. ______________
7. Our current liability insurance in view of the new law that went into effect April 1 needs to be increased. ______________
8. On Wednesday our sales hit a new all-time record. ______________

TEAR HERE

9. The transport of the shipment was delayed at the border but the driver expects to make up time between Brockville and Oshawa. ______

10. In a file drawer we found several books of old stamps. ______

11. Having been selected to serve as our chair Patrick Leong made valuable contributions to our committee's work. ______

12. You have purchased from us often and your payments in the past have always been prompt. ______

13. Before a policy is issued a prospective policyholder is thoroughly investigated. ______

14. A meeting will be called after the CEO reviews the findings of our research. ______

15. The research although it is subject to interpretation seems to suggest that wearable technology may still be too expensive for the market. ______

C. In the following sentences, add any necessary commas. In the space provided, indicate briefly the reason for the comma(s). Write *C* if a sentence is correct.

1. Although it represents a small share of our total sales the loss of the Regina territory would negatively affect our profits. ______

2. Mike Lazaridis who is one of the founders of Research In Motion (RIM) was born in Turkey but came to Canada when he was just five years old. ______

3. Once the invoices are put into QuickBooks the bookkeeper will reconcile them against the bank account. ______

4. Only college graduates will be considered and only those with technical skills will be hired. ______

5. Having earned Progressive Aboriginal Relations certification the company partnered with the Chippewa nation to build up the business on traditional territory. ______

6. The gas company offers a plan to equalize monthly bills although some people may prefer to pay for the gas they use in the month that they use it. ______

7. We hope that the new year will be prosperous for you and that we may have many more opportunities to serve you. ______

8. For at least the next six months we cannot increase salaries. ______

9. We do not see any reason for continuing this inefficient profitless practice at this time. ______

10. Because the model became unavailable the photographer had to reschedule the shoot. ______

11. By 2025 Internet privacy is expected by many experts to be nonexistent. ______

12. We risk lost sales if the telephone is not answered by the third ring. ______

TEAR HERE

13. If a good reason for your lateness is not forthcoming you risk getting a warning. ____________________

14. Focused on preparing for the upcoming trade show Maya decided to postpone the radio advertising campaign. ____________________

15. Any increase in salaries as you might have expected is presently impossible because of declining profits. ____________________

TEAR HERE

NAME ____________________

LEVEL III

A. **(Self-check)** In the following sentences, add any necessary commas. In the space provided, indicate briefly the reason for the comma(s). Write *C* if a sentence is correct.

1. Boeing announced that it will cut over 10000 jobs this year. ____________
2. What it is is a matter of principle. ____________
3. The first shift starts at 7 a.m.; the second at 4 p.m. ____________
4. "I am having your policy amended" said Mrs. Bennett "and you will receive the paperwork soon." ____________
5. In the fall we will need only six operators not the eight we have. ____________
6. In November 2019 11 Canadian cities were found to have unsafe lead levels due to antiquated pipes. ____________
7. We are issuing Policy No. 2176800394 in your name. ____________
8. What we need most to succeed as opposed to lower overhead is an increased customer base. ____________
9. "A résumé is a balance sheet without any liabilities" said personnel specialist Robert Half. ____________
10. Marie-Anne Day Walker-Pelletier has served as chief of the Okanese First Nation for a long long time. ____________

Check your answers.

B. In the following sentences, add any necessary commas. In the space provided, indicate briefly the reason for the comma(s). Write *C* if a sentence is correct.

1. "Next to trying and winning" said Lucy Maud Montgomery "the best thing is trying and failing." ____________
2. On October 23 16 additional workers will be hired. ____________
3. On January 1 our office is moving to 23689 Main Street North. ____________
4. In December 2019 Paul Desmarais Jr. and his brother stepped down as co-CEOs of Power Corp. ____________
5. On paper business plans can seem more complex than they are. ____________
6. The company has chosen to offer executives company cars rather than increases in salary to ensure its compensation package remains competitive. ____________
7. Level 6 secretaries are eligible for promotion after 12 months of probation; Level 5 secretaries after 18 months. ____________

8. Our special training program is just one year long not two years. ____________

9. Motion-picture producer Samuel Goldwyn said "A verbal contract isn't worth the paper it's written on." ____________

10. Before long online stores may outnumber brick-and-mortar stores. ____________

11. Scott Frehner MBA was hired as a consultant. ____________

12. In May 2016 88000 people in Fort McMurray were forced from their homes due to wildfires. ____________

13. Many employees who can donate a weekend of their time to Habitat for Humanity. ____________

14. What it was was an international power struggle. ____________

15. Selwa Khan D.C. and Annette Bellotti M.D. both have offices in the Queensland Medical Building. ____________

16. Although bored students managed to stay awake during the lecture. ____________

17. The government has announced repairs to more than 21 000 km of highway. ____________

18. In Room 201 32 computers and 16 printers are operating. ____________

19. Cooperation not criticism is what is needed. ____________

20. The accountant told us that it was very important to save all our receipts. ____________

C. Review of Levels I, II, and III. To make sure you have mastered the use of commas, try your skill on these challenging sentences that cover all levels. Add any necessary commas, and in the space provided, write the number that you added. Write *C* if a sentence is correct. Be prepared to discuss the rule for each comma you add.

1. Hiawatha Osawamick owner of Hiawatha's Catering won the Indigenous Entrepreneur of the Year award in 2020. ____________

2. John D. Rockefeller Sr. who founded Standard Oil was known as a driven determined and philanthropic man. ____________

3. Sold at auction the two properties recouped $55000 in lost tax money for the City of St. John's Newfoundland. ____________

4. Writing a business plan helps an aspiring entrepreneur determine whether a business idea once fleshed out is viable or if competition market size or finance needs may prove to be insurmountable roadblocks. ____________

5. Writing a business plan the aspiring entrepreneur determined her idea was viable but she learned she would have to find a more central easily accessible location. ____________

6. At a recent meeting of our team we decided that members should at their convenience complete an online training module. ____________

7. The safety guidelines require everyone to wear a hard hat safety goggles and closed-toe footwear on the worksite even if no work is in progress. ____________

8. If you work in an office with open cubicles it is rude to listen to music or podcasts without headphones. ____________________

9. It is important that employees treat one another with respect and kindness in both verbal and written communications. ____________________

10. Our yearly budget for equipment supplies and utilities was over $2000000. ____________________

11. "There is no such thing" said Tom Peters "as a minor lapse in integrity." ____________________

12. Documents were destroyed computers were hacked and employee files were stolen during the recent break-in. ____________________

13. The hacked computers were quickly secured; the stolen employee files however were never recovered. ____________________

D. Writing Exercise. Your instructor may ask you to complete this exercise of ten sentences on a separate sheet.

Select ten comma rules that you think are very important. Name each rule; then write an original sentence illustrating each.

POSTTEST

Add any necessary commas in the following sentences.

1. Successful entrepreneurs must have vision and creativity and drive.
2. The restaurant sponsors several baseball hockey and lacrosse teams in the community and it offers discounts for team events.
3. Please let us know Mrs. Youngblood what we can do to ensure a pleasant smooth transition.
4. The manager thinks on the other hand that all service calls must receive prior authorization and that current service contracts must be honoured.
5. Speaking with the client Marjorie offered two different solutions to the issue he had with the setup.
6. To meet the deadline make sure your application fee is received by the end of business on December 14.
7. When trained all employees in this company should be able to offer logical effective advice to customers.
8. Rick Skrenta who created the first computer virus wrote the malicious code in 1982 as a harmless prank.
9. Sitwat Majid BSc spoke at the Banff Alberta conference in June 2021.
10. If you are unsure you may ask Mrs. Carlson not Mr. Ray for additional information.

TEAR HERE

EDITOR'S CHALLENGE

The following letters contain errors in spelling, punctuation, and language principles covered thus far, as well as other common errors. Use proofreading marks to make all necessary corrections.

Adventure Sports, Inc.

8550 Old Dairy Road
Juneau, AK 99801

Email: troy@alaska.net
FAX: 907-789-2319

March 7, 202x

Mr. Kevin M. Simpson
433 East Albert
Edmonton, AB T9E 7X5

THANKS FOR YOUR INTEREST IN KAYAK TOURS

Enclosed is a list of current trips and other information, that you requested about our Kayak tours in Alaska. To ensure a quality wilderness experience the number of guests on a tour are limited to six people. No special experience is neccesary, many of our guests have never been in a sea kayak, and are surprised to find that they are very stable. Moreover we teach you safe efficient operation of a kayak.

All equipment, meals, and safety gear, is included in the trip price. We provide charter transportation from Juneau to the trip location, however you are responsible for getting to Juneau, and for your meals and lodging before and after the trip. To reserve a trip you must make a 50 percent deposit. We will hold reservations for your party for two weeks. Anyone who must request a refund, will be charged a $50 handling fee. In some instances, we must cancel a trip because of to few participants, or dangerous weather. If we must cancel you will receive a full refund.

Our most popular trip is whale watching and kayaking at Pt. Adolphus. This four day trip costs US$750 which includes boat charter and fairy. We also recommend the glacier tour at Tracy Arm and our island tour of Pt. Couverdon. By the way custom dates is available for family's or group's of three or more.

Call, write or fax to make your reservations. We look forward to providing you with the wilderness adventure of a lifetime!

Troy M. Donohue

TROY M. DONOHUE, ADVENTURE SPORTS INC.

Enclosure

TEAR HERE

Briggs Mills Inc.

440 Vine Street
Fredricton, NB E3C 5G7

www.briggsmills.com
506-579-3100

May 12, 202x

Ms. Julie Perzel
Director Human Resources
Clayton Manufacturing
10001 East Industrial Park Road
Fredricton, NB G2B 4B8

Dear Ms. Pretzel:

Mr. Martin A. Anderson whom is applying for the position of manger of manufacturing support at your organization requested that I write this confidential letter of of reccommendation. Mr. Anderson has worked under my supervision as a manufacturing support supervisor at Briggs Mills Inc. for three year's.

As a supervisor of manufacturing support Mr. Anderson helped to hire, evaluate, and supervise a team of four machine technicians. Him and his team was responsible for the preventive maintance, troubleshooting and repair of machines on three production lines. Because of his strong interpersonal skills Mr. Anderson expected and obtained high performance from his machine technicians. Each technician that was evaluated, ranked in the upper two levels of performance for the past three years'. In addition Mr. Andersons own performance was evaluated at our highest level for the last two years.

Mr. Anderson's team developed a highly-effective maintenance and calibration program, that reduced line shutdowns by 10 percent. Furthermore, in addition to his supervisory work Mr. Anderson initiated improvements in machine documentation.

Mr. Anderson's changes enabled support personal to repair machines without relying on production engineers. Although documentation changes were cumbersome for our engineers Mr. Anderson brang about needed change without alienating engineers or technicians. His enthusiastic upbeat personality has had a positive affect on the entire organization.

Im sorry that Mr. Andersen may leave Briggs Mills but I am confident that his technical, interpersonal and leadership skills will serve you well in your organization. I recommend him highly, and would be happy to have him return to us in the future.

Sincerely,

Cheng Lim
Vice President, Operations

CHAPTER

SEMICOLONS AND COLONS

16

OBJECTIVES

When you have completed the materials in this chapter, you will be able to do the following:

LEVEL I

- Use semicolons correctly in punctuating compound sentences
- Use semicolons when necessary to separate items in a series

LEVEL II

- Distinguish between the proper and improper use of colons to introduce listed items
- Correctly use colons to introduce quotations and explanatory sentences

LEVEL III

- Distinguish between the use of commas and semicolons before expressions such as *namely, that is,* and *for instance*
- Understand why semicolons are sometimes used to separate independent clauses joined by coordinating conjunctions
- Use colons appropriately in special situations and know whether to capitalize words following colons

PRETEST

Add any necessary semicolons, colons, and commas in the following sentences.

1. Three of the world's most innovative companies are Apple Google and Toyota.
2. Many companies offer employees a work-from-home option as a result these companies save money on overhead.
3. The Insurance Institute for Highway Safety has one primary criterion for its designation "top safety pick" the cars must be best in class at protecting their occupants.

(continued)

PRETEST *(CONTINUED)*

4. The following experts were invited to speak Tom Woods Mount Royal College Beverly Linnell Southern Alberta Institute of Technology and Judy O'Shea Lethbridge Community College.
5. Speakers for the morning session are now scheduled speakers for the afternoon session have not yet been arranged.
6. The programming committee however must proceed with plans for the entire conference.
7. Although the committee had many cities from which to choose it decided to limit the selection to larger centres namely Vancouver, Toronto, or Montréal.
8. "Green" technologies have been gaining a strong following consequently many industries have introduced green products and recycling programs.
9. Cedric's son has one major educational goal he wants to earn his law degree.
10. The meeting will begin promptly at 10 45 a.m.

This chapter introduces semicolons and colons, which can be two powerful punctuation marks in business writing. Skilled writers use semicolons and colons to signal readers about the ideas that will follow. You can improve your writing and look more professional if you know how to use colons and semicolons correctly. In this chapter you will learn basic uses and advanced applications of these two important punctuation marks.

LEVEL I

STUDY TIP

Remember that a comma follows only a conjunctive adverb of two syllables or more.

BASIC USES OF THE SEMICOLON

Semicolons tell readers that two closely related ideas should be thought about together. The most common use of the semicolon occurs in compound sentences. The semicolon is a stronger punctuation mark than a comma, which signifies a pause; but the semicolon is not as strong as a period, which signifies a complete stop.

Understanding the use of the semicolon will help you avoid fundamental writing errors, such as the *comma splice* (separating two independent clauses with only a comma) and the *run-on sentence* (running two independent clauses together without punctuation). Many business and professional communicators mistakenly use a comma when they should use a semicolon and vice versa.

STUDY TIP

Don't capitalize the word after a semicolon unless it's a proper noun.

Independent Clauses Separated by Conjunctive Adverbs

Semicolons are used primarily when two independent clauses are separated by a conjunctive adverb or a transitional expression (Chapter 13). Here are some examples for review:

Companies make no profits until they recover costs; *therefore,* most companies use a cost approach in pricing. (A semicolon separates two independent clauses joined by the conjunctive adverb *therefore.*)

Advertising is aimed at increasing sales; *thus* an advertising policy must be formulated with that objective. (A semicolon separates two independent clauses joined by the conjunctive adverb *thus*.)

Independent Clauses Without Coordinating Conjunctions or Conjunctive Adverbs

Two or more closely related independent clauses not separated by a conjunctive adverb or a coordinating conjunction (*and, or, nor, but, so, yet, for*) require a semicolon.

The licensing company is called the *franchisor;* the dealer is called the *franchisee.*
Our inside teller service closes at *4 p.m.; outside* ATM service is available 24 hours a day.

As you learned in Chapter 2, a serious punctuation error results if separate independent clauses are joined by only a comma (a comma splice) or without any punctuation whatsoever (a run-on sentence).

Comma splice: The licensing company is called the franchisor, the dealer is called the franchisee.
Run-on sentence: The licensing company is called the franchisor the dealer is called the franchisee.

Series Containing Internal Commas or Complete Thoughts

Semicolons are used to separate items in a series when one or more of the items contain internal commas. Using a semicolon this way will make your sentence clearer to your reader.

Only the company branches in St. John's, Newfoundland; Sherbrooke, Québec; and Mississauga, Ontario, are showing substantial profits.
Attending the conference were Teresa Caruana, executive vice president, Cabrillo Industries; Martin Manheim, president, Servex Corporation; and Joyce Moran, program director, Club Mediterranean.

STUDY TIP

When using a semicolon between items in a series, don't forget the final one before *and.* Note that this semicolon is not ever optional, unlike the final comma in a series.

Semicolons may also be used to separate three or more independent clauses in a series.

The first step consists of surveying all available information related to the company objective so that an understanding of all problems can be reached; the second step consists of interviewing consumers, wholesalers, and retailers; and the third step consists of developing a research design that indicates the actual methods and procedures to be used.

CAREER TIP

Using the semicolon skilfully is one mark of an educated writer.

A series of short independent clauses with no internal punctuation, however, may be separated by commas (Chapter 15).

Amazon.com was founded in 1994, it unveiled its website in 1995, and it went public in 1997.

Complete the reinforcement exercises for Level I on pages 310–311.

LEVEL II

BASIC USES OF THE COLON

Although it has a variety of functions, the **colon** most often introduces lists, quotations, and explanatory sentences.

Formally Listed Items

Use a colon after an independent clause that introduces one item, two items, or a list of items. A list may be shown vertically or horizontally and is frequently introduced by such words as *the following, as follows, these,* or *thus*. Even when such words are implied but not stated, use a colon after an independent clause introducing a list.

> Jan created a company intranet in hopes of *the following:* improved internal communication. (Independent clause introducing single item)
>
> Some of the most commonly used manufacturers' discounts are *the following:* trade, cash, quantity, and seasonal. (Formal list with introductory expression stated)
>
> Our business uses several delivery services: UPS, Purolator, and Federal Express. (Formal list with introductory expression implied)
>
> *These* are a few of the services that a correspondent bank performs for other banks:
>
> **1.** Collecting cheques and payments
> **2.** Accepting letters of credit and travellers' cheques
> **3.** Making credit investigations (Formal list shown vertically)

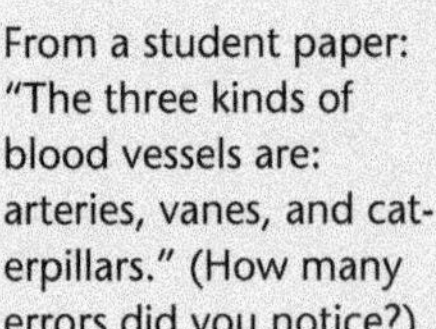

BE THE EDITOR

From a student paper: "The three kinds of blood vessels are: arteries, vanes, and caterpillars." (How many errors did you notice?)

Do not use a colon unless the list is introduced by an independent clause. Lists often function as sentence complements or objects. When this is the case, the statement introducing the list is not complete and no colon should be used. It might be easiest to remember that lists introduced by verbs or prepositions require no colons (because the introductory statement is incomplete). Therefore, generally do not place a colon after a verb or preposition.

> Three courses in this program are Accounting 103, Business English 210, and Computer Science 220. (No colon is used because the introductory statement is not complete; the list is introduced by a *to be* verb and functions as a complement.)
>
> Awards of merit were presented to Professor Loncorich, Ms. Harned, and Dr. Konishi. (No colon is used because the introductory statement is not an independent clause; the list functions as the object of the preposition *to*.)

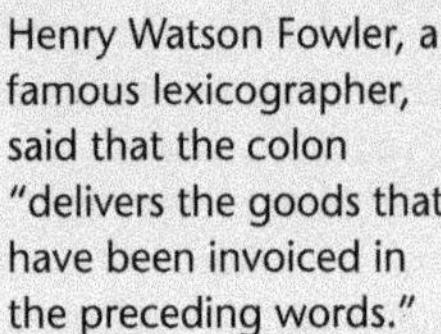

DID YOU KNOW?

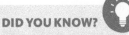

Henry Watson Fowler, a famous lexicographer, said that the colon "delivers the goods that have been invoiced in the preceding words."

Do not use a colon when an intervening sentence falls between the introductory statement and the list.

> According to a recent survey, these are the top convention cities in North America. The survey was conducted by *Tradeshow Week*.
>
> Las Vegas New York
> Vancouver Toronto

ASK AN EDITOR

Question:

When I list items vertically, should I use a comma or semicolon after each item? Should a period be used after the final item? For example,

Please inspect the following rooms and equipment:

1. *The control room*
2. *The power transformer and its standby*
3. *The auxiliary switchover equipment*

Answer:

Generally, do not punctuate items listed vertically. However, if the listed items are complete sentences, you may use periods after each item.

Long Quotations

A colon instead of a comma may be used to introduce long one-sentence quotations and quotations of two or more sentences.

> Consumer advocate Sandra Hersh said: "Historically, in our private-enterprise economy, consumers determine what and how much is to be produced through their purchases in the marketplace; hence the needs of consumers are carefully monitored by producers."

Incomplete quotations not interrupting the flow of a sentence require no colon, no comma, and no initial capital letter.

> The columnist described the Jackson-Triggs winery as "a vintner's heaven."

Explanatory Sentences

Use a colon to separate two independent clauses if the second clause explains, illustrates, or supplements the first.

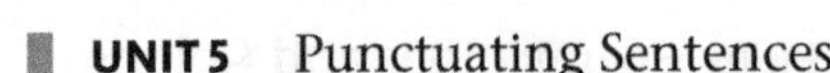

The company's newly elected directors immediately faced a perplexing dilemma: they had to choose between declaring bankruptcy and investing additional funds in an attempt to recoup previous losses.

To succeed in this job, you must remember one thing: you are here to serve the customer.

Complete the reinforcement exercises for Level II on pages 312–313.

LEVEL III

SPECIAL USES OF THE SEMICOLON

You have just studied the basic uses for semicolons and colons. Occasionally, though, these punctuation marks are used in circumstances demanding special attention. First we will look at special uses of the semicolon.

Introductory Expressions Such as *Namely, for Instance,* and *That Is*

When introductory expressions (such as *namely, for instance, that is,* and *for example*) immediately follow independent clauses, they are preceded by either commas or semicolons. Generally, if the words following the introductory expression form a series or an independent clause, use a semicolon before the introductory expression and a comma after it.

STUDY TIP

Notice that a comma follows *namely, for instance, that is,* and *for example* when these words are used as introductory expressions.

Numerous fringe benefits are available to employees*; namely,* stock options, life insurance, health insurance, dental care, and vision care. (A semicolon is used because *namely* introduces a series at the end of the sentence.)

We offer outstanding prices on flights to Europe*; for example,* flights to Glasgow and Belfast begin at $469. (A semicolon is used because *for example* introduces an independent clause.)

If the list or explanation that follows the introductory expression is not a series or an independent clause, use commas before and after the introductory expression.

Our company is considering better ways to evaluate employees*, for example,* an objective performance appraisal system. (A comma is used because *for example* introduces neither a series nor an independent clause.)

We value one trait in our employees above all others*, that is,* integrity. (A comma is used because *that is* introduces neither a series nor an independent clause.)

These same introductory expressions (*namely, for instance,* etc.) may introduce parenthetical words within sentences. Commas usually punctuate parenthetical words within sentences. If the introductory expression introduces several items punctuated by internal commas, however, use dashes or parentheses. (Dashes and parentheses are treated in detail in Chapter 17.)

The biggest health problems facing workers, *namely,* drug abuse and alcoholism, cost industry over one billion dollars a year. (Commas are used because the parenthetical words contain only two items joined by *and.*)

The pursuit of equity—for instance, in wages, job security, and working conditions—was the main concern of workers. (Dashes are used because the introductory expression introduces a series with internal commas.)

Independent Clauses With Coordinating Conjunctions

Normally, a comma precedes a coordinating conjunction (*and, or, but,* etc.) when it joins two independent clauses. If either of the independent clauses contains an additional comma, however, the reader might be confused as to where the second independent clause begins. For this reason you may use a semicolon instead of the normally expected comma.

BE THE EDITOR

Advertisement for a car wash: "We do not scratch your paint finish with machinery, we do it by hand." (Do you see two errors?)

We have considered your suggestions carefully, *and* it appears that they have considerable merit. (A comma precedes the coordinating conjunction because no additional punctuation appears within either clause.)

The first three cities recommended by the relocation committee were Atlanta, Toronto, and Detroit*; but* Vancouver, Calgary, and Seattle were also mentioned. (A semicolon precedes the coordinating conjunction to show where the second independent clause begins and to prevent confusion.)

SPECIAL USES OF COLONS

Colons also have other uses that are common in business writing.

ASK AN EDITOR

Question:

If I am using a fragment to introduce a vertical list, should I use a colon, as in the following sentence:

On today's schedule are appointments with:

- *Dr. Tim Berger at 10:30 a.m.*
- *Selena Malik at 1 p.m.*
- *Vita Sedgwick at 3:30 p.m.*

Answer:

Generally, avoid introducing vertical lists with fragments. In your example above, you could write "On today's schedule are the following appointments:" before the list.

Business Letter Salutations

Colons are placed after the salutation of a business letter with mixed punctuation.

Dear Mr. Nguyen: Dear Mike: Dear Customer Service:

Time

In expressions of time, use a colon to separate hours from minutes.

2:45 p.m. 12:01 a.m. 17:40 (24-hour clock)

Publication Titles

Place a colon between titles and subtitles of books, articles, and other publications.

HOW: A Handbook for Office Professionals (book title)
"Oil Prices: How High Can They Go?" (article title)

Capitalization Following Colons

When you use a colon to introduce a series in sentence format, do not capitalize the first word after the colon unless it is a proper noun.

The six *C*s of effective business communication are the following: clarity, courtesy, conciseness, completeness, correctness, and confidence.

These cities will receive heavy promotional advertising: Dauphin, Portage la Prairie, and Selkirk.

STUDY TIP

Generally, no punctuation follows fragments (incomplete statements) listed vertically.

Do, however, capitalize the first letter of each item in a vertical list.

To be legally enforceable, a contract must include at least three elements:

1. Mutual assent of competent parties
2. A consideration
3. A lawful purpose

The listening comprehension section of the test has three parts:

- Question and response
- Short conversations
- Short talks

Do not capitalize the first letter of an independent clause following a colon if that clause explains or supplements the first one (unless, of course, the first word is a proper noun).

> You will be interested in our credit card for one special reason: we offer you the opportunity of a full refund of the low annual fee.

Capitalize the first letter of an independent clause following a colon if that clause states a formal rule or principle.

> Experienced negotiators adhere to this principle: Never cut what you can untie.

For a quotation following a colon, capitalize the initial letter of each complete sentence.

> Commenting on the importance of incorporation, historians Krooss and Seropian said: "A strong case can be made for the proposition that the increased use of the corporation was the most important institutional innovation of the century. The corporate form permeates American business."

A FINAL WORD

Semicolons are excellent punctuation marks when used carefully and knowledgeably. After reading this chapter, though, some students are guilty of semicolon overkill. They begin to string together two—and sometimes even three—independent clauses with semicolons even if the clauses are not closely related. Remember to use semicolons in compound sentences *only* when two ideas are better presented together.

Complete the reinforcement exercises for Level III on pages 314–315.

NAME ______________________

CHAPTER 16 ■ Reinforcement Exercises

LEVEL I

A. (Self-check) For each of the following sentences, underline any errors in punctuation. In the space provided, write the correct punctuation mark plus the word preceding it. Write *C* if a sentence is correct.

EXAMPLE: Breeding and raising horses can be profitabl<u>e,</u> consequently, more landowners are investing in horses. ___profitable;___

1. Michael found it difficult to get used to working in a cubicle, at his previous job he'd had an office. ______
2. Texting is a leap backward in the science of communication, in fact, it is similar to Morse code. ______
3. By September 2018 TikTok had more monthly installs than Facebook, Instagram, YouTube, and SnapChat. ______
4. Many people buy and sell items on eBay, it is the most widely used online auction site. ______
5. Jim checked the order against the packing slip, everything came in as ordered. ______
6. Our equipment costs have tripled in the last five years, salary expenses have increased even more. ______
7. Canadians have embraced online shopping in recent years, as a matter of fact, e-commerce sites are performing better than many brick-and-mortar stores. ______
8. *Chatelaine*'s list of the "dreamiest" bookstores in Canada includes The Bookshelf in Guelph, Ontario; The Odd Book in Wolfville, Nova Scotia; Librairie Drawn & Quarterly in Montréal, Québec, and Whodunit in Winnipeg, Manitoba. ______
9. Communications is the largest sector on the list Internet services make up the second-largest sector. ______
10. Consumers are looking for alternative sources of power, thus some companies are offering such products as paper-thin batteries for compact devices. ______

Check your answers.

B. Add any necessary commas or semicolons to the following sentences. In the space provided, write the number of punctuation marks you inserted. Write *C* if a sentence is correct.

EXAMPLE: New equipment was ordered eight weeks ago; delivery is expected within two weeks. ___1___

1. Tomiko identified the problem Raeanne offered suggestions and Mallory critiqued each idea. ______

TEAR HERE

2. Toyota wants to expand beyond automobiles hence the company has moved into health care support, consulting, prefab houses, advertising, and sweet potatoes. ____________

3. Twenty-one-year-old Shadunjen van Kampen is the first Indigenous woman to complete training to become a commercial pilot in Yukon. ____________

4. Some of the most famous product failures in history, along with the companies responsible, have included the Hula Burger McDonald's the Betamax Sony and Breakfast Mates Kellogg's. ____________

5. Our cabin rentals are suitable for businesses planning company retreats meetings or special events families needing accommodations to attend weddings reunions or other celebrations or school groups organizing overnight field trips in a natural setting. ____________

6. Your account is now several months past due as a result it is not possible for us to grant you further extensions. ____________

7. All items should be input into the computer bar-coded and priced before being put on shelves. ____________

8. We must write an ad to get applicants for the temporary jobs available in December then we must figure out how to reach those applicants. ____________

9. Maxwell arrived he clocked in and he began serving customers. ____________

10. The hotel has sent us many discount coupons for local attractions but we won't have an opportunity to take advantage of any of them. ____________

11. Dawson City was full of fortune hunters at the turn of the century it is now full of tourists, at least during the summer. ____________

12. Computer hackers can easily decode short passwords thus passwords should be at least eight characters long and be a mix of letters and numerals. ____________

13. Web advertising attempts to reach large international audiences television advertising is aimed at national or local audiences. ____________

14. If you want to decrease theft in your store install security cameras they act as a deterrent for all but the most brazen of shoplifters. ____________

15. Five applicant cities—Paris France Hamburg Germany Budapest Hungary Rome Italy and Los Angeles U.S.A.—were competing to host the 2024 Summer Olympics. ____________

16. Smart companies assume their computer networks will be broken into consequently they develop computer-use policies to limit the damage. ____________

17. This bank branch is closing on April 30 please visit the branch located at 2025 Harwood Avenue. ____________

18. Our training can usually be completed in six to ten months therefore you can begin earning a full wage in less than a year. ____________

19. If you adopt our automatic payroll system employees can download our app to check their hours pay rate and the status of their paycheques moreover our system allows you to produce countless useful reports with the touch of a button. ____________

20. At this time we are allowing curbside pickup of orders Mondays 10 a.m. to 2 p.m. Wednesdays noon to 4 p.m. and Fridays 10 a.m. to 2 p.m. ____________

TEAR HERE

NAME ____________________

LEVEL II

A. **(Self-check)** For each of the following sentences, underline any errors in punctuation. In the space provided, write the correct punctuation plus the preceding word. If a colon should be omitted, write *Omit colon.* Write *C* if a sentence is correct.

EXAMPLE: Business model patents were awarded to: Netflix, TiVo, and Priceline. ___Omit colon___

1. In order to be awarded a business model patent, the idea must be: concrete, useful, new, and unique. ____________
2. The Canadian Federation of Independent Business provides the following services to small business owners; advocating on their behalf with multiple levels of government, business counselling, and helping businesses ensure compliance. ____________
3. During the presentation the realtor explained; "If you purchase before the start of construction, you can choose from 20 suite layouts; you can also customize your suite. Best of all, you can still take advantage of pre-construction prices." ____________
4. The head of the computer security firm admitted one big problem: it is difficult to find good people without criminal records. ____________
5. *Fortune* selected five companies as the most socially responsible; Vodaphone, General Electric, HSBC Holdings, France Télécom, and HBOS. ____________
6. Other socially responsible companies include the following. Please check the *Fortune* website for the complete list: ____________
   Nokia
   Électricité de France
   GDF Suez
7. The services offered by the spa include: facials, manicures and pedicures, laser hair removal, and specialized skin treatments. ____________
8. Because of the urgency of the problem, we have left phone messages for: Chief Joseph Wallace, Patricia Longbranch, and William Spencer. ____________
9. The shipment has been detained at the border, bugs were discovered in the pallets. ____________
10. Shane proposed a solution to our daycare problem: open a home office and share child care duties. ____________

Check your answers.

B. For the following sentences, add any necessary punctuation. In the space provided, write the number of punctuation marks you inserted. Write *C* if a sentence is correct.

EXAMPLE: Shipments of computer components will be sent to Dallas, Vancouver, Barcelona, and Zurich. ___3___

1. Polygraph examinations generally consist of four elements a pre-examination interview, a demonstration, questioning of the examinee, and a post-examination interview. ____________

TEAR HERE

2. Many young applicants today are making one big mistake they are sharing too much information about their personal lives online. ______________

3. B. J. Fogg, director of Stanford University's Persuasive Technology Lab, said "Finding the right balance will take time, if it is ever achieved. Unlike face-to-face conversations, there's really no good way yet for people to let one another know that they are being too revealing." ______________

4. Many companies are augmenting their marketing efforts with social media activity on sites such as Facebook Twitter and Instagram. ______________

5. The records of the following employees will be reviewed for salary evaluation Please send the records by October 1

   Vicky Peck   Julie Mauer
   Tony Watkins   Ivan Krakowski ______________

6. Before reopening after COVID-19, businesses took several precautions having hand sanitizer at the entrance putting up Plexiglas barriers by the cash requiring employees to wear face masks and ensuring surfaces were disinfected several times a day. ______________

7. These are the three types of business structures sole proprietorship, partnership, and incorporation. ______________

8. A sole proprietor claims income for the business on his or her personal tax form whereas a corporation files taxes separately. ______________

9. Our engineers are creating a new wheelchair design with these features lighter weight, height-adjustable arm rests, swing-away leg rests, and elevating seat. ______________

10. The law of supply and demand can function under only one condition producers must know what consumers want. ______________

11. Professor Charlotte Cohen asked that research reports contain the following parts introduction body summary and bibliography. ______________

12. Additional costs in selling a house are title search, land transfer tax, preparation of documents, and closing fee. ______________

13. Henry Ford said "If money is your hope for independence, you will never have it. The only real security that a man can have in this world is a reserve of knowledge, experience, and ability." ______________

14. Copyright gives the creator of an original work domain over how that work is used a trademark protects a word, name, or symbol and distinguishes the associated product from like products and a patent prevents others from reproducing an invention in any form. ______________

15. Facebook has acquired many tech products since 2004, including Bloomsbury AI, Redkix, and Oculus VR. ______________

TEAR HERE

NAME ________________________

LEVEL III

A. **(Self-check)** In the following sentences, add any necessary punctuation. In the space provided, write the number of punctuation marks you inserted. Write *C* if a sentence is correct.

1. The meeting started promptly at 1:15 p.m. and ended at 3:45 p.m. ________

2. Sales personnel may be assigned to other countries we have offices in; for example, India, Brazil, France, and South Africa. ________

3. If she accepts the transfer to Calgary, she will have a better chance of promotion but if she declines the transfer, her family will not be uprooted. ________

4. Canada's Top Employers for Young People are selected based on the programs they've implemented to attract younger workers namely tuition assistance work-study programs mentorship programs and advancement opportunities. ________

5. Nutrien Ltd. a fertilizer company in Saskatoon for example has an Aboriginal Internship Program it gives Indigenous students an opportunity to be mentored, meet peers, and participate in community initiatives. ________

6. All employees are urged to observe the following rule When in doubt, consult the company style manual. ________

7. For the opening session of the convention, the keynote speaker will be Norma Patterson, systems analyst; and for the afternoon general membership meeting, the speaker will be Judith R. Rice, union representative. ________

8. A must-read book for retail managers is *Why We Buy the Science of Shopping.* ________

9. When calculating holiday pay, you must count only regular hours worked that is do not include vacation pay or overtime pay. ________

10. You may pay your invoice using any of the following methods: credit card, cheque, or online payment. ________

Check your answers.

B. In the following sentences, add any necessary punctuation. In the space provided, write the number of punctuation marks you inserted. Write *C* if a sentence is correct.

EXAMPLE: If she completes the proposal, Ms. Upchurch will fly to Ottawa on Tuesday; if not, she will leave on Thursday. 3

1. We are looking for a number of traits in our new sales associate good communication skills outgoing personality and patience. ________

2. Because of his extended service abroad Edward Mautz was selected to head the export division and because of her outstanding sales experience Piya Malom was selected to head the marketing division. ________

3. An author, a composer, or a photographer may protect his or her product with a government-approved monopoly namely a copyright. ________

TEAR HERE

4. The book club will discuss Stacy Perman's *In-N-Out Burger A Behind-the-Counter Look at the Fast-Food Chain That Breaks All the Rules* at next week's meeting. ____________

5. The writer of a research report should include a variety of references; for instance, books, periodicals, government publications, and newspapers. ____________

6. Three times have been designated for the interviews Thursday at 630 p.m. Friday at 330 p.m. and Monday at 10 a.m. ____________

7. Companies that plan to expand in China should be aware of several important factors for example regulatory environment cultural differences and technologies in use. ____________

8. The FedEx work culture includes an Open Door program that is the company encourages its employees to interact openly with management. ____________

9. Franca Santin a sales representative for Bombardier enjoyed her position very much but when a competing company offered her a substantial increase in salary she found it very tempting. ____________

10. Fascinating stories circulate about Henry Ford founder of the Ford Motor Company Lee Iacocca former CEO Chrysler Motor Company and Shoichiro Toyoda former chief Toyota Motor Company. ____________

C. Insert a colon, a semicolon, or a comma in the space in each of the following sentences.

1. If you want to apply for a Visa card for your business, contact one of the following banks__ CIBC, RBC, Scotiabank, or TD.
2. Although approximately 90 percent of private-sector employees work in small and medium-sized enterprises__ these businesses are the least likely to receive government bailouts when in trouble.
3. Some employees may be required to work on public holidays__ those in hospitality, health care, and businesses with continuous operations, for example, may have to work their regular shift but be paid a premium to do it.
4. A significant benefit of Square's point-of-sale system is that it is free__ Shopify, on the other hand, requires a paid subscription but offers lower credit card processing fees.
5. Companies across North America are reconsidering their real estate needs__ that is, a fixed physical space for all their employees.

D. **Writing Exercise.** Your instructor may ask you to complete this exercise on a separate sheet.

According to the instructions that follow, write eight sentences about the software programs you use. Here is an example: *I use Microsoft Word for most documents I create; however, I have recently found several uses for Excel.*

(a) Write three original sentences illustrating basic uses of semicolons.

(b) Write one sentence using *namely* with a semicolon preceding it.

(c) Write three original sentences illustrating basic uses of colons.

(d) Compose a list arranged vertically, and write an introduction to it using an independent clause that requires a colon.

Label each of the eight items with (a), (b), (c), or (d).

TEAR HERE

POSTTEST

In the following sentences, add any necessary semicolons, colons, and commas.

1. The Ford Edsel was one of the most famous business failures in history Coca-Cola's New Coke was another well-known disappointment.
2. Nick Hahn, advertising consultant, said "Placing the product in the past is comforting to consumers. It grounds them in a time when things were better."
3. Companies must have one goal when using nostalgia in advertising campaigns they must evoke a brand's heritage in a contemporary way.
4. Have you read Robert K. Greenleaf's book *Servant Leadership A Journey Into the Nature of Legitimate Power and Greatness*?
5. Gas prices are rising dramatically therefore more people are riding their bikes or walking.
6. The best leaders possess one important trait integrity.
7. The following instructors have been chosen to represent their schools at the professional meeting Ian Mason Cégep de Jonquière Patricia Parnall Sir Sandford Fleming College and Richard Almonte George Brown College.
8. Items in the conference kits include granola bars, branded reusable water bottles, a book, and a vendors' guide.
9. Farm Credit Canada is a Crown corporation that is a business created by government but operating outside of it.
10. Google offers unique benefits to its employees for instance an on-site hairstylist, meals prepared by gourmet chefs, financial planning classes, a shuttle service, and an outdoor volleyball court.

EDITOR'S CHALLENGE

The following memos contain errors. Use proofreading marks to indicate corrections.

TO: Patrick M. Young

FROM: Kellie Whitford

DATE: May 2, 202x

SUBJECT: Sites for *Bodega Bay* Telefilm

This memo describes the progress of my search for a appropriate rustic home, villa, or farmhouse. To be used for the wine country sequences in the upcoming telefilm *Bodega Bay.* As you requested three sites has been selected for you to inspect on May 21.

Background. To prepare for this assignment I consulted Director Mario Polero who gave me his preferences for the sight. He wants a picturesque home, that is located near vineyards, moreover he would like woods in the background. I also consulted Producer Tucker Setterberg who told me that the site must accommodate 55 to 70 production crew members for approximately three weeks' of filming. Jocelyn Garcia who is our telefilm accountant requested that the cost of the site not exceed $24,000, for a three week lease.

Work Completed. For the past eight days I have searched the Niagara Peninsula in the southern Ontario wine country. Since this area is rich with history I was able to locate many possibilities including: turn-of-the-century estates, Victorian mansions and rustic farmhouses. One of the best sites are the Country Meadows a 97 year old farmhouse, with a breathtaking view of vallies and woods. The most promising towns are the following Niagara-on-the-Lake, St. Catharines and Pelham.

Work to Be Completed. In the next few days I'll search the Ontario countryside, and inspect winerys such as: Jackson-Triggs, Hillebrand, and Inniskillin. Many of the older winerys has charming structures, however they also attract tourists, and crowds of people.

By May 14, you'll have my final report, that will describe the three better locations.

TEAR HERE

CompuFix

Interoffice Memo

DATE: February 3, 202x

TO: Doug Brent

FROM: Sonya Takado ST

SUBJECT: Hiring Interns for Summer Program

The Human Resources' Department was recently contacted by Mr. Bruce Tang P.Eng. an administrator of the computer systems technician program at Camosun College. Camosun prides themselves on the one main aspect that differentiates their program from other's, it's students get a guaranteed internship. Mr. Tang has asked weather CompuFix are willing to take part in Camuson's internship program therefore I want to inform you that HR is offering its support to you if your interested in adding an intern to your group.

An intern can offer sevral advantages to your department; help ease the workload as technicians take vacations through the summer months, bring a fresh prospective, youthfull enthusiasm, and recent learning too a team, and potentially fill a future vacancy while requiring less-training post-internship.

Should you chose to hire a intern for a two-month work placement, HR will help by providing interns with: an interview experience, feedback on their resumé, a workstation, and an honorarium at the end of the placement.

To discuss this oportunity please contact me at extention 261, or by email at your earliest convience.

For additional resources, please visit MindTap at login.cengage.com. Cengage | MINDTAP

TEAR HERE

OTHER PUNCTUATION

CHAPTER

17

OBJECTIVES

When you have completed the materials in this chapter, you will be able to do the following:

LEVEL I

- Use periods to correctly punctuate statements, commands, indirect questions, and polite requests
- Use periods to correctly punctuate abbreviations and numerals
- Use question marks and exclamation marks correctly

LEVEL II

- Recognize acceptable applications for dashes and parentheses
- Correctly punctuate and capitalize material set off by parentheses

LEVEL III

- Use double and single quotation marks properly
- Correctly place other punctuation marks in relation to quotation marks
- Use brackets, underlines, and italics appropriately

PRETEST

Use proofreading marks to insert appropriate punctuation and formatting in the following sentences.

1. Wow What a presentation
2. I wonder whether all candidates for the C E O position completed M B A degrees
3. Will you please send certificates to Wanda Allenton and P M Brin
4. Ms Graf has an appointment for 4 p m doesn't she

(continued)

PRETEST (CONTINUED)

5. Dr Lee Ms Adams and Mr Khan have been appointed to the Y M C A committee
6. Was the Canadian Business article you wanted me to read called How to Rebrand Your Company's Image the Right Way
7. Please invite Radene Schroeder Ph D and M L Vasquez M D
8. Three industries pipelines construction and petroleum refining are experiencing the most growth
9. The best chapter in Thomas L Friedman's book The World Is Flat was How Companies Cope
10. Did Lavina just ask Why haven't we got the website specs yet

As you have already learned, punctuation can make all the difference in your writing. This chapter continues our discussion of punctuation by teaching you how to use periods, question marks, and exclamation marks correctly. It also includes guidelines for using dashes, parentheses, single and double quotation marks, brackets, underlines, and italics.

LEVEL I

USES FOR THE PERIOD

The period is used to punctuate sentences, abbreviations, initials, and numerals. Guidelines for each use are covered in this section.

To Punctuate Statements, Commands, and Indirect Questions

Most sentences in business and professional writing end with periods. Use a period at the end of a statement, a command, or an indirect question.

Ali Mazahri was promoted to a new position with increased salary and responsibilities. (Statement)
Send them our latest catalogue and price list. (Command)
Marilyn asked whether we had sent the price list. (Indirect question)

To Punctuate Polite Requests

Use a period, not a question mark, to punctuate a polite request. A **polite request** is a command or suggestion phrased as a request. Such a request asks the reader to perform a specific action instead of responding with a *yes* or a *no*.

Could you please turn your cellphone off during the meeting.
May I suggest that you follow the instructions on page 6 of your manual.
Will you be sure to lock the door when you leave.

If you are uncomfortable using a period at the end of a polite request, rephrase the sentence so that it is more clearly a command.

Will you please mail your cheque in the enclosed envelope. (Polite request)
Please mail your cheque in the enclosed envelope. (Polite request rephrased as a command)
You should mail your cheque in the enclosed envelope. (Polite request rephrased as statement)

ASK AN EDITOR

Question:
In email messages is it acceptable to use abbreviations such as IMHO (in my humble opinion), LOL (laughing out loud), and TIA (thanks in advance)?

Answer:
Among close friends who understand their meaning, such abbreviations are certainly acceptable. But in business messages, these abbreviations are too casual and too obscure. Not all readers would know what they mean. Emoticons (or smileys) such as :-) are also too casual for business messages. Worst of all, such abbreviations and emoticons make business messages look immature and unprofessional.

To Punctuate Abbreviations

Abbreviations are shortened versions of words. Because of their inconsistencies, abbreviations sometimes present problems for writers. The following suggestions will help you organize certain groups of abbreviations and will provide many models. In studying these models, note the spacing, capitalization, and use of periods. For a more thorough list of acceptable abbreviations, consult an up-to-date dictionary or style manual.

Use periods after most abbreviations beginning with lowercase letters. Notice that the internal periods are not followed by spaces.

a.m. (ante meridiem) p.m. (post meridiem)
doz. (dozen) i.e. (that is)
e.g. (for example) etc. (et cetera or and so on)
misc. (miscellaneous) enc. (enclosure)

Use periods for most abbreviations containing both uppercase and lowercase letters.

Dr. (Doctor) No. (Number)
Esq. (Esquire) Rev. (Reverend)
Ms. (blend of Miss and Mrs.) Sat. (Saturday)
Mr. (Mister) Feb. (February)

Use periods with abbreviations that represent initials of a person's first and middle names. Note that a person's initials are separated by a space when they appear with a surname.

Ronald J. Gilmore J. A. Jones (initials)

Some terms that began as abbreviations have become accepted as words over time and do not take periods.

fax (facsimile) perk (perquisite)
tech (technology, technologist) rep (representative)
ad (advertisement) specs (specifications)
phone (telephone) gas (gasoline)

Do *not* use periods or internal spaces for most other capitalized abbreviations, such as these.

BA (bachelor of arts)
CBC (Canadian Broadcasting Corporation)
CEO (chief executive officer)
CFO (chief financial officer)
CPU (central processing unit)
EST (Eastern Standard Time)
FYI (for your information)
IBM (International Business Machines)
ID (identification)
IPO (initial public offering)
MBE (Member of the Order of the British Empire)
MD (doctor of medicine)
PDF (portable document format)
PhD (doctor of philosophy)
RRSP (registered retirement savings plan)
SASE (self-addressed, stamped envelope)
SIDS (sudden infant death syndrome)

ASK AN EDITOR

Question:
What is the name of a group of initials that form a word? Is it an abbreviation?

Answer:
A word formed from the initial letters of an expression is called an **acronym** (pronounced *ACK-ro-nim*). Examples include *scuba*, from *self-contained underwater breathing apparatus*, and *PIN*, from *personal identification number*. Acronyms are pronounced as words, unlike abbreviations, which are pronounced letter by letter. *RCMP* and *NHL*, for example, are abbreviations.

SOP (standard operating procedure)
UNEF (United Nations Emergency Force)
URL (universal resource locator)
USA (United States of America)
YYZ (Toronto Pearson International Airport code)

STUDY TIP

Most abbreviations fall into this group: capitalized letters, no periods, and tight spacing.

(Readers of previous editions of this text may notice a change in the treatment of academic degrees. Current prevalent practice is to use no periods.)

If the last word in a sentence is an abbreviation that takes a period, do not add an extra period to end the sentence.

The meeting was scheduled for 9 a.m. (Not *a.m.*.)
The company offers many perks: an on-site gym, discounted tickets to certain events, free-pizza Fridays, etc. (Not *etc.*.)

Do *not* confuse metric symbols with abbreviations. As symbols, they require no periods and no *s* in their plural form.

cm (centimetre/s)
g (gram/s)
kg (kilogram/s)
km (kilometre/s)
m (metre/s)
mm (millimetre/s)

To Punctuate Numerals

For a monetary sum, use a period (decimal point) to separate dollars from cents.

The two items in question, $13.92 and $98.07, were both charged in the month of October.

BE THE EDITOR

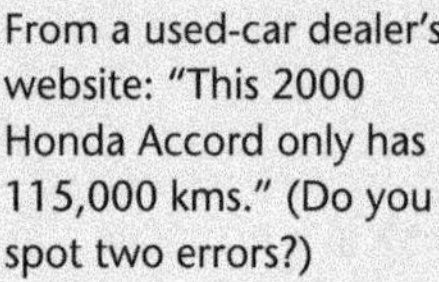

From a used-car dealer's website: "This 2000 Honda Accord only has 115,000 kms." (Do you spot two errors?)

Use a period (decimal point) to mark a decimal.

Only 38.6 percent of registered voters actually voted in Wednesday's election.

USES FOR THE QUESTION MARK

The question mark punctuates direct questions and questions added to statements.

To Punctuate Direct Questions

Use a question mark at the end of a direct question. A **direct question** requires an answer.

Have you sent the price list?
What can we do to improve communication among departments?

To Punctuate Questions Added to Statements

Place a question mark after a question that is added to the end of a statement (a tag question). Use a comma to separate the statement from the question.

The laptop and cellphone charging stations at the airport are free to use, aren't they?
This HR announcement should be sent by email, don't you think?

STUDY TIP

Don't be tempted to punctuate statements that suggest uncertainty as questions. For example, "I wonder whether he called" is a statement, not a question.

To Indicate Doubt

A question mark within parentheses may be used to indicate a degree of doubt about some aspect of a statement.

After Google went public (2004?), its stock price increased dramatically.
Shaun said he was late because his car (a hybrid?) wouldn't start in the cold weather.

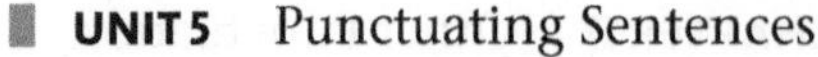

USE FOR THE EXCLAMATION MARK

After a word, phrase, or clause expressing strong emotion, use an exclamation mark. The exclamation mark is an emphatic mark of punctuation reserved for strong feelings. Business, professional, and academic writers use it sparingly.

> Impossible! We understood the deadline to be tomorrow.
> What a day! It seems as though closing time will never come.
> It is incredible that my Apple watch is still working after such punishment!

Do not use an exclamation point after mild interjections such as *oh* and *well*.

> Well, it seems we have little choice in the matter.

Complete the reinforcement exercises for Level I on pages 328–329.

LEVEL II

USES FOR THE DASH

The dash is often used to show emphasis. As an emphatic punctuation mark, however, the dash loses effectiveness when it is overused. In a word processing program, you form a dash by typing two hyphens with no space before, between, or after the hyphens. In printed or desktop publishing-generated material, a dash appears as a solid line that is longer than a hyphen (called an *em* dash—it is the width of the capital letter *M*). Study the following suggestions for and illustrations of appropriate uses of the dash.

To Set Off Parenthetical Elements and Appositives

Within a sentence parenthetical elements are usually set off by commas. If, however, the parenthetical element itself contains internal commas or deserves emphasis, use dashes to set it off. (As discussed later in this section, parentheses may be used instead if the information should be de-emphasized.)

> Sources of raw materials—farming, mining, fishing, and forestry—are all dependent on energy.
> Four legal assistants—Priscilla Alvarez, Vicky Evans, Yoshiki Naka, and Edward Botsko—received cash bonuses for outstanding service.
> All employees—and that includes Ann Patterson—must work overtime this weekend. (Although the parenthetical element doesn't contain commas, it is set off to add emphasis.)

To Indicate an Interruption or Afterthought

An interruption or abrupt change of thought or afterthought may be separated from the rest of a sentence by dashes. However, sentences with abrupt changes of thought or with appended afterthoughts can usually be improved through rewriting.

> The shipment will be on its way—you have my word—by Wednesday. (Interruption of thought)
> You can submit your report Friday—no, we must have it by Thursday at the latest. (Abrupt change of thought)

To Set Off a Summarizing Statement

Use a dash (not a colon) to separate an introductory list from a summarizing statement.

Variety of tasks, contact with people, opportunity for advancement—these are traits I seek in a job.

Cross-country skiing, hiking, and reading—those are Rudy's favourite pastimes.

To Attribute a Quotation

Place a dash between a quotation and its source.

BE THE EDITOR

From a box of cereal: "Everyday's a new adventure with Katy."

"Live as if you were to die tomorrow. Learn as if you were to live forever." —Mahatma Gandhi

"English is the language of men ever famous and foremost in the achievements of liberty." —John Milton

USES FOR PARENTHESES

Parentheses are used in pairs. Parentheses can be used to enclose a complete sentence or to enclose a word or an expression within a sentence. This section covers guidelines for using parentheses correctly.

STUDY TIP

Parentheses say to the reader, "This is not that important; you can wait until you finish the sentence to read it." Dashes say, "Hey, this is important; pay attention!"

To Set Off Non-essential Sentence Elements

Generally, non-essential sentence elements may be punctuated as follows: (a) with commas, to make the lightest possible break in the normal flow of a sentence; (b) with dashes, to emphasize the enclosed material; and (c) with parentheses, to de-emphasize the enclosed material.

Figure 17, which appears on page 9, shows the internal structure of the engine. (Normal punctuation)

Figure 17—which appears on page 9—shows the internal structure of the engine. (Dashes emphasize enclosed material.)

Figure 17 (which appears on page 9) shows the internal structure of the engine. (Parentheses de-emphasize enclosed material.)

Explanations, references, and directions are usually enclosed in parentheses when used as non-essential sentence elements.

The bank's current business hours (10 a.m. to 3 p.m.) will be extended soon (to 6 p.m.).

We recommend that you use hearing protectors (see our comment on p. 618) when using this electric drill.

To Show Numerals and Enclose Enumerated Items

In legal documents and contracts, numerals commonly appear in both word and figure form. Parentheses enclose the figures in such documents. However, business writers seldom use this wordy technique.

Your contract states that the final instalment payment is due in ninety (90) days.

When using numbers or letters to enumerate lists within sentences, enclose the numbers or letters in parentheses. Use letters for items that have no particular order; use numbers for items that suggest a sequence.

To pay your bill online, (1) log on to our secure website, (2) click the Pay Bill link, (3) select the bill you want to pay, (4) input the amount you want to pay, (5) select the date on which you want to make payment, (6) click the Pay button, and (7) click the Confirm button.

Punctuating Around Parentheses

If the material enclosed by parentheses is embedded within another sentence, a question mark or an exclamation mark may be used where normally expected. Do not, however, use a period after a statement embedded within another sentence.

I visited the new business travel website (have you seen it?) last night.

The fire alarm sounded (but no one moved!) in the middle of our annual general meeting.

This air conditioner cools 800 square metres of space (if used as outlined in the user manual).

If the material enclosed by parentheses is not embedded in another sentence, use whatever punctuation is required. Note that the item in parentheses begins with a capital letter in this case.

Report writers must document all references. (See Appendix C for a guide to current documentation formats.)

In less than ten years, the price of that article has tripled. (Who would have thought it possible?)

In sentences involving expressions within parentheses, a comma, semicolon, or colon that would normally occupy the position occupied by the second parenthesis is then placed after that parenthesis.

When I return from my trip (in late June), I will begin work on the feasibility study. (Comma follows closing parenthesis.)

Your application for a credit card was received before the deadline (November 1); however, you did not supply two financial references. (Semicolon follows closing parenthesis.)

Complete the reinforcement exercises for Level II on pages 330–332.

BE THE EDITOR

From globalnews.ca: "The person was just curious and looking at information, there was nothing illegal going on per say." (Do you see two errors?)

LEVEL III

USES FOR QUOTATION MARKS

Quotation marks help readers understand what words were written or spoken by somebody else. They may also be used to enclose short expressions, definitions, and titles.

To Enclose Direct Quotations

Quotation marks are used to enclose direct quotations. Unless the exact words of a writer or speaker are being repeated, however, do not use quotation marks.

"I think there is a world market for about five computers," said IBM founder Thomas J. Watson. (Direct quotation enclosed.)

Dwight Moody said that character is what you are in the dark. (Indirect quotation requires no quotation marks.)

BE THE EDITOR

Sign in a public washroom: "Employees must 'wash hands.'"

Capitalize only the first word of a direct quotation.

"The office staff," said Ms. Rogers, "has now reached its full complement." (Do not capitalize the word *has* since it continues the sentence.)

To Enclose Quotations Within Quotations

Use single quotation marks (apostrophes on most keyboards) to enclose quoted passages cited within quoted passages.

Sharon Miles remarked, "In business writing I totally agree with Aristotle, who said, 'A good style must, first of all, be clear.'"

STUDY TIP

In North American style (which differs from European style), periods and commas are always *inside* quotation marks. Semicolons and colons are always outside. The position of question marks and exclamation marks depends on the material quoted.

To Enclose Short Expressions

Slang, jargon, words used in a special sense such as for humour or irony, and words following *stamped, labelled,* or *marked* are usually enclosed within quotation marks.

Did you know our CEO was so "woke"? (Slang)
In web terminology robots are referred to as "bots." (Jargon)
Once "charged," my phone's battery lasts less than five minutes. (Irony)
The package was stamped "Handle with care." (Words following *stamped*)

To Enclose Definitions

Quotation marks are used to enclose formal definitions of words or expressions. The word or expression being defined should be underlined or set in italics.

The Latin word *ergo* means "therefore" or "hence."
Business people use the term *working capital* to indicate an "excess of current assets over current debts."

ASK AN EDITOR

Question:
We can't decide whether a period should go inside quotation marks or outside. At the end of a sentence, I have typed the title "Positive Vs. Negative Values." The author of the document wants the period outside because she says the title does not have a period in it.

Answer:
In North America when a period or comma falls at the same place quotation marks would normally fall, the period or comma is always placed inside the quotation marks, regardless of the content of the quotation. (In Britain a different style is observed; a few Canadian publishers may use that style.)

To Enclose Titles

Quotation marks are used to enclose titles of subdivisions of literary and artistic works, such as magazine and newspaper articles, book chapters, poems, lectures, TV show episodes, and songs. However, titles of entire books, magazines, pamphlets, newspapers, plays, movies, music albums, and television series are set in italics (or underlined).

Business communication students should regularly reread the section of *Canadian Business English* entitled "Sentence Faults."
Rob left the *Canadian Business* article "Here's What Happens When You Get a Treadmill Desk" in his boss's office as a subtle hint.
In the episode of *The Office* called "Diversity Day," the boss, played by Steve Carell, managed to offend everyone.

Punctuating Around Quotation Marks

Periods and commas are always placed inside closing single or double quotation marks.

Betty said, "I'm sure the package was marked 'Fragile.'"
The article is called "Bad Business of Banks," but I don't have a copy.

Semicolons and colons are, on the other hand, always placed outside quotation marks.

The contract stipulated that "both parties must accept arbitration as binding"; therefore, the decision reached by the arbitrators is final.

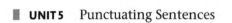

Three dates have been scheduled for the seminar called "Successful E-Business": April 1, May 3, and June 5.

Question marks and exclamation marks may go either inside or outside closing quotation marks. If the question mark or exclamation mark belongs to the text in quotation marks, place it inside; if the punctuation belongs to the surrounding text, place it outside.

Stefan can identify with the *Forbes* article "If You Don't Trust Me, Why Did You Hire Me?" (Question mark belongs to the quoted text.)
"The next time your cellphone rings," fumed the CEO, "we will ask you to leave!" (Quotation is an exclamation.)
Do you know who said, "Money is more trouble than it's worth"? (Surrounding text asks a question; quotation does not.)
I can't believe that the invoice had a stamp saying "Overdue"! (Surrounding text is an exclamation; quotation is not.)

If both the quoted and surrounding text ask questions, use only one question mark, and place it inside the quotation marks.

When did the manager ask, "Who wants to reserve a summer vacation?"

USES FOR ITALICS

Use italics (or underline if italics are not available) for titles of books, magazines, newspapers, pamphlets, albums, movies, plays, and other complete published or artistic works that contain subdivisions. In addition, italicize words under discussion in a sentence and used as nouns.

Bank on Yourself, a book by Pamela G. Yellen, was favourably reviewed in *The Wall Street Journal*. (Complete published works)
Two of the most frequently misspelled words are *calendar* and *separate*. (Words used as words under discussion)

USES FOR BRACKETS

Within quotations, brackets are used by writers to enclose their own inserted remarks. Such remarks may be corrective, illustrative, or explanatory. Brackets are also used within quotations to enclose the word *sic*, which means "thus" or "so." This Latin word emphasizes the fact that an error actually appears thus in the quoted material.

"A British imperial gallon," reported Miss Sedgewick, "is equal to 1.2 US gallons [4.54 litres]." (Explanatory remark)
"The company's reorganization program," wrote President Theodore Bailey, "will have its greatest affect *[sic]* on our immediate sales."

Complete the reinforcement exercises for Level III on pages 333–334.

ASK AN EDITOR

Question:
I'm not sure where to place the question mark in this sentence: *His topic will be "What Is a Good Health Plan (?)"* Does the question mark go inside the quotation marks? Also, should a comma precede the title of the talk?

Answer:
First, the question mark goes inside the quotation mark because the quoted material is a question. Be sure that you do not use another end punctuation mark after the quotation mark. Second, do not use a comma preceding the title because the sentence follows normal subject–verb–complement order. No comma is needed to separate the verb and the complement (the title).

DID YOU KNOW?

Italic type was invented in the fifteenth century in Italy for use in courts.

ASK AN EDITOR

Question:
Where should the word *sic* be placed when it is used?

Answer:
Sic means "thus" or "so stated" and is properly placed immediately after the word or phrase to which it refers. For example, *The article said that "the past few weeks have been unusually peaceful for Steven* [sic] *Harper and his government." Sic* is used within a quotation to indicate that a quoted word or phrase, though inaccurately used or spelled, appeared thus in the original. *Sic* is italicized and placed within brackets.

NAME ________________

CHAPTER 17 ■ Reinforcement Exercises

LEVEL I

A. **(Self-check)** In the space provided after each of the following sentences, indicate whether a period, a question mark, or an exclamation mark is needed. Use proofreading marks.

EXAMPLE: May I please have your answer by return mail ⊙

1. Will you be sure to log off before you leave ________
2. What a great sales day ________
3. I wonder who the keynote speaker will be ________
4. Has anyone tracked the package on the Purolator website ________
5. Contact us today for a free estimate ________
6. Wow! How inspirational ________
7. Graham asked what our next Instagram giveaway will be ________
8. Oh, I don't believe we should worry about it at this time ________
9. The meeting is at 2 p.m., isn't it ________
10. Would you please sign on pages two and six ________

Check your answers.

B. In the following sentences, all punctuation has been omitted. Insert necessary commas, periods, question marks, colons, and exclamation marks. Some words have extra space between them so that punctuation may be inserted easily; however, a space does not mean that punctuation is necessary. Use a caret (‸) to indicate most insertions. In the space provided, indicate the number of punctuation marks you inserted. Consult a dictionary or a reference manual for abbreviation style if necessary.

EXAMPLE: Will you please add Mr⊙ T⊙ G⊙ Skaggs Jr⊙ to the address list⊙ 5

1. Neve asked whether Murray J Lewis was hired as C I O at Dolby Laboratories Inc ________
2. Can you please leave a message for me on my cell ________
3. The client asked whether a new C P U is needed ________
4. Well we did a fantastic job didn't we ________
5. It was Ms Jenkins not Mr Reed who was appointed educational consultant to C N I B ________

TEAR HERE

6. How do you think the changes the C R T C has made to its Canadian content regulations will affect T V viewers ______

7. Stop Save that file before changing it ______

8. Please deliver the signed contracts to Mr C P Ryan before 5 p m ______

9. If I B M were to offer a full-service contract we would be interested ______

10. What a great choice for V P ______

11. Darren asked whether most automobiles were delivered f o b ______

12. Must the candidate have an M B A ______

13. The Toronto office pipes in radio station C F M X because the manager Ms Sim prefers that station ______

14. Does he often confuse the abbreviations e g and i e in his email messages ______

15. Will you be able to R S V P by Fri Sept 30 ______

16. Do any of the open positions require I Q testing ______

17. Has the erroneous charge of $45 95 been removed from my account ______

18. The guest list includes Dr Lyn Clark Ms Deborah Kitchin and Prof Sonya Chin ______

19. Beata asked whether in her absence we've watered her plants, fed her goldfish, etc ______

20. Why we have not heard from the C F O is a mystery to me ______

21. You did change your P I N for your entry card didn't you ______

22. Among the speakers are the following Michael Hartman M D and Gail Nemire R N ______

23. The strongest candidate earned his B A at U B C ______

24. Indigenous Corporate Training Inc which specializes in working effectively with people of Indigenous descent is hosting today's training session ______

25. Wow I have no response to that ______

TEAR HERE

NAME ______________________

LEVEL II

A. (Self-check) In the space provided, write the letter of the best version of each sentence.

1. (De-emphasize parenthetical element.)
(a) Four features—camera, text messaging, web access, and voice mail—are what consumers want most in their cellphones.
(b) Four features, camera, text messaging, web access, and voice mail, are what consumers want most on their cellphones.
(c) Four features (camera, text messaging, web access, and voice mail) are what consumers want most on their cellphones. ______________

2. (a) "The greatest glory in living lies not in never falling, but in rising every time we fall." —Nelson Mandela
(b) "The greatest glory in living lies not in never falling, but in rising every time we fall," Nelson Mandela
(c) "The greatest glory in living lies not in never falling, but in rising every time we fall": Nelson Mandela ______________

3. (a) Our figures show that employees raised more than $52,000 (was that part cash, part food donations) for the food bank.
(b) Our figures show that employees raised more than $52,000 (was that part cash, part food donations?) for the food bank.
(c) Our figures show that employees raised more than $52,000 (was that part cash, part food donations) for the food bank? ______________

4. (Emphasize.)
(a) Currently our basic operating costs: rent, utilities, and wages, are 10 percent higher than last year's.
(b) Currently our basic operating costs (rent, utilities, and wages) are 10 percent higher than last year's.
(c) Currently our basic operating costs—rent, utilities, and wages—are 10 percent higher than last year's. ______________

5. (a) Our operating revenue for 2019 (see Appendix A) exceeded our expectations.
(b) Our operating revenue for 2019, see Appendix A, exceeded our expectations.
(c) Our operating revenue for 2019: see Appendix A, exceeded our expectations. ______________

6. (a) When the roof leaked, (spring 2020), the landlord had it re-shingled right away.
(b) When the roof leaked (spring 2020), the landlord had it re-shingled right away.
(c) When the roof leaked (spring 2020,) the landlord had it re-shingled right away. ______________

7. (a) Sales, sales, and more sales, that's what we need to succeed.
(b) Sales, sales, and more sales—that's what we need to succeed.
(c) Sales, sales, and more sales; that's what we need to succeed. ______________

TEAR HERE

8. (a) *Business News Daily* suggests businesses take these three steps when rebranding: (1) identify their goals, (2) articulate why they do what they do, and (3) act on their plan.
   (b) *Business News Daily* suggests businesses take these three steps when rebranding: 1. identify their goals, 2. articulate why they do what they do, and 3. act on their plan.
   (c) *Business News Daily* suggests businesses take these three steps when rebranding: a) identify their goals, b) articulate why they do what they do, and c) act on their plan. __________

Check your answers.

B. Insert dashes or parentheses in the following sentences. In the space provided, write the number of punctuation marks you inserted. Count each parenthesis and each dash as a single mark.

EXAMPLE: (Emphasize.) Three of the biggest problems with email — privacy, overuse, and etiquette — will be discussed. 2

1. (De-emphasize.) Having a presence on social media sites for example, Facebook, Twitter, Instagram helps businesses gain information about their customers. __________
2. (Emphasize.) A benefit of social media is access to instant feedback positive or negative from customers. __________
3. "Over 60 percent of management problems result from faulty communications." Peter Drucker __________
4. (Emphasize.) Three branch assistant managers Celia Guinto, James Redman, and Candi Herman will be promoted this month. __________
5. Retirement savings plan contributions and an employee share purchase plan these are just two financial benefits all our employees are entitled to. __________
6. (De-emphasize.) As soon as you have the blood test try to do so before December 20, we will process your insurance forms. __________
7. To read actively, 1 skim the document or chapter; 2 write down the headings, changing them into questions; 3 read the document, and write down answers to your questions; 4 put the highlights of what you've read into your own words; and 5 review the document to ensure you've recalled the information correctly. __________
8. Funds for the project will be released on the following dates see Section 12.3 of the original grant: January 1, March 14, and June 30. __________
9. (De-emphasize.) More than half the survey respondents all of whom work in the tourism sector fear for their jobs. __________
10. The warranty contract is limited to sixty 60 days. __________

TEAR HERE

C. Using three different forms of punctuation, correctly punctuate the following sentence. In the space provided, explain the differences among the three methods you have employed.

1. Numerous considerations all of which are fully described in our report prompted the closure of the outlet.

2. Numerous considerations all of which are fully described in our report prompted the closure of the outlet.

3. Numerous considerations all of which are fully described in our report prompted the closure of the outlet.

Explanation:

1. ______________________________

2. ______________________________

3. ______________________________

TEAR HERE

NAME ______________________

LEVEL III

A. (Self-check) In the space provided, indicate whether the following statements are true (*T*) or false (*F*).

1. Double quotation marks enclose the exact words of a writer or speaker. ______
2. Names of books, magazines, movies, television series, and newspapers should be italicized. ______
3. Periods and commas are placed inside or outside closing quotation marks, depending on their relationship to the quoted material. ______
4. Brackets are used by writers to enclose their own remarks inserted into a quotation. ______
5. *Parentheses* is another word for *brackets*. ______
6. A quotation within a quotation is shown with single quotation marks. ______
7. Semicolons and colons are always placed before closing quotation marks. ______
8. If both a quotation and the sentence it is within are questions, use a question mark before the closing quotation marks and another one after. ______
9. A word or an expression being defined should be italicized or underlined. ______
10. The word *sic* shows that a quotation is free of errors. ______

Check your answers.

B. Many, but not all, of the following sentences contain direct quotations. Insert all necessary punctuation. Underlines may be used for words that would be italicized in print.

EXAMPLE: (ital) The word asset means "an item of monetary value."

1. I recently read an article titled Are There Any Rules in the Bailout Game
2. I have yet to hear a man, said Gloria Steinem, ask for advice on how to combine marriage and a career
3. The term preferred shares means shares having priority over common shares in the distribution of dividends
4. Bill Gates's favourite business book, Business Adventures, includes a chapter simply called Xerox Xerox Xerox Xerox.
5. Did Richard Branson really say Money is a poor indicator of success
6. In his speech the software billionaire said Our goal is to link the world irregardless sic of national boundaries and restrictions
7. Oprah Winfrey said, The best jobs are those we'd do even if we didn't get paid
8. The manager said that we may have to work overtime this weekend to get everything ready for inventory taking.
9. The postal worker asked Should I stamp your package Fragile

TEAR HERE

10. Did you read the Forbes article Can We Just Work From Home Forever

11. The expression persona non grata means one who is not acceptable

12. While banging repeatedly on the elevator doors, Mrs Lowe shouted, Please help us

13. José Cil, C E O of Tim Hortons' parent company, said the uptick in sales is partly because of the new home delivery offering

14. The working title of Jim's article is Automation in the Office however he may change the title later

15. In the arena of human life, said Aristotle, the honours and rewards fall to those who show their good qualities in action

C. Review of Levels I, II, and III. In the following sentences, add all necessary punctuation.

1. Would you please forward Mr. Dhawan's email message to me

2. Ergonomic chairs, keyboards, and monitors all employees should have these.

3. Removing the back panel see the warning on page 1 should be done only by authorized repair staff

4. (Emphasize.) Three primary themes flexible work schedules, encouraged volunteerism, and reward and recognition programs are recurrent among Canada's top fifty employers.

5. (De-emphasize.) Time-tracking software e.g., Toggl, RescueTime, ATracker can help a business increase its employees' productivity.

6. (Direct quotation.) Was it President Martin who said What can't be cured must be endured

7. The word copyright literally means right to copy

8. Mary Gooderham's fascinating article on virtual reality in The Globe and Mail was entitled The Next Best Thing to Being

9. The envelope marked Confidential was delivered to the wrong office

10. (Direct quotation.) Did Azir ask where our supply of printer cartridges is

D. Writing Exercise. On a separate sheet, write a paragraph describing your ideal job. Try to include as many of the punctuation marks you have studied as possible: commas, semicolons, colons, periods, question marks, exclamation marks, dashes, parentheses, quotation marks, italics, and possibly even brackets. Include a quotation from your boss. Make up the name of a book or an article that you could publish about this job.

TEAR HERE

POSTTEST

In the following sentences, use proofreading marks to insert necessary punctuation and formatting.

1. The C F O wondered whether the rise in G D P would affect his company's share price
2. (De-emphasize.) Purolator Inc owned mostly by Canada Post operates more than 500 hybrid-electric vehicles
3. Taking pictures, surfing websites, watching T V shows these are just some of the things people do with their cellphones
4. Did Dr Yee give you the test results before she left at 5 p m
5. Will you please send me a copy of the article titled Winning Negotiation Strategies
6. When did we receive this package marked Confidential
7. The only guests who have not sent R S V P s are Ms Lee Ms Gold and Mr Vila
8. The word principal was misused in the chapter titled Writing Persuasive Letters
9. Who said The secret of business is to know something no one else knows
10. (Emphasize.) Three of the most powerful women in business Indra Nooyi, Anne Mulcahy, and Meg Whitman are all well over fifty

TEAR HERE

EDITOR'S CHALLENGE

The following letters contain errors in concepts that you have studied thus far. They also contain a few spelling or typographical errors. Use proofreading marks to show all necessary corrections. Notice that the first letter is addressed to a company; hence the writer doesn't know whom to address in the salutation. The simplified style avoids this problem.

GLOBAL IMPORTERS INC.

814 John Street, Suite 205

Kelowna, BC V1Y 5S7

May 15, 202x

West Coast Foods Ltd

729 Leland Street

Maple Ridge, BC. V2X 7L3

YOUR MAY 3 PURCHASE ORDER NO 14902

All the in stock items requested in your recent purchase order were ship to you Friday May 8 from our Vancouver warehouse.

Because of unseasonably wet weather in February; this springs supply of black teas from Sri Lanka are extremely limited. We have none of these fine tea on hand at present, however, we expect a small shipment to arrive by August 1.

We do have in our warehouse a stock of select black teas from the following sources, south China Japan and south India. Indian teas as you are well aware do not always meet some of our customers high standards, Chinese and Japanese teas though are generally well regarded.
In fact one of our customers recently said "Our best sales are now from Chinese black tea". Moreover an article in the January 8, 202x issue of The Globe and Mail described the healthful affects of Japanese tea.

Please call us toll free at 1-800-321-8993 to tell us whether you wish to wait for the Sri Lankan black tea; or whether you prefer the immediate supply of black tea from China, Japan, or India?

YUKO KIMURA

YUKO KIMURA, MANAGER

2419 Branch Lane SW
Calgary, AB T2W 3L1
August 23, 202x

Mr. Doug Young, Manager
Longhorn Grill
3210 South Homer Avenue SE
Calgary, AB T2P ON5

Dear Mr. Young,

Even when us servers has given good service some customers don't leave a tip. This is a serious problem for we at Longhorn Grill. Many of us has gotten together and decided to bring the problem—and a possible solution, to your attention in this letter. Please read our ideas with a open mind, then suggest a meeting time to discuss them.

Some restaurants (such as the Coach House in Toronto—now automatically adds a 15 percent tip to the bill. Other restaurants are printing gratuity guideline's on checks. As well many portable terminals now provides a calculation feature so customers can chose the percentage tip they want to leave; 10, 15, or 20 percent. You can read about these procedures in an article titled Forcing the Tip, which appeared in "The New York Times." Ive enclosed a copy.

A mandatory tip printed on checks would work good at Longhorn don't you think. We give good service and receive many complements, however some customers forget to tip. By printing a suggested tip on the check we remind customers, a printed mandatory tip also does the math for customers which is an advantage for those who are not to good with math!

Printing mandatory tips on checks not only would help customers but also prove to the staff that you support them in there goal to recieve decent wages for the hard work they do. A few customers might complain but these customers can always cross out the printed tip if they wish. If you have any doubts about the plan we could try and implement it for a six month period and monitor customer's reactions.

Will you please let us know your feelings about this proposal as soon as possible. Its a serious concern to we servers.

Sincerely,

Brenda Stewart

Brenda Stewart
Server

Enclosure

TEAR HERE

NAME ____________________

UNIT 5 REVIEW ■ Chapters 15–17 (Self-Check)

Begin your review by rereading Chapters 15 through 17. Then, check your comprehension of those chapters by completing the exercises that follow and comparing your responses with those shown on page 531.

LEVEL I

Add any necessary punctuation in the following sentences. In the space provided, write the number of punctuation marks you inserted. Write *C* if a sentence is correct.

1. Professor how can I clean up my "digital dirt" before I look for a job ____________
2. However the matter is resolved, the goodwill of the customer is paramount. ____________
3. Deepfakes videos edited to produce a message different from the original are a growing concern for individuals and businesses alike. ____________
4. In business deepfakes can be used for example to defraud C E O s to sully reputations or to manipulate world markets. ____________
5. Experts who can determine the authenticity of videos have developed products and services to help companies detect deepfake attacks. ____________
6. With this level of artificial intelligence (A I) technology out there however we all have to learn to be sceptical of video content. ____________
7. Audio also can be faked in fact one test proved that even a mother didn't recognize the A I that replicated her son's voice on the phone. ____________
8. The trade show begins January 26 202x at 10 a m ____________
9. Employers want to hire the right people the first time therefore many conduct web searches to learn more about job candidates. ____________
10. Mr Deerchild would you please schedule the e-newsletter for distribution as soon as it's ready ____________

In the space provided, write the letter of the correctly punctuated sentence.

11. (a) Some employees would prefer better benefits others would choose more vacation days.
    (b) Some employees would prefer better benefits, others would choose more vacation days.
    (c) Some employees would prefer better benefits; others would choose more vacation days. ____________

12. (a) Reports have arrived in our offices from Geneva, Switzerland, Munich, Germany, and Vienna, Austria.
    (b) Reports have arrived in our offices from Geneva, Switzerland; Munich, Germany; and Vienna, Austria.
    (c) Reports have arrived in our offices from Geneva, Switzerland; Munich, Germany, and Vienna, Austria. ____________

TEAR HERE

13. (a) Social media sites help businesses share information faster, additionally, they can increase traffic to company websites.
(b) Social media sites help businesses share information faster; additionally, they can increase traffic to company websites.
(c) Social media sites help businesses share information faster; additionally they can increase traffic to company websites. ____________

14. (a) Would you please check the CBC website.
(b) Would you please check the C.B.C. website.
(c) Would you please check the CBC website? ____________

15. (a) She said she held BA and MFA degrees didn't she?
(b) She said she held B.A. and M.F.A. degrees, didn't she?
(c) She said she held BA and MFA degrees, didn't she? ____________

LEVEL II

In the space provided, write the letter of the correctly punctuated sentence.

16. (a) When I last saw him (was it in June?), he had just started a new job.
(b) When I last saw him (was it in June) he had just started a new job.
(c) When I last saw him (was it in June?); he had just started a new job. ____________

17. (a) Wow! A total of 89.9 percent of the voters approved!
(b) Wow, a total of 89.9 percent of the voters approved.
(c) Wow. A total of 89.9 percent of the voters approved! ____________

18. (a) We are looking for three qualities in an employee; honesty, intelligence, and a good work ethic.
(b) We are looking for three qualities in an employee, honesty, intelligence, and a good work ethic.
(c) We are looking for three qualities in an employee: honesty, intelligence, and a good work ethic. ____________

19. (a) Of the companies he interviewed with, he was most interested in Compaq, IBM, and Dell.
(b) Of the companies he interviewed with, he was most interested in: Compaq, IBM, and Dell.
(c) Of the companies he interviewed with, he was most interested in Compaq; IBM; and Dell. ____________

20. (a) Jack Welch said, "I've learned that mistakes can often be as good a teacher as success."
(b) Jack Welch said: "I've learned that mistakes can often be as good a teacher as success."
(c) Jack Welch said; "I've learned that mistakes can often be as good a teacher as success." ____________

21. (a) The spokesperson compared three other railways: Canadian National, Canadian Pacific, and Amtrak, with VIA Rail.
(b) The spokesperson compared three other railways—Canadian National, Canadian Pacific, and Amtrak—with VIA Rail.
(c) The spokesperson compared three other railways—Canadian National, Canadian Pacific, and Amtrak with VIA Rail. ____________

TEAR HERE

22. (a) Apple, Microsoft, Amazon, Alphabet, Berkshire Hathaway—these are the five largest companies in the world.
(b) Apple, Microsoft, Amazon, Alphabet, Berkshire Hathaway: these are the five largest companies in the world.
(c) Apple, Microsoft, Amazon, Alphabet, Berkshire Hathaway, these are the five largest companies in the world. ____________

23. (a) Several Canadian biotech firms, Medicago, based in Quebec City, Que., Entos, based in Edmonton, Alta., and AbCellera Biologics, based in Vancouver, B.C., were key players in the race to a COVID-19 vaccine.
(b) Several Canadian biotech firms (Medicago, based in Quebec City, Que.; Entos, based in Edmonton, Alta.; and AbCellera Biologics, based in Vancouver, B.C.) were key players in the race to a COVID-19 vaccine.
(c) Several Canadian biotech firms, Medicago, based in Quebec City, Que.; Entos, based in Edmonton, Alta.; and AbCellera Biologics, based in Vancouver, B.C., were key players in the race to a COVID-19 vaccine. ____________

24. (a) Notable members of the fund's honorary committee have been Ewa Ninkovic, Chief Claire Balfour, and Paul Beeston.
(b) Notable members of the fund's honorary committee have been: Ewa Ninkovic, Chief Claire Balfour, and Paul Beeston.
(c) Notable members of the fund's honorary committee have been—Ewa Ninkovic, Chief Claire Balfour, and Paul Beeston. ____________

25. (a) The pilot project, which you can read about on page 6 of the report, may help us justify the new system.
(b) The pilot project which you can read about on page 6 of the report may help us justify the new system.
(c) The pilot project that you can read about on page 6 of the report, may help us justify the new system. ____________

LEVEL III

In the space provided, write the letter of the correctly punctuated sentence.

26. (a) Our goal is to encourage, not hamper, good communication.
(b) Our goal is to encourage—not hamper, good communication.
(c) Our goal is to encourage, not hamper good communication. ____________

27. (a) Only one department submitted its report on time, that is the Legal Department.
(b) Only one department submitted its report on time, that is, the Legal Department.
(c) Only one department submitted its report on time: that is the Legal Department. ____________

28. (a) The location of the convention has been narrowed to three sites, namely, Victoria, Vancouver, and Seattle.
(b) The location of the convention has been narrowed to three sites; namely, Victoria, Vancouver, and Seattle.
(c) The location of the convention has been narrowed to three sites; namely Victoria, Vancouver, and Seattle. ____________

TEAR HERE

29. (a) Sudbury, Ontario, is often called "The Big Nickel".
(b) Sudbury, Ontario, is often called 'The Big Nickel.'
(c) Sudbury, Ontario, is often called "The Big Nickel." ______________

30. (a) The computer was producing "garbage," that is, the screen showed gibberish.
(b) The computer was producing "garbage"; that is, the screen showed gibberish.
(c) The computer was producing "garbage;" that is, the screen showed gibberish. ______________

31. (a) A cartel is defined as a "group of companies acting to control prices."
(b) A "cartel" is defined as a 'group of companies acting to control prices.'
(c) A *cartel* is defined as a "group of companies acting to control prices." ______________

32. (a) Although published in 1937, How to Win Friends and Influence People by Dale Carnegie still offers valuable insights, especially in the chapter "An Easy Way to Become a Good Conversationalist."
(b) Although published in 1937, *How to Win Friends and Influence People* by Dale Carnegie still offers valuable insights, especially in the chapter "An Easy Way to Become a Good Conversationalist."
(c) Although published in 1937, "How to Win Friends and Influence People" by Dale Carnegie still offers valuable insights, especially in the chapter *An Easy Way to Become a Good Conversationalist.* ______________

33. (a) "The only place where success comes before work, said Vince Lombardi, is in the dictionary."
(b) "The only place where success comes before work," said Vince Lombardi, "is in the dictionary."
(c) "The only place where success comes before work," said Vince Lombardi "is in the dictionary." ______________

34. (a) Who was it who said, "If I'm going to do something, I do it spectacularly or I don't do it at all."?
(b) Who was it who said, "If I'm going to do something, I do it spectacularly or I don't do it at all"?
(c) Who was it who said, "If I'm going to do something, I do it spectacularly or I don't do it at all?" ______________

35. (a) Catherine O'Hara said, "Even before you've earned it, treat yourself and your career with the level of respect that you hope to one day deserve."
(b) Catherine O'Hara said; "Even before you've earned it, treat yourself and your career with the level of respect that you hope to one day deserve."
(c) Catherine O'Hara said, "Even before you've earned it, treat yourself and your career with the level of respect that you hope to one day deserve". ______________

36. (a) The daily draws take place throughout May, the grand prize draw, in June.
(b) The daily draws take place throughout May; the grand prize draw, in June.
(c) The daily draws take place throughout May; the grand prize draw in June. ______________

TEAR HERE

ASK AN EDITOR REVIEW

In the space provided, write the letter of the word or phrase that correctly completes each sentence.

37. Before opening, we need to purchase the following:

(a)
- Cash register
- Receipt printer
- Bar code reader

(b)
- Cash register,
- Receipt printer,
- Bar code reader.

____

38. The Public Relations (a) department too (b) department, too, has been understaffed for some time. _______

39. The speaker's topic today (a) is, (b) is "Radio Advertising in the Internet Era." _______

40. Did you hear the keynote address "Radio Advertising in the Internet (a) Era"? (b) Era?" _______

TEAR HERE

PROFESSIONAL BUSINESS LETTERS

Business letters are important forms of external communication; that is, they deliver information to individuals outside an organization. Although email has become incredibly successful for both internal and external communication, many important messages still require written letters. Business letters are necessary when a permanent record is required, when formality is significant, or when a message is sensitive and requires an organized, well-considered presentation. Business letters may request information, respond to requests, make claims, seek adjustments, order goods and services, sell goods and services, recommend individuals, develop goodwill, apply for jobs, or achieve many other goals. All business people have to write letters of various kinds, but a majority of those letters will be informational.

CHARACTERISTICS OF BUSINESS LETTERS

Writers of good business letters—whether the messages are informational, persuasive, or negative—are guided by six *C*s: conciseness, clarity, correctness, courtesy, completeness, and confidence. In earlier Writer's Workshops, you learned techniques for making your writing concise and clear. You've also studied many guidelines for correct grammar and usage throughout this textbook. At this point we will review some of these techniques briefly as they relate to business letters.

CONCISENESS. Concise letters save the reader's time by presenting information directly. You can make your letters concise by avoiding these writing faults: (a) wordy phrases (such as *in addition to the above* and *in view of the fact that*), (b) excessive use of expletives or fillers (such as *There are four reasons that explain . . .* or *It is a good plan*), (c) long lead-ins (such as *This message is to inform you that* or *I am writing this letter to*), (d) needless adverbs (such as *very, definitely, quite, extremely,* and *really*), and (e) old-fashioned expressions (such as *attached please find* and *pursuant to your request*).

CLARITY. Business letters are clear when they are logically organized and when they present enough information for the reader to understand what the writer intended. Informational letters are usually organized directly with the main idea first. Clarity can be enhanced by including all the necessary information. Some authorities estimate that one-third of all business letters are written to clarify previous correspondence. To ensure that your letters are clear from the start, put yourself in the reader's position and analyze what you have written. What questions may the reader ask? Does your information proceed logically from one point to another? Are your sentences and paragraphs coherent?

CORRECTNESS. Two aspects of correctness are accuracy of facts and accuracy of form. In regard to facts, good writers prepare to write by gathering relevant information. They collect supporting documents (previous letters, memos, and reports), make inquiries, jot down facts, and outline the message. Correct letters require thorough preparation. In the same manner, correct letters require careful proofreading and attention to form. Typographical errors, spelling irregularities, and grammatical faults distract the reader and damage the credibility of the writer. Correct business letters also follow one of the conventional formats, such as block or modified block, shown in Appendix C.

COURTESY. You develop courtesy in business letters by putting yourself in the place of the reader. Imagine how you would like to be treated, and show the same consideration and respect for the individual receiving your message. The ideas you express and the words used to convey those ideas create an impression on the reader. Be alert to words that may create a negative feeling, such as *you claim, unfortunately, you neglected, you forgot,* and *your complaint.* Create a positive feeling by presenting your message from the point of view of the reader. Try to use the word *you* more than the words *I* and *we.*

COMPLETENESS. In order for a letter to be complete, it should answer all questions your reader might have. When formulating your message, consider the who, what, when, where, why, and how. The goal in writing complete letters is to avoid unnecessary follow-up. You don't want to waste your reader's time or your own.

CONFIDENCE. Employers want employees who are confident in themselves and in what they do. Therefore, avoid using words that make you sound weak such as *I think, I feel,* and *I believe.* Just come right out and say it with confidence!

Skill Check 5.1: Reviewing the Six Cs

1. Which of the following is most concise?
- (a) Due to the fact that we had a warehouse fire, your shipment is delayed.
- (b) This is to inform you that your shipment will be delayed.
- (c) Because of a warehouse fire, your shipment is delayed.
- (d) There was a warehouse fire, which explains why your shipment is delayed. ____________

2. Which of the following is clear and logical?
- (a) If the strike is not settled quickly, it may last a while.
- (b) Flying over the rain forests of Indonesia, the trees form a solid and menacing green carpet.
- (c) This is not to suggest that Kingston, Oshawa, and London are not the most affordable areas for housing.
- (d) Prince Charles complained that the citizens of Britain speak and write their language poorly. ____________

3. Which of the following is grammatically correct?
- (a) We hope that you and he will be in town for our next seminar.
- (b) Business leaders today confront a host of ethical issues; including email privacy, whistleblowing, and exploitation of overseas labourers.
- (c) We must develop a policy on returning merchandise. So that they know about it before they are made.
- (d) Jeffrey has 20 years experience in the software industry. ____________

4. Which of the following is most courteous?
- (a) During your interview, I informed you that if we were not successful in finding a suitable candidate, I would contact you.
- (b) We appreciate receiving your letter describing your treatment by our store security personnel.
- (c) In your letter of June 1, you claim that you were harassed by our store security personnel.
- (d) Unfortunately, we are unable to complete your entire order because you neglected to provide a shirt size. ____________

5. Which of the following is most nearly complete?
   (a) The form you requested will be mailed to you.
   (b) We are forwarding Form A11, as you requested.
   (c) We are sending the form you requested.
   (d) You'll receive Form A11 by mail within three business days. ____________________

6. Which of the following sounds most confident?
   (a) I hope to hear from you soon about the available position.
   (b) Our committee thinks that this is the best way to handle the problem.
   (c) I look forward to speaking with you about my proposal.
   (d) We believe that our product will best meet your needs. ____________________

WRITING PLAN

Most business letters have three parts: opening, body, and closing. This three-part writing plan will help you organize the majority of your business messages quickly and effectively.

OPENING. The opening of a business letter may include a subject line that refers to previous correspondence or summarizes the content of the message. If you decide to include a subject line, it should make sense but should not be a complete sentence; it is not followed by a period.

The first sentence of a business letter that requests or delivers information should begin directly with the main idea. If you are asking for information, use one of two approaches. Ask the most important question first, such as *Do you have a two-bedroom cottage on Devil's Lake available for the week of July 8–15?* A second approach involves beginning with a summary statement, such as *Please answer the following questions regarding. . . .* If the letter delivers information, begin with the most important information first, such as *Yes, we have a two-bedroom cottage on Devil's Lake available for . . .* or *Here is the information you requested regarding . . .* Most informational business letters should NOT begin with an explanation of why the letter is being written.

BODY. The body of the letter provides explanations and additional information to clarify the first sentence. Use a separate paragraph for each new idea, being careful to strive for concise writing.

If the message lends itself to enumeration, express the items in a bulleted or numbered list. Be certain, of course, to construct the list so that each item is parallel.

Think about the individual reading your message. Will that person understand what you are saying? Have you included enough information? What may seem clear to you may not be so evident to your reader. In responding to requests, don't hesitate to include more information than was requested—if it is on topic and you feel it would be helpful.

Maintain a friendly, conversational, and positive tone.

CLOSING. Business letters that demand action should conclude with a specific request, including end dating if appropriate. That is, tell the reader when you would like the request complied with, and, if possible, provide a reason (e.g., *Please send me this information by June 1 so that I can arrange my vacation*).

Letters that provide information may end with a summary statement or a pleasant forward-looking thought (e.g., *We are happy to provide this information to help you plan your summer vacation*). Business organizations may also use the closing to promote products or services.

Avoid ending your letters with mechanical phrases such as *If I can be of further service, don't hesitate to call on me* or *Thanks for any information you can provide.* Find a fresh way to express your desire to be of service or to show appreciation.

Figure 5.1 illustrates the application of the writing plan to an information request. Notice that the subject line summarizes the main topic of the letter, while the first paragraph provides more information about the reason for writing. The body of the letter explains the main idea and includes a list of questions so that the reader can see quickly what information is being requested. The closing includes an end date with a reason.

Figure 5.1

Information Request

GraphicPros

264 South Halsted St.

Mississauga, ON L5T 3K8

FAX (905) 568-2210 VOICE (905) 568-8319 INTERNET: http://www.graphicpros.com

March 5, 202x

Ms. Kesha Scott

Micro Supplies and Software

4671 Main Street

Saskatoon, SK S7K 3G3

Dear Ms. Scott:

Summarizes main idea → SUBJECT: Availability and Price of Equipment Security Devices

Introduces purpose immediately → Please provide information and recommendations regarding security equipment to prevent the theft of office computers, keyboards, monitors, faxes, and printers.

Explains need for information → Our office now has 18 computer workstations and 6 printers that we must secure to desks or counters. Answers to the following questions will help us select the best devices for our purpose:

Groups open-ended questions into list for quick comprehension and best feedback →

1. What device would you recommend to secure a workstation consisting of a computer, monitor, and keyboard?
2. What expertise and equipment are required to install and remove the security device?
3. How much is each device? Do you offer quantity discounts; if so, how much?

Courteously provides end date and reason → Because our insurance rates will be increased if the security devices are not installed before May 12, we would appreciate your response by March 26.

Sincerely,

Karina Levitt

Office Manager

Skill Check 5.1: Reviewing the Writing Plan

In the space provided, write *a*, *b*, or *c* to identify the letter part where each of the following might logically be found.

a = opening   b = body   c = closing

1. Explanation and details ________

2. Subject line that summarizes main idea ________

3. End date with reason ________

4. Numbered or bulleted list ________

5. Main idea ________

6. Summary statement or forward-looking thought ________

Writing Application 5.1

Revise the following poorly written letter. Use block style (every line starts at the left margin) and mixed punctuation. This is a personal business letter; follow the format shown in Figure C.2 in Appendix C (see p. 441), inserting your own address in the return address block. Remember that the following letter is poorly written. Improve it!

Writer's street address
City, Province Postal Code
Current date

Ms. Barbara L. George
Manager, Rainbow Resort
1102 West Island Road
Omemee, ON K0L 2W1

Dear Ms. George:

I saw an advertisement recently in *Sunset* magazine where Rainbow Resort rents houseboats. My family and I (there are three kids and my wife and me) would like to take a vacation on a houseboat from July 17 through July 24 on the Trent-Severn Waterway. We've never done this before, but it sounds interesting.

Please send me any information you may have. I'll have to make my vacation plans soon. I have no idea how much this might cost. If we rent a houseboat, we want to know do you provide bedding, dishes, pots and pans, and the like? I'm wondering about navigating a houseboat. Will we have to take a course or training on how to operate it? It may be too difficult for us to operate. Where can we travel on the waterway in one of your houseboats? What if we decide to stay on more than one week? I actually have two weeks of vacation, but we may want to travel in our RV part of the time. Does insurance come with the rental fee? Our kids want to know if it has a TV.

Yours,

Leslie E. Childers

Leslie E. Childers

Writing Application 5.2

Assume you are Barbara George. Write a response to Mr. Childers's letter. Use block style and mixed punctuation. Tell Mr. Childers that the rental fee, which is $220 per day or $1,500 per week, does include insurance. You have a houseboat available for July 17–24, but definite reservations must be made for that time and for the week following, if Mr. Childers decides to stay two weeks. Your houseboats can travel through 20 lakes, canals, and rivers. Rainbow Resort provides bedding, dishes, and kitchenware. Yes, each houseboat has a TV set. You also provide an AM/FM radio and a DVD player. Your houseboats accommodate four to ten people, and you require a deposit of $800 for a one-week reservation. Reservations must be received by June 1 to ensure a July vacation. Your houseboats are easy to operate. No special training is required, but you do give each operator about 30 minutes of instruction. Send Mr. Childers a brochure describing Rainbow Resort and the memorable holiday he and his family can enjoy. The scenery and attractions are good.

Writing Application 5.3

Write a personal business letter in response to the following problem. For your home office, you ordered a VoIP phone system called the Plantronics Calisto Pro Series DECT 6.0. This hands-free system includes a Bluetooth headset that allows you to answer your land line, mobile, and VoIP phone calls with one device. It has many other attractive features, and you were eager to try it. When it arrived, however, you installed it according to the instructions and discovered that an irritating static sound interfered with every telephone call you made or received. You don't know what caused the static, but the product description promised the following: "Thanks to the system's superior noise-cancelling Bluetooth headset with extended mouthpiece, you will always sound professional. The Calisto Pro phone operates on DECT 6.0 frequency, which means that call clarity is not affected by Wi-Fi networks or home appliances such as a microwave, and you can roam up to 90 metres from the base without suffering any degradation in sound quality."

Because you need a clear signal for your business, you returned the VoIP phone system January 15 by UPS Next Business Day shipping service to ElectroWare Ltd., the Web-based supplier from whom you purchased the system. You still have a copy of the invoice, which states that merchandise may be returned for any reason within 30 days after purchase. You also have the UPS receipt proving that you returned it. However, your MasterCard statement (Acct. No. 5390-3390-2219-0002) has not shown a credit for the return. Your last two monthly statements show no credit for $249.95. You are wondering what happened. Did ElectroWare receive the returned VoIP phone system? Why hasn't your account been credited? If ElectroWare did not receive the shipment, you want UPS to trace it. Write to ElectroWare Ltd., 22121 Crystal Creek Boulevard, Lethbridge, Alberta T9L 3T2. You have complied with ElectroWare's instructions regarding returning merchandise, and you want the company to credit your account. You do not want another phone system from ElectroWare. Be sure to open your letter with a direct request for the action you want taken.

For additional resources, please visit MindTap at login.cengage.com. Cengage | MINDTAP

UNIT 6

Writing With Style

CHAPTER 18
Capitalization

CHAPTER 19
Numbers

CHAPTER 20
Effective Sentences

CAPITALIZATION

CHAPTER

18

OBJECTIVES

When you have completed the materials in this chapter, you will be able to do the following:

LEVEL I

- Properly capitalize sentence beginnings, the pronoun *I*, proper nouns, and proper adjectives
- Determine when to capitalize geographic locations, organization names, academic courses and degrees, common nouns with abbreviations, and seasons

LEVEL II

- Understand how to capitalize business correspondence components and personal titles
- Correctly capitalize numbered items; points of the compass; departments, divisions, agencies, and committees; government terms; product names; and published and artistic titles

LEVEL III

- Capitalize beginning words; celestial bodies; ethnic, cultural, language, and religious references; and words following *marked*, *labelled*, and *stamped*
- Apply special rules in capitalizing personal titles and terms

PRETEST

Use proofreading marks (≡) to show any letters that should be capitalized in the following sentences.

1. If i were you, i would transfer to vancouver island university.
2. In his book *the naked future: what happens in a world that anticipates your every move*, Patrick Tucker wrote, "we will not win by shaking our fists in the air at technology."

(continued)

PRETEST *(CONTINUED)*

3. Subject: sales meeting next thursday
4. The week before mother's day is one of the busiest times of the year for canada post.
5. Last spring father travelled to the east coast to visit his mother.
6. This semester I have classes in history, computer technology, french, and psychology.
7. The canadian medical association's executive will meet in the manitoba room of the hilton hotel on march 25.
8. While uncle Gilles was studying for his master's degree, he lived in the city of montréal.
9. Our company president and vice president met with several supervisors on the west coast to discuss how to compete against google's new online offerings.
10. The revenue canada booklet our accountant gave me explains the use of form T2202.

One difficult thing about writing is learning the rules that will help you write with style. In this chapter you will learn the rules for capitalization. They reflect conventional practices; that is, they have been established by custom and usage. By following these conventions, a writer tells a reader, among other things, what words are important. In earlier times writers capitalized most nouns and many adjectives at will; few conventions of capitalization or punctuation were consistently observed. Today most capitalization follows definite rules that are widely accepted and practised.

Within many large organizations, a stylebook prescribes capitalization style. Dictionaries are also helpful in determining capitalization practices, but they do not show all capitalized words. To develop skill in controlling capitals, study the rules and examples in this chapter.

LEVEL I

CAREER TIP

Many large companies publish style manuals showing their preferred capitalization and the spelling of frequently used terms. One of the first tasks of new employees is becoming familiar with the company style manual.

BASIC RULES OF CAPITALIZATION

Beginning of a Sentence

Capitalize the first letter of a word beginning a sentence.

When Rawlings Men's Wear closed its downtown store, it opened an online store.
In recent years many retailers have made the switch from brick-and-mortar to e-commerce.

The Pronoun *I*

Capitalize the pronoun *I*, no matter where it appears or how it is used in a sentence.

If *I* were you, *I*'d continue my education.
If you gave me a chance, *I*'m sure that *I* could change your mind.

Proper Nouns

Capitalize proper nouns, including the names of *specific* persons, places, schools, streets, parks, buildings, holidays, months, days, nicknames, agreements, websites, historical periods, and so forth. Do *not* capitalize common nouns that make general reference.

Proper Nouns	**Common Nouns**
Jackson Turner	a young man on the basketball team
United States of America	neighbouring country of Canada
Canadore College, University of British Columbia	a college and a university
Grand Avenue Park	a park in the town
Empire Room, Royal Inn	a room in the hotel
Canada Day, Easter	holidays
January, February, March	first three months of the year
Saturday, Sunday	weekend days
Humber River Bridge	a bridge over a river
Polo Park Shopping Centre	a mall
Parliament, the Senate	components of government
the Great One, the Big Apple	nicknames of people and places
Stipulation of Interest Agreement	an agreement between companies
Wikipedia, Google, Facebook	popular websites
PowerPoint, Photoshop	software programs
Great Depression, Digital Age	historical periods

STUDY TIP

Most proper nouns retain their capital letters when they become adjectives; for example, Italian marble, French toast, Shakespearean sonnet, Elizabethan collar, and Pythagorean theorem.

Proper Adjectives

Capitalize most adjectives that are derived from proper nouns.

Arabic alphabet	Renaissance art
Danish pastry	Richter scale
Heimlich manoeuvre	Roman numeral
Keynesian economics	Victorian furniture

Do not capitalize those few adjectives originally derived from proper nouns that have become common adjectives (without capitals) in certain phrases through popular usage. Consult your dictionary when in doubt.

china dishes	italic type
diesel engine	mandarin collar
french fries	manila folder
homburg hat	venetian blinds

DID YOU KNOW?

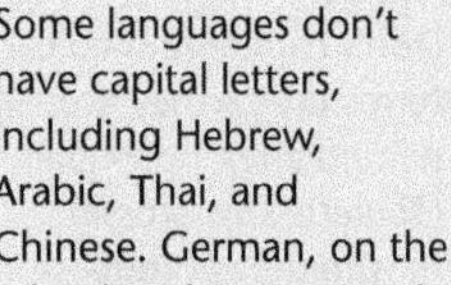

Some languages don't have capital letters, including Hebrew, Arabic, Thai, and Chinese. German, on the other hand, uses capital letters for all nouns.

Geographic Locations

Capitalize the names of *specific* places such as continents, countries, provinces and territories, cities, mountains, valleys, lakes, rivers, oceans, and geographic regions. Capitalize *county*, *state*, and *region* only when they follow proper nouns.

South America, Asia
Ontario, British Columbia
Port Hood, Québec City
Rocky Mountains
Lake Michigan, James Bay
the Prairies, the Maritimes
Huron County, York Region
Manitoba Escarpment
Red River, Mississippi River
Rivière des Prairies
Atlantic Ocean, Black Sea
Northwest Passage
Okanagan Valley
New York State

ASK AN EDITOR

Question:
I work for the National Therapy Association. When I talk about "the association" in a letter, should I capitalize it?

Answer:
No. When a common noun is used as a shortened form to refer to an organization, it is generally not capitalized. In formal or legal documents (contracts, bylaws, etc.), however, it may be capitalized.

Organization Names

Capitalize the principal words in the names of all business, civic, educational, governmental, labour, military, philanthropic, political, professional, religious, social, and sports organizations. Capitalize an introductory *the* only when it is part of an organization's official name (as it appears on the organization's website).

Bank of Montreal
B'nai Brith
Canadian Red Cross
Canadian Union of Public Employees
Federation of Saskatchewan Indian Nations
Liberal Party, New Democrats
National Hockey League
Royal Canadian Legion
The Bay
The World Bank

Generally, do NOT capitalize *committee, company, association, board,* and other shortened name forms when they are used to replace full organization names. If these shortened names, however, are preceded by the word *the* and are used in formal or legal documents such as contracts, bylaws, or minutes, they may be capitalized.

Did you know that the *company* will pay certain medical benefits? (Ordinary document)
The *Association* is herein authorized to disburse funds. (Formal document)

STUDY TIP

Course titles with numbers are usually capitalized (*Marketing 101*) because they refer to specific courses. Those without numbers usually are not capitalized (*marketing*) unless the full course title is used.

Academic Courses and Degrees

Capitalize the names of numbered courses and specific course titles. Do not capitalize the names of academic subject areas unless they contain a proper noun.

Marina took *Accounting* 186, *English* 122, and *Principles of Management* last semester.
All accounting majors must take business English and business law.
My most interesting classes are *history, business management,* and *French.*

ASK AN EDITOR

Question:
I'm writing a paper for my biology class on *in vitro fertilization*. Since this is a medical term, shouldn't I capitalize it?

Answer:
Don't capitalize medical terms unless they are named after individuals (*Tourette's syndrome*). *In vitro* means "outside the living body." Incidentally, specialists in the field use the abbreviation *IVF* after the first introduction of the term *in vitro fertilization*.

Capitalize abbreviations of academic degrees whether they stand alone or follow individuals' names. Do not capitalize general references to degrees.

Aleksandar hopes to earn *BSc* and *MSc* degrees.
Sylvia Sasot, *PhD*, teaches psychology in the fall.
New employees include Joanne Duncan, *MSW*, and Thomas Wong, *RN*.
The university offers *bachelor's* and *master's* degrees.

Common Nouns With Abbreviations

Although abbreviations often use capitalized initials, terms are not capitalized when spelled out unless they are proper nouns.

Are you contributing to the company-subsidized registered retirement savings plan? (*RRSP* spelled out is not a proper noun.)

Where is our chief executive officer? (*CEO* spelled out is generally not treated as a proper noun. Some companies' styles do capitalize job titles, so you will want to confirm your company's style. See also the section in Level II called "Titles of People.")

Seasons

Generally, do not capitalize seasons. When combined with a year to refer to a distinct period, such as a semester in school or a business quarter, however, a season is often capitalized.

Last *winter* we drew lots for *summer* vacations.
Eric Spiesel began working on his degree online during the *Fall 2020* semester.

Complete the reinforcement exercises for Level I on pages 360–361.

LEVEL II

SPECIAL RULES OF CAPITALIZATION

Business Correspondence Components

Capitalize the first word of the salutation and complimentary close of business letters, memos, and email messages.

Dear Mr. Hemingway: (Capitalize the first word and all nouns in a salutation.)
Sincerely yours, (Capitalize the first word of a complimentary close.)

Capitalize all the main words in subject lines of memos and email messages. Do NOT capitalize articles, coordinating conjunctions (*for, and, nor, but, or, yet, so*), or prepositions of three or fewer letters unless they appear at the beginning or end of the subject line.

SUBJECT: *Monthly Sales Meeting on June 9* (Capitalize the first letter of all main words in a subject line.)

Titles of People

Many rules exist for capitalizing personal and professional titles of people.

1. Capitalize courtesy titles (such as *Mr., Ms.,* and *Dr.*) and other personal titles when they immediately precede names.

Ms. Liane Goodale	Dr. Laurier Roberge
Aunt Gertrude	Professor Magee
Councillor Cheng	Mayor Rasmussen
Commander Chris Hadfield	Chief Dan George
Rabbi David Cohen	Prince William

2. Do not capitalize a person's title—professional, business, military, religious, political, family, or related to nobility—when the title is followed by the person's name used as an appositive. (You may recall that appositives rename or explain previously mentioned nouns or pronouns.)

Only one *professor*, Nalini Ravel, was available to serve as club advisor.
University employees asked their *president*, Mary Sue Coleman, to help raise funds.
Reva Hillman discovered that her *uncle*, Paul M. Hillman, had named her his heir.

3. Do not capitalize titles or offices following names unless they appear in a displayed list.

Gary Bauer, *vice president*, controls all hiring.

After repeated requests, Kay Carver, *supervisor*, Document Services, announced extended hours.

The following employees will represent Sun Microsystems at the annual conference:
Peter Li, *Director of Research*
Radia Perlman, *Software Designer*
Tim Bray, *Director of Web Technologies*

STUDY TIP

People's titles used alone or with an appositive are not capitalized. However, when used as part of a high-ranking official's name, the title is capitalized.

4. Capitalize titles in addresses and closing lines of business correspondence.

Mr. Kenneth Miller	Very sincerely yours,
Executive Vice President, Planning	
Energy Systems Technology	
112 Ellery Street	Patricia Barr
Victoria, BC V8W 3K5	Sales Supervisor

5. Do not capitalize the titles of high-ranking national or international officials except when the title is used as part of the official's name.

	But
the prime minister	the visit of the Pope
the president (of the United States)	an audience with the Queen
the chief justice	the Governor General

Note these three common exceptions: *Queen* (referring to the Queen of England), Governor General (referring to the Queen's representative in Canada), and *Pope* are capitalized in all uses.

CAREER TIP

The honorific *Ms.* is preferred by most women these days, rather than *Mrs.* or *Miss*, titles that denote a woman's marital status.

6. Do not capitalize family titles used with possessives or articles.

my mother	the aunt	Lee's uncle
his father	a cousin	Mike's dad

But do capitalize titles of close relatives when they are used without modifiers—as names are used.

Please call *Father* and *Mother* immediately.
This is *Grandmother's* brooch.

Numbered and Lettered Items

Capitalize nouns followed by numbers or letters (except in page, paragraph, line, and verse references).

Gate 68, Flight 238	Form 2900-4	Building I-63-B
Invoice No. 15891	Volume II, Appendix A	Supplement No. 3
Order 1034	County Road 56	page 6, line 12

Points of the Compass

Capitalize *north, south, east, west,* and other points of the compass when they represent *specific* regions. Do not capitalize the points of the compass when they are used in directions or in general references.

the Middle East, the Far East	heading east on Eglinton Avenue
the West, the Midwest (of the United States)	to the west of town
the East, the West Coast	eastern Ontario, southern Manitoba

STUDY TIP

A clue to the capitalization of a region is the use of *the* preceding it: *the East Coast, the West, the Pacific Rim.*

Departments, Divisions, and Committees

Generally, capitalize the principal words in the official names of departments, divisions, or committees within *your own* organization. Outside your organization capitalize only *specific* department, division, or committee names. (Company styles may differ from these general guidelines.)

I will be sending résumés to the *human resources departments* of several companies.
A *steering committee* has not yet been named.
Dr. Nguyen is director of the *Northern Division* of Barco. (Specific division)
Sue works in our *Communication Services Department.* (Insider reference)
Grievances are referred to our *HR Practices Committee.* (Insider reference)

Government Terms

Do not capitalize words like *federal, government, national, provincial, territorial,* or *state* unless they are part of a specific title.

Neither the *provincial government* nor the *federal government* would fund the proposal.
The legislative body in Québec is called the *National Assembly.*

ASK AN EDITOR

Question:
My manager routinely asks me to "xerox" documents. It seems to me this term is outdated. Is there a better term to use?

Answer:
Xerox is a brand of copy machine, so the term your manager uses is a trademark infringement, not just outdated language. The correct request would be to "photocopy" or simply "make a copy" of the document.

Product Names

Capitalize product names only when they represent brand names or trademarks of products. Frequently used product names, like many in the following list, are shown in dictionaries and labelled as trademarked or proprietary terms. Common nouns following manufacturers' names are not capitalized.

Band-Aid	Jeep	PowerPoint
Coke, Coca-Cola	Kleenex	Q-tip swab
Crock-Pot	Magic Marker	Rollerblade
Dell computer	Plasticine	Scotch tape
Formica counter	Popsicle	Styrofoam cup

Published and Artistic Titles

Capitalize the main words in the titles and subtitles of books, magazines, newspapers, articles, movies, plays, albums, songs, poems, websites, and reports. Do *not* capitalize articles (*a, an, the*), coordinating conjunctions (*and, but, or,* etc.), or prepositions with three or fewer letters (*in, to, by, for,* etc.) unless they begin or end the title or subtitle.

BE THE EDITOR

On Rogers' on-screen TV guide: Whose Line is it Anyway?

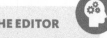

STUDY TIP

Don't make the mistake of using lowercase for all short words in titles. *Is* and *are* are verbs, and *it* is a pronoun; these are important words that should always be capitalized in titles.

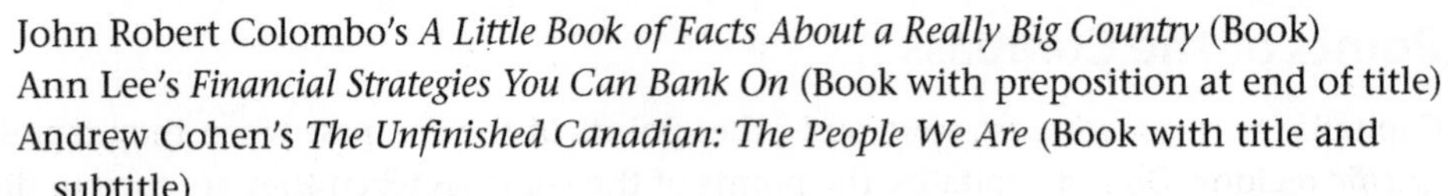

John Robert Colombo's *A Little Book of Facts About a Really Big Country* (Book)
Ann Lee's *Financial Strategies You Can Bank On* (Book with preposition at end of title)
Andrew Cohen's *The Unfinished Canadian: The People We Are* (Book with title and subtitle)
The Globe and Mail (Newspaper with *The* as part of masthead)
"How to Get the Most From a Placement Service" in *Newsweek* (Magazine article)
Late Show With Stephen Colbert (TV Series)
Life Is Beautiful (Movie)
The Tragically Hip's "New Orleans Is Sinking" on *Up to Here* (Song and album)

Complete the reinforcement exercises for Level II on pages 362–363.

LEVEL III

ADDITIONAL RULES OF CAPITALIZATION

Beginning Words

CAREER TIP

Once you're working in your chosen field, continue to expand your skill set. Continuing education is greatly valued by business leaders and will reflect well on you when promotions are being considered.

In addition to capitalizing the first word of a complete sentence, capitalize the first words in quoted sentences, independent phrases, bulleted or enumerated items, and formal rules or principles following colons.

John F. Kennedy said, "*Man* is the most extraordinary computer of all." (Quoted sentence)
No, not at the present time. (Independent phrase)
Big utilities formed an alliance to sell the following:

1. *Electricity*
2. *Natural gas*
3. *Energy management services (Enumerated items)*

Our office manager responded with his favourite rule: *Follow* the company stylebook for correct capitalization. (Rule following colon)

Celestial Bodies

Capitalize the names of celestial bodies such as planets, stars, asteroids, and constellations. Do not capitalize the terms *earth, sun,* or *moon* unless they appear in a context with other celestial bodies in the solar system.

Venus and Mars are the closest planets to *Earth.*
Global warming is changing the climate on *earth.*

Ethnic, Cultural, Language, and Religious References

Capitalize terms that relate to a particular culture, language, race, or religion.

The *Dene* are the *Athapaskan*-speaking *First Nations* peoples, including the *Chipewyan, Dogrib, Gwich'in,* and *Slavey* groups.
In Hawaii *Asian* and *Western* cultures merge.
Both *English* and *Hebrew* are spoken by *Jews* in Israel.
The candidate wasn't popular with *French-Canadian* voters.

Words Following *Marked* and *Stamped*

Capitalize words that follow the words *marked* and *stamped.*

For greater care in transport, the package was stamped *Fragile.*
That bill was marked *Paid in Full* on September 15.

Special Uses of Personal Titles and Terms

1. Generally, titles are capitalized according to the specifications set forth earlier. However, when a title of an official appears in that organization's minutes, bylaws, or other such official documents, it is capitalized.

   The *Controller* will have authority over departmental budgets. (Title appearing in bylaws)
   By vote of the shareholders, the *President* is empowered to implement a stock split. (Title appearing in annual report)

2. When the terms *ex, elect, late,* and *former* are used with capitalized titles, these terms are not capitalized.

   The projections of *ex-Vice President* Baldwin have proven exceedingly accurate.
   Chief-elect Okemow addressed the First Nations council.

3. Titles are capitalized when used in direct address, except for the terms *sir, madam, ladies,* and *gentlemen.*

   May I ask, *Doctor,* what my mother's prognosis is?
   What can I do, *Professor,* to improve my grade before the end of the semester?
   You'll soon learn, *ladies and gentlemen,* how this new procedure can reduce your workload.

Complete the reinforcement exercises for Level III on pages 364–365.

ASK AN EDITOR

Question:
I work for a provincial agency, and I'm not sure what to capitalize or hyphenate in the underlined phrase in this sentence: *Provincial agencies must make forms available to non-English-speaking applicants.*

Answer:
When a prefix is joined to a word that must be capitalized, the prefix is usually followed by a hyphen and the capital letter is retained, as in *anti-American, mid-July, or pre-Confederation.* In your example, because the word *speaking* also combines with *non-English* to form a single-unit adjective, it, too, should be hyphenated. Thus, the expression as you've written it is correct.

NAME ____________________

CHAPTER 18 ■ Reinforcement Exercises

LEVEL I

A. **(Self-check)** In the following sentences, use proofreading marks to correct errors you find in capitalization. Use three short lines (_) under a lowercase letter to indicate that it is to be changed to a capital letter. Draw a diagonal (/) through a capital letter you want to change to a lowercase letter. In the space provided, write the total number of changes you made in each sentence. Write *0* if a sentence is correct. When in doubt about capitalizing a word, refer to a Canadian dictionary.

EXAMPLE: The Bandit Henry McCarthy was also known as Billy the kid. ____2____

1. The entire Staff is invited to attend a Time Management seminar on monday, june 4. ________
2. To this day, Bell remains a dominant force in the Telecommunications Industry. ________
3. The Company is developing its facebook presence to try to reach new Customers. ________
4. In the Fall i plan to begin my Master's Degree in Marketing at Simon Fraser University. ________
5. Use India ink to make dark headings on the manila folders. ________
6. The customer lives on Pelee island, which is on the canadian side of lake erie. ________
7. On its website, transport Canada offers Safety Guidelines for flying any type of Remotely Piloted Aircraft System (RPAS), commonly referred to as *Drones*. ________
8. Starbucks ensures high standards by training its Baristas in Coffee Preparation techniques and Customer Service. ________
9. All our Sales Representatives met in the Sheraton room of the red lion inn for a Training Session on Stress Management. ________
10. Our new Security team is composed of Jim the Basset Hound and Joe the Cocker Spaniel. ________

Check your answers.

B. Use proofreading marks to correct any capitalization errors in these sentences. In the space provided, write the total number of changes you made. Write *0* if a sentence is correct.

1. Because he was interested in Computer Technology, Craig took computer mathematics I, general physics I, and computer circuitry II. ________
2. The Post Office has discontinued home delivery in the City of Winnipeg, Manitoba. ________
3. Many people with Email now get all their Bills delivered online. ________

TEAR HERE

4. The Keen Family, who bought their Recreational Vehicle from us, now travel exclusively by RV and are heading to cowtown this month for the Calgary stampede. ______________

5. Did you notice the freudian slip made by the Arbitrator? ______________

6. Representatives from the Fishing, Mining, and Forestry Industries will take part in a National Natural Resources conference in Halifax. ______________

7. The Canadian cancer society sells Daffodils every april to raise money for Research. ______________

8. A labrador retriever is the popular Store Mascot of a shop in Downtown Dartmouth. ______________

9. Last Summer Tricia Adams took out a policy with the Co-operators. (The word *the* is part of the company name.) ______________

10. Work schedules in november will be adjusted for employees to attend a remembrance day ceremony. ______________

11. Most End Users of our product live in the americas, but we also have several in a few european countries. ______________

12. Once again the Toronto maple leafs will not be in the Playoffs and will not be taking home the stanley cup. ______________

13. The company's facebook page and instagram feed are getting more Likes than ever. ______________

14. His report on diesel engines contained many greek symbols in the engineering equations. ______________

15. The Hip-Hop mogul's customized lincoln navigator sported big wheels, satellite radio, three dvd players, six tv screens, a sony ps5, and vibrating front seats. ______________

TEAR HERE

NAME ____________________

LEVEL II

A. (Self-check) In the following sentences, use proofreading marks to correct errors in capitalization. In the space provided, write the total number of changes you made. Write *0* if a sentence is correct.

EXAMPLE: General manager Cooper was promoted to Vice President. ______3______

1. SUBJECT: new payroll processing procedure ______
2. Please consult figure 52D in appendix B for instructions for computing the depreciation of equipment. ______
3. Martin Cooper, a General Manager of Motorola, created the first true cellphone. ______
4. Shoppers Drug Mart was founded by Murray Koffler, a Pharmacist, in 1962. ______
5. Both mother and uncle George are engineers working in the wind power division of Suncor. (Assume this is an official division name.) ______
6. We've suggested that mr. and mrs. Amato contact the office of the federal ombudsman for victims of crime. ______
7. My Aunt recommended that before I apply to Colleges I read this year's "Canadian university report" from *the globe and mail.* ______
8. Address the envelope to Ms. Maris Sheaffer, director, employee services, Omega Corporation, 304 Hilyard Street, Edmonton, Alberta T6J 5G4. ______
9. The Western boundary of treaty 8 was determined to be along the arctic-pacific divide. ______
10. Illy, a company founded in the Northern part of Italy during world war I, produces coffee made from pure arabica beans. ______

Check your answers.

B. Use proofreading marks to correct errors in the sentences below. In the space provided, write the total number of changes you made. Write *0* if a sentence is correct.

1. All Federal and Provincial Government agencies must make their websites accessible to the blind, and Businesses should as well. ______
2. The Prime Minister tasked labour minister Tassi with leading the implementation of the Pay Equity Act. ______
3. My Mother, a highly respected Business Strategist, suggested that I read the book *Lean in: Women, work, and the will to lead.* ______
4. At Amazon Canada, we are looking to hire a Specialist in Automatic Speech Recognition (ASR) in our digital products department. (Assume this is an official department name.) ______
5. To locate the exact amount of provincial funding, look on Line 7, Page 6 of supplement no. 4. ______

TEAR HERE

6. Steve Chen, one of the Founders of YouTube, hurried to gate 16 to catch flight 263 to Vancouver. __________

7. The director of purchasing, Harvey Gross, ordered an Epson Document Camera and a MasterVision Interactive Whiteboard for the boardroom. __________

8. Send all inquiries in writing to Paul Jorgensen, director, mining operations, Goldcorp Canada limited, p.o. box 58, Thunder bay, ontario P7B 5Z8. __________

9. SUBJECT: new health and safety protocols in effect immediately __________

10. To learn how to be a Business Leader, read the article "Why should anyone be led by you?" __________

11. Because of her allergies, Kristen had to run out at lunch to buy kleenex and benadryl. __________

12. Yours Truly,

    Fatima Mala

    Project manager, Information technology __________

13. My uncle Brian is moving to the West Coast to take a job as Managing Director of a large hotel chain. __________

14. The lunch our Executive Assistant ordered in consisted of reuben sandwiches, caesar salad, and cans of coca-cola for everyone. __________

15. The Media were visibly surprised when councillor Gaspar, the Mayor's biggest supporter, openly disagreed with the proposed transit plan. __________

NAME ______________________

LEVEL III

A. **(Self-check)** In the following sentences, use proofreading marks to make necessary changes. In the space provided, write the total number of changes you made. Write *0* if a sentence is correct.

EXAMPLE: The Late Prime Minister Lester Pearson is remembered for his efforts at the united nations toward the goal of world peace. ___3___

1. In South America most Brazilians speak portuguese, most Surinamese speak dutch, and most Guyanese speak english. ______
2. Because the letter was marked "confidential," Sandy delivered it personally to the Boss. ______
3. Google's first guiding principle is this: focus on the user and all else will follow. ______
4. Mercury, venus, earth, and mars are dense and solid. ______
5. The most common lies job seekers use on their résumés are the following:
   1. inflated job titles
   2. false employment dates
   3. fake academic credentials ______
6. How on Earth do these job seekers think they will get away with it? ______
7. Our website charges europeans in euros. ______
8. We have Ex-Councillor Lupus and Mayor-Elect Lanham scheduled for the Remembrance Day ceremonies. ______
9. You, Sir, have made an impression on our hiring committee. ______
10. Our organization's bylaws state, "the Secretary of the Association will submit an agenda two weeks before each meeting." ______

Check your answers.

B. In the following sentences, use proofreading marks to make necessary changes. In the space provided, write the total number of changes you made. Write *0* if a sentence is correct.

1. As the Sun beat down on the crowd, the Vice-Chancellor continued his graduation address to the students of the University of Manitoba. ______
2. Would you like me to proofread your presentation? yes, thank you very much. ______
3. As a Human Resources Manager, Jill received many letters that began "Dear Sir or Madam." ______
4. Most jobs in government require working knowledge of both english and french. ______
5. The accountant marked the invoice "paid." ______
6. The minutes of our last meeting summed up what happened: "The Vice President acted on behalf of the President, who was attending a conference in the far East." ______

TEAR HERE

7. Please present the feedback from constituents, councillor. ________

8. You need to stamp each piece of mail "received" as you open it. ________

9. The important steps to remember when doing CPR are the following:
   1. call 911
   2. push down in the centre of the victim's chest
   3. blow into victim's mouth until you see the chest rise ________

10. Thomas Watson Sr., Former CEO of IBM, said "to be successful, you have to have your heart in your business, and your business in your heart." ________

C. **Review of Levels I, II, and III.** Write *a* or *b* in the space provided to indicate correct capitalization. Assume that each group of words except No. 2 is part of a complete sentence.

	(a)	(b)	
1.	conduct a google search	conduct a Google search	________
2.	SUBJECT: 2020 annual report available	SUBJECT: 2020 Annual Report Available	________
3.	Starbucks Coffee	Starbucks coffee	________
4.	Welcome, ladies and gentlemen	Welcome, Ladies and Gentlemen	________
5.	british counterpart	British counterpart	________
6.	awarded a Bachelor's degree	awarded a bachelor's degree	________
7.	courses in French and anatomy	courses in French and Anatomy	________
8.	the Federal Government	the federal government	________
9.	a file marked "urgent"	a file marked "Urgent"	________
10.	avoid the sun's rays	avoid the Sun's rays	________
11.	the governor general's speech	the Governor General's speech	________
12.	exit from highway 5	exit from Highway 5	________

D. **Writing Exercises.**

1. Write ten original sentences that contain at least 20 properly capitalized words (not counting the first word) that illustrate a variety of capitalization rules.

2. Write one or two paragraphs summarizing an article from a local newspaper. Choose an article with as many capital letters as possible. Apply the rules of capitalization you learned in this chapter.

POSTTEST

In the following sentences, use proofreading marks to correct errors in capitalization.

1. Will the company pay for courses I take toward my M.B.A. Degree?
2. SUBJECT: employee retreat this friday
3. I really enjoyed the book *The Snowball: Warren Buffett And The Business Of Life.*
4. As an Equal Opportunity Employer, we offer accommodations for christian, jewish, and muslim holiday observances.
5. Applicants for the Controller position should address their résumé to Mika Palalas in our human resources department.
6. Alvin Toffler, a Writer and Futurist, once said, "it is better to err on the side of daring than the side of caution."
7. Judy took night courses in english literature, accounting, and sociology at the University.
8. The engineers will meet in the algonquin room of the four points Sheraton next thursday.
9. Tell me, doctor, which hospital has the best Cancer centre.
10. My mother and my uncle Michael will spend the christmas holidays with us.

TEAR HERE

EDITOR'S CHALLENGE

The following letters contain errors reflecting the concepts you have studied thus far, as well as other common errors. Use proofreading marks to show all necessary corrections.

HOLST BROTHERS CONSTRUCTION

2230 DUNSMUIR AVE.

OTTAWA, ON K1A 2J7 (613) 828-4493

January 4, 202x

Ms. Danielle M. Forrester
President, Interior Design Institute
504 Richmond street
Ottawa, ON K1N 7B7

Dear Ms. Forrester:

Here is a breif report about our work with the cheviot hills residence being prepared as the show-case house for the Interior Design Institute. The renovation and remodelling is progressing on schedule, and should be ready for the photographers from metropolitan home magazine june 1.

Past Progress

During the Fall the work crew completed the following tasks, removal of all wood shingles, repair of the plywood roof base and installation of a permawear tile roof. In december we replaced damaged window facings we also repaired the plumbing in two baths and the kitchen. As you requested we investigated italian marble for the entry and spanish tiles for the patio. A price sheet for those items are enclosed.

Current Progress

At present we are concentrating on the Living Room which required ceiling repair and electrical rewiring, see page 6 of your blueprints. The pyramid skylight has been installed in the library, however, we had to alter two bookcases in doing so. After consulting the President and General Manager of our company, we decided to absorb some of the extra costs involved, however; other off budget items will be your responsibility.

Future Schedule

In February we expect to complete all the interior finish work, and the painters will apply two coats of anderson no. 343 wall primer. I believe that Ms. Chin and Mr. Darwin whom you sug-gested would be decorating the downstairs, could begin there work february 15. Just have them call my Supervisor or I to arrange the exact date.

Sincerely yours,

Irena Overmeyer

Irena Overmeyer

Brant Property Management

620 Mumford Rd.

Saint John, NB E2J 2B5 **(506) 652-6526** **www.brantproperty.ca**

June 15, 202x

Ms. Monika Harding
Fibre Festival
240 Atlantic Avenue, unit 16
Saint John, NB E2L 1U8

Dear Ms. Harding:

You have been a good tenant of Brant Properties for the past eight years and we are pleased that your retail store in unit 16 at our 240 Atlantic avenue location has thrived.

As you know the Plaza is in need for updating and repair. we have aranged for Bristol construction to do work on the building though the Month of September, as a result, Stores in the plaza will have to closed on a rotating schedule. The work effecting your Unit will be completed form Monday September 19 to Friday September 23, and will include the following;

1. reinforcement of the roofs waterproofing system
2. re-drywalling of damaged ceiling in unit
3. updating of electrical wiring
4. exterior re-facing with Stucco
5. installation of a awning above doorway

Additionally we are asking tenants to pay a fee for inclusion on a Pylon Sign that will be near to the road, to draw in more customers. These signs are said to "Pay for (themselves) through increased traffic within three months."

To fund the upgrades to the building you will see a 3 percent increase in your rent as off January 1.

I trust that you will see the benefit of the proposed construction despite the impending disruption to business, nevertheless, I am available by phone or email to address any concerns you have.

Sincerely,

Uday Basara

Uday Basara, property manager
Brant Property Management
ubasara@brantproperty.ca

For additional resources, please visit MindTap at login.cengage.com. Cengage | MINDTAP

TEAR HERE

CHAPTER

19

NUMBERS

OBJECTIVES

When you have completed the materials in this chapter, you will be able to do the following:

LEVEL I

- Choose correctly between figure and word forms to express general numbers and numbers beginning sentences
- Properly place hyphens in numbers when needed
- Express money, dates, clock time, addresses, and telephone and fax numbers appropriately

LEVEL II

- Use the correct form in writing related numbers, consecutive numbers, periods of time, ages and anniversaries, and round numbers
- Use the correct form in expressing numbers used with words, abbreviations, and symbols

LEVEL III

- Correctly express weights, measurements, and fractions
- Use the correct form in expressing percentages and decimals and ordinals

PRETEST

Examine the expression of numbers in the following sentences. Should the word or figure form of the numbers be used? Underline any incorrect or unconventional form, and write an improved form in the space provided (e.g., *$10* or *ten dollars*?). Write *C* if a sentence is correct.

1. Worldwide, there are now seventy-three countries producing products for Fairtrade, 1707 producer organizations, and more than 35000 Fairtrade products on the market. ________
2. As many as 2/3 of teens admit that an informal texting style has crept into their school assignments. ________

(continued)

PRETEST (CONTINUED)

3. In addition, 50 percent of teens said they use text message abbreviations such as LOL in school assignments. ________
4. The main office is at 1 Broadway Lane. ________
5. 12 department members had to send their regrets because they were double-booked for ten a.m. ________
6. When Roxanne reached 18 years of age, she assumed ownership of over fifty ha of property in two provinces. ________
7. Take twenty dollars to pick up 20 ninety-two-cent stamps at the post office. ________
8. Of the twenty cars we had available on May 2nd, we have only four cars left today. ________
9. The art treasure measures only twenty-three cm by thirty cm, but it is said to be worth nearly $2 million dollars. ________
10. The smallest winged insect is the Tanzanian parasitic wasp, which has a wingspan of point two mm. ________

Just as capitalization is governed by convention, so is the expression of numbers. Usage and custom determine whether to express a number in the form of a figure (e.g., *5*) or in the form of a word (e.g., *five*). Numbers expressed as figures are shorter and easier to comprehend, so you'll see these used in business documents such as invoices, statements, and purchase orders. However, numbers used as words are necessary in certain instances. Observe the following guidelines in expressing numbers that appear in written sentences.

LEVEL I

BASIC GUIDELINES FOR EXPRESSING NUMBERS

STUDY TIP

To remember it better, some people call this the "rule of ten": words for one through ten; figures for 11 and above.

General Rules for Numbers

WRITING NUMBERS IN WORD OR FIGURE FORM. The numbers one through ten are generally written as words. Numbers above ten are written as figures.

The committee consisted of *nine* regular members and *one* chair.

The *37* spoiled questionnaires were discarded.

NUMBERS THAT BEGIN SENTENCES. Numbers that begin sentences are written as words. If a number involves more than two words, however, the sentence should be rewritten so that the number no longer falls at the beginning.

Twenty-three investors provided capital for the down payment.

A total of *320* distributors agreed to market the product. (Not *Three hundred twenty* distributors agreed to market the product.)

HYPHENATING NUMBERS. Compound numbers from *21* through *99* are hyphenated when written in word form.

Thirty-nine people applied for the forensic science technician position.

Forty-six companies performed below expectations last quarter.

LARGE NUMBERS. Numbers of four digits or more (except years, house numbers, room numbers, and the like) usually require a comma to divide each set of thousands. An alternative style—and one preferred when using SI measures (*Système international d'unités*, commonly referred to as the metric system)—is to use a space in place of the comma.

The contest attracted *11,362* entries.
The 50/50 prize awarded was nearly *$16 000*.

Money

Sums of money $1 or greater are expressed as figures. If a sum is a whole dollar amount, most business writers omit the decimal and zeros (whether or not the amount appears with other fractional dollar amounts).

Although he budgeted only *$25*, Mike spent *$34.50* for the gift.
The statement showed purchases of *$7.13*, *$10*, *$43.50*, *$90*, and *$262.78*.

Sums less than $1 are written as figures that are followed by the word *cents*. However, if they appear in a series with sums greater than $1, use a dollar sign and a decimal instead. If a sentence contains unrelated amounts of money, treat each amount separately.

Lisa said that she had only *65 cents* with her.
Our *monthly* petty cash statement showed purchases of *$7.13*, *$.99*, *$2.80*, *$1*, and *$.40*. (Related numbers)
For every *$10* you spend in our restaurant, we will donate *50 cents* to the Special Olympics. (Unrelated numbers)

Dates

In dates, numbers that appear after the name of the month are written in **cardinal figures** (*1*, *2*, *3*, etc.). Those that stand alone or appear before the name of a month with *of* are written in **ordinal figures** (*1st*, *2nd*, *3rd*, etc.).

The meeting is scheduled for *October 5* in our office.
On the *2nd* of January and again on the *18th*, we called for service.

Most Canadian and American communicators express dates in the following form: *month day, year* (a comma separates the day and the year). An alternative form, used primarily in military and international correspondence, uses this order without a comma: *day month year*. Some business organizations, especially those doing business globally, prefer the international date style for its clarity since it separates the numerals of the day and the year.

By *October 1, 2022*, all construction on the subway must be completed. (General date format)
The rental contract was originally signed *25 June 2019*. (Military and international format)

Clock Time

Use figures when expressing clock time with *a.m.*, *p.m.*, *noon*, or *midnight*. Omit the colon and zeros with whole hours. When exact time is expressed with *o'clock*, either figures or words may be used (but be consistent). Note that phrases such as *in the afternoon* or *in the morning* may follow clock time expressed with *o'clock* but not time expressed with *a.m.* or *p.m.*

The first shift starts at *8 a.m.*; the second, at *3:30 p.m.*
At *four* (or *4*) *o'clock* in the afternoon, we'll announce the winner.

ASK AN EDITOR

Question:
I'm never sure when to hyphenate numbers with other words; for example, are the hyphens correct in *ten-years-old*?

Answer:
Numbers are hyphenated with other words when together they form a compound adjective that precedes a noun. In your example, you would not use hyphens because the phrase *ten years old* would not be used as a compound adjective before a noun. However, you would use hyphens in a phrase such as *ten-year-old child*. (Note singular *year*.)

STUDY TIP

A common error is the use of both $ and the word *dollars*. Watch for it in your writing.

DID YOU KNOW?

The dollar sign ($) first appeared in business correspondence among the British, Canadians, Americans, and Mexicans in the 1770s.

ASK AN EDITOR

Question:
Should I put quotation marks around figures to emphasize them? For example, *Your account has a balance of "$2,136.18."*

Answer:
Certainly not! Quotation marks should not be used as a mechanical device for added emphasis.

Addresses

Except for the number *One*, house and building numbers are expressed as figures. Apartment numbers, suite numbers, box numbers, and route numbers are also written in figure form. Do not use commas to separate digits in these numbers.

805 Fiske Avenue	*27321* Riverside Drive
One Victoria Boulevard	*1762* Cone Street, Apt. *2B*
PO Box *8935*	Rural Route *19*

ASK AN EDITOR

Question:
A fellow team member wants to show dollar amounts in two forms, such as the following: *The consultant charges two hundred dollars ($200) an hour.* I think this is overkill. Do we have to show figures in two forms?

Answer:
In formal legal documents, amounts of money may be expressed in words followed by figures in parentheses. However, business writers do not follow this practice because it is unnecessary, wordy, and pretentious. In fact, some readers are insulted because the practice suggests they are not bright enough to comprehend just one set of figures.

Telephone and Fax Numbers

Telephone and fax numbers are expressed with figures. The area code is frequently placed in parentheses preceding the telephone number. Be sure to include a space after the closing parenthesis. Common alternative forms include separating all three parts of the phone number with hyphens or with periods. When including an extension, separate it from the phone number with a comma. If your company has a style guide, it may dictate a style for writing phone numbers.

Please call us at *647-828-1100* for further information.
You may reach me at *(306) 685-4321, Ext. 281,* after 9:30 a.m.
Call our toll-free number at *1-800-340-3281* for the latest sports updates.
Please fax your order to *902.937.5594.*

Complete the reinforcement exercises for Level I on pages 376–378.

LEVEL II

SPECIAL GUIDELINES FOR EXPRESSING NUMBERS

Related Numbers

Related numbers are those used similarly in the same document, often in reference to the same noun. They should all be expressed as the largest number is expressed. Thus, if the largest number is greater than ten, all the numbers should be expressed as figures.

Only *3* companies out of *147* failed to return the survey form.
Of the *98* email documents Casey received today, *19* were marked "Urgent" and *7* were marked "Confidential."
Nearly *20* employees will be expected to share the *15* computers, *8* printers, and *3* fax machines. (Note that items in a series are always considered to be related; the number of employees is, in fact, an unrelated number.)

Unrelated numbers within the same document are written as words or figures according to the general guidelines presented earlier in this chapter.

The *two* bridges carry at least *10,000* cars during the *four* peak traffic hours.
Twenty-three contract changes will be discussed by *89* employees working in *eight* departments.

Consecutive Numbers

When two numbers appear one after another and both modify a following noun, readers may misread the numbers because of their closeness. You should express one number in word form and the other in figure form. Use word form for the first number unless the second number would make a much shorter word.

The economist divided the era into *four 25*-year periods.
Erich purchased *twelve* 64 GB flash drives for his team.
We'll need at least *150 sixty*-watt bulbs. (Use word form for the second number as it is a significantly shorter word.)

STUDY TIP

Numbers included in a series (three or more items) are always considered related.

Periods of Time

Periods of time (seconds, minutes, hours, days, weeks, months, and years) are treated as any other general number. That is, the "rule of ten" applies: numbers ten and below are written in word form. However, figures are used to achieve special emphasis in expressing business concepts such as discount rates, interest rates, warranty periods, credit terms, loan periods, and payment terms.

Mrs. Martino has been with our firm for *35* years.
We agreed to hold the booking for only *15* days.
After a *183-day* strike, workers returned to their jobs.
Pay your invoice within *10 days* to receive a *2 percent* discount. (Figure form used for business concepts)
Higher interest rates are offered on *6*- to *9*-month certificates of deposit.

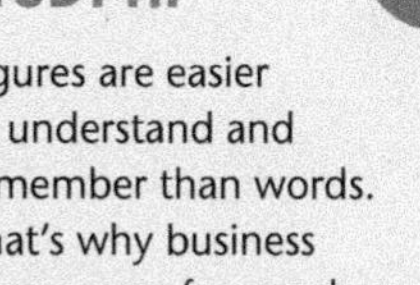

STUDY TIP

Figures are easier to understand and remember than words. That's why business terms, even for numbers under ten, are generally written as figures.

Note that legal documents usually show periods of time twice, first in words and then in figures enclosed in parentheses: *period of sixty (60) days.*

Ages and Anniversaries

Ages and anniversaries that can be written out in one or two words are generally expressed in word form. Those that require more than two words (101+) are written in figures. Figures are also used when an age (a) appears immediately after a person's name; (b) is expressed in exact years, months, and sometimes days; or (c) is used in a technical, legal, or statistical sense.

When he was *forty-one,* Mr. Selnig became the company's president.
This year marks the *twenty-fifth* anniversary of the company's founding.
Grace Siebold, *63,* plans to retire in two years.
The child was adopted when he was *3* years *8* months and *24* days old.

Numbers Used With Words, Abbreviations, and Symbols

Numbers used with words are expressed as figures.

page 4	Policy 04-168315	Area Code 819
Room 14	Volume 5	Section 16
Option 3	Form 1040	Bylaw 96-221

Numbers used with abbreviations are also expressed as figures.

Apt. 16	Serial No. 265188440	Nos. 199 and 202
Ext. 245	Account No. 286-32-5891	Social Insurance No. 412 434 456

Notice that the word *number* is capitalized and abbreviated (*No.*) when it precedes a number. However, if the word *number* begins a sentence, do not abbreviate it.

Avoid symbols (such as #, %, ¢) in contextual business writing (sentences). In other business documents where space is limited, however, symbols are frequently used. Numbers appearing with symbols are expressed as figures.

15%	44¢	#10 nails	2/10, n/60

BE THE EDITOR

From *The Denver Post*: "The Allied Jewish Federation, which overseas the fund drive, hopes to raise $5.5 million."

Round Numbers

Round numbers are approximations. They may be expressed in word or figure form, although figure form is shorter and easier to comprehend.

Approximately *400* (or *four hundred*) employees signed the petition.
At last count we had received about *20* (or *twenty*) reservations.

For ease of reading, round numbers in the millions or billions should be expressed with a combination of figures and words.

The prime minister asked for a budget cut of *$2 billion*.
In its lawsuit IBM made *69 million* documents available to the government.
Nearly *1.2 million* imported cars were sold last year.

Complete the reinforcement exercises for Level II on pages 379–380.

LEVEL III

ADDITIONAL GUIDELINES FOR EXPRESSING NUMBERS

CAREER TIP

If your company has a style manual, check it for number preferences. Larger companies may prescribe the figure or word form they prefer for often-used numbers.

Weights and Measurements

Weights and measurements, including temperatures, are expressed as figures.

The truck used *80* L of gasoline and *2* L of oil on the trip.
A postcard ad measures *4* by *6* inches (about *10* by *15* cm).
The announcement gave the baby's weight as *7* pounds *14* ounces.
The highest temperature ever recorded was 56.7 degrees Celsius in 1913 in Death Valley, California.

In sentences, the nouns following weights and measurements are spelled out if they refer to traditional units of measurement (e.g., 7 *pounds* 14 *ounces*) but should not be spelled out if they refer to metric units of measure (10 by 15 cm). For business forms, charts, and technical writing, symbols or abbreviations are generally used.

57 kg	17°C	100 km	2 lb.
5 tbsp.	9' × 12'	#10	7 oz.

Canada adopted the metric/SI system in 1971, but examples here include traditional forms such as *pound* and *foot* because they are still in common use. Note that SI uses symbols rather than abbreviations. No periods are used unless the symbol falls at the end of a sentence. Abbreviations for traditional units of measure are now sometimes written without periods as well. Note, however, that if abbreviating *inches* (*in.*), a period is always necessary to differentiate it from the word *in*.

Fractions

Simple fractions are fractions in which both the numerator and the denominator are whole numbers. They are expressed as words and are hyphenated.

Over *three-fourths* of the students attended the lecture.
A *two-thirds* majority is needed to carry the motion.

Long or awkward fractions appearing in sentences may be written either as figures or as a combination of figures and words.

The computer will execute a command in *1 millionth* of a second. (A combination of words and figures is easier to comprehend.)

Flight records revealed that the emergency system was activated *13/200* of a second after the pilot was notified. (The figure form is easier to comprehend.)

Mixed fractions (whole numbers combined with fractions) are always expressed as figures.

The office desks were expected to be *35¼* inches long, not *35½* inches. (Notice that no space follows a whole number when a keyboard fraction is used.)

The envelope measured *3 5/8* inches by *6 1/2* inches. (Notice that fractions that must be keyed with slashes are separated with a space from their related whole numbers.)

When fractions that are constructed with slashes appear with key fractions, be consistent by using the slash construction for all the fractions.

Percentages and Decimals

Percentages are expressed with figures that are followed by the expression *percent* (or *per cent*). The percent sign (%) is used primarily on business forms or in statistical presentations.

Interest rates have been as low as *0.25 percent* and as high as *16 percent.*

The report states that *52 percent* of the workers joined the union.

Decimals are expressed with figures. If a decimal does not contain a whole number and does not begin with a zero, a zero should be placed before the decimal. An exception is made for decimals used with a dollar sign.

Daryl Thomas set a record when he ran the race in *9.86* seconds. (Contains a whole number)

Close examination revealed the settings to be *.005* of an inch off. (Begins with a zero)

Less than *0.1* percent of the operating costs will be borne by taxpayers. (Zero placed before decimal that neither contains a whole number nor begins with a zero)

Each fastener costs $.95. (Decimal with dollar sign)

Ordinals

Ordinal numbers show position in an ordered sequence. Although ordinal numbers are generally expressed in word form (*first, second, third,* etc.), two exceptions should be noted: (1) figure form is used for dates appearing alone or appearing before a month preceded by *of,* and (2) figure form is used when the ordinal would require more than two words.

MOST ORDINALS.

The company is celebrating its *fortieth* anniversary.

Before the *eighteenth* century, spelling was not standardized.

Of 237 sales representatives, Joanna ranked *second* in total sales.

Jeanne Sauvé became the *twenty-third* Governor General in 1984.

DATES.

Your payment must be received by the *30th* to qualify for the cash discount.

We experienced a power outage on the *2nd* of June.

LARGER ORDINALS.

Our bank ranks *103rd* in terms of capital investments.

Complete the reinforcement exercises for Level III on pages 381–382.

NAME ______________________________

CHAPTER 19 ■ Reinforcement Exercises

LEVEL I

A. (Self-check) In the space provided, write the letter of the correct answer.

1. All (a) 11, (b) eleven restaurant managers said that they had problems with employees' coming in late for their shifts. ________
2. (a) 23, (b) Twenty three, (c) Twenty-three call centres in India announced that they will be switching from customer service to mortgage processing. ________
3. On the (a) 13th, (b) 13, (c) thirteenth of April, two Domino's employees posted a prank video on YouTube that made the company look bad. ________
4. It took the management of Domino's (a) 2, (b) two days to respond publicly to the prank. ________
5. My bank charges service fees of $5, $1.50, and (a) 95 cents, (b) $.95 for various transaction types. ________
6. The office address is listed as (a) Three, (b) 3 Meadowlark Drive. ________
7. Department mail is usually distributed at (a) 10 a.m., (b) ten a.m. ________
8. Organizers expect (a) 38,000, (b) 38000 people to attend the Macworld Conference & Expo. ________
9. Be sure you have (a) $8, (b) eight dollars in cash to pay for parking. ________
10. We plan to meet at (a) 9:00 a.m., (b) 9 a.m. Tuesday. ________

Check your answers.

B. Assume that the following phrases appear within sentences (unless otherwise noted) in business correspondence. Write the preferred form in the space provided. Write *C* if a phrase is correct.

EXAMPLE: Twenty new blog entries ___20 new blog entries___

1. (beginning of sentence) 15 photocopies ________
2. on April 9 ________
3. charged $.10 per copy ________
4. sent 10 email messages ________
5. on the seventh of May ________
6. call 800/598-3459 ________
7. a charge of $39.00 ________
8. on August 31st ________
9. meeting at 11:00 a.m. ________
10. eight o'clock breakfast meeting ________
11. arrived at 10 p.m. at night ________
12. 22 July, 2021 ________
13. has sixty-six rooms ________
14. costs $49 dollars ________
15. hired 5 new employees ________
16. exactly twenty dollars ________

TEAR HERE

17. 12655 Centre Street ____________

18. 1 Hampton Square ____________

19. (beginning of sentence) Twenty seven interviewers ____________

20. at 7 o'clock ____________

21. May 15, 2019 ____________

22. at six thirty p.m. ____________

23. the fourth of May ____________

24. cheque for one hundred dollars ____________

25. exactly 90¢ ____________

C. Rewrite these sentences, correcting any errors.

1. Please call me at (403)685.1230 Ext. 309.

2. On January 13th Alex submitted the following petty cash disbursements: $2.80, 99 cents, $3.00, and 76 cents.

3. The insurance broker located at 11,261 Ashland Drive is getting us quotations from 4 different companies.

4. 8 pages of *The Canadian Press Stylebook* are devoted to dealing with sensitive subjects.

5. On the 28 of March, twenty representatives from partner companies are touring our facility.

6. If you have only thirty dollars, why are you considering the model that costs $49.99?

TEAR HERE

7. Regular work breaks are scheduled at 10:00 a.m. in the morning and again at 3:30 p.m. in the afternoon.

8. COVID-19 forced the business to close on the sixteenth of March, and it didn't reopen until the thirteenth of June.

9. 24 different wireless packages are available from our 3 local dealers.

10. Although the small size of french fries costs only ninety-nine cents from the chip truck, most customers spend between four dollars and four dollars and ninety-nine cents on lunch.

TEAR HERE

NAME ____________________

LEVEL II

A. (Self-check) Write *a* or *b* in the space provided to complete each of the following sentences.

1. The Mayrs submitted two (a) forty-page, (b) 40-page income tax returns. ____________
2. Your flight will depart from (a) Gate Nine, (b) Gate 9. ____________
3. It is rare these days for an employee to stay with one company for (a) twenty-five, (b) 25 years. ____________
4. Of the 235 emails sent, only (a) nine, (b) 9 bounced back. ____________
5. Saima knew from age (a) 16, (b) sixteen that she wanted to be an entrepreneur. ____________
6. Google paid (a) $4.95 million, (b) $4,950,000 to settle a click-fraud case. ____________
7. In the past hour, (a) three, (b) 3 people donated $500 each. ____________
8. For the store's (a) 25th, (b) twenty-fifth anniversary, it is offering a (c) 25 percent, (d) twenty-five percent discount on all merchandise. ____________
9. Your short-term loan comes due in (a) 60, (b) sixty days. ____________
10. The serial number on my monitor is (a) 85056170, (b) 85,056,170. ____________

Check your answers.

B. For the following sentences, underline any numbers or words that are expressed inappropriately. Write the correct form in the space provided. Write *C* if a sentence is correct.

EXAMPLE: The documentation group has prepared <u>4 twenty-page</u> reports. four 20-page

1. Our board of directors is composed of 15 members, of whom three are doctors, four are nurses, and eight are other health care professionals. ____________
2. For the focus group, we need 20 50-year-olds. ____________
3. The founder of Birch Bark Coffee Company was one of 40 recipients of the Canada Innovation & Entrepreneurship Award, distributed in 5 separate online ceremonies. ____________
4. We would like to confirm our insurance policy covers our 15 laptops, five printers, and four tablets. ____________
5. The following invoice Nos. have been outstanding for three months: Nos. 1355801, 1355826, and 1355882. ____________
6. Model 8,400 costs $10,000 to buy or can be leased for $275 a month for a 3-year term. ____________
7. Accounts not paid within sixty days will be suspended. ____________
8. Of the 385 manuscript pages, ten pages require minor revisions and eight pages demand heavy revision. ____________
9. John Edwards, forty-one, and Maria Gomez, thirty-three, are two of our company's youngest VPs. ____________
10. On page twenty-two of Volume two, the total deficit is listed at nearly $34,000,000,000. ____________
11. Warranties on GPS devices are limited to ninety days. ____________

TEAR HERE

12. Line eight of the contract states that you have four days to change your mind. ____________

13. Only two of the 78 staff members took sick days last month. ____________

14. The offer expires in three days, six hours, and 27 minutes. ____________

15. Taking 7 years to construct, the 3,700-square-metre home reportedly cost more than fifty million dollars. ____________

16. Of the people who liked our Facebook post, 76% were women. ____________

17. It took 10 inspection teams to review and rewrite thirty thousand pages of deeds, options, leases, and bills of sale. ____________

18. At seventy-eight years old, Peter Buckman doesn't want to retire. ____________

19. With 4 pickups daily, the delivery service serves two thousand employees in 45 departments. ____________

20. The government pledged some forty billion dollars in aid to small businesses. ____________

C. Assume that the following phrases appear in business or professional correspondence. Write the preferred form in the space provided. Write *C* if a phrase is correct.

1. sold for $1,500,000

____

2. one hundred seven five-page essays

____

3. a law that is one year two months and five days old

____

4. about three hundred voters

____

5. Stage Two of reopening

____

6. Account No. 362,486,012

____

7. seventy-two-month car loan

____

8. Highway Twenty-three

____

9. a period of seventeen years

____

10. 9 2-bedroom condos

____

NAME ______________________

LEVEL III

A. (Self-check) Write *a*, *b*, or *c* in the space provided to show the correct answer.

1. More than (a) one half, (b) one-half, (c) 1/2 of drivers say they are driving less to keep gas expenses down. ______

2. Less than (a) 3 percent, (b) three percent of cars sold in Canada in 2019 were electric. ______

3. To make tassels, first cut yarn into (a) 15 cm, (b) fifteen centimetre lengths. ______

4. The amusement park rides are restricted to people taller than (a) 4'10", (b) 4 feet 10 inches. ______

5. Canada celebrated its (a) 150th, (b) one hundred fiftieth anniversary in 2017. ______

6. The first (a) four and a half, (b) 4½ pages of the document provide background information. ______

7. To ensure customer safety at the front entrance in winter, we need a mat measuring at least (a) 4 by 8 m, (b) four by eight metres. ______

8. This year's maintenance costs are only (a) 0.5, (b) .5 percent above last year's. ______

9. Did you order (a) four, (b) 4 L of hand sanitizer? ______

10. Did you know that many high-rise buildings have no (a) 13th, (b) thirteenth floor? ______

Check your answers.

B. Review of Levels I, II, and III. Underline any errors in the following sentences, paying special attention to appropriate number usage. Rewrite the sentences correctly.

1. Futurpreneur Canada offers aspiring entrepreneurs ages 18 through 39 up to $45000 dollars in financing and 2 years of mentorship.

____

____

2. Of the small businesses owned by Canadians under age 30, 55% are fully owned by men, 15% are fully owned by women, and 14% are fully owned by a visible minority.

____

____

3. Manitobah Mukluks are rated to thirty-two degrees Celsius below freezing.

____

____

TEAR HERE

4. Take note of the following maximum letter dimensions by weight:

Category	Weight	Dimensions
Standard	Up to fifty grams	245 mm. by 156 mm.
Nonstandard/oversize	Up to five hundred grams	380 mm. by 270 mm.

5. The cash register was out only $0.05 at the end of Deena's 1st shift.

6. Our company ranks one hundred seventh in terms of total exports.

7. The business in Unit Six at 1 Foote Street asked for a rent deferral to the tenth of the month.

8. At least seven-tenths of the members attended the May sixth meeting, at which we approved the budget of $35000.

9. Eleven hundred twenty-seven square feet of office space will comfortably fit twelve desks.

10. We open in the morning at 10:00 a.m. and close at 6:00 p.m. in the evening.

C. Writing Exercises.

1. Select 15 number rules from this chapter. Write one sentence illustrating each rule. Label each rule.
2. In your local newspaper (online or print), find ten sentences with numbers. Write those sentences on a separate sheet. After each one, explain what rule the number style represents. Strive to find examples illustrating different rules.

TEAR HERE

POSTTEST

In the following sentences, underline numbers that are expressed inappropriately. Write the corrected form in the space provided.

1. 58 restaurants were nominated for the city's People's Choice Award.

2. We can offer you high-speed Internet for just thirty dollars a month.

3. The author Julia Flynn Silar tries to post at least 4 140-character updates on Twitter every day.

4. On the ninth of August, 2,500 computer programmers will attend a convention in Toronto.

5. The coldest temperature ever recorded was minus eighty-nine point two degrees Celsius in 1983 in Antarctica.

6. It took the Canada Revenue Agency seven years to collect the 750,000 dollars owed by the 2 companies.

7. Before the third of the month, we had received seventeen calls regarding the bicycle we advertised for twenty dollars.

8. The department's eighteen employees share four gender-inclusive bathrooms, two boardrooms, and one lunchroom.

9. Manjit Khan, thirty-three, is earning 200 thousand dollars a year doing a job she loves.

10. We will need ten fifty-page booklets before December 1st.

TEAR HERE

EDITOR'S CHALLENGE

The following messages contain errors representing language principles covered thus far, as well as other common errors. Use proofreading marks to make corrections.

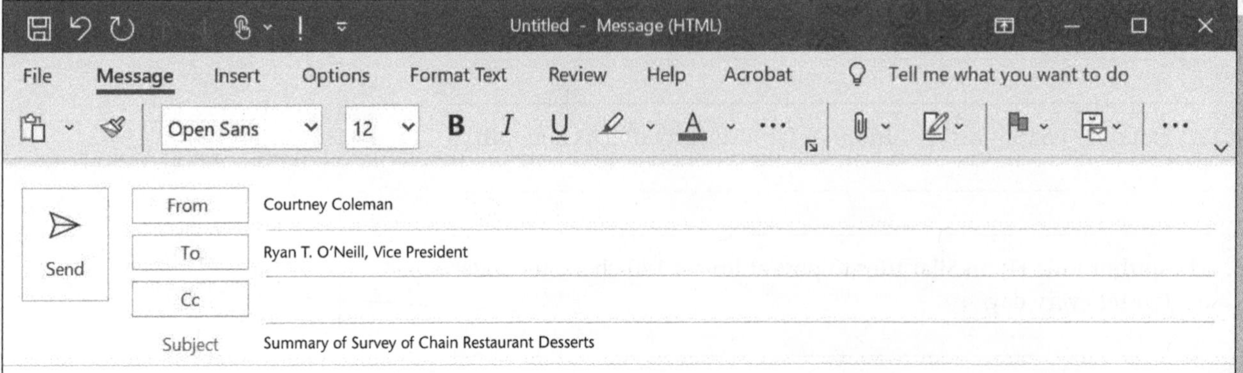

As an intern here at Midland Food Services I appreciate the opportunity you have give me to informally investigate desserts offered by major chain restaurants. At our October 20th meeting of interns you mentioned that desserts are suppose to be fun. And that many of the chains were missing a big opportunity to develop a dessert business.

To complete my Project No. three I visited 10 of the biggest and best chains in the metropolitan area and bought and taste all there desserts. I rated them on a scale of one to ten. Over a period of 5 weeks I tryed over fifty desserts in 12 restaurants. Although I will submit my full report shortly here is a brief summary of the dramatic, but disappointing, results.

- Surprisingly the average dessert score was only four point two on a 10-point scale. I rated the desserts for taste, texture, portability, healthfulness and freshness of concept.
- 1/2 of the chains still have "hot apple pies." A leftover from the 1960's. These "pies" are largely dough with an overpowering taste of cinnamon and sugar. They have 280 calories and fifteen grams of fat, more then a Cheeseburger or a order of French Fries!
- 1/3 of the chains offered chocolate chip cookies, they cost between ninety-nine cents and two dollars and contain another 15 grams of fat and three hundred or more calories.

The best chain dessert I have ever encounter was "Fudge Grande, Choco Taco" from Taco bell. Available as a special last year, it was innovative, fun, tasty, portably, relevant, and refreshing. However the best restaurant dessert I've ever ate is a Chewy- Choco-Caramel-Marshmallo-Popcorn Bar offered by my college cafeteria.

The full findings of my informal survey is in three eleven-page reports. That I will distribute at the next Midland internship meeting Tuesday December 12th.

TEAR HERE

October 1, 202x

CERTIFIED MAIL, RETURN RECEIPT REQUESTED

Mr. Charles Smith
Customer Relations
Sony Canada

115 Gordon Baker Road
Toronto, ON M2H 3R6

Dear Mr. Smith,

Pictures from a once in a lifetime trip are irreplaceable. Thats why I put my trust in Sonys Cybershot DSC-W100 Digital Camera, which I bought for a cruise I took to the french caribbean last Summer to celebrate my 40th birthday. Experience, dependability and customer service, these are the quality's that I associate with the name "Sony."

I took 100's of pictures on my twenty day trip. Although I checked some of the early shots using the lcd screen I didn't check any pictures for the last 1/2 of the trip in order to conserve my battery. When I come home however I learned that most of the pictures I took latter in the trip did not turn out because the camera had malfunctioned. 98 of the pictures I took the last week of my trip were faded to a near white colour. Enclosed is the camera, the memory card I used, the printed photos and my receipt for the camera.

As you must realize the value of these photographs are far greater then the cost of the printing, or the purchase price of the camera. The real loss is the complete record of a beautiful trip. Without pictures, I will not remember how I felt and looked standing in front of diamond rock in the Southern part of Martinique or shopping in the town of marigot in St. Martin. I will not remember dancing with children around a fire in a Guadalupe Village. 11 days of my dream vacation went essentially unrecorded. This period represents more than 50% of my vacation.

Replacing the film or camera are not enough. Without pictures I feel like I never took the trip. I have suffered a tremendous emotional loss and I am requesting that sony pay me $7500 so that I may repeat my trip, and replace the pictures lost because of this faulty camera.

I know that Sony enjoys a excellent reputation with consumers, therefore, I trust that you will do the right thing in helping me replace my lost memories. Please contact me by October 30th so that I may begin making plans for a Spring cruise.

Sincerely,

Daniella Davidson

Daniella Davidson
Enclosures: Sony Cyber-shot camera, memory card, printed photos, receipt

CHAPTER 20

EFFECTIVE SENTENCES

OBJECTIVES

When you have completed the materials in this chapter, you will be able to do the following:

LEVEL I

- Eliminate wordy phrases and redundant words
- Use the active voice of verbs in writing efficient sentences
- Compose unified sentences by avoiding excessive detail and extraneous ideas

LEVEL II

- Write clear sentences using parallel construction for similar ideas
- Place words, phrases, and clauses close to the words they modify
- Avoid ambiguous pronoun references when using pronouns such as *this*, *that*, *which*, and *it*

LEVEL III

- Achieve emphasis by subordinating secondary ideas to primary ideas
- Recognize and use concrete words instead of abstract words
- Use transitional expressions (such as *therefore*, *however*, and *for example*) to develop coherence between thoughts

PRETEST

Rewrite the following sentences to eliminate problems in parallelism, redundancy, modification, reference, conciseness, and coherence.

1. We expect growth in the neighbourhood of 20 percent.

____

____

(continued)

PRETEST *(CONTINUED)*

2. A motion to invite emeritus association members to attend the conference at no cost was introduced by Aziz Yadav.

3. Our objectives are to make our stock profitable, to operate efficiently, and developing good employee relations.

4. Waiting in line outside the store, the open sign finally went on.

5. Combine together the first four ingredients in a medium mixing bowl.

6. In view of the fact that we are moving, we are not renewing the rental agreement.

7. After illegally removing documents from his Toronto office, a jury convicted Conrad Black of obstruction of justice.

8. After closing, Lisa had to empty the cash register, count the cash, close out the payment terminal, and the doors had to be locked.

9. I would like your final decision by June 1.

10. The company has discontinued its benefits plan, which has angered employees.

The business world, where time is valuable, demands efficient writing that is meaningful and coherent. Wordy communication wastes the reader's time; unclear messages confuse the reader and are counterproductive. You can improve your writing skills by emulating the practices of good writers. Most good writers begin with a rough draft that they revise to produce a final version. This chapter shows you how to revise your rough-draft sentences to make them efficient, clear, emphatic, and coherent.

LEVEL I

WRITING EFFICIENT SENTENCES

Revising Wordy Phrases

Sentences are efficient when they convey a thought directly and economically—that is, in the fewest possible words. Good writers excise all useless verbiage from their writing. Some common examples of wordiness follow.

Wordy Phrases	Concise Substitutes
along the lines of	like
at all times	always
at the present time	now
at this point in time	now
by the name of	named
due to the fact that	because
for the purpose of	for
in all probability	probably
in connection with	about
in spite of the fact that	even though
in the amount of	for
in the event that	if
in the final analysis	finally
in the near future	soon
in the neighbourhood of	approximately
in view of the fact that	since
until such time as	until
with a view to	to
with reference to	about
with regard to	about

Notice that the revised versions of the following wordy sentences are more efficient.

Wordy: *Due to the fact that* fire damaged our warehouse, we must delay some shipments.

More efficient: *Because* fire damaged our warehouse, we must delay some shipments.

Wordy: Please send your cheque *in the amount of* $45.

More efficient: Please send your cheque *for* $45.

Wordy:	We expected *in the neighbourhood of* 25 applicants.
More efficient:	We expected *approximately* 25 applicants.

Eliminating Redundant Words

Words that are needlessly repetitive are called "redundant." Writers can achieve greater efficiency (and thus more effective sentences) by eliminating redundant words or phrases. Some common redundant expressions follow:

advance planning	erode away	original source
basic essential	few in number	past history
close proximity	final outcome	refer back to
collaborate together	free gift	repeat again
completely unanimous	join together	sufficient enough
consensus of opinion	large (or small) in size	true facts
cooperate together	lift up	unite together
end result	mix together	visible to the eye

This list, however, is not exhaustive. People use redundant expressions all the time, and new ones are constantly created. When reviewing your own work, think about the meanings of words and try to identify repetition of *meanings*, not just of words.

Redundant:	The *examples shown* in Figure 2 *illustrate* letter styles.
More efficient:	Figure 2 shows (or illustrates) letter styles.
Redundant:	The seminar covers only the *fundamental basics.*
More efficient:	The seminar covers only the basics (*or* only the fundamentals).
Redundant:	*As a rule,* we *generally* approve all such requests.
More efficient:	We generally approve all such requests.
Redundant:	The committee *cooperated together* to settle the issue.
More efficient:	The committee cooperated to settle the issue.

ASK AN EDITOR

Question:
I received a magazine advertisement recently that promised me a *free gift* and a *15 percent off discount* if I subscribed. What's wrong with this wording?

Answer:
You have a double winner here in the category of redundancies. The word *gift* suggests *free*; therefore, to say *free gift* is like saying *I'm studying English English.* It would be better to say *special gift*. In the same way, *15 percent off discount* repeats itself. Omit *off.*

Using the Active Voice

Sentences that use active verbs are more economical—and, of course, more direct—than those using passive verbs. (See Chapter 8, Level II, for a review of passive and active voices.)

Passive:	Your account *has been credited* with your recent payment.
Active:	We *credited* your account with your recent payment.
Passive:	At our next meeting, your request *will be considered.*
Active:	At our next meeting, *we will consider* your request.
Passive:	Our Products Division *was informed* by you that you want an office copier.
Active:	*You informed* our Products Division that you want an office copier.

Writing Unified Sentences

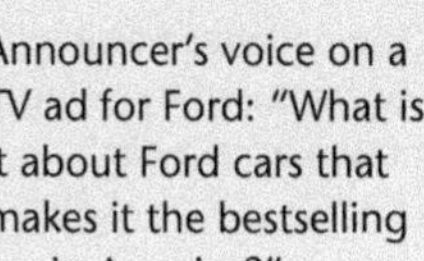

BE THE EDITOR

Announcer's voice on a TV ad for Ford: "What is it about Ford cars that makes it the bestselling car in America?"

A sentence is unified if it contains only closely related ideas. When extraneous or unrelated ideas appear in a sentence, they confuse the reader. Sentences lacking unity can be improved by clarifying the relationship between the ideas, by excising the extraneous ideas, or by shifting the unrelated ideas to separate sentences.

Lacks unity: It is easy for you to do your holiday shopping, and we offer three unique catalogues.

Improved: It is easy for you to do your holiday shopping because we offer three unique catalogues.

Lacks unity: I certainly appreciate the time you spent with me in our interview last week, and I am enrolling in a computer science course this summer.

Improved: I certainly appreciate the time you spent with me last week. Because of our interview, I am enrolling in a computer science course this summer.

Lacks unity: Retailers must have a system of inventory control, and they must keep current on reorders.

Improved: To be able to keep current on reorders, retailers must have a system of inventory control.

Including excessive detail can also damage sentence unity. If many details are necessary for overall clarity, put them in an additional sentence.

Excessive detail: One of the nation's leading suppliers of pure bottled water mails thousands of computerized statements every month, along with a variety of inserts, including overdue payment notices and pieces that are meant to be advertising and promotions, which became very costly in terms of both cash flow and personnel time.

Improved: One of the nation's leading suppliers of pure bottled water mails thousands of monthly computerized statements, overdue notices, and promotional information. This mailing operation has become costly and time-consuming.

Excessive detail: A report can be important, but it may not be effective or be read because it is too long and bulky, which will also make it more difficult to distribute, to store, and to handle, as well as increasing its overall cost.

Improved: An important report may be ineffective because it is too long. Its bulk may increase its cost and make it difficult to read, handle, distribute, and store.

Complete the reinforcement exercises for Level I on pages 396–398.

BE THE EDITOR

"The patient's pelvis was fractured by being thrown from a car."

LEVEL II

WRITING CLEAR SENTENCES

Clear sentences immediately convey their central thought. Good writers achieve sentence clarity through the use of parallel construction, the avoidance of misplaced modifiers, and the use of unambiguous pronoun references.

Developing Parallel Construction

Clarity can be improved by using grammatically similar structures to express related parts of a sentence. For example, do not use *ing* words for two of the ideas in a list and an infinitive (*to* verb) for the third idea: *reading, eating, and studying* (not *to study*). Use nouns with nouns, verbs with verbs, phrases with phrases, and clauses with clauses. Each item in the following list, for instance, is an active verb: *the machine sorted, stamped, and counted* (not *and had a counter*). List items should flow smoothly into one another and have a clear relationship to one another, not just to the introductory words. These phrases, for example, all name settings: *safety must be improved in the home, in the classroom, and on the job* (not *and for office workers*).

Faulty:	Steel filing cabinets are best for durability, ease of cleaning, and they resist fire better.
Improved:	Steel filing cabinets are best for durability, ease of cleaning, and fire resistance. (All nouns)
Faulty:	Composing, revising, and then to proofread—these are necessary steps in report writing.
Improved:	Composing, revising, and proofreading—these are necessary steps in report writing. (All *ing* nouns, or gerunds)

Avoiding Misplaced Modifiers

You will recall that **modifiers** are words, phrases, or clauses that limit or restrict other words, phrases, or clauses. To be clear, modifiers must be placed carefully so that the words they modify are obvious. When a modifier is placed so that it appears to be modifying the wrong word or words, that modifier is said to be *misplaced*. In Chapter 10 introductory verbal modifiers were discussed. An introductory verbal modifier is sometimes misplaced simply by being at the beginning of the sentence. Consider how the introductory verbal modifier makes the following sentence nonsensical: *Walking down the street, the building was the tallest I had ever seen.* After all, the building was not doing the walking. In positions other than the beginning of a sentence, misplaced modifiers may also interfere with sentence clarity.

Faulty:	We provide a map for all visitors reduced to a one-inch scale.
Improved:	For all visitors we provide a map reduced to a one-inch scale.
Faulty:	Employees did not hear the alarm working busily on the rush printing job.
Improved:	Employees working busily on the rush printing job did not hear the alarm.
Faulty:	The boss is only offering us $15 an hour.
Improved:	The boss is offering us only $15 an hour.

BE THE EDITOR

From globalnews.ca: "A baby survived a car crash in a frigid Utah river after being strapped in a car seat upside-down for about 14 hours before being found by a fisherman."

Improving Pronoun References

Sentence confusion results from the use of pronouns without clear antecedents. An **antecedent** is a specific noun or pronoun to which a pronoun refers (see Chapter 6). Be particularly careful with the pronouns *this, that, which,* and *it.* Confusion often results when these pronouns have as their antecedents an entire clause; such confusion can usually be avoided by substituting a noun for the pronoun or by following the pronoun with a clarifying noun (or nouns).

Faulty: Installation of a computerized billing system has improved our cash flow and reduced our accounts receivable. *This* helps our entire operation run more efficiently and profitably.

Improved: Installation of a computerized billing system has improved our cash flow and reduced our accounts receivable. *The new system* helps our entire operation run more efficiently and profitably.

Faulty: We have a policy of responding to customer inquiries and orders on the same day they are received. *That* keeps us busy and keeps our customers satisfied.

Improved: We have a policy of responding to customer inquiries and orders on the same day they are received. *That policy* keeps us busy and keeps our customers satisfied.

Faulty: Our engineering projects require work on thousands of details that need constant updating and access to technical data, supplies, and references, *which* is why an open office design allowing team interaction is essential.

Improved: Our engineering projects require work on thousands of details that need constant updating and access to technical data, supplies, and references. *These needs* explain why an open office design allowing team interaction is essential.

Faulty: If you participate on the committee, *it* will reflect well on you at review time.

Improved: Your participating on the committee, should you get involved, will reflect well on you at review time.

Complete the reinforcement exercises for Level II on pages 399–401.

ASK AN EDITOR

Question:
I just typed this sentence: *You will see in our manual where multiple bids must be obtained.* Somewhere from my distant past I seem to recall that *where* should not be used this way. Can you help me?

Answer:
You're right. *Where* should be used only to refer to location. In your sentence the relative pronoun *that* is the correct word.

BE THE EDITOR

From *The Boston Globe*: "Then her hair caught fire while sitting in a front seat during a fireworks display."

LEVEL III

WRITING EMPHATIC AND COHERENT SENTENCES

You can achieve emphasis and coherence in your writing by using clause subordination, concrete words, and effective transitions.

Emphasis Through Subordination

Subordination is a technique skilful writers use to show the relationship between unequal ideas. Appropriate emphasis can be achieved by using subordinate conjunctions, such as *if, because, since,* and *when,* and relative pronouns, such as *who, which,* and *that,* to introduce secondary ideas or incidental information. Principal ideas should appear in independent clauses, and less important ideas should be expressed in subordinate or dependent clauses.

Principal idea:	Compucorp recently entered the microcomputer market.
Secondary idea:	Compucorp is a division of Intel.
Sentence:	Compucorp, which is a division of Intel, recently entered the microcomputer market.
Principal idea:	Your account is now three months overdue.
Secondary idea:	You have been a good customer in the past.
Sentence:	Although you have been a good customer in the past, your account is now three months overdue.
Principal idea:	A credit card holder is not liable for more than $50 in unauthorized purchases.
Secondary idea:	The credit card holder must give notice to the issuer of the card.
Sentence:	If a credit card holder gives notice to the issuer of the card, the holder is not liable for more than $50 in unauthorized purchases.

Emphasis Through the Use of Specificity

As you know, concrete words (see Chapter 3, pp. 38–39) refer to specific persons, places, concepts, qualities, and actions. They bring to mind sharp images and arouse strong feelings. Abstract words, such as *honesty*, *freedom*, and *utilization*, are less likely to call forth immediate sensory reactions because they refer to general ideas. Use concrete, specific words and constructions to make your writing emphatic, persuasive, and clear.

Abstract:	Your shipment will be sent *soon*.
Concrete:	Your shipment will be sent *October 1*.
Abstract:	Our candidate won by a *substantial margin*.
Concrete:	Our candidate won by a *2-to-1 margin*.
Abstract:	The *utilization of computer capabilities* helped us reduce costs.
Concrete:	*Computerized filing and billing* helped us reduce costs.
Abstract:	The Model DC-161 copier produces your first copy *quickly*.
Concrete:	The Model DC-161 copier produces your first copy *in five seconds*.

When an abstract word is necessary, its meaning can often be enhanced by adding clarifying words.

Abstract:	During the hearing no one questioned Mr. Turner's *loyalty*.
Concrete:	During the hearing no one questioned Mr. Turner's *loyalty to the company*.

CAREER TIP

Use *concrete* words when you want to emphasize or promote an idea. Use *abstract* words to soften bad news.

Coherence Through the Use of Transitional Words or Phrases

Orderly and consistent development of ideas leads to coherence. Coherence between sentences can be attained by the use of transitional expressions such as *therefore, in this way, in addition, for example, however, moreover, for this reason,* and *on the other hand*. Such words and phrases serve as flags to signal the reader that ideas are being contrasted or amplified. Notice that transitional words and phrases in the following sentences help the reader connect successive ideas.

We improved customer service as a result of spending less time on clerical chores. *Moreover*, we reduced storage charges for shipments held up because of incorrect documentation.

A blank endorsement enables anyone in possession of a cheque to cash the cheque. A special endorsement, *on the other hand,* enables only a specific person to cash it.

When the federal government purchases goods on a cost-plus contract, it requires detailed accounting reports. *In this way,* the government can monitor the production operations and costs.

Complete the reinforcement exercises for Level III on pages 402–403.

NAME ______________________________

CHAPTER 20 ■ Reinforcement Exercises

LEVEL I

A. **(Self-check)** In the following sentences, inefficient phrases have been underlined. In the space provided, suggest a more efficient substitute for each underlined phrase.

EXAMPLE: In the event that your package doesn't arrive, we will file a claim and ship the order again. ___if___

1. We have no positions open at the present time. ______________
2. We are referring you to a sales representative by the name of Saul Epstein. ______________
3. Kateri is looking to build an online store along the lines of Francine's. ______________
4. Due to the fact that we have not received payment for three months, we must cancel your service. ______________
5. We will not reopen fully until such time that it is deemed safe to allow large groups to convene. ______________
6. The lawyer refused to comment with regard to the charges against her client. ______________
7. We are attaching an invoice in the amount of $450. ______________
8. The documents have in all probability been shredded. ______________
9. In spite of the fact that we've filled the position you applied for, we'd like to meet with you to discuss another opening. ______________
10. We are paying in the neighbourhood of $100,000. ______________

Check your answers.

B. Rewrite the following sentences to eliminate redundancies.

EXAMPLE: This paragraph is exactly identical to that one.

This paragraph is identical to that one.

1. The reason why we are discussing the issue is to reach a consensus of opinion.

____

____

2. Our modern office equipment is up to date in every feature.

____

____

TEAR HERE

3. The security guard circled around the car several times.

4. In an explanation at the beginning of the article, the author explained his position.

C. Make the following sentences more efficient and more direct by using the active voice.

EXAMPLE: The invoice was sent by our organization ten days ago.

We sent the invoice ten days ago.

1. Strong leadership was provided by the general manager.

2. Your order is now being processed by our Shipping Department.

3. Everyone's tasks were scheduled by the project manager overseeing the website redesign.

4. The Employee of the Month award has been won by Robert Wedman.

D. The following sentences lack unity. Improve them by reorganizing the ideas or by shifting extra details to separate sentences.

EXAMPLE: We are installing an optical character recognition system, and our website will contain all the documents we published before going online.

Once we have installed the optical character recognition system, we will be able to post to our website all the documents we published before going online.

1. Companies that communicate with customers by bulk email are required to provide unsubscribe options, and in 2019 the Canadian Radio-Television and Telecommunications Commission fined nCrowd Inc. $100,000 for not complying.

TEAR HERE

2. We have placed a lien on your property, and your payment is 60 days past due, which explains the lien.

3. In 2020 a Québec resident went to a Lids store in Ottawa to have the slogan "Black Lives Matter" embroidered on a hat, and the store refused to do it because it claimed it was a political message, but the company's rules are that only registered trademarks can't be put on customized products, so the company responded that the manager misunderstood the policy.

4. Award-winning chef Sean Sherman, of the Oglala Lakota Sioux nation, is a cookbook author and Indigenous cuisine educator, and he's working toward opening The Indigenous Food Lab, which will be both a restaurant and a training centre that educates about Indigenous foods.

TEAR HERE

NAME ______________________________

LEVEL II

A. (Self-check) In the following sentences, the underlined words illustrate one of the following sentence faults:

a = faulty parallel construction
b = faulty phrase placement
c = faulty pronoun reference

In the space provided, write the letter that best indicates the sentence fault.

EXAMPLE: Our objectives are to increase production, reduce costs, and improving the quality of our work. ____a____

1. Aafia doesn't write English well. This is causing her difficulty in finding a job. ________
2. Our visitor's package for Timmins includes one night's accommodation, continental breakfast, and you'll receive passes for the gold mine tour and the Shania Twain Centre. ________
3. Stuart read about modern customers' expectations for businesses to have multi-channel options in a trade magazine. ________
4. In an effort to reduce plastic waste, the company serves lunch to visiting guests on paper plates. ________
5. As a business grows, its founder needs to step away from day-to-day tasks, which can be difficult to do. ________
6. Automatic cash transfers can be made only on the written authority of the customer from a chequing account. ________
7. Tax write-offs, less commuting time, and working more flexible hours—these are advantages to working from home. ________
8. There are cables everywhere under my desk; it makes my cubicle look messy all the time. ________
9. Reasons for a company to relocate can be cheaper real estate, lower taxes, or regulations may be less cumbersome. ________
10. Profitable shares, efficient operations, and developing good customer relations are our objectives. ________

Check your answers.

B. Rewrite the following sentences so that they demonstrate parallel construction.

1. In our class we have studied punctuation, spelling, and when to use capital letters.

____

____

TEAR HERE

2. Tilley's travel shorts for men are lightweight, can be washed and dried overnight, and available in small to XXXL sizes.

3. Business letters should be written concisely, clearly, and with accuracy.

4. For businesses that don't accept cash, transactions are automatically reconciled, they need to make fewer trips to the bank, and are less likely to be robbed.

C. Rewrite these sentences to remedy misplaced modifiers.

1. We have received several complaints about the stiffness of the reclining mechanism from customers.

2. Any person may recover damages from the manufacturer of a product who is injured by the product.

3. Our coat resembles the original trench coat for the soldiers of the First World War designed by Englishman Thomas Burberry.

4. An instrument technician is needed for the Kensington Eye Institute with two years' recent experience.

D. Rewrite the following sentences to avoid faulty pronoun references.

1. The cost of postsecondary education continues to rise, which is the reason students sometimes work more hours than is advisable.

TEAR HERE

2. Mrs. Valdez suggested that we try a four-day work week on an experimental basis for one month. That received considerable employee support.

3. LifeLabs suffered a cyber-attack in 2019 resulting in the largest data breach in Canadian history. This prompted the company to invest $50 million in information security management.

4. Our equipment is outmoded, production is costly, and orders are slow, which is why we are forced to cut back.

NAME ______________________________

LEVEL III

A. **(Self-check)** In the space provided after each of the following sentences, write *T* (true) or *F* (false).

1. Subordination is a technique writers use to show the relationship between unequal ideas. ________
2. The word *if* may be used to introduce a principal idea in an independent clause. ________
3. Transitional expressions serve as flags to signal the relationship between ideas. ________
4. When an abstract word is necessary, its meaning can often be enhanced by adding clarifying words. ________
5. *Courage* is an example of a concrete word. ________
6. Coherence is achieved when sentences and their parts are related logically. ________
7. Secondary ideas should appear in dependent clauses. ________
8. Abstract words refer to specific persons, places, concepts, and actions. ________
9. *Utilization* is an example of an abstract word. ________
10. The transitional expression *consequently* signals a contrast between two ideas. ________

Check your answers.

B. Below are sets of principal ideas and secondary ideas. For each set, write a sentence combining, with appropriate emphasis, the two ideas.

	Principal Idea	**Secondary Idea**
1.	Rosemary Fraser didn't show up for her appointment this morning.	We had scheduled Rosemary Fraser for a job interview.

____

____

	Principal Idea	**Secondary Idea**
2.	Ron Joyce and Tim Horton founded their coffee-and-doughnut business in Hamilton, Ontario, in the 1960s.	Tim Horton was a professional hockey player until his death in 1974.

____

____

	Principal Idea	**Secondary Idea**
3.	Mattel has sold more than a billion dolls from its long-lived Barbie line.	Critics say Barbie promotes unhealthy stereotypes.

____

____

TEAR HERE

4. Only 14 directors identified as belonging to a visible minority. | Twenty-three Canadian boards composed of 255 directors were surveyed.

5. George Klein invented the electric wheelchair in 1952. | George Klein was working as a mechanical engineer at the National Research Council of Canada laboratories in 1952.

C. Rewrite the following sentences, making the italicized words concrete. Supply any information needed.

EXAMPLE: The Bank of Canada *increased* its key rate.

The Bank of Canada increased its key rate by a quarter of a point.

1. We will send your order *as soon as possible.*

2. When we have further information, we will *contact* you.

3. To *succeed* in this job, you will have to *work hard.*

4. Deena's *workspace* is always *disorganized.*

D. **Writing Exercises.** Your instructor may ask you to complete this exercise on a separate sheet.

Write four original sentences, one for each of the following transitional expressions: (a) *therefore*, (b) *however*, (c) *consequently*, and (d) *in addition.*

Then write a sentence with a misplaced modifier (e), along with a corrected version (f). Label each sentence with its corresponding letter.

TEAR HERE

POSTTEST

Rewrite the following sentences to address problems in parallelism, redundancy, modification, reference, conciseness, and coherence. Note that not all sentences contain errors; however, all can be improved.

1. With multiple lenses and many features, I don't understand why he can't get expert-quality photos with that camera.

2. The mail must have been picked up by Momen.

3. We always take the age of the patient into consideration.

4. The customer service representative said he would adjust my bill, changed my service plan, and is sending me a new modem.

5. Employees must always wear their ID badges at all times.

6. Due to the fact that most Canadians are highly indebted, an increase in interest rates could have serious consequences.

7. The global pandemic of 2020 hit small businesses hard, which required many to change business models altogether.

8. First and foremost, you must reserve a meeting room.

9. Reports must be complete, correct, and contain appropriate detail.

10. One of our delivery vehicles was involved in an accident, and the accident happened within 10 km of its destination.

TEAR HERE

EDITOR'S CHALLENGE ■

The following abstract and letter contain errors reflecting the concepts you have studied. Use proofreading marks to show all necessary corrections. Be especially alert to wordy expressions that could be condensed.

ABSTRACT

On the date of November 10th Dennis W. Wilbur, director, human resources development authorized a study for the purpose of learning whether or not employment equity guidelines for women is being met at Globex enterprises.

A research program was developed to make investigation into each divisions hiring practises. In the neighbourhood of twenty-three thousand employee records was searched to determine date of employment, division and gender. Statistics Canada data were examined by way of comparison.

The following findings in regard to the aforementioned study resulted;

- Halifax is five % above the numerical goals for the three year period
- Regina is seven % below the numerical goals for the three year period
- St. John's is two % above the numerical goals (but figures were available for only five hundred of 2,256 employees

On the basis of these findings the compliance committee recommend the development of (1) a intensive recruiting program to search for and bring qualified females into the Regina division and (2) the development of a training program to train females for drafting and design positions in Regina. The Regina Division should hire two females for every 1 male until such time as 16 extra females are hire. In view of the fact that a training program may cost as much as five hundred thousand dollars, we further recommend that a committee be established at this point in time to investigate funding.

TEAR HERE

580 East Leffels Street
Regina, SK S4S 3T5
November 7, 202X

Ms. Ellen Rabkin
Retail Credit Department
Union National Bank
PO Box 2051
Edmonton, AB T5W 4B3

Dear Ms. Rabkin:

My wife and I hope that you will be able to help us solve a problem with charges on our Visa card account. Two years ago me and my wife became cardholders of your bank's visa card, our account number is 4002-3422-8910-3299. We were happy with the service until recent charges that we would like to discuss with you.

Between the period of August 7 and September 17, we made 12 small purchases. Ten of these purchases received telephone approval. When we received our October statement, a copy of which is enclosed with this letter we were surprised to see that we had been charged a penalty in the amount of ten dollars for each of these purchases due to the fact that our account was over the limit. The whole charge totalled $120.

Of course, we should of been more aware of of the status of our account. In view of the fact that our purchases were approved however, we assumed that we were still within our credit limit.

Upon receipt of our October statement we immediately went to our bank branch and spoke with Mr Jonathan Walker, who listened patiently to our story. He was unable to wave the charges, and referred us to you.

Please examine our account, Ms. Radkin, and reconsider this penalty. Since we have never before exceeded our credit limit and having received telephone approval for most of the charge in question, we feel that the $120 charge should be removed. We appreciate Mr. Walkers attention and yours and look forward to a speedy resolution of this problem.

Sincerely,

Phillip M. Stevenson

Phillip M. Stevenson

Enclosure

TEAR HERE

NAME ______________________

UNIT 6 REVIEW ■ Chapters 18–20 (Self-Check)

Begin your review by rereading Chapters 18 through 20. Then check your comprehension of those chapters by completing the following exercises. Compare your responses with those provided at the end of the book, page 531.

LEVEL I

Write *a* or *b* in the space provided to identify the group of words that is more acceptably expressed.

1. (a) courses in Business Law, Spanish, and sociology (b) courses in business law, Spanish, and sociology ________

2. (a) works in Albert county (b) works in Albert County ________

3. (a) a lake in Manitoba (b) a Lake in Manitoba ________

4. (a) a fall promotional event (b) a Fall promotional event ________

5. (a) Cyrillic alphabet (b) cyrillic alphabet ________

6. (a) the 22nd of June (b) the 22 of June ________

7. (a) ten dollars (b) $10 ________

8. (a) sixty eight (b) sixty-eight ________

9. (a) on November 28th (b) on November 28 ________

10. (a) in spite of the fact that (b) although ________

11. (a) about (b) with reference to ________

12. (a) in the near future (b) soon ________

LEVEL II

Write *a* or *b* in the space provided to identify the group of words that is more acceptably expressed.

13. (a) my Grandma and Grandpa (b) my grandma and grandpa ________

14. (a) travel west on Highway 20 (b) travel West on Highway 20 ________

15. (a) our manager, Joe Bertuccio (b) our Manager, Joe Bertuccio ________

16. (a) Plum Johnson's *They Left us Everything* (b) Plum Johnson's *They Left Us Everything* ________

17. (a) a message from Mia Petrovic, Sales Manager (b) a message from Mia Petrovic, sales manager ________

TEAR HERE

18. (a) a message from Managing Director Cook (b) a message from managing director Cook ____________

19. (a) for the next six weeks (b) for the next 6 weeks ____________

20. (a) 2 twenty-five page booklets (b) two 25-page booklets ____________

21. (a) nine couriers serving 14 offices (b) 9 couriers serving 14 offices ____________

Each of the following sentences illustrates one of these sentence faults:

a = faulty parallel construction (such as *running*, *walking*, and *to ride*)
b = faulty phrase placement (phrase not close to word(s) it modifies)
c = faulty pronoun reference (pronoun such as *this*, *that*, *which*, or *it* with no clear antecedent)

In the space provided, write the letter that best describes the sentence fault. Then, rewrite the sentences to rectify their faults.

22. We installed fabric divider panels in the office to provide privacy, reduce sound, and they added colour to the office. ____________

23. Poor ventilation, inadequate light, and hazardous working conditions were cited in the complaint. It must be improved before negotiations continue. ____________

24. Seated in the back of the room, the keynote speaker's address was hard for Yasmin to hear. ____________

LEVEL III

Select the correct group of words below, and write its letter in the space provided.

25. (a) Have a seat, sir. (b) Have a seat, Sir. ____________

26. (a) Mayor-Elect Jeet Kumar (b) Mayor-elect Jeet Kumar ____________

27. (a) a parcel stamped "fragile" (b) a parcel stamped "Fragile" ____________

28. (a) our 28th year in business (b) our twenty-eighth year in business ____________

29. (a) less than 0.2 percent (b) less than .2 percent ____________

30. (a) only two km to go (b) only 2 km to go ____________

31. (a) 80% of the votes (b) 80 percent of the votes ____________

32. (a) when he became 21 (b) when he became twenty-one ____________

33. (a) a 1/3 interest (b) a one-third interest ____________

34. (a) the rising sun (b) the rising Sun ____________

35. (a) a Hindu wedding (b) a hindu wedding ____________

ASK AN EDITOR REVIEW

In the space provided, write the letter of the word or phrase that correctly completes each sentence.

36. The (a) Coronavirus, (b) coronavirus of 2020 shut down businesses nationwide. __________

37. I see it in the policy handbook (a) that, (b) where a job must be posted internally first. __________

38. The policy handbook is (a) six years old, (b) six-years-old and in need of an update. __________

39. We will move to the new office by (a) mid-September, (b) mid September. __________

40. Show your employee identification to get a discount of (a) 30 percent off, (b) 30 percent. __________

SHORT REPORTS

Reports are a fact of life in the business world today. They are important because they convey needed information and because they help decision makers solve problems. Organizing information into a meaningful report is a skill you will want to acquire.

CHARACTERISTICS OF REPORTS

As an introduction to report writing, this workshop focuses on the most important characteristics of reports. You'll learn valuable tips about the format, data, headings, and writing plan for short business reports and internal proposals.

FORMAT. How should a business report look? Three formats are common. *Letter format* is appropriate for short reports prepared by one organization for another. A letter report, as illustrated in Figure 6.1, is like a letter except that it is more carefully organized. It includes side headings and lists where appropriate. *Memo format* is common for reports written within an organization. These internal reports look like memos—with the addition of side headings. *Report format* is used for longer, more formal reports. Printed on plain paper (instead of letterhead or memo forms), these reports begin with a title followed by carefully displayed headings and subheadings.

DATA. Where do you find the data for a business report? Many business reports begin with personal observation and experience. If you were writing a report on implementing flextime for employees, you might begin by observing current work schedules and by asking what schedules employees prefer. Other sources of data for business reports include company records, surveys, questionnaires, and interviews. If you want to see how others have solved a problem or if you need to collect background data on a topic, you can consult magazines, journals, and books. Also, of course, much information is available electronically—search online library indexes or databases.

HEADINGS. Good headings in a report highlight major ideas and categories. They guide the reader through a report. In longer reports they divide the text into inviting chunks, and they provide resting places for the eyes. Short reports often use *functional headings* (such as *Problem*, *Summary*, and *Recommendations*). Longer reports may employ *talking headings* (such as *Short-Term Parking Solutions*) because they provide more information to the reader. Whether your headings are functional or talking headings, be sure they are clear and parallel. For example, use *Visible Costs* and *Invisible Costs* rather than *Visible Costs* and *Costs That Don't Show*. Don't enclose headings in quotation marks, and avoid using headings as antecedents for pronouns. For example, if your heading is *Laser Printers*, don't begin the next sentence with *These produce high-quality output . . .*

Skill Check 6.1: Reviewing the Characteristics of Short Reports

In the space provided, write the letter to indicate the best format for the report described in the first three questions.

a = memo format   b = letter format   c = report format

1. A short report to a company from an outside consultant ________

2. A short report from a product manager to her boss ________

(continued)

TEAR HERE

Figure 6.1

Short Report—Letter Format

Liberty Environmental Inc.

2593 North Glebe Road

Calgary, AB T2T 4T1 (403) 356-1094

October 9, 202x

Ms. Sharon J. Goode

Richmond Realty Inc.

3390 Chester Avenue

Calgary, Alberta T3S 1K7

Dear Ms. Goode:

Explains purpose, outlines sources of information

At the request of Richmond Realty, I have completed a preliminary investigation of its Mountain Park property listing. The following findings and recommendations are based on my physical inspection of the site, official records, and interviews with officials and persons knowledgeable about the site.

Includes headings to show report organization

Findings and Analyses

Describes findings and explains their significance

My preliminary assessment of the Mountain Park listing and its immediate vicinity revealed rooms with damaged floor tiles on the first and second floors of 2539 Mountain View Drive. Apparently, in recent remodelling efforts, these tiles had been cracked and broken. Examination of the ceiling and attic revealed possible contamination from asbestos. The insulation material surrounding the hot-water storage tank was in poor condition.

Located on the property is Mountain Technology, a possible hazardous waste generator. Although I could not examine its interior, this company has the potential for producing hazardous waste material contamination. Moreover, several large dumpsters in the parking lot collect trash and debris from surrounding businesses. Because these dumpsters are uncovered, they pose a risk to the general public.

Concludes with recommendations for solving the problem

Recommendations

To reduce its potential environmental liability, Richmond Realty should take the following steps in regard to its Mountain Park listing:

Uses bulleted list to improve readability and comprehension

Begins each recommendation with a verb for consistency

- Conduct an immediate asbestos survey at the site, including inspection of ceiling insulation material, floor tiles, and insulation around a gas-fired heater vent pipe at 2539 Mountain View Drive.
- Prepare an environmental audit of the generators of hazardous waste currently operating at the site, including Mountain Technology.
- Obtain lids for the dumpsters situated in the parking areas, and ensure that the lids are kept closed.

If you would like to discuss the findings or recommendations in this report, please call me and I will be glad to answer your questions.

Sincerely,

Scott R. Evans

Scott R. Evans

Environmental Assessment Specialist

3. A long report describing a company's diversity program ________

4. If you were writing a report to persuade management to purchase more computers, which of the following is the best way to begin collecting data?

   (a) Observe current use
   (b) Consult books and journals
   (c) Search the Internet ________

5. Which combination of report headings is best?

   (a) Delivery costs, Suppliers
   (b) Reduction of delivery costs, Recommendations
   (c) "Delivery costs," "Supply Costs"
   (d) Reducing Delivery Costs, Finding New Suppliers ________

WRITING PLAN FOR A SHORT REPORT

Short reports often have three parts: introduction, findings, and recommendations. If the report is purely informational, a summary may be used instead of recommendations.

INTRODUCTION. This part of a report may also be called *Background.* In this section you'll want to explain why you are writing. You may also (a) describe what methods and sources were used to gather information and why they are credible, (b) provide any special background information that may be necessary, and (c) offer a preview of your findings.

FINDINGS. This section may also be called *Observations, Facts, Results,* or *Discussion.* Important points to consider in this section are organization and display. You may wish to organize the findings (a) chronologically (for example, to describe the history of a problem), (b) alphabetically (if you were, for example, evaluating candidates for a position), (c) topically (for example, discussing sales by regions), or (d) from most to least important (such as listing criteria for evaluating equipment). To display the findings effectively, you could (a) use side headings, (b) number or bullet each finding, (c) underline or boldface the key words, or (d) merely indent the paragraphs.

SUMMARY OR RECOMMENDATIONS. Some reports just offer information. Such reports may conclude with an impartial summary. Other reports are more analytical, and they generally conclude with recommendations. These recommendations tell readers how to solve the problem and may even suggest ways to implement the necessary actions. To display recommendations, number or bullet each one and place it on a separate line.

Notice that the letter report in Figure 6.1 includes an introduction, findings and analyses, and recommendations.

WRITING PLAN FOR AN INTERNAL PROPOSAL

Both managers and employees must occasionally write reports that justify or recommend something such as buying equipment, changing a procedure, hiring an employee, consolidating departments, or investing funds. Here is a writing plan for an internal proposal that recommends a course of action.

TEAR HERE

INTRODUCTION. In this section identify the problem briefly. Use specific examples, supporting statistics, and authoritative quotations to lend credibility to the seriousness of the problem. If you think your audience will be receptive, announce your recommendation, solution, or action immediately and concisely. If you think your audience will need to be persuaded or educated, do not announce your solution until after you have explained its advantages.

BODY. In writing the body of an internal proposal, you may want to include all or some of the following elements. Explain more fully the benefits of the recommendations or steps to be taken to solve the problem. Include a discussion of pros, cons, and costs. If appropriate, describe the factual and ethical negative consequences of the current situation. For example, if your internal proposal recommends purchasing new equipment, explain how much time, effort, money, and morale are being lost by continuing to use outdated equipment that needs constant repairs. Quantification through accurate facts and examples builds credibility and persuasive appeal. Explain the benefits of your proposal. A bulleted list improves readability and emphasis. Anticipate objections to your proposal and discuss ways to counter those objections. The body should also provide a plan and schedule for implementing your proposal. If many people will be included in implementing the proposal, prepare a staffing section. Describe who will be doing what. You may also describe alternative solutions and show how they will not work as well as your proposal.

CONCLUSION. In the conclusion summarize your recommendations. Describe the specific action to be taken. Ask for authorization to proceed. To motivate the reader, you might include a date for the action to take place and a reason for the deadline.

An internal proposal is generally formatted as a memo such as the one shown in Figure 6.2. In this memo report, the writer expects the reader to be receptive to the recommendation of pilot-testing smart tires. Thus the proposal begins immediately with the recommendations. The body discusses how the recommendations would work, and it itemizes benefits. It anticipates objections and counters them. The closing summarizes what action is to be taken and presents a deadline.

Writing Application 6.1

Organize the following information into a short letter report. As Cory M. Chavez, president, Chavez and Associates, you have been hired as a consultant to advise the St. Catharines City Council. The City Council has asked you and your associates to investigate a problem with Willow Park Beachway.

In 1979 St. Catharines constructed a 4-m pathway, now called the Willow Park Beachway. It was meant originally for cyclists, but today it has become very popular for joggers, walkers, cyclists, in-line skaters, skateboarders, sightseers, and people walking their dogs. In fact, it's become so popular that it is dangerous. Last year the St. Catharines Police Department reported an amazing 65 collisions in the area, not counting the close calls and minor accidents that no one reported. The City Council wants your organization to identify the problem and come up with some workable recommendations for improving safety.

As you look into the matter, you immediately decide that the council is right. A problem definitely exists! In addition to the many pedestrians and riders, you see that families with rented pedal-powered surreys clog the beachway. Sometimes they even operate these vehicles on the wrong side. Your investigation further reveals that cyclists with rental bikes do not always have bells to alert walkers and that poor lighting makes nighttime use extremely dangerous. You've noticed that conditions seem to be the worst on Sundays. This congestion results from nearby arts and crafts fairs and sales, attracting even more people to the crowded area.

Your investigation confirms that the beachway is dangerous, but what to do about it? In a brainstorming session, your associates make a number of suggestions for reducing the dangers to users. By the way, the council is particularly interested in lessening the threat of liability to

(continued on p. 415)

Figure 6.2

Internal Proposal—Memo Format

DATE: September 20, 202x
TO: Kevin West, Vice President
FROM: James Worthington, Operations Manager
SUBJECT: Pilot-Testing Smart Tires

Introduces problem briefly but with concrete facts

Next to fuel, truck tires are our biggest operating cost. Last year we spent $211,000 replacing and retreading tires for 495 trucks. This year the cost will be greater because prices have jumped at least 12 percent and because we've increased our fleet to 550 trucks. Truck tires are an additional burden since they require labour-intensive paperwork to track their warranties, wear, and retread histories. To reduce our long-term costs and to improve our tire tracking system, I recommend that we do the following:

Presents recommendations immediately

- Purchase 24 Goodyear smart tires
- Begin a one-year pilot test on six trucks

How Smart Tires Work

Justifies recommendation by explaining the proposal and benefits

Smart tires have an embedded computer chip that monitors wear, performance, and durability. The chip also creates an electronic fingerprint for positive identification of a tire. By passing a hand-held sensor next to the tire, we can learn where and when a tire was made (for warranty and other identification), how much tread it had originally, and what its serial number is.

How Smart Tires Could Benefit Us

Offers counterargument to possible objection

Although smart tires are initially more expensive than other tires, they could help us improve our operations and save us money in four ways:

Enumerates items for maximum impact and readability

1. **Retreads.** Goodyear believes that the wear data are so accurate that we should be able to retread every tire three times, instead of the current two times. If that's true, in one year we could save at least $27,000 in new tire costs.

2. **Safety.** Accurate and accessible wear data should reduce the danger of blowouts and flat tires. Last year, drivers reported six blowouts.

3. **Record keeping and maintenance.** Smart tires could reduce our maintenance costs considerably. Currently, we use an electric branding iron to mark serial numbers on new tires. Our biggest headache is manually reading those serial numbers, decoding them, and maintaining records to meet safety regulations. Reading such data electronically could save us thousands of dollars in labour.

4. **Theft protection.** The chip can be used to monitor each tire as it leaves or enters the warehouse or yard, thus discouraging theft.

Summary and Action

Specifically, I recommend that you do the following:

Specifies action to be taken

- Authorize the special purchase of 24 Goodyear smart tires at $450 each, plus one electronic sensor at $1,200
- Approve a one-year pilot test in our Winnipeg territory to equip six trucks with smart tires and track their performance

Concludes with deadline and reason

Please let me have your authorization by September 30 so that I can begin the pilot test before the winter driving season is upon us.

TEAR HERE

the city. One of your associates thinks that the beachway should be made at least 5 m wide or more. Another suggests that the beachway be lighted at night. Someone thinks that a new path should be built on the beach side of the existing beachway; this path would be for pedestrians only. Educating users about safety rules and etiquette would certainly be wise for everyone. One suggestion involves better striping or applying colours to designate different uses for the beachway. And why not require that all rental bicycles be equipped with bells? One of the best recommendations involves hiring uniformed "beach hosts" who would monitor the beachway, give advice, offer directions, and generally patrol the area.

In a short report, outline the problem and list your recommendations. Naturally, you would be happy to discuss your findings and recommendations with the St. Catharines City Council.

Writing Application 6.2

Assume that your office needs a piece of equipment such as a photocopier, digital camera, computer, printer, scanner, or the like. Do the research necessary to write a convincing internal proposal to your boss. You feel that your boss will be receptive to your request, so you can use the direct approach.

For additional resources, please visit MindTap at login.cengage.com. Cengage | MINDTAP

DEVELOPING SPELLING SKILLS

APPENDIX A

WHY IS ENGLISH SPELLING SO DIFFICULT?

No one would dispute the complaint that many English words are difficult to spell. Why is spelling in our language so perplexing? For one thing, our language has borrowed many of its words from other languages. English has a Germanic base upon which a superstructure of words borrowed from French, Latin, Greek, and other languages of the world has been erected. For this reason, its words are not always formed by regular patterns of letter combinations. In addition, spelling is made difficult because the pronunciation of English words is constantly changing. Today's spelling was standardized nearly 300 years ago, but many words are pronounced differently today than they were then. Therefore, pronunciation often provides little help in spelling. Consider, for example, the words *sew*, *dough*, *hoe*, and *row*.

Other complications were introduced when Noah Webster wrote the first American English dictionary. Webster made several changes from the British spellings, for example, dropping the *u* in *our* endings (as in *honor*), transposing the *r* and *e* in *re* endings (as in *center*), and changing some *s*'s to *z*'s (as in *analyze* and *realization*). Canadian spelling blends British and American preferences: we largely use *our* and *re* endings, as the British do, but we prefer the American *z* over the *s* in *yze, ize,* and *ization* endings. The *Canadian Oxford Dictionary* and *Gage Canadian Dictionary* indicate that both styles are acceptable. The spelling style chosen depends on custom and on the preference of the individual or on the requirements of the workplace. Above all, consistency within any single piece of writing is important. If you choose *our* and *re* spellings, you must use these throughout a document; it is incorrect to have, for example, both *honour* and *valor* in the same piece.

WHAT CAN YOU DO TO IMPROVE YOUR SPELLING?

Spelling is a skill that can be developed, just as arithmetic, keyboarding, swimming, and other skills can be developed. Because the ability to spell is a prerequisite for success in business and in many other activities, effort expended to acquire this skill is effort well spent.

Three traditional approaches to improving spelling have met with varying degrees of success.

Rules or Guidelines

The spelling of English words is consistent enough to justify the formulation of a few spelling rules—perhaps more appropriately called guidelines because the generalizations in question have exceptions. Such guidelines are, in other words, helpful but not infallible.

Mnemonics

Another approach to improving your ability to spell involves the use of mnemonics or memory devices. For example, you might associate the word *principle* with the word *rule* to form in your mind a link between the meaning and the spelling of *principle*. Mnemonics can be an effective device for the improvement of spelling only if the speller makes a real effort to develop the necessary memory hooks.

Rote Learning

A third approach to the improvement of spelling centres on memorization. Study the word until you can readily reproduce it in your mind's eye. Writing the word several times will also help you memorize its correct spelling.

THE 1-2-3 SPELLING PLAN

Proficiency in spelling is not attained without concentrated effort. Here's a plan for mastering the correct spelling of the 400 commonly misspelled words and word pairs included in this appendix. For each word, try this 1-2-3 approach.

1. Is a spelling guideline applicable? If so, select the appropriate guideline and study the word in relation to that guideline.
2. If no guideline applies, can a memory device be created to aid in the recall of the word?
3. If neither a guideline nor a memory device will work, the word must be memorized. Look at the word carefully. Pronounce it. Write it or repeat it until you can visualize all its letters in your mind's eye.

Before you try the 1-2-3 plan, become familiar with the six spelling guidelines that follow. These spelling guidelines are not intended to represent all the possible spelling rules appearing in available spelling books. These six guidelines are, however, among the most effective and helpful of the recognized spelling rules.

Guideline 1: Words Containing *ie* or *ei*

Although there are exceptions to it, the following familiar rhyme can be helpful:

Write *i* before *e*
Except after *c*
Or when sounded like *ay*
As in *neighbour* and *weigh.*

Study the following three lists of words illustrating the three parts of the rhyme.

(1) *i* Before *e*		**(2) Except After *c***	**(3) or When Sounded Like *ay***
achieve	ingredient	ceiling	beige
belief	mischief	conceit	eight
believe	niece	conceive	freight
brief	piece	deceit	heir
cashier	relief	deceive	neighbour
chief	shield	perceive	reign
convenient	sufficient	receipt	sleigh
field	thief	receive	their
friend	view		vein
grief	yield		weight

Exceptions: These exceptional *ei* and *ie* words must be learned by rote or with the use of a mnemonic device. Note that many of them contain the long *e* sound.

ancient	foreign	neither
caffeine	forfeit	protein
either	height	seize
financier	leisure	weird

Guideline 2: Words Ending in *e*

For most words ending in an *e*, the final *e* is dropped when the word is joined to a suffix that begins with a vowel (such as *ing, able,* or *al*). The final *e* is retained when a suffix that begins with a consonant (such as *ment, less, ly,* or *ful*) is joined to such a word.

Final *e* Dropped	**Final *e* Retained**
advise, advisable	approximate, approximately
arrive, arrival	arrange, arrangement
believe, believing	care, careless
care, caring	definite, definitely
cure, curable	hope, hopeless
desire, desirable	like, likely
disperse, dispersal	require, requirement
hope, hoping	safe, safely
move, movable	sincere, sincerely
receive, receiving	time, timeless
value, valuable	use, useful

Exceptions: The few exceptions to this spelling guideline are among the most frequently misspelled words. As such, they deserve special attention. Notice that they all involve a dropped final *e*.

argument	ninth	wholly
judgment	truly	

Guideline 3: Words Ending in *ce* or *ge*

When *able* or *ous* is added to words ending in *ce* or *ge*, the final *e* is retained if the *c* or *g* is pronounced softly (as in *service* or *change*).

advantage, advantageous
courage, courageous
outrage, outrageous
change, changeable
service, serviceable
manage, manageable

Guideline 4: Words Ending in *y*

Words ending in a *y* that is preceded by a consonant normally change the *y* to *i* before all suffixes except those beginning with an *i*.

Change *y* to *i* Because *y* Is Preceded by a Consonant

accompany, accompaniment
apply, appliance
carry, carried, carriage
company, companies
dry, drier, driest
duty, dutiful
empty, emptiness
forty, fortieth
hurry, hurries
industry, industrious
secretary, secretaries
study, studied, studious
try, tried

Do Not Change *y* to *i* Because *y* Is Preceded by a Vowel

annoy, annoying, annoyance
attorney, attorneys
employ, employer, employs
stay, staying, stayed
valley, valleys

Do Not Change *y* to *i* When Adding *ing*

accompany, accompanying
accompany, accompanying
apply, applying
satisfy, satisfying
study, studying
try, trying

Exceptions:

day, daily
gay, gaily
mislay, mislaid
pay, paid
lay, laid
shy, shyly

Guideline 5: Doubling a Final Consonant

If one-syllable words or two-syllable words accented on the second syllable end in a single consonant preceded by a single vowel, the final consonant is doubled before adding a suffix beginning with a vowel.

Although complex, this spelling guideline is extremely useful and therefore well worth mastering. Many spelling errors can be avoided by applying this guideline.

One-Syllable Words

bag, baggage
can, canned
drop, dropped
fit, fitted
get, getting

Two-Syllable Words

acquit, acquitting, acquittal
admit, admitted, admitting
begin, beginner, beginning
commit, committed, committing
control, controller, controlling

(continued)

(continued)

One-Syllable Words	Two-Syllable Words
man, manned	defer, deferred (BUT deference*)
plan, planned	excel, excelled, excelling
run, running	occur, occurrence, occurring
shut, shutting	prefer, preferring (BUT preferable*)
slip, slipped	recur, recurred, recurrence
swim, swimming	refer, referring (BUT reference*)
ton, tonnage	regret, regrettable

*Because the accent shifts to the first syllable, the final consonant is not doubled.

Here is a summary of conditions necessary for application of this guideline:

1. The word must end in a single consonant.
2. The final consonant must be preceded by a single vowel.
3. The word must be accented on the second syllable (if it has two syllables).

Words derived from *offer, differ, suffer, widen, deepen,* and *benefit* are not governed by this guideline because they are accented on the first syllable. In the United States, the same is true of *cancel, equal,* and *travel;* however, British and Canadian spelling conventions require a doubling of the final *l* in these words before endings that begin with vowels (e.g., *travelled, travelling, traveller*). If you are unsure, it is always a good idea to check a Canadian dictionary for the preferred Canadian spelling.

Guideline 6: Prefixes and Suffixes

For words in which the letter that ends the prefix is the same as the letter that begins the main word (such as in *dissimilar*), both letters must be included. For words in which a suffix begins with the same letter that ends the main word (such as in *coolly*), both letters must also be included.

Prefix	Main Word	Main Word	Suffix
dis	satisfied	accidental	ly
il	literate	clean	ness
ir	responsible	cool	ly
mis	spell	even	ness
mis	state	incidental	ly
trans	sexual	keen	ness
un	necessary	mean	ness

On the other hand, do not supply additional letters when adding prefixes to main words.

Prefix	Main Word
dis	appearance (not dissappearance)
dis	appoint
mis	take

Probably the most important guideline you can follow in spelling correctly is to use the dictionary whenever in doubt.

400 MOST FREQUENTLY MISSPELLED WORDS AND WORD PAIRS* (DIVIDED INTO 20 LISTS OF 20 WORDS EACH)

LIST 1	LIST 2	LIST 3
absence	afraid	applying
acceptance	against	approaches
accessible	aggressive	appropriate
accidentally	all right	approximately
accommodate	almost	arguing
accompaniment	alphabetical	argument
accurately	already	arrangement
accustom	although	article
achievement	amateur	athlete
acknowledgement/acknowledgment†	among	attack
acquaintance	amount	attendance, attendants
acquire	analysis	attitude
across	analyze	attorneys
actually	angel, angle	auxiliary
adequately	annoyance	basically
admitted	annual	beautiful
adolescence	answer	before
advantageous	apologized	beginning
advertising	apparent	believing
advice (noun), advise (verb)**	appliance	benefited

*Compiled from lists of words most frequently misspelled by students and business people.

†This type of listing (with a slash) indicates that British and American versions are both accepted in Canada. The first of each pair is the version more frequently used, according to the *Canadian Oxford Dictionary*.

**Pairs listed in this manner (separated by commas) are homonyms or commonly confused word pairs. Consult your dictionary for meanings.

LIST 4

biggest
breath, breathe
brief
business
calendar
capital
career
careless
carrying
cashier
ceiling
certain
challenge
changeable
chief
choose, chose
cloths, clothes
column
coming
committee

LIST 5

companies
competition
completely
conceive
conscience
conscientious
conscious
considerably
consistent
continuous
controlling
controversial
convenience
council, counsel
cylinder
daily
deceive
decision
define
dependent

LIST 6

description
desirable
destroy
development
difference
dining
disappearance
disappoint
disastrous
discipline
discussion
disease
dissatisfied
distinction
divide
doesn't
dominant
dropped
due
during

LIST 7

efficient
eligible
embarrass
encourage
enough
environment
equipped
especially
exaggerate
exceed
excellence
except
exercise
existence
experience
explanation
extremely
familiar
fascinate
favourite

LIST 8

February
fictitious
field
finally
financially
foreigner
fortieth
forty
forward, foreword
freight
friend
fulfill
fundamentally
further
generally
government
governor
grammar
grateful
guard

LIST 9

happiness
hear, here
height
heroes
hopeless
hoping
huge
humorous
hungry
ignorance
imaginary
imagine
immediately
immense
importance
incidentally
independent
indispensable
industrious
inevitable

LIST 10

influential
ingredient
initiative
intelligence
interest
interference
interpretation
interrupt
involve
irrelevant
irresponsible
island
jealous
judgment/judgement
kindergarten
knowledge
laboratory
labourer
laid
led, lead

LIST 11

leisurely
library
licence (noun), license (verb)
likely
literature
lives
loneliness
loose, lose
losing
luxury
magazine
magnificence
maintenance
manageable
manoeuvre
manner
manufacturer
marriage
mathematics
meant

LIST 12

mechanics
medicine
medieval
mere
miniature
minutes
mischief
misspell
mistake
muscle
mysterious
naturally
necessary
neighbour
neither
nickel
niece
ninety
ninth
noticeable

LIST 13

numerous
obstacle
occasionally
occurrence
offered
official
omitted
operate
opinion
opportunity
opposite
ordinance
organization
origin
original
paid
pamphlet
parallel
particular
passed, past

LIST 14

pastime
peaceable
peculiar
perceive
performance
permanent
permitted
persistent
personal, personnel
persuading
phase, faze
philosophy
physical
piece
planned
pleasant
poison
political
possession
possible

LIST 15

practice (noun), practise (verb)
precede
preferred
prejudice
preparation
prevalent
principal, principle
privilege
probably
proceed
professor
prominent
proving
psychology
pursuing
quantity
quiet, quite
really
receipt
receiving

LIST 16	LIST 17	LIST 18
recognize	scenery	specimen
recommend	schedule	stationary, stationery
reference	science	stopped
referring	secretaries	stories, storeys
regard	seize	straight, strait
relative	sense, since	strenuous
relieving	sentence	stretch
religious	separation	strict
reminiscent	sergeant	studying
repetition	serviceable	substantial
representative	several	subtle
requirement	shining	succeed
resistance	shoulder	success
responsible	sight, site, cite	sufficient
restaurant	significance	summary
rhythm	similar	supposed
ridiculous	simply	surprise
sacrifice	sincerely	suspense
safety	source	swimming
satisfying	speak, speech	syllable

LIST 19	LIST 20
symbol	tremendous
symmetrical	tried
synonymous	truly
technique	undoubtedly
temperament	unnecessary
temperature	until
tendency	unusual
than, then	useful
their, there, they're	using
themselves	vacuum
theories	valuable
therefore	varies
thorough	vegetable
though	view
through	weather, whether
together	weird
to, too	were, where
tomorrow	wholly, holy
tragedies	writing
transferred	yield

APPENDIX B

DEVELOPING VOCABULARY SKILLS

If you understand the meanings of many words, you can be said to have a "good vocabulary." Words are the basis of thought. We think with words, we understand with words, and we communicate with words.

A large working vocabulary is a significant asset. It allows us to use precise words that say exactly what we intend. In addition, we understand more effectively what we hear and read. A large vocabulary also enables us to score well on employment and intelligence tests.

In the business world, where precise communication is extremely important, surveys show a definite correlation between vocabulary size and job performance. Skilled workers, in the majority of cases, have larger vocabularies than unskilled workers. Supervisors know more words than the workers they direct, and executives have larger vocabularies than employees working for them.

Having a good vocabulary at our command doesn't necessarily ensure our success in life, but it certainly gives us an advantage. Improving your vocabulary will help you expand your options in an increasingly complex world.

Vocabulary can be acquired in three ways: accidentally, incidentally, and intentionally. Setting out intentionally to expand your word power is, of course, the most efficient vocabulary-building method. One of the best means of increasing your vocabulary involves the use of index cards: when you encounter an unfamiliar word, write it on a card and put the definition of the word on the reverse side of the card. Just five to ten minutes of practice each day with such cards can significantly increase your vocabulary.

Your campaign to increase your vocabulary can begin with the 20 lists of selected business terms and words of general interest included in this appendix. You may already know partial definitions for some of these business terms and words. Take this opportunity to develop more precise definitions for them. Follow these steps in using the word lists:

1. Write the word on an index card.
2. Look up the word in your dictionary. Compare the dictionary definitions of the word with the definition choices shown in this appendix. Select the correct definition, and write its letter in the space provided. (The definitions provided in the textbook are quite concise but should help you remember the word's most common meaning.)
3. On the reverse side of your card, write the phonetic spelling of the word and the word's part of speech. Then write its definition, using as much of the dictionary definition as you find helpful. Try also to add a phrase or sentence illustrating the use of the word.
4. Study your index cards often.
5. Try to find ways to use your vocabulary words in your speech and writing.

LIST 1

1. adjacent = (a) previous, (b) similar, (c) overdue, (d) nearby ______
2. ambivalence = having (a) uncertainty, (b) ambition, (c) compassion, (d) intelligence ______
3. belligerent = (a) overweight, (b) quarrelsome, (c) likeable, (d) believable ______
4. cusp = (a) peak, (b) molar, (c) curse, (d) drinking vessel ______
5. decadent = in a state of (a) repair, (b) happiness, (c) decline, (d) extreme patriotism ______
6. entitlement = (a) label, (b) tax refund, (c) screen credit, (d) legal right ______
7. equivalent = (a) subsequent, (b) identical, (c) self-controlled, (d) plentiful ______
8. paramount = (a) foremost, (b) high mountain, (c) film company, (d) insignificant ______
9. plausible = (a) quiet, (b) believable, (c) notorious, (d) negative ______
10. unilateral = (a) powerful, (b) harmonious, (c) one-sided, (d) indelible ______

LIST 2

1. affluent = (a) rich, (b) slippery, (c) persistent, (d) rebellious ______
2. autocrat = one who (a) owns many cars, (b) is self-centred, (c) has absolute power, (d) collects signatures ______
3. benevolent = for the purpose of (a) religion, (b) doing good, (c) healing, (d) violence ______
4. entrepreneur = (a) business owner, (b) traveller, (c) salesperson, (d) gambler ______
5. impertinent = (a) stationary, (b) bound to happen, (c) obsolete, (d) rude or insolent ______
6. imprudent = (a) unwise, (b) crude, (c) vulnerable, (d) lifeless ______
7. mediator = one who seeks (a) overseas trade, (b) profits, (c) safe investment, (d) peaceful settlement ______
8. preponderance = (a) thoughtfulness, (b) exclusive right, (c) superiority, (d) forethought ______
9. recipient = (a) receiver, (b) respondent, (c) voter, (d) giver ______
10. reprehensible = (a) disobedient, (b) independent, (c) blameworthy, (d) following ______

LIST 3

1. affable = (a) cheap, (b) pleasant, (c) strange, (d) competent ______
2. consensus = (a) population count, (b) attendance, (c) tabulation, (d) agreement ______
3. criterion = (a) standard, (b) command, (c) pardon, (d) law ______
4. diligent = (a) gentle, (b) industrious, (c) prominent, (d) intelligent ______
5. hydraulic = operated by means of (a) air, (b) gasoline, (c) liquid, (d) mechanical parts ______
6. hypothesis = (a) triangle, (b) prologue, (c) highest point, (d) theory ______
7. phenomenon = (a) imagination, (b) rare event, (c) appointment, (d) clever saying ______
8. reticent = (a) reserved, (b) strong-willed, (c) inflexible, (d) disagreeable ______
9. sanctuary = a place of (a) healing, (b) refuge, (c) rest, (d) learning ______
10. stimulus = something that causes (a) response, (b) light, (c) pain, (d) movement ______

LIST 4

1. beneficiary = one who (a) receives a licence, (b) creates goodwill, (c) receives proceeds, (d) makes friends ______
2. constrain = (a) restrict, (b) filter, (c) use, (d) inform ______
3. corroborate = (a) contradict, (b) recall, (c) erode, (d) confirm ______
4. dun = a demand for (a) legal action, (b) payment, (c) credit information, (d) dividends ______
5. equitable = (a) fair, (b) profitable, (c) similar, (d) clear ______
6. fluctuate = (a) rinse out, (b) magnetize, (c) violate, (d) rise and fall ______
7. indolent = (a) self-indulgent, (b) lazy, (c) pampered, (d) uncertain ______
8. nullify = (a) disappear, (b) imitate, (c) invalidate, (d) enhance ______
9. obsolete = (a) ugly, (b) outmoded, (c) audible, (d) scant ______
10. stabilize = to make (a) pleasant, (b) congenial, (c) traditional, (d) firm ______

LIST 5

1. arbitrate = (a) decide, (b) construct, (c) conquer, (d) ratify ______
2. coalition = (a) deliberation, (b) allegiance, (c) adherence, (d) alliance ______
3. collate = (a) assemble, (b) denounce, (c) supersede, (d) discuss ______
4. conglomerate = combination of (a) executives, (b) companies, (c) investments, (d) countries ______
5. franchise = (a) fictitious reason, (b) right, (c) obligation, (d) official announcement ______
6. logistics = (a) speculations, (b) analytic philosophy, (c) reasonable outcome, (d) details of operation ______
7. proxy = authority to (a) act for another, (b) write cheques, (c) submit nominations, (d) explain ______
8. subsidiary = (a) performance below expectations, (b) country dominated by another, (c) company controlled by another, (d) depressed financial condition ______
9. termination = (a) end, (b) inception, (c) identification, (d) evasive action ______
10. virtually = (a) absolutely, (b) precisely, (c) almost entirely, (d) strictly ______

LIST 6

1. affiliate = (a) trust, (b) attract, (c) effect, (d) join ______
2. alter = (a) perform religious ceremony, (b) isolate, (c) attribute, (d) modify ______
3. boisterous = (a) noisily exuberant, (b) masculine, (c) cheerful, (d) rotund ______
4. configuration = (a) stratagem, (b) foreign currency, (c) form, (d) comprehension ______
5. conveyance = (a) vehicle, (b) transformation, (c) baggage, (d) consortium ______
6. infringe = (a) ravel, (b) embroider, (c) encroach, (d) margin ______
7. jurisdiction = (a) science of law, (b) enunciation, (c) justice, (d) authority ______
8. non-partisan = (a) unbiased, (b) antisocial, (c) ineffective, (d) untenable ______
9. parity = (a) price index, (b) justice under law, (c) plenitude, (d) equality of purchasing power ______
10. usury = (a) method of operation, (b) implementation, (c) illegal interest, (d) customary ______

LIST 7

1. anonymous = (a) multiplex, (b) powerless, (c) vexing, (d) nameless ________
2. cartel = (a) combination to fix prices, (b) ammunition belt, (c) partnership to promote competition, (d) placard ________
3. conjecture = (a) coagulation, (b) gesticulation, (c) guesswork, (d) connection ________
4. disparity = (a) unlikeness, (b) separation, (c) lack of emotion, (d) repudiation ________
5. environment = (a) urban area, (b) zenith, (c) surroundings, (d) latitude ________
6. impetus = (a) oversight, (b) stimulus, (c) hindrance, (d) imminence ________
7. portfolio = a list of (a) books, (b) security analysts, (c) corporations, (d) investments ________
8. quiescent = (a) presumptuous, (b) motionless, (c) immoderate, (d) volatile ________
9. surrogate = (a) substitute, (b) accused, (c) authentic, (d) suspended ________
10. tariff = (a) marsupial, (b) announcement, (c) ship, (d) duty ________

LIST 8

1. accrue = (a) conform, (b) accumulate, (c) diminish, (d) multiply ________
2. amortize = (a) pay off, (b) reduce, (c) romance, (d) kill ________
3. commensurate = (a) infinitesimal, (b) erroneous, (c) reliable, (d) proportional ________
4. consortium = (a) configuration, (b) partnership or association, (c) royal offspring, (d) rental property ________
5. discernible = (a) perceptive, (b) pretentious, (c) recognizable, (d) dissident ________
6. frugal = (a) thrifty, (b) wasteful, (c) judicious, (d) profligate ________
7. pecuniary = (a) rudimentary, (b) eccentric, (c) financial, (d) distinctive ________
8. retract = (a) disavow, (b) reorganize, (c) reciprocate, (d) hide ________
9. scrutinize = (a) cheerfully admit, (b) baffle, (c) persist, (d) examine carefully ________
10. tenacious = (a) falling apart, (b) persistent, (c) immobile, (d) chagrined ________

LIST 9

1. amiable = (a) brusque, (b) impetuous, (c) feasible, (d) likeable ________
2. credible = (a) plausible, (b) deceitful, (c) religious, (d) financially sound ________
3. defendant = one who (a) sues, (b) answers suit, (c) judges, (d) protects ________
4. dissipate = (a) accumulate, (b) partition, (c) liquefy, (d) scatter or waste ________
5. incentive = (a) impediment, (b) support, (c) impressive, (d) remuneration ________
6. innocuous = (a) harmless, (b) injectable, (c) facetious, (d) frightening ________
7. morale = (a) productivity, (b) truthful, (c) lesson, (d) emotional condition ________
8. motivate = (a) encourage, (b) languish, (c) force, (d) award ________
9. oust = (a) install, (b) instigate, (c) shout, (d) expel ________
10. superfluous = (a) extraordinary, (b) very slippery, (c) shallow, (d) redundant ________

LIST 10

1. adroit = (a) ideal, (b) resilient, (c) witty, (d) skilful ________
2. derogatory = (a) minimal, (b) degrading, (c) originating from, (d) devious ________
3. escrow = (a) international treaty, (b) public registration, (c) reprobate, (d) type of deposit ________
4. facsimile = (a) principle, (b) prototype, (c) exact copy, (d) counterfeit ________
5. inordinate = (a) unwholesome, (b) excessive, (c) unimportant, (d) treacherous ________
6. logical = (a) reasoned, (b) irrelevant, (c) lofty, (d) intricate ________
7. malfeasance = (a) prevarication, (b) injury, (c) superstition, (d) misconduct ________
8. noxious = (a) harmful, (b) unusual, (c) pleasant, (d) inconsequential ________
9. résumé = (a) budget report, (b) minutes of meeting, (c) photo album, (d) summary of qualifications ________
10. sustainable = (a) valuable, (b) lasting, (c) edible, (d) conscious ________

LIST 11

1. animosity = (a) happiness, (b) deep sadness, (c) hatred, (d) study of animals ________
2. caveat = (a) headwear, (b) warning, (c) neckwear, (d) prerogative ________
3. conscientious = (a) meticulous, (b) productive, (c) cognizant, (d) sophisticated ________
4. cosmopolitan = (a) provincial, (b) multicoloured, (c) intoxicating, (d) worldly ________
5. decipher = (a) preclude, (b) decode, (c) demise, (d) reproach ________
6. euphemism = (a) religious discourse, (b) grimace, (c) figure of speech, (d) mild or indirect expression ________
7. fraudulent = (a) loquacious, (b) candid, (c) deceitful, (d) despotic ________
8. peripheral = (a) marginal, (b) imaginary, (c) visionary, (d) supernatural ________
9. pungent = (a) knowledgeable, (b) uncouth, (c) acrid, (d) vulnerable ________
10. requisite = (a) essential, (b) demanding, (c) skilful, (d) discreet ________

LIST 12

1. ad valorem = (a) esteemed, (b) genuine, (c) precious, (d) proportional ________
2. carte blanche = (a) white carriage, (b) credit terms, (c) full permission, (d) geographical expression ________
3. de facto = (a) prejudicial, (b) actual, (c) routine, (d) unlawful ________
4. esprit de corps = (a) group enthusiasm, (b) strong coffee, (c) central authority, (d) government overturn ________
5. modus = (a) method of procedure, (b) compromise, (c) business transaction, (d) flexible arbitration ________
6. per capita = per unit of (a) income, (b) population, (c) birth, (d) household ________
7. per diem = (a) daily, (b) weekly, (c) yearly, (d) individually ________
8. prima facie = (a) self-taught, (b) apparent, (c) principal, (d) artificial ________
9. status quo = (a) haughty demeanour, (b) steadfast opinion, (c) position of importance, (d) existing condition ________
10. tort = (a) rich cake, (b) extended dream, (c) wrongful act, (d) lawful remedy ________

LIST 13

1. acquit = (a) absolve, (b) pursue, (c) interfere, (d) impede ________
2. annuity = (a) yearly report, (b) insurance premium, (c) tuition refund, (d) annual payment ________
3. complacent = (a) appealing, (b) self-satisfied, (c) sympathetic, (d) scrupulous ________
4. contraband = (a) discrepancy, (b) opposing opinion, (c) smuggled goods, (d) ammunition ________
5. insolvent = (a) uncleanable, (b) inexplicable, (c) bankrupt, (d) unjustifiable ________
6. malicious = marked by (a) good humour, (b) ill will, (c) great pleasure, (d) injurious tumour ________
7. negligent = (a) careless, (b) fraudulent, (c) unlawful, (d) weak ________
8. nominal = (a) enumerated, (b) beneficial, (c) extravagant, (d) insignificant ________
9. rescind = (a) consign, (b) oppose, (c) repeal, (d) censure ________
10. stringent = (a) rigid, (b) expedient, (c) compliant, (d) resilient ________

LIST 14

1. affirm = (a) make secure, (b) assert strongly, (c) elevate, (d) encircle ________
2. exonerate = (a) commend, (b) declare blameless, (c) banish, (d) emigrate ________
3. expedite = (a) elucidate, (b) get rid of, (c) amplify, (d) rush ________
4. hamper = (a) impede, (b) delineate, (c) release, (d) assuage ________
5. implement = (a) suppress, (b) ameliorate, (c) carry out, (d) attribute ________
6. induce = (a) teach, (b) construe, (c) persuade, (d) copy ________
7. obliterate = (a) obstruct, (b) prevent, (c) minimize, (d) erase ________
8. quandary = a state of (a) doubt, (b) certainty, (c) depression, (d) apprehension ________
9. surmount = (a) hike, (b) overcome, (c) interpret, (d) specify ________
10. veracity = (a) truthfulness, (b) swiftness, (c) efficiency, (d) persistence ________

LIST 15

1. aggregate = a collection of (a) hostile individuals, (b) foreign words, (c) disparate elements, (d) sticky liquids ________
2. ambiguous = (a) peripatetic, (b) uncertain, (c) enterprising, (d) deceptive ________
3. amend = (a) alter, (b) pray, (c) praise, (d) utter ________
4. apportion = (a) sanction, (b) ratify, (c) estimate, (d) divide ________
5. collaborate = (a) scrutinize, (b) cooperate, (c) surrender, (d) accumulate ________
6. ingenuity = (a) innocence, (b) torpor, (c) cleverness, (d) self-composure ________
7. irretrievable = not capable of being (a) sold, (b) identified, (c) explained, (d) recovered ________
8. lenient = (a) liberal, (b) crooked, (c) benevolent, (d) explicit ________
9. retrench = (a) dig repeatedly, (b) reduce, (c) reiterate, (d) enlighten ________
10. trivial = (a) composed of three parts, (b) momentous, (c) paltry, (d) economical ________

LIST 16

1. audit = (a) examine, (b) speak, (c) exchange, (d) expunge __________
2. arrears = (a) retreat, (b) gratuity, (c) overdue debt, (d) option __________
3. curtail = (a) obstruct, (b) restore, (c) rejuvenate, (d) cut short __________
4. encumber = (a) grow, (b) substantiate, (c) burden, (d) illustrate __________
5. exemplify = (a) segregate, (b) divulge, (c) illustrate, (d) condone __________
6. extension = (a) unusual request, (b) prolonged journey, (c) haphazard results, (d) extra time __________
7. fortuitous = (a) lucky, (b) courageous, (c) radical, (d) assiduous __________
8. innovation = (a) reorganization, (b) occupancy, (c) introduction, (d) solution __________
9. syndicate = (a) union of writers, (b) council of lawmakers, (c) group of symptoms, (d) association of people __________
10. venture = (a) speculative business transaction, (b) unsecured loan, (c) stock split, (d) gambling debt __________

LIST 17

1. acquiesce = (a) gain possession of, (b) confront, (c) implore, (d) comply __________
2. enumerate = (a) articulate, (b) list, (c) enunciate, (d) see clearly __________
3. erratic = (a) pleasurable, (b) inconsistent, (c) exotic, (d) serene __________
4. expedient = serving to promote (a) fellowship, (b) one's own interests, (c) good of others, (d) speedy delivery __________
5. feasible = (a) authentic, (b) profuse, (c) practicable, (d) extraneous __________
6. literal = (a) exact, (b) devout, (c) apropos, (d) noticeable __________
7. lucrative = (a) providential, (b) swift, (c) pleasant, (d) profitable __________
8. negotiable = (a) essential, (b) adequate, (c) transferable, (d) economical __________
9. nonchalant = (a) dull, (b) cool, (c) unintelligent, (d) sagacious __________
10. reconcile = (a) settle or resolve, (b) calculate, (c) modify, (d) remunerate __________

LIST 18

1. byte = (a) dental occlusion, (b) computer storage, (c) digits processed as a unit, (d) type font __________
2. encrypt = (a) convert into code, (b) print, (c) commit fraud, (d) inter __________
3. execute = (a) eradicate, (b) inquire, (c) oppose, (d) carry out __________
4. memory = (a) printer logic, (b) computer information-storage capacity, (c) automatic printout, (d) software __________
5. menu = list of (a) parts, (b) options, (c) serial numbers, (d) vendors __________
6. morph = (a) combine, (b) alter by computer, (c) scan, (d) exchange data __________
7. program = (a) alphabetical list, (b) computer log, (c) coded instructions, (d) microprocessor __________
8. prompt = (a) reminder, (b) code, (c) function, (d) format __________
9. retrieve = (a) acquiesce, (b) instruct, (c) remove code, (d) recover information __________
10. tentative = (a) sporting, (b) hesitant, (c) permanent, (d) repetitive __________

LIST 19

1. apprehensive = (a) knowledgeable, (b) fearful, (c) reticent, (d) autonomous ________
2. circumspect = (a) cautious, (b) uncertain, (c) co-operative, (d) frugal ________
3. collateral = (a) revenue, (b) secret agreement, (c) book value, (d) security for a loan ________
4. insinuation = (a) disagreeable proposal, (b) indirect suggestion, (c) elucidating glimpse, (d) flagrant insult ________
5. liaison = (a) legal obligation, (b) treaty, (c) connection between groups, (d) quarantine ________
6. procrastinate = (a) predict, (b) reproduce, (c) postpone, (d) advance ________
7. ratification = the act of (a) confirming, (b) reviewing, (c) evaluating, (d) inscribing ________
8. renovate = (a) renegotiate, (b) restore, (c) supply, (d) deliver ________
9. saturate = to fill (a) slowly, (b) dangerously, (c) as expected, (d) to excess ________
10. vendor = (a) seller, (b) manufacturer, (c) tradesperson, (d) coin collector ________

LIST 20

1. abhorrent = (a) extremely disagreeable, (b) attractive, (c) valueless, (d) addictive ________
2. appraisal = (a) general information, (b) certification, (c) estimation, (d) approval ________
3. collusion = (a) secret agreement, (b) direct conflict, (c) partial exclusion, (d) original artwork ________
4. commingle = (a) swindle, (b) mix, (c) separate, (d) communicate ________
5. dissolution = (a) intemperance, (b) solubility, (c) subversion, (d) separation ________
6. ensue = (a) change subtly, (b) relinquish, (c) track down, (d) follow ________
7. rejuvenate = to make (a) youthful, (b) slender, (c) sturdy, (d) impregnable ________
8. stipulation = (a) permission, (b) requirement, (c) rejection, (d) concurrence ________
9. subsidy = (a) scholarship, (b) financial assistance, (c) payment due, (d) unacknowledged payment ________
10. tenuous = (a) flimsy, (b) indecisive, (c) cautious, (d) firm ________

APPENDIX

REFERENCE GUIDE TO DOCUMENT FORMATS

Business documents carry two kinds of messages. Verbal messages are conveyed by the words chosen to express the writer's ideas. Nonverbal messages are conveyed largely by the appearance of a document. If you compare an assortment of letters and memos from various organizations, you will notice immediately that some look more attractive and more professional than others. The nonverbal message of professional-looking documents is that these documents were sent by people who are careful, informed, intelligent, and successful. Understandably, you're more likely to take seriously documents that use attractive stationery and professional formatting techniques.

Over the years certain practices and conventions have arisen regarding the appearance and formatting of documents. Although these conventions offer some choices (such as letter and punctuation styles), most business documents follow standardized formats. To ensure that your documents carry favourable nonverbal messages about you and your organization, you'll want to give special attention to the appearance and formatting of your letters, envelopes, memos, email messages, and fax cover sheets.

APPEARANCE

Two important elements for achieving a professional appearance are stationery and placement of the message on the page.

Stationery

Most organizations use high-quality stationery for printed business documents. This stationery is printed on select paper that meets two qualifications: weight and cotton-fibre content.

Paper is measured by weight per ream (500 sheets) and may range from 9 pounds/4.1 kg (thin onionskin paper) to 32 pounds/14.5 kg (thick card and cover stock). Most office stationery is in the 16- to 24-pound (7.3- to 10.9-kg) range. Lighter 16-pound (7.3-kg) paper is generally sufficient for internal documents, including memos. Heavier 20- to 24-pound (9.1- to 10.9-kg) paper is used for printed letterhead stationery and is recommended for résumés.

Paper is also judged by its cotton-fibre content. Cotton fibre makes paper stronger, softer in texture, and less likely to yellow. Good-quality stationery contains 25 percent or more cotton fibre.

Letter Placement

The easiest way to place letters on the page is to use the defaults of your word processing program. These are usually set for side margins of 2.5 to 3 cm (1 inch to 1¼ inches). Most companies find these margins acceptable.

If you want to adjust your margins to better balance shorter letters, use the following chart:

Words in Body of Letter	Side Margins	Blank Lines After Date
Under 200	3.5–4 cm/1½ in.	4 to 10
Over 200	2.5 cm/1 in.	2 to 3

Experts say that a "ragged" right margin is easier to read than a justified (even) margin. You might want to turn off the justification feature of your word processing program if it automatically justifies the right margin.

LETTER PARTS

Professional-looking business letters are arranged in a conventional sequence with standard parts. The following sections discuss how to use these letter parts properly, and Figure C.1 illustrates the parts in a block-style letter.

Letterhead

Most business organizations use 8½- by 11-inch (21.6- by 27.9-cm) paper printed with a letterhead displaying their official name, street address, website address, and telephone number.

Dateline

On letterhead paper you should place the date two blank lines below the last line of the letterhead (5 cm [2 inches] from the top edge of the paper [line 13]). If you are using plain paper, place the date immediately below your return address. Since the date appears 5 cm (2 inches) from the top, start the return address an appropriate number of lines above it. The most common dateline format is as follows: *June 9, 2020.* Don't use *th,* etc., when the date is written this way. For European or military correspondence, use the following dateline format: *9 June 2020.* Notice that no commas are used.

Addressee and Delivery Notations

Delivery notations such as *CONFIDENTIAL* or *CERTIFIED MAIL* are typed in all capital letters two blank lines above the inside address.

Inside Address

Type the inside address—that is, the address of the organization or person receiving the letter—single-spaced, starting at the left margin. The number of lines between the dateline and the inside address depends on the size of the letter body and the font size. To balance the letter on the page, generally one to nine blank lines are appropriate.

Be careful to duplicate the exact wording and spelling of the recipient's name and address on your documents. Usually, you can copy this information from the letterhead of the correspondence you are answering. If, for example, you are responding to *Jackson & Perkins Company,* don't address your letter to *Jackson and Perkins Corp.*

Figure C.1

Letter and Punctuation Styles

island graphics
893 Dillingham Boulevard, Victoria, BC V6R 2L3
(205) 493-2310 http://www.islandgraphics.com

↓ 2 inches or 2 blank lines below letterhead

September 13, 202x

↓ 1 to 9 blank lines

Mr. T. M. Wilson, President
Visual Concept Enterprises
1901 West Broadway
Vancouver, BC V6C 2R6

↓ 1 blank line

Dear Mr. Wilson:

↓ 1 blank line

SUBJECT: Block Letter Style

↓ 1 blank line

This letter illustrates block letter style, about which you asked. All typed lines begin at the left margin. The date is usually placed 2 inches from the top edge of the paper or two blank lines below the last line of the letterhead, whichever position is lower.

This letter also shows mixed punctuation. A colon follows the salutation, and a comma follows the complimentary close. Open punctuation requires no comma or colon, but we find that most of our customers prefer mixed punctuation.

If a subject line is included, it appears two lines below the salutation. The word *SUBJECT* is optional. Most readers will recognize a statement in this position as the subject without an identifying label. The complimentary close appears one blank line below the end of the last paragraph.

↓ 1 blank line

Sincerely,

Mark H. Wong

↓ 3 blank lines

Mark H. Wong
Graphic Designer

↓ 1 blank line

MHW:pil

Letterhead

Dateline

Inside address

Salutation

Subject line

Body

Complimentary close and signature block

Block Style, Mixed Punctuation

Modified Block Style, Mixed Punctuation

Always be sure to include a courtesy title such as *Mr., Ms., Mrs., Dr.,* or *Professor* before a person's name in the inside address—on both the letter and the envelope.

Remember that the inside address is not included for readers (who already know who and where they are). It's there to help writers accurately file the message.

Attention Line

An attention line allows you to send your message officially to an organization but to direct it to a specific individual, office, or department. Here are two common formats for attention lines:

MultiMedia Enterprises	MultiMedia Enterprises
2931 St. Laurent	Attention: Marketing Director
Montreal, QC H2F 3C2	2931 St. Laurent
ATTENTION: MARKETING DIRECTOR	Montreal, QC H2F 3C2

Attention lines may be typed in all caps or with mixed uppercase and lowercase letters. The colon following *Attention* is optional. Notice that an attention line may be placed two lines below the address block or printed as the second line of the inside address. You'll want to use the latter format if the address block will be copied to the envelope so that the attention line will not interfere with the last-line placement of the postal code.

Whenever possible, use a person's name as the first line of an address instead of putting that name in an attention line. Some writers use an attention line because they fear that letters addressed to individuals at companies may be considered private or that if the addressee is no longer with the company, the letter may not be opened. Actually, unless a letter is marked *Personal* or *Confidential,* it will very likely be opened as business mail.

Salutation

For most letter styles, place the letter greeting, or salutation, one blank line below the last line of the inside address or the attention line (if used). If the letter is addressed to an individual, use that person's courtesy title, if known, and last name (*Dear Mr. Lanham*). Even if you are on a first-name basis (*Dear Leslie*), be sure to add a colon (not a comma or a semicolon) after the salutation. Do not use an individual's full name in the salutation unless you are unsure of gender or gender identification (*Dear Leslie Lanham*).

It is always best to address a letter to a specific person. Do your research to identify to whom a letter should be sent. If you can't find the name of the person who should receive the letter, you can use the salutation *Dear [Job Title].* If you have cause to address a letter to an organizational team as a whole, use the team name in the salutation (*Dear Executive Team*).

Subject and Reference Lines

Although experts suggest placing the subject line one blank line below the salutation, many organizations place it above the salutation. Use whatever style your organization prefers. Reference lines often show policy, account, or file numbers; they generally appear one blank line above the salutation. Use initial capital letters as in a title, or use all capital letters.

Body

Most business letters and memoranda are single-spaced, with double-spacing between paragraphs. Very short messages may be double-spaced with indented paragraphs.

Complimentary Close

Typed one blank line below the last line of the letter, the complimentary close may be formal (*Very truly yours*) or informal (*Sincerely yours* or *Cordially*).

Signature Block

In most letter styles, the writer's typed name and optional identification appear two to three blank lines below the complimentary close. The combination of name, title, and organization information should be arranged to achieve a balanced look. The name and title may appear on the same line or on separate lines, depending on the length of each. Use commas to separate categories within the same line but not to conclude a line.

Sincerely,	Cordially yours,
Jeremy M. Wood	*Casandra Baker-Murillo*
Jeremy M. Wood, Manager	Casandra Baker-Murillo
Technical Sales and Services	Executive Vice President

Some organizations include their names in the signature block. In such cases the organization name appears in all caps one blank line below the complimentary close, as shown here:

Cordially,

LITTON COMPUTER SERVICES
Shelina A. Simpson
Shelina A. Simpson
Executive Assistant

Reference Initials

If the author of the letter does not actually prepare the letter, reference initials identify who keyed the letter. If used, the initials of the writer and typist are typed one blank line below the writer's name and title. Generally, the writer's initials are capitalized and the typist's are lowercase, but this format varies. Today the writer's initials are often omitted.

Enclosure Notation

When an enclosure or attachment accompanies a document, a notation to that effect appears one blank line below the reference initials. This notation reminds the sender to insert the enclosure in the envelope, and it reminds the recipient to look for the enclosure or attachment. The notation may be spelled out (*Enclosure, Attachment*), or it may be abbreviated (*Enc., Att.*). It may indicate the number of enclosures or attachments, and it may also identify a specific enclosure (*Enclosure: Form 1099*).

Copy Notation

If you make copies of correspondence for other individuals, you may use *cc* to indicate courtesy copy or carbon copy or merely *c* for any kind of copy. A colon following the initial(s) is optional.

Second-Page Heading

When a letter extends beyond one page, use plain paper of the same quality and colour as the first page. Identify the second and succeeding pages with a heading consisting of the name of the addressee, the page number, and the date. Use either of the following two formats:

Rachel Lawson   2   May 3, 202x

Rachel Lawson
Page 2
May 3, 202x

Both headings appear 2.5 cm (1 inch) from the top of the paper, followed by two blank lines to separate them from the continuing text. Avoid using a second page if you have only one line or the complimentary close and signature block to fill that page.

LETTER STYLES

Business letters are generally prepared in one of two formats. The more popular is the block style.

Block Style

In the block style, shown in Figure C.1, all lines begin at the left margin. This style is a favourite because it is easy to format.

Modified Block Style

The modified block style differs from block style in that the date and closing lines appear in the centre, as shown at the bottom of Figure C.1. The date may be (a) centred, (b) begun at the centre of the page (to align with the closing lines), or (c) backspaced from the right margin. The signature block—including the complimentary close, writer's name and title, or organization identification—begins at the centre. The first line of each paragraph may begin at the left margin or may be tabbed 1.25 cm (½ inch). All other lines begin at the left margin.

Personal Business Style

When business and professional writers prepare letters on plain paper, they often use the personal business style. It includes the writer's street and city address on two lines above the date, as shown in Figure C.2. Notice that the writer's name does not appear here; it is typed and signed at the end of the letter. The personal business letter may be formatted in (a) full block style with all lines starting at the left margin, (b) modified block style with blocked paragraphs, or (c) modified block style with indented paragraphs.

Figure C.2

Personal Business Style

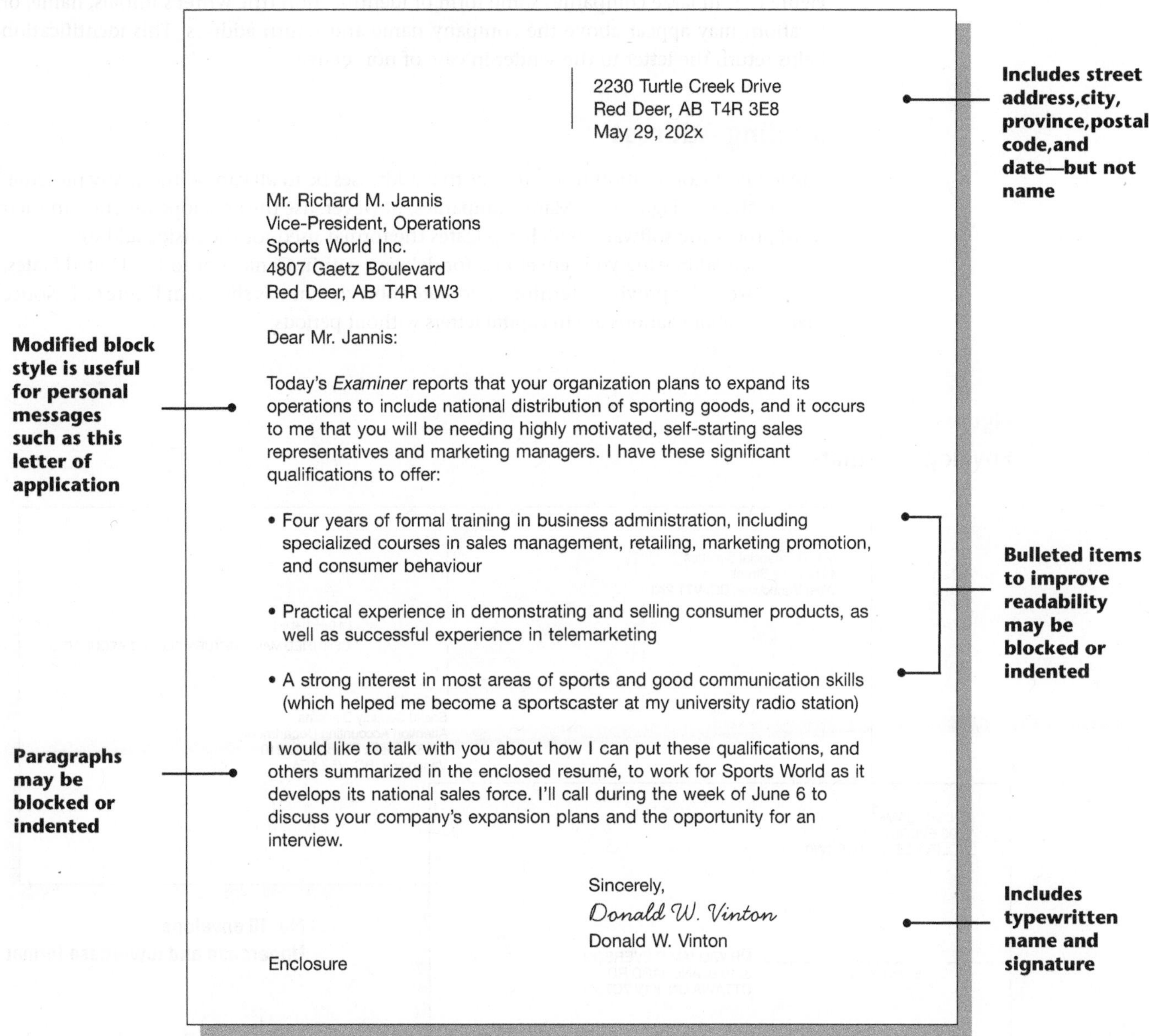

2230 Turtle Creek Drive
Red Deer, AB T4R 3E8
May 29, 202x
Includes street address,city, province,postal code,and date—but not name
Mr. Richard M. Jannis
Vice-President, Operations
Sports World Inc.
4807 Gaetz Boulevard
Red Deer, AB T4R 1W3
Dear Mr. Jannis:
Modified block style is useful for personal messages such as this letter of application
Today's *Examiner* reports that your organization plans to expand its operations to include national distribution of sporting goods, and it occurs to me that you will be needing highly motivated, self-starting sales representatives and marketing managers. I have these significant qualifications to offer:
• Four years of formal training in business administration, including specialized courses in sales management, retailing, marketing promotion, and consumer behaviour
• Practical experience in demonstrating and selling consumer products, as well as successful experience in telemarketing
• A strong interest in most areas of sports and good communication skills (which helped me become a sportscaster at my university radio station)
Bulleted items to improve readability may be blocked or indented
I would like to talk with you about how I can put these qualifications, and others summarized in the enclosed resumé, to work for Sports World as it develops its national sales force. I'll call during the week of June 6 to discuss your company's expansion plans and the opportunity for an interview.
Paragraphs may be blocked or indented
Sincerely,
Donald W. Vinton
Donald W. Vinton
Includes typewritten name and signature
Enclosure

PUNCTUATION STYLES

Two punctuation styles are commonly used for letters. *Mixed* punctuation, shown in Figures C.1 and C.2, requires a colon after the salutation and a comma after the complimentary close. *Open* punctuation contains no punctuation after the salutation or complimentary close.

ENVELOPES

An envelope should be of the same quality and colour of stationery as the letter it carries. Because the envelope introduces your message and makes the first impression, you need to be especially careful in addressing it. Moreover, how you fold the letter is important.

Return Address

The return address is usually printed at the upper left corner of an envelope, as shown in Figure C.3. In large companies some form of identification (the writer's initials, name, or location) may appear above the company name and return address. This identification helps return the letter to the sender in case of non-delivery.

Mailing Address

Canada Post Corporation recommends that addresses be in all caps without any punctuation, as show in Figure C.3. Many companies, however, use the envelope function in their word processing software, which replicates the format used for the inside address.

When addressing your envelopes for delivery within Canada or to the United States, use the two-letter province, territory, and state abbreviations, as shown in Figure C.4. Notice that these abbreviations are in capital letters without periods.

Figure C.3
Envelope Formats

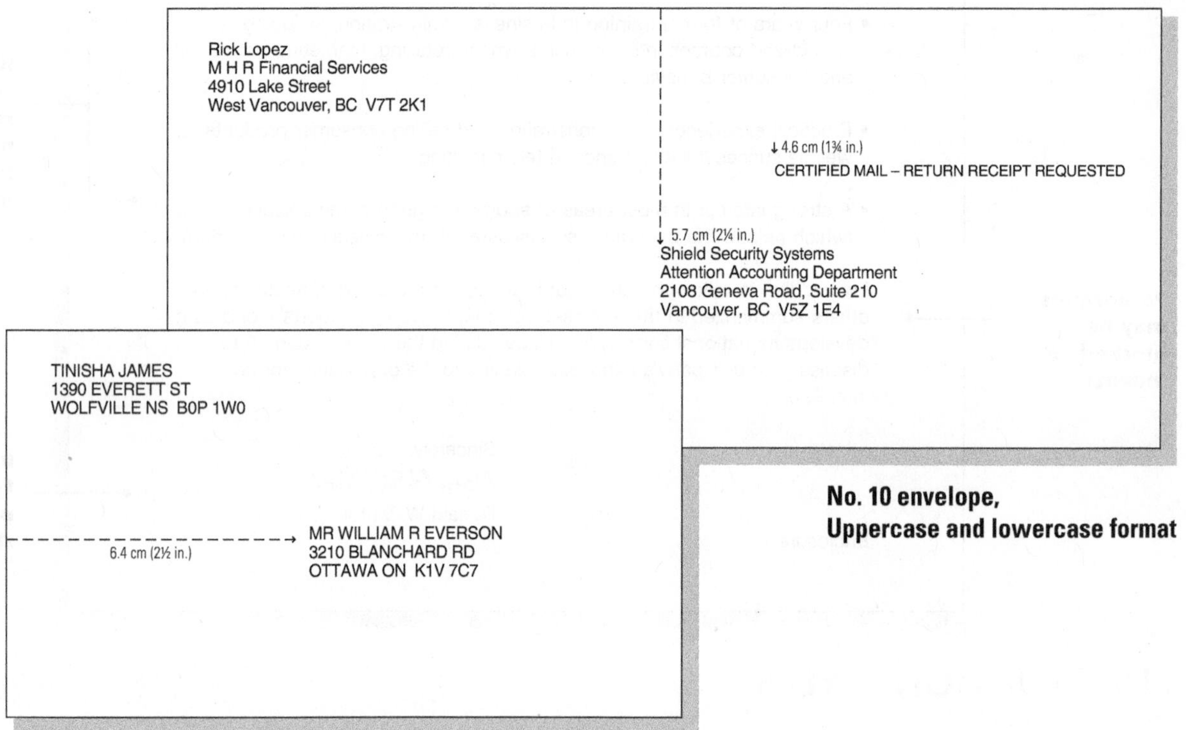

Rick Lopez
M H R Financial Services
4910 Lake Street
West Vancouver, BC V7T 2K1
4.6 cm (1¾ in.)
CERTIFIED MAIL – RETURN RECEIPT REQUESTED
5.7 cm (2¼ in.)
Shield Security Systems
Attention Accounting Department
2108 Geneva Road, Suite 210
Vancouver, BC V5Z 1E4
TINISHA JAMES
1390 EVERETT ST
WOLFVILLE NS B0P 1W0
6.4 cm (2½ in.)
MR WILLIAM R EVERSON
3210 BLANCHARD RD
OTTAWA ON K1V 7C7

No. 10 envelope, Uppercase and lowercase format

No. 6¾ envelope, CPC uppercase format

Figure C.4

Abbreviations of Provinces, Territories, and States

Province or Territory	Two-Letter Abbreviation
Alberta	AB
British Columbia	BC
Manitoba	MB
New Brunswick	NB
Newfoundland and Labrador	NL
Northwest Territories	NT
Nova Scotia	NS
Nunavut	NU
Ontario	ON
Prince Edward Island	PE
Quebec	QC
Saskatchewan	SK
Yukon Territory	YT

State or Territory	Two-Letter Abbreviation
Alabama	AL
Alaska	AK
Arizona	AZ
Arkansas	AR
California	CA
Canal Zone	CZ
Colorado	CO
Connecticut	CT
Delaware	DE
District of Columbia	DC
Florida	FL
Georgia	GA
Guam	GU
Hawaii	HI
Idaho	ID
Illinois	IL
Indiana	IN
Iowa	IA
Kansas	KS
Kentucky	KY

State or Territory	Two-Letter Abbreviation
Louisiana	LA
Maine	ME
Maryland	MD
Massachusetts	MA
Michigan	MI
Minnesota	MN
Mississippi	MS
Missouri	MO
Montana	MT
Nebraska	NE
Nevada	NV
New Hampshire	NH
New Jersey	NJ
New Mexico	NM
New York	NY
North Carolina	NC
North Dakota	ND
Ohio	OH
Oklahoma	OK
Oregon	OR
Pennsylvania	PA
Puerto Rico	PR
Rhode Island	RI
South Carolina	SC
South Dakota	SD
Tennessee	TN
Texas	TX
Utah	UT
Vermont	VT
Virgin Islands	VI
Virginia	VA
Washington	WA
West Virginia	WV
Wisconsin	WI
Wyoming	WY

Folding

The way a letter is folded and inserted into an envelope sends additional nonverbal messages about a writer's professionalism and carefulness. Most business people follow the procedures shown here, which produce the fewest creases to distract readers.

For No. 10 envelopes, begin with the letter face up. Fold slightly less than one-third of the sheet toward the top, as shown below. Then fold down the top third to within 0.5 cm of the bottom fold. Insert the letter into the envelope with the last fold toward the bottom of the envelope.

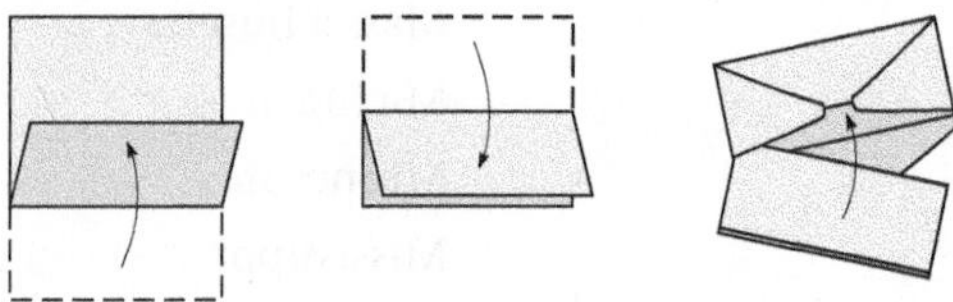

For smaller No. 6¾ envelopes, begin by folding the bottom up to within 1.25 cm of the top edge. Then fold the right third over to the left. Fold the left third to within 1.25 cm of the last fold. Insert the last fold into the envelope first.

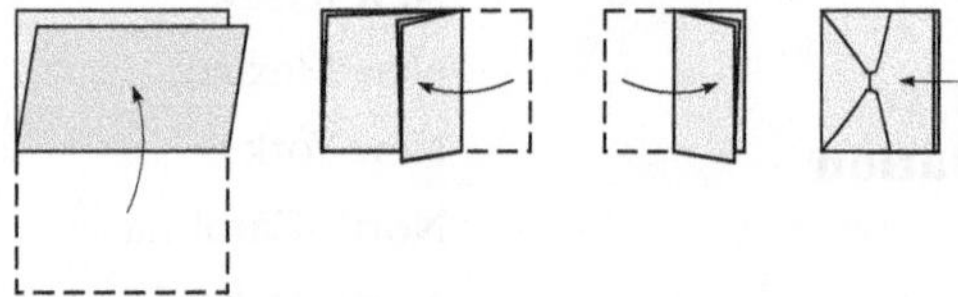

MEMORANDA

Memoranda deliver messages within organizations, although email has replaced the use of printed memos in most places. The design and arrangement of memo forms vary; however, they usually include the basic elements of *TO*, *FROM*, *DATE*, and *SUBJECT*. Large organizations may include other identifying headings, such as *FILE NUMBER*, *FLOOR*, *EXTENSION*, *LOCATION*, and *DISTRIBUTION*.

Business writers today typically use a standardized memo template. This template automatically provides attractive headings with appropriate spacing and formatting. Other writers store their own preferred memo formats.

If no printed or stored computer forms are available, memos may be printed out on company letterhead or on plain paper, as shown in Figure C.5. On a full sheet of paper, leave a top margin of 3.5 cm; on a half sheet, leave a top margin of 2.5 cm. Double-space and type in all caps the guide words: *TO:*, *FROM:*, *DATE:*, *SUBJECT:*. Align all the fill-in information two spaces after the longest guide word (*SUBJECT:*). Leave two blank lines after the last line of the heading, and begin typing the body of the memo. Like business letters, memos are single-spaced.

Memos are generally formatted with side margins of 3 cm, or they may conform to the printed memo form.

Figure C.5
Memo on Plain Paper

↓ 3.8 cm (1½ in.)

DATE: February 3, 202x

TO: Dawn Steward, Manager
Sales and Marketing

FROM: Jay Murray, Vice President
Operations

SUBJECT: Telephone Service Request Forms

↓ 2 blank lines

To speed telephone installation and improve service within the Bremerton facility, we are starting a new application procedure.

Service request forms will be available at various locations within the three buildings. When you require telephone service, obtain a request form at one of the locations that is convenient for you. Fill in the pertinent facts, obtain approval from your division head, and send the form to Brent White. Request forms are available at the following locations:

EMAIL MESSAGES

Email is the most popular form of communication in today's workplace. The following suggestions, illustrated in Figure C.6, may guide you in setting up the parts of an email message, but always check with your organization so that you can follow its practices.

To Line

Include the receiver's email address after *To*. If the receiver's address is recorded in your address book, you usually just have to begin typing his or her name. For an address not yet in your address book, be sure to key it very carefully since one mistyped character can redirect or prevent delivery.

Cc

Insert the email address of anyone who is to receive a copy of the message. *Cc* stands for *carbon copy* or *courtesy copy*. Don't be tempted, though, to send needless copies just because it's easy.

Bcc

Include here the email address of anyone who is to receive a copy of the message without other receivers' knowledge. *Bcc* stands for *blind carbon copy*. Writers use the *bcc* line for mailing lists or for sending messages to a number of people. The *bcc* line works well to conceal the names and addresses of all receivers for privacy purposes.

Subject

Identify the subject with a brief but descriptive summary of the topic. Be sure to include enough information to be clear and compelling. Capitalize the subject line as you would a title. Subject lines in all lowercase letters look unimportant and unprofessional. Most important, never leave a subject line blank.

Figure C.6
Typical Email Message

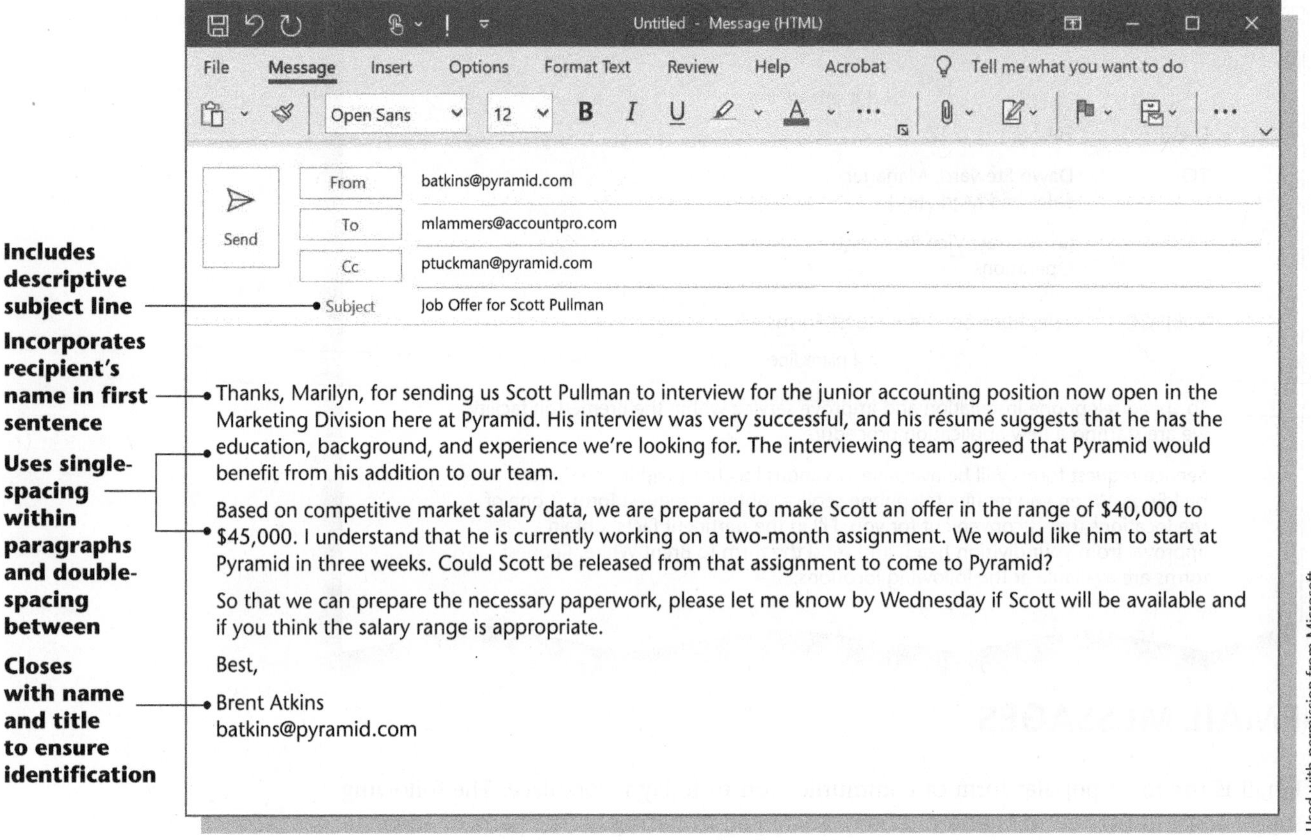

Untitled - Message (HTML)
File
Message
Insert
Options
Format Text
Review
Help
Acrobat
Tell me what you want to do
Open Sans
12
Send
From
batkins@pyramid.com
To
mlammers@accountpro.com
Cc
ptuckman@pyramid.com
Subject
Job Offer for Scott Pullman
Thanks, Marilyn, for sending us Scott Pullman to interview for the junior accounting position now open in the Marketing Division here at Pyramid. His interview was very successful, and his résumé suggests that he has the education, background, and experience we're looking for. The interviewing team agreed that Pyramid would benefit from his addition to our team.
Based on competitive market salary data, we are prepared to make Scott an offer in the range of $40,000 to $45,000. I understand that he is currently working on a two-month assignment. We would like him to start at Pyramid in three weeks. Could Scott be released from that assignment to come to Pyramid?
So that we can prepare the necessary paperwork, please let me know by Wednesday if Scott will be available and if you think the salary range is appropriate.
Best,
Brent Atkins
batkins@pyramid.com
Includes descriptive subject line
Incorporates recipient's name in first sentence
Uses single-spacing within paragraphs and double-spacing between
Closes with name and title to ensure identification

Used with permission from Microsoft

Salutation

Include a brief greeting, if you like. A formal salutation such as *Dear Sondra* followed by a comma or a colon is suitable for people outside your organization or those you are less familiar with. Many people use a more informal greeting like *Hi, Sondra!* or *Good morning* or *Greetings* within an organization or with known colleagues. Some writers simulate a salutation by including the name of the receiver in the first line, as shown in Figure C.6. Other writers treat an email message like a memo and skip the salutation entirely.

Message

Cover just one topic in your message, and try to keep your total message under two screens in length. Single-space and be sure to use both uppercase and lowercase letters. Double-space between paragraphs.

Closing

Conclude an external message, if you like, with a closing such as *Sincerely, Best wishes,* or *Warm regards,* followed by your name. If the recipient is unlikely to know you, it's a good idea to include your title and organization. Some email users include a *signature file* with identifying information that is automatically inserted at the end of each message. Writers of email messages sent within organizations may omit a closing but should still type at least their first names at the end of email messages to personalize them.

Attachment

Use the attachment window or button to select the path and file name of any file you wish to send with your email message, and call attention to the attachment in the body of your message.

FAX COVER SHEET

Documents transmitted by fax are usually introduced by a cover sheet, as shown in Figure C.7. As with memos, the format varies considerably. Important items to include are (a) the name and fax number of the receiver, (b) the name and fax number of the sender, (c) the number of pages being sent, and (d) the name and telephone number of the person to notify in case of unsatisfactory transmission.

When the document being transmitted requires little explanation, you may prefer to attach an adhesive note (such as a Post-it fax transmittal form) instead of a full cover sheet. These notes carry essentially the same information as shown in the printed fax cover sheet. They are perfectly acceptable in most business organizations and can save considerable paper and transmission costs.

Figure C.7

Fax Cover Sheet

FAX TRANSMISSION

DATE: ______________________ FAX

TO: ______________________ NUMBER: ________________

____

____

FAX

FROM: ______________________ NUMBER: ________________

____

____

NUMBER OF PAGES TRANSMITTED INCLUDING THIS COVER SHEET: ________

MESSAGE:

If any part of this fax transmission is missing or not clearly received, please call:

NAME: ______________________

PHONE: ______________________

CONTENTS SELF-HELP EXERCISES

NAME ______________________________

Nearly every student who takes this English course says, "I wish I had more exercises to try my skills on." Because of the many requests, we provide this set of self-help exercises for extra reinforcement. Immediate feedback is an important ingredient in successful learning. Therefore, a key to these exercises begins on page 520. Don't check the key, of course, until you complete each exercise.

Worksheet 1

This exercise is designed to help you develop a better understanding of the parts of speech. Using Chapter 1, write a brief definition or description of the eight parts of speech listed here. Then list three words as examples of each part of speech.

	Brief Definition	Three Examples		
1. noun	names person, place, thing, concept	Anthony	paper	truth
2. pronoun				
3. verb				
4. adjective				
5. adverb				
6. preposition				
7. conjunction				
8. interjection				

Fill in the parts of speech for all the words in these sentences. Use a dictionary if necessary.

We sent an email message to Jennifer, but she was very busy.

9. We ______________

10. sent ______________

11. an ______________

12. email ______________

13. message ______________

14. to ______________

15. Jennifer ______________

16. but ______________

17. she ______________

18. was ______________

19. very ______________

20. busy ______________

Gosh, no one on our team or in our department read the president's memo!

21. Gosh ______________

22. no one ______________

23. on ______________

24. our ______________

25. team ______________

26. or ______________

27. in ______________

28. our ______________

29. department ______________

30. read ______________________ 32. president's ______________________

31. the ______________________ 33. memo ______________________

Although Taylor arrived late, the committee meeting started promptly.

34. Although ______________________ 37. late ______________________ 40. meeting ______________________

35. Taylor ______________________ 38. the ______________________ 41. started ______________________

36. arrived ______________________ 39. committee ______________________ 42. promptly ______________________

NAME ______________________

Worksheet 2

Fill in the parts of speech for all the words in these sentences. Use a dictionary if necessary.

I sold property in Fredericton, but one transaction may not clear escrow.

1. I ______
2. sold ______
3. property ______
4. in ______
5. Fredericton ______
6. but ______
7. one ______
8. transaction ______
9. may ______
10. not ______
11. clear ______
12. escrow ______

Oh, did Lee really think he could change that method of operation?

13. Oh ______
14. did ______
15. Lee ______
16. really ______
17. think ______
18. he ______
19. could ______
20. change ______
21. that ______
22. method ______
23. of ______
24. operation ______

Our company recently joined Facebook and Twitter, so now we need active followers.

25. Our ______
26. company ______
27. recently ______
28. joined ______
29. Facebook ______
30. and ______
31. Twitter ______
32. so ______
33. now ______
34. we ______
35. need ______
36. active ______
37. followers ______

Fifteen minutes into the meeting, Mae and her assistant quietly slipped into the room.

38. Fifteen ______
39. minutes ______
40. into ______
41. the ______
42. meeting ______
43. Mae ______
44. and ______
45. her ______
46. assistant ______
47. quietly ______
48. slipped ______
49. into ______
50. the ______
51. room ______

NAME ______________________________

Worksheet 1

LOCATING SUBJECTS AND VERBS

Action verbs tell what the subject is doing or what is being done to the subject. For each of the following sentences, locate the action verb and underline it twice. Then locate the simple subject of the verb and underline it once.

To locate the subject, use the verb preceded by *who?* or *what?* In the example the verb is *answered.* To help you find the subject, ask *Who answered?*

EXAMPLE: A group of applicants answered the advertisement.

1. One of our top salespeople sold $2 million worth of life insurance.
2. The e-commerce boom is causing many brick-and-mortar stores to close their doors.
3. Our telephones rang constantly during the sales campaign.
4. In the winter we will hire four new workers for this department.
5. Front-line workers and management reached an agreement late last night.
6. The most successful salespeople received trips to Cuba.
7. With the reorganization several positions were eliminated.
8. Last week we released our new line of upscale, stylish cellphones.
9. One of the reviewers really disliked the software changes.
10. A committee consisting of 11 employees plus the manager was appointed to investigate.
11. The applicant with the best qualifications received the first interview.
12. Everything except labour and parts is covered by your warranty.

Linking verbs (such as *am, is, are, was, were, be, being,* and *been*) often join to the sentence words that describe or rename the subject. In the following sentences, underline the linking verbs twice and the subjects once.

EXAMPLES: E. J. Todd was president of the organization last year.
In the morning the air is cool.

13. The team members seem to work well together.
14. The new copiers are very dependable.
15. June and Ian both feel unwell today.
16. Dul Youn Hu has been office manager for nine years.
17. Our new offices are much brighter than our previous ones.

NAME ____________________

Worksheet 2

SENTENCE PATTERNS

Finish the sentences below in the patterns indicated.

Subject–Verb

EXAMPLE: Cellphones ring.

1. Shareholders ____________________.
2. Some changes ____________________.
3. Employees ____________________.
4. The security alarm ____________________.
5. The team leader ____________________.
6. Last year's sales ____________________.

Subject–Action Verb–Object

EXAMPLE: The sales director made a call.

7. Our salesperson sold ____________________.
8. The assistant sent ____________________.
9. An event coordinator organized ____________________.
10. I recommended ____________________.
11. Someone locked the ____________________.
12. The clerk filed all the ____________________.

Subject–Linking Verb–Complement

EXAMPLES: She is very friendly.
Jim could have been the manager.

13. Sales have been ____________________.
14. Selena feels ____________________.
15. The new owner is ____________________.
16. The consultant seems ____________________.
17. The writer could have been ____________________.
18. The caller was ____________________.

Compose original sentences in the following patterns.

19. (Subject–verb) ____________________
20. (Subject–verb) ____________________
21. (Subject–action verb–object) ____________________
22. (Subject–action verb–object) ____________________
23. (Subject–linking verb–complement) ____________________
24. (Subject–linking verb–complement) ____________________

NAME ______________________________

Worksheet 3

SENTENCE FAULTS

From the list below, select the letter that accurately describes each of the following groups of words. Write it in the space provided.

c = correctly punctuated sentence   cs = comma splice
f = fragment   ro = run-on sentence

1. The management of a multinational corporation with branch offices in several cities. ______
2. Send me a brochure and a price list for your latest camping equipment. ______
3. To compete with Apple, Samsung offers a trade-in program. ______
4. Brazil, Chile, and Australia are located in the southern hemisphere their summers and winters are the opposite of ours. ______
5. A training session on our new email program will be held Monday, January 14, all employees should plan to attend. ______
6. Because it is difficult to improve your language skills on your own. ______
7. Individuals and families who may have hereditary conditions such as a predisposition to certain cancers. ______
8. It wasn't the company's fault, it was the salesperson's. ______
9. Successful candidates for the positions will be motivated and energetic good communication skills will be essential. ______
10. I'll have the answer soon, first I must make a telephone call. ______
11. If you consider all the pros and cons before you make a decision. ______
12. A credit will be applied to your account therefore your next bill will require no payment. ______
13. Your entire department is entitled to overtime compensation. ______
14. You check the current address list, and I'll check the old one. ______
15. You check the current address list, I'll check the old one. ______
16. You check the current address list I'll check the old one. ______
17. Whether or not the product is returned in its original packaging. ______
18. When you return from the conference, please submit a brief report describing what you learned. ______
19. Our online sales are thriving, however, our retail sales are not meeting expectations. ______
20. If you agree that this memo accurately reflects our conversation. ______

NAME ______________________

LEVEL I

Write the preferred plural forms of the nouns shown below. Use a dictionary if necessary.

1. tissue ______________________
2. foot ______________________
3. latch ______________________
4. Bush ______________________
5. myth ______________________
6. language ______________________
7. fax ______________________
8. sandwich ______________________
9. valet ______________________
10. child ______________________
11. success ______________________
12. chorus ______________________
13. stock ______________________
14. branch ______________________
15. idea ______________________
16. woman ______________________
17. mismatch ______________________
18. taxi ______________________
19. Shiraz ______________________
20. annex ______________________
21. klutz ______________________
22. Ross ______________________
23. storm ______________________
24. alibi ______________________
25. Jones ______________________
26. Chavez ______________________
27. ox ______________________
28. business ______________________
29. computer ______________________
30. wish ______________________

LEVEL II

Write the preferred plural forms of the nouns shown below. Use a dictionary if necessary.

1. wharf ______________________
2. heir apparent ______________________
3. 2010 ______________________
4. Wolf ______________________
5. embargo ______________________
6. cm ______________________
7. attorney ______________________
8. amt. ______________________
9. faculty ______________________
10. by-product ______________________
11. entry ______________________
12. runner-up ______________________

13. alto ____________________

14. knife ____________________

15. notary public ____________________

16. A ____________________

17. Brady ____________________

18. memo ____________________

19. ally ____________________

20. zero ____________________

21. loaf (of bread) ____________________

22. yr. ____________________

23. Mistry ____________________

24. well-wisher ____________________

25. oz. ____________________

26. journey ____________________

27. MBA ____________________

28. wolf ____________________

29. studio ____________________

30. 21 ____________________

LEVEL III

Write the preferred plural forms of the nouns shown below. Use a dictionary if necessary.

1. datum ____________________

2. thesis ____________________

3. bacterium ____________________

4. Chinese ____________________

5. series ____________________

6. alumnus ____________________

7. alumna ____________________

8. genus ____________________

9. axis ____________________

10. news ____________________

11. p. (page) ____________________

12. f. (and following page) ____________________

13. vertebra ____________________

14. phenomenon ____________________

15. criterion ____________________

Select the correct word in parentheses, and complete the sentences in your own words.

16. The goods produced in that factory (is, are) ____________________.

17. The statistics (is, are) ____________________.

18. Several (formula, formulas) ____________________.

19. Four separate (analysis, analyses) ____________________.

20. In the business curriculum, economics (is, are) ____________________.

NAME ______________________

LEVEL I

Worksheet 1

Before you begin this exercise, review the five-step plan for placing apostrophes:

1. Look for possessive construction. (Usually two nouns appear together.)
2. Reverse the nouns. (Use a prepositional phrase, such as *interest of three years*.)
3. Examine the ownership word. (Is it singular or plural?)
4. If the ownership word is singular, add an apostrophe and *s*.
5. If the ownership word is plural and ends in *s*, add only an apostrophe. If the ownership word is plural but does not end in *s*, add both an apostrophe and an *s*.

Using apostrophes, change the following prepositional phrases into possessive constructions.

EXAMPLE: interest of three years — three years' interest

1. books of all students ______________
2. responsibility of my manager ______________
3. uniforms of the women ______________
4. rent of two months ______________
5. signature of an employee ______________
6. yards of our neighbours ______________
7. the landing of the pilot ______________
8. agreement of all partners ______________
9. parents of the children ______________
10. strengths of the department ______________
11. time of five years ______________
12. cars of those people ______________
13. merger of last week ______________
14. parent company of the two businesses ______________
15. opinions of citizens ______________
16. mountains of Canada ______________
17. requirements of the employer ______________
18. résumés of all candidates ______________
19. policies of the government ______________
20. fees of both agents ______________

NAME ______________________________

Worksheet 2

In the space provided, write the correct possessive form of the word in parentheses.

1. Applicants will have at least a (year) wait for an apartment. ____________

2. Several (drivers) complaints prompted the posting of a better sign. ____________

3. The (vehicle) security system is faulty. ____________

4. The electronics store installed a hidden video camera to observe a suspected (thief) activities. ____________

5. We catch up on the (day) news by watching *CBC Newsworld* every night at 5. ____________

6. No matter the time of day, the (visitors) parking lot is always full. ____________

7. Did you look at (Jess) activity log for last week? ____________

8. Most (readers) letters supported the magazine's editorial position. ____________

9. Where is the (caller) message? ____________

10. All (authors) rights are protected by copyright law. ____________

Underline any errors in the following sentences, and write the correct form in the space provided. Write *C* if a sentence is correct.

11. The Gaps headquarters are as simple, clean, and comfortable as the company's clothing. ____________

12. The names of these customers are not alphabetized. ____________

13. Some of the countrys biggest manufacturers are being investigated. ____________

14. The common area's of the building were updated last year. ____________

15. Your organizations voice mail system is excellent. ____________

16. The vice presidents resignation left a vital position unfilled. ____________

17. Are all our clients records now electronic? ____________

18. I am prepared to protest the bill of my lawyer, William Glass. ____________

19. In three years time, the software paid for itself. ____________

20. Not a single farmers crop was undamaged by the storm. ____________

21. A citizens committee was formed to address parking problems. ____________

22. One years interest on the account amounted to $120. ____________

23. Each customers complimentary game tickets were mailed today. ____________

24. Our office is entering a womens baseball team in the insurance brokers league. ____________

25. New benefits for employees were announced in the supervisors memo. ____________

NAME ____________________

LEVEL II

Underline any errors in the following sentences, and write the correct form in the space provided. Write *C* if a sentence is correct.

1. The document required the notary publics signature and seal. ____________
2. Please contact our Sales' Department for a brochure. ____________
3. Olivia was sent to the printers to pick up her new business cards. ____________
4. My lawyer, Sandra Thom's, suggestion is to drop the lawsuit. ____________
5. The desk's top had to be refinished by a skilled woodworker. ____________
6. We borrowed my aunt's and uncle's motor home. ____________
7. All RNs' uniforms must now be identical. ____________
8. This month's expenses are somewhat less than last months. ____________
9. Debbie's and Julie's phones have similar song lists. ____________
10. The president's secretary's telephone number has been changed. ____________
11. Many CEO's, presidents, and other executives attended the event. ____________
12. My two brothers-in-law's beards are neat and well trimmed. ____________
13. The committee meeting will be held at Larrys. ____________
14. We spent our vacation enjoying Québecs' historical sights. ____________
15. Can you stop at the Phillipses to look at their clogged sink? ____________
16. The CBC's report on the vote was better than any other network's. ____________
17. Clark's and Clark's reference manual is outstanding. ____________
18. The Los Angeles' symphony planned an evening of Beethoven. ____________
19. The two architects licences were issued together. ____________
20. Our sales this year are greater than last years. ____________
21. Two PhDs applied for the job. ____________
22. Leo's and Ambreen's marriage licence was lost. ____________
23. The prime minister answered all the reporters questions carefully. ____________
24. Workers said they expected a days pay for an honest days work. ____________
25. Mei-Ling and Thien's new car came with a five-year warranty. ____________

NAME ____________________

LEVEL III

In the space provided, write the correct forms of the words shown in parentheses.

EXAMPLE: The (Jarvis) cat is missing. Jarvises'

1. When are the (Amara) expected? ________
2. Lee (Ross) office is on the south side of the campus. ________
3. Both (class) test results were misplaced. ________
4. Beth (Saunders) home is farther away than anyone else's. ________
5. Is anyone overseeing (Alex) work? ________
6. The (Cadiz) response is the only one we haven't received yet. ________
7. Only my (boss) desk is cluttered. ________
8. The other (boss) desks are rather neat. ________
9. Have the (Abramovich) picked up their order yet? ________
10. Several (actress) costumes were so valuable that insurance policies were taken out on them. ________
11. I think that is Mr. (Harris) parking spot you just took. ________
12. Ms. (Abbas) raise will be retroactive to February 1. ________
13. Who is (Elias) partner for the laboratory experiment? ________
14. That (waitress) section consists of four tables. ________
15. None of the (Garvey) belongings were missing. ________
16. Have you visited the (Morris) vacation home? ________
17. Only Mrs. (Betz) car remained in the parking lot. ________
18. Do you know if the (Vargas) house has sold yet? ________
19. Miss (Simons) new Internet connection provides better access. ________
20. Mr. (Jones) property is on Kelton Avenue. ________
21. The professor (emeritus) office was recently vacated. ________
22. Have you seen the (Williams) four-room tent that they took camping last weekend? ________
23. We heard that the (Kimball) house may be sold. ________
24. Visitors at Graceland swore they saw (Elvis) ghost. ________

NAME ______________________________

LEVEL I

Worksheet 1

List seven pronouns that could be used as subjects of verbs.

1. ____________ **4.** ____________ **7.** ____________

2. ____________ **5.** ____________

3. ____________ **6.** ____________

List seven pronouns that could be used as objects of verbs or objects of prepositions.

8. ____________ **11.** ____________ **14.** ____________

9. ____________ **12.** ____________

10. ____________ **13.** ____________

PRONOUNS AS SUBJECTS

Select the correct pronoun to complete each sentence below. All the omitted pronouns function as subjects of verbs.

15. I don't remember if (I, me) submitted any purchase requisitions. ____________

16. In the afternoon training session, (she, her) will make presentations. ____________

17. Will (he, him) be going to the sales meeting? ____________

18. It seems that (they, them) expect to see you Saturday. ____________

19. It is difficult to explain why (her, she) quit. ____________

20. Of all the applicants, only (we, us) agreed to be tested now. ____________

21. We believe that (she, her) deserves a raise. ____________

22. After (he, him) had returned, customers were handled more rapidly. ____________

23. Only (her, she) will participate in the demonstration. ____________

24. After the spring sales campaign, (he, him), along with two others, will be promoted. ____________

25. Because I am most familiar with the project, (I, me) should complete the report. ____________

NAME ________________

Worksheet 2

PERSONAL PRONOUNS AS OBJECTS

Select the correct pronoun to complete each sentence below. All the omitted pronouns function as objects of verbs or prepositions. Prepositions have been underlined to help you identify them.

1. Just <u>between</u> you and (I, me), our branch won the sales trophy. ________

2. Has anyone contacted (he, him)? ________

3. We hope to show (they, them) the billing procedure this afternoon. ________

4. Everybody <u>but</u> (I, me) is ready to leave. ________

5. Have you talked <u>with</u> (her, she) about this change? ________

6. We need more workers <u>like</u> (him, he) to finish the job. ________

7. All supervisors <u>except</u> (her, she) approved the plan. ________

8. This insurance program provides (they, them) with equal benefits. ________

9. Terms of the settlement were satisfactory <u>to</u> (we, us). ________

10. Every operator <u>but</u> (I, me) had an opportunity for overtime. ________

POSSESSIVE-CASE PRONOUNS

Remember that possessive-case pronouns (*yours, his, hers, its, whose, theirs,* etc.) do not contain apostrophes. Do not confuse these pronouns with the following contractions: *it's* (it is, it has), *there's* (there is, there has), *who's* (who is, who has), and *you're* (you are). In the following sentences, select the correct word.

11. Do you think (its, it's) necessary for us to sign in? ________

12. Is (theirs, their's) the white house at the end of the street? ________

13. The contract and all (its, it's) provisions must be examined. ________

14. They admitted that the mistake was (there's, theirs). ________

15. Jack's car and (hers, her's) are the only ones left in the lot. ________

16. The cheque is good only if (its, it's) signed. ________

17. (You're, Your) taking Don's place, aren't you? ________

18. (Who's, Whose) umbrella is that lying in the corner? ________

19. Most car registrations were sent April 1, but (our's, ours) was delayed. ________

20. The bank dropped (its, it's) lending rate overnight. ________

NAME ______________________________

LEVEL II

Select the correct pronoun to complete these sentences.

1. Do you expect Mr. Jefferson and (they, them) to meet you? ______________
2. No one could regret the error more than (I, me, myself). ______________
3. These photocopies were prepared by Ari and (she, her). ______________
4. (We, Us) policyholders are entitled to group discounts. ______________
5. Gil thought the advertisement to be as effective as (I, me, myself). ______________
6. Universal Parcel is hiring James and (I, me, myself) for the summer. ______________
7. Have you corresponded with the authors, Dr. Lee and (she, her)? ______________
8. On that project no one works as hard as (he, him, himself). ______________
9. Everyone but Mr. Foster and (he, him) can help customers if necessary. ______________
10. My winning the customer service award pleased my manager as much as (I, me, myself). ______________
11. Only Erik (he, himself, hisself) knows what is best for him. ______________
12. We asked two women, Denise and (she, her), to come along. ______________
13. The responsibility for making the decision belongs to Aideen and (she, her). ______________
14. Miss Greerson thinks that Mr. Campbell is a better salesperson than (she, her). ______________
15. All property claims must be submitted to my lawyer or (I, me, myself) before April 15. ______________
16. The new contract is acceptable to both management and (us, we, ourselves). ______________
17. None of the other managers are as difficult to please as (he, him). ______________
18. The best time for you and (he, him) to enrol is in January. ______________
19. You, (I, me, myself), and Laura should meet soon about the project. ______________
20. Everyone except Kevin and (I, me, myself) was able to join the program. ______________
21. It seems as though (they, them) in Marketing have already made the decision. ______________
22. (She and I, Her and me, Her and I) are among the best-qualified candidates. ______________
23. Have you invited Jon and (she, her, herself) to our picnic? ______________
24. Most of the email messages sent to (us, we) employees are considered spam. ______________
25. Only Gurpreet and (I, me, myself) were given company cellphones. ______________

NAME ______________________

LEVEL III

Worksheet 1

Remember that pronouns that rename the subject and that follow linking verbs must be in the subjective case (it *was he who placed the order*). When the infinitive *to be* has no subject (which must immediately precede the infinitive *to be*), the pronoun that follows must be in the subjective, or nominative, case (*my sister is often taken to be I*). *No* subject = *no*minative.

In the following sentences, select the correct word.

1. It must have been (her, she) who called this morning. ____________

2. I certainly would not like to be (he, him). ____________

3. Do you think that it was (they, them) who complained? ____________

4. The store's owner is (she, her). ____________

5. The employee to get the promotion was expected to be (he, him). ____________

6. If you were (she, her), would you take the job? ____________

7. No one had guessed the culprits to be (they, them). ____________

8. Shirati said that yesterday's driver could have been (he, him). ____________

9. Miss Soriano asked Frank and (I, me, myself) to help her. ____________

10. Was it (they, them) who made the contribution? ____________

11. The hardest worker seems to be (he, him). ____________

12. Producer Edwards would not allow me to be (he, him) in the production. ____________

13. Mr. Fox wants to assign you and (her, she) the project. ____________

14. Are you sure it was (I, me) who was called to the phone? ____________

15. The surprise guest was thought to be (she, her). ____________

16. If it had not been (she, her) who made the announcement, I would not have believed it. ____________

17. How could anyone have thought that Margaret was (I, me)? ____________

18. I do not wish to discourage either you or (he, him). ____________

19. If anyone is disappointed, it will be (I, me, myself). ____________

20. If the real estate agent were (I, me, myself), the house would have sold by now. ____________

21. Do you think it was (her, she) who made the large contribution? ____________

22. Mr. Egal selected you and (he, him) because of his confidence in your abilities. ____________

23. If it had been (she, her), we would have recognized her immediately. ____________

24. None of us were surprised to learn the recipient of the award was (she, her). ____________

NAME ______________________

Worksheet 2

Select the correct word to complete the following sentences.

1. Only the president and (he, him) can grant leaves of absence. ________
2. The manager mistook Danielle to be (I, me). ________
3. The Roomba vacuum has sensors that guide it back to (its, it's) docking station. ________
4. Our staff agreed that you and (she, her) should represent us. ________
5. How can you believe (us, we) to be guilty? ________
6. Was the chosen campaign (their's, theirs, there's)? ________
7. An announcement was made that the new manager is (he, him). ________
8. My friend and (I, me) looked for jobs together. ________
9. This matter will be kept strictly between you and (I, me). ________
10. Good students like you and (she, her) are always prepared. ________
11. We need someone to speak up for (we, us) users of the product. ________
12. We agreed that (your, you're) the best person for the job. ________
13. Send the announcement to Ms. Nguyen and (she, her) today. ________
14. All office staff except Kim and (he, him) have requested that week off. ________
15. Many locker combinations are listed, but (your's, yours) is missing. ________
16. Apparently the message was intended for you and (I, me, myself). ________
17. Was it (he, him, himself) who ordered the sample? ________
18. The bank is closed, but (it's, its) ATM is open. ________
19. Please submit the report to (him or me, he or I) before May 1. ________
20. When (there's, theirs) help needed at the cash, a customer service associate can jump in. ________
21. For you and (he, him), I would suggest careers in marketing. ________
22. These personnel changes affect you and (I, me, myself) directly. ________
23. Do you or (she, her) have first-aid training? ________
24. Only two branches plan to expand (they're, their) display rooms. ________
25. The operator thought it was (she, her) calling for assistance. ________
26. Because you are a member of the audit review team, you have a better overall picture of the operations than (I, me, myself). ________
27. Though you may not agree with our decision, I hope you'll support Todd and (I, me, myself) in our effort to get the job done. ________

6 PRONOUNS AND ANTECEDENTS SELF-HELP EXERCISES

NAME ______________________________

LEVEL I

Pronouns must agree with the words for which they substitute. Don't let words and phrases that come between a pronoun and its antecedent confuse you.

EXAMPLES: Every one of the women had *her* forms ready. (Not *their.*)
The supervisor, along with four assistants, offered *his* support. (Not their.)

Select the correct word(s) to complete these sentences.

1. Cheng told Mr. Mei that (he, Cheng) needed his eyes checked. ____________

2. Employees must have (his, her, his or her, their) physical examinations completed by December 31. ____________

3. After a job well done, everyone appreciates (his, her, his or her, their) share of credit. ____________

4. A soldier puts (his, her, his or her, their) life on the line just by enlisting. ____________

5. Individuals like Mr. Herndon can always be depended on to do (his, his or her, their) best in all assignments. ____________

6. If a policyholder has a legitimate claim, (he, she, he or she, they) should contact us immediately. ____________

7. An employee who is paid hourly and takes public transit to work can be reimbursed a percentage of (his, her, his or her, their) monthly travel expenses. ____________

8. If one of the interns is in today, I have some work (he, she, he or she, they) can do. ____________

9. Carolyn Davis, along with several other company employees, volunteered to donate some of (his, her, his or her, their) time this weekend to the fund-raiser. ____________

10. A few members of the touring group, in addition to the guide, wanted (his or her picture, their pictures) taken. ____________

11. One of the team members left (his, her, his or her, their) notebook in the boardroom. ____________

12. Leah, as well as several of the store's sales associates, has asked that (her, his or her, their) wages be reviewed. ____________

Rewrite this sentence to avoid the use of a common-gender pronoun. Show three versions.

Every employee must obtain his parking permit in the supervisor's office.

13. ______________________________

14. ______________________________

15. ______________________________

NAME ______________________

LEVEL II

Underline any pronoun–antecedent errors in the following sentences. Then write a corrected form in the space provided. Write *C* if a sentence is correct.

1. Last Friday either Miss Monahan or Miss Chavez left their machine on. ____________

2. Every player on the men's team enjoys their time on the field. ____________

3. Every clerk, manager, and executive will be expected to do their part in making the carpooling program a success. ____________

4. Somebody left his cellphone in the tray at the airport security check. ____________

5. Neither one of the men wanted to have their remarks quoted. ____________

6. Anyone who takes public transit to work can be reimbursed a percentage of his monthly travel expenses. ____________

7. Mrs. Nagar, along with many other members of the staff, sent her best wishes. ____________

8. Each of the pieces of equipment came with their own software. ____________

9. The firm of Higgins, Thomas, & Keene is moving their offices to Warner Plaza. ____________

10. Every manager expects the employees who report to them to be willing to earn their salaries. ____________

11. Neither of the women had her driver's licence in the car. ____________

12. We hoped that someone in the office could find their copy of the program. ____________

13. We look forward to speaking to either a board member or the board chair and getting their input. ____________

14. If everybody will please take their seats, we can get started. ____________

15. The faculty agreed to publicize their position on budget cuts. ____________

16. Did you see that HomeCo reduced their prices on lawn mowers? ____________

17. Few of the colour printers had the sale price marked on it. ____________

18. Every one of the office employees, as well as many of the executives, agreed to let students ask them about the experience of working here. ____________

19. The marketing team is asking other departments for feedback on their idea. ____________

20. All managers and employees know that she or he must boost productivity. ____________

NAME ______________________________

LEVEL III

Worksheet 1

In selecting *who* or *whom* to complete the sentences below, follow these five steps:

EXAMPLE: We do not know (who, whom) the contract names.

1. Isolate the *who* clause: (*who, whom*) the contract names.
2. Invert to normal subject–verb order: the contract names (*who, whom*).
3. Substitute pronouns: the contract names *him*/the contract names *her.*
4. Equate: the contract names *whom.*
5. Complete: We do not know *whom* the contract names.

1. (Who, Whom) will you invite to your party? ____________

2. Rick Nash is the employee (who, whom) the CEO asked to present to the board. ____________

3. Do you know (who, whom) will be taking your place? ____________

4. To (who, whom) did she refer in her letter? ____________

5. Has Ling told you (who, whom) she nominated for the customer service award? ____________

6. Dr. Truong is a man (who, whom) everyone respects. ____________

7. I know of no one else (who, whom) plays so well. ____________

8. With (who, whom) do you want to work? ____________

9. (Who, Whom) has the best chance to be elected? ____________

10. The person (who, whom) I'm taking to the banquet is Teresa. ____________

In choosing *who* or *whom* to complete these sentences, ignore parenthetical clauses such as *I think, we know, you feel,* and *I believe.*

11. Julie is a person (who, whom) I know will be successful in that role. ____________

12. The human resources director hired an individual (who, whom) he thought would be the best performer. ____________

13. Is Luke Hastings the dealer (who, whom) you think I should call? ____________

14. The entrepreneur (who, whom) I feel should win the contest is Nadia. ____________

15. (Who, Whom) do you believe will be given the job? ____________

NAME ______________________

Worksheet 2

In the following sentences, selecting *who, whom, whoever,* or *whomever* first requires isolating the clause within which the pronoun appears. Then, within the clause, determine whether a subjective-case (*who, whoever*) or objective-case (*whom, whomever*) pronoun is required.

EXAMPLE: Give the package to (whoever, whomever) opens the door. (*He* or *she* opens the door = *whoever* opens the door.) whoever

1. A bonus will be given to (whoever, whomever) sells over $100,000. ______
2. Discuss the problem with (whoever, whomever) is in charge of the program. ______
3. We will interview (whoever, whomever) you recommend. ______
4. You may give the tickets to (whoever, whomever) you wish. ______
5. Johnson said to give the parking pass to (whoever, whomever) asked for it. ______
6. (Whoever, Whomever) the manager called in to take Joey's shift didn't show up. ______
7. Please call (whoever, whomever) you believe can repair the machine. ______
8. (Whoever, Whomever) accepts the job must agree to a police check. ______
9. I would like to meet with (whoever, whomever) Professor Hammond provided a reference for. ______
10. (Whoever, Whomever) is chosen to lead the delegation will command attention at the convention. ______

In choosing *who* or *whom* to complete these sentences, be especially alert to pronouns following the linking verbs. Remember that the subjective *who* is required as a subject complement.

EXAMPLE: Was it (who, whom) I thought it was? (It was *he* = *who*.) who

11. (Who, Whom) needs the replacement battery? ______
12. The visitor who asked for me was (who, whom)? ______
13. Is the newly appointed CEO (who, whom) we thought it would be? ______
14. As a career counsellor, Cheryl will coach (whoever, whomever) is at a professional crossroads. ______
15. For (who, whom) is this new printer? ______

NAME ____________________

Worksheet 3

In the following sentences, select the correct word.

1. (Who, Whom) did you call for assistance? ____________
2. Edward Lincoln, (who, whom) we thought would never be hired, did well in his first assignment. ____________
3. To (who, whom) did you send your résumé? ____________
4. You should hire (whoever, whomever) you feel has the best qualifications. ____________
5. Did the client say (who, whom) he wanted to see? ____________
6. The man (who, whom) I talked to yesterday came in again today. ____________
7. (Whoever, Whomever) is first on the list will be called next. ____________
8. The sales rep sent notices to customers (who, whom) she felt should be notified. ____________
9. The Marketing Department has not yet figured out exactly (who, whom) the target customer is. ____________
10. The manager praised the clerk (who, whom) worked late. ____________
11. She is the one (who, whom) Jenny helped yesterday. ____________
12. Several people have speculated to (who, whom) Mr. Huong's email was directed. ____________
13. (Who, Whom) is Stacy often mistaken to be? ____________
14. (Who, Whom) did you say to call for reservations? ____________
15. Please make an appointment with (whoever, whomever) you consider to be the best dentist. ____________
16. Here is a list of satisfied customers (who, whom) you may wish to contact. ____________
17. (Whoever, Whomever) is suggested by Mr. Arthur must be interviewed. ____________
18. No matter (who's, whose) name is on the ballot, I know which party will get my vote. ____________
19. Jan is one person on (who, whom) I have come to depend. ____________
20. (Who, Whom) do you think the government will offer the contract to? ____________
21. Do you know (whose, who's) jacket this is? ____________
22. Do you know (who, whom) their sales representative is? ____________
23. We're not sure (whose, who's) signed up for Friday's seminar. ____________
24. The copywriter is a man (who, whom) Sibyl knows from her previous job. ____________
25. You'll never guess (whose, who's) running for city council! ____________

NAME ______________________

LEVEL I

Select the correct verb.

1. Did you tell me that your brother's name (is, was) Martin? ______________

2. The accident (occured, occurred) late last evening. ______________

3. Nobody I asked knew where your office (is, was) located. ______________

4. Are you sure that her maiden name (is, was) Spitnale? ______________

5. We were taught that an ounce of prevention (is, was) worth a pound of cure. ______________

In the space provided, write the correct form of the verb indicated in parentheses.

EXAMPLE: Joan (carry) a heavy workload every day. (present tense) carries

6. The first Kentucky Fried Chicken franchise (open) in Japan in 1970. (past) ______________

7. Each year KFC's best sales in Japan (occur) on Christmas Eve. (present) ______________

8. Because of the restaurant's popularity at Christmas, many people (reserve) a bucket two months in advance. (future) ______________

9. The marketing director (study) possible sales sites in foreign countries. (past) ______________

10. We (analyze) such factors as real estate, construction costs, and local attitudes toward fast food. (future) ______________

11. Management (apply) a complex formula to forecast the profitability of the new business. (past) ______________

12. We (consider) the vast differences between the two cultures. (past) ______________

13. Each local franchise (vary) the side dishes to accommodate cultural preferences. (present) ______________

14. Kentucky Fried Chicken (insist) on retaining its original recipe in foreign stores. (present) ______________

15. Because of a potato shortage, however, KFC (have) to stop offering french fries. (future) ______________

16. Doing business in Japan (require) appreciation of rituals and formalities. (present) ______________

17. When you visit East Asia, the presentation of business cards (demand) special attention to ceremony. (future) ______________

18. Western business people (try) to observe local customs. (past) ______________

NAME ____________________

LEVEL II

Select the correct helping verb from the options in parentheses.

EXAMPLE: We all (were, had, will) wanted to attend, but there was room for only three. had

1. The notice left on the door (is, has, will) need to be brought to the post office. ____________
2. The managers (are, have, will) meeting secretly down the hall. ____________
3. Most of our employees (are, have, will) replied to the workplace satisfaction survey. ____________
4. Chief Hacquin (was, had, will) commenting on our leadership in his speech. ____________
5. None of the proposed solutions (were, had, will) work. ____________

Keep your textbook handy so that you can look up the verb forms required in the following sentences.

EXAMPLE: By June 1 you (employ) here one full year. (future perfect, passive) will have been employed

6. McDonald's (open) many restaurants in foreign countries. (present perfect) ____________
7. The committee (plan) several team activities. (present progressive) ____________
8. We (call) for service at least three times before a technician arrived. (past perfect) ____________
9. She (work) on that project for the past six months. (present perfect) ____________
10. We (shop) when the storm began. (past progressive) ____________
11. The mayor (sign) the proclamation at this afternoon's public ceremony. (future progressive) ____________
12. The bulldozer working on street repairs (broke) the water main. (present perfect) ____________
13. I (see) two buses pass me by the time I reached the bus stop. (past perfect) ____________
14. We (consider) the installation of a new email system. (present progressive) ____________
15. The Queen's message (hear) all across Canada. (past progressive, passive) ____________

NAME ______________________

LEVEL III

Worksheet 1

Select the correct verb.

1. The condition of the streets has (became, become) intolerable. ______
2. Water (froze, freezed) in the pipes last night. ______
3. Have you (seeked, sought) work with our company in the past? ______
4. Has a location for the new equipment been (chose, chosen)? ______
5. Three new homes were recently (build, built) on Fairfax Avenue. ______
6. The TV commercial was (sang, sung) by an actress whose lips didn't match the soundtrack. ______
7. We must have (forgot, forgotten) the keys. ______
8. Nobody else I know has (took, taken) the Medical College Admission Test. ______
9. André and the others had (went, gone) for lunch earlier. ______
10. Celine was sick for a week after she was (bit, bitten) by an insect in the tropics. ______

Underline any errors in the following sentences. Write the correct form in the space provided. Write *C* if a sentence is correct. Do not add helping verbs.

EXAMPLE: After we <u>run</u> out of food, we had to return to camp headquarters. ran

11. We had ate a small snack before we ordered dinner. ______
12. When Mario went to the fridge for his lunch, he found that half his iced tea had been drank. ______
13. Mr. Gazdik was stricken just as he left the witness stand. ______
14. Hundreds of mushrooms sprung up after the rain. ______
15. Many people were shook by the company's sale yesterday. ______
16. Tracy has wore her stylish new boots only twice. ______
17. He had already wrote a large portion of his report before leaving. ______
18. Jamal's car was stole from the parking lot. ______
19. Since the traffic was so bad, you should have took the subway to work. ______
20. If we had went to the conference, we would have received free concert tickets, too. ______

NAME ______________________________

Worksheet 2

LIE–LAY

Use the chart below to help you select the correct form of *lie* or *lay* in these sentences.

Present	Past	Past Participle	Present Participle
lie (rest)	lay (rested)	lain (have, has, or had rested)	lying (resting)
lay (place)	laid (placed)	laid (have, has, or had placed)	laying (placing)

EXAMPLE: This afternoon I must (rest) down before dinner. lie

1. I am sure that I (placed) the report on your desk yesterday. ____________
2. The obedient dog (rested) down on command. ____________
3. This month's bills have been (resting) in the drawer for weeks. ____________
4. Bill has (placed) his receipts in Rumi's receipts folder. ____________
5. The worker was (placing) concrete blocks for the foundation. ____________
6. This evening I must (rest) down before we leave. ____________
7. Yesterday I (rested) on my bed for an hour before dinner. ____________
8. (Place) the papers in the stack over there. ____________
9. The files in that cabinet have (rested) there for years without anyone looking at them. ____________
10. Let the painting (rest) there for several hours until it dries completely. ____________

Now try these sentences to test your skill in using the forms of *lie* and *lay.*

11. Will you be able to (lie, lay) down before dinner? ____________
12. How long have these papers been (laying, lying) here? ____________
13. You can just (lie, lay) your bag there. ____________
14. Will the mason (lay, lie) bricks over the concrete patio? ____________
15. The contract has (laid, lain) on his desk for over two months. ____________
16. Yesterday I (laid, lay) back in my chair and fell asleep. ____________
17. It is important not to leave sensitive documents (laying, lying) around. ____________
18. Returned books (lie, lay) in a pile at the library until the staff can return them to the stacks. ____________
19. I'm sure I (laid, layed, lied) my keys on this counter. ____________
20. When you were (lying, laying) the new carpet, did you remove the baseboards? ____________

NAME ____________________

LEVEL I

Fill in the answers to the following questions with information found in your text.

1. What kind of action verb directs action toward a person or thing (transitive or intransitive)? ____________
2. What kind of action verb does not require an object to complete its action (transitive or intransitive)? ____________
3. What kind of verb joins the subject to a word or words that rename or describe the subject (action, linking, or helping)? ____________
4. What do we call the nouns, pronouns, and adjectives used with linking verbs to complete the meaning of a sentence by renaming or describing the subject? ____________

In each of the following sentences, indicate whether the underlined verb is transitive (*T*), intransitive (*I*), or linking (*L*). In addition, if the verb is transitive, write its object. If the verb is linking, write its complement. The first two sentences are followed by explanations to assist you.

5. James ran along the dirt path back to his home. (The verb *ran* is intransitive. It has no object to complete its meaning. The prepositional phrase *along the dirt path* tells where James ran; it does not receive the action of the verb.) ______I______
6. The caller might have been Fran. (The verb phrase ends with the linking verb *been*. The complement is *Fran*, which renames the subject *caller*.) ______L______
7. Jane added the addresses of our most recent customers to our records. ____________
8. Customers crowded into the store at the beginning of the sale. ____________
9. Sherry was a consultant on the software conversion project. ____________
10. Levi Strauss first sold pants to miners in San Francisco in the 1800s. ____________
11. The house sold for $30,000 above the asking price. ____________
12. Chocolate fudge ice cream tastes better than chocolate mint. ____________
13. Do you think it was he who suggested the improvement? ____________
14. Our new business cards arrived just in time for the conference. ____________
15. Our company recruiter asks the same questions of every candidate. ____________
16. Many corporations present gifts to important foreign clients. ____________
17. This dictionary is the best on the market for office workers. ____________
18. Vijay listened carefully to the customer's concerns about the product. ____________
19. Ellen feels justified in asking for a raise. ____________
20. Customers have high expectations for most advertised products. ____________

NAME ______________________________

LEVEL II

Worksheet 1

Transitive verbs direct action toward something. In the active voice, the subject performs the action; in the passive voice, the subject receives the action. Writing that incorporates active-voice verbs is more vigorous and more efficient than writing that contains many passive-voice verbs. To convert a passive-voice verb to the active voice, look for the doer of the action. (Generally the agent of the action is contained in a *by* phrase.) In the active voice, the agent becomes the subject.

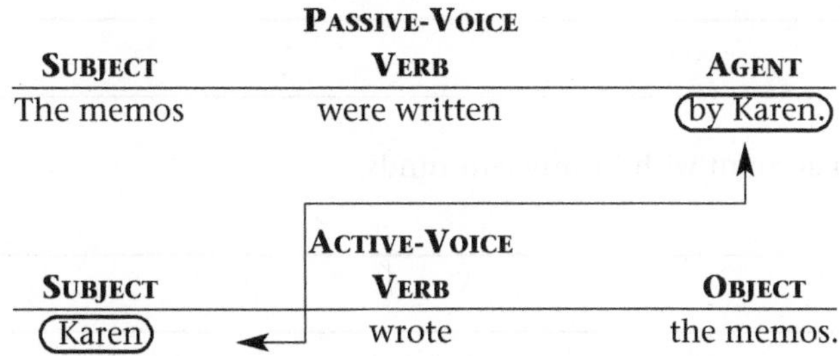

For each of the following sentences, underline the agent (doer of the action). Write that word in the space provided. Then rewrite the sentence changing the passive-voice verb to active voice. Your rewritten version should begin with the word (and its modifiers) that you identified as the doer of the action.

Agent

1. The text message was not picked up by Mariam until Monday morning. ____________

____

____

2. Several franchises were visited last week by head office. ____________

____

____

3. Withdrawals must now be authorized by Mrs. Bradford. ____________

____

____

4. Sandip was asked by Mr. Stern to be responsible for turning out the lights at the end of the day. ____________

____

____

5. Employees who travel a great deal were forced by management to surrender their frequent-flyer awards. ____________

____

____

NAME ____________________

Worksheet 2

Some sentences with passive-voice verbs do not identify the doer of the action. Before these sentences can be converted, a subject must be provided. Use your imagination to supply subjects, and rewrite the sentences in the spaces provided.

Passive: Interest will be paid on all deposits. (*By whom?* By CIBC.)
Active: CIBC will pay interest on all deposits.

By Whom?

1. The transition must be completed by 3 p.m. ____________

2. Cheques were written on an account with insufficient funds. ____________

3. Our computer was programmed to total account balances. ____________

4. Decisions are made in the courts that affect the daily lives of all Canadians. ____________

5. Cash discounts are given for payments made with cash or debit card. ____________

6. Employees working with computers were warned to change their passwords frequently. ____________

7. Our accounting records were scrutinized during the audit. ____________

NAME ______________________

LEVEL III

Write the correct answers in the space provided.

1. If I (was, were) you, I would complete my degree first. ______
2. The human resources director recommended that Jeff (be, is) hired with the condition that he continue college courses at night. ______
3. If Mr. Greer (was, were) in the office yesterday, he did not sign the cheques. ______
4. One of the shareholders moved that a committee (be, is) constituted to study the problem immediately. ______
5. If the manager were here, he (will, would) sign the work order and we could proceed. ______
6. Government officials recommend that all homes (are, be) stocked with an emergency supply of food and water. ______
7. Téo wishes that he (was, were) qualified for the job. ______
8. It is important that you (are, be) on time for the interview. ______
9. Dr. Washington suggested that the patient (rest, rests) for the next two days. ______
10. If the sale of the company (was, were) to go through, would you stay? ______
11. If Mrs. Balfour (was, were) in my position, she would probably do the same thing. ______
12. Liz suggested that the driver's route (is, be) changed to incorporate a stop at Quikmart. ______
13. Under the circumstances, even if the voter registration drive (was, were) successful, we might lose the election. ______
14. The professor recommended that everyone (meet, meets) in the parking lot before the field trip. ______
15. He acts as though he (was, were) the only employee who has to work this weekend. ______
16. It is important that Gene (receives, receive) your full co-operation during the audit. ______
17. If the fax machine (was, were) working, you could have the figures immediately. ______
18. If Ron (was, were) at the sales meeting, I missed him. ______
19. Laurie uses credit cards as if she (was, were) an heiress. ______
20. It has been moved and seconded that the meeting (is, be) adjourned. ______

NAME ______________________________

LEVEL I

Worksheet 1

For each of the following sentences, cross out any phrase that comes between a verb and its subject. Then select the correct verb and write it in the space provided.

EXAMPLE: One ~~of the most interesting books on all the lists~~ (is, are) *Becoming a Millionaire at 21.* ___is___

1. Many websites on the prohibited list at our office (provide, provides) games or amusement. ______
2. The supervisor, together with two technicians, (is, are) working on the faulty circuit. ______
3. The problem with the fuel injectors (seem, seems) to be too much sediment buildup. ______
4. A good many workers in addition to Mirva (think, thinks) the work shifts should be rearranged. ______
5. Everyone except you and John (is, are) being sent out of province for further training. ______
6. The table as well as two chairs (was, were) damaged. ______
7. A list with all the customers' names and addresses (is, are) being sent. ______
8. Other equipment, such as our terminals and printers, (need, needs) to be re-evaluated. ______
9. One of our best customers (comes, come) in every Saturday. ______
10. Several copies of the report (is, are) being prepared for distribution. ______
11. The furniture, as well as all the printers and computers, (is, are) for sale. ______
12. Adverse effects of the medication (is, are) not yet known. ______
13. Mr. Nakamura and his daughter and wife (is, are) moving to Fredericton. ______
14. The profits from his home-based business (is, are) surprising. ______
15. Every one of the potential businesses that you mention (sounds, sound) good. ______
16. A shipment of 8,000 drill sets (was, were) sent to the warehouse. ______
17. Everyone other than the evening employees (is, are) coming. ______
18. Replacement of the printer's four toner cartridges (costs, cost) nearly $400. ______
19. Officials in several levels of government (has, have) to be consulted. ______
20. A letter together with several enclosures (was, were) mailed yesterday. ______

NAME ____________________

Worksheet 2

For each of the following sentences, underline the simple subject. Then select the correct verb and write it in the space provided.

EXAMPLE: Here (is, are) a <u>copy</u> of the findings for your files. ___is___

Suggestion: If you know that a subject is singular, temporarily substitute *he, she,* or *it* to help you select the proper verb. If you know that a subject is plural, temporarily substitute *they* for the subject.

1. Industrial goods (travel, travels) through different distribution channels than do consumer goods. ________
2. Here (is, are) the book and magazines you ordered. ________
3. Coleman, Harris & Juarez, Inc., one of the leading management consultant firms, (is, are) able to accept our business. ________
4. Our new division in the Prairies (open, opens) next month. ________
5. There (appear, appears) to be many significant points omitted from the report. ________
6. The various stages in the life cycle of a product (is, are) instrumental in determining profits for that product. ________
7. Hydro bills, because of a fixed-rate distribution charge, (is, are) rising. ________
8. "14 Interview Questions That Are Actually Illegal" (offer, offers) important information for job seekers and interviewers alike. ________
9. The size and design of its container (is, are) influential in the appeal of a product. ________
10. Just one representative from each of the seven teams (has, have) to approach the podium. ________
11. WestJet (has, have) been able to increase service while cutting costs. ________
12. Only two seasons of the year (provide, provides) weather that is suitable for gliding. ________
13. (Has, Have) the Wongs' moving van arrived yet? ________
14. At present the condition of the company's finances (is, are) extremely strong as a result of the recent bond sale. ________
15. Incoming mail from three flights (is, are) now being sorted. ________
16. Sitting with our CEO and president at Table 1 (is, are) the mayor. ________
17. One of the best designs (appear, appears) to belong to your student. ________
18. Aggressiveness and delinquency in boys (is, are) linked to high levels of lead in their bones, according to a recent study. ________
19. Certainly the ease and convenience of shopping at any hour of the day or night—and getting fast delivery without ever leaving home—(is, are) very appealing. ________

NAME ______________________

LEVEL II

For each of the following sentences, underline the simple subject. Then select the correct verb and write it in the space provided.

1. Most of the salary compensation to which he referred (is, are) beyond basic pay schedules. ________
2. The Committee on Youth Activities (has, have) enlisted the aid of several well-known athletes. ________
3. Each of the young men and women (deserve, deserves) an opportunity to participate in local athletics. ________
4. Either your company or one of your two competitors (is, are) going to win the government contract. ________
5. No one except the Cunninghams (was, were) able to volunteer. ________
6. Neither of the two small businesses (is, are) able to secure a loan. ________
7. Every employee and guest (receive, receives) a gift bag at the party. ________
8. Neither the packing list nor the two invoices (mention, mentions) the missing ottoman. ________
9. Every one of your suggestions (merit, merits) consideration. ________
10. Our survey shows that every one of the owner-managed businesses (was, were) turning a profit. ________
11. Either Steven or you (is, are) expected to return the call. ________
12. None of the ceiling sprinklers (seem, seems) to be working. ________
13. Mrs. Roberts said that most of the credit for our increased sales (belong, belongs) to you. ________
14. The group of Indo-European folk dancers (is, are) first on the program. ________
15. Some of the enthusiasm (is, are) due to the coming holiday. ________
16. After 10 p.m. the staff (has, have) to use the front entrance only. ________
17. (Is, Are) any of the resort's pools saltwater? ________
18. The union (has, have) come to an agreement with management. ________
19. The employees and management (has, have) to do their part to make the workplace better. ________
20. Most of the packages that were sent out four days ago (has, have) been signed for. ________

NAME ______________________

LEVEL III

Select the correct word for each of the following sentences.

1. Reed says that 25 metres of plastic pipe (has, have) been ordered. ______
2. The number of women in executive positions (is, are) steadily increasing. ______
3. Phillip said that he is one of those individuals who (enjoy, enjoys) a real challenge. ______
4. Over two-thirds of the stock issue (was, were) sold immediately after it was released. ______
5. One of the caterers who (is, are) bidding on the job hosts a cooking show. ______
6. That most offices are closed on weekends (put, puts) a wrench in our plans. ______
7. The majority of the employees (favour, favours) the reorganization plan. ______
8. Plants (is, are) a nice addition to any room. ______
9. At least four-fifths of the women in the audience (is, are) willing to participate in the show. ______
10. How could it be I who (am, is) responsible when I had no knowledge of the agreement until yesterday? ______
11. A number of shipments (has, have) been detained at the border. ______
12. Employee health and safety (is, are) a top priority of ours. ______
13. Are you one of those people who (like, likes) to sleep late? ______
14. I'm sure that it is you who (is, are) next on the list. ______
15. It looks as if 50 centimetres of extra cord (is, are) what we need. ______
16. The market for our jeans that (flatters, flatter) every shape is boundless. ______
17. At least one-third of the desserts purchased for the party (was, were) uneaten. ______
18. Hiking in Europe and sailing to Scandinavia (is, are) what I plan for my future vacations. ______
19. Rajina Paramanathan is the only one of our customers who consistently (respond, responds) to our surveys. ______
20. Whoever submitted an application earliest (has, have) the right to be interviewed first. ______

NAME ____________________

LEVEL I

A verb form ending in *ing* and used as a noun is a **gerund**.

Passing the examination is important. (Gerund used as a subject.)

A noun or pronoun modifying a gerund should be possessive.

Your passing the examination is important.

Don't confuse verbals acting as nouns with those acting as adjectives.

The man *selling* the car is good at his job. (*Selling* functions as an adjective describing *man*.)

The man's *selling* the car is necessary for him to be paid. (Verbal noun *selling* functions as the subject of the verb *is*.)

In the following sentences, underline any gerunds and write their modifiers in the space provided. If a sentence contains no gerund, write *None*.

EXAMPLE: It is your smoking that disturbs the others. ____Your____

1. This job offer is contingent on your passing our physical examination. ________
2. Our office certainly did not approve of his investing in high-risk securities. ________
3. It was Mr. Cortina's gambling that caused him to lose his job. ________
4. The delivery driver running the red light was stopped by police. ________

Some of the remaining sentences contain gerunds. If any error appears in the modifier, underline the error and write the correct form in the space provided. Write *C* if a sentence is correct.

EXAMPLE: Mrs. Feng was instrumental in us acquiring the Collins account. ____our____

5. His recent award is directly related to Mr. Frank receiving a promotion. ________
6. The person sitting beside me wouldn't stop talking throughout the presentation. ________
7. Do you think you criticizing the manager had anything to do with your transfer? ________
8. We appreciate him calling to give us the news. ________
9. Was the bank handling of the situation satisfactory? ________
10. It appears that us contacting the company directly is the only logical action to take at this time. ________
11. An employee taking a message must write clearly. ________
12. Mrs. Fackler said that me working overtime this weekend is unnecessary. ________
13. The employees working overtime this week will receive their overtime pay in next month's cheques. ________

NAME ______________________________

LEVEL II

A verbal form used as an adjective (to describe or modify nouns or pronouns) is a **participle**. When a participle, either as a separate word or as part of a phrase, introduces an independent clause, the participle or its phrase should be followed by a comma. When a phrase containing a participle interrupts the flow of a sentence with non-essential information, it should be set off with commas. The following sentences are punctuated correctly. Underline the participles and participial phrases.

1. Constructed in 2018, MPK 21 is the second building Canadian architect Frank Gehry designed for Facebook's Menlo Park campus.
2. Surrounded, the enemy troops raised a white flag.
3. Mr. Wilson, seeing his opportunity, brought up the subject of employee fringe benefits.
4. Our new records management system, installed just two months ago, is saving us money.
5. Miss Strawn, rereading the article several times, could not believe her eyes.
6. Speaking in front of the large crowd, Mike felt more nervous than he'd expected to.
7. Irritated, the manager raised his voice.
8. A person opening a new account is required to have a valid signature card on file.

For each of the following sentences, add any commas necessary to punctuate verbal forms or phrases. In the space provided, write the comma(s) and preceding words. Write *C* if a sentence is correct.

EXAMPLE: Comptroller Duffy restricted by federal guidelines revised many budget procedures. ____Duffy, guidelines,____

9. After choosing a model we placed our equipment order. ____________
10. The Hammonds having cashed in their tax-free savings accounts went shopping for a recreational vehicle. ____________
11. Reading a stock market tickertape requires some training. ____________
12. Displaying security transactions large tickertape screens may be found in most brokerage houses. ____________
13. An executive representing a local brokerage firm called me. ____________
14. Terry downloading the feature sheet wanted more information about the boat. ____________
15. Encouraged by his manager Darryl applied for the supervisory position. ____________
16. Growing in popularity co-working spaces give freelance workers and those with home-based businesses an office outside the home. ____________
17. Using a global positioning system (GPS) can be important to drivers, boaters, and even hikers. ____________
18. Circling the earth twice a day GPS satellites transmit precise information. ____________

NAME ____________________

LEVEL III

From the pairs of sentences that follow, select the sentence that is more logically stated. Write its letter in the space provided.

1. (a) Hurriedly proofreading the report, three errors were found by Minako.
   (b) Hurriedly proofreading the report, Minako found three errors. ________

2. (a) To ensure non-biased feedback, names were withheld from the proposals.
   (b) To ensure non-biased feedback, the company asked that names be withheld from the proposals. ________

3. (a) In investing money in the stock market, one must expect risks.
   (b) In investing money in the stock market, risks must be expected. ________

4. (a) While looking for Ann's number, the telephone rang and I heard Ann's voice.
   (b) While looking for Ann's number, I answered the phone and heard Ann's voice. ________

5. (a) After filling out an application, the personnel manager gave me an interview.
   (b) After filling out an application, I was given an interview by the personnel manager. ________

6. (a) Designed by Frank Gehry, the new Facebook building fits 2,900 employees.
   (b) Designed by Frank Gehry, 2,900 employees fit into the new Facebook building. ________

7. (a) To receive a certificate, 30 hours of training must be completed.
   (b) To receive a certificate, a student must complete 30 hours of training. ________

Check your answers. Using the better versions of the above sentence pairs as models, rewrite the following sentences to make them logical. Add words as necessary, but retain the verbal expressions as sentence openers.

8. Completing the examination in only 20 minutes, a perfect score was earned by Maria.

____

____

9. To locate the members' names and addresses, an Internet search was done.

____

____

10. Seated at the back of the stadium, the band could hardly be seen.

____

____

11. To appear well educated, good communication skills are important.

____

____

12. Addressing an audience for the first time, my knees shook and my voice wavered.

____

____

NAME ______________________________

LEVEL I

Write the correct comparative or superlative form of the adjective shown in parentheses.

EXAMPLE: Carmen is (neat) than her sister. neater

1. We hope that the new procedures prove to be (effective) than previous procedures. ____________
2. Of all the suggestions made, Mr. Bradley's suggestion is the (bad). ____________
3. Are any of the notes (easy) to read than these are? ____________
4. Of the three sisters, Roshani is the (friendly). ____________
5. The rhododendron is the (beautiful) plant in our garden. ____________
6. We make many printers, but the Model SX6 is the (fast). ____________
7. No restaurant makes (good) hamburgers than Tommy's. ____________
8. Located next to the airport, Malton is probably the (noisy) area in the city. ____________
9. Living in the suburbs usually provides (quiet) surroundings than living in the city. ____________
10. Of all the letters we have received, this one seems the (sincere). ____________
11. For this job we need the (skilled) employee in the department. ____________
12. I'm afraid Hanh has the (less) chance of being selected for the position. ____________
13. No one at work is (slow) than Andreas. ____________
14. DataSource is (likely) to be awarded the contract than CompuPro. ____________
15. Loblaw tends to jump on consumer trends (early) than its competitors do. ____________
16. Pierre has had (few) citations than any other driver. ____________
17. The weather is certainly looking (good) today than yesterday. ____________
18. Everyone watching the video thought that Yong looked (credible) than any other actor. ____________
19. The results were (bad) than we expected. ____________
20. Sharon's report had the (few) errors of all those submitted. ____________

NAME ________________________________

LEVEL II

Write *C* if the underlined word or words in the sentences below are correctly expressed. If they are incorrect, write a corrected form in the space provided.

EXAMPLE: Because less people made contributions, we failed to reach our goal. fewer

1. He played his music so loud that we couldn't work. ______
2. We have decided to increase our point-of-purchase advertising. ______
3. How much further will we proceed in our study of business ethics? ______
4. We insist that our delivery persons know the rules of the road and drive careful. ______
5. The machine is running quieter since we installed a hood. ______
6. Gerald and I felt badly about John's accident. ______
7. The general manager should not become involved in this conflict of interest issue. ______
8. She finished her diploma when she was nineteen-years old. ______
9. At present we're searching for a source of inexpensive, accessible raw materials. ______
10. My organization has selected the later of the two proposals you submitted. ______
11. The applicant did good on the test of communication skills. ______
12. Most everyone offered congratulations to Kenneth on his promotion. ______
13. We are conducting the campaign from house-to-house. ______
14. Mrs. Wharton appeared to be looking quite well despite her recent illness. ______
15. You can sure depend on my help whenever you need it. ______
16. No one behaved different when the representative from head office was here. ______
17. The employees seem real concerned about the new parking fee. ______
18. You are a preferred charge-account customer at our store. ______
19. We expect a signed contract in the not too distant future. ______
20. Unfortunately, we've had less applications this year than ever before. ______

NAME ______________________

LEVEL III

In the following sentences, select the correct word(s).

1. Only the (a) two last, (b) last two speakers made relevant comments. ____________
2. Our team did better than (a) any other, (b) any team in the province. ____________
3. Don is more stubborn than (a) anyone else, (b) anyone I know. ____________
4. The charity was disappointed to (a) only recruit, (b) recruit only one volunteer from our company. ____________
5. Applications will be given to the (a) first five, (b) five first job candidates. ____________
6. To get a representative vote, the committee (a) needs almost, (b) almost needs all members to take part. ____________
7. Syed (a) merely said, (b) said merely that the proposal could be better. ____________

For each of the following sentences, underline any errors in the use of adjectives and adverbs. Then write the correct form. Write *C* if a sentence is correct.

8. Meryl asked her assistant to print her messages neater when she takes her calls. ____________
9. The uniform you are required to wear certainly fits you good. ____________
10. Because we have less work to do this week, we should finish soon. ____________
11. The recently-enacted law has received great support. ____________
12. Apparently we have picked the worse time of the year to list an office for rent. ____________
13. Winning an award from the Customer Service Professionals Network was a honour for our organization. ____________
14. Liz didn't hardly touch her lunch yesterday or today. ____________
15. One method of increasing sales is to provide high value incentives to staff. ____________
16. Because of their many kindnesses to us, I feel badly that we cannot reciprocate in some way. ____________
17. If less people were involved, the new procedures could have been implemented earlier. ____________
18. He won't even go to that restaurant if it's my treat. ____________
19. Festival promoters rented a 840 acre farm in Ulster County. ____________

NAME ______________________________

LEVEL I

Underline any errors in the following sentences. Then write the correct form. Write *C* if a sentence is correct.

1. You should of seen the looks on their faces! ____________

2. Only Mr. Levine and he had access to the company records. ____________

3. I read the book and plan to attend the lecture too. ____________

4. Between you and I, we should be able to get the job done. ____________

5. Sue got a new cellphone off of Kijiji. ____________

6. The chair is to heavy for one person to lift. ____________

7. The director of human resources, along with the office manager and she, is planning to improve hiring procedures. ____________

8. If we had known about the error earlier, we could of done something about it. ____________

9. Is Kaseem going to the seminar to? ____________

10. If it weren't for Ms. Berk and he, Neve wouldn't have kept her job. ____________

11. Did you obtain your copy of the team proposal off him? ____________

12. Please get your passes from either Tom or she. ____________

13. See whether you can get some change for the machine off of her. ____________

14. Both the project coordinator and he should have verified the totals before submitting the bid. ____________

15. The commission for the sale has to be divided between Ms. Carpenter and he. ____________

16. Because to few spaces are available, additional parking must be found on nearby streets. ____________

17. If you and he had discussed the proposal, we might of been able to submit it today. ____________

18. So that we may better evaluate your application, please supply references too. ____________

19. You could have had complimentary tickets if you had called Joan or she. ____________

20. The marketing manager assigned too many customers to Anwar and I. ____________

NAME ____________________

LEVEL II

For each of the following sentences, underline any errors in the use of prepositions. Then write a correct form. Write *C* if a sentence is correct.

1. We think that beside salary the major issue is working conditions. ____________

2. Your interest and support of this new web program will be greatly appreciated. ____________

3. The warranty period was over with two months ago. ____________

4. Please come into see me when you are finished your meeting. ____________

5. Just inside of the office entrance is the receptionist. ____________

6. Between the three of them, they should be able to figure out how to put the desk together. ____________

7. Will you be able to deliver the goods like you said you would? ____________

8. For most of us, very few opportunities like this ever arise. ____________

9. Exactly what type software did you have in mind? ____________

10. Some of the trucks were moved in to the garage at dusk. ____________

11. All of the performance reviews are now complete. ____________

12. Because of your concern and involvement in our community action campaign, we have received thousands of dollars in contributions. ____________

13. I know the time and date of our next committee meeting, but I do not know where it will be held at. ____________

14. His management book is one among many, but it is worth reading. ____________

15. Joanna could not help from laughing when she saw her email. ____________

16. Please hurry up so that we may submit our proposal quickly. ____________

17. What style furniture is most functional for the waiting room? ____________

18. Carla was unsure where our office is. ____________

19. All parking lots opposite to the corporate headquarters are being resurfaced. ____________

20. Immediately after Kathy graduated high school, she started college. ____________

NAME ____________________

LEVEL III

In the following sentences, select the correct word. Write its letter in the space provided. Use your text or a dictionary if necessary.

1. Customer service skills really come into play when a customer becomes angry (a) at, (b) with the service representative. ____________
2. Elise is a proven expert (a) in, (b) with cellphone technology. ____________
3. Candidates are expected to adhere (a) to, (b) with the fund-raising rules. ____________
4. After corresponding (a) to, (b) with their home office, I was able to clear up the error in my account. ____________
5. Yusef intends to work with the client independent (a) from, (b) of the company. ____________
6. If you (a) plan to attend, (b) plan on attending the summer session, you'd better register immediately. ____________
7. A few of the provisions are retroactive (a) for, (b) to January 1. ____________
8. Jeff talked (a) to, (b) with his boss about the company's future plans. ____________
9. While standing (a) on, (b) in line for the tickets, I worked on my tablet. ____________
10. She made every effort to reason (a) to, (b) with the unhappy customer. ____________
11. Apparently the letters in the ad do not sufficiently contrast (a) with, (b) against the background. ____________
12. His behaviour is no different (a) from, (b) than a schoolchild's. ____________
13. Do you dare to disagree (a) to, (b) with him? ____________
14. Being the leader of a business team is similar (a) with, (b) to coaching a sports team. ____________
15. I am becoming bored (a) with, (b) of my job. ____________
16. Would you prefer a standing desk (a) to, (b) over a traditional desk? ____________
17. He went on working oblivious (a) from, (b) to the surrounding chaos. ____________
18. The figures on the balance sheet could not be reconciled (a) to, (b) with the actual account totals. ____________
19. A number of individuals agreed (a) to, (b) with the plan. ____________
20. Our office is convenient (a) for, (b) to many cafés and restaurants. ____________

NAME ______________________________

LEVEL I

Name four coordinating conjunctions:

1. ______________________ **3.** ______________________

2. ______________________ **4.** ______________________

When coordinating conjunctions connect independent clauses (groups of words that could stand alone as sentences), the conjunctions are preceded by commas. The two independent clauses form a compound sentence.

COMPOUND SENTENCE: We hope to increase sales in the East, *but* we need additional sales personnel.

Use a comma if the sentence is compound. When the words preceding or following the coordinating conjunction do not form an independent clause, do not use a comma; this is a simple sentence.

SIMPLE SENTENCE: The bank will include the cheque with your monthly statement *or* will send the cheque to you immediately.

In the following sentences, selected coordinating conjunctions appear in italics. Write (a) or (b) for each sentence.

a = no punctuation needed b = insert a comma before the italicized conjunction

5. Mr. Green is a specialist in information systems *and* he will be responsible for advising and assisting all our divisions. ______

6. Mr. Green is a specialist in information systems *and* will be responsible for advising and assisting all our divisions. ______

7. This is a sales meeting *but* other topics of interest may also be discussed. ______

8. The plan you are developing looks well-thought-out *and* may actually turn sales around in your division. ______

9. We seek the reaction of the council *and* of others who have studied the plan. ______

10. The company hopes to boost sales by introducing environmentally friendly products *or* it will have to find other ways to increase profits. ______

11. I think that the plan will be effective *and* that it will save us time and money. ______

12. This new benefit plan will cost the employee more money *but* the expanded benefits will more than offset the increased costs. ______

13. We are taking over a portion of the fourteenth floor but we will not be moving into that area until March. ______

14. Send me your latest price list for all digital camera equipment *and* add my name to your mailing list. ______

15. Our travel costs were very high last year *and* may become even more exorbitant if the cost of air travel continues to rise. ______

NAME ______________________

LEVEL II

1. Name six conjunctive adverbs:

(a) ______________ (c) ______________ (e) ______________

(b) ______________ (d) ______________ (f) ______________

2. When a conjunctive adverb joins independent clauses, what punctuation mark precedes the conjunctive adverb? ______________

3. Many words that serve as conjunctive adverbs can also function as parenthetical adverbs. When used parenthetically, adverbs are set off by what punctuation marks? ______________

In the following sentences, words acting as conjunctive or parenthetical adverbs are underlined. Add necessary commas and semicolons to punctuate the sentences. In the space provided, write the number of punctuation marks you added.

4. The company is planning <u>nevertheless</u> to proceed with its expansion. ______________
5. The price of the tour is contingent upon double occupancy <u>that is</u> two people must share accommodations. ______________
6. The new uniforms <u>on the other hand</u> are wash and wear. ______________
7. Our bank is extending its service until 6 p.m. <u>hence</u> we are better able to accommodate your banking needs. ______________
8. The new bicycle uses technology to warn riders of approaching cars <u>however</u> riders must still remain vigilant on city streets. ______________
9. The business began online <u>then</u> it opened brick-and-mortar stores. ______________
10. The manager has <u>consequently</u> requested a leave of absence. ______________
11. We have few summer jobs available in our organization <u>consequently</u> we do not advertise at colleges. ______________
12. When they graduate <u>however</u> these same young people will find a different employment picture with our organization. ______________
13. We know you are not yet ready to make a large order <u>nevertheless</u> we are sending you samples of our principal products. ______________
14. The shipment should be sent from the Detroit warehouse <u>otherwise</u> duties will be charged to the customer. ______________
15. Today's job market is extremely competitive <u>however</u> recent graduates can find jobs if they are well trained and persistent. ______________
16. Having a different résumé for each job opening <u>furthermore</u> will show that a candidate understands the needs of the various positions. ______________
17. Most recruiters prefer chronological résumés <u>consequently</u> we advise our graduates to follow the traditional résumé format. ______________
18. Human resources professionals spend little time reading a cover letter <u>therefore</u> it is wise to keep your letter short. ______________
19. A cover letter <u>moreover</u> stresses what you can do for an employer. ______________
20. During an employment interview, recruiters try to uncover negative information <u>however</u> job candidates try to minimize faults and weaknesses. ______________

NAME ____________________

LEVEL III

The correlative conjunctions *both . . . and, either . . . or, neither . . . nor,* and *not only . . . but (also)* should be used in parallel constructions. That is, the words these conjunctions join should be similarly patterned. Compare the words that *follow* the conjunctions. For example, if a verb follows *either,* a verb should follow *or.* If the active voice is used with *neither,* then the active voice should be used with *nor.* Study the following examples.

Not Parallel: Either Suk Ying is typing the Collins report or proofreading it. (A subject and verb follow either, but only a verb follows or.)

Parallel: Suk Ying is either typing the Collins report or proofreading it. (Similar verb forms follow both conjunctions.)

Not Parallel: Neither have I pumped the gas, nor was the oil checked. (An active-voice construction follows neither while a passive-voice construction follows nor.)

Parallel: I have neither pumped the gas nor checked the oil.

In the following exercise, write the letters of the sentences that are constructed in parallel form.

1. (a) We have neither the energy to pursue this litigation, nor do we have the finances. ____________
(b) We have neither the energy nor the finances to pursue this litigation.

2. (a) You may either write a research report, or a book report can be done. ____________
(b) You may write either a research report or a book report.

3. (a) He is not only clever but also witty. ____________
(b) He is not only clever, but he is also witty.

4. (a) The company maintains both a website and a blog. ____________
(b) The company both maintains a website, and it keeps a blog.

Revise the following sentences so that the correlative conjunctions are used in efficient parallel constructions.

5. You can either fax him your response, or you can send him an email message. ____________

____

____

6. Relocating the business will both increase our parking capacity, and we will be able to warehouse more.

____

____

7. Neither does Tony have a job offer, nor does he even have an interview lined up.

____

____

8. We can either list the house low and postpone taking offers, or we can start out at a higher price and take offers immediately. ____________

____

____

NAME ____________________

LEVEL I

In the space provided, write *T* (true) or *F* (false) for each of the following statements.

1. A phrase is a group of related words without both a subject and a verb. ________
2. A clause is a group of related words containing both a subject and a verb. ________
3. An independent clause has a subject and a verb and makes sense by itself. ________
4. A dependent clause is missing either a subject or a verb. ________
5. Conjunctions such as *after, because, if,* and *when* are used at the beginning of independent clauses. ________

Indicate whether the following groups of words are phrases (*P*), independent clauses (*I*), or dependent clauses (*D*). If you indicate that a group of words is an independent clause, capitalize the first word (use ≡) and place a period at the end of the group of words.

EXAMPLE: he stood in a very long line. I

6. on Tuesdays throughout the month ________
7. although she came every meeting ________
8. a notice was posted ________
9. during the period from April to October ________
10. if sales continue to climb as they have for the past four months ________
11. the director asked for additional personnel ________
12. as soon as we can increase our production ________
13. he responded ________
14. because your organization has financial strength ________
15. as part of our commitment to you ________
16. satellite telephone service is now available ________
17. in order that we may improve service to our customers ________
18. you will need your receipt to make a return ________
19. when he returns to the office ________
20. fill out and mail the enclosed card ________
21. it is the end of the quarter ________
22. reworking our original plans ________
23. five essential elements for a good résumé ________
24. because your old résumé listed your work history and then went on to describe previous jobs in grim and boring detail ________
25. a good résumé is a joy for an employer to read ________

NAME ____________________

LEVEL II

Add necessary commas to the following sentences. Write *C* if a sentence is correct.

1. If we follow the consultant's suggestions we will improve our department's efficiency. ____________

2. We will if we follow the consultant's suggestions improve our department's efficiency. ____________

3. We will improve our department's efficiency if we follow the consultant's suggestions. ____________

4. When completed the renovation should make the seventh floor much more attractive. ____________

5. Let's discuss the problem when Ms. Dale returns. ____________

6. The motorist who parked his car in the restricted area is in danger of being ticketed. ____________

7. Our latest company safety booklet which was submitted over six weeks ago is finally ready for distribution. ____________

8. As you may know we are changing manufacturing facilities for some of our products. ____________

9. Housing prices provided interest rates remain low are expected to continue to rise. ____________

10. If necessary you may charge this purchase to your credit card. ____________

11. Ursula who is working as an intern in Purchasing has applied for the Finance Department job. ____________

12. Any employee who responds to an internal posting automatically gets an interview. ____________

13. I assure you that you will hear from Ms. Habib as soon as she returns. ____________

14. Because the website was temporarily down we did not receive your order. ____________

15. May I look through the catalogue before you throw it out? ____________

16. The additional premium you were charged which amounted to $175.12 was issued because of your recent accident. ____________

17. As expected the proposal should help us more clearly define long-term objectives. ____________

18. We will submit the proposal within four working days if that schedule meets with your approval. ____________

19. Before we sign any contract we must make site visits and verify all information. ____________

20. In this proposal I have outlined a seven-step purchasing program that meets all the objectives you indicated were important to you. ____________

NAME ____________________

LEVEL III

Use the information provided within parentheses to construct dependent clauses for the following sentences. Add relative pronouns or subordinating conjunctions such as *who, which, although,* and *since.*

EXAMPLE: Dr. Cushman recently moved his practice to Victoria. (Dr. Cushman specializes in pediatrics.)

Dr. Cushman, who specializes in pediatrics, recently moved his practice to Victoria.

1. The original agreement was drawn between Mr. Hightower and Columbia Communications. (The agreement was never properly signed.) ____________________

2. Shopify helps businesses develop online stores. (Many entrepreneurs do not have the expertise to build their own websites.) ____________________

3. Thank you for informing us that your credit card is missing. (This credit card has an expiration date of April 2020.) ____________________

Combine the following clauses into single sentences.

4. (Your account is four months past due.) We will be forced to take legal action. We must hear from you within seven days. ____________________

5. Sally Horton won an award as this month's outstanding employee. (She works in our Quality Control Department.) Ms. Horton is secretary to the manager in that department. ____________________

6. (Office hours end at 5 p.m.) Many employees work late. Better lighting needs to be installed in the parking lot. ____________________

7. We are sending you four poster advertisements. They will appear in magazines in April. (April marks the beginning of a national campaign featuring our sports clothes.) ____________________

8. Mr. Girard plans to retire at the end of this year. (Mr. Girard has worked at Rocketwell for thirty-seven years.) After he retires, Mr. Girard plans to devote more time to his orchid collection. ____________________

NAME ______________________

LEVEL I

Add necessary commas to the following sentences. For each sentence indicate the number of commas that you have added. Write *C* if a sentence is correct.

1. Your present insurance Mr. Isaq does not cover the care and custody of property belonging to others. ______
2. By the way have you updated the fire insurance coverage on your home and its contents? ______
3. Have you met Abigail Olson our controller? ______
4. Our team leader is from Calgary Alberta but is now working in Edmonton. ______
5. The CEO's son Mark will be joining our team for the summer. ______
6. The proposed plan unfortunately will not improve employee profit-sharing benefits. ______
7. Send the shipment to MicroTech Systems 750 Grant Road Burnaby British Columbia V5E 4B2 as soon as possible. ______
8. Thank you Mr. Singh. ______
9. You have until Friday April 30 to make complete payment on your past-due account. ______
10. The print ad will appear on the subway in bus shelters and in select magazines and newspapers. ______
11. In February 2015 we outgrew our office and moved to these larger premises. ______
12. I hope that your brother Gary will be able to join us. ______
13. You will in addition receive a free brochure outlining our wireless devices. ______
14. The coffee is made the pastries have arrived and the boardroom is ready. ______
15. All things considered the company will be obligated to pay only those expenses directly related to the installation. ______
16. Only Mr. Hudson a specialist in information systems is qualified to write that report. ______
17. You can avoid patent trademark and copyright problems by working with an intellectual property lawyer. ______
18. We are convinced incidentally that our lawyer's fees are most reasonable. ______
19. Yes Mr. Van Alstyne developed the policy. ______
20. On the form you will see two places where you are to sign. ______

NAME ______________________________

LEVEL II

Add necessary commas to the following sentences. For each sentence indicate the number of commas that you have added. Write *C* if a sentence is correct.

1. We must find a practical permanent solution to our Internet access problems. ____________
2. For a period of about six months it will be necessary to reduce all expenditures. ____________
3. Mr. Desai speaking on behalf of the company announced its purchase of two smaller drugstore chains. ____________
4. We held a marketing meeting last week and representatives from all divisions were on hand to provide their input. ____________
5. I am looking forward to getting together with you when you are again in Halifax. ____________
6. We have decided as I have told you to downscale the advertising campaign. ____________
7. Consumer patterns for the past five years are being studied carefully by our marketing experts. ____________
8. Having studied the changing demographics of the community the agency has several recommendations to help us grow our business. ____________
9. After you have examined my calculations please send the report to Bill Thompson. ____________
10. Please send the report to Bill Thompson after you have examined my calculations. ____________
11. Mr. Ebadi listening to his employees' input pondered the best solution to the problem. ____________
12. Our human resources director is looking for intelligent articulate young people who desire an opportunity to grow with a start-up company. ____________
13. Read the brochure at your leisure and call me if you have any questions. ____________
14. Beginning on the 15th of June Dell is slashing prices on laptop computers. ____________
15. I mentioned to him at that time that we could not locate the monitor. ____________
16. As soon as I can check the inventory we will place an order. ____________
17. On October 25 the president and I visited Sandra Goodell who is president of Sandra Goodell Public Relations. ____________
18. You may at your convenience submit a report describing when where and how we should proceed. ____________
19. To begin the transfer process we will need a purchase order for the inventory. ____________
20. Any student who has not signed up for a team yet must see the instructor. ____________

NAME ______________________________

LEVEL III

Add necessary commas to the following sentences. For each sentence indicate the number of commas that you have added. Write *C* if a sentence is correct.

1. Michael Ferrari PhD has written another book on consumer buying. ____________
2. In 2010 our company expanded its marketing to include the United Kingdom. ____________
3. By 2019 12 of our competitors were also selling in Great Britain. ____________
4. The bike's body is titanium; its seat post steel. ____________
5. It was a large manila envelope not a white folder that held the contract. ____________
6. Long before our president conducted his own research into marketing trends among youthful consumers. (Tricky!) ____________
7. "We prefer not to include your name" said the auditor "when we publish the list of inactive accounts." ____________
8. You may sign your name at the bottom of this sheet and return it to us as acknowledgment of this letter. ____________
9. Enclosed is Policy No. 850000611 for your records. ____________
10. Irving Feinstein MD will be the speaker at our next meeting. ____________
11. The essay contest awarded a prize of a $10000 scholarship. ____________
12. Ever since we have been very careful to count the number of boxes in each shipment. ____________
13. In her lecture Dr. Hawkins said "One species of catfish reproduces by hatching eggs in its mouth and growing them to about three inches before releasing them." ____________
14. The customer files will always be in the bottom drawer never in the top drawer. ____________
15. Ten computers were sold in January; nine in February. ____________
16. Our figures show that 17365000 separate rental units were occupied in September. ____________
17. The more challenging the problem the more determined Mr. Iverson becomes to solve it. ____________
18. By the way it was the president not the vice president who ordered the cutback. ____________
19. The therapist said "A diamond is a chunk of coal that made good under pressure." ____________
20. Whoever signs signs at his or her own risk. ____________

NAME ______________________________

LEVEL I

Punctuate the following groups of words as single sentences. Add commas and semicolons. Do not add words or periods to create new sentences.

EXAMPLE: Come in to see our new branch office^, our friendly manager^, and our customer service representatives.

1. Our principal function is to help management make profits however we can offer advice on staffing problems as well.
2. Delegates came from as far away as Charlottetown Prince Edward Island Mount Pearl Newfoundland and Fort McMurray Alberta.
3. Jerry looked up names Andrea addressed envelopes and Janelle stuffed envelopes.
4. Thank you for your interest in our products a catalogue will be sent to you this week.
5. Although employees often complain about lack of parking space little interest was shown in a proposed carpooling program.
6. The clients will be out of town the rest of the week therefore we will have to schedule the presentation for next week.
7. This sale is not open to the general public we are opening the store to preferred customers only.
8. Some of the employees being promoted are Jill Roberts secretary Legal Department Lea Lim clerk Human Resources and Mark Cameron dispatcher Transportation Department.
9. Many business experts say it's best to do one thing and do it well on the other hand companies like Loblaw have been extremely successful with diversified businesses.
10. In the morning I am free at 10 a.m. in the afternoon I have already scheduled an appointment.
11. Rogers is working to improve customers' opinions as a result complaints have decreased by 28 percent.
12. Look over our online catalogue make your selections and click to submit your order.
13. We hope that we will not have to sell the property but selling may be our only option.
14. The film that you requested is now being shown to law students in Ontario it will be shown during June in Manitoba and it will be used during July and August in the provinces of Alberta and British Columbia.
15. We do not sell airline seats we sell customer service.
16. Our convention committee is considering the Hyatt Regency Hotel Vancouver British Columbia the Hotel Halifax Halifax Nova Scotia and the Chelsea Inn Toronto Ontario.
17. As requested the committee will meet on May 4 it will not however make any announcements until September.
18. Market research involves the systematic gathering recording and analyzing of data about consumer and product issues.

NAME ______________________________

LEVEL II

Add colons, semicolons, or commas to the following sentences. Do not add words or periods. Write *C* after the sentence if it is correct.

1. Three phases of our business operation must be scrutinized purchasing, production, and shipping.
2. The candidates being considered for supervisor are Ned Bingham, Sean Davis, and Anna Donato.
3. Senator Zoubek said "The economy can continue its recovery only if prices are controlled. In addition, inflation must remain below 7 percent."
4. The following dates are reserved for counselling

   September 28 January 4

   September 30 January 6
5. At its next meeting, the board of directors must make a critical decision should the chief executive officer be retained or replaced?
6. This year's seminar has been organized to give delegates an opportunity to exchange ideas, plans, techniques, and goals.
7. The three Cs of credit are as follows character, capacity, and capital.
8. Our Boston Massachusetts tour package included visits to these interesting historical sites the House of Seven Gables, Bunker Hill, the Boston Tea Party Ship and Museum, and Paul Revere's home.
9. Plasticity is a company that aims to boost happiness in the workplace based on four factors hope efficacy resilience and optimism.
10. The speaker said that membership is free but that contributions would be greatly appreciated.
11. Several of the tax specialists on the panel were concerned with the same thought government spending continues to rise while taxes are being reduced.
12. For a charitable organization to qualify for registration it must have one of the following purposes relieving poverty, furthering education, advancing religion, or benefiting the community in certain ways.
13. Scholarships will be awarded to Adeena Kanaan Jeremy Stone and Carolena Garay.
14. Our favourite Alberta resort is noted for fly fishing, mountain biking, tennis, and hiking.
15. Our favourite Alberta resort is noted for the following fly fishing, mountain biking, tennis, and hiking.

NAME ______________________________

LEVEL III

Add colons, semicolons, dashes, or commas as needed. If a word following a colon should not be capitalized, use a proofreading mark (/) to indicate lowercase. Show words to be capitalized with a capitalization mark (≡). Write *C* if a sentence is correct.

1. There are three primary ways to pay for goods purchased online namely by credit card on the vendor's website, by email money transfer, or through PayPal.
2. Please order the following supplies Cartridges, paper, and staples.
3. Although we are expanding our services we continue to do business according to our original philosophy that is we want to provide you with flexible and professional investment services on a highly personal basis.
4. Computer-savvy business people always follow this unwritten rule Save your document often!
5. Dr. Ruglio's plane departed at 2 15 and should arrive at 6 45.
6. When he filed his taxes, Tony missed claiming expenses for advertising, insurance, postage, and fuel and, as a result, he ended up owing money.
7. Three of our top executives namely Mr. Gabereau, Mr. Wright, and Mrs. Stranahan are being transferred to the Winnipeg office.
8. On our list of recommended reading is *Investment an Introduction to Analysis.*
9. Canadians who are self-employed may now be eligible to receive for instance maternity, sickness, and compassionate care benefits.
10. Our airline is improving service in several vital areas for example baggage handling, food service, and weather forecasts.
11. Julie Schumacher was hired by a brokerage house and given the title of "registered representative" that is she is able to buy and sell securities.
12. Professor Wilson listed five types of advertising Product, institutional, national, local, and corrective.
13. We considered only one location for our fall convention namely Montréal.
14. Many important questions are yet to be asked concerning our program for instance how can we meet our competitor's low prices on the West Coast?
15. Jessica Pryce-Jones says that her research shows that happiness on the job makes one more productive "If you're really happy at work, you'll solve problems faster, be more creative, adapt fastest to change, receive better feedback, get promoted quicker, and earn more over the long-term."

NAME ____________________

LEVEL I

Add any necessary punctuation to the following sentences.

1. Will you please review the F A Q s (frequently asked questions) posted on our website
2. You did say the meeting is at 10 a m didn't you
3. Mrs Kephart is a C A working for Berman Ltd
4. I wonder whether the old photocopier will be replaced or just fixed
5. Help The door is jammed
6. Shoe widths increase by 5 mm intervals
7. Our C E O and C F O normally make all budget decisions
8. Although most candidates had B A degrees two applicants had M A degrees
9. What a day this has been
10. Cynthia asked if invitations had been sent to Miss Tan Mr Roe and Ms Rich
11. My brother-in-law Rudy who has his M B A manages my R R S P
12. Alan Bennett M D and Gina Hawtin Ph D were our keynote speakers
13. Because Susanne typed 80 w p m she was hired as a word processing specialist for C I D A
14. We're expanding marketing efforts in China France and the U K
15. Have you seen the ads for that market
16. The sales representative did say that the price of the car was f o b Windsor didn't he
17. Would you please check Policy Nos 44657001 and 44657002 to see if each includes $50 000 comprehensive coverage
18. Did you say the order was received at 5 p m
19. Wow How much was the lottery prize
20. May I suggest that you fax the request to the attention of Mr Seth Harcourt Jr

NAME ____________________

LEVEL II

Write *T* (true) or *F* (false) after the following statements.

1. In typewritten or simple word processing–generated material, a dash is formed by typing two successive underscores. ____________

2. Parentheses are often used to enclose explanations, references, and directions. ____________

3. Dashes must be avoided in business writing since they have no legitimate uses. ____________

4. Question marks and exclamation marks may be used to punctuate parenthetical statements (enclosed within parentheses) within other sentences. ____________

5. If a comma is meant to fall at the same point where words enclosed by parentheses appear, the comma is deleted. ____________

Circle the letter of the correctly punctuated sentence.

6. (a) I am busy on all those dates—oh, perhaps October 18 is free.
(b) I am busy on all those dates: oh, perhaps October 18 is free.
(c) I am busy on all those dates, oh, perhaps October 18 is free.

7. (De-emphasize)
(a) Directions for assembly, see page 15, are quite simple.
(b) Directions for assembly—see page 15—are quite simple.
(c) Directions for assembly (see page 15) are quite simple.

8. (a) Prosthetic limbs, insoles, face shields, tracheas, and jewellery, these are just some examples of 3-D printer innovations.
(b) Prosthetic limbs, insoles, face shields, tracheas, and jewellery—these are just some examples of 3-D printer innovations.
(c) Prosthetic limbs, insoles, face shields, tracheas, and jewellery: these are just some examples of 3-D printer innovations.

9. (a) To file a complaint with the Better Business Bureau (BBB), call during regular business hours.
(b) To file a complaint with the Better Business Bureau, (BBB) call during regular business hours.
(c) To file a complaint with the Better Business Bureau (BBB) call during regular business hours.

10. (Normal emphasis)
(a) The company's CEO (who is a known philanthropist) spends his Saturday mornings helping at a soup kitchen.
(b) The company's CEO, who is a known philanthropist, spends his Saturday mornings helping at a soup kitchen.
(c) The company's CEO—who is a known philanthropist—spends his Saturday mornings helping at a soup kitchen.

11. (a) "What is needed for learning is a humble mind." (Confucius)
(b) "What is needed for learning is a humble mind.": Confucius
(c) "What is needed for learning is a humble mind." —Confucius

12. (a) The due date is past (July 1;) however, we will waive the interest.
(b) The due date is past; (July 1) however, we will waive the interest.
(c) The due date is past (July 1); however, we will waive the interest.

13. (a) Only one person was in my office—Denise Powell, and I trust her.
(b) Only one person was in my office (Denise Powell), and I trust her.
(c) Only one person was in my office; Denise Powell, and I trust her.

14. (Emphasize)
(a) Our current mortgage rates: see page 10 of the enclosed booklet—are the lowest in years.
(b) Our current mortgage rates (see page 10 of the enclosed booklet) are the lowest in years.
(c) Our current mortgage rates—see page 10 of the enclosed booklet—are the lowest in years.

NAME ____________________

LEVEL III

Write *T* (true) or *F* (false) for each of the following statements.

1. When the exact words of a speaker or writer are repeated, regular (double) quotation marks enclose the words. ____________

2. To indicate a quotation within another quotation, single quotation marks (apostrophes on most keyboards) are used. ____________

3. When a word is defined, its definition should be underlined. ____________

4. The titles of books, magazines, newspapers, and other complete works published separately may be either underlined or italicized. ____________

5. The titles of book chapters and of magazine articles may be underlined, italicized, or enclosed in quotation marks. ____________

6. Periods and commas are always placed outside closing quotation marks. ____________

7. Brackets are used when a writer inserts his or her own remarks inside a quotation. ____________

8. The Latin word *sic* may be used to call attention to an error in quoted material. ____________

9. Semicolons and colons are always placed outside closing quotation marks. ____________

10. If both the quotation and the surrounding text are questions, two question marks are used, one inside the quotation marks and one outside. ____________

Write the letter of the correctly punctuated statement.

11. (a) "When Mr. Davis calls," my manager said, "tell him I'll meet him at 2 p.m."
(b) "When Mr. Davis calls, my manager said, tell him I'll meet him at 2 p.m."
(c) "When Mr. Davis calls", my manager said, "tell him I'll meet him at 2 p.m." ____________

12. (a) The director said, "This memo is clearly marked Confidential."
(b) The director said, "This memo is clearly marked 'Confidential'."
(c) The director said, "This memo is clearly marked 'Confidential.'" ____________

13. (a) A *chattel* is defined as a "piece of movable property."
(b) A "chattel" is defined as a *piece of movable property.*
(c) A "chattel" is defined as a "piece of movable property." ____________

14. (a) Do you know who it was who said, "Forewarned is forearmed."
(b) Do you know who it was who said, "Forewarned is forearmed"?
(c) Do you know who it was who said, "Forewarned is forearmed."? ____________

15. (a) A meeting was scheduled to 'ideate' marketing tag lines.
(b) A meeting was scheduled to "ideate" marketing tag lines.
(c) A meeting was scheduled to *ideate* marketing tag lines. ____________

NAME ____________________

Complete Punctuation Review

Insert all necessary punctuation in the following sentences. Correct any incorrect punctuation. Do not break any sentences into two sentences.

1. Did you see the article entitled Soaring Salaries of C E O s that appeared in *The New York Times*

2. This years budget costs are much higher than last years, therefore I will approve overtime only on a case by case basis.

3. The board has three new members Dr. Carla Chang Professor Mark Rousso and Robert Price Esq

4. Needless to say upper management expects all employees to arrive by 9 a m E S T

5. We formerly depended on fixed-rate not variable rate mortgages.

6. The fleet manager is considering the following vehicles for safety, an Isuzu box truck for gas mileage, a Nissan cargo van and for getting attention, the Fiat Doblo.

7. Last year we moved corporate headquarters to Vancouver British Columbia but maintained production facilities in Calgary Alberta.

8. (Quotation) Did I just hear Dr. Tran say There will be no more tests.

9. Graduation ceremonies for B A candidates are at 11 a m, graduation ceremonies for M B A candidates are at 2 p m.

10. As we previously discussed the reorganization will take effect on Monday August 8.

11. We have reached the conclusion as you may have heard that e-commerce is inevitable in the twenty first century.

12. Will you please send copies of our annual report to Anna Golan and D A Rusterholz?

13. Although the manufacturer was working hard to meet government requirements certain mechanisms remained a pain point.

14. In the event of inclement weather we will close the base and notify the following radio stations CFRB CHIN and CHUM.

15. (Emphasize) Three excellent employees Gregorio Morales, Dawna Capps, and DaVonne Williams will be honoured at a ceremony Friday June 5.

16. (Quotation) Your attitude not your aptitude will determine your altitude, said Zig Ziglar.

17. By May 15 our goal is to sell 15 cars, by June 15 20 additional cars.

18. The full impact of the C R T C ruling is being studied you will receive information as it becomes available.

19. The goal here is to get a larger share of wallet i e more money from each customer.

20. Send the contract to Ms Courtney Phillips Administrative Assistant Globex Industries 7600 Normandale Boulevard Scarborough ON M1K 5G4 as soon as possible.

21. (De-emphasize) Please return the amended budget proposal see page 2 for a summary of the report to the presidents office by Friday March 4.

22. Prospective entrepreneurs were told to read a Success magazine article entitled A Venture Expert's Advice.

23. Larry Zuckerman our former manager now has a similar position with I B M.

24. Employees are concerned primarily with three job issues namely wages, security, and working conditions.

25. As expected this years expenses have been heavy, consequently we may have to freeze hiring for the next six months.

26. Would you please read the rebranding memo then provide me with three ideas for promotion

NAME ____________________

LEVEL I

Write the letter of the group of words that is correctly capitalized.

1.	(a) a dinner of swedish meatballs	(b) a dinner of Swedish meatballs	________
2.	(a) in the field of marketing	(b) in the field of Marketing	________
3.	(a) the Richardson Building	(b) the Richardson building	________
4.	(a) for Sikhs in our community	(b) for sikhs in our community	________
5.	(a) an order for china and crystal	(b) an order for China and crystal	________
6.	(a) both Master's and Doctorate degrees	(b) both master's and doctorate degrees	________
7.	(a) Welland Canal	(b) Welland canal	________
8.	(a) a class in conversational French	(b) a class in Conversational French	________
9.	(a) our Summer vacation	(b) our summer vacation	________
10.	(a) a German shepherd	(b) a German Shepherd	________
11.	(a) the Russian revolution	(b) the Russian Revolution	________
12.	(a) traffic in the big apple	(b) traffic in the Big Apple	________
13.	(a) the King Edward room	(b) the King Edward Room	________
14.	(a) on Remembrance Day	(b) on Remembrance day	________
15.	(a) the waters of the bay of Fundy	(b) the waters of the Bay of Fundy	________

Use proofreading marks to capitalize (≡) or to show lowercase (/) letters in the following sentences.

16. Bob's Esso Station is located on Speedway Avenue in the next County.

17. Many employees of the Meredith Corporation plan to participate in the Company's profit-sharing plan.

18. Sponsors of the gala benefit for the Animal Guardian society included a local Canadian tire store.

19. During the Winter I will enrol in management, business english, and accounting.

20. The bevelled glass insert is available through Special Order from Clearview glass and mirror.

21. Our persian cat and russian wolfhound cohabit quite peacefully.

22. Last Fall my family and I visited epcot center in orlando, florida.

23. The two companies signed a stipulation of interest agreement last april.

24. Interior designers recommended italian marble for the entry and mexican tiles for the patio.

25. A Limousine will take guests from the Airport directly to the Royal York hotel.

NAME ______________________

LEVEL II

Write the letter of the group of words that is correctly capitalized.

1.	(a) my uncle and my aunt	(b) my Uncle and my Aunt	______
2.	(a) Very sincerely yours,	(b) Very Sincerely Yours,	______
3.	(a) Send it to Corporal Lee.	(b) Send it to corporal Lee.	______
4.	(a) Volume II, Page 37	(b) Volume II, page 37	______
5.	(a) located in northern Alberta	(b) located in Northern Alberta	______
6.	(a) fourth floor, unit 402	(b) fourth floor, Unit 402	______
7.	(a) within our Human Resources Department	(b) within our human resources department	______
8.	(a) the World Wildlife Federation	(b) the world wildlife federation	______
9.	(a) in appendix III	(b) in Appendix III	______
10.	(a) heading South on Highway 5	(b) heading south on Highway 5	______
11.	(a) the book *Love and Will*	(b) the book *Love And Will*	______
12.	(a) both federal and provincial laws	(b) both Federal and Provincial laws	______
13.	(a) Q-tips and kleenex	(b) Q-tips and Kleenex	______
14.	(a) orders from Sales Director Jared Ali	(b) orders from sales director Jared Ali	______
15.	(a) a trip to the east coast	(b) a trip to the East Coast	______

Use proofreading marks to capitalize (≡) or to show lower case letters (/) in the following sentences.

16. We received a directive from Ruth MacVean, Supervisor of our Administrative Services Division.

17. The President of our Company gave an address titled "Leadership: What Effective Managers do and how They do it."

18. Gina Schmidt, customer service representative, attended a convention in the Eastern part of the province.

19. Stay on highway 10 until you reach exit 7; then head North.

20. Mayor Bruno visited the Capital in an attempt to increase the city's share of Provincial funding.

21. The best article in the magazine is "Does your training measure up?" by Leslie Brokaw.

22. John placed his ray-ban sunglasses on the formica counter.

23. Sue's Mother and Father were scheduled to leave on flight 37 from gate 6 at Gander international airport.

24. We have suggested that a Committee be formed to discuss the issues that Councillor Peterson raised in his talk with our Director of Corporate Communications last week.

NAME ____________________

LEVEL III

Write the letter of the group of words that is correctly capitalized.

1.	(a) photographs sent from Mars to Earth	(b) photographs sent from Mars to earth	________
2.	(a) a room marked "private"	(b) a room marked "Private"	________
3.	(a) the Egyptian Room and the Sahara Room	(b) the Egyptian room and the Sahara room	________
4.	(a) the best coffee on earth	(b) the best coffee on Earth	________
5.	(a) from President-Elect Ross	(b) from President-elect Ross	________
6.	(a) What are your office hours, professor?	(b) What are your office hours, Professor?	________
7.	(a) some asian cultures	(b) some Asian cultures	________
8.	(a) an envelope stamped "confidential"	(b) an envelope stamped "Confidential"	________
9.	(a) our sales director, Joe Hines	(b) our Sales Director, Joe Hines	________
10.	(a) to ex-Premier Davis	(b) to Ex-Premier Davis	________

Use proofreading marks to capitalize (≡) or to show lower case letters (/) in the following sentences.

11. The box was marked "fragile."

12. A paddleboat was seen travelling west along the Fraser river.

13. No one recognized ex-minister Thurston when he toured the Okanagan valley.

14. We wonder, commander, if the gravity of Mars might be similar to that of earth.

15. The Organization's bylaws state, "On the third Monday of every month, the Club's Treasurer will prepare the financial report."

16. Representatives from Pacific Rim Countries are willing to meet with us to discuss exporting goods for our Distribution.

17. The Minister of foreign affairs met with the prime minister to discuss this country's National policy toward african nations.

18. yes, at 9 a.m.

19. In malaysia we soon learned that muslims do not eat pork and that buddhists and hindus do not eat beef.

20. We will take both your regular income and bonuses into account, Sir.

NAME ____________________

LEVEL I

In the space provided, write the letter of the correctly expressed group of words.

1.	(a) for 24 employees	(b) for twenty-four employees	________
2.	(a) only 9 rooms left	(b) only nine rooms left	________
3.	(a) twenty-five dollars	(b) $25	________
4.	(a) on the thirtieth of May	(b) on the 30th of May	________
5.	(a) the change is 20 cents	(b) the change is twenty cents	________
6.	(a) (military style) 5 April 2005	(b) 5th April 2005	________
7.	(a) $2.05, 85¢, and $5.00	(b) $2.05, $.85, and $5	________
8.	(a) we start at 9 a.m.	(b) we start at 9 a.m. in the morning	________
9.	(a) One Feint Drive	(b) 1 Feint Drive	________
10.	(a) 226 Sixth Street	(b) 226 6th Street	________

Underline any errors in the expression of numbers in the following sentences. In the space provided, write the correct form.

11. 194 businesses were sent the ethics survey December 1st. ________

12. We just learned that 2 companies have moved their corporate offices to twenty-fifth Avenue. ________

13. Three of the least expensive items were priced at $5.00, $3.29, and 99 cents. ________

14. Your payment of $100.00 must be received by the second of February. ________

15. We have invited 6 candidates for interviews on June 1st. ________

16. Our office, formerly located at Two Ford Place, is now located at One Kent Avenue. ________

17. Please call me at (815)-611-9292, X 3, before 4:30 p.m. ________

18. I can meet you at eight o'clock p.m. ________

19. 3 of our employees start at 8:00 a.m., and 5 start at 8:30 a.m. ________

20. If reservations are made before the fifteenth of the month, the fare will be $204 dollars. ________

21. Grossmont College offers a fifteen-hour training course that costs just under one hundred dollars. ________

22. Classes meet Monday through Thursday from 11:45 a.m. to one p.m. ________

23. The Werners moved from 1,762 Milburn Avenue to 140 Rural Route Eight. ________

24. Lisa had only $.25 left after she purchased supplies for forty-four dollars. ________

25. On the third of January and again on the 18th, our machine needed service. ________

NAME ______________________

LEVEL II

Write the letter of the correctly expressed group of words.

1.	(a) for 82 students in 3 classes	(b) for 82 students in three classes	________
2.	(a) interest of three percent	(b) interest of 3 percent	________
3.	(a) over the past thirty years	(b) over the past 30 years	________
4.	(a) two 35-minute walks	(b) 2 thirty-five-minute walks	________
5.	(a) he is 45 years old	(b) he is forty-five years old	________
6.	(a) line three	(b) line 3	________
7.	(a) nearly 2.6 billion units	(b) nearly 2,600,000,000 units	________
8.	(a) 9 taxi receipts, 18 meal receipts, and 2 baggage receipts	(b) nine taxi receipts, 18 meal receipts, and two baggage receipts	________
9.	(a) Lois Lamb, 65, and John Lamb, 66	(b) Lois Lamb, sixty-five, and John Lamb, sixty-six	________
10.	(a) the business's 15th anniversary	(b) the business's fifteenth anniversary	________

Underline any errors in the expression of numbers in the following sentences. Write the corrected forms. Write *C* if a sentence is correct.

11. We have received 50 reservations over the past 14 days. ________

12. Please order twenty-five two-ring binders large enough to hold 100 pages each. ________

13. 33 of the corporations had operating budgets that exceeded one million dollars. ________

14. Because many telecommute, twenty employees share ten workspaces. ________

15. Chapter eight in Volume two provides at least three references to pumps. ________

16. About 100 pallets need to be removed from Warehouse 11, and another eight pallets, from Warehouse Two. ________

17. We ordered two seventy-centimetre desks and three chairs. ________

18. Of the twenty requests we received, five were acted on immediately, three were tabled, and the rest were outside our domain. ________

19. The 2 loans must be repaid within 90 days. ________

20. When she was only 24 years old, Mrs. Ibrahim supervised more than 120 employees. ________

21. Only two of the 125 mailed surveys were undeliverable. ________

22. Frank Morris, sixty-four, plans to retire in one year. ________

23. Linda Hannan and her fifteen-person company signed a four million dollar contract. ________

24. Payment must be received within thirty days. ________

25. The thirty-year mortgage carries an interest rate of eight percent. ________

NAME ______________________

LEVEL III

Assume that all the following phrases appear in complete sentences. Write the letter of the phrase that is appropriately expressed.

	(a)	(b)	
1.	(a) the tank holds just 35 L	(b) the tank holds just thirty-five litres	________
2.	(a) only a three percent gain	(b) only a 3 percent gain	________
3.	(a) $^4/_5$ of the voters	(b) four-fifths of the voters	________
4.	(a) a 50% discount	(b) a 50 percent discount	________
5.	(a) a one-half share	(b) a one half share	________
6.	(a) a decline of .5 percent	(b) a decline of 0.5 percent	________
7.	(a) a 3rd-place finish	(b) a third-place finish	________
8.	(a) in the nineteenth century	(b) in the 19th century	________
9.	(a) a 5-pound limit	(b) a five-pound limit	________
10.	(a) on Canada's one hundred twenty-fifth anniversary	(b) on Canada's 125th anniversary	________

Underline any errors in the expression of numbers. Write the corrected forms.

11. A No. Ten envelope actually measures four and a half by nine and a half inches. ________

12. All the drivers in the 33rd Grand Prix finished the race. ________

13. Tests show that the driver responded in less than seven two hundredths of a second. ________

14. The pillow is accented with two mm cording. ________

15. The desk top measured seventy-eight and a half centimetres by one hundred fifty three and three-quarters centimetres. ________

16. To qualify for a three percent discount, submit your payment by the thirtieth. ________

17. The office was moved about fifty blocks on the tenth of December. ________

18. Place the date of a business letter on line 13, which is five centimetres from the top edge of the paper. ________

19. The notebook computer weighs just three point six kilograms and is thirty-nine and a half centimetres wide. ________

20. Appropriation measures must be passed by a 2/3 majority. ________

21. She ordered a nine by twelve rug, which would cover ½ the floor. ________

22. After completing Form Ten Forty, the accountant submitted his bill for $800 dollars. ________

23. By the year 2,020, the number of employees over the age of 55 will have increased by 52%. ________

24. Nine different airlines carry over one hundred thousand passengers daily. ________

25. The company car took twenty-five litres of gasoline and cost 26 dollars and twenty-five cents. ________

NAME ______________________

LEVEL I

Revise the following sentences to eliminate wordy phrases and needless repetition.

1. In the event that the shares rise, please sell my holdings. ______________________

2. In a summary at the end of her report, Catherine Perkins reported increased service costs. ______________________

3. The document we need you to sign is along the lines of a waiver of liability. ______________________

4. In spite of the fact that a tall fence surrounded the parking lot on all sides, security was a problem. ______________________

5. As a rule in the contemporary workplace of today, all employees without exception need good computer skills. ______________________

Revise the following sentences to avoid passive-voice verbs.

6. Apparently this letter was written by an employee from your office. ______________________

7. The lights were left on by whoever used the room last. ______________________

8. We were informed by your electronics division that your prices will be raised. ______________________

9. Credit cannot be extended because your bills have not been paid. ______________________

10. Several reviews of our products have been posted by bloggers. ______________________

Revise the following sentences to make them more unified.

11. Phil will be taking a two-week vacation, and your work assignment has been changed. ______________________

12. We need to land some new accounts, and each of us must do what we can to save funds. ______________________

NAME ____________________

LEVEL II

Revise the following sentences to avoid faulty parallel construction.

1. Figures were checked, corrections were made, and we sent the report. ____________________

2. The duties will include supervising office workers, organizing meetings, correspondence, and the candidate will be responsible for travel arrangements.

3. We are looking for new premises that are centrally located, of suitable size for 20 employees, and that have parking for approximately 15 cars. ____________________

4. Consumer activists seek to ensure that products perform as advertised, they are safe, and the physical environment is not harmed. ____________________

5. The policy affected all vendors, suppliers, and those involved with consulting. ____________________

Revise the following sentences to avoid misplaced modifiers.

6. The busy human resources director interviewed only candidates who had excellent computer skills in the morning.

7. You and your staff will have no trouble in any of the 21 countries you visit with exchange rates and red tape.

8. The package is on your desk that was delivered yesterday. ____________________

Revise the following sentences to avoid unclear pronoun references. Be particularly careful with the pronouns *this, that, which,* and *it.* Be sure they refer to clear antecedents.

9. Computers and new software helped us reduce personnel costs, increase productivity, and improve quality. That justifies the cost of this investment. ____________________

10. The account had to be sent to Collections, which will unfortunately tarnish the client's credit rating. ____________________

11. Both data and word processing functions are performed with the new software; therefore, this should reduce overall costs.

NAME ____________________

LEVEL III

Use subordinate conjunctions (such as *if, because, although,* and *since*) or relative pronouns (such as *who, that,* and *which*) to create one sentence from the two ideas.

	Primary Idea	Secondary Idea
1.	The Time Book Club will send you a free bestseller if you join now.	Time has given over $30 million worth of books to its members.

____

____

	Primary Idea	Secondary Idea
2.	Taxpayers can claim charitable donations made in the previous five years.	Donations must be made to a registered charity to be eligible for tax credit.

____

____

	Primary Idea	Secondary Idea
3.	Business executives have difficulty forecasting future sales and profits.	Complex variables such as income, unemployment, and taxes influence buying power.

____

____

	Primary Idea	Secondary Idea
4.	The RCMP has more than 20,000 members and handles problems of national significance.	The force began as the North-West Mounted Police in 1873.

____

____

Improve the coherence of the following sentences by adding appropriate transitional expressions (such as *therefore, however, for example,* and other expressions discussed in the chapter).

5. Our bank has experienced unprecedented growth in the past five years; ____________, we plan to expand our facilities to meet the growing demand for our services.

6. You could be enjoying the many conveniences that Imperial Credit Card holders enjoy; ____________, you must first complete the enclosed application to receive one of our cards.

7. Employees must familiarize themselves with the company's policies and procedures; ____________, employees are expected to help ensure a positive working environment for colleagues.

8. Only a few of our salespeople have made reservations for the April 10 seminar; ____________, we are sending this reminder of the seminar.

9. Our college savings plan will help you finance more than your children's tuition costs; ____________, fees for room, board, books, and other expenses may be covered.

ANSWERS TO SELF-HELP EXERCISES

CHAPTER 1

Worksheet 1

Answers will vary. 2. substitutes for a noun; he she it 3. shows action or joins words that describe the subject; jumps works is 4. describes nouns or pronouns; tall soft five 5. modifies verbs, adjectives, or other adverbs; hurriedly very tomorrow 6. joins nouns and pronouns to the sentence; to for at 7. connects words or groups of words; and but or 8. shows strong feelings Wow! Gosh! No! 9. pronoun 10. verb 11. adj 12. adj 13. noun 14. prep 15. noun 16. conj 17. pronoun 18. verb 19. adv 20. adj 21. interj 22. pronoun 23. prep 24. adj 25. noun 26. conj 27. prep 28. adj 29. noun 30. verb 31. adj 32. adj 33. noun 34. conj 35. noun 36. verb 37. adv 38. adj 39. adj 40. noun 41. verb 42. adv

Worksheet 2

1. pronoun 2. verb 3. noun 4. prep 5. noun 6. conj 7. adj 8. noun 9. verb 10. adv 11. verb 12. noun 13. interj 14. verb 15. noun 16. adv 17. verb 18. pronoun 19. verb 20. verb 21. adj 22. noun 23. prep 24. noun 25. adj 26. noun 27. adv 28. verb 29. noun 30. conj 31. noun 32. conj 33. adv 34. pronoun 35. verb 36. adj 37. noun 38. adj 39. noun 40. prep 41. adj 42. noun 43. noun 44. conj 45. adj 46. noun 47. adv 48. verb 49. prep 50. adj 51. noun

CHAPTER 2

Worksheet 1

1. (S) one (V) sold 2. (S) boom (V) is causing 3. (S) telephones (V) rang 4. (S) we (V) will hire 5. (S) workers and management (V) reached 6. (S) salespeople (V) received 7. (S) positions (V) were eliminated 8. (S) we (V) released 9. (S) one (V) disliked 10. (S) committee (V) was appointed 11. (S) applicant (V) received 12. (S) Everything (V) is covered 13. (S) members (V) seem 14. (S) copiers (V) are 15. (S) June and Ian (V) feel 16. (S) Dul Youn Hu (V) has been 17. (S) offices (V) are

Worksheet 2

Answers will vary. 1. voted 2. were requested 3. arrived 4. rang 5. will decide 6. dropped 7. a policy 8. an email 9. the party 10. him 11. door 12. letters 13. good 14. unwell 15. Mr. Jones 16. competent 17. Mr. Smith 18. John 19–23.

Worksheet 3

1. f 2. c 3. c 4. ro 5. cs 6. f 7. f 8. cs 9. ro 10. cs 11. f 12. ro 13. c 14. c 15. cs 16. ro 17. f 18. c 19. cs 20. f

CHAPTER 3

LEVEL I

1. tissues 2. feet 3. latches 4. Bushes 5. myths 6. languages 7. faxes 8. sandwiches 9. valets 10. children 11. successes 12. choruses 13. stocks 14. branches 15. ideas 16. women 17. mismatches 18. taxis 19. Shirazes 20. annexes 21. klutzes 22. Rosses 23. storms 24. alibis 25. Joneses 26. Chavezes 27. oxen 28. businesses 29. computers 30. wishes

LEVEL II

1. wharves 2. heirs apparent 3. 2010s 4. Wolfs 5. embargoes 6. cm 7. attorneys 8. amts. 9. faculties 10. by-products 11. entries 12. runners-up 13. altos 14. knives 15. notaries public 16. A's 17. Bradys 18. memos 19. allies 20. zeros 21. loaves 22. yrs. 23. Mistrys 24. well-wishers 25. oz. 26. journeys 27. MBAs 28. wolves 29. studios 30. 21s

LEVEL III

1. data 2. theses 3. bacteria 4. Chinese 5. series 6. alumni 7. alumnae 8. genera 9. axes 10. news 11. pp. 12. ff. 13. vertebrae 14. phenomena 15. criteria *Answers will vary.* 16. are 17. are 18. formulas 19. analyses 20. is

CHAPTER 4

LEVEL I

Worksheet 1

1. all students' books 2. my manager's responsibility 3. the women's uniforms 4. two months' rent 5. an employee's signature 6. our neighbours' yards 7. the pilot's landing 8. all partners' agreement 9. the children's parents 10. the department's strengths 11. five years' time 12. those people's cars 13. last week's merger 14. the two businesses' parent company 15. citizens' opinions 16. Canada's mountains 17. the employer's requirements 18. all candidates' résumés 19. government's policies 20. both agents' fees

Worksheet 2

1. year's 2. drivers' 3. vehicle's 4. thief's 5. day's 6. visitors' 7. Jess's (or Jess') 8. readers' 9. caller's 10. authors' 11. Gap's 12. C 13. country's 14. areas 15. organization's 16. vice president's 17. clients' 18. C 19. years' 20. farmer's 21. citizens' 22. year's, amounts 23. customer's 24. women's, brokers' 25. supervisor's

LEVEL II

1. public's 2. Sales 3. printer's 4. The suggestion of my lawyer, Sandra Thom, is 5. desk top or top of the desk 6. aunt and uncle's 7. C 8. last month's 9. C 10. telephone number of the president's secretary 11. CEOs 12. beards of my two brothers-in-law 13. Larry's 14. Québec's 15. Phillipses' 16. C 17. Clark and Clark's 18. Angeles 19. architects' 20. last year's 21. C 22. Leo and Ambreen's 23. reporters' 24. day's, day's 25. C

LEVEL III

1. Amaras 2. Ross's or Ross' 3. classes' 4. Saunders's or Saunders' 5. Alex's 6. Cadizes' 7. boss's 8. bosses' 9. Abramoviches 10. actresses' 11. Harris's or Harris' 12. Abbas' or Abbas's 13. Elias' or Elias's 14. waitress's 15. Garveys' 16. Morrises' 17. Betz's 18. Vargases' 19. Simons's or Simons' 20. Jones's or Jones' 21. emeritus' or emeritus's, or office of the professor emeritus 22. Williamses' 23. Kimballs' 24. Elvis's or Elvis'

CHAPTER 5

LEVEL I

Worksheet 1

1.–14. *Order of answers may vary.* 1.–7. I, you, he, she, it, we, they 8.–14. me, you, him, her, it, us, them 15. I 16. she 17. he 18. they 19. she 20. we 21. she 22. he 23. she 24. he 25. I

Worksheet 2

1. me. 2. him 3. them 4. me 5. her 6. him 7. her 8. them 9. us 10. me 11. it's 12. theirs 13. its 14. theirs 15. hers 16. it's 17. You're 18. Whose 19. ours 20. its

LEVEL II

1. them 2. I 3. her 4. We 5. I 6. me 7. her 8. he 9. him 10. me 11. himself 12. her 13. her 14. she 15. me 16. us 17. he 18. him 19. I 20. me 21. they 22. She and I 23. her 24. us 25. I

LEVEL III

Worksheet 1

1. she 2. he 3. they 4. she 5. he 6. she 7. them 8. he 9. me 10. they 11. he 12. him 13. her 14. I 15. she 16. she 17. I 18. him 19. I 20. I 21. she 22. him 23. she 24. she

Worksheet 2

1. he 2. me 3. its 4. she 5. us 6. theirs 7. he 8. I 9. me 10. her 11. us 12. you're 13. her 14. him 15. yours 16. me 17. he 18. its 19. him or me 20. there's 21. him 22. me 23. she 24. their 25. she 26. I 27. me

CHAPTER 6

LEVEL I

1. Cheng 2. their 3. his or her 4. his or her 5. their 6. he or she 7. his or her 8. He or she 9. her 10. their pictures 11. his or her 12. her 13.–15. *in any order.* 13. Every employee must obtain his or her . . . 14. Every employee must obtain a parking permit . . . 15. All employees must obtain their parking permits . . .

LEVEL II

1. use her instead of their 2. his instead of their 3. his or her instead of their 4. his or her for his 5. his for their 6. his or her for his 7. C 8. its for their 9. its for their 10. him or her for them 11. C 12. his or her for their 13. his or her for their 14. his or her seat for their seats 15. its for their 16. its for their 17. them for it 18. him or her for them 19. its for their 20. they for she or he

LEVEL III

Worksheet 1

1. Whom 2. whom 3. who 4. whom 5. whom 6. whom 7. who 8. whom 9. Who 10. whom 11. who 12. who 13. whom 14. who 15. Who

Worksheet 2

1. whoever 2. whoever 3. whomever 4. whomever 5. whoever 6. Whomever 7. whoever 8. Whoever 9. whomever 10. Whoever 11. Who 12. who 13. who 14. whoever 15. whom

Worksheet 3

1. Whom 2. who 3. whom 4. whoever 5. whom 6. whom 7. Whoever 8. who 9. who 10. who 11. whom 12. whom 13. Who 14. Whom 15. whomever 16. whom 17. Whoever 18. whose 19. whom 20. Whom 21. whose 22. who 23. who's 24. whom 25. who's

CHAPTER 7

LEVEL I

1. is 2. occurred 3. is 4. is 5. is 6. opened 7. occur 8. will reserve 9. studied 10. will analyze 11. applied 12. considered 13. varies 14. insists 15. will have 16. requires 17. will demand 18. tried

LEVEL II

1. will 2. are 3. have 4. was 5. will 6. has opened 7. is planning 8. had called 9. has worked 10. were shopping 11. will be signing 12. has broken 13. had seen 14. are considering 15. was being heard

LEVEL III

Worksheet 1

1. become 2. froze 3. sought 4. chosen 5. built 6. sung 7. forgotten 8. taken 9. gone 10. bitten 11. eaten 12. drunk 13. C 14. sprang 15. shaken 16. worn 17. written 18. stolen 19. taken 20. gone

Worksheet 2

1. laid 2. lay 3. lying 4. laid 5. laying 6. lie 7. lay 8. Lay 9. lain 10. lie 11. lie 12. lying 13. lay 14. lay 15. lain 16. lay 17. lying 18. lie 19. laid 20. laying

CHAPTER 8

LEVEL I

1. transitive 2. intransitive 3. linking 4. complements 5. I 6. L—Fran 7. T—addresses 8. I 9. L—consultant 10. T—pants 11. I 12. L—better 13. L—he 14. I 15. T—questions 16. T—gifts 17. L—best 18. I 19. L—justified 20. T—expectations

LEVEL II

Worksheet 1

1. Mariam (Mariam did not pick up the text message . . .)
2. head office (Head office visited several franchises . . .)
3. Mrs. Bradford (Mrs. Bradford must now authorize withdrawals.)
4. Mr. Stern (Mr. Stern asked Sandip to be responsible . . .)
5. management (Management forced employees who . . .)

Worksheet 2

Revised sentences will vary. 1. The IT Department must complete . . . 2. Mr. Smith wrote cheques . . . 3. John programmed . . . 4. Judges make decisions . . . 5. We give cash discounts . . . 6. Management warned employees . . . 7. Our CGA scrutinized our accounting records . . .

LEVEL III

1. were 2. be 3. was 4. be 5. would 6. be 7. were 8. be 9. rest 10. were 11. were 12. be 13. were 14. meet 15. were 16. receive 17. were 18. was 19. were 20. be

CHAPTER 9

LEVEL I

Worksheet 1

1. provide 2. is 3. seems 4. think 5. is 6. was 7. is 8. needs 9. comes 10. are 11. is 12. are 13. are 14. are 15. sounds 16. was 17. is 18. costs 19. have 20. was

Worksheet 2

1. travel 2. are 3. is 4. opens 5. appear 6. are 7. are 8. offers 9. are 10. has 11. has 12. provide 13. Has 14. is 15. is 16. is 17. appears 18. are 19. are

LEVEL II

1. Most is 2. Committee on Youth Activities has 3. Each deserves 4. your company, one is 5. No one was 6. Neither is 7. employee, guest receives 8. list, invoices mention 9. one merits 10. one was 11. Steven, you are 12. None seems 13. credit belongs 14. group is 15. Some is 16. staff has 17. Are any 18. union has 19. employees, management have 20. Most have

LEVEL III

1. has 2. is 3. enjoy 4. was 5. are 6. puts 7. favour 8. are 9. are 10. am 11. have 12. are 13. like 14. are 15. is 16. flatter 17. were 18. are 19. responds 20. has

CHAPTER 10

LEVEL I

1. your passing 2. his investing 3. Mr. Cortina's gambling 4. None 5. Mr. Frank's receiving 6. C 7. your criticizing 8. his calling 9. bank's handling 10. our contacting 11. C 12. my working 13. C

LEVEL II

1. Constructed in 2018 2. Surrounded 3. seeing his opportunity 4. installed just two months ago 5. rereading the article several times 6. Speaking in front of the large crowd 7. Irritated 8. opening a new account 9. model, 10. Hammonds, accounts, 11. C 12. transactions, 13. C 14. Terry, sheet, 15. manager, 16. popularity, 17. C 18. day,

LEVEL III

1. b 2. b 3. a 4. b 5. b 6. a 7. b 8.–12. *Answers may vary.*

8. Completing the examination in only 20 minutes, Maria earned a perfect score.
9. To locate the members' names and addresses, you can do an Internet search.
10. Seated at the back of the stadium, Lydia and Ian could hardly see the band.
11. To appear well educated, a person must have good communication skills.
12. Addressing an audience for the first time, I felt my knees shake and my voice wavered.

CHAPTER 11

LEVEL I

1. more effective 2. worst 3. easier 4. friendliest 5. most beautiful 6. fastest 7. better 8. noisiest 9. quieter 10. most sincere 11. most skilled 12. least 13. slower 14. more likely 15. earlier 16. fewer 17. better 18. more credible 19. worse 20. fewest

LEVEL II

1. loudly 2. C 3. C 4. carefully 5. more quietly 6. bad 7. conflict-of-interest 8. nineteen years old 9. C 10. latter 11. well 12. Almost 13. house to house 14. C 15. surely 16. differently 17. really 18. charge account 19. not-too-distant 20. fewer

LEVEL III

1. b 2. a 3. a 4. b 5. a 6. a 7. b 8. more neatly 9. well (for *good*) 10. C 11. recently enacted 12. worst (for *worse*) 13. an (for *a*) 14. hardly touched 15. high-value 16. bad (for *badly*) 17. fewer people 18. even if 19. an 840-acre farm

CHAPTER 12

LEVEL I

1. should have (for *should of*) 2. C 3. C 4. me (for *I*) 5. from (for *off of*) 6. too heavy (not *to heavy*) 7. her (for *she*)

8. could have (for *could of*) 9. too (for second *to*) 10. him (for *he*) 11. from (for *off*) 12. her (for *she*) 13. from (for *off of*) 14. C 15. him (for *he*) 16. too (for *to*) 17. might have (for *might of*) 18. C 19. her (for *she*) 20. me (for *I*)

LEVEL II

1. besides (for *beside*) 2. interest *in* 3. omit *with* 4. in to (for *into*) 5. omit *of* 6. among (for *between*) 7. as (for *like*) 8. C 9. type *of* software 10. into (for *in to*) 11. omit *of the* 12. concern *for* 13. omit *at* 14. C 15. omit *from* 16. omit *up* 17. style *of* 18. unsure *of* 19. omit *to* 20. graduated *from*

LEVEL III

1. b 2. a 3. a 4. b 5. b 6. a 7. b 8. b 9. b 10. b 11. a 12. a 13. b 14. b 15. a 16. a 17. b 18. b 19. a 20. b

CHAPTER 13

LEVEL I

The order of Answers 1–4 may vary. 1. and 2. or 3. nor 4. but (also acceptable for 1–4: for, so, yet) 5. b 6. a 7. b 8. a 9. a 10. b 11. a 12. b 13. b 14. b 15. a

LEVEL II

1. *Answers for this item may vary.* therefore, however, consequently, moreover, then, hence, thus 2. semicolon 3. commas 4. planning, nevertheless, (2) 5. occupancy; that is, (2) 6. uniforms, on the other hand, (2) 7. 6 p.m.; hence (1) 8. cars; however, (2) 9. online; then (1) 10. has, consequently, (2) 11. organization; consequently, (2) 12. graduate, however, (2) 13. order; nevertheless, (2) 14. warehouse; otherwise, (2) 15. competitive; however, (2) 16. opening, furthermore, (2) 17. résumés; consequently, (2) 18. letter; therefore, (2) 19. letter, moreover, (2) 20. information; however, (2)

LEVEL III

1. b 2. b 3. a 4. a

5. You can either fax him your response or send him an email message.

6. Relocating the business will increase both our parking and warehousing capacity.

7. Tony has neither a job offer nor even an interview lined up.

8. We can either list the house low and postpone taking offers or list it at a higher price and take offers immediately.

CHAPTER 14

LEVEL I

1. T 2. T 3. T 4. F 5. F 6. P 7. D 8. I 9. P 10. D 11. I 12. D 13. I 14. D 15. P 16. I 17. D 18. I 19. D 20. I 21. I 22. P 23. P 24. D 25. I

LEVEL II

1. suggestions, 2. will, suggestions, 3. C 4. completed, 5. C 6. C 7. booklet, ago, 8. know, 9. prices, low, 10. necessary, 11. Ursula, Purchasing, 12. C 13. C 14. down, 15. C 16. charged, $175.12, 17. expected, 18. days, 19. contract, 20. C

LEVEL III

Answers may vary.

1. Although it was never properly signed, the original agreement was drawn between Mr. Hightower and Columbia Communications.

2. Shopify helps businesses develop online stores because many entrepreneurs do not have the expertise to build their own websites.

3. Thank you for informing us that your credit card, which has an expiration date of April 2020, is missing.

4. Because your account is four months past due, we will be forced to take legal action unless we hear from you within seven days.

5. Sally Horton, who works as secretary to the manager in our Quality Control Department, won an award as this month's outstanding employee.

6. Even though office hours end at 5 p.m., many employees work late, so better lighting needs to be installed in the parking lot.

7. We are sending you four poster advertisements that will appear in magazines in April, which marks the beginning of a national campaign featuring our sports clothes.

8. Mr. Girard, who has worked at Rocketwell for thirty-seven years, plans to retire at the end of this year and devote more time to his orchid collection.

CHAPTER 15

LEVEL I

1. (2) insurance, Mr. Isaq, 2. (1) By the way, 3. (1) Olson, 4. (2) Calgary, Alberta, 5. C 6. (2) plan, unfortunately, 7. (4) Systems, 750 Grant Road, Burnaby, British Columbia V5E 4B2, 8. (1) you, 9. (2) Friday, April 30, 10. (2) subway, shelters, 11. C 12. C 13. (2) will, in addition, 14. (2) made, arrived, 15. (1) considered, 16. (2) Hudson, systems, 17. (2) patent, trademark, 18. (2) convinced, incidentally, 19. (1) Yes, 20. C

LEVEL II

1. (1) practical, 2. (1) months, 3. (2) Desai, company, 4. (1) week, 5. C 6. (2) decided, you, 7. C 8. (1) community 9. (1) calculations, 10. C 11. (2) Ebadi, input, 12. (1) intelligent, 13. (1) leisure, 14. (1) June, 15. C 16. (1) inventory, 17. (1) Goodell, 18. (2) when, where, 19. (3) process, 20. C

LEVEL III

1. (2) Ferrari, PhD, 2. C 3. (1) 2019, 12. (1) post, 5. (2) envelope, folder, 6. (1) before, 7. (2) name," said the auditor, 8. C 9. C 10. (2) Feinstein, MD, 11. (1)$10,000 (or $10 000) 12. (1) since, 13. (1) said, 14. (1) drawer, 15. (1) nine, 16. (2) 17,365,000 (or 17 365 000) 17. (1) problem, 18. (3) way, president, vice president, 19. (1) said, 20 (1) signs, signs

CHAPTER 16

LEVEL I

1. profits; however, 2. Charlottetown, Prince Edward Island; Mount Pearl, Newfoundland; and Fort McMurray, 3. names, envelopes, 4. products; 5. space, 6. week; therefore, 7. public; 8. Roberts, secretary, Legal Department; Lea Lim, clerk, Human Resources; and Mark Cameron, dispatcher, 9. well; hand, 10. 10 a.m.; 11. opinions; result, 12. catalogue, selections, 13. property, 14. Ontario; Manitoba; 15. seats; 16. Hyatt Regency Hotel, Vancouver, British Columbia; the Hotel Halifax, Halifax, Nova Scotia; and the Chelsea Inn, Toronto, 17. requested, May 4; not, however 18. gathering, recording,

LEVEL II

1. scrutinized: 2. C 3. said: 4. counselling: 5. decision: 6. C 7. follows: 8. Boston, Massachusetts, sites: 9. factors: hope, efficacy, resilience, 10. C 11. thought: 12. registration, purposes: 13. Kanaan, Stone, 14. C 15. following:

LEVEL III

1. online; namely, 2. supplies: cartridges, 3. services, philosophy; that is, 4. rule: 5. 2:15 6:45 6. fuel; 7. executives—namely, Mr. Gabereau, Mr. Wright, and Mrs. Stranahan— 8. *Investment: An* 9. receive, instance, 10. areas; for example, 11. representative"; that is, 12. advertising: product, 13. convention, namely, 14. program; for instance, 15. productive:

CHAPTER 17

LEVEL I

1. FAQs website. 2. 10 a.m., didn't you? 3. Mrs. CA Ltd. 4. fixed. 5. Help! jammed! 6. intervals. 7. CEO CFO decisions. 8. BA degrees, MA degrees. 9. been! 10. Tan, Mr. Roe, and Ms. Rich. 11. Rudy, MBA, RRSP. 12. Bennett, MD, Hawtin, PhD, speakers. 13. 80 w.p.m., CIDA. 14. China, France, and the UK. 15. market? 16. f.o.b. Windsor, didn't he? 17. Nos. $50,000 (or $50 000) coverage. 18. 5 p.m.? 19. Wow! prize? 20. Mr. Jr.

LEVEL II

1. F (use two hyphens) 2. T 3. F 4. T 5. F 6. a 7. c 8. b 9. a 10. b 11. c 12. c 13. b 14. c

LEVEL III

1. T 2. T 3. F 4. T 5. F 6. F 7. T 8. T 9. T 10. F 11. a 12. c 13. a 14. b 15. b

Complete Punctuation Review

1. "Soaring Salaries of CEOs" *The New York Times*? 2. This year's last year's; therefore, case-by-case 3. members: Chang, Rousso, Price, Esq. 4. say, 9 a.m. EST. 5. fixed-rate, not variable-rate, 6. vehicle: truck; van; 7. Vancouver, British Columbia, Calgary, 8. say, "There tests"? 9. BA 11 a.m.; MBA 2 p.m. 10. discussed, Monday, August 8. 11. conclusion, heard, twenty-first 12. D. A. Rusterholz. 13. requirements, "pain point." 14. weather, stations: CFRB, CHIN, and CHUM. 15. employees—Gregorio . . . Williams—Friday, June 5. 16. "Your attitude, aptitude, altitude," 17. cars; by June 15, 18. CRTC studied; 19. "share of wallet" (i.e., customer). 20. Ms. Courtney Phillips, Administrative Assistant, Globex Industries, 7600 Normandale Boulevard, Scarborough, ON M1K 5G4, 21. (see report) president's Friday, 22. *Success* "A Venture Expert's Advice." 23. Zuckerman, manager, IBM. 24. issues; namely, 25. expected, year's heavy; consequently, 26. memo; promotion.

CHAPTER 18

LEVEL I

1. b 2. a 3. a 4. a 5. a 6. b 7. a 8. a 9. b 10. a 11. b 12. b 13. b 14. a 15. b 16. station county 17. company's 18. Society Tire 19. winter English 20. special order Glass and Mirror 21. Persian Russian 22. fall Epcot Center Orlando, Florida 23. Stipulation of Interest Agreement April 24. Italian Mexican 25. limousine airport Hotel

LEVEL II

1. a 2. a 3. a 4. b 5. a 6. b 7. a 8. a 9. b 10. b 11. a 12. a 13. b 14. b 15. b 16. supervisor 17. president company Do How Do It 18. eastern 19. Highway Exit north 20. capital provincial 21. "Does Your Training Measure Up?" 22. Ray-Ban Formica 23. mother and father Flight 37 Gate 6 International Airport 24. committee director of corporate communications

LEVEL III

1. a 2. b 3. a 4. a 5. b 6. b 7. b 8. b 9. a 10. a 11. Fragile 12. River 13. Minister Valley 14. Commander Earth 15. organization's 16. countries distribution 17. minister national African 18. Yes 19. Malaysia Muslims Buddhists Hindus 20. sir

CHAPTER 19

LEVEL I

1. a 2. b 3. b 4. b 5. a 6. a 7. b 8. a 9. a 10. a 11. (*Answers will vary.*) A total of 194 December 1 12. two 25th Avenue 13. $5 $.99 14. $100 2nd 15. six June 1 16. 2 Ford Place

17. (815) 611 Ext. 3 18. 8 p.m. (or eight o'clock in the evening) 19. Three 8 a.m. five 20. 15th $204 21. 15-hour $100 22. 1 p.m. 23. 1762 Rural Route 8 24. 25 cents $44 25. 3rd

LEVEL II

1. b 2. b (business concept) 3. b 4. a 5. b 6. b 7. a 8. a 9. a 10. b 11. C 12. 25 two-ring 13. Thirty-three $1 million 14. 20 15. Chapter 8 Volume 2 16. 8 pallets Warehouse 2 17. 70-centimetre 18. 20 requests 5 3 19. two 20. twenty-four years 21. Only 2 22. 64 23. 15-person $4 million 24. 30 days (business concept) 25. thirty-year or 30-year 8 percent

LEVEL III

I. a 2. b 3. b 4. b 5. a 6. b 7. b 8. a 9. a 10. b 11. No. 10 4½ by 9½ inches 12. thirty-third 13. $^{7}/_{200}$ 14. 2 mm 15. 78½ by 153¾ cm 16. 3 percent 30th 17. 50 blocks 10th 18. 5 cm 19. 3.6 kg 39½ cm 20. two-thirds 21. 9 by 12 half 22. Form 1040 $800 23. 2020 fifty-five 52 percent 24. 100,000 or 100 000 25. 25 L $26.25

CHAPTER 20

LEVEL I

Answers will vary.

1. If the shares rise, please sell my holdings.
2. In her summary, Catherine Perkins reported increased service costs.
3. The document we need you to sign is like a waiver of liability.
4. Although a tall fence surrounded the parking lot, security was a problem.
5. In today's workplace all employees need good computer skills.
6. An employee from your office apparently wrote this letter.
7. Whoever used the room last left the lights on.
8. Your electronics division informed us that you are going to raise your prices.
9. We cannot extend credit because you have not paid your bills.
10. Bloggers have posted several reviews of our products.
11. Because Phil will be taking a two-week vacation, your work assignment has been changed.
12. Until we land some new accounts, each of us must do what we can to save funds.

LEVEL II

Answers will vary.

1. We checked figures, made corrections, and sent the report.
2. The duties will include supervising office workers, organizing meetings, preparing correspondence, and making travel arrangements.
3. We are looking for new premises that are centrally located, that are of suitable size for 20 employees, and that have parking for approximately 15 cars.
4. Consumer activists seek to ensure that products perform as advertised, are safe, and do not harm the environment.
5. The policy affected all vendors, suppliers, and consultants.
6. In the morning the busy human resources director interviewed only candidates . . .
7. You and your staff will have no trouble with exchange rates and red tape in any of the . . .
8. The package that was delivered yesterday is on your desk.
9. Computers and new software helped us reduce personnel costs, increase productivity, and improve quality. These results justify the cost of this investment.
10. The account had to be sent to Collections; unfortunately, the account's delinquency will tarnish the client's credit rating.
11. Both data and word processing functions are performed with the new software; therefore, this software should reduce overall costs.

LEVEL III

Answers will vary.

1. The Time Book Club, which has given over $30 million worth of books to its members, will send you a free bestseller if you join now.
2. Taxpayers can claim charitable donations made in the previous five years if those donations were made to a registered charity.
3. Because complex variables such as income, unemployment, and taxes influence buying power, business executives have difficulty forecasting future sales and profits.
4. The RCMP, which began as the North-West Mounted Police in 1873, has more than 20,000 members and handles problems of national significance.
5. therefore (or consequently) 6. however 7. in addition (or moreover) 8. consequently (or therefore) 9. for example (or in fact)

ANSWERS TO CHAPTER EXERCISES

CHAPTER 1

Pretest

1. (c) pronoun 2. (b) adverb 3. (c) verb 4. (a) adjective 5. (d) noun 6. (b) conjunction 7. (b) pronoun 8. (a) verb 9. (c) preposition 10. (d) noun

Reinforcement Exercises

A. 1. b 2. a 3. a 4. c 5. b 6. d 7. a 8. d 9. c 10. b 11. c 12. a

Posttest

1. d 2. c 3. d 4. a 5. a 6. b 7. d 8. b 9. c 10. b

CHAPTER 2

Pretest

1. f 2. cs 3. c 4. ro 5. f 6. c 7. cs 8. f 9. ro 10. f

Reinforcement Exercises

A. 1. T 2. F 3. F 4. F 5. T 6. F 7. T 8. T 9. F 10. T 11. T 12. T

Posttest

1. ro 2. c 3. f 4. cs 5. f 6. f 7. c 8. cs 9. c 10. ro

CHAPTER 3

Pretest

1. proofs of purchase 2. boxes 3. attorneys 4. leaves of absence 5. diagnoses 6. logos 7. potatoes 8. Februarys 9. 1970s 10. suits

Reinforcement Exercises

LEVEL I

A. 1. assistants 2. viruses 3. pitches 4. mice 5. taxes 6. bananas 7. businesses 8. blocks 9. children 10. couches

LEVEL II

A. 1. bills of lading 2. chiefs 3. currencies 4. folios 5. IDs 6. Sundays 7. lives 8. proofs 9. runners-up 10. pros and cons

LEVEL III

A. 1. stimuli 2. phenomena 3. series 4. alumnae 5. criteria 6. pp. 7. analyses 8. data 9. vertebrae 10. crises

D. 1. booths 2. diagnoses 3. franchisees 4. Wilcoxes 5. studios 6. women 7. C 8. RNs and NPs 9. C 10. ins and outs 11. Fitches 12. valleys 13. boards of directors 14. C 15. shelves 16. Pulleys 17. Equinoxes 18. tariffs 19. higher-ups, bonuses 20. C

Posttest

1. knives 2. typos 3. alleys 4. companies 5. crises 6. *u*'s 7. sisters-in-law 8. DVDs 9. women 10. Thomases

CHAPTER 4

Pretest

1. students' 2. runner-up's 3. months' 4. property's 5. editor-in-chief's 6. companies' 7. Assan's 8. Sales 9. dollars' 10. Horowitzes'

Reinforcement Exercises

LEVEL I

A. 1. a day's labour 2. patients' meals 3. a learner's permit 4. ten months' interest 5. the purchasing manager's office 6. the world's economies 7. competitors' prices 8. the treasurer's duties 9. a month's delay 10. Heba's gift

LEVEL II

A. 1. editor-in-chief's 2. Thomas 3. Jones 4. company's 5. runner-up's 6. C 7. Communications 8. C 9. ladies', men's 10. sister-in-law's

LEVEL III

1. a 2. b 3. b 4. b 5. a 6. b 7. a 8. b 9. a 10. a

Posttest

1. managers' 2. last month's 3. companies' 4. Collections 5. makes, Valentine's 6. witnesses' 7. father-in-law's 8. years' 9. Lopezes' 10. parties'

CHAPTER 5

Pretest

1. her 2. I 3. she 4. she 5. him 6. We 7. her 8. me 9. him 10. me

Reinforcement Exercises

LEVEL I

A. 1. he 2. there's 3. them 4. your 5. her 6. her 7. we 8. she 9. him 10. him

LEVEL II

A. 1. her and me 2. he 3. we 4. us 5. We 6. I 7. her 8. me 9. she 10. her

LEVEL III

1. she 2. he 3. me 4. she 5. they 6. he 7. he 8. she 9. her 10. he

Posttest

1. I 2. us 3. we 4. they 5. he 6. she 7. We 8. me 9. us 10. I

CHAPTER 6

Pretest

1. her 2. its 3. its 4. whom 5. whoever 6. his 7. her 8. who 9. Meteorologists 10. his or her

Reinforcement Exercises

LEVEL I

A. 1. his or her 2. his or her 3. his 4. Human resources experts 5. he, his 6. his or her 7. his or her 8. their 9. her 10. he or she reaches

LEVEL II

A. 1. his or her 2. their 3. its 4. their 5. his or her 6. her 7. his or her 8. its 9. his 10. its

LEVEL III

A. 1. Whose 2. who 3. Whom 4. whom 5. whoever 6. whom 7. whom 8. who 9. who's 10. Whoever

E. 1. its TV campaign 2. VPs, his or her time 3. Itineraries, employees', Rick or me 4. it was she 5. faxes, you and he 6. tenants' and landlords' 7. we Canadians, America's 8. father-in-law's, transactions. One 9. his or her 10. Breaches of contract, contract's 11. he, years' 12. businesses', customers' 13. exam, she will 14. companies, it's, week's 15. C 16. jobs; half 17. That company will, whoever applies to work there 18. her seat belt 19. Weiszes 20. needs them

Posttest

1. her 2. his or her 3. its 4. Who 5. whoever 6. his or her 7. their 8. its 9. its 10. Whose

CHAPTER 7

Pretest

1. future 2. past 3. present 4. present 5. past 6. came 7. gone 8. lying 9. drank 10. sat

Reinforcement Exercises

LEVEL I

A. 1. carried 2. is 3. jammed 4. is 5. is 6. transferred 7. submitted 8. sells 9. wants 10. tried

LEVEL II

A. 1. future perfect 2. present progressive, passive 3. future 4. present progressive 5. past perfect 6. future progressive 7. present perfect progressive 8. past perfect 9. future perfect progressive 10. present progressive

LEVEL III

A. 1. risen 2. seen 3. flown 4. begun 5. written 6. shook 7. broke 8. spoken 9. known 10. gone

Posttest

1. present 2. past 3. present perfect 4. past participle 5. present participle 6. seen 7. rung 8. lain 9. rise 10. sat

CHAPTER 8

Pretest

1. a 2. c 3. b 4. b 5. a 6. c 7. b 8. b 9. b 10. a

Reinforcement Exercises

LEVEL I

A. 1. L 2. T 3. I 4. L 5. T 6. L 7. I 8. L 9. T 10. I

LEVEL II

A. 1. passive 2. active 3. passive 4. active 5. active 6. passive 7. passive 8. passive 9. active 10. active

LEVEL III

A. 1. were 2. be 3. were 4. was 5. be 6. attend 7. would 8. be 9. were 10. receive

Posttest

1. a 2. b 3. a 4. b 5. a 6. b 7. c 8. b 9. b 10. b

CHAPTER 9

Pretest

1. are 2. intimidates 3. has 4. plans 5. was 6. are 7. understands 8. lie 9. is 10. is

Reinforcement Exercises

LEVEL I

A. 1. are 2. is 3. are 4. Have 5. seems 6. was 7. is 8. provides 9. has 10. appears

LEVEL II

A. 1. was 2. is 3. attends 4. provides 5. is 6. are 7. Every one 8. does 9. are 10. admits

LEVEL III

A. 1. is 2. speaks 3. is 4. have 5. is 6. have 7. are 8. have 9. is 10. is

Posttest

1. was 2. have 3. dictates 4. qualifies 5. were 6. has 7. makes 8. are 9. has 10. are

CHAPTER 10

Pretest

1. b 2. c 3. b 4. b 5. c 6. a 7. b 8. c 9. b 10. b

Reinforcement Exercises

LEVEL I

A. 1. your 2. Mardi 3. Mardi's 4. his 5. company's 6. clerk 7. colleagues' 8. Hepler's 9. their 10. Rachel

LEVEL II

1. d 2. c 3. a 4. a 5. d 6. a 7. b 8. c 9. b 10. c

LEVEL III

1. b 2. b 3. a 4. b 5. a 6. b 7. a 8. a 9. b 10. b

Posttest

1. a 2. c 3. a 4. b 5. a 6. b 7. c 8. b 9. c 10. b

CHAPTER 11

Pretest

1. better 2. carefully 3. These sorts 4. could 5. worse 6. An 7. well 8. fewer 9. six-year-old 10. newly repaired

Reinforcement Exercises

LEVEL I

A. 1. worst 2. worse 3. this 4. an 5. can 6. hottest 7. These 8. a 9. has 10. harder

LEVEL II

A. 1. good 2. farther 3. face-to-face 4. fewer 5. nervous 6. surely 7. bad 8. latter 9. year to year 10. suspiciously

LEVEL III

A. 1. first 50 2. C 3. any other manager 4. even our IT department 5. just two more 6. last 12 7. wanted merely one 8. cost the company nearly 9. only with 10. any other business

Posttest

1. more smoothly 2. bad 3. These kinds 4. further 5. could 6. fewer 7. A 8. well 9. page-by-page 10. enthusiastic, hard-working

CHAPTER 12

Pretest

1. her 2. go 3. too 4. as if 5. from 6. to 7. beside 8. among 9. in to 10. about

Reinforcement Exercises

LEVEL I

A. 1. from 2. should have 3. too 4. her 5. me 6. him 7. would have 8. from 9. to 10. them

LEVEL II

A. 1. among 2. besides 3. inside 4. into 5. as if 6. accept 7. like 8. between 9. off 10. beside

LEVEL III

A. 1. plan to stay 2. comply with 3. talk to 4. conform to 5. C 6. stand in line 7. expert in 8. adhere to 9. prefers taking . . . to driving 10. angry with

Posttest

1. him 2. except 3. could have 4. in to 5. outside 6. as if 7. with 8. among 9. Besides 10. for

CHAPTER 13

Pretest

1. C 2. relocate; nevertheless, 3. Kitchener, but 4. effectively; consequently, 5. reviews, therefore, 6. important, however, 7. ago; therefore, 8. defect; then 9. b 10. b

Reinforcement Exercises

LEVEL I

A. 1. a 2. b (not compound because no subject follows *nor*) 3. b 4. a 5. b 6. a 7. c 8. b 9. b 10. a

LEVEL II

A. 1. (1) background; thus 2. (2), consequently, 3. (2) back; therefore, 4. (2) theft; however, 5. (2) learn, however, 6. (2) distributed; on the other hand, 7. (2) did, nevertheless, 8. (1) overdue; hence 9. (2) Liam, on the other hand, 10. (2) one; nevertheless,

LEVEL III

A. 1. b 2. b 3. b 4. a 5. a 6. a 7. b 8. a 9. b 10. a

Posttest

1. month; 2. C 3. increasing; consequently, 4. convinced, nevertheless, 5. relocating, 6. sure, however, 7. rapidly; therefore, 8. industry; 9. b 10. b

CHAPTER 14

Pretest

1. attachment, 2. C 3. year, 4. college, 5. possible, 6. Kala, Department, 7. account, month, 8. test, 9. C 10. C

Reinforcement Exercises

LEVEL I

A. 1. P 2. I 3. P 4. D 5. I 6. I 7. D 8. D 9. P 10. I

LEVEL II

A. 1. (2) Fishbourne, Manulife, 2. (1) decision, 3. (0) 4. (0) 5. (2) model, drastically, 6. (0) 7. (1) desired, 8. (0) 9. (2) Relations, firm, 10. (1) available,

LEVEL III

A. 1. a 2. c 3. d 4. b 5. d 6. c 7. b 8. c 9. c 10. a

Posttest

1. C 2. industry, 3. necessary, 4. Kaul, Products, 5. C 6. opened, 7. C 8. meat, 9. profit, 10. DiPasqua, position,

CHAPTER 15

Pretest

1. Cleveland, Chemnitz, 2. Jr., Companies, Dublin, Ireland, Toronto, 3. interview, Ms. Cordero, Tuesday, June 9, 4. province, 5. meeting, 6. is, expect, 7. ago, 8. tired, evening, morning, 9. Iqaluit, Nunavut, Minkevich, MBA, Monday, 10. said, headache,

Reinforcement Exercises

LEVEL I

1. Tuesday, September 11, 2001, (elements of a date) 2. circumstances, (parenthetical expression) 3. trunks, briefcases, airplane luggage, (series) 4. Kingston, Ontario, Gatineau, Québec, (elements of geographical item) 5. C (no commas with appositive containing essential information) 6. Bernstein, (appositive with non-esssential information) 7. C (no comma with short introductory phrase that answers *When?*) 8. shipped, Ms. Stillwater, (direct address) 9. C 10. C (no comma in series joined by conjunctions)

LEVEL II

1. honest, (independent adjectives) 2. life, (intro. verbal phrase) 3. C (no comma after short prep. phrase) 4. quit, (intro. dependent clause) 5. doctor, form, (non-essential dependent clause) 6. June 15, (intro. verbal phrase) 7. weekend, (independent clauses with coord. conj.) 8. confidential, (non-essential dependent clause) 9. C (essential dependent clause) 10. orders, (intro. dependent clause)

LEVEL III

A. 1. 10,000 or 10 000 (numeral more than four digits) 2. is, is (clarity) 3. second, (omitted words) 4. amended," Bennett, (short quotation) 5. operators, (contrasting statement) 6. 2019, (adjacent numerals) 7. C 8. succeed, overhead, (contrasting statement) 9. liabilities," (short quotation) 10. a long, long (clarity)

Posttest

1. C 2. baseball, hockey, community, 3. know, Mrs. Youngblood, pleasant, 4. thinks, hand, 5. client, 6. deadline, 7. trained, logical, 8. Skrenta, virus, 9. Majid, BSc, Banff, Alberta, 10. unsure, Carlson, Ray,

CHAPTER 16

Pretest

1. Apple, Google, 2. option; as a result, 3. pick": 4. speak: Woods, College; Linnell, Technology; O'Shea, 5. scheduled; 6. committee, however, 7. choose, centres; namely, 8. following; consequently, 9. goal: 10. 10:45

Reinforcement Exercises

LEVEL I

A. 1. cubicle; 2. communication; 3. C 4. eBay; 5. slip; 6. years; 7. years; 8. Québec; 9. list; 10. power;

LEVEL II

A. 1. Omit colon 2. Owners: 3. explained: 4. C 5. responsible: 6. list. 7. Omit colon 8. Omit colon 9. border: 10. C

LEVEL III

A. 1. C 2. C 3. (1) promotion; but 4. (5) workers; namely, assistance, programs, programs, 5. (4) Ltd., Saskatoon, for example, Program; 6. rule: 7. C 8. (1) Buy: 9. worked; that is, 10. C

Posttest

1. history; 2. said: 3. campaigns: 4. Leadership: 5. dramatically; therefore, 6. trait: 7. meeting: Mason, Jonquière; Parnall, College; Almonte, 8. C 9., that is, 10. employees; for instance,

CHAPTER 17

Pretest

1. Wow! presentation! 2. MBA degrees. 3. P.M. Brin. 4. Ms. p.m., she? 5. Dr. Lee, Ms. Adams, Mr. committee. 6. *Canadian Business* "How Way"? 7. Schroeder, PhD, M.L. Vasquez, MD. 8. industries—pipelines, construction, petroleum refining— growth. 9. Thomas L. Friedman's *The World Is Flat* "How Cope." 10. ask, "Why yet?"

Reinforcement Exercises

LEVEL I

A. 1. . 2. ! 3. . 4. ? 5. . 6. ! 7. . 8. . 9. ? 10. .

LEVEL II

A. 1. c 2. a 3. b 4. c 5. a 6. b 7. b 8. a

LEVEL III

A. 1. T 2. T 3. F 4. T 5. F 6. T 7. F 8. F 9. T 10. F

Posttest

1. CFO GDP price. 2. Inc. (owned Post) vehicles. 3. shows—their cellphones. 4. Dr. p.m.? 5. "Winning Strategies." 6. "Confidential"? 7. RSVPs Ms. Lee, Ms. Gold, Mr. Vila. 8. *principal* "Writing Letters." 9. said, "The knows"? 10. business—Indra Whitman—are fifty.

CHAPTER 18

Pretest

1. I I Vancouver Island University 2. *The Naked Future: What Happens in a World That Anticipates Your Every Move* We 3. Sales Meeting Next Thursday 4. Mother's Day Canada Post 5. Father East Coast 6. French 7. Canadian Medical Association's Manitoba Room Hilton Hotel March 8. Uncle Montréal 9. West Coast Google's 10. Revenue Canada Form

Reinforcement Exercises

LEVEL I

A. 1. staff time management Monday June (5) 2. telecommunications industry (2) 3. company Facebook customers (3) 4. fall I master's degree marketing (5) 5. (0) 6. Island Canadian Lake Erie (4) 7. Transport safety guidelines remotely piloted aircraft system *drones* (8) 8. baristas coffee preparation customer service (5) 9. sales representatives Room Red Lion Inn training session stress management (10) 10. security basset hound cocker spaniel (5).

LEVEL II

A. 1. New Payroll Processing Procedure (4) 2. Figure Appendix (2) 3. general manager (2) 4. pharmacist (1) 5. Mother Uncle Wind Power Division (4) 6. Mr. Mrs. Office of the Federal Ombudsman for Victims of Crime (7) 7. aunt colleges University Report *The Globe and Mail* (7) 8. Director, Employee Services (3) 9. western Treaty Arctic-Pacific Divide (5) 10. northern World War (3)

LEVEL III

A. 1. Portuguese Dutch English (3) 2. "Confidential" boss (2) 3. Focus (1) 4. Venus, Earth, Mars (3) 5. Inflated False Fake (3) 6. earth (1) 7. Europeans (1) 8. ex-Councillor Mayor-elect (2) 9. sir (1) 10. The (1)

Posttest

1. degree 2. Employee Retreat This Friday 3. *and the Business of* 4. equal opportunity employer Christian Jewish Muslim
5. controller Human Resources Department 6. writer futurist It 7. English university 8. Algonquin Room Four Points Thursday 9. Doctor, cancer 10. Christmas

CHAPTER 19

Pretest

1. 73 1,707 (or leave as is) 35,000 2. two-thirds 3. 50 percent 4. One 5. Twelve 10 a.m. 6. eighteen 50 ha 7. $20 twenty 92-cent 8. 20 cars May 2 4 cars 9. 23 cm by 30 cm $2 million 10. 0.2 mm

Reinforcement Exercises

LEVEL I

A. 1. a 2. c 3. a 4. b 5. b 6. b 7. a 8. a 9. a 10. b

LEVEL II

A. 1. b 2. b 3. a 4. b 5. b 6. a 7. a 8. b, c 9. a 10. a

LEVEL III

A. 1. b 2. a 3. a 4. b 5. a 6. b 7. a 8. a 9. b 10. b

Posttest

1. Fifty-eight 2. $30 a month 3. four 140-character 4. 9th 5. 89.2 degrees 6. $750,000 two companies 7. 3rd 17 $20 8. 18 employees 9. 33 $600,000 10. 50-page December 1

CHAPTER 20

Pretest

Answers may vary. 1. growth of approximately 20 percent 2. Aziz Yadav introduced a motion to . . . 3. and to develop good employee relations. 4. While we were waiting in line . . . 5. Combine the first . . . 6. Since we are moving, we are not renewing the rental agreement. 7. After illegally removing documents from his Toronto office, Conrad Black was convicted of obstruction of justice. 8. and lock the doors. 9. I would like your decision by June 1.
10. The company's discontinuation of its benefits plan has angered employees.

Reinforcement Exercises

LEVEL I

A. 1. currently 2. named 3. like 4. Because 5. until 6. about 7. for 8. probably 9. Although/Even though 10. approximately/about

LEVEL II

A. 1. c 2. a 3. b 4. b 5. c 6. b 7. a 8. c 9. a 10. a

LEVEL III

A. 1. T 2. F. 3. T 4. T 5. F 6. T 7. T 8. F 9. T 10. F

Posttest

1. I don't understand why he can't get expert-quality photos with that camera; after all, it has multiple lenses and many features. 2. Momen must have picked up . . . 3. We always consider the age . . . 4. would adjust my bill, change my service plan, and send me a new modem 5. must always wear their ID badges. 6. Because most Canadians . . . 7. Because the global pandemic of 2020 hit small businesses hard, many changed operating models altogether. 8. First, you must reserve a meeting room. 9. complete, correct, and detailed. 10. . . . in an accident within 10 km of its destination.

ANSWERS TO UNIT REVIEW EXERCISES

UNIT 1 REVIEW Chapters 1–2

1. b 2. c 3. b 4. c 5. a 6. c 7. b 8. a 9. c 10. a 11. c 12. d 13. d 14. c 15. a 16. a 17. b 18. c 19. cs 20. c 21. c 22. f 23. cs 24. f 25. c 26. ro 27. cs 28. cs 29. ro

Ask an Editor Review

30. a 31. b 32. b 33. b 34. c

UNIT 2 REVIEW Chapters 3–6

LEVEL I

1. b 2. b 3. a 4. c 5. a 6. a 7. b 8. a 9. d 10. c 11. b 12. a

LEVEL II

13. a 14. b 15. c 16. a 17. a 18. b 19. b 20. a 21. b 22. c 23. b 24. c

LEVEL III

25. b 26. c 27. a 28. b 29. a 30. a 31. a 32. b 33. b 34. a 35. a 36. b 37. b 38. b

Ask an Editor Review

39. b 40. b 41. a 42. a 43. b

UNIT 3 REVIEW Chapters 7–10

LEVEL I

1. b 2. a 3. c 4. a 5. b 6. b 7. a 8. b 9. a 10. a 11. a 12. b 13. a 14. b 15. a

LEVEL II

16. b 17. b 18. b 19. a 20. a 21. b 22. a 23. 2 24. 0 25. 1

LEVEL III

26. b 27. b 28. b 29. b 30. a 31. a 32. b 33. a 34. b 35. a 36. b 37. b 38. a 39. b 40. b

Ask an Editor Review

41. a 42. b 43. b 44. a

UNIT 4 REVIEW Chapters 11–14

LEVEL I

1. a 2. a 3. b 4. a 5. b 6. a 7. b 8. b 9. c 10. 0 11. 1 12. 0 13. 1

LEVEL II

14. a 15. a 16. b 17. a 18. a 19. a 20. d 21. e 22. b 23. a 24. c 25. c 26. e 27. e

LEVEL III

28. a 29. b 30. a 31. b 32. a 33. a 34. b 35. a

Ask an Editor Review

36. b 37. b 38. a 39. a 40. a

UNIT 5 REVIEW Chapters 15–17

LEVEL I

1. (2) Professor, job? 2. C 3. (2) "Deepfakes," original, 4. (4)used, for example, CEOs, reputations, 5. C 6. (2) there, however, 7. (2) faked; in fact, 8. (4) January 26, 202x, at 10 a.m. 9. (1) time; therefore, 10. Mr. Deerchild, ready? 11. c 12. b 13. b 14. a 15. c

LEVEL II

16. a 17. a 18. c 19. a 20. a 21. b 22. a 23. b 24. a 25. a

LEVEL III

26. a 27. b 28. b 29. c 30. b 31. c. 32. b 33. b 34. b 35. a 36. b

Ask an Editor Review

37. a 38. b 39. b 39. b 40. a

UNIT 6 REVIEW Chapters 18–20

LEVEL I

1. b 2. b 3. a 4. a 5. a 6. a 7. b 8. b 9. b 10. b 11. a 12. b

LEVEL II

13. b 14. a 15. a 16. b 17. b 18. a 19. a 20. b 21. a 22. a (. . . sound, and add colour.) 23. c (. . . complaint. These problems must be improved . . .) 24. b (Seated in the back of the room, Yasmin . . .)

LEVEL III

25. a 26. b 27. b 28. b 29. a 30. b 31. b 32. b 33. b 34. a 35. a

Ask an Editor Review

36. b 37. a 38. a 39. a 40. B

ANSWERS TO APPENDIX B EXERCISES

LIST I
1. (b) 2. (a) 3. (b) 4. (a) 5. (b) 6. (d) 7. (b) 8. (a) 9. (b) 10. (c)

LIST II
1. (a) 2. (c) 3. (b) 4. (a) 5. (d) 6. (a) 7. (d) 8. (c) 9. (a) 10. (c)

LIST III
1. (b) 2. (d) 3. (a) 4. (b) 5. (c) 6. (d) 7. (b) 8. (a) 9. (b) 10. (a)

LIST IV
1. (c) 2. (a) 3. (d) 4. (b) 5. (a) 6. (d) 7. (b) 8. (c) 9. (b) 10. (d)

LIST V
1. (a) 2. (d) 3. (a) 4. (b) 5. (b) 6. (d) 7. (a) 8. (c) 9. (a) 10. (c)

LIST VI
1. (d) 2. (d) 3. (a) 4. (c) 5. (b) 6. (c) 7. (d) 8. (a) 9. (d) 10. (c)

LIST VII
1. (d) 2. (c) 3. (c) 4. (a) 5. (c) 6. (b) 7. (d) 8. (b) 9. (a) 10. (d)

LIST VIII
1. (b) 2. (a) 3. (d) 4. (b) 5. (c) 6. (a) 7. (c) 8. (a) 9. (d) 10. (b)

LIST IX
1. (d) 2. (a) 3. (b) 4. (d) 5. (d) 6. (a) 7. (d) 8. (a) 9. (d) 10. (d)

LIST X
1. (d) 2. (b) 3. (d) 4. (c) 5. (b) 6. (a) 7. (d) 8. (a) 9. (d) 10. (b)

LIST XI
1. (c) 2. (d) 3. (c) 4. (d) 5. (b) 6. (c) 7. (c) 8. (a) 9. (c) 10. (a)

LIST XII
1. (d) 2. (c) 3. (b) 4. (a) 5. (a) 6. (b) 7. (a) 8. (b) 9. (d) 10. (c)

LIST XIII
1. (a) 2. (d) 3. (b) 4. (c) 5. (c) 6. (b) 7. (a) 8. (a) 9. (c) 10. (a)

LIST XIV
1. (a) 2. (b) 3. (d) 4. (a) 5. (c) 6. (c) 7. (d) 8. (a) 9. (b) 10. (a)

LIST XV
1. (c) 2. (b) 3. (a) 4. (d) 5. (b) 6. (c) 7. (d) 8. (a) 9. (b) 10. (c)

LIST XVI
1. (a) 2. (c) 3. (d) 4. (c) 5. (c) 6. (d) 7. (a) 8. (a) 9. (d) 10. (a)

LIST XVII
1. (d) 2. (b) 3. (b) 4. (b) 5. (c) 6. (a) 7. (d) 8. (c) 9. (b) 10. (a)

LIST XVIII
1. (c) 2. (a) 3. (d) 4. (b) 5. (b) 6. (b) 7. (c) 8. (a) 9. (d) 10. (b)

LIST XIX
1. (b) 2. (a) 3. (d) 4. (b) 5. (c) 6. (c) 7. (a) 8. (b) 9. (d) 10. (a)

LIST XX
1. (a) 2. (c) 3. (a) 4. (b) 5. (d) 6. (d) 7. (a) 8. (b) 9. (b) 10. (a)

GLOSSARY

abbreviations Shortened versions of words (p. 321)

abstract nouns Nouns that name qualities and concepts that may be difficult to visualize (p. 38)

acronym Word formed of initials (pp. 147, 321)

active voice The voice the verb is in when the subject of a sentence performs an action; the "voice of business" (p. 148)

adjectives Words that describe nouns or pronouns (p. 5)

adverbs Words that describe verbs, adjectives, or other adverbs (p. 6)

antecedent The noun or pronoun to which a pronoun refers (pp. 74, 90, 393)

appositives Words or groups of words that explain or rename previously mentioned nouns or pronouns (p. 74)

article A type of adjective that identifies, or marks, nouns; sometimes called "noun markers" (p. 5)

auxiliary verb See *helping verb* (p. 16)

cardinal figures 1, 2, 3, etc. (p. 371)

case The grammatical form a pronoun takes depending on its purpose in a sentence—subjective case, objective case, possessive case (p. 72)

clause A word group that contains a subject and a predicate (pp. 112, 241)

coherence A quality of good writing achieved through effective organization and skilful use of writing devices (p. 201)

collective nouns Words that refer to a collection of people, animals, or objects; treated as singular when operating as a single unit and plural when acting individually (e.g., *staff, team, herd*) (p. 93)

colon A punctuation mark that most often introduces lists, quotations, and explanatory sentences (p. 305)

comma A punctuation mark that indicates a pause in the flow of a sentence (p. 284)

comma splice The incorrect joining of two or more complete sentences with a comma (p. 21)

common nouns Nouns that name *generalized* persons, places, and things (p. 39)

comparative statements Statements introduced by *than* or *as* (p. 74)

complement A noun, a pronoun, or an adjective that renames or describes the subject; always follows a linking verb (p. 18)

complete predicate The verb or verb phrase and its modifiers, objects, and complements (p. 16)

complete subject The simple subject and all its modifiers (p. 16)

compound nouns Nouns formed by joining two or more words; may be written as one word, separate words, or hyphenated words (p. 41)

compound sentence A sentence with two or more independent clauses (p. 241)

concrete nouns Nouns that name specific objects that you can actually see, hear, feel, taste, touch, or smell (p. 38)

conjunctions Words that connect other words or groups of words (p. 6)

conjunctive adverb A word or group of words used to effect a transition from one thought to another from one clause to another (p. 242)

contractions Shortened (contracted) forms of subjects and verbs (e.g., *it's, they're*) (p. 73)

coordinating conjunctions Joining words and phrases that connect words, phrases, and clauses of equal grammatical value or rank (p. 240)

correlative conjunctions A pair of words used to connect grammatically equal sentence elements and to provide emphasis (p. 243)

dangling modifier A modifier not followed immediately by a word it can logically modify (p. 184)

degrees (of adjectives and adverbs) The forms adjectives and adverbs take: positive, comparative, and superlative (p. 208)

demonstrative pronouns Pronouns that designate specific persons or things (p. 77)

dependent clause A group of words with a subject and a verb that cannot stand by itself; it is introduced by a *subordinating conjunction* and requires an independent clause to complete its meaning (p. 257)

direct object A noun or pronoun that answers the question *What?* or *Whom?* (p. 18)

direct question A question that requires an answer from the person asked (p. 322)

essential clause A clause that is needed to identify the noun to which it refers; this clause limits the meaning of the noun (p. 258)

forms (of adjectives and adverbs) See *degrees* (p. 208)

future tense The verb tense that shows actions that are expected to occur at a later time (p. 123)

gender The sex of the person being spoken about (pp. 72, 91)

gerund A verb form that ends in *ing* and is used as a noun (p. 180)

helping verb A verb that comes before the principal verb and expresses timing, shows emphasis, or demonstrates necessity or possibility; the most common helping verbs are forms of *to have, to be,* and *to do* (pp. 16, 124)

idioms Word combinations unique to a particular language or dialect (p. 227)

imperative mood The verb mood used to express a command or give advice (p. 149)

indefinite pronouns Pronouns that replace nouns in a non-specific way (p. 77)

independent adjectives Two or more adjectives that independently modify a noun that follows (p. 212)

independent clause A group of words with a subject and a verb that can stand by itself as a complete sentence (p. 256)

indicative mood The verb mood used to express a fact (p. 149)

indirect object A noun or pronoun that answers the question *To whom?, To what?, For whom?,* or *For what?* (p. 18)

infinitive The base form of a verb, usually preceded by *to* (pp. 75, 181)

inflection The form a verb takes depending on number, person, voice, and tense (p. 122)

interjections Words that express strong feelings (p. 6)

interrogative pronouns Pronouns that replace nouns in a question (p. 77)

intransitive The type of verb that does not require an object to complete its action (p. 147)

inverted order A sentence structure in which at least one part of the verb comes before the subject (p. 19)

irregular nouns Nouns whose plural is formed by changing the spelling of the word (p. 39)

irregular verbs Verbs whose past tense is not formed with the addition of *d* or *ed* (p. 128)

linking verbs Verbs that express a state of being and generally link the subject to words in the predicate that describe it or rename it (pp. 75, 147)

mixed fractions Whole numbers combined with fractions (p. 375)

modifiers Words that describe or limit (pp. 16, 392)

non-essential clause A clause that contains information that is not needed to identify its antecedent (p. 259)

nouns The names of persons, places, things, qualities, concepts, and activities (p. 4)

number How many people or things are being spoken about (p. 72)

object of a preposition A noun or pronoun that usually follows the preposition (p. 224)

ordinal figures Numbers that show position in an ordered sequence (*1st, 2nd, 3rd,* etc.) (p. 371)

parallel (in construction) Having the same grammatical form (p. 243)

parenthetical adverb A word or group of words used to effect a transition from one thought to another within a single clause (p. 242)

parenthetical clause A clause that is unnecessary for the grammatical completeness of the sentence but that adds additional information for the reader (p. 258)

passive voice The voice the verb is in when the action of the verb is received by the sentence's subject, rather than directed by the subject; the "voice of tact" (p. 148)

past participle May be used as part of a verb or as an adjective; when used as a verb, it is preceded by a helping verb (a form of *to have*); usually formed by adding *d* or *ed* to the root verb (p. 125)

past tense The verb tense that shows action that has been completed (p. 122)

perfect tenses Tenses that show actions that are already completed, or *perfected;* formed with a form of *to have* + past participle (p. 126)

person Who is speaking or being spoken about (p. 72)

personal pronouns Pronouns used to replace nouns or other pronouns (pp. 72, 76)

phrase A group of related words without a subject and a verb (p. 240)

polite request A command or suggestion phrased as a request (p. 320)

possession The state of one noun (or pronoun) possessing another (p. 56)

prepositional phrase A group of two words or more that begins with a preposition and ends with its object (pp. 6, 224)

prepositions Connecting words that show the relationship of a noun or pronoun to other words in a sentence (pp. 6, 224)

present participle May be used as part of a verb or as an adjective; when used as a verb, it is preceded by a helping verb (a form of *to be*); formed by adding *ing* to the root verb (p. 125)

present tense The verb tense that expresses current or habitual action and facts that are true at all times; may also be used in constructions showing future action (p. 122)

primary tenses Tenses that indicate the simple present, past, and future (p. 122)

principal verb The verb identifying the action or state of being; it is the last verb in a verb phrase (p. 16)

progressive tenses Tenses that indicate action in progress now, in progress in the past, or in progress in the future; usually formed with a form of *to be* + present participle (p. 125)

pronouns Words used in place of nouns (p. 4)

proper nouns Nouns that name *specific* persons, places, and things; always capitalized (p. 39)

reciprocal pronouns Pronouns that indicate mutual relationship (p. 77)

reflexive pronouns Pronouns that end in *self* or *selves* and emphasize or reflect on their *antecedents* (p. 74)

regular nouns Nouns whose plural is formed with the addition of *s* or *es* (p. 39)

related numbers Numbers used similarly in the same document, often in reference to the same noun or listed together in a series (p. 372)

relative pronoun clauses Clauses that begin with *that, which, who, whom,* or *whose;* the verb that follows *that, which,* or *who* must agree with the antecedent of the relative pronoun (p. 167)

relative pronouns The pronouns *who, whom, whose, which,* and *that* when used to introduce dependent clauses; may introduce essential or non-essential clauses (pp. 77, 257)

round numbers Approximations (p. 374)

run-on sentence The fusion of two or more complete sentences without punctuation (p. 20)

semicolon A punctuation mark that indicates two closely related ideas that should be thought about together (p. 304)

sentence fragment An incomplete sentence punctuated as if it were a complete sentence (p. 19)

serial comma A comma before the conjunction (usually *and* or *or)* in a list of three or more items (p. 284)

simple fractions Fractions in which both the numerator and the denominator are whole numbers (p. 374)

simple predicate A verb or verb phrase that tells what the subject is doing or what is being done to the subject (p. 16)

simple sentence A sentence with one independent clause (p. 241)

simple subject A noun or pronoun that tells who or what the sentence is about (p. 16)

simple tenses See *primary tenses* (p. 122)

subjunctive mood The verb mood used to express a doubt, a conjecture, or a suggestion (p. 149)

subordinating conjunction A word that joins a dependent clause to an independent clause, denoting limitations on the meaning of the independent clause (p. 256)

terminal dependent clause A dependent clause that is at the end of the sentence (p. 258)

topic sentence A sentence that summarizes what a paragraph is about, usually placed at the beginning of a paragraph (p. 200)

transitional expression See *conjunctive adverb* (p. 242)

transitive The type of verb that expresses an action directed toward a person or thing (p. 146)

verb phrase A helping verb (or more than one helping verb) + a main verb (p. 124)

verbs Words that express an action, an occurrence, or a state of being (p. 5)

INDEX